EGYPT "THE HOLY LAND"
THE QUINTESSENTIAL BOOK

EGYPT THE "HOLY LAND"

THE QUINTESSENTIAL BOOK

AFRICAN AMERICANS IN ANCIENT KEMET/EGYPT: "THE HOLY LAND"

FREDERICK MONDERSON

SUMON PUBLISHERS

FREDERICK MONDERSON

SuMon Publishers
PO Box 160685
Brooklyn, New York 11216

sumonpublishers.com@sumonpublishers.com
blackfolksbooks.com@blackfolksbooks.com
fredsegypt.com@fredsegypt.com   blackegyptbooks.com@blackegyptbooks.com

Copyright Frederick Monderson/ SuMon Publishers, 2014 All Rights Reserved.

No part of this book may be reproduced, stored in a retrieval system, or transmitted by any means without the written permission of the author.

ISBN – 978-1-61023-045-2
LCCN - 2012952275

In the Tribute to Professor George Simmonds, "Unsung Hero," Dr. Fred Monderson sat at the feet of his heroes, Brother X, Michael Carter, Dr. Leonard Jeffries, El Hombre Brath, Dr. Lewis, Prof. George Simmonds, Dr. ben-Jochannan, Sister Camille Yarbrough, among others.

EGYPT "THE HOLY LAND"
THE QUINTESSENTIAL BOOK

ABOUT THE AUTHOR

Dr. Frederick Monderson is a retired *college* professor and school teacher who taught African History in the City University of New York and American History and Government in the NY public schools. He has written more than 1000 articles in the NY Black Press, *Daily Challenge, Afro Times* and *New American* newspapers. Very active in community service he has also written several books on Egypt including *Who were the Ancient Egyptians?*; *The Awesome Egyptian Temple*; *Eternal House: The Egyptian Tomb*; *Grassroots View of Ancient Egypt*; *Celebrating Dr. Ben Jochannan*; *Michael Jackson: The Last Dance*; as well as *Barack Obama: Ready, Fit to Lead*; *Barack Obama: Master of Washington, DC*; and *Obama: Master and Commander*; *Where are the Kamite Kings?*; *Medinet Habu: Mortuary Temple of Rameses III*; *Temple of Karnak: The Majestic Architecture of Ancient Egypt*; *An Egyptian Resurrection*; *Intrigue Through Time* (*a novel on Ancient Egypt*); *Egypt Essays on Ancient Kemet*; *The Majesty of Egyptian Gods and Temples* (a book of Egyptian Poems); *The Ramesseum: Mortuary Temple of Rameses II*; *Hatshepsut's Temple at Deir el Bahari*; *Research Essays on Ancient Egypt*; *The Colonnade: Then and Now*; *Reflections on Ancient Kemet*; *Seven Letters to Mike Tyson on Egyptian Temples*; *10 Poems Praising Great Blacks for Mike Tyson*; also *Sonny Carson: The Final Triumph* (5 Volumes); *and Glory of the Ancestors: 19 Letters to O.J. Simpson on Ancient African History*. A student of the esteemed Dr. Yosef ben-Jochannan, Dr. Monderson conducts tours to Egypt annually. Next Tour is scheduled for July 12-26, 2014.

For tour information, please contact Orleane Brooks-Williams at Nostrand Travel, 726 Nostrand Avenue, Brooklyn, New York 11216. Phone Number 718-756-5300.

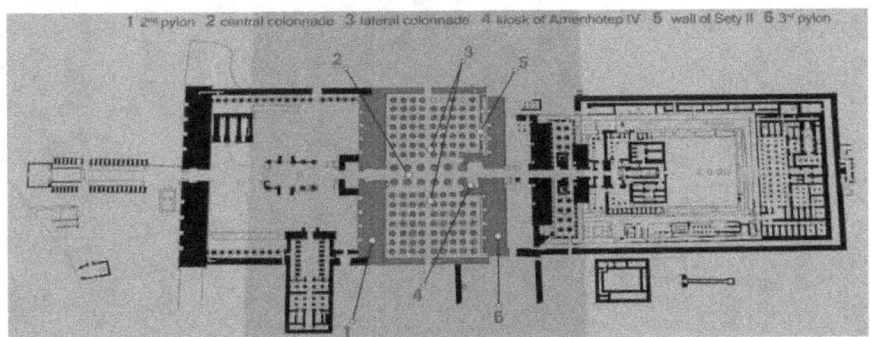

Plan view of Karnak temple emphasizing various features of the Hypostyle Hall.

FREDERICK MONDERSON

In Karnak's Hypostyle Hall, Seti I kneels to present two ointment jars to Amon as Min. Notice how Min's creative organ, from his navel not scrotum, is defaced.

The Middle Kingdom "White Chapel," reconstructed and on view in the "Open Air Museum" at Karnak Temple.

QUINTESSENTIAL BOOK
"THE HOLY LAND"

Cast of Characters

1. James Morrison, young College Professor, theologian, at the University of Michigan, 30 years old.

2. Michael Montout, Christian Pastor, 56 years old, Ypsilanti, Michigan.

3. Dr. Oswald Benjamin, author, historian, lecturer, tour guide.

4. Farouk Ghorab, Egyptian guide based in Luxor.

5. Mr. John and Mrs. Joy Brown, Newark, New Jersey, real estate investors.

6. Mr. Frank and Mrs. Jessie James, Princeton, New Jersey. Mr. James is an electrical contractor and Mrs. James teaches grades 4 and 5 in elementary school.

7. Ms. Stephaniea McCall, 36 years old, schoolteacher, 9th grade, Rochdale, Queens, New York.

8. Carmelitiea Shabazz, 32 years old, graduate student, Bronx, New York. Art and Architecture, History of Architecture, Egyptian Architecture.

9. Kashmoney Malone, 28 years old, MBA, contributing editor for a major *Business* magazine.

10. Dr. James and Mrs. Ada Madison, Ypsilanti, Michigan.

11. Dr. Sylvester and Mrs. Regina Singleton, celebrating their 50th wedding anniversary, emeritus history and political science Professors.

12. Mr. John and Mrs. Glenda Stewart, retired educators, Washington, District of Columbia.

13. Mr. Walter and Mrs. Juliet Brown retired postal worker, Atlanta, Georgia. Mrs. Brown is a department store sales manager.

14. Leonel Nelson Escobar, Dominican Republic, banker.

15. Michelliea Georges, 26 years old, Philadelphia, Penn. Senior, history major, Temple University.

16. Regina Hendricks. Senior, psychology major, University of Michigan.

FREDERICK MONDERSON

17. George Washington, 48 years old, BA and MA, graduate of Hunter College of the City University of New York.

18. Peter Monderson, BA graduate, Hunter College of the City University of New York.

19. Robert Matthews, Businessman, Brooklyn, New York.

20. Mr. Charles and Mrs. Shirley Palmer.

21. Michael and Mary Palmer (son and wife).

22. Cosmo Palmer (grandson).

23. Frederick Maloney, MD, Resident Surgeon, Kings County Hospital Center, Brooklyn, New York.

24. Henrietta Potter, Registered Nurse, Kings County Hospital Center, Brooklyn, New York.

25. Lesley Jacobs, 50 years old, Businessman, electronics.

26. Jack Bender, 36 years old, musician.

27. Dr. Benjamin's Man.

28. Lady from California.

29. Dr. and Mrs. Mc Flair, Philadelphia Pastor.

30. Hattie Guerre and Jerome Ford, soul mates from California.

31. Bryce Menkheperre Raymond and Eric Joel Brown, New York City Middle School students entering their final grade.

32. Dr. Leonard and Mrs. Marilyn James, Professor Emeritus, Atlanta, Georgia.

33. Esperanza Rodriguez, Dr. Monderson's assistant.

34. Teddy Cubia. New York City, retired educator, poet.

35. Michael Sinclair, 35, Graduate of Temple University's Afrocentric Institute of African Studies.

QUINTESSENTIAL BOOK "THE HOLY LAND"

36. Joshua Monderson, Mechanical Engineer.

37. Cherise Maloney, Lady from Brooklyn, New York.

38. Dr. Alexander and Mrs. Holly Pushkin.

39. Sharon Montgomery, Librarian from Washington, DC.

40. Dr. Frederick Monderson.

Day 1. DEPARTURE FROM JFK AIRPORT NEW YORK

Ring! Ring! Ring!
Hello!
Daughter: Hi daddy. Are you going to Egypt today?
Father: Yes, Keisha, my sweet. I'm leaving this evening.
Daughter: Well, I just called to wish you a safe and enjoyable trip. Hope you take lots of pictures and do bring me back some interesting mementos, perhaps a small pyramid, maybe an obelisk, and some beautiful papyrus.
Father: Well, you certainly remember and I'll see you when I get back. The taxi is here to take me to the airport. Bye.
Father: Howdy. Take me to John F. Kennedy Airport, Egypt Air Airlines.
Taxi Driver: No problem. The traffic is light this afternoon. What time is your flight?
Father: My flight is 7:00 PM, but I must check in by 5:00 PM.
Taxi Driver: It's 4:15 PM. We won't have a problem getting there on time. Is this your first time going to Egypt?
Father: Oh no! I have been to Egypt perhaps about twenty times. I'm part of a tour group going to Egypt for 15 days. This is a wonderful experience that I enjoy very much. There is so much to see. It's an enjoyable experience, I recommend it to everyone, and you should make the trip yourself some day.
Taxi Driver: I certainly will. I've heard about it. I'm going to retire next year and I will do my best to try to get there. Well, traffic was easy, so here we are, Egypt Air.
Father: Thanks. I think I see some of my friends standing in line before the Egypt Air counter. I'll go straight to the check-in-counter.

FREDERICK MONDERSON

CHECK IN PROCESS

Hi. I am Dr. Fred Monderson. I'm here to check in for the flight to Cairo, Egypt, with the tour group. Here's my passport.
Attendant: Very good. The travel agent has submitted your name. We have arranged a block of seats for your group. Everything's ok. You're in seat 9B. Boarding is 6:15 at Gate 41. Here are the other seating arrangements for your group.

Esperanza Rodriguez is in 9A; Dr. Oswald Benjamin, 9C; Dr. John Africa, 9D; Mr. John and Mrs. Joy Brown, 9 F; G; Mr. Frank and Mrs. Jessie James, 9 H, J; Stephaniea McCall, 15D; Carmelitiea Shabazz, 10A; Kashmoney Malone, 10 B; Dr. James and Mrs. Ada Madison, 10 C, D; Mr. Sylvester and Regina Singleton, 10 F, G; Mr. John and Mrs. Glenda Stewart, 10 H, J; Mr. and Mrs. Walter and Josephine Brown, 11 A, B; Regina Samuels, 11 C; Michelliea Georges, 11D; George Washington 11F; Peter Monderson, 11 G; Robert Matthews, 11 H; Mr. Michael and Mrs. Mary Palmer 12 A, B; Mr. Charles and Shirley Palmer 12 C, D; Cosmos Palmer 12 F; Dr. Frederick Maloney, 12 G; Henrietta Potter, 12 H; Lesley Jacobs, 12 J; Musician Jack Bender, 14 A; Dr. Benjamin's man 14B; Sharon Montgomery, 14 C; Dr. and Mrs. Mc Flair, 14 D, F; Hattie Guerre and Jerome Ford, 14 G, H; Dr. Leonard and Mrs. Marilyn James, 15 A, B; James Morrison 15 C. Michael Montout, 15 D; Teddy Cubia, 11J; Brother Sabuba, 14J; Lady from California 16 A; Dr. Alexander and Mrs. Holly Pushkin, 15 G,H; Joshua Monderson, 15E; Cherise Maloney, 15F; Michael Sinclair, 16B.

Attendant: That is your group. You can now proceed through the checkpoint to your gate No. 41. Boarding will commence in forty-five minutes. Have a wonderful flight.

With that, the group moved through the security check-point and into the lounge areas passing duty free shops, deli, restaurants, telephones, newsstands, camera and perfume shops, etc. A few people stopped to purchase some of these items.

Day 1 (Continued).

Esperanza Rodriguez. Good Day, Mi Amor. Everything looks good. The check-in went without a hitch. I have Xeroxed a copy of your tribute to your mentor Dr. ben-Jochannan for distribution to the group as they boarded the plane.

Dr. Fred Monderson: Thank you, my dear. You are such an efficient assistant. Hopefully, with you by my side, things will go pretty easy and this trip should be a success.

QUINTESSENTIAL BOOK
"THE HOLY LAND"

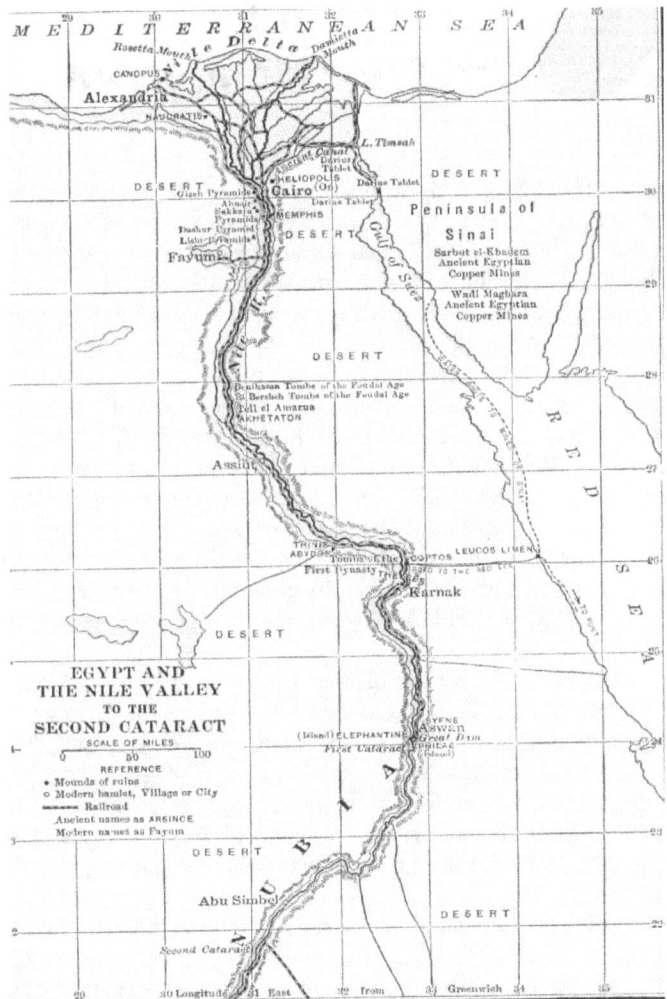

Holy Land - Map of Egypt and the Nile Valley to the Second Cataract.

FREDERICK MONDERSON

Dr. YOSEF A. A. BEN-JOCHANNAN
By
Dr. Fred Monderson

Sitting and listening recently to one of Dr. Ben's lectures given back in 1997, I realized he is near 95 years old, at least! Equally, and considering he has had more than half a dozen heart attacks and strokes, and as a student of his, I thought he certainly deserved a tribute from me, before it's too late! Most people believe Dr. Ben is an extraordinary man of many talents, but principally a man who held the African woman in the highest esteem. He taught us in the beginning was the African woman! Human creation came out of the African woman! As the obelisk is a small pyramid on a tall base, this is the pedestal upon which Dr. ben-Jochannan placed the African woman. He honored the Black Woman who is the source of the Black Family! He taught us the Black Woman is a Goddess! He also led the light to the Nile Valley. He took Egypt to destroy white supremacy! It's like Marcus Garvey said: "The cubs are running free out there," and, thanks to Dr. Ben, intellectual cubs are challenging the distortions, omissions and putting Africa in its proper place in world civilization history through its accomplishments in Nubian and Egyptian, Nile Valley, cultures that gave so much to the world.

The twentieth century has been blessed with great African and African-American writers and historians. These include Dr. W.E.B. DuBois, Dr. Carter G. Woodson, Dr. Kwame Nkrumah, Dr. Ivan Van Sertima, J. A. Rogers, Cheikh Anta Diop and Dr. Leonard James of New York City Technical College of the City University of New York, among others. This reservoir of brainpower has equally extended into the Twenty-First Century. However, none of these giants surpass the literary production, commitment, tirelessness, and sincere dedication to Africa, its people and cultural history more than Dr. Yosef Alfredo Antonio ben-Jochannan. Outspoken visionary, ahead of his time, controversial but he is not afraid to take an iconoclastic and individualistic if a somewhat idiosyncratic point of view and defend it irrespective. His friends and students, affectionately call this father, teacher, historian, friend and Egyptologist, "Doc Ben." In fact, back in the early 1970s when even "Black folks" did not readily accept "Dr. Ben," one should wonder how he got his name. It was a young man named "Barney" and I, Fred Monderson who first started calling him not "Dr. Ben" but "Ben Jo" while we were first at New York City Technical College in 1973 and then at Hunter College in 1976 and the name stuck. Finally, Curtis Dunmoodie, a fellow student of both the Tech and Hunter joined and we began calling him "Dr. Ben" out of respect in defiance of those "feather bedders" who said "Dr. Ben has no Ph.D."

QUINTESSENTIAL BOOK
"THE HOLY LAND"

Ever cried for Dr. Ben? This statement once made me cry at New York City Technical College. I hurriedly took the train to 125th Street in Harlem, before Prof. George Simmonds calmed me down, showing me Dr. Ben's Doctorate in Anthropology from the University of Havana, with the Spanish designation, on the wall. That is what some of the "false prophets" still do today in academia to him and others! And so you ask them to match their literary production with their in-clandestine vituperativeness and they cannot! Period!

Here is a serious scholar, Dr. ben-Jochannan, who spent a lifetime researching, writing, and defending the integrity and intellectual capabilities of African people worldwide. Dr. Ben pioneered in indigenous ancient African terminology. Imagine a European-American scholar discovering an African woman in Ethiopia and naming her "Lucy" after an Englishman's song "Lucy in the Sky with Diamonds." Dr. Ben said no! Her name is *Denk Nesh* not Lucy!

In 1989, "Doc Ben" celebrated fifty years of visiting ancient Kemet, Ta-merry (Egypt), and the Nile Valley cultures. This prolonged involvement has powerfully under-girded the basis of his researches, speeches, writings and educational tours. In that experience, he began and for some time maintained archaeological digs on the Island of Elephantine and elsewhere. Alas, these have been discontinued.

This writer was happy to be a part of that epoch making 1989 Tour that marked "Doc Ben's" Fiftieth Anniversary visiting the ancient African "Holy-Land" and the next year 1990 for the First Nubian Festival. More importantly, I met "Doc Ben" in early 1972. This was right after the publication of his seminal works, *African Origins of the Major Western Religions (1970)*, *Africa: Mother of Western Civilization (1971)*; and *Black Man of the Nile (1972)*, later *Black Man of the Nile and His Family*. The style of his writings, copious nature of referents employed to defend things African, pointing the way for young scholars and his Afrocentric pioneering approach made "Doc Ben," a very well-respected elder, and formerly a sought after speaking attraction, a man who "tells it like it is!"

Dr. ben-Jochannan has compiled an impressive thirty odd publications. He helped set the stage for a whole new approach in interpreting Africa's contributions to civilization, its heritage and its legacy. He lit the fire of intellectual and cultural consciousness in Africans worldwide. The style of dress with an Afrocentric flavor is also credited to him. Establishing connections between Africans in America, the Caribbean, Africa, Asia and Europe are all attributed to Dr. ben-Jochannan, a man of vision, seer, and an intellectual giant. Many of his books challenged the distortions of Europeans in writing, publishing and disseminating knowledge about the arts, sciences, religion, etc., of the ancient people today called Egyptians. Dr. Ben has included omissions and corrected distortions

FREDERICK MONDERSON

systematically implanted and perpetrated by non-Afrocentric Western, European and American historiography that has falsified the historical past with a prejudiced interpretation. Many of his books challenged what he felt were the distortions of Europeans in writing, publishing and disseminating knowledge about the arts, sciences, religion, etc., regarding ancient Africa and modern interpretation. Dr. Ben dared to expose what he felt was the hypocrisy of western scholarship. He attacked the foundational pillars upon which he felt a false or stolen legacy rests.

Very early he also expressed the view that some scholars are confused because they were taught with a wrong premise. In his own right, and as a result of his teachings, he had no choice but to produce, publish and distribute his works without the aid of major publishing firms. He was thus a pioneer in self-publishing, launching Alkebu-Lan Publishing Company and appealing and winning the support of many upcoming nationalists as they purchased his books in first edition form.

Initiating a new approach to history, the result was an exposition and critical analysis of political, academic and scientific forces of Europe and Africa, each struggling to claim heritage of the ancient and modern historical record. Dr. Ben addressed professionals, laymen, clergy, students and educators. He stressed vitality, resilience and creative expressions that shaped the modern African personality and worldview. Such an approach found ready ears among a people yearning for factual information about their illustrious African past in effort to inspire their minds. They were enthused by the positive nature and potency of their cultural African heritage as "Ben" outlined it. He also took great pains to explain that there were lusterless pages in Africa's past. Nevertheless, his historical and political consciousness fueled their emerging aspirations. This outlook brought Dr. Ben well-deserved adulation and respect of many grateful people. They understood and welcomed his contributions among the litany of great African-American literary artists.

Important, Dr. Ben's writings, lectures and educational tours over the years have stressed two essential themes. The first is that civilization, through science, religion, government, architecture, agriculture, philosophy, and the arts first emerged in Africa. The voice of these utterances made manifest through the conduit of today's Egypt and the Nile Valley idea factory. He argued that Central Africa is the actual source of civilization. In his approach, Dr. Ben showed how the structural foundations of western civilization developed from discoveries and scientific applications in the Nile Valley. Lastly, he took great pains to show his perspective that the writing and teaching of modern history has been distorted to elevate Europe and degrade Africa, and that this distortion must be rectified. This fundamental view helped establish the need for African historical reconstruction and interpretation particularly as we navigate this new century and millennium.

QUINTESSENTIAL BOOK "THE HOLY LAND"

Holy Land Illustrations 1. The Falcon hitching a ride; and Sarcophagus with the Goddess Nut on the breast.

The second of Dr. Ben's themes has been that Africans worldwide should be proud of their ancestors' accomplishments. The arts and sciences that today govern the world are very much Africa's legacy. All African-related peoples should show great pride and dignity in their history and heritage. In this exercise they must respect themselves and carry themselves with dignity and pride, with a balanced view, and teach the young how to identify with Africa. In so doing, they must study and visit Africa. Yet, they must also be aware of the machinations of cultural imperialism and cultural genocide at work designed to stultify Africa's intellectual consciousness. The young must immerse themselves in an African-centered perspective of history and research, write and teach others in turn. They must study languages, French, German, Swahili, Greek, Latin, Coptic, Arabic and *Medu Netcher* or hieroglyphics. These are the languages in which Africa's history is recorded. They must struggle to correct the recent distorted history of Africa's past. In this way, future leaders would help to better the lot of humanity and save the world from its impending moral, spiritual and scientific destruction. To

FREDERICK MONDERSON

accomplish these objectives the good doctor has supplied a reservoir of information from his life's researches. A fundamental tenet of his is, in our research, we should "get the oldest material and work from there!"

Holy Land Ceramic Photo 1. Falcon as representative ceramic art.

Dr. ben-Jochannan's major thesis of his *African Origins of the Major "Western Religions"* is that African religious practices were denigrated and called "Fetishism" and "Paganism." In fact, he showed, in meticulously organized arguments that these early thought processes are the fundamental bases of Judaism, Christianity, and Islam. He argued that these ideas were first developed and nurtured in Central Africa among indigenous peoples and then extended throughout the Nile Valley. Having migrated down the Nile River, they found greatest fruition in Kemet (Egypt) and were preserved by its civilization advances and the nature of its geography. Thousands of years in formulation, the early knowledge was first compiled in the "Book of Gates," "Book of Knowing Ra," etc., "Pyramid Texts," then "Coffin Texts," and the later *Book of the Dead* or *Book of Going Forth By Day*, that is *Book of Going Forth By Day* and also the "Mysteries of Sais" (Egypt). He explained why Africa's second cultural daughter, Kemet, rose to greater prominence than did the eldest, Ethiopia. To repeat, he stressed and still maintains today, this is despite all the "new evidence," that civilization began in the south of Upper Egypt, in sub-Saharan or Central Africa!

QUINTESSENTIAL BOOK
"THE HOLY LAND"

Another of Dr. Ben's works is *Africa: Mother of Western Civilization*. Its major thesis holds that the fundamental laws, principles, philosophies, ideas, arts and crafts that educated the West, started in Africa through the Nile Valley cultural explosive experience. For critical teachers who face this dilemma he has some advice. For them, he wrote: "the only credentials necessary in the experience of African history, otherwise mis-nomered 'the Black Experience' and 'Black Studies,' are the documented proofs and the sources from whence they are taken."

For this reason, *Africa: Mother of Western Civilization* is an enormous compendium of facts, sources, illustrations, and analyses that challenge laymen and scholars alike. It suggests all educators and lay persons alike become involved. It opens new vistas and a wide array of historical sources relating to the significance of Africa in world civilization.

Black Man of the Nile and His Family marks the third of the trilogy of Dr. Ben's seminal works. This particular source represents the maturity of his thoughts and presentations. It also contains a number of objectives the author, ben-Jochannan, sought to accomplish.

The first of these objectives is, "an attempt to create in all African and African related peoples, especially the young African and African-American, a sense of belonging in the great African heritage." It is, writes Dr. Ben: "specifically directed to those who have criminally demasculinized, denuded, and otherwise denigrated the Africans of their **CULTURAL, ECONOMIC, POLITICAL, SCIENTIFIC, SPIRITUAL**, and all other forms of their heritage and human decency." To this we should add their intellectual heritage as represented in Egypt and Nubia.

This view also presents: **"AFRICAN ORIGINS OF EUROPEAN CIVILIZATION"** in a manner whereby, "scholars can find interesting use for it in their research; as much as the layman can for processing information."

Dr. Ben has viewed his role as gadfly presenting "pertinent information needed in the African peoples' **RE-IDENTIFICATION** with their great ancestral heritage." Lastly, he continued, the "major desired accomplishment this volume seeks to achieve, is to provide anthropological evidence of the ancient heritage of the Africans" and their contributions all over the world.

There are other books, including those which, as *Abu Simbel to Ghizeh: A Guide Book and Manual*, is in itself a useful piece of writing. But, there are others including as Sir Francis Bacon (1561-1626) informed: "Some books are to be tasted, others to be swallowed, and some few to be chewed and digested." This much can be said of the trilogy of Dr. ben-Jochannan's works, *Black Man of the Nile and His Family*; *Africa: Mother of Western Civilization*; and *The African Origins of the "Major Western" Religions*. The others are equally interesting! Everyone must buy and read these books and pass them on to others particularly the sons and daughters who as the next generation must be properly schooled in historical methodology, problem solving skills, etc.

Finally, as a supporter and student of his who has all his books in First Edition form, most of which the Author signed, and based on observations and analytic critique, this writer would like to add a 12-point summation of how one can view Dr. Yosef Alfredo Antonio ben-Jochannan's contribution as an unselfish and fearless elucidation of the historical record systematically distorted to elevate Europe and denigrate Africa designed to wreak psycho-social debasement of the African spirit and persona.

1.   Appreciation is required for the man who, for more than half a century, pursued an Afrocentric historical scholarship which challenged the behemoth of western intellectual oppression of Africa and her offsprings while simultaneously enlightening many to the wonders of a creative African cultural heritage and spirit.

2.   Commendation is due Dr. ben-Jochannan for the humanitarian work he did among the Nubians in Egypt and Sudan, viz., Aswan, Daboud, Wadi Halfa, Dongola Province and Fashoda.

3.   Giving credence to his call for racial solidarity we must recognize his call to action in what could be called cultural genocide in the African-American studies curriculum predating and in a way fueling the Afrocentric insistence on multi-culturalism.

4.   Emulation is needed of his style of critical analysis of unfolding and contemporary developments, whether it was historical omissions as in Alex Haley's *Roots*; misrepresentation in King Tut's exhibition that again took place in America recently; taking to task T. Eric Peet's "The Problem with Akhenaton;" criticism of Father Temple's *Bantu Philosophy*; challenge to another writer's description that Rameses II had "badly abscessed teeth;" and so forth.

5.   We can appreciate his identifying "They all look Alike, All!" thus linking peoples across the globe who were victims of imperialist machinations, racial hatred and cultural aggression.

6.   His clarification of the differences between the Black Nationalist and the Black Marxist was very timely and inspiring and still is.

QUINTESSENTIAL BOOK "THE HOLY LAND"

7. First to outline the *History of the Bible*, he challenged the "Black Clergy Without a Black Theology" and offered a "Black Bible for Black spiritual and religious consciousness."

8. We must acknowledge as human he may have made some mistakes, surely outweighed by the foundation of ethical and cultural Ma'at he implanted in the consciousness of African people worldwide.

9. His insistence that all African-Americans visit the Nile Valley to imbibe in the cultural heritage and grow from the intellectual exposure, but more particularly their dress code and mannerism among the people must not be construed as the "arrogance of Ugly Americans," was and is still timely, insightful and inspiring.

10. His outspoken nature, love for Marcus Garvey and Garvey's "Philosophy and Opinions," praise of "Black Goddesses," critique of Academics who are in disagreement, "fifth columns," so to speak, made him anathema to people who had more moderate historical interpretations.

11. Dr. ben-Jochannan had little respect for people in high positions who never promoted the capabilities of their subordinates, be their heritage Africa, Europe, Asian, or in solidarity with their adopted country or country of birth.

12. A staunch Pan-Africanist, he aspired to see accomplished, sustained and measurable economic, political and educational empowerment for people of African heritage worldwide. More important, he shined the light of truth and conscious intellectual awakening about Egypt that has fired an unrelenting Black intellectual challenge to misrepresentation that is beginning to make us free!

Therefore, we must recognize that Dr. ben-Jochannan has made a major contribution to African intellectual growth. He created an historical vision over time that allowed thousands to see the light. In fact, he was one of the lights of the African Diaspora! He taught us how to persevere to persevere! He asked us to standardize our learning, have a standard for our behavior, and don't fear, don't fear defeat, don't fear death! He said "Black man, worship your woman because she has done what you can't do!"

FREDERICK MONDERSON

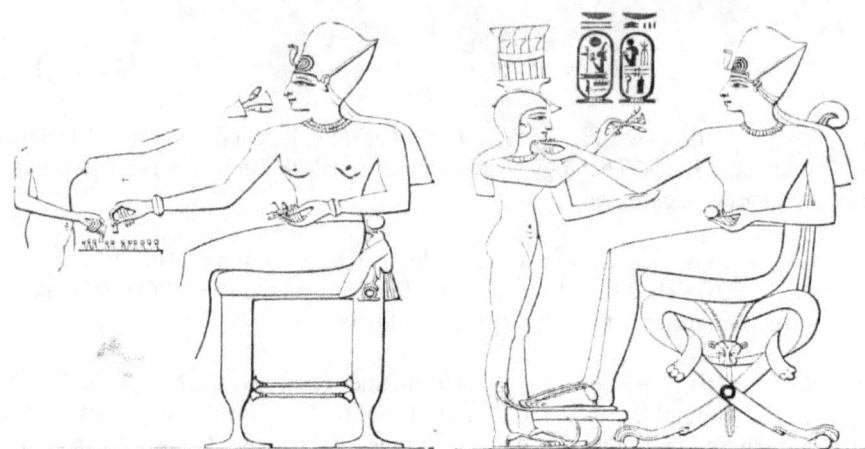

Holy Land Illustration 2. Rameses III, playing at draughts with his Ladies in the Medinet Habu Temple and seated in a Chair; on the principle of later camp-stools.

CONVERSATIONS IN THE AIRPORT LOUNGE

Dr. Leonard James: Hi. I'm Leonard James, my friends call me Lenny. This is my wife Marilyn. We are retired and making our first trip to Egypt. We're in seat 15 A and B.
Walter Brown: I'm Walter Brown. This is my wife Juliet. I'm a retired Postal Worker from Atlanta, Georgia. My wife was in sales. We're in seats 11 A and B.
Dr. Leonard James: Atlanta! We're from Atlanta! In fact, Stone Mountain. Isn't this a small world? We've been planning this trip for many years.
Walter Brown: So were we. I have heard much about ancient Egypt from my longtime friend Dr. Monderson, though I have not had time to do any serious reading about the culture.
Dr. Leonard James: I have been an educator for thirty years teaching African History and Sociology. At the foundation of much of my teaching Egypt has been a topic of great interest. Now I will be able to see firsthand some of the ideas spoken of and discussed in my classroom. My wife Marilyn was an executive secretary for a major company.
Walter Brown: I'm pretty sure I can learn a lot from you then. Fortunately, my son had done this trip before and insisted that I look, listen and learn and take lots of photographs.
Dr. Leonard James: Photographs! Yes! Egypt is a photographic paradise. As Dr. Monderson told me, it is also a historical, cultural, architectural and religious and

QUINTESSENTIAL BOOK
"THE HOLY LAND"

philosophic adventure. This trip can certainly open your eyes. I am certainly looking forward to it.

Walter Brown: Well, I can well imagine. I certainly hope to get as much out of this experience as I can. After a lengthy career as a Postal Worker, I bring a vastly different field of experience to this trip, so I may be able to benefit even more from simply being observant.

Dr. Leonard James: I tend to agree with you. I'm sure we will all grow from this experience.

Mr. Charles Palmer: Hi. I'm Charles Palmer. This is my wife Shirley. We're from Brooklyn, New York. This is our first trip to the land of ancient Kemet.

Mr. Frank James: Pleased to meet you. My name is Frank James and this is my wife Jessie. We're from Princeton, New Jersey.

Mr. Charles Palmer: This is my son Peter and his wife Mary Palmer and our grandson Cosmos Palmer. We thought making this trip together would be a wonderful experience.

Mr. Frank James: You bet'cha. This is a wonderful opportunity for you to network. It would be even easier for you as a support network. It's good that you brought the youngster along. How old is he?

Mr. Charles Palmer: He is nine years old. We have seats 12 A, B, C, D, and E. Where are you sitting?

Mr. Frank James: We're in seats 9 G and H. Well, I'm sure we will have a wonderful time. Have you been to Egypt before?

Mr. Charles Palmer: When we were first married we visited Jordan, Israel and spent two days in Cairo. However, we never had the opportunity to do much traveling, raising a family and so on. You know!

Mr. Frank James: I certainly do. I raised four children working as a mechanic and did some janitorial work also. But I have always wanted to come to Egypt. I did a little reading of it over the years. My wife worked in a bookstore and assisted my reading whenever there was some spear time.

Mr. Charles Palmer: I know how you feel and I think I know how you made it. I worked as an accountant but my wife spent a great many years caring for her sick mother so I was the principal breadwinner. Nevertheless, I'm sure we will not only get to know each other better as time goes by but this trip promises to be very enlightening and educational.

Mr. Frank James: Ok. Well nice meeting you.

Mr. Charles Palmer: Same here. See you in Egypt.

FREDERICK MONDERSON

Holy Land Papyrus 1. Goddess Isis extends her protective wings with the Cartouche of Tutankhamon, depicted within.

Mr. John Brown: Hello. I'm John Brown. This is my wife Joy. We're from Newark, New Jersey. We're in seats 9 E and F.
Dr. Madison: Hi. I'm Dr. James Madison. This is my wife, Ada. We're from Ypsilanti, Michigan. We're in 10 C and D. This is a big group we're traveling with.
Mr. John Brown: Yes. I'm told it's near fifty people.
Dr. Madison: Yes. Enough to fill a bus. Ha. Is this your first trip to Egypt? I was there ten years earlier and have wanted to get back there ever since. My practice has kept me so busy I have not been able to fulfill the promise to return. Well, finally, my wife insisted I take the time off and do this.
Mr. John Brown: I am told Egypt has a magnet that calls you back. I must certainly test this theory. Though I can't say I'll be back next year. I'm in real estate and there's an anticipated take-off in the industry. Well, if this materializes then within a few years I can probably make a return trip. Nevertheless, that is contingent on the 'theory of return' being valid.
Dr. Madison: Oh, the theory is valid enough. However, it's basically based on how much there is to see and the limited time on one of these tours. I have even heard if you drink water from the Nile River, you will definitely return.
Mr. John Brown. You seem to know a great deal about this culture.

QUINTESSENTIAL BOOK
"THE HOLY LAND"

Dr. Madison: I have been reading about Egypt since my trip ten years ago in preparation for this return. I was so impressed with the pyramids, temples and tombs I vowed to read as much as I can to validate the theory of return.
Mr. John Brown: What are some of the titles you have read? I think I need to begin collecting a bibliography of books I may find interesting.
Dr. Madison: There are standard books you can get in any of the popular Black Bookstores in any of the states. I hear New York has lots of these bookstores and that vendors even sell nothing but black books on the sidewalks. The first book I would recommend to you is one by the famous historian and Egyptologist, Dr. ben-Jochannan. It's called *Black Man of the Nile and His Family*. Another is *Abu Simbel to Ghizeh: A Guide Book and Manual*. They were described in the hand-out as part of the reading assignment and are basic history and sightseeing expositions on Egypt. They are written from within the prism of the Black experience. There are others that are of a religious and philosophical nature.
Mr. John Brown: You say we should read Dr. ben-Jochannan's as a source of broad intellectual thinking. I hear he lives in New York. I would certainly like to meet him. I did hear his name mentioned in some circles.

Ms. Malone: Dr. Benjamin, I have heard so much about you from my uncle Dr. Fred Monderson. He claims he has known you for over thirty years.
Dr. Benjamin: Yes. We go back a long way. He's a good friend and student of mine who has bought and read my books and traveled to Egypt with me on several occasions. He is very knowledgeable about Egypt. In a way I have watched him mature in understanding and writing about this culture. If I may say so, I used to say he was long winded, but in fact, he is properly equipped as a distance runner. Dr. Monderson is well equipped for the arduous task of defending Egypt as African.
Ms. Malone: These are some friends, Stephaniea McCall, Carmelitiea Shabazz, and Peter Monderson who are dying to meet you.
Stephaniea McCall: Hi, Dr. Benjamin, you are such an icon in our community; it is an honor for me to be in your presence. It means even more to speak with you and to be able to travel to Egypt with you.
Carmelitiea Shabazz: Equally too, Dr. Benjamin, it is also an honor to meet you. As a graduate student, I was required to read one of your books. It is such a powerful work that emphasizes the role of Black men in Egypt. Your outright insistence that Egypt is a Black culture of ancient Africa is troubling for some people but timely in that you pull no punches. Let me thank you for your unflinching insistence that Egypt is a Black culture!
Esperanza Rodriguez: Dr. Benjamin, you are a hero to my family. I am so thrilled to meet you and to travel to Egypt with you is an experience I will never forget.
Peter Monderson: Dr. Benjamin, nice to see you again. On two occasions you have lectured at my school, Hunter College where I studied architectural engineering, when you sat in for Dr. John Clarke. Both times your inspiring lectures were debated long after you left. To be traveling to Egypt with you is

FREDERICK MONDERSON

indeed an honor for me. For some of us who are Black conscious, you are quite an inspiration. Look for me to be in your presence throughout.

Robert Matthews: Hi. I am Bob Matthews, from Brooklyn, New York. I am seated in 11 D.
Lesley Jacobs: Hi. I'm Lesley Jacobs from Boston, Massachusetts. I'm in 12 H. Pleased to meet you. I own an electronics store. In fact, it's a Radio Shack franchise. You know, we sell gadgets of all types for the young at heart.
Robert Matthews: I am the Chief Executive of a Help Center in Brooklyn. We provide all sorts of service to the community, from counseling on public issues to computer training for all ages. I am seated in 11 D. This is my first trip to Egypt. I have heard so much of this culture that I decided to take my vacation and go to see for myself.

Frederick Maloney: Hi, Ms. Potter. What a surprise! Imagine seeing you on this trip. Are you still in Pediatrics in the Bed Tower?
Henrietta Potter: Hi, Dr. Maloney. What is the Resident Surgeon of Kings County Hospital doing going on a two-week trip to Egypt?
Frederick Maloney: I have been planning this trip for a long time. I've heard of a temple named Kom Ombo that depicts evidence of medical instruments. I would certainly like to verify this phenomenon from thousands of years ago.
Henrietta Potter: It certainly shows that the medical profession goes back a long way among those Blacks of ancient Africa. Where are you seated? I am in 12 G.
Frederick Maloney: How interesting. I'm in 12 F. We must continue this discussion on board.
Henrietta Potter: Without a doubt. Perhaps next year we can encourage some other medical people to make the trip.
Frederick Maloney: I agree. I need to get some duty-free items. See you on board.
Henrietta Potter: Ok.

Teddy Cubia: Hi I'm Teddy Cubia. I am a retired New York City educator, I'm in 11 J.
Dr. Alexander Pushkin: I'm Dr. Alexander Pushkin and this is my wife, Holly, we're in 15 G, H. We are returning to Egypt after a 15 year absence. This will be a very memorable experience for us, since it has been a constant topic in our home.
Teddy Cubia: There is a young man I want you to meet. Here he comes now. Hello Michael. This is Michael Sinclair. Michael, this is Dr. Alexander Pushkin and his wife, Holly.
Michael Sinclair: Please to meet you folks. I'm from the Philadelphia area and a graduate of Temple University.
Teddy Cubia: That's great. Isn't that where Afrocentricity originated?
Michael Sinclair: It certainly did. Dr. Molefi Asante is the contemporary author of that school of thought.

QUINTESSENTIAL BOOK
"THE HOLY LAND"

Dr. Pushkin: I have seen him on *Nightline*. There are some things I need to have clarified about his idea of Afrocentricity. Maybe you could be helpful.
Michael Sinclair: I will be glad to. As a graduate of Temple University's Afrocentric Institute there are a lot of questions I am forced to answer about that school of thought.
Teddy Cubia: We will be glad to have you answer any questions we have about the subject.
Michael Sinclair: One of the things I learnt from Dr. Asante is, always remain prepared and "Never let a historic situation pass you by without writing about it." He has sternly insisted we take the most copious notes, which I did!
Dr. Pushkin: That is so reassuring.

Michelliea Georges: Regina, I would like you to meet George Washington. He graduated from Hunter College in 1976. We met at a friend recently and he told me he was on this trip.
Regina Hendricks: Pleased to meet you. You don't look that old to me. Are you as smart as you are handsome? I'm a psych major at the University of Michigan. What was your major studying at Hunter?
George Washington: I studied History at Hunter College and was pleased to meet Dr. Clarke and Dr. ben-Jochannan. But the person who impressed me the most was the young Professor Donna Richards or Merimba Ani, who had just started teaching there. I did courses in art history, ancient history and "Black Studies," which is what Dr. Richards' and Prof. Clarke's Department was called at the time.
Michelliea Georges: At Temple University's Department of African-American Studies, my major is African-American History with a Minor in Egyptian Studies.
George Washington: I hear you have some heavy hitters at that school. Who is the Department head?
Michelliea Georges: Dr. Molefi Kete Asante is the Chairman of the Afrocentric Institute. In that school of thought, there is a great deal of emphasis on the role of the ancient Egyptians in establishing the parameters of knowledge in the ancient world and its impact on the modern. In fact, they do sponsor a trip to Egypt but I wanted to go on Dr. Monderson's trip because Dr. Benjamin is on this one.
Regina Hendricks: Yes, but I hear this elder is only along in a listening or advisory capacity.
Michelliea Georges: But I expect he may give a lecture or two. We have to see, but I feel we are so privileged to be able to be with such a distinguished scholar. This should be an extraordinary trip. Where are you guys seated?
George Washington: I'm in 11 B.
Michelliea Georges: I'm in 11 A.
Regina Hendricks: You guys are sitting together but I am in 10 J. Two seniors together on the same trip. This should be interesting. Perhaps we could prepare a paper each about our experiences that can be attached to our theses.
Michelliea Georges: I'm way ahead of you guys.

FREDERICK MONDERSON

George Washington: Since you guys have exams coming up, I figure I may be able to help you both. I have my lap-top computer with me and it has all my notes from my years at Hunter College. I did a course on "Ancient History" with Professor Richard Hogan and "African Religious Thought Systems" with Professor Donna Richards.
Regina Hendricks: That is great. You could "feed us" whenever we are together, on the bus, at dinner or wherever.
George Washington: Ok.

Holy Land Papyrus 2. Goddess Ma'at kneels and extends her protective wings before Isis with Hathor enthroned while Horus as Ra-Horakhty escorts Queen Nefertari.

Michael Montout: Say, aren't you that young theologian from the University of Michigan? I'm Michael Montout from Ypsilanti.
James Morrison: Well, yes. I teach religion at the University of Michigan. Small world that two Michigonians could be on the same trip. In fact, I think a pastor and his wife from Philadelphia are also traveling with us.
Michael Montout: Here they are right now. Sir, may I introduce you to a fellow "Man of the Cloth." This is Prof. James Morrison who teaches religion at the University of Michigan.
Dr. McFlair: Well, it's good to see young people interested in Biblical Studies.
Michael Montout: Dr. McFlair, I don't teach religion. I am a practicing minister myself. I have a church and school in Ypsilanti, Michigan.
Dr. McFlair: Good for you. I did not introduce my wife, this is Mrs. McFlair. We are in seats 14 B, C.
Michael Montout: I'm in 9 C.
James Morrison: I'm in 15 D. Perhaps we could exchange some ideas on this trip that would make interesting discussion when I return to class in September.

QUINTESSENTIAL BOOK
"THE HOLY LAND"

Michael Montout: Be glad to. I have a few questions about religion and philosophy that you may be able to help me with.
James Morrison: Ok. Perhaps during some of those breakfasts, lunches and dinners we can sit together and discuss such.
Michael Montout: Great.

Mr. Sylvester Singleton: Hi. This is my wife Regina. We are celebrating our Fiftieth Wedding Anniversary. I think we are seated next to you. We're in 10 E, F.
Mr. John Stewart: I think you are right. This is my wife Glenda. We have only been married fifteen years. We are in seats 10 G, H.

California Lady: Hi. Have we met before? I do a lot of traveling across the country to speak on motivational issues. I'm in 33 A.
Hattie Jones: Perhaps. This is Jerome Smith, my soul mate. We may have met before. Nevertheless, we are in 14 D, E.
Asantewaa Harris: Did I hear correctly that both Dr. Benjamin and Dr. John Africa are on this trip?
Hattie Jones: You certainly did. Both are here. Well, it's time to board. See you on the plane.

Joshua Monderson: Hello, Cherise. I did not know you were going on this trip? How's your family? Where are you seated?
Cherise Maloney: Hi, Joshua Monderson. Well fancy meeting you here. My family is fine. I see you are accompanying your brother on this trip. I am seated in 16 A.
Joshua Monderson: I am right next to you in 16 B. This should be an interesting flight. We can discuss some of my brother's work as time permits.
Cherise Maloney: Sure. It will be a great opportunity for me. I am also glad to return to Egypt with Dr. Monderson.
Joshua Monderson: I know you are.

Michael Sinclair: Hi Dr. Benjamin. I have heard so much about you. As a graduate of Temple University's Afrocentric Institute, we studied much of your work and it is thus an honor for me to be traveling to Egypt with you.
Dr. Benjamin: Thank you young man. John, so we are on another of those wonderful trips to the motherland. How many times have we done this?
Dr. John Africa: I can't remember. Do you remember the first trip we did together? When was it?
Dr. Benjamin: The first time I remember we traveled together to Egypt was in 1957. That first time was indeed memorable. There must have been six persons with us. That time I was able to purchase my illustrated copy of the *Book of the*

FREDERICK MONDERSON

Dead for a price that was extremely reasonable by today's standards. I don't even think you could get one today.

Dr. John Africa: Most of the antiquities they try to sell today are basically fakes. I was able to begin my book collection however. Do you remember the little bookstore, Aboudy, in Luxor? At that time they seemed to have everything.

Dr. Benjamin: One thing I seem to notice, being African-American; books published after 1960 seem to systematically exclude our people from their rightful place in the historical and philosophical narrative and processes of this important African culture. It's as if there was, and is a conspiracy to deny any meaningful role of African people not only in Egypt but also from the historical record. Had we not stayed the course our people probably would not have any meaningful record that gives the African people credit for the things they created.

Dr. John Africa: Let us not forget the work of J.A. Rogers and John Huggins and John Jackson and some of the younger writers like Van Sertima, Browder, Asante, and so on. It's like Molefi Asante wants to "Give Africans agency as subjects not objects of history." Hope you are taking notes young man!

Michael Sinclair: "I certainly am, sir."

Dr. Benjamin: True, but I refer to works that specifically dealt with Egypt. We must continue this on board; we have to take our seats. Remember this is an eleven-hour trip so there will be lots of time for us to move around the plane and to reminisce. Let's Go.

Dr. John Africa: Ok.

ON BOARD EGYPT AIR FLIGHT 988 TO CAIRO

Ladies and Gentlemen, this is Captain Farouk Mohammed. We just leveled off at 35,000 feet and will be cruising at a speed of 550 miles an hour. For those of you who so desire, you can plot the duration of our flight on the television between movies. The estimated flying time is 10 hours and 35 minutes. Our estimated time of arrival is 11:52 AM. The temperature in Cairo is 84 degrees and sunny. Indications are that we will have a smooth flight. So relax and enjoy. There is music on the channels and two movies are scheduled. There is no smoking on board. As soon as possible after we have leveled off, I will turn the seat-belt sign off for you to move about. However, while seated please keep your seat belt fastened and return to your seats promptly when the seat-belt sign comes back on. Refreshments will be served soon and we will also serve Dinner and Breakfast before arrival. Enjoy the flight.

Speed: **550 miles per hour**
Altitude   **35,000 feet**

QUINTESSENTIAL BOOK
"THE HOLY LAND"

Distance	**5, 857 miles**
Time - Destination	**10 hrs, 35 mins.**
Arrive – Destination	**11:52 Cairo Time**

Captain Mohammed: Ladies and gentlemen, we're on final approach to Cairo International Airport. We should be on the ground in 15 minutes. Cabin Crew, please cross check and prepare for landing.

Ladies and Gentlemen, This is the Captain. We have landed at Cairo International Airport. The time now is 11:00 AM. The temperature is 88 degrees Fahrenheit. After Immigration and Customs, please register any Video Cameras you have in your possession. Thank you for flying Egypt Air.

Day 2.   CAIRO

Esperanza Rodriguez: Hello, Mi Amor. The connecting flight to Luxor is about two hours from now. The luggage is to be transferred and we can perhaps visit the duty free shops in the airport. I have duplicated and handed out to the group your selection on the Nile Valley. As you indicated, when we get to Luxor and are checked in, then you will give the Introductory Briefing.

Dr. Fred Monderson: That is correct. I must remind the group that they have to register their video cameras with Customs after they have visited Immigration. Thank you, my dear.

THE NILE VALLEY
By
Fred Monderson

"The Nile Valley"

More and more as we move from celebrating *Black History Month*, *Women's History Month* and *April's Stand for Children* every year, lest we forget, the ancient African country called Kemet (today's Egypt) holds the keys to a rich African, African-American heritage in philosophy, science, astronomy, mathematics, medicine, religion and architecture and that women also made early contributions of significance. Now, there's an ever-present need to remind young brothers and sisters as well as their parents and grandparents, that they must read, "Form study groups," visit museums and if possible the Nile Valley. More importantly, they must sign on to defend Kemet (Egypt) as African! The strength of this resolve will buoy any intellectual quest and social up-lift effort by virtue of the great diversity of knowledge bases innovated by ancient Africans, that today provide the foundations for much of modern social thought and practice. Greece and Rome did this for Europe and still plays an important part in American education. However, let us not forget Egypt's influence on Greece and Greek thought.

The Nile Valley is one of Africa's and the ancient world's early centers of civilization. Taken together with Mesopotamia's "Tigris-Euphrates," India's "Indus Valley," and China's "Hwang Ho," the years of continuous government and cultural growth in these areas staggers the imagination.

However, the Nile River is unique. Of the world's major rivers, it's the only one flowing south to north. All others flow north to south! That river is fed by the White Nile from Uganda, the Blue Nile from Ethiopia and the Atbara which joins it below Khartoum in Nubia. During the Pleistocene Age (same as the Ice Age) lasting from one million to about 10,000 B.C., there were Nile River terraces, according to Fairservis, that have been traced at: "300, 200, 150, 100, 50, 30, and 10 feet above present level, each indicating an old bed of the Nile." This meant the river was more voluminous as far back into the past as one can imagine.

Walter A. Fairservis, Jr. in *The Ancient Kingdoms of the Nile* (New York: New American Library, 1962) explained, "traces of man are found beginning with the 100-foot terrace, indicating that during that part of the Pleistocene, when the Nile was one hundred foot higher than now, man began the long occupation of the valley that was to witness so much of human history."

The volume of the Nile attracted man and wild beasts to the oasis it had etched between the two deserts. The river first domesticated man and then animals. V. Gordon Childe's *New Light on the Most Ancient East* believed the Wadis along the desert were veritable gardens where could be found, "herds of wild asses, Barbary sheep, urus, antelope, gazelles, giraffes and the lions and leopards that preyed thereon." The swamps fringing the river supported elephants, kudu, and two kinds of wild pigs, hippopotami, crocodiles, and wild boars.

Science Magazine, in an article in the February 1982 issue, discussed the beginnings of agriculture along the Nile, from about 15,000 and 16,500 years ago – all this, while ice still covered much of Europe and America. At this early date these first humans, African peoples, were already raising crops of wheat, barley,

QUINTESSENTIAL BOOK
"THE HOLY LAND"

lentils, chickpeas, capers and dates, as well as moving towards creating laws, language and establishing cultural traditions. They were doing it in the flood-plains of the Nile and the bordering Eastern and Western Deserts, much as people would continue to do for perhaps 13,000 years until the classical Egyptian civilization arose, and on into modern times. While these dates may seem far-fetched, the people of ancient Kemet, in today's North Africa, however, claim to have an historical time-frame of 26,000 years, based on the astronomical great Precession. This phenomenon, notwithstanding, the argument that farming "began" in the "fertile crescent" and spread to Kemet/Egypt, about 4500 B.C., needs back-dating by thousands of years. Further, the argument for an 8,000-10,000 B.C. "Near Eastern origin" for cultivated agriculture needs new attention, as does the origination date of Egyptian civilization. This area of study may be thousands of years older than previously suspected.

Africans on the Nile around the Khartoum area are known to have practiced some form of planting of wild seeds in the Wadi catch basins at 12,000-11,000 B.C. This farming was seasonal and not extensive. They have, however, only left implements for grinding grains after the harvest that gives evidence of their level of technological sophistication.

An even more revolutionary find was the discovery published in *The New York Times* newspaper of February 8, 1970. Accordingly, South African archaeologists reported the discovery of a 43,000 year-old mine carbon dated at Yale and Groningen. Found in neighboring Swaziland in an iron-ore mountain, stone-age tools left by prehistoric man indicate that early ancient Africans had been mining hematite-a source of iron. The early miners had excavated for hematite rich in specularite-one of the most prized pigments and cosmetics of ancient times. Professor John H. Clarke, one of this writer's teachers and African Historian *Emeritus* of Hunter College, CUNY, when quizzed about this find, replied: "Since man had reached a level of cultural sophistication to do any form of mining he had to have had a large population." As such, Dr. Clarke posited the existence of agricultural practices to feed that population which must have been large. This, then, adds another dimension to the argument as to when agriculture really began in Africa, for the first sophisticated human or prototype human population.

FREDERICK MONDERSON

Holy Land Papyrus 3. The Great Pyramids at Ghizeh and the Sphinx, guardian of the Necropolis in the foreground.

Holy Land Papyrus 3a. Tutankhamon sits in his chair astride a papyrus boat as his wife, Ankh-es-en-pa-Aten before the return to Thebes and Ankh-en-en-Amen after the return to Thebes, who offers two lotus flowers and he admires the birds and other flowers.

QUINTESSENTIAL BOOK
"THE HOLY LAND"

Holy Land Photo 1. Abu Simbel Temple of Rameses II. Kashida Maloney of Brooklyn, New York, stands before the colossal seated statues of Rameses II entrancing his Temple.

CONFERENCE WITH ASSISTANT
Day 1. DEPARTURE FROM New York JFK AIRPORT

FREDERICK MONDERSON

        Check-In
Day 2.   **CAIRO**
        LUXOR: **Check-In at the SONESTA HOTEL**

Day 3.   **LUXOR: East Bank**
        KARNAK TEMPLE
        LUXOR TEMPLE

Day 4.   **LUXOR: West Bank I**
        VALLEY OF THE KINGS
        DEIR EL BAHARI
        THE RAMESSEUM

Day 5.   **LUXOR: West Bank II**
        MEDINET HABU
        ALABASTER FACTORY

Day 6.   **ABYDOS AND DENDERA**
        ABYDOS
        DENDERA

Day 7.   **LUXOR TO ASWAN**

QUINTESSENTIAL BOOK
"THE HOLY LAND"

ESNEH TEMPLE OF GOD KHNUM
EDFU TEMPLE OF GOD HORUS
KOM OMBO TEMPLE OF SOBEK AND HAROEIS

ASWAN

Check-In at the Oberoi Hotel at Aswan.

Day 8. **ASWAN**
ABU SIMBEL

Day 9. **ASWAN**
TEMPLE OF ISIS
KALABSHA TEMPLE OF GOD MENDULESE

Day 10. **ASWAN**
HIGH DAM

FREDERICK MONDERSON

**UNFINISHED OBELISK
LOTUS MEMORIAL**

**Day 11. ASWAN
TOMBS OF THE NOBLES
(Optional)
MAUSOLEUM OF AGA KHAN
KITCHENER GARDENS
(Optional)
OLD CATARACT GARDENS
(Optional)
BOATING ON THE NILE
(Optional)**

**Day 12. Free for afternoon travel to Cairo
CAIRO Check-in
CAIRO
SAKKARA
STEP-PYRAMID
MASTABA OF PTAH-HOTEP
MASTABA OF KA-GEMNI**

QUINTESSENTIAL BOOK
"THE HOLY LAND"

      MEMPHIS MUSEUM
      Rameses II's Statue
      The Alabaster Sphinx

Day 13 CAIRO
          GHIZEH PYRAMIDS
          PAPYRUS MUSEUM

Day 14. CAIRO
          EGYPTIAN MUSEUM OF ANTIQUITIES
          KHALILI BAZAAR
          GOODBYE CELEBRATION
          SUMMATION OF THE ENTIRE TRIP

Day 15. CAIRO AIRPORT
          FLIGHT TO NEW YORK
          NEW YORK
          JFK ARRIVAL HOME

FREDERICK MONDERSON

Holy Land Photo 2. Abu Simbel Temple of Rameses II. Bust of one of two right side seated colossal statues of Rameses and smaller figures of the King offering Ma'at to Ra Horakhty, tutelary deity of this Temple.

The year 4241 B.C. is the accepted date for the invention of the "Calendar" of the cultural history of ancient Kemet. This time register was based on an annual observation of the "inundation" of the Nile River. Such a calendar consisted of 3 seasons of 4 months each, and each month had 30 days, for a total 360-day year. Soon their priestly scholars intercalated or inserted by adding 5 days for a total 365-day year. However, while this was still short ¼-day, according to Cheikh Anta Diop, they had known this from as early as c. 4241 B.C. and corrected this disparity by adding 1-year every Sothic Cycle of 1460 years. This was the real "leap year" and not the present addition of a day every four years in February, which can really be considered a "leap day."

The *Inundation* lasted 4 months and covered the land. The river deposited a thick, rich, black, alluvial substance which acted as fertilizer. Equally Broderick's *Dictionary of Egyptian Archaeology* (1902) mentions "boat building" as one of the most important trades in the Nile Valley. Boats were made for fishing, leisure, funeral, and transport. Philosophically, the Sun God rode across the sky in a solar barque or sun-boat, allowing ceremonial as well as divine boats to be found in the religious writings and beliefs systems.

At various places, such as Abu Simbel, Aswan, Kom Ombo, and Memphis, Nilometers were set up to measure the river's volume, according to Wallis Budge. Through a viable post-Inundation strategy, engineers surveyed the lands to

QUINTESSENTIAL BOOK
"THE HOLY LAND"

demarcate land-holdings and to facilitate effective farming techniques. As a result, the prosperous Kemetic culture of the Nile Valley, with agriculture as a mainstay, gave the nation an enormous food surplus, and the development of arts and crafts that signaled establishment of cultural mores and traditions. Their ingenuity became a powerful bargaining asset for trade and other relations with neighboring states in and outside Africa. Thus, whether in trade, religion - with its Heaven/Hell concepts and moral demands, transportation, farming, division of labor and specialization of crafts, mathematics, art and architecture, mining and industry, and even defense, the Nile permeated every aspect of this ancient African civilization's way of life.

In a land essentially rainless, the first pharaohs were able to assure prosperity by harnessing the potent waters of the river through a system of irrigation. They transported water great distances, via, canals. These canals also served as waterways for light boat-travel. Importantly, through practical systems of maintenance, these canals more land was brought under effective cultivation. The multi-disciplinary bureaucracy that grew up around the required labor organization could predict and worship, harness and even store water from the bounty of the Nile. Rainfall along the Nile ranges from about 3 to 6 inches in Cairo to diminishing amounts as the boat sails from north to south. In contrast, we get as much as 76 inches, perhaps annually sometimes even more, in the United States.

After the water had receded from the Nile's flood, farmers planted. At the end of final harvest, the land again became parched and dry. The Pharaoh filled the gap, by providing water from his stored-up sources in lakes and reservoirs. In this desert-like time of need, his largess made him larger than life. The Pharaoh, in control of the Nile, had at his disposal an administrative network that conducted national, regional and local affairs and leveled taxes to support this work.

Hydraulic engineering was employed in raising dams, dikes and embankments; draining swamps; cutting canal sluices and transporting water. The water wheel and shaduf were used to raise water to higher levels. So, controlling and exploiting the river aided early man's innovative and scientific efforts to settle in the Nile Valley and to produce bountiful harvests. The Nile was rich in phosphates and the inundation thoroughly covered the land. Many times, if managed properly, this enriching process allowed two or three crops to be grown annually.

Magic was among the priests' repertoire for insuring a Nile flood of sufficient quantity. Many important religious ceremonies were connected with the river called "Hapi." For example, there were ceremonies of "Opening of the Dykes" and "Opening of the Basins." Here the Pharaoh and his religious bureaucracy of priests officiated by blessing the waters, the land and commencement of the farming season. This body, called the Priesthood, consisted of the learned scholars, intellectuals of their day, who not only administered to religious beliefs and practices, but also kept records and trained engineers and mathematicians to survey the land after the destruction of the inundation, which removed all boundary marks. Through this strategy, priests were then able to predict grain output, levy taxes, and store grain for their temples.

From this vantage point they observed the river for untold generations. They noticed patterns in opposites as nature unfolded. Around them they saw the Nile and desert juxtaposed, cultivation and wilderness side by side, fecundity and barrenness everywhere; life and death; and, good and evil ever-present. So, their theologians created religious thought, a primeval mound, and myths explaining creation, an important element of ancient religion. Out of worship of local gods, Heliopolis, Memphis, Abydos and Thebes, Hermopolis, became important theological centers, each perpetuating and seeking to assure the primacy of their god and that cult. The river, throughout it all, was paramount and lucrative.

Natural resources were bountiful and predictable while the Nile was unpredictable. The river fluctuated. Some years it was "too high" and this brought overflow and destruction. "Too low" a Nile meant insufficient grain production and difficult times. Yet still, an agricultural bounty pervaded the valley that, in addition to wheat, grain, barley and ember, farmed in the riverain plain, personal gardens were also used to good advantage. That is, as far as possible, every family kept a vegetable garden and a large tree in the yard, to provide shade from the sun.

Food stuff comprising the villager's diet included wheat, barley, vetch or legumes, and dates, together with what he was able to grow in kitchen gardens. They planted vegetables that included leeks, onions, lettuce, melons, cucumbers, beans, other pulses, radishes, and garlic. Vegetable oils were used in cooking, lighting and cosmetics. Medicine mostly came from the balanos and moringa trees, and from sesame and castor oil plants. Fruits included figs, date palms, grapes, pomegranates, and carob, a chocolate-type legume.

QUINTESSENTIAL BOOK "THE HOLY LAND"

Holy Land Illustration 3. Spearing the Hippopotamus (left); and Spear used in the chase of the Hippopotamus (right).

Trees grew along the Nile but not in sufficient quantity to provide wood for building and much of the cedars had to be imported from Lebanon, while other woods came from elsewhere. Nevertheless, ancient Kemet still had a varied flora that is worth mentioning. There were marsh plants, papyrus and three varieties of blue, white and pink lotus, that are sparse today. The sycamore and date palm trees were imported from Central Africa and adapted well to the environment of lower down the Nile. The tamarisk, nabk, moringa, and carob or locust trees also grew along the Nile. So too did several varieties of acacia and Mimosa-sont, mimosa habbas, white acacia. Farnesiana - and pomegranate trees increase in number with distance from the Mediterranean. There were also the dom-palm, willow and Persea trees.

Many trees were sacred to these Africans of ancient Kemet who began to use stone for building preferring to use their trees for shade from the hot sun, for fruit and for flowers. The sacred trees included the Persea, *Mimusops Schimperi*, and the *Ished* tree of Heliopolis, the *Sycamore*.

The papyrus is a most ubiquitous plant all along the Nile. From earliest times this plant provided materials for making paper and scrolls upon which much of the language, called *Medu Netcher*, was written. Still, inscriptions in stone are also abundant. The papyrus is memorialized in the decorated tombs of the monarchs and nobles showing daily life scenes, and on papyri found during excavations at Abydos, Thebes, and other locations where modern scholars and others searched and plundered. Strangely, plunder was a problem in the early kingdoms. Papyri tell of religious happenings and beliefs, stories, tales, poems, biographies, and even medical treatises. They also include laundry lists. There were tomb desecrations for purposes of robbery.

Herbs were an essential part of religious practices of embalming and preparing the dead, and also used in medicine. Plants found growing in many places include: woody nightshade, mandrake, wild cherry, olive, cornflower, and petals of blue and white lilies. Myrrh and incense trees were brought from Nubia and used in religious practices in temples. Domestic animals were available very early in the pre-historic period. While the dog was probably man's earliest companion, there were more domestic animals he came to rely on for food and labor, such as oxen and cows.

Serpents were mainly indigenous to Egypt/Kemet. Some were harmless, like the colubers and the haje viper. The asp was worshiped under the name of the uraeus. Philosophically and practically this snake was part of pharaonic regalia, worn on the forehead of the pharaoh as a symbolic protector. It occasionally attains a length of six and a half feet, and when approached will erect its head and inflate its throat in readiness for darting forward. The bite is fatal. The crocodile and hippopotamus have practically disappeared except in the extreme south, in Nubia.

Fish could be viewed as an extension of the river. The Nile catfish was sacred, because of its relationship to the God Osiris. There were other varieties of fish. Catching them generated an additional industry that was also a life giving sustenance and delighted the kitchens of both high and low. Some of the sea fish enter from the Mediterranean and inhabit the fresh water. These included Shad, Mullet, Perch and the Labrus. Many of the fish came from Ethiopia and Central Africa with the flow of the Nile. With the construction of the first and second Aswan Dam, this has been impeded. Nevertheless, early fish from the Upper Nile River include two kinds of Alesetes, the soft-shelled turtle, the Bagrus Docmac, and the Mormyrus. The Bagrus Bayad and the turtle grow to about one yard, and the Labrus to three and a half yards in length.

Birds from afar migrated to enjoy the oasis spanning the Eastern and Western Deserts. Such birds of Europe as swallows, quails, geese, wild ducks and herons make the trek annually. The Nile water was special, it had life giving virtues. The local bird population included geese, white and black ibises, red flamingoes, duck, quails, swans, pelicans, coromants, pigeons, and chickens. Birds that migrated and remained to acclimatize include turtledoves, mag-pipes, the kingfisher, the partridge and the sparrow. Birds of prey included the eagle and falcon, the merlin, the bald-headed vulture, the kestel, and the golden sparrow.

QUINTESSENTIAL BOOK "THE HOLY LAND"

Holy Land Illustration 4. The mythological cow of Hathor (left); and again carrying the Deceased and his Ba into the "Afterlife" (right).

Wine was made from sap, grapes, arrack and beer from barley. Game hunting was a longtime sport of men, especially the nobles. The wealthy could afford to go hunting and display in their tombs, pictures of wonderful times in the marshes. Prey included antelope, ibex, ostriches, hares, gazelles and oryx. These then added to the diversity of flora and fauna this region of Africa produced in the ancient history of man.

Minerals abound in the jewelry and beautiful works of art and architecture are a reflection of ancient African wealth, creations and achievements. The natural disposition of the geography lends itself to challenge the mind of ancient man to quarry and mine. Gold, silver, electrum, copper, tin and later bronze generated craftsmanship and artistry that have defied the ages. Semi-precious stones included carnelian, garnets, jaspers, rock crystal, amazonite, and amethyst. They were worked rather well and today adorn displays in museums around the globe in cities such as Brooklyn, Manhattan, Paris, London and elsewhere worldwide. A significant number of "private collections" of antiquities are known to exist.

Quarrying has been an industry ever since the first stone structure was erected along the Nile. Obelisks and other colossi erected at such sites as Karnak, Luxor, Abu Simbel, Heliopolis and a number of other places attest to quarrying, river transport of stone as well as architectural and artistic adroitness. These accomplishments impressed worshipers and visitors, who today continue to marvel at the religious significance of the structures where the gods could be reached.

The Nile Valley with its wide diversity of people, resources, natural phenomena, plant and animal life came together to speak Africa's conscience, philosophy, science and arts to the world. The impact then and now remain incalculable and poses a challenge for African-Americans who must defend the legacy of ancient Egypt, Kemet, as African. The rewards remain abundant since practically every genre of knowledge; Viz., philosophy, medicine, astronomy, agriculture, writing, architecture, art, government, mathematics and religion have all been formulated, rehearsed and played out on that important world stage. Thus, Mother Africa spoke through her two oldest daughters Ethiopia and Egypt/Kemet.

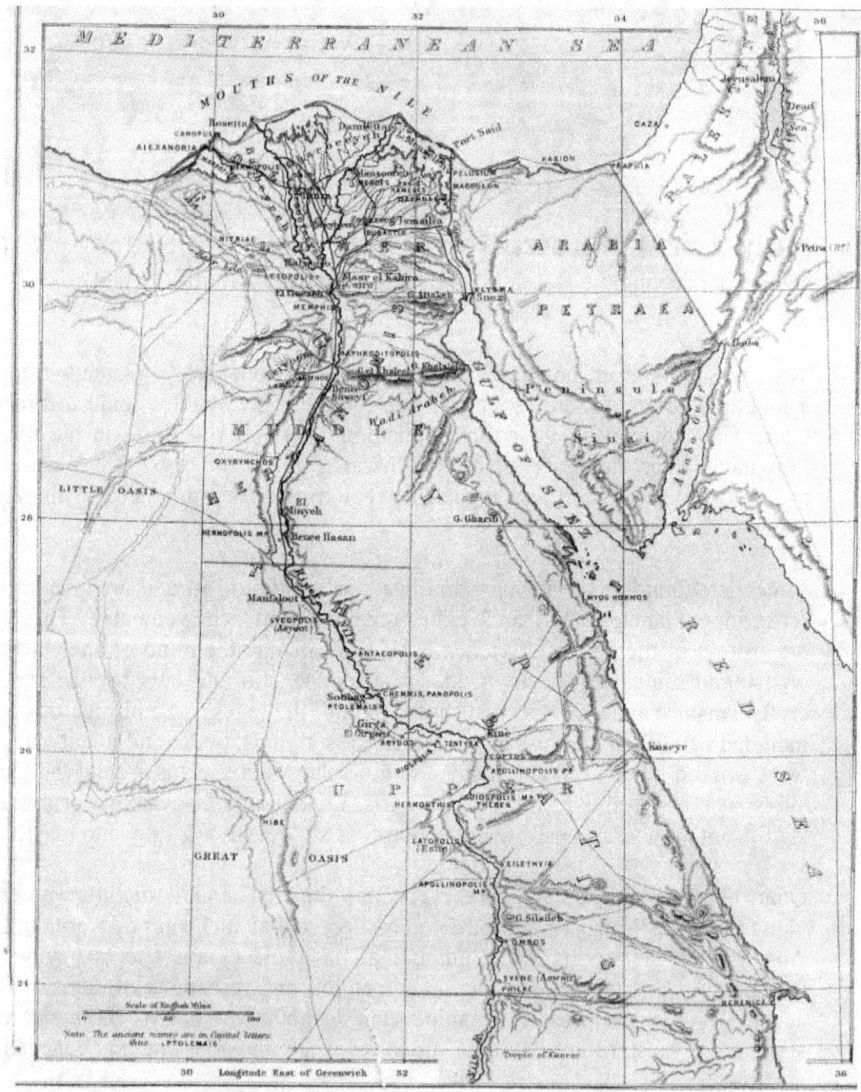

Holy Land - Map of Egypt and the Nile Valley showing (*Encyclopedia Britannica*, 9th Edition, 1911) principally Graeco-Roman names of sites used deliberately in 19th Century scholars' ingrained description as some have affirmed as "part of the conspiracy against ancient Egypt."

QUINTESSENTIAL BOOK "THE HOLY LAND"

REFERENCES

Aldred, Cyril. *The Egyptians.* New York: Thames and Hudson, (1961) 1987.
_____. *Egypt to the End of the Old Kingdom.* London: Thames and Hudson, 1965.
Baines, John and Jaromir Malek. *Atlas of Ancient Egypt.* New York: Facts on File, 1980.
Bartlett, John. *Familiar Quotations.* (Fourteenth Edition) (Emily Morison Beck, Editor). Boston: Little, Brown and Company, (1882) 1968 (Sixth Printing).
ben-Jochannan, Yosef A. A. *Blackman of the Nile and his Family.* Baltimore, MD: Black Classics Press, (1972) 1989.
Broderick, M. *Dictionary of Egyptian Archaeology.* New York: 1902.
Budge, E.A.W. *Dwellers on the Nile.* New York: Benjamin Bloom, Inc., (1885) 1972.
Childe, V. Gordon. *New Light on the Most Ancient East.* New York: W.W. Norton, 1933.
Diop, Cheikh Anta. "Africa: Cradle of Humanity" in *Nile Valley Civilizations.* Edited by Ivan Van Sertima. New Brunswick, New Jersey: *Journal of African Civilizations*, (1985) 1986.
Fairservis, Walter. *Ancient Kingdoms of the Nile.* New York: New American Library, 1962.
_____. *Egypt: Gift of the Nile.* New York: Macmillan, 1963.
Jackson, John. *Introduction to African Civilizations.* Secaucus, New Jersey: Citadel Press, (1970) 1974.

Arrival at Luxor Airport and met by representatives of the travel company Sunny Climes, then transported by bus to our hotel, the Sonesta at Luxor.

FREDERICK MONDERSON

DAY 2: LUXOR HOTEL CHECK IN AND ORIENTATION

Dr. Fred Monderson. Good Afternoon, my brothers and sisters. We made it to Luxor! We're staying at the Sonesta Hotel! This is a city of extraordinary historical importance. It has been around and dominated this nation and the world longer than any other nation on earth. Look around. Learn. Be wise. Many of you who are from such places as New York, California, Chicago and Detroit, know of slicksters. However, the slickest people I know of are in this African city. So be careful. When you go out do so in pairs or in groups. Try to do all your shopping in the daylight. There are not many places to go at nights, but do be careful if you go out at night. Be careful at all times. The Tourist Police make an extraordinary effort to aid tourists. Do not be too surprised by the escorts they provide for us. As I said they make a special effort to ensure our security.

This is an educational trip for you to become wiser. As the proverb says, we are seeking knowledge, wisdom and understanding. Let us share experiences, talk to each other at breakfast, dinner, on the bus and everywhere. Let us multiply our knowledge. Discuss the lectures, the temples, tombs, guides, Nile River, museums, pyramids and let us all gain from the experience. Take lots of photographs. Ask your questions; inject any and all words and ideas of wisdom you may have encountered in your various walks of life. Let us make this trip interesting and memorable, so that we can all grow from what I like to call an adventure. In fact, I have always considered Egypt to be an intellectual, spiritual, religious, artistic, historical, cultural and photographic adventure. Investigate and experience all of this and share with your roommates, dinner partners, those you sit next to on the bus, shop with and let us all share ideas to grow even more. We must transform ourselves intellectually and spiritually from simply being bold enough to travel to Egypt, cradle of civilization and the modern state, land of the ancestors. This mindset we must take home with us and educate our brethren. We owe this to the ancestors.

We could start with Imhotep (c. 2600 B.C.) who said, "Man, know thyself!" Then to Socrates (469-399 B.C.) who believed: "There is only one good, knowledge, and one evil, ignorance." Even further, Aristotle who said in his *Metaphysics*, "All men by nature desire knowledge." Ezekiel spoke of "The ancients of days" and that "many shall run to and fro, and knowledge shall be increased." We are no different! Let us also remember Sir Francis Bacon (1561-1626), who said in his *Meditations*: "Knowledge is power," and, in his *Letter to Lord Burleigh* (1592) he noted: "I have taken all knowledge to be my province." Let us do that! Equally too, Lord Tennyson implored: "Let knowledge grow from more to more." Even Proverbs offers: "Where there is no vision, the people perish," and that "A wise

QUINTESSENTIAL BOOK "THE HOLY LAND"

man is strong; yea, a man of knowledge increaseth strength." Therefore, let us all contribute elements of strength and make an effort to change ourselves, families, communities, country, and if possible, the world. Dr. ben-Jochannan always asked, in referring to the trip to Egypt: "Now that you have the knowledge, what are you going to do with it?" All the prized virtues must become part of our repertoire. We must imbibe and demonstrate wisdom, justice, fortitude, temperance, ambition, resourcefulness, creativity and devotion.

The *Psalms* offered: "So teach us to number our days, that we may apply our hearts to wisdom," and that "The fear of the lord is the beginning of wisdom."

Finally, Joseph Joubert (1754-1824) informed: "To teach is to learn twice," and "Ask the young; they know everything." Let us not forget our two young brothers Eric Joel and Bryce Menkheperre for they are the future. Talk to them, teach them, and learn from them and hopefully they will carry the well-lit torch we will so brilliantly light as we explore the knowledge of the ancients, and the glory and wisdom of the ancestors. Whenever we are asked as Job did: "Where shall wisdom be found, and where is the place of understanding," let them know it is here in Egypt. Let it be known, Charles William Eliot (1834-1926) once read an *Inscription on the 1890 Gate to Harvard Yard* that aptly describes what we are about: "Enter to grow in wisdom, depart better to serve thy country and wisdom." As for myself, I am apt to echo sentiments of Confucius (551-479 B.C.) in his *Analects*, Book VII: "I am not one who was born in the possession of knowledge; I am one who is fond of antiquity, and earnest in seeking it there." This is what we the privileged must teach others. With much modesty, I bequeath this work to my people, the Black People of America, the African Diaspora and those in Africa!

Holy Land Illustration 5. Catching a wild ox with the noose or lasso. Beni-Hassan; and bringing in fish and opening them, preparatory to their being salted. In a tomb near the Pyramids.

Even further, let us endeavor as Auguste Compte (1798-1857) insisted in his *System of Positive Philosophy*: "Love is our principle, order our foundation, progress our goal."

FREDERICK MONDERSON

However, when all is said and done, always remember Cheikh Anta Diop in *The African Origin of Civilization: Myth or Reality* (1974) has argued: "The African historian who evades the problem of Egypt is neither modest nor objective, nor unruffled; he is ignorant, cowardly, and neurotic. Imagine, if you can, the uncomfortable position of a Western historian writing of Europe without referring to Graeco-Latin antiquity and try to pass that off as a scientific approach." So therefore, we as African historians must deal with Egypt as the "gift of Africa to the world" or be guilty as charged. Even more, let us remember Prof. John H. Clarke who said in a speech at the Afro-American Conference in Detroit, Michigan, on May 13, 1967, entitled "A New Approach to African History" that "The final interpretation of African history is the responsibility of scholars of African descent." Nevertheless, Gordon Parks in *Voices in the Mirror* (1990) advises: "Steep yourself in black history, but don't stop there. I love Duke Ellington and Count Basie, but I also listen to Bach and Beethoven. Do not allow yourself to be trapped and snarled in limits set for you by someone else."

Then I say there is nothing new under the sun. Without punning, this does not necessarily refer to the Egyptian sun. Then again, perhaps it does. I wish to bring to your attention an interesting book of quotations. It is edited by Dorothy Winbush Riley and entitled *My Soul Looks Back*, '*Lest I forget*: *A Collection of Quotations by People of Color*, Harper Perennials, (1991) 1995. In her Introduction she wrote: "Senusert II of Egypt cried, 'Would I have words that are unknown, utterances and sayings in new languages, that have not yet passed away, and that have not already been said repeatedly by the ancestors.' The ancient ones knew as we know that original thought is limited, and many ideas are repeated from generation to generation. They also know the importance of keeping historical records detailing their deeds and accomplishments." We must look for those thoughts, learn them and teach our people so they can move forward and be successful in their ventures. As we stand on the shoulders of giants, as well as our ancestors, let us also provide the shoulders so future generations can stand on ours. After all, it is the shoulders of giants that are responsible for human progress. This is our god given responsibility. Let us not fail the people!

Let me also remind, particularly those of you who did some preliminary studies of hieroglyphics before you got here; as you go among and view the depictions on the walls of temples especially, notice names may spell with varied vowels. For example, the gods' names may be spelt Ra or Re. In case of the Theban deity, it could be Amon, Amen, Amun, or depending to the time referred to, Amun-Ra, Amen-Ra, Amon-Ra and so on. Amenhotep or Amenophis is another example regarding the New Kingdom monarchs. Thutmose, Thutmosis, Tutmose, Tutmosis, and so on are some of the ways in which soft vowels may be used in a language. Then there is Seti or Sety or Queen Thiy or Tiy, and so on. Know this and not be confused by various spellings of names. There is much to learn here. Also, remember to do the readings in the handouts, this is to further enhance what you learn.

QUINTESSENTIAL BOOK
"THE HOLY LAND"

Now, having said that, Ladies and Gentlemen, **Sunny Climes** has promised us a second bus rather than keep all of us on one bus. So therefore, I have divided up everyone into smaller groups and placed you on buses Number 1 and 2. I will also assign you your room number. Be careful with the hotel key. Please don't lose it for you will be billed for a replacement. All phone calls out of the country will be billed to you before we leave the hotel. Anything you use not covered in the food group will also be billed to your room number. We will not be able to leave until all bills are taken care of. Yet still, enjoy and have a wonderful trip. God is love!

Bus I — Groups I, II and III.

Group I - Bus Number 1.

Dr. Leonard James: Room 510
    Mrs. Marilyn James

Walter Brown: Room 512
    Mrs. Juliet Brown

Mr. Michael Palmer: Room 514
    Mrs. Mary Palmer
    and son Cosmos

Mr. Charles Palmer: Room 513
    Mrs. Shirley Palmer

Mr. Frank James: Room 522
    Mrs. Jessie James

Mr. John Brown: Room 526
    Mrs. Joy Brown

FREDERICK MONDERSON

Group II -   Bus Number 1.

Dr. Madison: Room 616
    Mrs. Ada Madison
Mr. John Brown: Room 618
    Mrs. Joy Brown
Ms. Kashmoney Malone: Room 620
Stephaniea McCall: Room 620
Carmelitiea Shabazz: Room 622
Esperanza Rodriguez: Room 622
Peter Monderson: Room 525
Leonel Nelson Escobar: Room 625
Dr. Fred Monderson: Room 503

Group III -   Bus Number 1.

Robert Matthews: Room 626
Lesley Jacobs: Room 626
Frederick Maloney: Room 624
Henrietta Potter: Room 624
Michelliea Georges: Room 430
Regina Hendricks: Room 430

QUINTESSENTIAL BOOK
"THE HOLY LAND"

George Washington: Room 525

Group IV   -   **Bus Number 2.**

Michael Montout: Room 527
James Morrison: Room 528
Dr. McFlair: Room 510
    Mrs. McFlair
Mr. Sylvester Singleton: Room 614
    Mrs. Regina Singleton
Mr. John Stewart: Room 516
    Mrs. Glenda Stewart
Asantewaa Harris: Room 428
Hattie Jones: Room 518
Jerome Smith: Room 518

Group V -   **Bus Number 2**

Dr. Oswald Benjamin: Room 432
Dr. John Africa: Room 434
Teddy Cubia: Room 523
Michael Sinclair: Room 523

FREDERICK MONDERSON

Dr. Alexander Pushkin: **Room 519**
Mrs. Holly Pushkin
Lady from California: **Room 615**

Holy Land Photo 3. Abu Simbel Temple of Rameses II. In Double Crown and with straight beard, Rameses pours libation and offers bouquet of flowers to Khnemu, God of the Cataracts.

Joshua Monderson: **Room 624**
Cherise Maloney: **Room 635**
Sharon Montgomery: **Room 517**
Jack Bender: **Room 515**

QUINTESSENTIAL BOOK
"THE HOLY LAND"

Dr. Fred Monderson: Having taken care of the registration just let me give you a few pointers on this important city.

Thebes of the Greeks, *Luxor* of the Arabs and *Waset* of the ancient Egyptians was an important city throughout the Middle and New Kingdoms. In fact, throughout Egyptian history this city was important but its fortunes rose and fell and when Egypt's enemies attacked, Thebes was the first city they felt they had to wreck. Clearly it was the city of Amon and later Amon-Ra. As such, then, it was the 'Throne of the Two Lands,' and 'City of the Lord of Eternity,' or 'City of the Hidden Name.' It's also been called 'The Mysterious City' and 'Mistress of the Temples.'

In this way, it enjoyed great status and was the recipient of not simply temple building, pharaonic philanthropy but also beautification. Anything that was pleasing to the god and to the priests was done to win favor for the pharaoh and thus the city benefitted.

The history of Egypt as we know it today, the pyramids aside, is primarily based on the remains of Thebes, whether tombs, temples, art, lakes and anything that has survived. We will be here for four days so I urge you to stay alert, visit with the people, look around you, be observant and try to take away from this city as memorable an experience as you can get. I would urge that you try to get to the Luxor Museum one afternoon since it is open from late afternoon until night.

Tomorrow we travel by bus first to Karnak then to Luxor temples with the rest of the day off. The purpose of the early morning wake up is to get us on the bus and to the site before many tourists are there as well as before the sun in its glory becomes too hot. Ask questions and pay attention to your guide. Any further questions you have will be answered later in the discussion. Dinner is at 7:00 in the Nubian Restaurant on floor B1, in the back. In the dining room, look for the section that says **Sunny Climes**. Enjoy the rest of your day.

FREDERICK MONDERSON

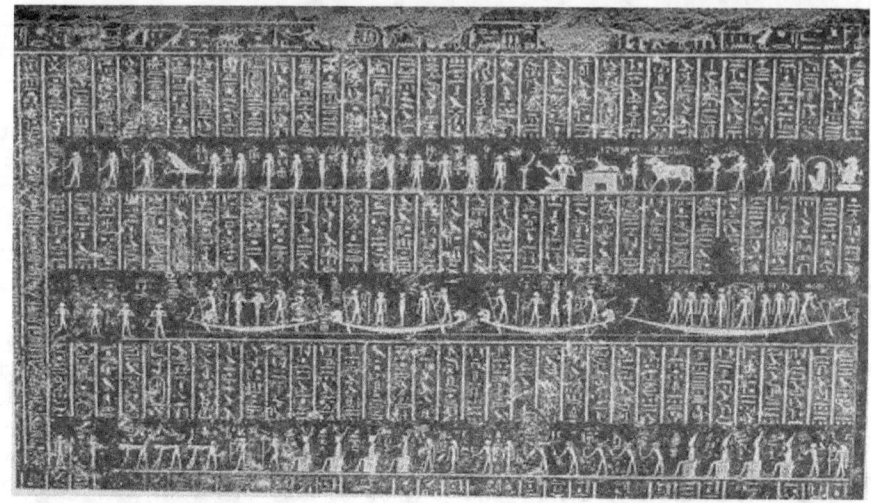

Holy Land Illustration 6. The Journey of the Sun-god through the Third Section of the Other World. From the sarcophagus of Nekht-Heru-het, King of Egypt, B.C. 378.

Day 3. KARNAK AND LUXOR
Wake up

Esperanza Rodriguez. Good Morning, Mi Amor. Your schedule for today takes you to Karnak and Luxor Temples.

I have prepared your selections "Egypt, Kush, Ethiopia" and "The Flow of the Nile" for distribution to the group. The important selection, *Karnak: The Majestic Architecture of Ancient Kemet* will be distributed on the bus. Please do remind them that this will be a separate posting that must be read and discussed later, after the site lecture. I am happy to be your assistant and will endeavor to help make this trip as memorable as possible. Please call on me any time.

There should also be questions pertaining to all the selections. These could be brought up at the discussion after the lecture on the day's site visit.

Dr. Fred Monderson: Thank you, my dear. I am confident you will do your best.

QUINTESSENTIAL BOOK "THE HOLY LAND"

EGYPT, KUSH, ETHIOPIA
By
Fred Monderson

Today, the history of North Africa - mainly Egypt, Kush and Ethiopia, is constantly being re-examined owing to the deluge of new information providing new analyses. In this we must pay some attention to familiarizing our youth with the significance of their continued interest in ancient Kemetic studies because of its relevance for the future. So that by the date of 2027, as the Afrocentrists would say, we'll be ready to understand the issues of historical distortion and defend Egypt as African; but more importantly we should be well on the road of cultural and historical redemption.

Now, we know, in the 19th Century and particularly the first half of the 20th Century, scholars from Great Britain, France, Turkey, Italy, Switzerland and Germany did extensive work of excavation in Egypt and the Nile Valley. The people who controlled such work, effectively created and emphasized an area called the "Middle East" and made Egypt a part of it. Employing existing geographic logic, they used the great desert, Sahara, as an artificial dividing line in Africa. This division was presented as existing for all time. The creators have tried to effectively block out any role for Ethiopia, Kush and Africans, in the Egyptian/Kemetic high culture. Here we see a coordinated, reinforced belief system between the workers in the field, the people who sponsored their expeditions, and those who published their reports and books. Through the reinforcement of newspapers and the new mass education systems, the general public came to accept their view as the truth and so what we call "misinformation" became the order of the day. The logical question then posed is: "On how many other historical events have people been misinformed?" This situation brings to mind one of the more interesting works in the Afrocentric literature entitled *What They Never Taught You in History Class* (1983), Indus Kamit Kush, published by Luxxor Publications.

FREDERICK MONDERSON

Holy Land Papyrus 4. The Psychostasia. As Anubis introduces the Deceased, he also adjusts the Scales atop which sits the feather of Thoth as Ammit, eater of the guilty, sits in readiness and Thoth records the results before Horus declares the subject "True of Voice," then to be introduced to Osiris (not in picture).

In addition, Herodotus, the "father of history" visited Egypt in c. 450 B.C. He wrote the *Histories* and devoted Book II, called *Euterpe*, to Egypt, ancient Kemet. This early traveler observed and commented the "Egyptians, Ethiopians and Colchians" were similar. They had "thick lips, broad noses, and woolly hair" and were "burnt of skin," or otherwise black. The Greek philosopher Aristotle in his book *Physiognomonica* is quoted as saying the "Egyptians and Ethiopians are cowards because they are black." He also argued that some northern whites were equally cowards, because they were white! He tried to find the middle ground in the debate on color and so found the Greeks as being the ideal. This may have had to do with their Mediterranean origin. Of course, we know his science was wrong! However, and fundamentally, he did label these Africans "black" and this too was based on his observations, as did Herodotus, even though these visitors to Egypt came at the end of Egypt's history. Still the people had retained their blackness despite invasions from Asia and the Mediterranean.

Diodorus Siculus, another ancient writer, claims the Ethiopians told him they had founded Egypt as a colony. In addition, many other writers of antiquity regarded the peoples of Africa, namely Egypt, Ethiopia, Kush, etc., as mainly one people. In this regard, critical contemporary scholarship on Egypt and the Nile Valley has shown that during the periods of the Old Kingdom, Middle Kingdom and New Kingdom, there were extensive contacts with the lands to the south of Egypt/Kemet, as well as the Mediterranean Sea. To the south, the pharaohs initiated, for the most part, peaceful economic and trade contacts with the land of Yam, Punt, Warit, Kush, etc. However, there were also during these periods, numerous military campaigns conducted to the south of Egypt/Kemet to secure

QUINTESSENTIAL BOOK
"THE HOLY LAND"

trade privileges and pre-empt military threats from that region. This was indeed a period of intensive interaction between all the peoples of the Nile River region. So much so, when Egypt was threatened from the north, the southlands remained a reservoir of military and economic support.

An article published in *The New York Times* on March 1, 1979, showed evidence of the world's earliest monarchy found in Nubia/Ethiopia, to the south of Egypt. Dr. Bruce Williams of the University of Chicago has shown how the symbols we associate with pharaonic power in Egypt/Kemet were found in Nubia in 3400 B.C. At the start of the Egyptian dynasties 3200 B.C., these power symbols were very much in use, including, enthroned pharaoh, white crown, disk of the sun, whip, flail, royal sailing barge, incense burner, Serekh or face of a building, falcon, etc. This interesting insight into kingly paraphernalia is partly explained by Aldred (1980: 96) who held, the "dignity of the king demanded that he should be seated upon a throne or standing upright, wearing his crowns and carrying his scepters." Particularly important, moreover, this evidence of monarchy is 200 years before such symbolism appeared in Egypt/Kemet. Such a discovery lent strong support to Diodorus' statement that Ethiopia founded Egypt as a colony.

Cheikh Anta Diop in *The African Origins of Civilization: Myth or Reality* has documented the cultural continuity of Egypt and Ethiopia. He has also posited the theory that Egypt was a Black civilization; the Egyptians were Black and whatever Whites in the Old Kingdom foundations, period of experimentation and creativity, were few and latecomers. In fact, the scholars Cheikh Anta Diop and Theophile Obenga were praised at UNESCO's final document for being the most prepared of all attendees at their conference on ancient Egypt where the fundamental Blackness of Ancient Egypt was affirmed.

Importantly, the demographic mix along the river has enabled early Nile Valley Blacks to found the Old Kingdom with its magnificence that has been so instrumental in later global cultural growth. Recently Bauval and Brophy have argued the impact of Nabta Playa as predecessors to the pharaohs Toby Wilkinson has equally outlined the influence of the Eastern Desert in Southern Upper Egypt before the dynastic period began.

In the history of African-American experience with Egypt/Kemet and the Nile Valley as a whole, the twentieth century has offered tremendous opportunities. This has resulted from an evolved and un-conquering intent to identify with Black "ancestors" and the ancient African cultural legacy that has advanced civilization. The Nineteenth Century, despite contemporary ignorance has provided evidence of early Black Nationalist identification with Egypt. In 1990, Dr. John Henrik Clarke of Hunter College of the City University of New York presented a wonderful lecture given at Aswan, Egypt, where he sketched a revealing picture of Caribbean and African-American nationalists' quest for Egypt. This provided a significant point of departure for today's nationalists, particularly the Afrocentrists. So, the work of these scholars set the stage for our young people to enter the Twenty-First Century with a sound understanding of their cultural history. So that by 2027, however arbitrarily chosen, this will become an important year to judge Black progress in any number of modalities of human social, political, educational and economic endeavors.

More importantly still, the African-American youth, particularly those of the inner city, have either not been educated or mis-educated about their connection with the Nile Valley and Egypt, the land of ancient Kemet. The urban schools, especially in the large industrial and economic centers as New York, Chicago and Detroit have not addressed the issue either. They have failed to integrate an understanding of the connection between the African-American youth particularly, and so many others in general.

Fortunately, however, there have been a number of credible African and African-American scholars who have labored unending to educate us all about our ancestors in Egypt. From the beginning of the century, W.E.B DuBois began articulating the intellectual nationalist movement of African-Americans in the country. Quite frankly, we could go back to the earlier stalwarts, David Walker, Martin Delaney, Frederick Douglass, Henry Highland Garnett, etc. W.E.B. Du Bois wrote *The Negro* in 1915. In spite of the paucity of source material available to him in the United States and despite the preponderance of archaeological and anthropological data, forming emerging histories, particularly those vitriolically distorted, DuBois argued for the role of Blacks in Egypt or Kemet, albeit of a mulatto type. Even more, he had followed in the footsteps of European writers whose iconoclastic attitudes pointed out and attacked the incubated process of systematic distortion of the relevant African historical record, wherein the fundamental Blackness of Kemet was underscored. In *The World and Africa*, Du Bois synthesized his earlier positions and much of his ideas have withstood the test of time. Marcus Garvey, Duse Mohammed, and Carter G. Woodson also educated us about the Blackness of Egypt, at a time when Blacks could hardly afford to study this ancient African culture.

The early scholars, in spite of their troubles with the times, had understood the significance of King Tut-ankh-Amon, when Howard Carter discovered his tomb in 1922. These critical scholars also worked so the ancestors of their day could read, research, study, and understand the fight to reclaim Egypt/ancient Kemet as African. Their work was undertaken and handed down as legacy to the next generation. Then along came another generation of critical African historians in the persons of J.A. Rogers, Dr. John H. Clarke, John Jackson, John Huggins, Dr. Y. ben-Jochannan, and Dr. Ivan Van Sertima. Cheikh Anta Diop came from Senegal in West African, Leonard Jeffries, and Leonard James from the New York area and Walter Rodney and G.M. James from Guyana, in the Caribbean, but more rightly South America. Dr. Carruthers, Wade Nobles, Na'im Akbar, and a host of

QUINTESSENTIAL BOOK
"THE HOLY LAND"

others, particularly from the *Association for the Study of Classical African Civilizations* were equally focused on the issue. They all preached, taught and wrote books in an attempt to educate the young and old of the African America community. Their message was clear, Egypt is African! Egypt is Kemet and Kemet is African! This is the philosophical stance from which we must wage the struggle to rightly educate our people and contribute to restoring Africa's proper place in the respectful narrative of the human experience.

African-American young people of today must come to a sense of understanding about the forces arrayed against them. They must develop critical operational problem solving skills that are essential for their survival. They must visit and utilize the great libraries and institutions of cultural and historical importance, that African ancestral artifactual evidence helps maintain. They must learn the difference between primary and secondary sources. They must understand the significance of critical comparative historical analysis. They must master the criteria for critical reading and reasoning as important tools in their intellectual growth. They must understand and operationalize the eight major social sciences in life situations that are critical to their development. This application of historical analysis will enable them to give purpose to the work that must be undertaken.

The African-American inner city youth must study, understand and claim the glories of Egypt/Kemet as their legacy. They must study art, architecture, anthropology, and archaeology. The languages French, German, Greek, Arabic, Coptic and Hieroglyphics are all fundamental disciplines in study of this glorious ancient African past, and these must be attempted at an early age. Only then will they be able to take their places as teachers, writers and defenders of their heritage and accomplishments for generations to come.

The African-American youth must therefore study Egypt/Kemet. They must research and teach in the twenty-first century just as their elders and ancestors have done in the twentieth and past centuries. Only then will they reclaim their cultural heritage and history, to be strong in a fast-paced and changing world.

2. Breakfast

Dr. Leonard James: Good Morning, my friend. Care to join Marilyn and me at our table?
Walter Brown: Good Morning, Dr. James. Delighted. Hello Mrs. James. You certainly look ready for this busy day. I heard last night this temple is one of the most important we will see on this trip so I intend to stick close to the guide, take my photos and listen to the post-site lecture very carefully.

FREDERICK MONDERSON

Mrs. Marilyn James: That is so true. Hopefully in the discussion later we could clarify some ideas that will certainly be generated after this day's temple visits are over. This culture is a topic my husband has taught about for years.

Dr. Leonard James: That is true, honey. That's some breakfast you are having, Brother Brown. I'm just having pancakes and eggs with my black coffee.

Walter Brown: Someone told me you could eat a lot and still lose weight on this trip. I intend to test this theory. That is why I am having peaches, some orange, grapefruit, and a piece of watermelon. Two eggs, with bacon, au-gratin potatoes, and two glasses of Kakadee or sorrel, as we know it. Don't forget to squeeze a little piece of lemon on your food for this might help you to combat the possibility of diarrhea.

Mrs. Juliet Brown: Strange, at home I know Walter leaves early for his job but he never eats that much at my table. Well, it's good to see him eat a hearty breakfast for a change.

Dr. Leonard James: Don't forget to drink some lemonade and squeeze some extra lemons just to keep the demon of diarrhea from getting you.

Walter Brown: I hear you. What is that you are writing, Dr. James?

Dr. Leonard James: Well, it's just some notes I am scribbling about Egyptian history to keep my mind active while I'm here, that would supplement and complement what we are being given in the lectures and readings as well as from critical observation. Perhaps I would share it with you for your critique.

Walter Brown: That is a good idea. I will be honored to read anything you write, homeboy! I'll read it on the bus and if you keep writing those I will keep reading them.

Dr. Leonard James: Thanks. That is certainly one way to motivate me.

Holy Land Photo 4. Abu Simbel Temple of Nefertari. Visitor admires the entrance façade of Nefertari's Temple to Goddess Hathor.

QUINTESSENTIAL BOOK
"THE HOLY LAND"

Mr. Peter Palmer: I'm having eggs, toast and coffee. Mrs. Palmer did not feel well last night and won't be joining us for this temple.

Mr. Frank James: Mr. Brown, I suppose over the years you have been ribbed about your name.

Mr. John Brown: John Brown? That is true, but as I reflect on that great ancestor, I think only of Plato's (427-347 B.C.) admonition in the *Republic*, Book V: "Until philosophers are kings, or the kings and princes of this world have the spirit and power of philosophy, and political greatness and wisdom meet in one, and those commoner natures who pursue either to the exclusion of the other are compelled to stand aside, cities will never have rest from their evils - no, nor the human race, as I believe - and then only will this one State have a possibility of life and behold the light of day."

Dr. Madison: Clearly John Brown was a man of great moral conviction for his actions challenged a society that was certainly not ruled by Plato's Philosophers or kings. He was a man of great wisdom who saw the evil of a system that was a cancer in the body politic and on a head-on collision with itself and history.

Mr. John Brown: Well, he certainly did as Aeschylus's (525-456 B.C.) extolled in his dictum: "Wisdom comes through suffering." I mean he suffered to show us wisdom!"

Ms. Malone: Who thought out the idea of building temples?

Carmelitiea Shabazz: Stratham (1912) tells us: "Herbert Spencer, indeed, laid it down that the first architects were priests, they alone understanding what kind of construction was required by the god."

Stephaniea McCall: So what do we look for when we get to the temple?

Carmelitiea Shabazz: The architecture is the important thing, how the building is constructed and so on.

Esperanza Rodriguez: Dr. Monderson mentions this in another of his books on the Colonnade. He says that Dr. ben-Jochannan emphasized the architecture as the most important feature of what we observe. He also quoted Garner Wilkinson (1850) who said the principal characteristics of Egyptian architecture are as follows: "The pyramidal, or inclining, line; which is particularly observable in the towers of the Propylon, the sides of the temple wall, and the gateways, where it terminates in the curve of the cornice. The towers themselves, which are of immense height and size, and are placed at the front of the larger temples. The flat stone roofs of the temples, without any pediment. The hieroglyphics, that covers the whole walls, within and without; explaining the subjects of the sculptures; the whole of the latter, as well as the moldings, and hieroglyphics, being colored, throughout the building. The globe with wings and asps, over the doors, signifying the 'good genius,' or protecting deity."

FREDERICK MONDERSON

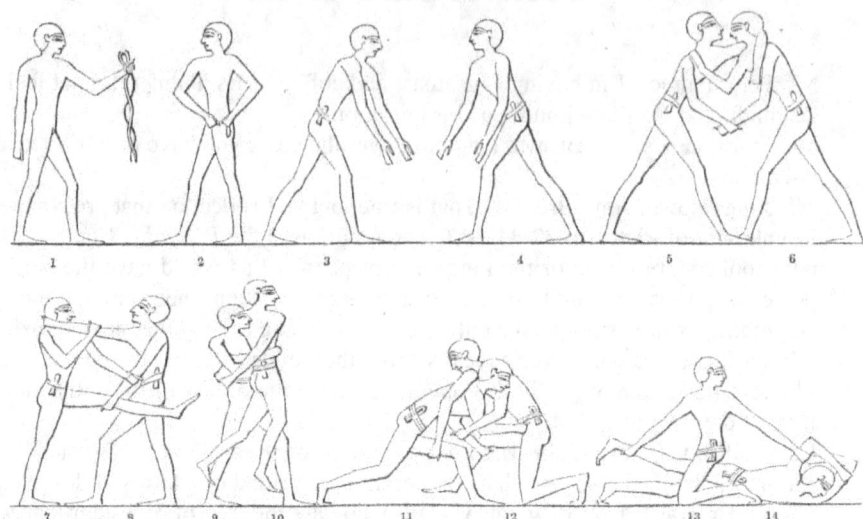

Holy Land Illustration 7. Some positions of wrestlers and more positions of wrestlers. Beni-Hassan.

Peter Monderson: Mr. Matthews, what do you think of Dr. Monderson's opening statement?

Robert Matthews: He certainly laid great emphasis on knowledge and wisdom. The belief is we can grow immensely if we seriously immerse ourselves in the task ahead. Observe, discuss, share, question and most of all respect yourselves, each other, and the culture that is so wonderful.

Lesley Jacobs: That is a beautiful camera you have Mr. Matthews. What is the name?

Robert Matthews: It's my son's camera. It's a Minolta. I just borrowed it so as to get some memorable photos as a reminder of my trip to Egypt. At my age, I don't think I will return to Egypt, so I need to have something to show my grandchildren and tell them of the memorable adventure I took as I explored the wonders of the Nile River culture.

Lesley Jacobs: I did not get one of those fancy cameras; I bought the Kodak one use camera. In fact, I bought a dozen of those. How many rolls of film did you bring?

Robert Matthews: My son who had been on one of those trips with Dr. ben-Jochannan told me to bring at least 25 rolls of 36 exposures. I hope that is enough. I always wanted to be a photographer and now my chance is here. I only want to get choice shots though.

Lesley Jacobs: Well perhaps we could share photos. I hear some of the developing shops give double prints. Perhaps we could swap the second sets.

Robert Matthews: That sounds good. That way we could get a wider coverage of scenes and objects.

QUINTESSENTIAL BOOK
"THE HOLY LAND"

Frederick Maloney: Hello my dear. How are you today? Let me introduce Leonel Escobar. He is a banker from the Dominican Republic.
Leonel Escobar: Pleased to meet you.
Henrietta Potter: Pleased to meet you. I am fine, Dr. Maloney. You look ready this morning. Today should be an interesting day for we visit some of the more important surviving temples in Egypt. The guide told me, one of these temples took two thousand years to build and it's somewhat well preserved. The second temple is also important.
Frederick Maloney: Yes. The first is Karnak and the second is Luxor. I hope your camera is ready for some spectacular photos that you could boast when you return to Kings County.
Henrietta Potter: I am ready. I wish to learn as much as I can on this trip. My mind is open.
Frederick Maloney: Good. Sir Francis Bacon (1561-1626) in *The Advancement of Learning*, Book I (1605) argued: "For all knowledge and wonder (which is the seed of knowledge) is an impression of pleasure in itself." So that fits you to a "T."
Henrietta Potter: I quite agree. However, I never thought I would be sitting with a banker. How different are they from other people whose money they handle?
Leonel Escobar: Ogden Nash (1907-1971) put it best when he said: "Bankers are just like anybody else, except richer."
Frederick Maloney: Very cute and true.
Leonel Escobar: Yes. However, Confucius (551-479 B.C.) said: "Have no friends not equal to yourself." I think we are on the same level and I am pleased to be paired with you two.
Frederick Maloney: Thanks.
Henrietta Potter: Me too.

Michelliea Georges: What I have learned at Temple University's Afrocentric Institute is that, as Harriet Tubman said, 'There is nothing more correct for African people than to struggle for freedom.'
Regina Hendricks: I can agree with such a philosophy.
George Washington: At Hunter College I was taught by Dr. John H. Clarke. I was rather impressed by Merimba Ani (Prof. Donna Richards) and also fortunate to have met the famous Dr. ben-Jochannan whom Dr. Monderson discussed in the first handout. The things I have learned from these four elders are simply this: Dr. Clarke told us history is like a road map that tells you where you have been, where you are and where you are going. Dr. ben-Jochannan told us to invest in books and educational materials so we can be well-informed. He also said, people interested in Africa should choose a country and specialize in it as opposed to being generalists on every country in Africa. Merimba Ani taught me philosophic understanding of the fundamentals of African religious thought and cultural processes. Dr. Monderson brought me to Egypt and spelled out much I intend to learn.

FREDERICK MONDERSON

Regina Hendricks: Does that mean you can't hop, skip, and jump all over the continent as I see some of the "guides" do.
George Washington: That is correct. Can you imagine doing four or five countries in two weeks? What can you see? Most of that time is taken to travel. So, choose one country and see it thoroughly. For those who want to be guides, choose one country and specialize in it. I think that makes sense.
Regina Hendricks: I will have to agree with you. It does make sense. What do you have for us in the notes?
George Washington: Well, I began an *Ancient History* class, 51-301 on September 8, 1975. My analysis of the day's work said the course will deal with *Ancient History* from the earliest times to possibly the time of Christ. It was on Egypt and Mesopotamia. Hieroglyphics or sacred writings can be the most ancient of written historical material. Demotic was the language of the people. Language fusion produced the lingua Franca. Aramaic was the language Jesus spoke. Coptic is a derivative of hieroglyphics. Early Christians destroyed much of Egypt.
Regina Hendricks: This is interesting. What texts did you use?
George Washington: We used J.A. Wilson's *The Culture of Ancient Egypt*; Moscati's *Faces of the Ancient Orient* and Frankfort's *Before Philosophy*.

Michelliea Georges: Were there others?
George Washington: I also used *Britannica Encyclopedia*. This gave me a hands-on feel of the land in both Egypt and Mesopotamia. We sought to find parallels between hieroglyphics or sacred writing; Demotic – the language of the people; and cuneiform – the wedge shaped inscriptions used in ancient Acadia, Babylonia, Assyria and Persia.

Around 540 B.C. Cyrus of Persia captured the Near East with the exception of Egypt.

Some of the sources for Egyptian history included Herodotus in whose time Mesopotamia was under Persian rule. Diodorus Siculus wrote on Laws and Politics. Strabo was a great ancient geographer. Nomes were Egyptian counties. Plutarch was an ancient geographer. Manetho listed dynasties from 3000-325 B.C. These were 31 dynasties. There were some errors in Manetho due to time difference he was writing about and changes in the hieroglyphic script. However, Manetho was fundamentally correct with much of what he wrote about. That is why modern scholars accept him as being credible. Renaissance travelers in the Middle East included Groefend for Mesopotamian history and Rawlinson for Assyriology. Elamite was a language of West Persia. In fact we could trace the evolution of that language from Old Persian – Elamite – Neo-Babylonian – Babylonian – Acadian and Sumerian.

I did not stop there for I was impressed very early with the work of Dr. Ben Jochannan. Prof. Clarke made us read 15 books and at least two of Dr. Ben's

QUINTESSENTIAL BOOK "THE HOLY LAND"

books entitled *Black Man of the Nile* and *Africa: Mother of Western Civilization*. He wanted us to read the third in the Trilogy, *African Origins of the Major Western Religions* but this was costly. However, I did when I took his class later on. We also had to read Cheikh Anta Diop's *African Origins of Civilization: Myth or Reality*, but this was very cerebral for first and second year students.

Michael Montout: Mr. Morrison, glad to have you join me for breakfast. Dr. McFlair and his wife are sitting with us. They are just getting their plates together. Perhaps we could get some of those questions asked and answered as you promised.
James Morrison: Delighted to join you. Let me get myself set up at the buffet table. I feel I could really eat a big breakfast today.
Dr. McFlair: Honey, Mr. Montout tells me James Morrison will join our table for breakfast. He is now fixing his plate.
Mrs. McFlair: Good. It's always good to hear from younger people particularly someone on the cutting edge of religious debates and practices. Here he is now.
James Morrison: Good morning to you, Dr. McFlair and Mrs. McFlair. Oh, Mrs. McFlair, how beautiful you look this wonderful morning, the Lord has made. How are you this morning, Dr. McFlair?
Dr. McFlair: Very well, young man. Honey, he certainly noticed your beauty. He could very well be a good talker.
Mrs. McFlair: Well, we'll see. This trip promises to be exciting and fact filled. Perhaps he can help us with some interpretations.

Holy Land Illustration 8. Two of the great faunal representatives, animal and bird, both having a stellar history in Egypt, symbolic and practical.

FREDERICK MONDERSON

Michael Montout: Perhaps you could explain to us. Mr. Morrison, 'What is the message of the religion of Egypt?'

James Morrison: I don't really teach Egyptian religion specifically but world religions and so don't know all the answers to questions you may pose, so please bear with me.

Michael Montout: We understand. Do your best.

James Morrison: As far as I remember, James H. Breasted, as early as 1907 offered the view that: "The moral aspirations which had come into the religion of Egypt with the ethical influences so potent in the Osiris myth, were now choked and poisoned by the assurance, that, however vicious a man's life, exemption in the hereafter could now be purchased at any time from the priests. In practical effect the sale of such rolls was identical with that of the sale of indulgences by Tetzel and his agents. Both devices failed, from the fact the penalty does not come from without, but operates within the offender. Neither perceived the ethical worthiness of a forgiveness affected by influences external to the life and character of the guilty. Their common idea of forgiveness is that of escape, and this not from the fatal inner consequences of evil conduct, but solely from external penalty. Nor does the magic roll of the Egyptian find its analogy solely in sale of papal indulgences."

Dr. McFlair: Let me get this clear. You are saying the priests were in a stage of moral decay similar to that in later Europe that spawned the Reformation.

James Morrison: I won't use the term moral decay but since they had access to the other world, they chose to capitalize on that. That in no way detracts from the seriousness and solemnity with which these people practiced worshipping and ritualizing their gods.

Michael Montout: We need to continue this on the bus because I think there needs to be more of an explanation. Looks like they are calling us to get on the bus.!

Mr. Sylvester Singleton: You two were educators; do you believe children go on sufficient trips to be able to understand the world about them?

Mr. John Stewart: That is a good question Mr. Singleton. I taught Public School and my wife taught in College. One thing my principal told me: 'Children do not do enough tripping,' so as often as possible, I would sponsor trips around the capital of our nation so they could get a grasp of the architecture, the cultural institutions and the government agencies and organizations in that wonderful city.

Mrs. John Stewart: John, honey, tell them of your experiences in the Library of Congress.

John Stewart: I made a special effort for them to know the difference between Independence Avenue, Constitution Avenue and Pennsylvania Avenue and the name of some of the government branches and agencies located on these historic streets. We did the Supreme Court, Congress and stood in front of the White House. I showed them the Smithsonian Institution, the National Art Gallery and the National Gardens. However, I was really impressed with the Library of Congress, particularly with the quote on the Madison Building wall: "Knowledge

QUINTESSENTIAL BOOK "THE HOLY LAND"

will forever govern ignorance; and a people who mean to be their own governors must arm themselves with the power which knowledge gives."
Mrs. Glenda Stewart: Well, they are calling us to board the bus. Let us continue this on the bus. I am sure they will be delighted to hear of what you saw in the Library of Congress and how it affected you.
John Stewart: Ok, my love. Will do.
Asantewaa Harris: I will love to hear what really impressed you in the Library of Congress, Mr. Stewart. I can't wait till you tell us on the bus.
John Stewart: Ok. However, I must visit the men's room before I board the bus.

Hattie Jones. My dear. Imagine us together in Egypt visiting Karnak and Luxor. What experiences we will have for our grand-children when we get old.
Jerome Smith: I certainly will remember this trip. Even more importantly I feel confident it will further cement our relationship. Perhaps one day we could bring our children to see what we saw.
Hattie: Yes. Maybe one day.

Teddy Cubia: Mr. Sinclair, you were giving us an explanation of Afrocentricity but this was not finished. Perhaps you could now continue.
Michael Sinclair: One of the most important of all questions we have had to deal with is whether Afrocentricity is a philosophy or a concept.
Dr. Alexander Pushkin: Well, what is it?
Michael Sinclair: Afrocentricity is both a concept and a philosophy. Anything which expresses an idea in language is a concept. Extension of concepts is called a class. A philosophy is different from a concept. Afrocentricity is a philosophic concept.
Teddy Cubia: You did well, Mr. Sinclair. Sort of brings back memories of my youth. Then I wrote one of my first poems called "The Game." Would you like to hear it? What do you think, Doc?
Dr. Alexander Pushkin: Go right ahead, Teddy.

"The Game"
By
Teddy Cubia

I lost to you – to gain from you – a knowledge of direction.
I have learned to win.
I must lose – not to you – or anyone –

FREDERICK MONDERSON

But to the play of the game.

You have mistaken the appearance of my occasional loss – to be proof of my failure.
But it will be the simple fact that I have lost now and then – and with the
Conscious effort of correcting my mistakes – that will cause me to be a champ among the best players.

You might beat me – but you will never defeat me.
Because only I myself can do that.

Michael Sinclair: Well done Mr. Cubia. Are there others, I would certainly like to hear them.
Teddy Cubia: There are a few others and as we go along, I will recite them to you particularly, on these long bus rides.

Holy Land Photo 5. Abu Simbel Temple of Rameses II. A closer look at the seated colossal statues, the miniature female figures at their feet and the statues and birds in foreground.

FLOW OF THE NILE
By
Fred Monderson

The flow of the Nile from south to north is the way Egypt/ancient Kemet and Nubia were oriented geographically, politically, religiously and socially. However, most Western, European and American historiographic representations

QUINTESSENTIAL BOOK
"THE HOLY LAND"

and teaching techniques orient the river and culture from north to south or foreign ascent of the river. In exploring this contradiction, Upper Egypt/Kemet, starting from Elephantine Island and the Temple of Isis on Philae Island, represented one of the two large divisions of the country of ancient Kemet. This region extended as far north above the Delta as Memphis, the Giza Plateau and Sakkara. In the Middle and New Kingdoms, the Southern border stretched deep into Nubian territory. The other large division of the United Upper and Lower Kingdoms, the north, comprised essentially the Delta region. We must keep in mind; the pharaoh is always King of Upper and Lower Egypt. It is always the south before the north, despite what the scholars have tried to foist on us.

Holy Land Ceramic Art 2. Beautiful display of jars in ceramic inlay within a kaleidoscope of further inlaid colors.

Throughout, the land was further subdivided into districts. The Greeks called these districts "nomes." From the first dynasty onwards, each nome was ruled by a noble family, in a feudal relationship, in the pharaonic system and each of these nobles was an aspirant to the crown. The number of these Nomes seems to have varied. Old Kemetic records generally gave 44. Pliny gave the same number; Strabo and Diodorus listed 36. The usually accepted number is 42. Of these 22 were in the South or Upper Egypt/Kemet and 20 were in the North or Lower Egypt/Kemet. Middle Egypt never came into play until much later. Importantly, however, each nome had its own capital. This was the seat of the hereditary governor. He was called a Nomarch. In the configuration of regional power from the Middle Kingdom onward, the south was supreme owing to its fighting ability and the primacy of Amun in religious, economic, political, architectural and artistic efforts and the daring, dreams and dramatics of men and women of great and noble aspirations.

H. Brugsch, in *Egypt Under the Pharaohs* tells us, the "capital" of "these nomes formed the central point of the particular divine worship of the district which belonged to it." He pointed out how the: "sacred name of the Nomes have handed down to us the names of the temple, of the chief deity, of the priests and priestesses, of the holy trees, and also the names of the town-harbor of the holy canal." Even further Brugsch indicated, ancient records provide evidence regarding: "… cultivated land, and the land which was only fruitful during the inundation, and much more information, in such completeness, that we are in a position, from the indications contained in these lists, to form the most exact picture of each Egyptian nome in all its details, almost without any gaps."

In the prehistoric period, nomes existed with their own peculiarities, viz., economic activities, arts and architecture industry, nome standards, deities, sacred animals, fortifications for defense, etc. They were parts of the north/south regional division of the country. The *Narmer Palette* informs of the conquest by this southern chieftain and warlord, over the northern region. The feat of Narmer's mobilization of a significant military force, the logistics of their descent of the Nile in sailing downstream, and conquering and collecting his enumerated booty, attests to the size of his own forces and the administrative genius that went into planning and execution, before and after the victory. It may be also significant that he had Inner Africa as his back-yard, where this provided the wherewithal for the great warrior tradition and the syncretized cultural creativity that lasted for duration of dynastic rule.

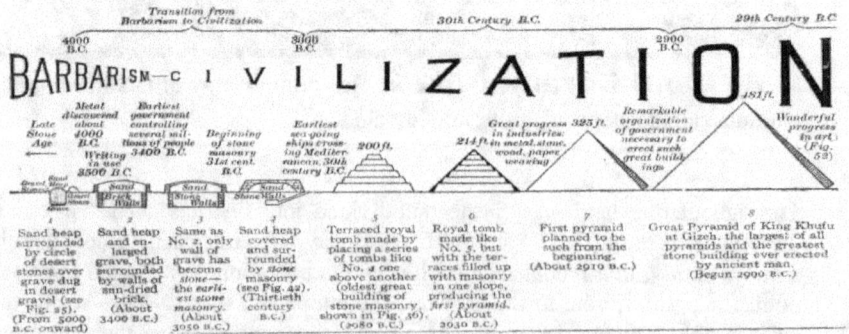

Holy Land Illustration 9. Civilization. At most 150 years, from the earliest stone masonry to the Great Pyramid. (Breasted)

QUINTESSENTIAL BOOK
"THE HOLY LAND"

A significant symbol of the unification was the White Crown to represent the Upper Kingdom, Red Crown to represent the Lower Kingdom, and a united Red and White Double-Crown to represent the United Kingdom of the North and South, in the sacred land of ancient Kemet. The Lotus plant symbolized the Upper Kingdom and Papyrus the Lower Kingdom, as other pharaonic symbols. There was no symbolic representation for Middle Egypt in the earliest geographic and political division of the land. In this, the *Suten Bat* titular designation King of the Upper and Lower Kingdoms remained one of the king's 5 names throughout dynastic times. The other names were his *Golden Horus*, *Horus*, *Two Ladies* and *Son of Ra*. Ever since, the north and south vied for supremacy in art, politics, agriculture, religion and economic relations from the Thinite Period, through the Middle Kingdom, New Kingdom, Late Period and Ethiopian Ascendancy in the XXVth Dynasty. While the north was generally represented by the Red Crown and the south the White Crown, the earliest example of the Red Crown has been found in the Eastern Desert of Upper Egypt.

The ruler of each nome performed a feudal obligation to the pharaoh. This relationship required the Nomarchs to pay taxes to the national treasury. They had to supply corvee' labor, through their underlings, slaves, serfs, etc., for national projects, as canal and road building and repairs, in their Nomes and to supply recruits for the national army, particularly in times of war. When the Pharaoh visited a nome, its Nomarch was responsible for the hospitality of the king. They were also responsible for maintaining local police, and a Judiciary.

In *Atlas of Ancient Egypt*, John Baines and Jaromir Malek point out the Nomes of Upper Egypt had their numbers fixed by the 5th dynasty. They cite as reference the *Kiosk of Senwosret I* (Twelfth Dynasty 1970-1936 B.C.) at Karnak that gives recorded lengths of each nome along the river. For Lower Egypt, the definitive number of 20 nomes was not set until the Graeco-Roman period. However, the 22 nomes of Upper Egypt/Kemet were well established by the beginnings of dynastic rule. Here is also compelling evidence of 'Southern Supremacy.'

Many pre-dynastic and early Dynastic cultures were located in the southern land, home of the first three Nomes. This area includes such ancient sites as Hierakonpolis, Naqada, Armant, Abadiyeh (Hu), Naga Ed-Der, El Kubaniya, El-Kab, Edfu, Badari, Mostagedda, Matmar, Ballas, Naqada, and Kharga and Dakhleh Oases and Gebelein. We should include the Eastern and Western Deserts of Upper Egypt. Thebes, in the fourth Nome, boasted twin cities of Luxor and Karnak as well. The sepulchral Valleys of the Kings, Queens, Nobles and Artisans are important repositories of funerary, artistic and architectural remains across the river in Upper Egypt/Kemet. This prominence, the God Amon, and its antiquity gave the south its powerful role in the affairs of the state. In addition, the Islands of Philae and Elephantine, and towns such as Aswan, Edfu, and El Kab provide valuable links to the origins of cosmological, theological, philosophic, scientific and mathematical beginnings along the Nile River in North-east Africa. Together with Tarkhan, Kom el-Ahmar and Abydos with its pre-dynastic forts, temples and cemeteries, these sites hold keys to earliest African origins in the Nile Valley and Egypt/Kemet.

For archaeologists, cemeteries proved virtual reservoirs of information, supplying enormous evidence of historical and cultural significance. Barbara Adams (1988) mentioned the preservative nature of the hot climate and dry sands in *Predynastic Egypt,* where she enumerated parts of the wealth found in graves of the pre-dynastic period. The category of pottery was decorated with "nature objects and geometric patterns." Coloring of pottery was by natural fire or hand painting. The "predynastic tombs revealed stone mace-heads; metal tools such as needles, chisels and adzes." Goldsmiths and other craftsmen worked jewelry and other items such as: "bracelets and rings; flint tools and weapons, both exotic and utilitarian ivory, pottery and stone human and animal figurines, ivory, stone shells and glazed composition (faience) beads and amulets; slate cosmetic palettes; ivory, bone and shell spoons, dishes, combs, bracelets and hairpins; leather and textile clothes and containers; and baskets, resins and plant food forms."

While most of these artifacts were recovered from graves, in settlements, on the other hand: "pottery sherds and stone implements are usually the most abundant finds, although some organic remains, particularly wooden posts and animal bones, can be salvaged by careful excavation."

Waset, of the indigenous peoples, became *Thebes* of the Greeks and *Luxor* of the Arabs. It was the religious capital for the significant years in the nation's development. As the center of an enormous empire, Upper Kemet orchestrated the affairs of state for the two lands during the Middle and New Kingdoms. This region also boasted some of the largest and most important temples in all of the land. The kings of the Middle and New Kingdom worshiped the Great God Amon-ra who resided at Thebes.

Luxor is situated on the east bank, and has temples of Amon, Mut, Khonsu, Montu and Ptah. There are others built chiefly by Amenhotep III and Rameses II. Amenophis or Amenhotep III, the 18th Dynasty Pharaoh, was the great-grandson of the military genius Thutmose III. Kemet reached the pinnacle of its cultural expansion during his reign. He built the Temple of Luxor close to the banks of the Nile, just south of the city. An Avenue of Sphinxes by way of the Temples of Mut and Khonsu connected it to the Karnak temples.

Even when Egyptian military strength was past its peak, economic conditions within the capital were sound. Jill Kamil in *Luxor*: *A Guide to Ancient Thebes* says of the New Kingdom: "Trade was connected with wealth pouring in from the

QUINTESSENTIAL BOOK
"THE HOLY LAND"

distant provinces of the empire." The empire then had come to encompass almost all West Asia including Palestine, Syria, Phoenicia and the northern parts of the Euphrates as well as Nubia and Libya. They contributed "great wealth brought by loaded caravans." Among the merchandise of exchange were, "gold, silver, metalware, ivory and timber, spices for the deity's taste and strange and exotic plants to roam in private gardens." Great wealth was lavished on the Amun priesthood who, in praising, worshiping and ritualizing the gods of ancient Kemet, brought great success and bounty to the state. Temple walls, ceilings and columns were encrested with religious, historical, cosmological and artistic inscriptional masterpieces that when applied to science, astronomy, mathematics, and medical practice, such industrious engines thrust humanity along the panoramic road of civilization development. All should be made aware, how wonderful it feels for the Diasporian African to know that people who looked like them were actively involved in the creation of knowledge and practice of ethical standards this early in man's development.

Karnak is also located on the east bank of the Nile at Thebes. It houses the Great Temple of Amon, and precincts to the deities Mut, the mother goddess, and Khonsu, the moon god, their son. A temple of the war god, Montu and numerous smaller temples and chapels round out the wide array of architectural works that date this temple to over two thousand years in construction. That is, from the time of the 12th Dynasty to after the Roman invasion in 30 B.C., *Nile Year* 4210, perhaps even earlier.

Western Thebes, across the river, contained numerous mortuary temples built by some of the most outstanding Pharaohs. Mentuhotep I, Mentuhotep II, Hatshepsut, Amenhotep I, Amenhotep II, Amenhotep III, Thutmose I, Thutmose II, Thutmose III, Thutmose IV, Seti I, Rameses I, Rameses II, Rameses III, Rameses VI, Merneptah, all built temples on the west bank of the Nile. Some kings erected palaces on the west bank as did Amenhotep III who built such a structure called Malcata for his wife Queen Tiy to reside on the west bank. He constructed a lake for her to sail her boat as a past-time. Also, Rameses III of the Twentieth Dynasty erected Medinet Habu, a temple and palace, considered the last major New Kingdom construction.

There are other temples and sites of significance to the visitor. In ancient times there was much activity during pharaonic and noble burials and during the "Opet Festival," the "Festival of the Valley" and others. The Temples of Medinet Habu and the Temple of Hathor at Deir el-Medina and all the others, when lit on those festive and holy days, convey an aura of African people at prayer, that added majesty making this region culturally, the most fertile archaeologically in all of Egypt, ancient Kemet, in all today's world. This is why young African-Americans need immersion in study to gain familiarity and knowledge of the ancient cultural heritage that lit up human history. They must also take their places in defense of Egypt as African.

In the Western Necropolis, or burial places, are located the Valley of the Kings ("*Biban el-Moluk*" in Arabic), the Valley of the Queens ("*Biban el-Harim*") and Valley of the Nobles. The Valley of the Kings today contains 65 royal tombs. In recent years, a huge tomb, KV 5 was found, previously discovered, containing the resting places of 36 sons of Rameses II. Perhaps the most well known pharaoh, the celebrated boy king, Tutankhamon, whose tomb was discovered by Howard Carter in 1922, and of whom Professor John H. Clarke liked to say, "Was a minor king who got a major funeral," was found in the Valley of the Kings. Dr. Clarke's remarks relate to circumstances surrounding religious conflict between Amun and the Aten worship of Amenhotep IV, Akhenaten, related to Tutankhamon.

Queens were interred in the Valley of the Queens (*Biban el-Harim*). However, while Queen Hatshepsut had a tomb there, and having also built the Deir el-Bahari mortuary temple, she constructed a tomb in the Valley of the Kings. This queen intended to build a tunnel from the mortuary temple to her tomb in the Valley of the Kings. Thus, she intended to be taken directly from the funerary ceremony to the internment in the Valley of the Kings. The architectural and engineering feat of such a venture was well within the capability of Kemetic technology, as the earliest tunnels date to the earlier Pyramid Age.

Primarily because she reigned as king from the time of her ascendancy to the pharaonic throne until Thutmose III ended her rule, Hatshepsut dressed as a man and wore a customary false beard. The nobleman, Senmut, her architect, built extensively for his mistress and shared great power and influence. Thutmose III was her younger brother whose throne she usurped. She reigned until his party of followers was strong enough to unseat hers. In vengeance, he removed all inscriptions with her name. He also destroyed many of her statues and works, though Deir el Bahari and the obelisk at Karnak, dedicated to her father Thutmose I and Amon, did not receive the full weight of his wrath. Deir el-Bahari was secondarily dedicated to the Goddess Hathor, and there was also a shrine for Anubis. Thutmose III built a ten-foot wall surrounding her obelisks at Karnak. While the wall has fallen, one obelisk still stands to this day. Piece of another obelisk lies nearby in front of the "Coca Cola Temple," beside the Sacred Lake. Its base remains in place beside the other standing one. Some scholars argue this wall protected the obelisk during the onslaught of the Aten revolution. A Sacred Lake was fed by underground springs linking the sacred Nile to this solemn place within the temple of Karnak, *Iput Isut*.

Rameses III also constructed a temple at Karnak and one in the Temple of Mut. Thus, Karnak, the "most select of places," boasted temples, courts, vestibules, decorated then ruined walls, altars, obelisks, kiosks, chapels, columns, statues,

QUINTESSENTIAL BOOK
"THE HOLY LAND"

stelae, a sacred lake, and reused blocks. Here we see the great art of Egypt/Kemet, its architecture, whether religious or civil, it's most enduring contribution to civilization boldly displayed.

There are Royal Tombs at el-Kurna dating back to the XIth Dynasty, Dra Abu el-Naga to the XVIIth Dynasty, and XVIII-XXth Dynasty Kings in the Valley, including the spectacular tomb of Tutankhamon. The village that housed workmen of the period is called Deir el-Medina. There are also rock-cut tombs dating from the 6th Dynasty down to the Greco-Roman period that are located at Beni Hasan in Middle Egypt/Kemet.

Located at Nagada and Tukh, are predynastic and early dynastic cemeteries. They contain mastaba tombs of the reign of Aha, of the First Dynasty. Coupled with Abydos, which had cemeteries of most of the nobility, including early Dynastic Royal tombs, they can represent important sources for history and early development of Upper Nile Valley culture. The prominence of Abydos, site of the head of Osiris, and where Rameses I, Seti I and Rameses II built temples, allowed it to boast wondrous inscriptions and some of the most beautiful artwork in all the land. It is also the only place one can still see the setting up of the Tet of Osiris, his backbone.

Dendera or the 6th Nome is part of an area that includes the 4th, 5th, 7th, and 8th and 9th Nomes. In this area are located Thebes, Koptos, Dendera, Diospolis Parva, Abydos and Thinis. Despite what has been recovered, these ancient sites still contain more remains, yet to be excavated.

The evidence therefore holds that Mother Africa and Ethiopia, her eldest daughter, spoke through Upper Egypt/ancient Kemet, and can be considered the anvil upon which Kemetic/Egyptian culture impacted so significantly throughout the ancient world, allowing that legacy to be foundational in western fields of thought and practice. Here is over-whelming evidence as to why, in most cases, the influence of the south always seemed to rule supreme over the north. While the south, however, held religious and economic relevance, the lower north-land had political and administrative significance. This northern region was the gateway to Asia as well as the entranceway into Africa, particularly as it related to lands further north, east and west. Yet still, when the nation was divided or invaded, help came in great abundance from the south as in the cases of personalities and experiences of Narmer, Mentuhotep, Ahmose, and Piankhy, Shabaka, and Taharka. These uniters of the two lands were great Africans whose ethics, mentality, courage and creativity, are worth emulating by today's young Black scholars and citizens.

FREDERICK MONDERSON

REFERENCES

Adams, Barbara. *Predynastic Egypt*. Bucks: Shire Publications, 1988.
Baines, John and Jaromir Malek. *Atlas of Ancient Egypt*. New York: Facts on File, 1980.
Brugsch, H. *Egypt Under the Pharaohs*.
Budge, E. A. Wallis. *Dwellers on the Nile*. New York: Robert Blum, Publishers, Inc., 1972.
Carpiceci, Alberto Carlo. *Art and History of Egypt*. Florence, Italy: Bonechi, 1994.

Everybody here? Got to go!

Holy Land Photo 6. Abu Simbel Temple of Rameses II. Close up of the two left side and the two right side statues and the other smaller figures before them.

3.   Bus ride

Dr. Leonard James: Mr. Brown, I have always taught my students, as Thomas Henry Huxley (1825-1895) explained: "The great end of life is not knowledge but action," and, "if a little knowledge is dangerous, where is the man who has so much as to be out of danger."

QUINTESSENTIAL BOOK
"THE HOLY LAND"

Walter Brown: I tend to agree with you. Equally, I have always tried to explain to my sons, why they should get an education. Do not just be a postman like me. I have nothing against this profession but you should be in charge of the post office instead. Get that education for with it comes knowledge and wisdom. For, as *Job 28* tells us: "The price of wisdom is above rubies," and, "Behold the fear of the lord, that is wisdom, and to depart from evil that is understanding."

Dr. Leonard James: Interestingly enough, Horace said something similar: "To flee vice is the beginning of virtue, and to have got rid of folly is the beginning of wisdom."

Dr. Madison: They tell us it took two thousand years to build this temple; I wonder how many men worked on it.

Mr. John Brown: Perhaps hundreds of thousands.

Dr. Madison: Without ribbing you further, my brother, did you hear of what Thomas Brigham Bishop (1835-1905) said of John Brown's Body?

Mr. John Brown: No. But perhaps you could tell me.

Dr. Madison: "John Brown's body lies a-moldering in the grave, His soul is marching on."

Mr. John Brown: Sounds interesting, so I will agree with it.

Holy Land Illustration 10. The proper attitude to approach the king (left); and an Old Kingdom nobleman seemingly coming out of a false door in his tomb at Sakkara.

Kashmoney Malone: Look at the size of those columns. I wonder how they were able to erect them.

FREDERICK MONDERSON

Stephaniea McCall: How did they get the idea to do such gigantic work and to move those heavy stones? It is amazing.

Carmelitiea Shabazz: Strathan tells (1912: 13-14) again: "It has been customary to speak of these Egyptian capitals, carved or painted with leafage, as derived from the imitation of the lotus bud and lotus flower, but if we take the bell capital here, in its unadorned state, we see nothing to indicate such naturalism imitation; and the conclusion should be obvious that the general form of the capital came first, and that the leafage which in the examples of the later and complete Egyptian style, give its semi-naturalistic appearance, is an ornament subsequently added to complete the decoration of the column, the whole surface of which was ornamented with figures and conventional design."

"From the earliest appearance of the column in built structures in Egypt or where it is introduced in rock-cut interiors, it is manifestly a stone form, and Egyptian architecture is essentially a stone architecture in its prevalent characters, as was natural in a country where timber was scarce and granite and stone abundant."

Even Further Strathan (1912: 15) says: "In the examples at Beni-Hasan, which are the most important and significant in an architectural sense, the column is found in a different form, or facets, a treatment which we may imagine to have arisen in the first instance from a desire to lighten the appearance of the square column by cutting off its angles and reducing it to an octagon; after which the further procedure of redesigning it to sixteen sides was obvious, and natural, as was also the hollowing of each side in order to give more emphasis to the angles."

Esperanza Rodriguez: Dr. Monderson dealt with the columns and colonnade in his 5-volume book with photographs from many countries on this subject. This work is entitled *The Colonnade: Then and Now*.

Star Jackson: What amazes me is how they were able to reach those heights without a scaffold as we know it.

Carmelita Shabazz: When we get to the Temple of Karnak, to the right behind the front face south of the First Pylon you will see a ramp left over when this entranceway was put up. Just beside the ramp, you will also notice the end column shows how they were essentially erected. Square blocks were first placed in position and then pounded smooth and round and this masonry without mortar is the science of their success in architecture.

Lepsius wrote: "The two columns in the portico being octagonal and the sides flat, the four intend columns sixteen-sided and with the sides slightly hollowed or fluted. Both forms of columns diminish slightly from the base to the tops, they have no capitals except a square slab or abacus, against the under-side of which the column abuts, but they stand on a large flat circular base stone, which became the same modification, the typical base of the Egyptian column through its whole

QUINTESSENTIAL BOOK
"THE HOLY LAND"

history. It has been argued that this large flat base stone is a reason for supposing that this form of column was originally a wooden post, which would require such a base to rest on. The argument, however, is not conclusive, as a stone column would be all the better for a wide base to distribute the pressure on the ground, and Egypt, as already observed is a stone not a timber country. It is to be noted that the abacus at the top of the column does not, as in Greek and all subsequent columnar architecture, project beyond the face of the beams above it, but is flush with the latter: and this characteristic obtains throughout Egyptian architecture of all dates."

Holy Land Illustration 11. Pigs; rarely seen in the sculptures. Thebes.

"It was almost commonplace with architectural historians, on the discovery of sixteen-sided columns, some of them fluted at Beni-Hasan, that here was the origin of the Greek Doric column; but rather, perhaps, as the true antiquity of the Beni Hasan tombs was not at first realized. Since then it has been pointed out that the interval of time between the Beni-Hasan caves and the earliest remaining structures in the Doric style was at least two thousand years and therefore there was no necessity or reason for assuming any relation between the two. On the other hand it must be remembered that, though we have the remains of the early Doric temples of Corinth, Paestum, and Selinus, we have no record of what kind of Greek record preceded them; the links in the chain wanting; and, moreover, the Egyptian sixteen-sided column (but without flushing) reappears on a large scale in the much more important monument at Deir el-Bahari, forming the mausoleum of

FREDERICK MONDERSON

Queen Hatshepsu dating about 1570 B.C., or 900 years subsequent to the Beni Hasan columns; and it appears again in a small but important portion of the great temple of Karnak. There was therefore an element of persistence in this form, though we cannot follow it from century to century; and in the absence of any other known origin of early Greek style, it seems reasonable to conclude that the form of Greek Doric is traceable to Egypt, although the intermediate states are wanting."

Robert Matthews: I have always been fascinated by what I read about Egyptian architecture. In my readings, very limited though they may be, Havelock Ellis (1859-1939) in the *Dance of Life* wrote: "The art of dancing stands at the source of all the arts that express themselves first in the human person. The art of building or architecture is the beginning of all the arts that lie outside the person; and in the end they unite."

Lesley Jacobs: How interesting, I was recently reading William Hickling Prescott's (1796-1859) *The Conquest of Peru* where he wrote: "The surest test of the civilization of a people - at least as sure as any - afforded by mechanical art is to be found in their architecture, which presents so noble a field for the display of the grand and the beautiful, and which, at the same time, is so intimately connected with the essential comforts of life."

Michelliea Georges: In a New York *Daily News* article of May 8, 1991, Molefi Asante on the subject of Afrocentricity entitled "Children must learn of History, Culture that shaped the Race," explained: "There is no public school system in which African-American children feel centered in the information they are learning in the classroom. Most of what children learn places them on the outside of information. This does not happen to the white child."

Regina Hendricks: I tend to agree. But I never thought of it that way.

George Washington: Black History Month does try to do much but still the culture should be taught all year long. According to my notes, the class I took at Hunter College's Black Studies Department, 29-322, under Dr. Donna Richards was entitled *African Religious Thought Systems*. Metaphysics is the branch of philosophy that deals with first principles and attempts to explain the nature of being or reality (ontology) and of the origin and structure of the world (cosmology): It is closely related to the theory of knowledge (epistemology). On September 10, 1975, I learned African cultural religious thought is the most complex in the world. Institutional religion and non-institutional religion exists in all cultures. In African society non-institutional religion exists for it is a part of the overall cultural way of life. Immortality, being remembered by posterity, is a way of life for the African. "Science" equals knowledge.

QUINTESSENTIAL BOOK
"THE HOLY LAND"

Christianity is a "sacred," "universal," "true," "world religion." God is omnipotent or all-powerful; omniscient - all knowing, extremely knowledgeable; omnipresence, all present or all seeing.

Michael Montout: As a young theologian what is the most important lesson you have learnt from your readings and in your teachings?
James Morrison: Interesting. Well, let me see. Beyond the wisdom of the religious totality, I think it's probably what Confucius said: "Hold faithfulness and sincerity as first principles." He also said in the *Analects*: "Without recognizing the ordinances of heaven, it is impossible to be a superior man."
Dr. McFlair: Good question. As the elder, let me ask you the same question, Mr. Montout.
Michael Montout: So you threw me my own curve ball. I have been a preacher for thirty years. I suppose it is something said by John Locke (1632-1704) in his *Second Treatise on Civil Government*: "Virtue is harder to be got than knowledge of the world; and, if lost in a young man, is seldom recovered."
Dr. McFlair: I guess I am forced to answer my own question: I suppose it is something Isaiah said that: "There shall come forth a rod out of the stem of Jesse, and a branch shall grow out of his roots. And the spirit of the Lord shall rest upon him, the spirit of wisdom and understanding, the spirit of counsel and might, the spirit of knowledge and of the fear of the Lord." We should not forget the idea of humility for this is indeed a wonderful virtue. The Proverbs says: "Before honor is humility."
Michael Montout: Thomas Stearns Eliot (1888-1965) made the case: "The only wisdom we can hope to acquire is the wisdom of humility" and "Humility is the most difficult of all virtues to achieve; nothing dies harder than the desire to think well of oneself."
James Morrison: I tend to agree, for John Selden (1584-1654) pointed out: "Humility is a virtue all preach, none practice; and yet everybody is content to hear."

Mr. Sylvester Singleton: I agree wholeheartedly.
Mrs. Glenda Stewart: Honey tells us about your experiences in the Library of Congress.
Mr. John Stewart: Ok. Well, I had to go to the Library of Congress to register a poem I once wrote and what I saw there made me decide to take as many kids as possible to let them enjoy the ambiance of the architecture, art and the inherent wisdom. There are really three buildings across from each other. The Jefferson Building is the main one. It is on Independence Avenue South East from the James Madison Building. The John Adams Building is to the east of, and across the street from, the Jefferson Building. The Jefferson building is to do research on African, Middle East, and Asian topics and for visitors to enjoy the scenery. The

FREDERICK MONDERSON

Adams building is to do research in business and other matters. The Madison Building is to register copyrights and a whole lot of other subjects.

I was really impressed with the columns in the architectural layout of the Jefferson Building as well as the painted ceiling and the writing on the walls. What I found there is the writings of the great literary giants such as Moses, Herodotus, Moliere, Shakespeare, Aristotle, Bacon, Milton, Homer and Dante. Of course I saw no names of individuals we would call African today and this was an issue of concern. However, the virtues of justice, fortitude, patriotism, courage, prudence, temperance, industry and Concordia were there.
Mrs. Glenda Stewart: Honey, tell them of the proverbs that really impressed you.
Mr. John Stewart: There were several such as "Beauty is truth, truth beauty" and "All are but parts of one stupendous whole whose body nature is and God the soul." The one that really impressed me is "The foundation of every state is the education of its youth." Another quote I found interesting also on the walls of the Madison Building read: "What spectacle can be more edifying or more reasonable than that of liberty and learning. Each leaning on the other for their mutual and surest support."

Holy Land Illustration 12. Gazelles and other animals belonging to the preserves. Tomb near the Pyramids.

Asantewaa Harris: I think that was really impressive. I must take a trip to Washington, DC, one day. I know it's a wonderful city.
Hattie Jones: I agree. But since we live in Los Angeles, it's a bit difficult. Perhaps I could purchase some books that detail the layout of the city.
Mr. John Stewart: "Books must follow sciences and not sciences books," and "Glory is acquired by virtue but preserved by letters" are some others. I will try to remember some more and perhaps share them at a later time.
Asantewaa Harris: Helmholtz (1821-1894) in *Academic Discourse*, in Heidelberg (1862) offered the view: "Whoever, in the pursuit of science seeks immediate practical utility, may generally rest assured that he will seek in vain. All that science can achieve is a perfect knowledge and a perfect understanding of the action of natural and moral forces." Of course, the quest for knowledge is a pure joy and every man must strive to unclog his memory of ignorance and pursue knowledge, understanding and ultimately wisdom.

QUINTESSENTIAL BOOK
"THE HOLY LAND"

Jerome Smith: Mr. Cubia, I did not get it earlier, you said you are retired but you look so young.

Teddy Cubia: You know, having worked twenty-five years in education, I chose to retire early so as to enjoy my later years.

Jerome Smith: I see. Hopefully, when I get to your age I could also retire and enjoy my later years, as well as look as well as you do.

Dr. Alexander Pushkin: Young man, I am a bit confused by your explanation of Afrocentricity as a philosophy and concept. Perhaps you could explain a bit further. I mean clarify yourself some more.

Michael Sinclair: Well, philosophy asks axiological, epistemological, aesthetic and ethical questions. Of course, aesthetic questions are different from factual questions. Factual questions ask size, color, members in a class, and so on.

What is meant when we say someone or something is centered? This is a philosophic question. We must keep in mind Afrocentrists are not rigid. Still, they insist that African people must be viewed as subjects not objects on the fringes of Europe.

Calif. Sister: This is interesting, but I am not sure you are clear in your explanation.

Michael Sinclair: Aesthetics, epistemology, axiology and ethics raise philosophic questions. These are the kinds of questions Afrocentrists ask. These are extensions of concepts or class. Philosophic questions are concrete and/or abstract. Philosophic questions are higher-level questions. Afrocentric inquiries are approaches to inquiries. What is meant by logical, semantics, ethical are all philosophical questions.

Teddy Cubia: I am a bit slow in catching up but can you explain some of those terms a bit further. I mean what is meant by cosmology, aesthetics, epistemology, axiology and ethics. I have an idea that the four virtues were wisdom, justice, fortitude and temperance. I also know that such other character traits as ambition, resourcefulness, courage and devotion are virtues that, while not classic, are everyday traits.

Michael Sinclair: While the virtues and traits are the up and down side of human nature, these previous terms try to explain the concepts we use in Afrocentricity. Some of the questions we ask are 'Where is a person placed?' 'How do you locate them?' 'How do you examine them?'

FREDERICK MONDERSON

For example, a question such as what is meant by centered is different from who has melanin or whether Cleopatra was black. These last two are not philosophical but factual questions. For instance, cosmological questions are of a universal nature or class of ideas, universe, and gender, social or economic class.

Epistemological questions require a nature of proof, investigating knowledge, knowing. Axiological questions are questions of value. We then ask, what is value? Aesthetics – What is good? How do you determine the good when good is not beautiful? Ethical – How do people behave or act in society. Thus these questions of a philosophic nature are of a higher level.

Even further, a philosophy may be a discipline or a world axiom. Systems differ from disciplines.

Kawaida is a system. Afrocentricity is a philosophic discipline. It is not readily discernible or obtainable. It is a way of knowing, or a training of the mind.

High-level questions about centeredness are intellectual ideas, not readily attainable. It demands study, reflection, and self-conscious motivation.

Another term we can be familiar with is paradigms or framework for inquiry. There are three aspects for obtaining a framework of Afrocentric understanding. These are ethnological, categorical, and functional. We ask ourselves: "Is this an Afrocentric text?" "What can I look for in this article that tells me it's Afrocentric?"

Dr. Alexander Pushkin: We have arrived at Karnak Temple. On the way back I will again put you on the spot, young brother. Nevertheless, I think you are holding it down philosophically and this adds another dimension to the spirituality and intellectual aspect of this trip.
Asantewaa Harris: That was good. Perhaps we could get Mr. Cubia to recite another one of his poems.
Teddy Cubia: Sure, but since we are getting to Karnak soon, I will make this a short one. It's called "Black is Light."

Black is Light

Blind?
Yes – the world is blind
To the power that is coming to light
Black is now
It's here
Would open your eyes
To see!

QUINTESSENTIAL BOOK "THE HOLY LAND"

4. Site

KARNAK TEMPLE
TEMPLE OF KARNAK: THE MAJESTIC ARCHITECTURE OF ANCIENT KEMET
BY
Frederick Monderson

In considering the world's most sacred places, with their artistic, architectural, philosophical, and religious mystique, none surpass the holy site of Karnak, home of Amon, head of the Theban triad. Amun, Mut and Khonsu, became supreme deities of the land during the Middle and New Kingdoms, of dynastic **K M T**. As such, the Temple of Karnak, 'Throne of Power,' in the city of Thebes, is one of the most spiritually profound and majestic architectural, or divine constructions, in all the land of ancient Kemet, today's Egypt, in Northeast Africa. What is interesting is that this theological, metaphysical and esoteric power remained a force for more than two thousand years. Another two thousand years later the awe and mysticism still mesmerizes the modern visitor who finds this structure an esoteric and spiritual Mecca and artistic and architectural photographic museum of bonanza proportions. Shaw and Nicholson (1995: 148) explained this with the view: "It is the largest and best-preserved temple complex of the New Kingdom, and its reliefs and inscriptions incorporate valuable epigraphic data concerning the political and religious activities of imperial Egypt." In fact, when we think of significant milestones in the history of art, architecture and development of mathematics, particularly in the Nile Valley, the Temple of Karnak, 'Throne of the World,' stands as a significant achievement for its creativity, beauty, majesty, and grandeur. Its preservation, sprawling nature, massive exactness, and double-axis, east and west, and north and south, duration of time in construction, and great array of builders and architects whose genius compounded here, all contribute to its memorable state. The sum total of the awesome dynamics viewed in today's remains, in superb defiance of the ravages of time that still evokes great reverence, awe and inspiration in the great mysteriousness of Karnak Temple. Comprising a

FREDERICK MONDERSON

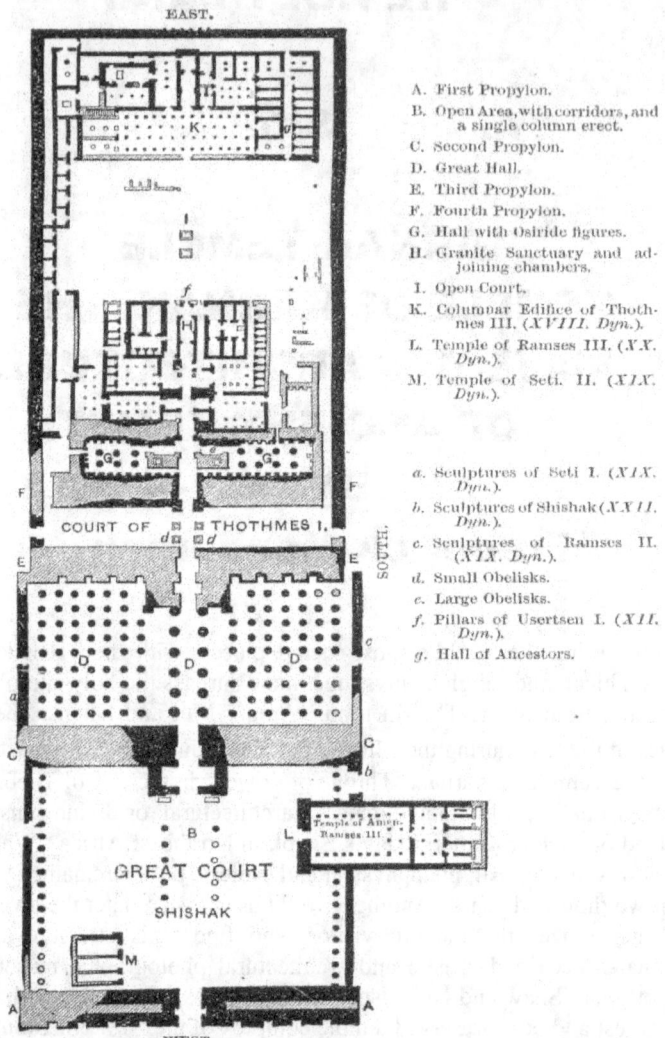

Plan of the Great Temple of Amon at Karnak

stupendous palace of spiritual, theological, metaphysical power and mystical beauty, the Temple of Karnak, within the Precinct of Amun, is an aggregate of worship temples whose buildings extended over a period of two thousand years. Here pharaohs vied with each other to erect structures in honor of the mighty deity Amon-Ra, 'Lord of the Thrones of Two Lands,' the sun god; his wife, Mut, the earth goddess; and their son, Khonsu, the moon god. These divinities comprised the Theban Triad. Weigall (1996: 61) supplied an explanation that: "To the Egyptians Thebes was known by many names. It was 'Victorious Thebes,' 'The Thrones of the Two Lands,' 'The Mysterious City,' 'The City of the Hidden

QUINTESSENTIAL BOOK "THE HOLY LAND"

Name,' 'The City of the Lord of Eternity,' 'The Mistress of Temples,' 'The Mistress of Might,' and so on."

Holy Land Illustration 13. Ploughing, sowing and reaping. Tombs of the Kings - Thebes; and Tritura, or threshing and winnowing. Thebes.

For architectural clarity of historical construction, Polyglot (1965: 41) supplies the names of rulers who glorified Amon at his innermost seat in Thebes, the Temple of Karnak. "The temple was built by Thutmosis I, Hatshepsut, Thutmosis III, Amenophis III, Rameses I, Seti I, Rameses II, Seti II, Rameses III, by the kings of the Bubastis and Taharka, and the Ptolemies." During this perennial experiment in creative religious art and architecture, Badawy's (1990: 11) explanation is that the New Kingdom rulers experimented in a variety of construction techniques and enterprises. "Building projects were characterized by large scale and deterioration in style, although some show originality and boldness. Queen Hatshepsut built her wonderful rock-cut temple at Deir el Bahari, with terraces and porticoes on polygonal columns, and decorated with beautiful low reliefs. Thotmes I,

FREDERICK MONDERSON

Amenophis III, Rameses I, and Rameses II carried out work at Karnak. Rameses busied himself with projects of dubious taste all over the country, but is responsible for the impressive rock-cut temples at Abu Simbel. A new style with realistic trend was inaugurated by Amenhotep III (Amenophis III) and brought to its apex by Amenhotep IV at his capital 'Amarna.'"

In tracing the evolution of the Karnak structure, Langenscheidt. (1990: 145) has provided a sketch showing some aspects of its history. "In subsequent generations it increased in size and magnificence and aligned itself with a number of other temples - to the north, the temples of Month and Ptah; to the south, the temple of Mut, with the long avenue of sphinxes leading to the temple of Luxor. As a result of these continual additions and alterations, the temple lacks unity; however, it offers a valuable overview of generations of Egyptian architecture and art."

Eames (1992: 223) expressed the following view on Karnak Temple that further underscores its importance and the magnitude of this precinct of Amun. "Unraveling the secrets of 2,000 years has been a major feat of Egyptology, made the more difficult by the fact that family rivalries and kingly jealousies were often the incentive behind new constructions. Often the reigning pharaoh would alter the royal cartouche of a predecessor and thereby take the credit for all the work that that predecessor had accomplished (which may be why Rameses II seems to have been so industrious in temple building). To add to the confusion, some parts of the building were raised from dismantled shrines or the walls of other temples. In addition, Karnak had to endure the degradation of Amon-Ra, first at the hands of the rebel pharaoh Akhenaten and then by the early Christians."

This and more Karnak endured!

The enclosure wall of this august temple had entrances on the north, south, east and west. Yet, since this was a riverside temple, entrance was generally from the west. However, within the enclosure wall, Smith (1991: 151) tells: "six gateways separate the front of the temple from the sanctuary, and obviously because they ran out of room at the front of the temple, four gateways were added on the side." This alignment comprised the two axes of the temple. Shaw and Nicholson (1995: 148) wrote accordingly: "The earliest axis stretches from west to east, incorporating the Great Hypostyle Hall of Rameses II (1279-1213 B.C.), which is over five hectares in area. The second axis extends the temple southwards towards the nearby precinct of the goddess Mut."

QUINTESSENTIAL BOOK
"THE HOLY LAND"

Holy Land Photo 7. Abu Simbel Temple of Rameses II. Entrance to Rameses' temple (left); and above the entrance on the cornice, the King is depicted offering his name as Ma'at to the titular deity, Ra-Horakhty.

The greatness of Karnak Temple is due to the assertive nature of the Theban princes who rose in the Middle and New Kingdoms and made their nome and nation great, under the inspiration, instigation and guidance of Amon, 'king of the gods.' Fragner (1994: 20) describes that two thousand year period of architectural trail blazing as "vegetative" construction. This form of construction occurs when a "building or even a whole complex grows organically, naturally and only acquires its final appearance over a long period of time." In this respect, and with Egypt/Kemet the world leader for more than a thousand years, Thebes prospered and the mighty temple of Karnak, home to Amun, was embellished with great buildings, whose architects excelled artistically and mathematically. In the ensuing growth of this site during a period of imperial expansion, Hart's (1996: 17) commentary is: "Treasure from successful military expeditions helped pay for the temple of Amun-Re at Karnak. Central columns, higher than a nine-story building, are crowned with carved papyrus heads. The walls are inscribed with records of Sethos I's battle victories. The grounds once included gardens, orchards and living quarters for temple workers." The aura of these creations were such that, they bloomed in majestic exuberance, while thousands of Priests and their property, and artistic and creative powers, glorified Amun, 'King of the Gods' in his palace at Karnak.

Gympel (1996: 8) adds even further the view that geography influences architecture, particularly as it relates to worship of the gods: "The procession temples in the Nile valley were carved into the rocks west of Thebes and the most famous are the Temple of Amon in Luxor and Karnak. They suggest that the religious and philosophical perspectives of the designing architects were influenced by the surrounding natural landscape."

FREDERICK MONDERSON

Equally, Mann (1993: 106) has added there's a higher force behind temple building in his statement: "The creation of sacred buildings echoes the creation of the universe, and both seek to follow similar mathematical laws. Therefore the Golden Section (phi) is found to govern the growth of plants and animals, and is also the primary proportion found in sacred buildings and monuments. In their use of numbers as a symbolic language, the Egyptians predate and influence Pythagoras and Plato."

Even further, Mann (1993: 106-07) allows a glimpse at how the multi-dimensionality of Kemetic science, allowed practitioner priests the opportunity to experiment in beating back the walls of ignorance. "The Egyptians communicated symbolic astrological and astronomical concepts beyond the actual form of the buildings. Similarly, their hieroglyphic language used symbols instead of mere signs. A sign has a limited meaning, while a symbol evokes correspondences and widens understanding. The Egyptians used their mythology to further understanding because it was more than simple history. Their gods came from the stars, bringing wisdom, understanding and power. Their myths were cosmic myths, describing planetary movements, and brought the mathematical reality of the stars to humanity."

Art was also a highly developed science, and artifacts easily portray profound ideas that under-gird this ancestral culture's religious and spiritual expression. Lurker (1991: 123) displayed a photograph that depicts how "Rames-Nakht, High Priest of Amun, kneels to present a small shrine upon which are represented the Theban Triad of Amun, Mut and their son, Khons. From Karnak. XX Dynasty, c. 1120 B.C. Egyptian Museum, Cairo." The war god Montu, himself a deity of the Theban nome, also had a temple to the north of Amon's at Karnak. Today these temples of Mut, Khonsu and Montu are closed to visitors. Yet still, the wonderful sights of the principal Karnak Temple are more than enough of a fascinating treat.

Holy Land Illustration 14. Sakkara. Tomb of Sekhemka, Vth Dynasty (left); and another scene showing the nobleman in different attitudes (right).

QUINTESSENTIAL BOOK "THE HOLY LAND"

For the modern visitor who disembarks from a bus, the walk to the temple is quite exhilarating. It's even more so when one realizes this is the path the ancestral monarchs ascended as they approached Karnak's revered place of divine and ancestral worship. Under girding this belief Baines and Malek (1980: 92) rightly points out the Karnak Temple was arranged in a manner that is reverse in its modern conception. "The layout of the great temple can be described as a series of pylons of various dates, with courts and halls between them, leading to the main sanctuary. The earliest are Pylon IV and V built by Tuthmose I; from then on the temple was enlarged in a westerly and a southerly direction."

Helping to comprehend the full scope and dimension of the Karnak Temple complex, Baines and Malek (1980: 92) added even further: "Nearly 20 other small chapels and temples are within the precinct of Amun, including a temple of Ptah built by Tuthmosis III, Shabaka, the Ptolemies and Tiberius (north of the Great Temple, close to the enclosure wall), and a chapel of Osiris Heqadjet 'Ruler of Time' of Osorkon IV and Shebitku (northeast of the Great Temple, close to the enclosure wall)."

Such grandeur in architectural construction, utilizing exact mathematical and scientific principles embodied in their work amazed young Champollion, 'father of modern Egyptology.' To this note, Sauernon (1962: 42) provides a quote echoing Champollion's own words of amazement in the following statement: "No ancient or modern people have thought of art or architecture on such a sublime scale so vast and so grandiose as that of the ancient Egyptians. They thought in terms of men 100 feet tall." Elsewhere, Aldred (1987: 33) mentions Belzoni, agent of Henry Salt, the British Consul. Belzoni was called the "strongman Egyptologist" who had written: "In the 19th Century the remains of Karnak and Luxor were like those of a city of giants, who after long conflict were all destroyed, leaving the ruins of their temples as the only proof of their former existence."

Shedding more light on such discussions, Habachi (1987: 52) has pointed to two recurring themes throughout the temple comprising the Precinct of Amun. "One showing the god Amon or Amon-Re presenting the king with a sword with which he might smite his enemies and the other portraying the king offering the gods rich tribute and prisoners captured during his visits."

While standing remains support the view the earliest temple began in the Middle Kingdom, Aldred (1987: 131) added: "The Theban buildings of the Middle Kingdom were used as quarries by later pharaohs and it is out of the foundations of the Third Pylon at Karnak that there has been reconstructed a white limestone kiosk which Sesostris I built at Thebes c. 1941 B.C. for a symbolical re-enactment of his main jubilee ceremonies at Memphis." Elsewhere, Aldred (1987: 85) displays a photograph of this temple with a caption reading: "Relief on a pillar of a temple erected by Sesostris I for one of his jubilees and demolished later as fill for a courtyard in the temple of Amun and Karnak. It shows the king and Ptah of Memphis mutually embracing within the god's shrine." All this notwithstanding, use of this site, in the 4th Upper Kingdom Nome, may extend to the beginnings of Pharaonic rule and into the prehistoric period. However, Weigall (1996: 61) has tempered this somewhat in his statement: "Diodorus says that Thebes is the most ancient city of Egypt, and, though this is evidently not correct, it may well be one of the most ancient cities of the country. There are some traces of prehistoric remains on the west-bank of the river opposite Karnak, and at Karnak itself relics of a period as early as the IInd Dynasty has been found."

Williams (1996: 91) adds to the unfolding mystery of the age of Karnak, as the 'Glory of ancient Thebes.' "The still interesting fact about Thebes is that many of its formerly great temples were prehistoric ruins even five thousand years ago. The most ancient temple at Karnak, for example, in what was the center of Nowe, goes back beyond the reach of man's records. No other city on earth ever had so many temples, and even today there are more ruins of temples there than anywhere in the world. Because of the splendor of their architectural designs and the colossal size of the structure, they, like the pyramids, became wonders of the world. Religion was not only the immediate occasion for the development of art and architecture, but it also inspired the drive for bigness, the grand design on a scale as huge as human skill and effort could achieve. Nothing less was befitting of the gods."

This site is contemporary with other centers and deities that emerged and held prominence in the early age of dynastic rule. The first twenty-two nomes stretched from Biga above Aswan and Elephantine to Memphis in the north.

We get a glimpse of this in Baines and Malek (1980: 15) as they throw light on these political divisions in the statement showing: "The 22 nomes of Upper Egypt were fixed by the 5th Dynasty, and their lengths along the river are recorded in the Kiosk of Senwosret I at Karnak. For Lower Egypt the definitive number of 20 nomes was not established until the Greco/Roman Period. The total number of 42 had a symbolic value: there were 42 judges of the dead, and the early Christian writer, Clemens of Alexandria (2nd Century A.D.), states that the Egyptians had 42 sacred books." These symbolic numbers notwithstanding, elsewhere Maspero has held the number of nomes were sometimes more, sometimes less than the number 42.

QUINTESSENTIAL BOOK "THE HOLY LAND"

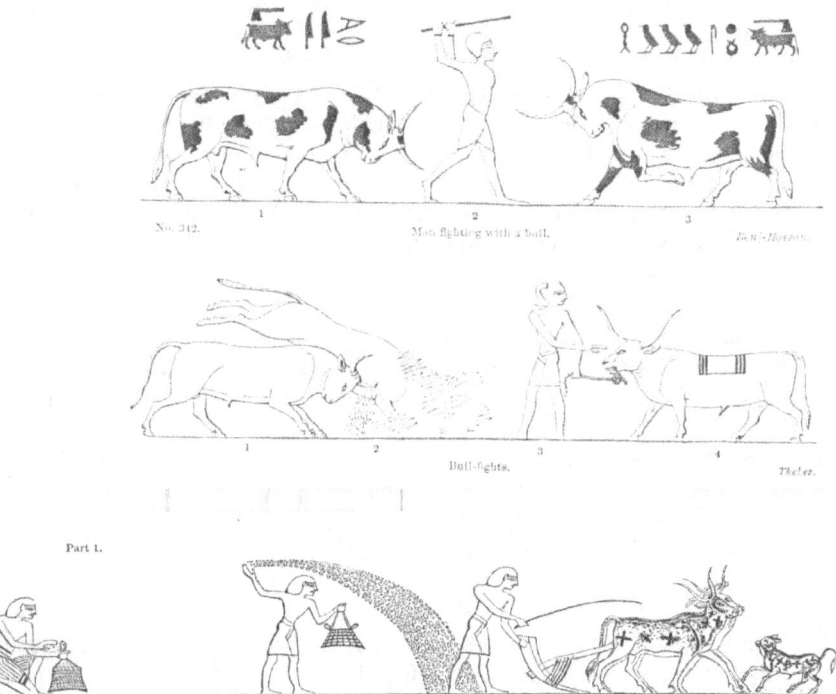

Holy Land Illustration 15. Man fighting with a bull (top); bull-fights; man puts seeds in basket and begins sowing and ploughing (bottom).

Additionally, in the position as seat of great learning and wisdom, during the Middle and New Kingdoms, Karnak as well as Thebes sparkled. This is further shown in Baines and Malek (1980: 90) who, beyond the artistry and functions, believe the "temple of Amun was ideologically and economically the most important temple establishment in the whole of Egypt." In its theological, cosmological and political dynamics, it was considered "the location of the emergence of the primeval mound at the beginning of time. It was the supreme 'city' and all other towns in Egypt could only try to imitate it and would only achieve pale reflections."

Significantly, if it could be imagined what the pathway to heaven would be like, the walk through the Processional Way of Karnak Temple seems just as exhilarating an inspiration, in this 'The Most select of places.' The aura, majesty and symbolism surrounding the home of the great Theban Triad, where 'Amun Lord of Karnak' resided, particularly intoxicates those privileged to behold this wonder as they are invigorated and rejuvenated by its intellectual promise and sacred and profound vitality. Knopf (1995: 404) says of the temple and its principal divinity: "The ancient name of Karnak *Ipet Sut* ('the most hallowed of places') designates the 'center of the world' where Amun, the creator of the universe, first created himself and then all things and living beings. He combined the power of the Theban demiurge (Amun) with that of the supreme sun god of Heliopolis (re). He was the guarantor of the continued survival of the universe that he had created and therefore of the kingdom ruled by his 'beloved son' pharaoh, the only official priest. Mankind, by worshiping in the temple, could help preserve cosmic harmony so essential to life, and encompassed by the Egyptian concept of *Ma'at*, which signified truth, order and justice. All this was part of the pharaoh's duty. Their watchword was 'Life, Stability and Strength.'"

Youssef (1991: 186) explained how in their layout: "Temples in general followed the same principles. For the ancient Egyptians the precinct represented a little replica of the cosmos at the time of creation. It was set apart from the everyday world and demarcated by a mud-brick girdle wall. Usually, but not always, the temple had an east-west axis, so that the rising or setting sun could strike right into its innermost recesses." There were many festivals throughout the year and Hart (1996: 8) showed how: "Processions, receptions, for foreign visitors and visits to the temple were opportunities to show the power of the pharaohs."

Even further Youssef (1991: 186) continued: "In the outer parts of the temple, the reliefs record historical events: the foundation and dedication of the temple itself and details of processions and ceremonies. The pharaoh is very much in evidence, leading the activities. He always faces the interior, while the resident god or goddess, often shown together with a consort and attendant gods, faces the outside world." Pharaoh looks in to worship, while the gods look out to bless and admire their creations, human and material.

This, as the visitor beholds the wondrous testaments of artistic and pictographic panorama at the root of epistemological, philosophic, religious and festive efforts of praise and ritualizing of the African god, Amon. Here then the modern visitor experiences an emotional, theosophical and intellectual transformation that sometimes African-Americans seem to come away experiencing as manifest in this pilgrimage. Clearly Amun was a good god for he blest his people and helped those ancient Africans prosper in mental faculty, perfection of the principles of Ma'at, that quintessential social elixir, and the proliferation of their artistic and architectural magnificence resulting in development of medicine, science, building practice, quarrying, technology and craftsmanship. This knowledge is important and underscores the effort of redemptive scholars so crucial to the necessary process of African historiographic reconstruction that is and must continue, particularly the work of contemporary black scholars and organizations such as ASCAC are trying to achieve.

QUINTESSENTIAL BOOK "THE HOLY LAND"

Nevertheless, to understand the nature of the temple, one has to familiarize oneself with the historical circumstances surrounding the emergence of the Amun priesthood and how this body influenced successive pharaohs to glorify their deity through works of architectural splendor. In furtherance of this aim, monarchs lavished enormous endowments of wealth in gold, cattle, spices, slaves, towns, buildings, gardens, etc., on Amun who brought success, fame and fortune to his most ardent supporters. Helping to trace the evolution of the worship of Amun, Steindorff and Seele (1971: 134) offers commentary that the: "cosmic god Amun was transferred from Hermopolis to Karnak in the Eleventh Dynasty so that he eventually became the local god of Thebes and later through identification with Re, as 'King of the gods' the national god of the New Kingdom."

Syncretism, or combining of gods, enabled "Hathor and Isis," wrote Steindorff and Seele (1972: 143), to be "considered the same person, while Amon of Karnak, Min of Coptos, and later even Khnum of Elephantine were combined into a single divinity."

Scholz (1997: 82) noted: "Min is one of the archaic ithyphallic gods, thought to be related to the darker-skinned Africans. Thus, he was sometimes portrayed as a 'black' god. He symbolized the bull-like potency of the one 'who fertilized his mother [Isis];' thus, they belonged to the circle of the royal gods." Wilkinson (1996: I, 327) added further in explanation of this concept regarding the deity and practice in this Nile River civilization: "The fundamental doctrine was the unity of the Deity, but this unity was not represented, and he was known by a sentence, or an idea, beings, as Iamblichus says, 'Worshiped in silence.' But the attributes of this being were represented under positive forms; and hence arose a multiplicity of gods, that engendered idolatry, and caused a total misconception of the real nature of the deity, in the minds of all who were not admitted to knowledge of the truth through the mysteries. The division of God in this attribute was in this manner. As soon as he was thought to have any reference to his works, or to man, he ceased to be quiescent; he became an agent; and he was no longer the One, but distinguishable and divisible, according to his supposed character, his actions, and his influences on the world. He was then the Creator, the Divine Goodness, (or the abstract idea of Good,) Wisdom, Power, and the like; and as we speak of Him as the Almighty, the Merciful, the Everlasting, so the Egyptians gave to each of his various attributes a particular name. But they did more: they separated them; and to the uninitiated they became distinct gods. As one of these, the Deity was Amun; probably, the divine mind in operation, the bringer of light of the secrets of its hidden will; and he had a complete human form, because man was the intellectual animal, and the principal design of the divine will in the creation."

FREDERICK MONDERSON

Holy Land Illustration 16. Sakkara. Nobleman Seker-Kha-Bau in different attitudes (left); and Stele of his Wife from the Tomb of Seker-Kha-Bau, IIIrd Dynasty (right).

This cosmological syncretism is a powerful reason why the mighty Amun, his precinct at Karnak, the city of Waset, the region of the Upper Kingdom, and the state of Kemet, all enjoyed the power it did for so long in the ancient world. Quirke (1992: 38-39) adds even further to this, in the statement: "Ra was a visible sovereign, as the sun-disk in the sky, but from the Middle Kingdom he was joined by a complement to express a concept more familiar to Judaism, Christianity and Islam, the invisible divinity that is present unseen everywhere in the world; this complement was Amun 'the hidden one.' In the Old Kingdom Amun appears only as one of the pre-existent aspects of nothingness, an opposite of the world of matter, like Keku, 'darkness.' His obscurity ends from the time that the rulers of Thebes began to claim the kingship of the Two Lands in C. 2000 B.C.; the local governor Intef set up a monument from which one octagonal column survives, reused in the foundations of a later construction, and one face of the column bears above the royal titles and name of Intef the identity of the new deity 'Amun-Ra, lord of the sky, power of the land, pillar of the Fighting (?) Province.' As the 'hidden' invisible divine power Amun provided the ideal cipher for the burgeoning ambitions of the Theban rulers. As a universal force Amun could be conceived in Egyptian terms as an aspect of Ra, in the compound form Amun-Ra and this deity became the principal god of empire in the New Kingdom, when Egypt controlled the gold mines of Nubia and trade routes of Syria-Palestine. Under the

QUINTESSENTIAL BOOK "THE HOLY LAND"

Thutmoside kings the treasuries of Amun in his main temple at Karnak filled with the spoils of war and the gains of international trade, and the cult center grew throughout the following millennium to become the largest religious complex on earth."

That is, Amun enjoyed all this, until challenged by the Amarna Heresy of Akhenaton. In building his temple beyond the eastern gate at Karnak the new king had to confront the grandeur of Amon. Girding himself for that battle, Amenhotep IV, 'Amon is Satisfied,' changed his name to Akhenaton, 'He who is Beneficial to Aton,' and became increasingly concerned with his new disk worship. With all the history of Amun worship at this site, the new religious visionary began to feel uncomfortable within the Precinct of Amon.

This is expressed in an opinion by Maspero (1904: V, 82) who held the view: "Thebes had belonged to Amen so long that the king could never hope to bring it to regard Atenu as anything but of inferior rank. Each city belonged to some god, to whom was attributed its origin, its development and its prosperity, and whom it could not forsake without renouncing its very existence. This belief forced Akhenaton to choose Amarna to build his new city Akhetaton 'City of the Horizon' and temple 'Mansion of the Obelisk,' 'Shadow of Ra.' He drew up the plans himself. Akhnaton also taught his artists new techniques of representing nature and the human form that contradicted the traditional mode of representing these subjects, particularly the Pharaoh. His mother Queen Tiy, and advisers Ay and Commander of the Egyptian Forces, General Horemhab, moved to strategic Amarna, along with a retinue of supporters, their families and property. There he began to write and praise the Aton, solar disk." Wilkinson (1971: 123) provides a personal insight into the king in his explanation: "Akhenaten, though never shown wearing earrings, is depicted with perforations in his ears on statues from Karnak."

FREDERICK MONDERSON

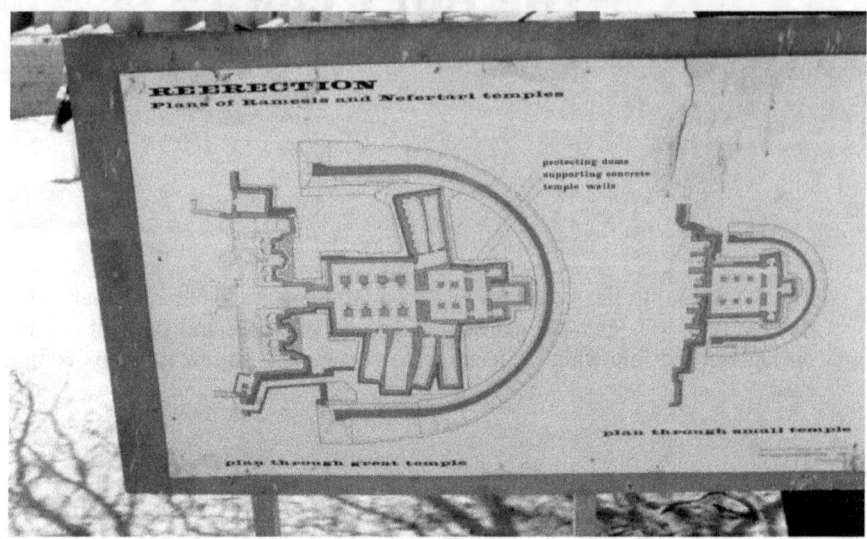

Holy Land Photo 8. Abu Simbel Temple of Rameses II. Plans of the twin Temples of Rameses and Nefertari in new sites after reconstruction and re-erection.

In Akhenaten's "Great Hymn to Aton," Obenga (1992: 19) wrote: "We see more than a text of monotheism and expressions of faith. It reveals an exact knowledge of nature which is surprisingly scientifically precise when compared to modern scientific knowledge."

However, after this Aton turned with a vengeance on Amon. Akhnaton decreed, according to Payne (1964: 128-29) that: "the name of the district where the Aton Temple was located was to be changed to 'The Brightness of Aton, the Great' and Thebes itself, the City of Amon, was to be renamed, 'The City of the Brightness of Aton.' His animosity was directed purely against Amon, for Prisse D'Avennes found at Karnak on fragments of the temple, the names of other divinities than Atonu worshiped by Khuniatonu." Maspero (1904: V, 89) pretty well summed up how the king felt. "The other gods, except Amon, were sharers with humanity in his benefits. Atonu prescribed him, and tolerated him only at Thebes; he required that the name of Amon should be effaced wherever it occurred, but he respected Ra, and Horus and Harmakhis - all, in fact but Amon: he was content with being regarded as their king, and he strove rather to become their chief than their destroyer."

Anger at the principal deity of the triad did not extend to the consort. For as Maspero (1904: V, 82) informed: "The proscription of Amon extended to inscriptions, so that while his name or figure, whatever could be got at, was chiseled out, the vulture, the emblem of Mut, which expresses the idea of mother,

QUINTESSENTIAL BOOK
"THE HOLY LAND"

was avoided." Overcoming the destruction of this period, in King Tutankhamon's return to Thebes following the death of Akhenaton, Amon re-emerged as principal deity under the succeeding dynasties of Ramesside kings. Amon's prosperity, power and respect were restored.

Arguably, it seems rather natural that Amon's adherents would return vengeance for the proscription they suffered. Erman (1907: 69-70) explained an attitude of Amon's priests in the following statement in exhortation of their deity. "Woe to him who injures thee! Thy city endures, but the city of him who injures thee has perished. Shame upon him who commits sacrilege against thee in any land. The sun of him who knew thee not has set; but he who knows thee, he shines; the sanctuary of him who injured thee lies in darkness, and the whole earth is in light."

In fact, Barnett (1996: 81) argued: "The cult of Amun lost power temporarily when Akhenaten transferred his capital to El-Amarna and worshiped Aten. The supreme position was soon regained but declined when the Assyrians destroyed Thebes... and the cult of Osiris became more popular and influential. Regarded by the Greeks as the equivalent of Zeus, the cult of Zeus Ammon spread to Greece, and then as Jupiter Ammon his cult spread to the Romans."

Powerful! Amon as Great God in universal beneficence!

Interestingly, that power, in its spiritual, intellectual, revitalizing and awe-inspiring significance is ever present today. The modern visitor is impressed by the stupendous remains with their timeless, esoteric mystique and artistic wonderment that reflect the deep sense of commitment of early Africans of ancient Kemet, in their communion with deity.

Secular and religious festivals as the Heb Sed, Opet and agricultural festivals were celebrated with great reverence. In one particular festival, the Feast of the Valley, wrote Bierbrier (1989: 97), the "sacred image of the god Amon was brought across the river to visit the mortuary temples of the deceased ruler. The Heb-Sed festival rejuvenated the king after years of rule. The Opet Festival represented Amun's journey to Luxor, the Southern Isut, to engage in worshiping Hathor/Mut, his wife. This feast involved extensive merriment."

Mention can now be made of Percy E. Newberry's "An Egyptian Gardener: The Tomb of Nakht" indicating the nobleman, under Thutmose III "held the office of head gardener of the gardens attached to the Temple of Karnak." One of his duties was to supply flowers daily to the main and subsidiary temples for their services and ceremonies. Nakht is depicted in his tomb: "presenting Thutmose III with a huge bouquet, five feet high, and composed of papyrus, lotus flowers, cornflowers, and poppies, interspersed here and there with fragrant fruits of the mimusopsi, a tree not now found in the gardens of Egypt, but well known at the present day in India. Some of these garlands have been found in the ancient cemeteries of Egypt, buried with the dead."

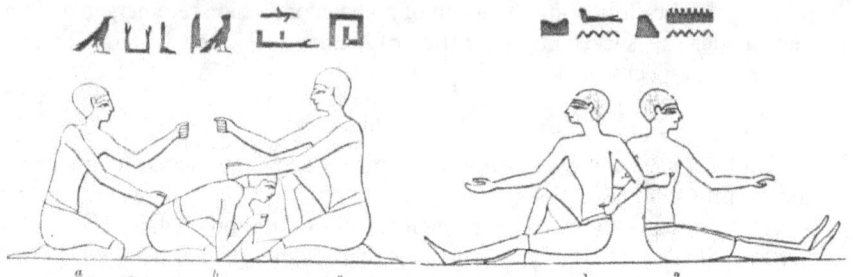

Holy Land Illustration 17. A game perhaps similar to the Greek Kollabism; and rising from the ground as they held each other. Beni-Hassan.

For the civil garden, a tomb of the nobleman Amten, who owned several estates, could be used as comparative reference. In another article "Ancient Egyptian Gardening," Newberry mentions this, the oldest garden yet discovered. "'The boundary wall,' wrote Amten, 'was 200 cubits (i.e. 350 feet) in breadth, and the same in width; the garden inside it was planted with beautiful trees, and a very great pond was excavated in its center, the surrounding garden being planted with fig-trees and vines. When the writing for the royal prescript had been made, a very great vineyard was planted, which yielded me wine in great quantity. I trained two acres of vine hidden in the interior of the wall, and I planted trees around it.'"

In this writer's examining this ancient culture, it ought not to be forgotten, racist scholarship, regarding Egypt and other places in Africa, have tried to falsely claim European authorship, under the banner of the "Hamitic Hypothesis," of many significant achievements made on this continent. This pseudo-scientific theory analyzed by my teacher and mentor Dr. Leonard James at New York City Technical College and now refuted, held that: "all evidence of civilization or high culture found in Africa was brought there by people of a white morphology." In that respect, activist pseudo-scientists have sought to claim as foreign, great Africans, whose influence on the world stage have been memorable. I say this to create an example of the enormous power of early African persona, spirituality, tenaciousness and creativity, to draw attention to attendant problems of ascribing their accomplishments to foreigners.

Dr. ben-Jochannan (1990: 40-41) strongly favored the African Rameses II, a great warrior pharaoh, high priest, military strategist, imperial colonizer, conqueror, engineer, builder, scientific patron, and father and husband. However, yet another authority claimed Rameses to be of Syrian origin! For, in addition to his stupendous building projects, this monarch was involved in the Battle of Kadesh,

QUINTESSENTIAL BOOK "THE HOLY LAND"

one of the most memorable military engagements of the ancient world. The events go like this. On an imperial expedition to Asia, the king set out with four regiments, Amun, Ra, Ptah, and Sutekh, himself in the vanguard force. Other Corps accompanying them were named the 'Tribes of Pharaoh,' and the 'Tribe of the Beauty of the Solar Disk.' The king pushed with great fervor and ran ahead of his troops. As night fell, the princes of the Kadesh Confederacy who had set an ambush sprung their trap on the unsuspecting and separated Egyptian/Kemetic force. Miraculously, and perhaps through divine intervention, Rameses II rose as the horde descended upon his encampment. He thereupon called upon Amon-Re, his father, beseeching the great Theban deity, reminding that he and his ancestors had praised and glorified Amun in the most stupendous manner and that Amun should never allow the likes of these foreigners to be the better of him. Listen carefully everyone!

With that the king sprang into action, seized his equipment, grabbed his chariot, rallied his forces and rode out of the orchestrated trap, linking up with his main force. Winning the day or night as it was, he was able to still broker a peace treaty in good terms with the Confederacy. This wonderful account was enshrined on the walls of his temples at Abu Simbel, the Ramesseum, Abydos, Beit Wali, and Luxor and at Karnak. They are also papyrus versions of the treaty with the Hittites. Importantly, this pharaoh, purportedly a Syrian, calling upon an African god while doing battle in Asia, is one aspect of the awe and might of Amun and the Theban social and religious system represented in his name. Is this a profound example of trilateralism or what? Of course, Rameses II, the great African, was not Syrian, though he did call upon his father, the ancestral god Amun, 'Lord of Karnak,' to give strength, courage and fortitude, while he battled foreigners and continued to propel the nation of Kemet, and Africa, to the prominence it enjoyed. There is might, power and wisdom in immersion in ancestral cultural heritage. Yet, throughout this experience, Maspero (1904) informs us, the "king practiced great reverence even on military expeditions." He carried a portable shrine where he could make morning presentations to the deity.

Aldred (1987: 166) on the other hand expressed another view in a section entitled "Decline of the Pharaonate," following the Amarna Revolution and Tutankhamon's counter-revolution resulting in restoration and praise of Amun and further glorifying Karnak.

"Despite this rehabilitation, and reforms in the army and fiscal service later introduced by Haremhab, it was left to the Ramessides of the next dynasty to repair much of the damage. Sethos I restored desecrated buildings at Thebes and embellished Abydos and other centers. His son, Rameses II, was the most vigorous builder to have worn the Double Crown, nearly half the temples remaining in Egypt date from his reign. His mortuary temple at Thebes, popularly known as the Ramesseum, the huge Hypostyle Hall at Karnak, the rock-hewn temples at Abu Simbel, and many other erections, would have contended lesser men; but in addition he usurped a great deal of the work of earlier kings to adorn the new capital city of Pi-Rameses on which he expended so much treasure. These appropriations have won him the reputation in modern times of being the arch-plunderer of other's monuments. This judgment, however, is too harsh. According to Egyptian beliefs a statue that had not received its annual consecration was deprived of its virtue, and belonged to no one." Is this akin to today's notion of public domain?

Even more, Aldred (1967: 167) continued: "There were still many monuments remaining from the reign of Akhenaten that had lain neglected and required re-consecration on new sites during the reign of Rameses II. Much of his work, particularly of the latter half of his long reign, is coarse, tasteless and tired, but he left so universal and impressive a legend of superhuman qualities that his successors could only attempt a pale reflection of. Rameses III, for instance, named his sons after those of his idol, and in his mortuary temple at Medinet Habu copied much of the decoration and texts of Ramesseum, a little to the north of Medinet Habu. The reliefs on the later site, however, showing the king hunting wild bulls and human foes, seem to be original in design. This temple included in its complex a palace, administrative buildings, military quarters, storerooms, gardens, bathrooms and pools. A great wall enclosed it and the main entrance was a fortified gate, built like a Syrian Migdol. It served, in fact, as a fortress for the protection of the populace of West Thebes in times of trouble during the later years of the Twentieth Dynasty when it was stormed at least twice in the fighting that broke out between the forces of Pinhasi and Herihor. Despite an evident decline in enterprise and intervention during this dynasty, the royal sepulchers continue to be vast excavations such as those of Rameses VI and VII. The architect's plan of the Tomb of Rameses IV, which has survived on a torn strip of papyrus at Turin, shows that it was designed to be equipped with a full set of furniture, including five gold-covered enclosures around the sarcophagus similar to the opulent provision made for Tutankhamon. The fine granite sarcophagus made for Rameses IV, and the one made for his father Rameses III, testify to the vigor of the pharaonic tradition which could still command such resources in what seems to be a period of decline."

In 1876 C. W. Goodwin published "Hymns to Amen" in the *Records of the Past*, Vol. 6. He dated the creation of these beautiful poems, contained in the *Anastasia Papyri* in the collection of the British Museum, to Ramesside times.

HYMN TO AMEN

1.   Oh! Amen, lend thine ear to him

QUINTESSENTIAL BOOK
"THE HOLY LAND"

2. who is alone before the tribunal
3. he is poor (he is not) rich.
4. The court oppresses him;
5. silver and gold for the clerks of the book,
6. garments for the servants. There is no other AMEN acting as a judge,
7. to deliver (one) from his misery;
8. when the poor man is before the tribunal,
9. (making) the poor to go forth rich.'

Another **HYMN TO AMEN** is as follows:

1. 'I cry, the beginning of wisdom is the way of Amen,
2. The rudder of (truth).
3. Thou art he that giveth bread to him who has none,
4. that sustaineth the servants of his house.
5. Let no Prince be my defender in all my troubles.
6. Let not my memorial be placed under the power
7. of any man who is in the house .... My lord is (my) defender
8. I know his power, to wit, (he is) a strong defender,
9. there is none mighty except him alone.
10. Strong is AMEN, knowing how to answer,
11. fulfilling the desire of him who cries to him;
12. the Sun is true King of gods,
13. the Strong Bull, the mighty lover (of power)'

A further **HYMN TO AMEN** is here included:

1. 'Come to me, O! thou Sun;
2. Horus of the horizon give me (help);
3. Thou art he that giveth (help);
4. there is no help without thee,
5. excepting thou (givest it).
6. Come to me, TUM, hear me thou great god.
7. My heart goeth forth towards An
8. Let my desires be fulfilled,
9. Let my heart be joyous, my inmost heart in gladness.
10. Hear my vows, my humble supplications every day,
11. my adorations by night;
12. my (cries of) terror .... prevailing in my mouth,
13. which come from my (mouth) one by one.
14. Oh! Horus of the horizon there is no other besides like him,

15. protector of millions, deliverer of hundreds of thousands,
16. the defender of him that calls to him, the Lord of An.
17. Reproach me not with my many sins.
18. I am a youth, weak of body.
19. I am a man without heart.
20. Anxiety comes upon me as an ox upon grass.
21. If I pass the night in .... and I find refreshment,
22. Anxiety returns to me in the time of lying down.'

[The previous compositions are addressed to the Supreme Being, under the names of Amen, Horus, and Tum, all identical with the Sun. But for the old Egyptians the ruling Pharaoh of the day was the living image and vice-regent of the Sun, and they saw no profanity in addressing the king in terms precisely similar to those with which they worshiped their god. The following address or petition, which also is found in the *Anastasi Papyri*, is a remarkable instance of this.]

The **HYMN OR ODE TO PHARAOH** is another treasure that needs to be included:

1. 'Long live the King!
2. This comes to inform the King.
3. to the Royal Hall of the lover of truth,
4. the great heaven wherein the Sun is.
5. (Give) thy attention to me, thou Sun that risest
6. to enligthen the earth with this (his) goodness.
7. The solar orb of men chasing the darkness from Egypt.
8. Thou art as it were the image of thy father the Sun,
9. who rises in heaven. Thy beams penetrate the cavern.
10. No place is without thy goodness.
11. Thy sayings are the law of every land.
12. when thou reposest in thy palace,
13. thou hearest the words of all the lands.
14. Thou hast millions of ears.
15. Bright is thy eye about the stars of heaven,
16. able to gaze at the solar orb.
17. If anything be spoken by the mouth of the cavern,
18. it ascends into thy ears.
19. Whatsoever is done in secret, thy eye seeth it,
20. O! BAENRA   MERIAMEN, merciful Lord, creator of breath.'

The king is Meneptah son of Rameses II, and his immediate successor. [This is not the language of a courtier. It seems to be a genuine expression of the belief that the king was the living representative of Deity, and from this point of view is

QUINTESSENTIAL BOOK "THE HOLY LAND"

much more interesting and remarkable, than if treated as a mere outpouring of empty flattery.]

Holy Land Papyrus 5. Bird hunting aboard a papyrus boat along with the family and a cat in the marshes.

In order to more properly experience the Temple of Karnak, one needs to understand the archaeological history surrounding the site. This may simply be, as Vercoutter (1992: 164) tells: "The vast citadel of the god Amun was likewise neglected and forgotten, its secrets veiled behind tumbling masonry and desert sand. Over the last four hundred years archaeologists have been uncovering those secrets little by little, bringing to light Karnak's original structures and piecing together what was once its great temple." Claude Traunecker and Jean-Claude Golvin, *History and Archaeology*, March 1982, as presented in Vercoutter (1992: 164-169) states: "As interest in the site unfolded, as early as 1589 European presence appeared at Karnak and an unknown traveler wrote: 'And as soon as I stepped inside and saw all those columns, I thought I must be dreaming! They were so thick! And all shaped like trees,' he wrote. Capuchin friars Fathers Francis and Protasius visited Karnak in 1668 and Father Protasius published a report in 1672. By 1722, the Jesuit scholar Claude Sicard identified 'the ruins of Luxor as the remains of ancient Thebes.'" Further, Vercoutter (1992: 166) noted that the Danish naval engineer Frederick Norden and the Anglican priest Richard Pococke: 'Were responsible for producing the first plans and drawings of Karnak.' Additionally, Vercoutter (1992) wrote: "In 1759 an Italian doctor by the name of Donati excavated at Karnak on behalf of various Italian princes. We owe the first truly scientific research and records, however, to the scholars who accompanied Napoleon to Egypt. In 1799 two young engineers, Jallois and Devilliers devoted a great deal of their time to studying Karnak, a vast palace, as they and their companions saw it, where a wise and powerful sovereign had once dwelled. And the European public discovered the wonders of Karnak through the *Description of Egypt's* magnificent illustrations - engravings which, though almost two centuries old, are still used by Egyptologists today."

"By 1828 Champollion copied inscriptions at Karnak as he hurriedly learned the new language he had deciphered six years earlier in 1822." Next, the German scholar Karl Lepsius worked at Karnak in 1843 as did, as Vercoutter (1992: 166) states, "Achile Prisse D'Avennes, part artist, part archaeologist, and part fortune hunter, dismantled the Tablet of the Kings at Karnak; in his eagerness to serve the 'interests of France,' he had it taken back to Paris." Watterson (1997: 4) showed how: "Forty-eight names of kings are legible in the Karnak Table, a chronological list compiled in the reign of Thutmose III (1479-1425 B.C.), which was carved on a wall in the temple of Amun at Karnak: it is now in the Louvre Museum. Fifty kings honored by Rameses II (1279-1213 B.C.) are named in a King-list in the Sakkara necropolis inscribed on a wall in the tomb of Tjunney, the king's overseer of works. Seventy-six kings are named in what is perhaps the most famous King-list that carved on a wall in the memorial temple of Rameses II's father, Seti (1294-1279 B.C.), at Abydos. The Abydos King-list is accompanied by a fine relief showing father and son making offerings to their ancestors; but only those kings who were considered worthy of honor were commemorated in this way." There was a *Second Abydos List* in the Temple of Rameses II at Abydos. This is now in the British Museum.

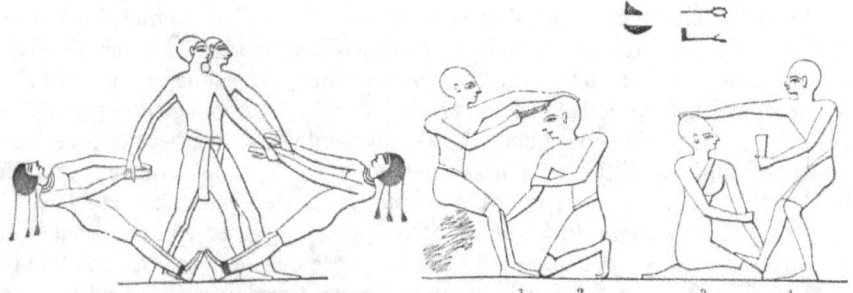

Holy Land Illustration 18. Men swinging women round by the arms. Beni-Hassan; and Barbers with above, *haq*, 'to shave.' Beni-Hassan.

Equally too, only names of kings who particularly benefited Karnak, up to the time of Thutmose III were engraved on the *Karnak Tablet*. However, though Mariette

QUINTESSENTIAL BOOK
"THE HOLY LAND"

had been working Karnak from as early as 1858 he only worked the Hypostyle Hall in 1860. Vercoutter (1992: 166) further on pointed out: "In 1861 a column in the recently excavated Hypostyle Hall had already collapsed. In 1865 it was a doorway situated between the 4th and 5th Pylons which caved in." A little later, in 1895, Jacques de Morgan helped set up the young French Egyptologist, Georges Legrain in charge of restoration at Karnak. After much work and even some showmanship for the visiting English royalties, eight years later he discovered the "Cachette Court." This was indeed a significant find of archaeological evidence particularly the statues that helped identify many pharaohs. Nevertheless, the fate of the temple got special attention with the fall of columns in the Hypostyle Hall on October 8, 1899, due to a mild earthquake.

Vercoutter (1992: 166-67) again tells: "From 1921 to 1925 a French architect by the name of Maurice Pillet took over where Legrain had left off. The 3rd Pylon incorporated numerous older structures and thus provided a wealth of documentary evidence. In 1924 Pillet narrowly avoided a fresh catastrophe in the southern half of the Hypostyle Hall. His successor, the architect H. Chevier, director of the *Travaux* de Karnak from 1926-1954 had the great good fortune to discover, carefully dismantle and reincorporate in the 3rd Pylon, an absolute gem of Egyptian architecture: the wayside station or chapel of Sesostris I [1971-1928 B.C.]"

We see, therefore, at Karnak, archaeologists had not simply repaired temples but they have also unveiled a wide array of ancient art in statues, stelae, obelisks, kiosks, altars, decorated blocks, columns, pylons, and walls. These were natural canvasses of divinely inspired creative expressions of literature and art in praise of Amon, revealed again after thousands of years. So much done, yet so much more to do! Claude Traunecker and Jean-Claude Golvin in Vercoutter (1992: 169) give a final admonition in pointing out that despite the successes at Karnak, so much is yet to be done. "The principal monuments have been excavated, but of the 300 acres of the archaeological zone, only about 35 have been excavated down to the ancient soil level (1.4%). The deep excavations represent no more than about 9 acres that is 2.9% of the total area excavated. So there may well be further surprises in store. Safeguarding Karnak, with all its architectural splendor, and continuing the work begun by Legrain must remain a major archaeological priority."

Adding clarity to this knowledge, we are informed by Woldering (1963: 148) who wrote: "The Egyptian word for Karnak is *Ipet Isut* or 'counter of the palaces' i.e., the assembly place of all the Egyptian deities, whose visiting gods had their chapels in the national temple, where they were worshiped."

FREDERICK MONDERSON

Holy Land Photo 9. Temple of Isis at Philae (now Agilka) Island. The thirty two columns of the Western Colonnade (left); and the seventeen columns of the Eastern Colonnade before the decorated First Pylon (right).

Holy Land Photo 9a. Temple of Isis at Philae (now Agilka) Island. A few visitors mill about in the Dromos to the Temple with the Western Colonnade to the left and the Eastern Colonnade to the right before the First Pylon and with Altars in the Walkway.

As noted, many archaeologists did extensive work to repair and clear this temple. Even today, Showker (1989: 1265) points out: "At Karnak, extensive restoration of the temple has been and continues to be made." However, as we saw, into the new twentieth century, Legrain was lucky to unearth several thousand statues in "their attitudes of the rank, in limestone, in black or pink granite, in yellow or red sandstone, in schist, in alabaster ...." in the "Cachette Court." Portman (1989: 39) reminds also, the Cachette Court was "erected by Tuthmose III, the walls were decorated by Rameses II and bear the text of the latter's treaty with the Hittite

QUINTESSENTIAL BOOK
"THE HOLY LAND"

King Metwallis. There is also a long list of the victories of Merenptah (1221-1214 B.C.)." Additionally, Bratton (1968: 178) discussed Le Grain's work at Karnak where: "From December 1903 to July 1904 he found 456 stone statues, seven sphinxes, and 8,000 bronzes. In the 1904-05 Season he recovered 200 stone statues and additional bronzes. All of these were drawn out of the water of the Cachette."

McGrath (1982: 170) added: "After this courtyard, there are four more pylons leading south, for a total of ten pylons in the temple complex. These four led to a ceremonial avenue to the Temple of Mut, Amon's wife. That temple has not been fully excavated yet. Archaeologists have recently discovered that, far from being simply an auxiliary temple to Karnak, the temple of Mut was almost as large and as grandiose as this companion."

Granted, modern archaeology did much for the recovery and systematization of the historical record of the Nile Valley. It exposed profound social, spiritual and scientific axioms that in their dynamism as engines of civilization development have guided the human experience along the pageantry of history. However, we must, in an effort at African historiographic reconstruction, recognize the hunger and limitations of many of the plunderers seeking ancient knowledge in the tombs of the sacred ancestors along the Nile. Modern analysis of the archaeological and anthropological record has also helped color the history of interpretation of this data, and thus projects a distorted view of the ancient African culture of Kemet. To this end, Afrocentric historiographic reconstruction needs only attempt a correction of the record through re-examination particularly records of a century ago. Then, the "records of the ancient records" were unearthed, analyzed, catalogued, distributed and disbursed to private collections, museums, and governments, where these entities now display their exhibits.

Yet, the religious significance of Amun can be seen in his Ennead or pantheon, whose composition included, Budge (1934: 162) wrote: "1. Amen-Ra at the head of the Southern Apt (Luxor), the Lord of Heaven, and his gods; 2. Mut, Lady of Heaven, Mistress of the World. 3. Khonsu, Nefer-hetep. 4. Min with symbol and temple. 5. Isis. 6. Neb Khemenu (Thoth). 7. Maat. 8. The Lady of Amenti (Hathor). 9. Osiris. 10. Un-Nefer-Khenti-Amenti. 11. Horus of the Two Horizons. 12. He of the Embalmment Chamber. 13. Het-Her (Hathor). 14. Governor of the House of the Physician. 15. Nephthys."

FREDERICK MONDERSON

Holy Land Illustration 19. Women tumbling, and performing feats of agility. Beni-Hassan; and Leveling, and squaring a stone and using the chisel and mallet. Thebes.

Concomitantly, in this respect, Hart helped supply an important view of numbers in Kemetic pantheism when he explained (1990: 13) the composition and number significance. "The nine deities can be restricted to the genealogy devised at Heliopolis, but the notion of a coterie of gods and goddesses was transferable; the temple of Abydos had an Ennead of seven deities, while there were fifteen members of the Ennead in the Karnak temple. Probably, because signs grouped in threes in Egyptian hieroglyphs conveyed the idea of an intermittent plural, the concept of nine gods and goddesses indicates a plural of plurals, sufficient to cover a pantheon of any number of deities in any temple."

Interestingly enough, though Mut was the wife of Amun, a title of "God's wife" came into the language, we are told, at the start of the New Kingdom. Apparently, Queen Tetisheri, wife of Sekenen-re Tao, was also known as Aahotep. Now, while her husband was away fighting the Hyksos invaders a palace coup broke out in Thebes under the instigation of "Tety the handsome." The queen gathered the loyalists and was able to put down the uprising, saving the throne for her family. His sons Kamose and then Ahmose followed her husband on the throne.

QUINTESSENTIAL BOOK "THE HOLY LAND"

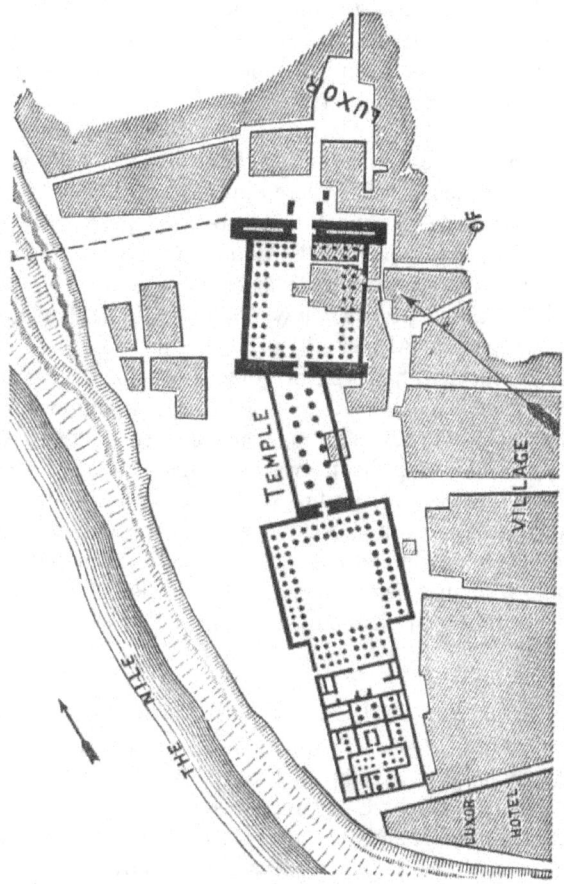

Holy Land – Plan of the Temple of Luxor.

We get a clearer understanding of these events from Aldred (1987: 144) who shed some light on the military developments of the time of the birth of the New Kingdom. Here he tells: "It was left to Kamose, the successor to Sekenen-re, to begin a war of liberation in earnest, and we are fortunate in having his account of the opening of the campaign in two texts, the second of which came to light in 1954 upon a stela among the foundations supporting a later colossus at Karnak. We learn that in his third regnal year, the new king sailed downstream with his forces and stormed the stronghold of a Hyksos collaborator, Teti, near Hermopolis, pushing his boundary to within a short distance of the entrance to the Faiyum. Kamose, next in line to the Theban principality, who carried on the struggle, was able to eventually reduce the Hyksos capital Avaris after a long siege. In order to deter further Asiatic incursions into Egypt, another campaign was necessary, and this was mounted as far as the town of Sharuhen in Southwestern Palestine, which was destroyed, thus advertising to the Asiatic princes the arrival of a vigorous new actor upon the international scene. This incursion into Palestine, however, was not followed up till later in the reign when the land of Syrian Fenkhu was invaded and their hump-backed cattle imported into Egypt."

However, a popular question regarding these invaders has for a long time been, "Who were the Hyksos?" and "Where did they come from?" Now, according to Samkange (1971: 64) regarding the Hyksos: "It was formerly thought that the Hyksos were 'Shepherd Kings,' a horde of invaders who suddenly erupted into Egypt, conquering it by spreading death and destruction. Now it is believed that they were, in fact, the people known in the Middle Kingdom as 'Rulers of Uplands.' These people, Aldred tells us, "were no more than wandering Semites trading their products with Egypt, or going down there for sanctuary, or to buy corn, or water their flocks according to an age-old tradition. The story of Joseph reveals how some of these Asiatics may have arrived, sold into serfdom for corn in time of famine, or offering themselves as menials in return for food and shelter. Famine or ethnic movements leading to large-scale infiltrations into the Delta of Semites, mixed perhaps with Hurrian elements, especially during the anarchy into which the Middle Kingdom lapsed, could have resulted in the founding of a Lower Kingdom State with an Asiatic king and officials taking over imperceptibly all the function and machinery of Pharaonic government."

Even further, Samkange (1971: 64) continued: "The Hyksos formed Fifteenth and Sixteenth Dynasties, adopted Egyptian titles, costumes, and culture, and even worshiped Egyptian gods. They ruled over Lower Egypt and their territories in Sinai and Palestine. Upper Egypt remained independent under Theban princes, while further south Nubia and the Sudan were under the prince of Kush. Both the Theban princes and the prince of Kush were, however, in alliance with the Hyksos."

Given credit for making tools and weapons of copper, as innovations, Samkange (1971: 64) credits the Hyksos with also making some peaceful additions to the culture they found in the Nile Valley. "More important than these weapons of destruction were certain abiding inventions of peace, such as improved methods of spinning and weaving, using an upright loom; new musical instruments, a lyre, the long-necked lute, the oboe, and tambourine. Humpbacked bulls were imported from an Asiatic source, probably brought by ship with the greatly increased trade that the Hyksos fostered. Other importations included the olive and pomegranate tree." Nevertheless, these conquerors had to go!

Ahmose, in following his brother to the throne completed the expulsion and founded the Eighteenth Dynasty. Ahmose married his sister, Aahmes-Nefertari, a

QUINTESSENTIAL BOOK
"THE HOLY LAND"

"coal-black Ethiopian," whose portrait is in the British Museum, London. The prominence of Amun was now set on the ascendancy.

Wilkinson (1971: 10) noted, "Amosis gave diadems and necklaces of gold and lapis lazuli to the temple of Amun at Karnak as part of the program of restoration of the temples after the defeat of the Hyksos." Like Aha, son of Narmer, founder of the first dynasty, this pharaoh, who cherished his mother and built a wonderful and ever larger tomb than that of his father Narmer, Ahmose also cared for his mother, Tetisheri or Aahotep. Robins (1993: 42-43) equally informs of the following about Queen Aahotep at the conclusion of hostilities. "Ahmose later set up a great stela at Karnak in which he included a passage praising Aahotep as 'one who cares for Egypt. She has looked after her [i.e. Egypt's] soldiers; she has guarded her; she has brought back her fugitives, and collected together her deserters; she has pacified Upper Egypt, and expelled her rebels.'"

She was indeed a remarkable woman and there were several others in this dynasty. Robins (1993: 43-44) noted that: "During his reign, Ahmose bestowed on her the title 'god's wife of Amun.' This event is known from a stela, which was set up in the temple of Amun at Karnak. It records what is basically a legal document establishing the office together with an endowment of goods and lands on Ahmose-Nefertari and her heirs in perpetuity. This office was a priestly one giving the bearer an important position in the cult of the god Amun at Thebes."

Elsewhere, Aldred (1987: 34) shows how: "... early in the Eighteenth Dynasty, Thebes had ceased to be the pharaoh's chief residence, and thereafter it gradually became the holy city of Amun, the king of the gods, and therefore a focus for pilgrimages. In the ancient world the feasts of Amun were sufficiently important to bring rulers to Thebes to take part in these joyous events. Thus the feast of Opet, during which the Amun triad were towed in their resplendent barges, amid rejoicings on both canal banks, from Karnak to Luxor during the second month of Inundation, was an occasion when the god gave oracular judgments on human affairs not capable of resolution by normal means. Several kings found it expedient to attend these events when their assumption of power, or nomination to the throne, received divine approval. A faint echo of the occasion still survives in the annual trundling of the boat of the local saint, Sheikh Abou'l Haggag, from his mosque in the Luxor Temple, around the town on a horse-drawn cart."

An even further reference was made when the ancestress of the 18th dynasty, later deified, passed away. This is referenced in Robins' (1993: 44) quote, "'when the god's wife Ahmose Nefertari, justified with the great god, lord of the west, flew to heaven.'"

FREDERICK MONDERSON

The union of Aahmose and Nefertari produced Amenhotep I, his successor. Equally too, in eternal gratitude the "Karnak School" of builders and their repertoire began the systematic restoration of the New plan of Karnak. Here history would witness the greatest display and expression of religiosity, in the union of spirituality in a sacred science that manifested a technical skill producing wondrous architectural testaments defying time in their survival.

Murray (1957: 235-36) provides a useful historical comparison of the growth of architectural form in the process of glorifying Amun at Karnak with, by providing a comparison of the other significant temple at the seat of this god's worship, the Temple of Luxor, particularly.

"As all the stone temples of the early periods suffered more or less complete destruction at the iconoclastic hands of the Hyksos, it is only on the analogy of the changes in the mortuary shrines of the kings that the changes in the god-temples can be followed. The simple plan was altered by degrees, beginning with a few store-chambers at the sides and perhaps a room for the priest. The sanctuary gradually became more difficult of access by the addition of vestibules and antechambers, and roofing of the inner court caused the darkness so desirable for the celebration of the mysteries."

"The outer court remained open to the sky, with sometimes a roofed colonnade round the sides. Hatshepsut's temple at Deir el Bahari is a good example of this transitional form, with an open colonnaded outer court, a pillared inner court (now a ruin), a vestibule, and a rock-cut shrine in the axis of the temple. Amenhotep III's temple at Luxor is a typical god-temple. Like all Egyptian temples it is oriented by the river, which here runs rather to the east of north and it was built on the site of an early shrine, probably one of the many temples of the XIIth dynasty which the Hyksos destroyed. The plan of Amenhotep's building was the usual one; the outer court originally was enclosed with a wall and had a roofed colonnade at the sides; but the inner court was the glory of the temple with its forest of pillars. The vestibules and shire have suffered much at the hands, first of the Romans, and then of the Christians, who altered the buildings and covered the ancient sculptures with figures of saints. All the walls of the temple were once richly sculptured and painted. Though the temple was very splendid and glorious the early plan is clearly visible."

"Later kings, however, added to it but without altering the fundamental design. Haremheb built a processional colonnade with seven pillars on each side and enclosed with a wall and roof. This led from Amenhotep's outer court into a much larger enclosure, which appears to be later in date."

QUINTESSENTIAL BOOK "THE HOLY LAND"

Murray (1957: 236-37) continued even further: "Like Karnak, the great temple of Dendera is the largest of a group of temples which cover a considerable area and are enclosed with a brick wall. It is one of the most stately and dignified of all the temples of Egypt. The entrance portico with its gigantic pillars has an impressiveness and glory beyond almost any other religious building. The number of little chapels and shrines on the roof and underground show that it was a temple for the celebration of the mysteries; and as it was a goddess-temple those mysteries were of the greatest of all mysteries, Life. Every part of the temple is decorated with sculpture which, though it cannot compare with any earlier work for beauty or technique, has the effect of great richness, and is in keeping with the general scheme of the building."

Returning to the "Queen Mother," apparently the next significant Queen to wield this title was Hatshepsut, who ruled in defiance of male domination. She built extensively to win the favor of the people.

We know little of Hatshepsut during the reigns of her father, Thutmose I, and of her half-brother and husband, Thutmose II. She appears on a stela of Thutmose as his principal wife and as god's wife, but she only seems to have come to prominence after the death of Thutmose II. The biography of an official of this time explicitly states that Thutmose II 'went up to heaven and was united with the gods. His son arose on his throne as king of the Two Lands and ruled on the seat of the one who begot him. His sister, the god's wife, Hatshepsut, controlled the affairs of the land.'

The success with which she was able to accomplish the latter was due to the party of influential men who allied with her. Chief among these was Senmut, sometimes spelled Senenmut, her architect.

James (1984: 32) speaks of a statue of Senmut now in the British Museum that was acquired from the Great Temple of Amon-Re at Karnak, with the following inscription. Here the word "king" refers to the queen. It states: "A boon which the King gives (to) Amun, Lord of the Seats of the Two Lands, chief of all the gods, that he may give all that proceeds from his offering-table of every day, on the day of the sixth-day festival, the month-festival, and the half-month festival, and on every festival of heaven and of earth, on the first day of the year, and on every calendar festival which happens in this temple; (may he also give) his sweet breath, which proceeds from him and his favor which exists on earth; all this, for the spirit of the hereditary prince, the count, follower of the King on his journeyings since his childhood, confidant of the king, the one who is in attendance on his feet, who is clear-sighted on the way to the palace, who adorns the Horus who is in this land [i.e. the King], the one who is intact of body, whom his lord has made intact, who understands thoroughly the character of the Lord of the Two Lands, who is pre-eminent of voice in privacy, vigilant in matters commanded him, who alone did what was profitable in the opinion of all, the overseer of all the building works of the King, the guider of him who works with his hands, who is skilled in every secret, who guides the man who knows towards what he does not know, the chamberlain, chief steward, and nurse of the Princess Neferure, the praised one of the Lady of the Two Lands, Senenmut, justified."

Holy Land Illustration 20. Sakkara. Sekhemka wears the Lion Skin and with his wife and son as various individuals perform different tasks, from his Tomb of the Vth Dynasty.

Elsewhere on the statue, we are told further, according to James (1984: 32-33) that Senmut enjoyed numerous titles bestowed by Hatshepsut, who some believe was her lover. "Hereditary prince, count, treasurer of the King of Lower Egypt, chief steward of the princess: He says, 'repeated for me the favors of the God's wife, Hatshepsut, may she live; magnified and enriched, I was promised before the companions, knowing that I was distinguished with her; they set me to be chief of her house, the Palace (may it live, be prosperous, be healthy), being under my supervision, being judge in the whole land, overseer of the granaries of Amun, Senenmut.' He says, 'O God's fathers, ordinary priests, lector priests of Amun, as you praise your gods, you will hand down your offices to your children inasmuch as you say a king's-boon-to-Amun pray for the spirit of Senenmut." He did much building in the name of the queen for the god Amon. In fact, Scholz (1997: 47) displays a photograph that read: "From a red granite block from the destroyed 'red

QUINTESSENTIAL BOOK "THE HOLY LAND"

Chapel' of Hatshepsut in Karnak depicting the ritual of the renewal of the powers of the ruler during the sed festival devoted to him. It is interesting to note that Hatshepsut and Thutmose III did great things for the god Amun."

Watterson (1997: 136) wrote that the cult of Amun grew with the incoming Eighteenth Dynasty when Amun was syncretized into the Sun god, Ra. However: "Under the patronage of Hatshepsut and Thutmose III, who both professed great devotion to him, Amun became Amun-Re, King of the Gods. An inscription in the temple of Amun at Karnak records that, when Thutmose III was a child, the statue of Amun sought him out and led him to stand in the place in the temple normally occupied by the king, an indication that the priesthood of Amun had made the young prince their protégée, engineering a divine oracle to proclaim him the next King of Egypt. Thutmose repaid them by pouring an enormous amount of the wealth gained from the empire into the treasury of Amun; and his immediate successors did likewise." Nevertheless, some scholars believe this synchronization of the god into Amon-Ra actually took place during the Middle Kingdom.

Nevertheless, in pursuit of their interests, the Theban Priesthood became a powerhouse, even though they were four principal religious sites where various deities were worshiped, as at Memphis, Ptah; Heliopolis, Ra; Osiris at Abydos; and Amen at Thebes, manifesting at Karnak and Luxor. The wealth, of Amon, entrenched particularly in the New Kingdom, included tens of thousands of individuals, specialists, enormous accumulated knowledge, scientists, artisans, astronomers, mathematicians, engineers, medical men, embalmers, with acres of land, buildings, ships, agricultural groves, and flower gardens. Great learning flourished here and this made Karnak the intellectual, religious and spiritual capital of ancient Kemet, and as such, "light of the ancient world." Even from great distances, men looked with confidence to the promise and symbolism of Karnak, this great and holy mound of creation. One could well imagine Amenhotep I, Thutmose I, Thutmose III, Amenhotep II, Amenhotep III, Seti I, Rameses II, Rameses III, on any one of their many military expeditions, before the day's battle, praising Amen in morning devotion, at their portable shrines. All this while the wheels of learning, language, ethics and science at Karnak guided education, architecture, astronomy, art, music, gaiety and reverence. Explaining the great hunger for learning to accommodate social mobility, Hart (1996: 42) noted: "Scribes would tell their sons that to be a scribe 'is greater than any other profession.' Student scribes took up to ten years to memorize the several hundred hieroglyphic signs. They also had lessons in astronomy, mathematics, astrology, practical arts and games and sports. Classroom discipline was strict and teachers believed that 'the ears of a boy are on his back. He listens only when he is beaten.' The boys who did not become scribes followed in their fathers' footsteps, becoming perhaps farmers or carpenters. Girls stayed at home and learned music, dancing and house-keeping skills from their mothers."

FREDERICK MONDERSON

Holy Land Photo 10. Temple of Isis at Philae (Now Agilka) Island. Another look at twenty six of the thirty two decorated columns of the Western Colonnade in the Dromos to the Temple and showing the watermarks from the time the Temple was inundated by the Nile.

KARNAK: THE POWER

Though the history of Thebes dates to the earliest formation of the Nomes, the buildings still standing at Karnak and those that have provided inscriptions of a historical significance tell us the temple was begun by the Middle Kingdom pharaohs. This may be because, we see signs of the primacy of Amen, during the XIIth Dynasty when kings took his name as Amenemenes, and became his staunchest adherents. Still, there is reason to believe the site of Karnak is built on even earlier foundations that were made of more perishable materials, possibly extending the sacredness of the site to the emergence of time measurement, the very beginning of the Calendar, *Nile Year*, 1, at 4240 B.C. However, Pier (1916: 91) is less ancient saying: "The prehistoric implements which have been found within site of the great Karnak pylons [and] Karnak itself provides relics which take us back to the period of the Second Dynasty or about 3000 B.C."

In-as-much as the Middle Kingdom was a period of consolidation, reorganization, expansion and artistic, linguistic and cultural growth, the glory days of the New Kingdom in imperialistic ventures, increased trade, extensive building undertakings, lavish art decoration in temples, tombs, and private and kingly residences, and so much more, represented another "golden age" of pharaonic rule. While Tetisheri and Sekenen-Ra began the war of liberation against the Hyksos, it

QUINTESSENTIAL BOOK
"THE HOLY LAND"

was their son Kamose and his brother Ahmose who expelled the "Shepherd Kings." Aahmes married Ahmes-Nefertari whom the British Museum artifact depicts as a "coal-black Ethiopian" Queen, bejeweled in long-flowing fashionable attire, wearing the Red, White and Blue Tricolor, 1500 years before Christ and thousands before the 20 or so modern nations whose flags are so designed.

Establishing the capital at Thebes at the start of the New Kingdom, Ahmose reaffirmed the primacy of the south, for as Payne (1964: 76-77) would write: "Ahmose announced that Amon, the Theban city-god, was henceforth to be worshiped as 'King of the Gods.' For it was Amon, Ahmose believed, who had led him to victory against the 'vile' Hyksos." After this, warrior pharaohs, Amenhotep I, his son Thutmose I, the latter's daughter Hatshepsut, and sons, Thutmose II and Thutmose III; the last king's son Amenhotep II, then Thutmose IV, Amenhotep III, and Horemheb, Rameses I, Seti I, his son Rameses II, Seti II and Rameses III, Bubastites, as well as Taharka, and the Greeks and Romans, all built at Karnak. These kings, whose efforts sought to enhance and placate the various shrines of the deities, contributed their unique part to the whole structure.

Particularly, the late period was one of continued expansion of the temple and a continuation of the artistic representation of the earliest periods. Greek pharaohs encouraged the religious and political significance of this site, through their repairs and erection of small structures at Karnak. They built principally at Philae, Kom Ombo, Edfu, Esna, Dendera, Elephantine, and Kalabsha.

In ancient times, a quay at the riverside allowed pharaoh to visit the temple Precinct of Amun for presentations at festivals, holy days, and important constructions. The same way that a canal connected the Temple of Karnak with the Nile River, a canal also connected Karnak with Luxor Temple, the 'Southern Isut.'

Accordingly, to Hart (1996: 8) writes, at the Quay of Karnak, "Officials, and tribute bearers, soldiers and slaves stood by the immense columns of the temple to welcome their pharaoh." Next, the pharaoh entered an Avenue of Sphinxes that entranced to the First Pylon of the Temple of Karnak where two now broken and buried statues stood. In modern times, two small obelisks of Seti II remain, before the entrance is approached from a raised platform. Here a double row 200 feet long Avenue of Criosphinxes or sphinxes with ram's heads, bearing the name of Rameses II, leads to the temple. Quirke (1992: 78) explains how: "At the temple of Amun at Karnak the sphinxes do not have the head of the king but that of the ram, symbol of Amun. They were set up between the temple and the river quay to the west by Rameses II and by Amenhotep III on the direct land-route from the temple toward Luxor temple. Other sphinxes' alleys include that between the Amun and Mut temples at Karnak, set up by Tutankhamon or his second successor

FREDERICK MONDERSON

Horemheb, and the avenue approaching the Amun temple at Luxor, set up by Nekhtnebef who had the head of the sphinx modeled more regularly as that of a king; the sphinxes in these avenues protect between their paws and under their chins, an image of the reigning king."

As the Sanctuary of the original temple dates to the Middle Kingdom, therefore in the approach from the west, there's a reverse order in the history of the buildings one encounters in a visit to Karnak Temple. The enormous structure's complexity is best underscored by Sauernon (1962: 142) who tells "Karnak is a world in which one could be completely lost." So it's best to stay with the guide or valuable sites and monuments could be easily overlooked.

The First Pylon

The **First Pylon** was built by the Ethiopians to wall the Great Court, and stands 370 feet wide, with the standing tower 140 feet high, and the structure 50 feet thick. We can quote Simpkins (1989) for "comparison, the west front of St Paul's Cathedral in London is 170 feet wide and 137 feet high." One of the two Propylon-towers retains a great part of its original height, but has lost its summit and cornice. Taharka and other Ethiopian rulers of the XXVth Dynasty built this pylon. Budge (1974: 53) says of this group of rulers: "The first king, Shabaka, is known from the Egyptian monuments to have beautified the temple of Karnak, and his name is found on many buildings there to which he made additions or repairs."

Applying his extensive knowledge of the religion of Kemet/Egypt, Budge (1969, II: 22-23) further explained: "The worship of Amen-Ra was introduced into Nubia by its Egyptian conquerors early in the XIIth Dynasty, and the inhabitants of that country embraced it with remarkable fervor; the hold which it had gained upon them was much strengthened when an Egyptian viceroy, who bore the title of 'royal son of Cush,' was appointed to rule over the land, and no efforts were spared to make Napata a second Thebes. The Nubians were, from the poverty of their country, unable to imitate the massive temples of Karnak and Luxor, and the festivals which they celebrated in honor of the Nubian Amen-Ra, and the processions which they made in his honor, lacked the splendor and magnificence of the Theban capital; still, there is no doubt that, considering the means which they had at their disposal, they erected temples for the worship of Amen-Ra of very considerable size and solidity. The hold which the priesthood of Amen-Ra of Thebes had upon the Nubians was very great, for in the troublous times which followed after the collapse of their power as priest kings of Egypt, the remnant of the great brotherhood made its way to Napata, and settling down there made plans

QUINTESSENTIAL BOOK "THE HOLY LAND"

and schemes for the restoration of their rule in Egypt; fortunately for Egypt their designs were never realized."

In the past, the tower on the north (left) of the pylon could be climbed for a spectacular view of the temple and the surrounding area. The full breadth of the wall was perforated with holes for fastening timbers that secured flagstaffs of the various representatives gods, usually placed in front of these propyla. No sculptures have ever been added to either face of the pylon, nor was the surface leveled to receive such decorations. Therefore, the structure can be considered unfinished. At the doorway, Kamil (1976: 39) mentions an inscription, "recording the latitude and longitude of the chief temples of the Pharaohs as calculated by the group of scholars accompanying the army of Napoleon to Egypt." There is an aerial photograph and a plan of the entire area at this entrance. On the inner-face of the southern Propylon an embankment remains and provides clues as to how these higher structures were erected. It is interesting that when DuBois wrote on Egypt, so little resources were available to him. Yet, he produced such penetrating analyses of the role of Africans in this early time. This is particularly why his work is significant. Interestingly enough, DuBois (1971: 137) says of the illustrious Taharka: "His building at Karnak was planned as one of the most striking in the ancient world. The temple built at Thebes had a relief representing the four corners of the four quarters of the Nilotic world: Dedun, the great God of Ethiopia, represents the south; Sopd, the eastern desert; Sedek, the western desert; and Horus, the north. According to Petrie: 'This shows how southern was the center of thought when the whole of Egypt is reckoned as the north.' Some writers say that Taharka led expeditions as far as the Strait of Gibraltar."

The Great Court

The **Great Forecourt**, called the "Court of the Bubastites" is 376 feet long and 338 feet wide, for an area of 93,000 square feet. Shishak of the XXIInd Dynasty built this Court and Maspero considers that he intended to roof over the columns but never completed the work. In the southeast angle of the court, there is a set of sculptures containing the names of the XXIInd Dynasty. Here Kamil (1980: 42) tells: "this scene commemorates the victory of Shishak of the Bible over Rehoboan, son of Solomon, the King of Judah, when Solomon's temple was robbed of its riches. Beneath Amon is the goddess Mut holding a club, bow and quiver, leading five rows of captives carved in perfect symmetry. To the right Sheshonk is grasping a group of captives by the hair and striking them with his raised club."

FREDERICK MONDERSON

Holy Land Papyrus 6. His wife does the flower bit for Tutankhamon while he stands, aided by a walking stick.

There are covered corridors on either side of the Court and two colonnades to the north and south. Budge (1974: 53) explained: "Taharka contributed a Kiosk of a double line of ten columns down the center, of which only one remains. At the other end of the temple, at its easternmost gate, Taharka also constructed another kiosk. This Taharka column stands 69 feet tall with open papyrus capitals. It took two years to dismantle and to re-erect the Taharka column by modern restoration

QUINTESSENTIAL BOOK
"THE HOLY LAND"

efforts. Beside the Sacred Lake Taharka built his temple." In addition, Ruffle (1977: 93) wrote, Taharka also built "two smaller colonnades at the Temple of Khonsu and Montu." There was much prosperity during the reign of Taharka and this success enabled the pharaoh to build extensively as he did at Thebes and elsewhere.

The corridors of the Court are 50 feet high. The temple of Rameses III interrupted the colonnade of the south. At the western and eastern end, of this southern colonnade, an embankment of evidence remains and indicates how the columns were erected. The colonnade on the North presents an even front of 18 columns. A chapel for the barque of the Theban Triad was dedicated by Seti II and located in the northwest corner of the court. When the visitor faces north or looks at the Shrine, Mut's compartment is to the left, Amun's in the center and Khonsu's to the right. Or, the god's wife is to his left and his son to his right. Beside this shrine is a flight of seven steps, on either side of which were granite statues of Rameses II, only one of which now remains, much mutilated. Double rows of Sphinxes lie in front of the northern and southern colonnades. These in part belonged to the Avenue of Criosphinxes at the entrance. Towards the Second Pylon on the northern side, stands a monumental statue, thought to be Rameses II and Nefertari. Some called her Lady Binta Anta. Scholz (1997: 43) identified this artifact in a photograph as: "The monumental sculpture of Rameses II in the first court of the Karnak temple, later usurped by Pinudjen I, 21st dynasty." There is a corresponding, though mutilated, statue to the right.

Rohl (1995: 373) mentions: "On the inner west side wall of the Bubastite Portal at Karnak there is a long inscription known as the Chronicle of Prince Osorkon. It details the career of the High Priest of Amon (HPA) and Crown Prince Osorkon, son of King Takelot II and great-grandson of Osorkon II." Accordingly, "The chronological data in the Chronicle of Prince Osorkon" wrote Rohl (1995: 373-74) are as follows: "Prince Osorkon is first attested as high priest at Karnak in Year 11 of his father Takelot II. He travels upstream to Thebes from his headquarters at El-Hiba - presumably for his induction. There appears to be political unrest in the Nile valley. A potential revolt is quickly suppressed. Osorkon is back at Karnak in Year 12 of Takelot to officiate at temple festivities ...."

"The offerings made by HPA Osorkon to the Karnak temples during his father's reign span a period of 14 years between Years 11 and 24. Finally, a Nile Level Text recorded on the west Quay at Karnak mentions Osorkon as high priest in the 29th year of Sheshonk III. The high priest made gifts to the temple of Amun at Karnak from Year 11 to Year 24 of Takelot II and then from years 22 to 29 of Sheshonk. There is no mention of offering between Years 1 and 21 of Sheshonk. The implication is that Year 22 of Sheshonk III followed directly on from Year 24 of Takelot II (perhaps in the same calendar year). The two kings may thus have ruled contemporaneously for 21 years."

In the southeast corner of the Great Court, intersecting the southern colonnade is the 170-foot long Temple of Rameses III of the XXth Dynasty, on a perpendicular axis to the main temple. It was built as a single unit without any additions, therefore different from the larger Karnak structure. It is, according to McGrath (1982) in referring to Rameses III's structure, "an entire mini-temple, with a courtyard, hypostyle hall, and triple sanctuary - a classic case of Pharaonic one-upmanship." At this point, Maspero (1926: 107) helps by pointing out: "The temple was built as an image of the world, as the Egyptians imagined it to be."

Two sandstone statues of King Rameses III were placed in front of the pylon, wearing the double Crown above the Nemes headdress. Osiride figures of the monarch stand proudly. In this temple, stands a Peristyle Court and Hypostyle Hall, Simpkins (1987: 6) has written, "eight bud-capital-decorated columns with reliefs showing the monarch, making offerings before various gods." On the west wall, Murnane (1983: 238) points to scenes, "illustrating the yearly progress of the ithyphallic form of Amun, who was related to the god Min of Coptos and represented the principle of exuberant fertility in nature." All stand before the Sanctuary.

The wealth of Amun during the later New Kingdom was immense and for comparison purposes we could use the Later Ramesside Period. Pier (1916: 100) mentions an inscription of Rameses III regarding gifts to Karnak: "'Its beauty is unto the dome of heaven, its august pillars are of electrum,' and Amenhotep II says: 'I made for Amon a hall in Karnak, a thing of wonder unnumbered in decorations of gold unnumbered in decorations of malachite and lapis lazuli, bright with flowers and filled with slaves.'"

Erman (1907: 71) further informs: "Under Rameses III the temple of Amon at Thebes possessed 926 square miles of land and 81,322 serfs, as well as 421,362 head of cattle. Heliopolis had 166 square miles of land, 12,963 serfs, and 45,544 head of cattle; while the respective numbers for Memphis, which was far behind, were nearly 11 square miles, 3,079 serfs, and 10,047 cattle."

Management of such wealth, Erman (1907: 71) wrote, needed "complete administrative organization, where distinguished persons served as superintendents of the treasury, of the land, granaries, cattle, or peasantry, with scribes and soldiers, architects, sculptors, painters, and all classes of minor officials." Of course, the 'Garden of Amon' is included for it bloomed with beautiful and varied flowers that the gardener prepared for every day's ritual.

QUINTESSENTIAL BOOK "THE HOLY LAND"

The Second Pylon

Horemheb built the **Second Pylon** at the close of the Eighteenth Dynasty, after the Amarna Heresy. Rameses I also gets credit for this pylon. He used blocks from Akhenaton's dismantled sun temple in its construction. His actions are rationalized in the statement of Portman (1989: 30) in the argument: "The re-use of blocks served a triple function: first, they make convenient filling for the pylon; second, the outrageous stones had to be hidden somewhere; and third, the inscriptions, being so recently dedicated to a solar deity, could not be sullied with a burial beyond the gates. All in all, a neat solution to an awkward heresy, and eminently Egyptian." The Pylon had four groves for flagstaffs. Ptolemy VI Philometer and Ptolemy IX Euergetes II of the Greek Period erected an intervening door. The lintel of this doorway is missing, but the jambs are well preserved. Simpkins also mentions sculptures showing Horemheb, the "king sacrificing to the gods of the temple and the sacred barque of Amun going to the temple."

At this entranceway, Brunton (1980: 218) wrote: "Gone were the seven steps which the builders had placed before the entrance, seven symbolical graduations of man's progress from the lower world of everyday existence to the highest sphere of spiritual attainment. For the Egyptians - numbering as many of the ancients- understood with the mysterious numbering which underlie the whole constructed universe; they knew that the seventh day or grade brought Rest, the highest peace for man, no less than for other created beings and things. I had found this sevenfold numbering in all their temples throughout the land, while it had appeared in clear and startling expression within the grand Gallery of the Great Pyramid. Therefore they had fittingly placed those steps, which time and man have all but torn from the ground, at the very entrance to the vestibule of Karnak's grandest and most impressive feature, the Great Hypostyle Hall of the Temple of Amen-Ra."

The Hypostyle Hall

Beyond this entranceway lies the **Hypostyle** masterpiece, a stupendous work of artistry and science that required quarrying, transportation, coordination and erection of untold tonnage of stone. The great hall was cleared and its columns strengthened in the winter of 1885.

However, eleven columns in the **HYPOSTYLE HALL** fell in October of 1899. As a result, efforts to re-erect them and preserve the wonderful structure have enabled moderns to obtain a better perspective of the significance of these 54,000 square feet of architectural magnificence. This Hypostyle Hall, Maspero (1904: V) has informed "measures one hundred and sixty-two feet in length, by three hundred and twenty-five in breadth. A row of twelve columns, the largest ever placed inside [any] building runs up the center having capitals in the form of inverted bells. One hundred and twenty-two columns with lotiform capitals fill the aisles in rows of nine each. The whole of the central bay is seventy-four feet above the ground, and the cornice of the two towers rises sixty-three feet higher."

Light penetrated into this hall through a sort of "clerestory," or "clear story," remains of which may still be seen on the south and eastside. Simpkins compares the columns "with Trajan's Column in Rome." Each of the open flower capitals has room for about 100 persons to stand.

Dr. ben-Jochannan (1989: 175) has probably written, particularly for African-American visitors to the land of ancient Kemet, the best insight of Karnak in the statement: "The Great Northern Temple of Warit (Karnak), Upper Egypt, North-East Africa is too much for anyone to try and complete in ten [10] years, and much less in a cordial single day by any group. This can only be considered the 'appetizer' for the 'main-course' your fifth [5th] or sixth [6th] return visit to this colossal wonder of the world by Africa's sons and daughters from the Americas or so-called Diaspora."

Holy Land Photo 10a. Temple of Isis at Philae (Now Agilka) Island. The First Pylon as seen from the Nile with the river's entrance to the Mammisi and the temple's true First Pylon further to the center right.

QUINTESSENTIAL BOOK
"THE HOLY LAND"

Maspero (1904: V, 172) also expressed the provocative inquiry: "We long to know who was the architect possessed of such confidence in his powers that he ventured to design and was able to carry out this almost superhuman undertaking. His name would be held up to almost universal admiration besides those of the great masters that we are familiar with, for no-one in Greece or Italy has left us any work which such simple means could produce a similar impression of boldness and immensity."

Credit for building this hall goes to several persons. To begin, Amenhotep III, "the Magnificent," who also built the "Temple of Luxor" as well as the "Temple of Mut," built the 12 massive columns of the Processional Way. Here and elsewhere he ushered in new forms of architecture, particularly in the "Temple of Soleb" in Nubia. Barnett (1996: 26) exhibits a photograph from a small temple of this ruler showing: "The defaced head of Amenhotep III in his chariot at the Temple of Amun at Karnak." In the Temple of Mut, evidently, Sekhmet, the lion goddess was a favorite of his, for as Armour says (1989: 130) he "placed several hundred statues of her in his temple dedicated to Mut." The king also created extensive tracts of land nearby to serve as gardens supplying flowers to the temple daily, all this after he had ascended the 'Golden Horus Throne of his Ancestors' to rule for thirty-six years.

However, assigning more extensive ownership to the Hypostyle Hall, Maspero (1926: 93) explained: "Rameses I conceived the plan, Seti I finished the building, Rameses II almost completed the decoration." Pier (1916: 97) added: "Rameses I inscribed his name upon one column, Seti's name appears upon seventy-nine and the remaining fifty-four bear the names of a number of later kings." The image of the god Min appears 16 times in this Hall. Ruffle (1977: 173) also added: "Merenptah recorded his victory in a relief at Karnak in the foundation of the Hypostyle Hall." Others such as Payne believed Horemheb, their predecessor first conceived of the idea of the entirety of the hall.

This notwithstanding, Portman described the Hypostyle Hall as a "mysterious mixture of the delicate and the massive, the exuberant and the overwhelming; the light of faith wrapped in the gloom of formalism." Cosmologically, he believed the: "petrified forest has its roots in the idea of the temple as a microcosm of the world. Out of the primeval waters Nun emerged the first island; on this island creation took place. The sky, the air, the dew, the plants and animals, all in their turn, took form at the beginning of time. This ideal world is shown in the typical decorations of a temple hall - a midnight sky with stars and astral beings on the ceiling, a riot of vegetation and animal life (quick or dead) on the walls and their growth of columns topped with papyrus or lotus buds."

FREDERICK MONDERSON

Fedden (1986: 81) offers a critical perspective of the work at Karnak, in her statement of comparison: "A Greek temple is coordinated; each part bears a relationship of balance to every other. The building is also proportioned to the human figure. The scale of the celebrants relates to the architecture; they do not creep, as must have done the priests of Amon-Ra, like mites, round the base of towering masonries. It is significant that the Egyptians in their temples never explored the possibilities of enclosed space. Their weighty hypostyles remained crowded halls of passage. Nowhere is insensibility to architectural form more apparent than in the famous hypostyle hall at Karnak. This gigantic chamber is said to be large enough to contain Notre-Dame, yet here is weight without mass, and size without splendor. The vast swollen pillars are flabby and spine-less, and their proximity destroy any sense of height or perspective. It remains a monument to all that determination, labor and craftsmanship can fail to achieve. The gods at Karnak were more grandiloquently, but less adequately, served than they had been in Zoser's mortuary temple at Sakkara over 1,500 years earlier."

Holy Land Illustration 21. Sedment Stele of Nebenkemt and family (left); and Steles and sacrificial altar (right).

Still, and even further, Maspero (1904: V, 172) would add in summation: "It is impossible to convey by words to those who have not seen it, the impression which it makes on the spectator."

QUINTESSENTIAL BOOK
"THE HOLY LAND"

The Third Pylon

At the east end of the Great Hall, the **Third Pylon** built by Amenhotep III, became the entrance to the temple and remained so up to the reign of Rameses I. Baines and Malek (1980) mention numerous blocks from earlier buildings reused in this pylon: "A sed-festival shrine of Senwosret I (the 'White Chapel') now re-erected to the north of the hypostyle hall, shrines of Amenhotep I and Amenhotep II; the 'red chapel' so-called for its material (red quartzite) and Thutmose IV, and a pillared portico of the same king." This quote is interesting for we know it was Hatshepsut who created the "Red Chapel."

Muller (1963: 670) explained how in the early Eighteenth Dynasty makeover: "Thutmosis I expanded the plan of the Middle Kingdom sanctuary towards the West in order to gain space for a new shrine and subsidiary rooms. He enclosed the expanded sanctuary on three sides with a wall, and the fourth became the pylon." Thutmose I's architect Ineni, who had served Amenhotep I, also helped Thutmose III to erect some of his structures. Ineni erected 4 obelisks in the Central Court between the Fourth and Fifth Pylon. Today only 1 obelisk stands here. We are given some statistics by Simpkins that the "shaft is of red Aswan granite, 71 feet high, weighs 143 tons. It is the second highest of the greater extant obelisks - the Mararius (Heliopolis) obelisk of Senusert I weighs 22 less."

KARNAK: THE GLORY!
The Fourth Pylon

The **Fourth Pylon** built by Thutmose I, is of smaller size and stands before 20 wooden truncated columns built by the king. Here a 40-foot vestibule leads to the Hall of Osiride Figures where Thutmose III placed 26 engaged-Osiride statues against the western wall. "In it are Two Obelisks of red granite like the others, but of large dimensions, the one now standing being 97 feet 6 inches high. This is the second tallest obelisk in the world, being surpassed in height by that of St. John Lateran at Rome. Thutmose I erected the former obelisk at Heliopolis. It is 105 feet 7 inches high."

While this part of the building bears the name of Thutmose I, the other standing obelisk in it bears the name of his daughter Hatshepsut, while another of hers lies fallen beside the Sacred Lake. Altogether the queen erected two pairs of obelisks at Karnak. The first pair was placed between Pylons IV and V and the second pair between Pylons V and VI.

"On the north side of the base of one of her still standing obelisks, Hatshepsut, who though Karnak, 'a holy place from immemorial time,' had written, Pier (1916: 99) has noted: "Having smelted electrum, I placed one half upon their shafts unheeding the mutterings of men for since the utterance of my mouth is law in all that cometh out of it, I cannot retract that which I have already uttered. So hear me then! I placed on them the finest electrum, and I weighed it by the bushel even as if it was corn. My majesty myself did cry the number of the weight."

During the retaliation against Hatshepsut, Thutmose encased this standing obelisk to shield it from public view. This act by Thutmose III, some people believe, protected and preserved it from destruction, particularly during the Amarna Period. Altogether Hatshepsut erected two pairs of obelisks at Karnak. At Deir el Bahari 4 obelisks are depicted on a wall. Her first pair of obelisks was cut at Aswan, shipped, transported and erected by Senmut her architect in seven months. Regarding other efforts in praise of Amon the king went to great lengths to please Amun her "father." Murray (1957: 50) mentions an account regarding Hatshepsut's thoughts on setting up these "needles" in Karnak temple: "'I was sitting in the palace of my Creator, when my heart urged me to make for him in the Hall of Columns two obelisks whose points should reach the sky. Verily, these two great obelisks that my majesty has wrought with electrum, they are of a single stone of hard granite without any join or division. My Majesty commanded this work in the 15th year on the first day of the month Mechir till the 16th year and the last day of the month Mesore, making seven months since ordering it in the quarry.'"

Michalowski (ND: 530) adds even more on work done by Hatshepsut at Karnak in the following statement: "The queen added a quartzite chamber for the sacred barge in the central section built by Thutmose I; on both sides of it there are several chambers known as the Queen's Apartments."

She had other works near the temple's east wall-as well as Pylon VIII on the south side of the temple. Senmut built extensively to win favor for her rule where at Karnak she worshiped her father and god Amun. To win public support for her rule, Hatshepsut proclaimed herself a child of virgin birth and this event was recorded in her Mortuary Temple at Deir el Bahari, on the west bank, across the river from Karnak. Khnum, who made man on his potter's wheel, according to Armour (1989: 142) is made to say to Hatshepsut: "I am forming you of substance of Amun, god of Karnak. I give you the land of Egypt and her people, and I will have you appear in glory as king in the name of Horus. You will be supreme among men, as has been commanded by your father Amen-Ra."

QUINTESSENTIAL BOOK
"THE HOLY LAND"

A very astute ruler, Hatshepsut went to great lengths to show legitimacy for her rule and in so doing erected many monuments. Commentary by Quirke (1992:77) as to the celebration of the Opet Festival is as follows: "The passage for the festive procession seems to have been marked first by Hatshepsut, in whose reign so many features of Pharaonic civilization took on new forms, but the temple complexes first formed an architectural unity embracing the Karnak temples of Amun and Mut and the Luxor temple of Amun under Amenhotep." Adding even further, Habachi (1987: 66) mentions a statement by Queen Hatshepsut where she boastfully affirms: "I have not been neglected of the city of the Lord of the Universe, rather I have paid attention to it. I know that Karnak is the Horizon [of heaven] Upon Earth, the august ascent of the First Occasion, the Sacred Eye of the Lord of the Universe."

The many successes of the Queen were attributed to a party of powerful men who accomplished much in their time. In the building department, Amenhotep replaced Senmut as architect and erected the second pair of obelisks between the fifth and sixth pylons on occasion of the queen celebrating her jubilee. As previously noted, Senmut had erected two obelisks between Pylons Four and Five where Thutmose I had placed his four.

Budge (1914: 145-48) recounts from "The Autobiography of Tehuti: The Erpa," a great noble, who in the eighteenth dynasty: "assisted in carrying out the great building schemes of Queen Hatshepsut and Thutmose III. Tehuti was a hereditary chief (*erpa*), and a Duke, and the Director of the Department of the Government in which all the gold and silver that were brought to Thebes as tribute were kept, and he controlled the distribution of the same in connection with the Public Work Department."

"Thanks be to Amen-[Ra, the King of the Gods], and praise be to His Majesty when he riseth in the eastern sky for the life, strength, and health of the King of the South, the King of the North, Maatkara (Hatshepset), and of the King of the South, the King of the North, Menkheperre (Thothmes III), who are endowed with Life, Stability, Serenity, and Health like Ra forever. I performed the office of chief mouth (i.e. director), giving orders. I directed the artificers who were engaged on the work of the great boat of the head of the river [called] Userhatamen. It was (inlaid) or overlaid with the very best gold of the mountains, the splendor of which illumined all Egypt, and it was made by the King of the South, the King of the North, Maatkara, in connection with the monuments which he made for his father Amen-Ra, Lord of the Thrones of the Two Lands, who is endowed with life like Ra forever, I performed the office of chief mouth, giving orders, I directed the artificers who were engaged on the work of the God-house, the horizon of the god, and on the work of the great throne, which was [made] of the very best silver-gold of the mountains, and of perfect work to last forever, which was made by Maatkara in connection with the monuments which he made for his father Amen-Ra, &c. I performed the office of chief mouth, giving orders. I directed the artificers who were engaged on the work of the shrine (?) of Truth, the framework of the doors of which the silver-gold made by Maatkara, &c. I performed the office of chief mouth, giving orders. I directed the artificers who were engaged on the works of *Tcheser-Tcheseru*, the Temple of Millions of Years, the great doors of which were made of copper inlaid with figures of silver-gold, which was made by Maatkara, &c."

"I performed the office of chief mouth, giving orders. I directed the artificers who were engaged on the work of Khakhut, the great sanctuary of Amen, his horizon in Amentet, whereof all the doors [were made] of real cedar wood inlaid (or overlaid) with bronze, made by Maatkara, &c. I performed the office of chief mouth, giving orders. I directed the artificers who were engaged on the works of the House of Amen, it shall flourish to all eternity! Whereof the pavement was inlaid with blocks of gold and silver, and its beauties were like unto those of the horizon of heaven, made by Maatkara, &c. I performed the office of chief mouth, giving orders. I directed the artificers who were engaged on the work of the great shrine, which was made of ebony from Kenset (Nubia), with a broad, high base, having steps, made of translucent alabaster [from the quarry] of Het-nub, made by Maatkara, &c. I performed the office of chief mouth, giving orders, I directed the artificers who were engaged on the works of the Great House of the god, which was plated with silver in which figures were inlaid in gold - in splendor lighted up the faces of all who beheld it - made by Maatkara, &c. I performed the office of chief mouth, giving orders. I directed the artificers who were engaged on the work of the great broad, high doors of the temple of Karnak, which were covered with plates of copper inlaid with figures in silver-gold, made by Maatkara, &c. I performed the office of chief mouth, giving orders. I directed the artificers who were engaged on the works in connection with the two great obelisks, [each of which] was one hundred and eight cubits in height (about 162 feet) and was plated with silver-gold, the brilliance whereof filled all Egypt, made by Maatkara, &c. I performed the office of chief mouth, giving orders. I directed the artificers who were engaged on the work of the holy gate [called] "Amen-shef," which was made of a single slab of copper, and the images (?) that belonged thereto, made by Maatkara, &c. I directed the artificers who were engaged on the works of the store-chests, which were plated with copper and silver-gold and inlaid with precious stones, made by Maatkara, &c. I directed that artificers who were engaged on the works of the Great Throne, and the God-house, which is built of granite and shall last like the firmly fixed pillars of the sky made by Maatkara, &c. And as for the wonderful things, and all the products of all the countries, and the beasts of the wonderful products of Punt, which His Majesty presented to Amen, Lord of the Apts, for the life, strength, and health of His Majesty, and with which

QUINTESSENTIAL BOOK "THE HOLY LAND"

he filled the house of this holy god, for Amen had given him Egypt because he knew that he would rule it wisely (?), behold, it was I who registered them, because I was of strict integrity. My favor was permanent before [His Majesty], it never diminished, and he conferred more distinctions on me than on any other official about him, for he knew my integrity in respect of him. He knew that I carried out works, and that I covered my mouth (i.e. held my tongue) concerning the affairs of his palace. He made me the director of his palace, knowing that I was experienced in affairs. I held the seal of the Two Treasuries, and of the store of all the precious stones of every kind that were in the God-house of Amen in the Apts [The temples of Karnak and Luxor], which were filled up to their roofs with the tribute paid to the god. Such a thing never happened before, even from the time of the primeval god. His Majesty commanded to be made of silver-gold for the Great Hall of the festivals. [The metal] was weighted by the heqet measure for Amen, before all the people, and it was estimated to contain 88 1/2 heqet measures, which were equal to 8,592 1/2 teben. It was offered to the god for the life, strength, and health of Maatkara, the ever living. I received the Sennu offerings, which were made to Amen-Ra, Lord of the Apts; these things, all of them, took place in peace in the mountain of the spirit-bodies who are in the Other World (Khert-Neter). I wish my memory to be perpetuated on the earth. I wish my soul to live before the Lord of Eternity. I wish that the doorkeepers of the gates of the Tuat (Other World) may not repulse my soul, and that it may come forth at the call of him that shall lay offerings in my tomb, that it may have bread in abundance and ale in full measure, and that it may drink after from the source of the river. I would go in and come out like the Spirits who do what the gods wish, that my name may be held in good repute by the people who shall come in after years, and that they may praise me at the two seasons (morning and evening) when they praise the god of the city."

The Fifth Pylon

Next is the ruined **Fifth Pylon** of Thutmose I. Thutmose III built the Hall of Records and here his priests recorded tribute to the temple. The hall originally had 16 columns and Osiris statues. Thutmose I's architect Ineni left an inscription in which he wrote, as Habachi (1987: 57) states: "I saw to the erection of two [great] obelisks, having built an august boat 120 cubits in length and 40 cubits in width in order to transport these obelisks. They arrived safe and sound, and landed at Karnak." One of these is the still standing obelisk that Thutmose I placed between the Fourth and Fifth Pylons.

FREDERICK MONDERSON

THE SIXTH PYLON

Both Thutmose I and Thutmose III built the small **Sixth Pylon**. On the west face are some of the celebrated **Geographical Lists**, containing the names of 1200 towns, king Thutmose III conquered, of which 628 remain. Not to be outdone by Hatshepsut or their father, Habachi (1991: 72) has written: "Thutmosis III set up at least seven obelisks in Karnak and two more in Heliopolis, but none of these still stand in their original places. They seem to have been erected for his first five Jubilees, celebrated successively in the thirtieth, thirty-fourth, thirty-seventh, fortieth, and forty-third years of his reign; although two of the obelisks (apparently, from the numbers written below, meant to represent two pairs of his obelisks at Karnak) are depicted in a scene showing the treasure which he offered to Amun-Re in celebration of the military campaigns in which the god had given him success." For further clarification, Habachi (1991: 73-76) adds more on Thutmose III's work: "Of the three pairs of obelisks erected at Karnak, one stood to the south of the Seventh Pylon; the upper part of one of these is now in Istanbul, while fragments of its mate remain at Karnak. A second pair stood to the west of the obelisks raised by Thutmosis III's grandfather Tuthmosis I. The pedestals of these were recently unearthed from beneath the foundations of the Third Pylon. The seventh and last of the Karnak obelisks of Tuthmosis III, a single one, is the largest surviving obelisk, with a height of 36 meters. Only its foundation remains in the eastern part of the Great Temple at Karnak."

Holy Land Illustration 22. The Noble Ti sailing and fishing in the marshes.

A small **Vestibule** in front of the granite gateway of the towers forms the facade of the court before the **Sanctuary**. In a hall before the **Sanctuary** stood two heraldic granite columns that, according to Murnane (1983) were "carved with the Egyptian Lotus (north) and the Papyrus of Upper Egypt (South) - thus expressing the union of the two lands before Amun. There

QUINTESSENTIAL BOOK "THE HOLY LAND"

are also statuettes of Amon and Amunet, erected by Tutankhamon and later usurped by Horemheb." After the 'Amarna Heresy,' Steindorff and Seele (1971: 224) quoted Tutankhamon who spearheaded the **Restoration** as declaring he was "beloved of Amen-Re, Lord of the Thrones of the Two Lands, the foremost of Karnak."

The actual **Sanctuary** or "Holy of Holies" is a mass of ruin, considering the number of assaults it suffered at the hands of invading forces. Yet, some of the chambers are still standing, and are covered with sculptures of the XVIII Dynasty.

In the large **Open Court** immediately beyond are some polygonal columns with the cartouches of Osirtasen I, of the XIIth Dynasty, in the midst of fallen architraves of the same era; showing that the original construction of the sanctuary dated from that era.

Muller (1963: 670) believed: "The nature of this god and his cult and the ceremonial procession in his honor determined the initial form and subsequent development of the sanctuaries. Sanctuaries were constructed at Karnak and in the Theban area, at Tod and Medamud, as early as the Middle Kingdom. The structures of the New Kingdom could therefore fall back on local tradition." So, while the construction of the Sanctuary dates to Senusert I, Thutmose III rebuilt it; the one *in situ* bears the name of Philip Arrhidaeus, half-brother of Alexander the Great, who restored it.

Muller explained how the inner shrine at Karnak consists of an elongated granite-walled room that is accessible from the west through a portal and has a window opening toward the east. The barge of the god rested on a support in this chamber. Murnane (1983: 231) mentioned: "The walls are covered with scenes illustrating the episodes of the offering rite with Amun appearing in his usual anthropomorphic guise and also in the ithyphallic form he shares with Min, the god of fertility." Pier (1916: 100) also notes how the gold figure of the Sun-god Amon was "taken from this building on some such grand occasion as the accession of a Pharaoh, the New Year's Feast or a Feast of Victory." Further clarifying, Murnane adds "from the suite of rooms just south of the sanctuary it is possible to see the full sequences of scenes showing the progress of the rituals during the annual feast."

FREDERICK MONDERSON

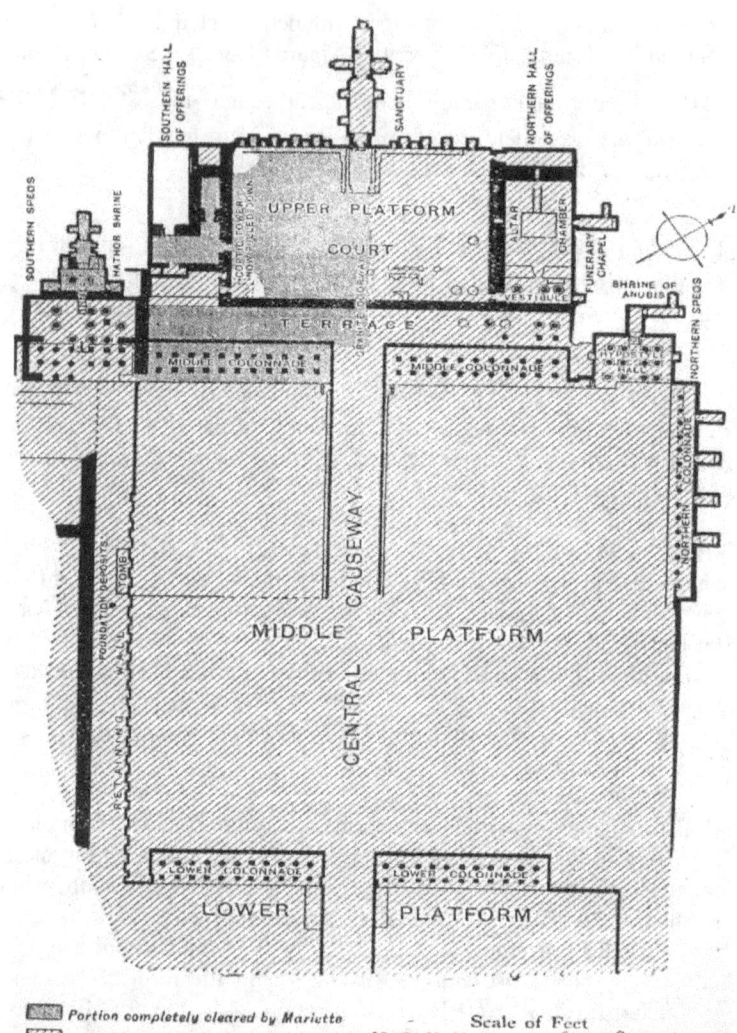

Holy Land – Plan of Hatshepsut's Temple at Deir el Bahari, Thebes.

QUINTESSENTIAL BOOK "THE HOLY LAND"

Holy Land Photo 11. Temple of Isis at Philae (Now Agilka) Island. The Second East Colonnade in the Courtyard fronting the First Pylon proper to the Temple. The inner face of the visible First Pylon was added by Nectanebo II to wall the then outer Courtyard and First Pylon.

From remains of architraves it shows Senusret I's temple was decorated. Manfred Lurker's illustration (1991: 32) depicts the: "Sedge and Bee symbols of Upper and Lower Egypt, aspects of the titles of Senusret I (1971-1928) carved on the processional Kiosk he built in the temple of Amun at Karnak, Middle Kingdom, XII Dynasty." In another picture we are further informed by Lurker (1991: 86) how, "The vulture goddess Nekhbet, together with her companion, the snake goddess Wadjet, symbolized the 'two ladies,' protectors of the two lands. They are shown resting on two baskets. XII Dynasty. Detail from a Processional Shrine of Senusert I."

To the East of the **Central Court** is Thutmose III's columnar edifice, the **Akh Menu**, the last significant building along the central east-west axis. Taharka and Rameses II did build temples further to the east of this structure. This "Festival Hall" of Thutmose III measures 144 feet wide and 52 feet deep and stands at a right angle to the sanctuary. The exterior wall is entirely destroyed except on the North side.

FREDERICK MONDERSON

Holy Land Photo 12. Temple of Isis at Philae (Now Agilka) Island. The actual Inner Face of the "true" First Pylon to the Temple proper depicts the King on the same plane as Horus and the Goddess Isis.

Murray's *Handbook for Egypt* (1888) supplies the following description for this festival temple. "Parallel to the four outer walls is a row of square pillars, going all round, within the edifice, 32 in number; and in the center are 20 columns, disposed in two lines, parallel to the back and front row of pillars. But the position of the latter does not accord with the columns of the center. An unusual caprice has changed the established order of the architectural details, the capitals and cornices being reversed, without adding to the beauty or increasing the strength of the building. The latter, however, had the effect of admitting more light to the interior."

Muller (1963: 670) explained even further: "It is the earliest basilica with the nave elevated above the side aisles, and its ceiling was supported by 'tent pole' columns. The fenestrated exterior walls rest on square pillars that also supported the stone ceiling beams covering the two aisles." Murnane (1983: 233) has argued the *Akh Menu* as a memorial temple, "encompasses a number of features - jubilees, reliefs, suites dedicated to chthonic and solar deities, chapels for ancestor worship - that are normally found in shrines dedicated to the cult of the ruler, particularly the king's mortuary temples." To underscore the significance of this, Diop (1991: 87) believed the world-view of Thutmose III essentially stated read: "The king in the righteousness of his heart, reigns, accomplishing the divine will."

On some of the columns of Thutmose III's "Festival Hall" are traces of evidence of a Christian church, and pictures of saints, between whom is a conventional representation of St. Peter.

QUINTESSENTIAL BOOK
"THE HOLY LAND"

Holy Land Papyrus 7. With fishes below in the water, Tutankhamon and his wife sail their boat on the Nile and enjoy the birds and lotus flowers.

In the southwest corner of the Festival Hall is where the famous **Karnak Tablet of Kings** or "Hall of Ancestors" rested. It listed 62 of Thutmose III's predecessors. When it was discovered in 1825, only 48 of these names were legible. In 1843 this prized artifact was stolen and shipped to *Bibliotheque Nationale de Paris*, by Prisse D'Avennes, and now rests in the Louvre Museum. Still, adding to a broader understanding of ancient Kemetic chronology, Spencer (1993: 14) wrote, the "monumental lists which include the kings of the early dynastic period are known as the Karnak, Saqqara and Abydos lists, the last of which, located in the temple of Seti I, is best preserved."

Now, further east of the **Hall of the Ancestors** lies the **Zoological Garden** of Karnak, showing birds, flowers, fruit, cattle and other animals seized by Thutmose III in a South-West Asia campaign during his 25th year. Thaneni, Thutmose III's military historian or chief scribe, wrote the **Annals of Thutmose III**, primarily about the "Battle of Megiddo." Steindorff and Seele (1971: 60) give three different lists of the conquered cities. One of these, on the north/south Axis, a list on the Seventh Pylon, is a "Catalogue of the Southern lands and Nubian peoples which his majesty subjugated."

Meanwhile, at the **Festival Hall**, Clarke and Engelbach (1990: 158-59) point out there is no drainage system for the roof. "The blocks have no joint-troughs between them, and are not cut to facilitate the flow of water over them. Possibly there was a thick layer of mortar or plaster over the whole roof."

On the southern side adytum are the vestiges of a colossal hawk, seated on a raised pedestal, and within sculptures containing the name of Alexander, who did restoration work to it.

Elsewhere, Budge (1990: 151) mentions: "Thutmose IV, the grandson of Thotmes III, found a great granite un-inscribed obelisk lying near Karnak, and caused it to be inscribed in his grandfather's name, and set it up in front of the great upper gate of Karnak opposite Thebes. Some think that the obelisk was actually made for Thothmes I, who died leaving it un-inscribed, and that it was annexed by Thothmes III, who either deliberately or through death left it as he had found it."

The **Sacred Lake** is located to the east of Pylons Seven and Eight and south of Rameses II's "Girdle Wall." It is 600 feet long and 360 feet wide and 12 feet deep. It was "connected by underground channels to the Nile." Here priests of Amon cleansed themselves for the temple ritual. *Time-Life* (1997: 66) tells this Sacred Lake was indeed important in the whole scheme of cleanliness, reverence and worship. "Three times a day - at dawn, midday, and dusk - the high priest of the god Amun disturbed the still waters of the sacred lake at Karnak to wash and purify himself before entering Amun's innermost sanctuary. Then, intoning prayers, the priest and his retinue would bathe and dress the god's statue and leave offerings of bread, meat, beer, and wine. These time-honored rituals secured the god's favor toward the people of Egypt and held back the forces of chaos for another day."

Simpkins (1987: 20) informs, in the Lake, the "sacred barques of the Theban Triad floated in the festival of Opet at flood time. The sacred boats were decorated, and statues of the gods were placed upon their canopies." Additionally, in enumerating works under Thutmose III, Maspero (1904: V, 70) mentions the "outline of the sacred lake, on which the mystic boats were launched on the nights of festivals, was also more symmetrical and its margin edged with masonry." Sauernon places a tomb of Osiris to the south of the Sacred Lake. Flower gardens also stood in this area while rooms for Osiris were placed to the north of the *Akh Menu*.

A statue in the Munich Museum found at Karnak contains an inscription of Bekenkhonsu, of the XIXth Dynasty, where he was described as "skilled in art, and the first prophet of Amen."

"I performed the best I could for the people of Amen, as architect of my lord. I executed the pylon 'of Rameses II, the friend of Amen, who listens to those who pray to him' (thus he is named), at the first gate of the Temple of Amen. I placed

QUINTESSENTIAL BOOK "THE HOLY LAND"

obelisks at the same made of granite. Their height reached the vault of heaven. The Propylon is before the same in sight of the city of Thebes, and ponds and gardens, with flourishing trees. I made two great double doors of gold. Their height reached to heaven. I caused to be made a double pair of great masts. I set them up in the splendid court in sight of his temple." This is actually the Temple of Luxor.

The earliest name found on any of the buildings of the Great Temple of Amon of Karnak is that of Osirtasen I. By his other name Amenemenes I, Grimal (1992: 160) informs: "He undertook important building works at Karnak, from which a few statues and a granite naos (which must have contained a cult statue) have survived. It is even possible that it was Ammenemes I who established the original temple of Mut to the south of the precinct of Amon-Re. Traces of his building works have also survived at Koptos, where he partly decorated the temple of Min; at Abydos, where he dedicated a granite altar to Osiris; at Dendera, where he consecrated a gateway, also in granite, to Hathor; and at Memphis, where he built the temple of Ptah. He also had a pyramid built for himself at el-Lisht, about fifty kilometers south of Memphis."

Equally, while Amenemenes may have built at Luxor, Amenhotep III or possibly other Pharaohs tore down this earlier structure and that king erected the now standing Temple of Luxor. Even more, we know that Senmut started the Temple of Mut in Asher during Hatshepsut's reign. This is consistent with Breasted's view (1923: 344) that credits Amenhotep III with building "a temple to Mut, the goddess of Thebes, where his ancestors had begun it, on the south of Karnak, and excavated a lake beside it. He then laid out a beautiful garden in the interval of over a mile and a half, which separates the Karnak from the Luxor temple and connected the great temples by avenues of rams carved in stone, each bearing a statue of the Pharaoh between the fore-paws."

Royal palaces and villas lined the Avenue of Sphinxes connecting Karnak with Luxor. Illustrations in the Temple of Amenhotep III show the water procession to Luxor, when Amon would visit during the Opet Festival. On the return trip, priests in white robes shouldered the god's bark along the Avenue of Sphinxes. Cottrell (1965: 174-75) speaks of another time of joyous celebrations in praise of Amun by Horemheb. He was the last king of the Eighteenth Dynasty, a usurper to the throne who exercised subterfuge to justify his right to the crown.

On the sculptured reliefs he had made on the side walls of his colonnade (north of the forecourt of Amenhotep) he depicts his arrival at Thebes during one of the greatest religious festivals of the Theban year, the 'Feast of Amun in the Apts;' it lasted twenty-four days and took place during the time of the Inundation. In the inscriptions which accompany the scenes we read that 'Horus proceeded with rejoicing to Thebes, city of the Lord of Eternity, with his son (Horemheb) in his embrace, to Karnak, to introduce him before Amun, to assign to him his office as king .... Behold they came with rejoicing at his beautiful feast in Luxor.'

Even further, Cottrell (1965: 175) could add: "This festival, which so conveniently coincided with Horemheb's arrival in Thebes, was one in which the sacred barge of Amun, carrying the image of the god, sailed from Karnak to Luxor, while processions accompanied it on shore carrying models of the sacred barque. It is this procession, which we see, vividly depicted on the temple reliefs set up by Horemheb. At the head of the procession march soldiers and standard-bearers, then come two royal chariots followed by men hauling on the sacred barge, women shaking systra (sacred rattles often depicted in the hands of priestesses), priests bearing the models of the sacred barge, and a representation of the great gate of the Karnak temple with its flag-staffs. On the east angle of the north wall we see sacrificial bulls, three sacred barges, and galleys. This relief depicts the procession returning to Karnak. Again we see the king's chariots, marching soldiers, the sacred barges floating downstream, and at last the Pharaoh offering his final sacrifice to the god." We do know Tutankhamon executed the illustrations of the Opet Festival on the walls beside the Processional Colonnade at Luxor Temple!

The third type of temple, the Kiosk or Processional, after the worship and mortuary temples, that Sesostris I erected was in an unknown spot at Karnak. It was dismantled and stuffed into the Third Pylon, and can now be seen with special permission in the "Open Air Museum," north of the Great Court. Trigger, et. al. (1989: 189) mentions a "Thirteenth Dynasty stele from Karnak records the flooding of the temple of Amen."

QUINTESSENTIAL BOOK
"THE HOLY LAND"

Holy Land Illustration 23. Sedment. Stele. Alone and smelling the lotus flower; with the Ms. and being attended to by servants; and being doused with holy water (left) ; and (right), Foreign pottery, Group 263. G. Ghurab. K. Kahun.

Scientific American Supplement No. 1208 (February 25, 1899: 19361) in covering the fall of the columns, tells: "The Nile, up to that time, had been Karnak's greatest enemy and the great inundation of 1887 submerged the hypostyle hall under ten feet of water. It was the Nile itself that was forced to repair the damage that it had done. Its water, diverted by a small canal, again came to lave the columns and pylons, and to dissolve the calcareous deposits that were corroding them at a point flush with the ground." However, whereas another, *Scientific American Supplement* No. 1252 (December 30, 1899: 20064) article argued: "It is said that many structures are endangered by the infiltration of the waters of the Nile, and that the destruction of the hypostyle hall is to be attributed thereto." On the other hand, it reported: "The commission appointed by the Egyptian government to inquire into the catastrophe is of the opinion that an earthquake caused the falling of the columns."

Nevertheless, Jordan (1976: 28) has shown how water seepage has affected the temple over the years, particularly in modern times. He states: "The Nile's river bed, however, has been independently rising over the years due to the deposition of silt (though the Aswan High Dam may now largely remove these silts from the water) and this raised water level has threatened some monuments which were originally built well above the water-table: the great Hypostyle Hall at the Karnak temple has suffered badly from damp."

Equally too, in a footnote Murray (1957: 229) speaks of the problem of flooding in the temple. She writes: "I have myself seen floods in the temple of Karnak due entirely to seepage, for though the river was running bank-high it had not over-flooded. And there is always the danger that the river may rise above its banks, then 'the emboldened floods link arms and flashing forward drown' whole villages. Two records of such an event are found. The first is the inscription of Smendes of the XXIst dynasty, engraved in the quarry at Gebelein: 'His Majesty sat in the hall of his palace in the city of Memphis, when there came messengers to inform his Majesty that the canal-work, which forms the boundary of Thothmes III's temple at Luxor, had begun to go to ruin, [on account of the waters] making a great flood and a mighty current therein on the great pavement of the house of the temple, it encircled the facade. His Majesty said, 'There has been nothing like this in the time of my Majesty, or from of old.' 'His Majesty sent master-builders and three thousand men with them to the choicest of the people.' The rest of the inscription is broken away."

Even further, Murray (1957: 229) continued: "The other record is of the reign of Osorkon II of the XXIst dynasty, and narrates not only the effect of the flood but the carrying out of the image of Amon by the priests to quell the rise of the waters: 'The floods came on in the whole land, it invaded the two shores as in the beginning; the land was in its power like the sea; there was no dyke of the people to withstand its fury. All the people were like birds, all the temples of Thebes were like marshes.' The resemblance of the people to birds was because they had to take refuge from the flood on the branches of trees. The height of the inundation is recorded in the Nile levels on the quay at Karnak Temple, and they show that the water must have risen and flooded the temples to the depth of two feet above the pavement."

In addition, Trigger et. al. (1989: 173) have deduced the "main source for the Theban revolt is a pair of stelae (and a scribal copy of one of them) erected in Karnak temple by Kamose and dated to his year 3" in the era of the war of liberation, the expulsion of the Hyksos and founding of the New Kingdom with Amun triumphant. The latest name appearing at the Temple of Amon "Lord of Karnak, Master of Heaven" is that of Alexander II, in a small chamber in the *Akh Menu* of Thutmose III. Hurry (1987: 104) tells of a mural painting, where: "In the

QUINTESSENTIAL BOOK "THE HOLY LAND"

temple of Ptah and Hathor at Karnak, Imhotep with Ptah and his consort Hathor are seen sculptured on the walls and worshiped by King Thutmosis III."

Here then is recounted a wonderful artistic, cultural, as well as theological, epistemological, and metaphysic and spiritual heritage, that African people can connect with. Knowledge of this cultural history that gave birth to science, mathematics, medicine, engineering, river transportation, quarrying, construction, and agriculture, can provide significant inspiration for children of the ancestors residing in urban and rural settings across America. Karnak lasted as long as it did and was influential because beneath its religious base, Ma'atian ethics and morality, were prime factors in Amon's efforts to uplift humanity, as he bid those glorious African Pharaohs and warrior kings and nobles, take prisoners the world over and bring them along with booty to Karnak, seat of the greatest of the Gods, Amon-Ra. Therein was born the relationship of the human and the divine, the religious and spiritual that fueled the intellectual consciousness and social growth and expression of man's capabilities that produced the wonderful panorama sketched above.

Very appropriate here friends, is Rev. McNair's dictum: "I cannot teach my people there is no God, I can only show them where God came from!" In this he meant, that God first appeared along the Nile River and the seat of his greatest manifestation was at Karnak, where Amon dwelt as Lord of the Gods!

Cottrell (1965: 180-81) after praising the pair of obelisks that Hatshepsut had her architect quarry at Aswan and set up at Karnak, seat of the king of the gods, incisively declares: "As for the rest of Karnak, each visitor will make his choice from the many wonders it contains. Some will carry in their memories the sacred lake on which the barque of Amun used to ride; others will remember the forest of columns in the hypostyle hall, the seventy-ton architraves poised against the blue Egyptian sky, and the enormous reliefs depicting Pharaonic conquests and sacrifices. My own memory is of a small dark chamber at the far end of the temple of Ptah (the artificer-god) and Hathor. You enter one of the dim mysterious cell-like rooms of the sanctuary and the bronze door gate as they close behind you. The sunlight has disappeared, and your eyes at first can see nothing in the dank, chilly darkness. Then, as light filters down through a tiny hole in the ceiling, you become aware of a female figure standing quite close to you. The body is that of a young woman with rounded hips and firm breast. But the face is that of a lioness. This is the only sanctuary in the whole of Karnak, which still houses the image of a deity. You are standing, as only the most privileged of the priests were permitted to stand, in the sanctuary of the goddess Sekhmet."

FREDERICK MONDERSON

Holy Land 12a. Prof. Donna Richards, Dr. Merimba Ani, prepares the "Holy Water" to make the Libation and help make successful ASCAC's 1999 Conference in New York.

Thus, Karnak is indeed a wonderful experience full of theological, intellectual, philosophical and scientific mystique and aura, ideas and practice, as represented

QUINTESSENTIAL BOOK "THE HOLY LAND"

in the building craft still evident in standing structures and the attendant religious ritual and practice.

Clearly, the effort these ancient Africans made to ritualize, worship and create sweet communion with their Gods, is reflective of how their descendants were able to religiously and spiritually express their feeling despite the many challenges, because they were in-tune with the divine. Now, to quote Dr. ben-Jochannan, regarding the creativity of those Nile Valley Africans, one should "visit Karnak and you will experience some semblance of how the ancients expressed themselves while setting standards in medicine, building, art, agriculture, language, navigation, science, etc., that propelled subsequent civilizations along the paths of human experience and development. Upon the sixth return to the Hypostyle Hall in Karnak, one gets a more profound understanding of the effort and achievement of these early Africans. More significantly, however, there is an intellectual, spiritual, psychic and moral transformation that occurs after one of these pilgrimages, when one engenders oneself in the paths of Ma'atian ethics and practice that can be tremendously helpful in meeting the challenges of modern existence."

REFERENCES

Aldred, Cyril. *The Egyptians*. New York: Thames and Hudson Inc., (1961) 1987.
Armour, Robert A. *Gods and Myths of Ancient Egypt*. Cairo: American University in Cairo Press, (1986) 1989.
Badawy, Alexander. *A History of Egyptian Architecture*. Vol. I. London: Histories and Mysteries of Man, Ltd., 1990.
Baines, John and Jaromir Malek. *Atlas of Ancient Egypt*. New York: Facts on File, 1980.
Barnett, Mary. *Egypt: Gods and Myths of Ancient Egypt*. London: Smithmark Publishers Inc., 1996.
ben-Jochannan, Yosef. *Abu Simbel to Ghizeh: A Guide Book and Manual*. Baltimore, MD: Black Classics Press, (1987) 1989.
_____. *The African Called Rameses ("The Great") II and the African Origin of "Western Civilization."* New York: Alkebu-Lan Book Associates, 1990.
Bierbrier, Morris. *The Tomb Builders of the Pharaohs*. Cairo: American University in Cairo Press, (1982) 1989.

FREDERICK MONDERSON

Holy Land 13. Temple of Isis. Kiosk of Trajan. Elevated columns, varied capitals, extended abacus or die under the architrave.

Breasted, John H. *A History of Egypt*. New York: Charles Scribner's Sons, (1905) 1923.
Brunton, Paul. *A Search in Secret Egypt*. New York: Samuel Weiser, (1935) 1980.
Budge, E. A. Wallis. *The Literature of the Ancient Egyptians*. London: J. M. Dent and Sons, 1914.
_____. *From Fetish to God in Ancient Egypt*. Oxford University Press and London: Humphrey Milford, 1934.
_____. *The Gods of the Egyptians*. Vol. II. New York: Dover Publications Inc., (1904) 1969.
_____. *The Mummy*. New York: Causeway Books, (1894) 1974.
_____. *Dwellers on the Nile*. New York: Dover Publishers, Inc., 1972.
Carpiceci, Alberto Carlo. *Art and History of Egypt*. Florence, Italy: Case Editrice Bonechi, 1994.
Clarke, Summers and R. Engelbach. *Ancient Egyptian Construction and Architecture*. New York: Dover Publications, Inc., (1930) 1990.
Cottrell, Leonard. *Egypt*. New York: Oxford University Press, 1966.
David, Rosalie. *Discovering Ancient Egypt*. New York: Facts on File, 1993.
Diop, Cheikh Anta. *Civilization or Barbarism*: *An Authentic Anthropology*. Brooklyn, New York: Lawrence Hill, 1991.
DuBois, W.E.B. *The World and Africa*. New York: International Publishers, (1946) 1971.
Eames, Andrew. Editor and Producer. *The Nile*: *Insight Guides*. Hong Kong. APA Publications, Ltd., 1992.
Erman, Adolf. *A Handbook of Egyptian Religion*. London: Archibald Constable and Co., Ltd., 1907.
Fedden, Robin. *Egypt: Land of the Valley*. London: Michael Haag, (1977) 1986.

QUINTESSENTIAL BOOK
"THE HOLY LAND"

Fragner, Benjamin. *The Illustrated History of Architecture*. London: Sunburst Books, 1994.
Goodwin, C. W. "Hymns to Amen" in *Records of the Past*. Vol. VI. Editor Samuel Birch. London: Samuel Bagster and Sons, 1876.
Grimal, Nicolas. *A History of Ancient Egypt*. Oxford/Cambridge, USA: Blackwell, 1988 (1993).
Gympel, Jan. *The Story of Architecture: From Antiquity to the Present*. Cambridge: Goodfellow and Egan, Cambridge, 1996.
Haag, Michael. *Guide to Egypt*. London: Michael Haag, (1987).
Habachi, Labib. *The Obelisks of Egypt: Skyscrapers of the Past*. Cairo: The American University in Cairo Press, (1984) 1987.
Hart, George. *Egyptian Myths*. London: British Museum Publications, 1990.
_____. *Ancient Egypt*. London: Time-Life Books, (1995) 1996.
Hobson, Christine Hobson. *The World of the Pharaohs*. London: Thames and Hudson, 1987.
Hurry, Jamieson B. *Imhotep: The Egyptian God of Medicine*. Ares Publishers, Inc., (1926) 1987.
James, T.G.H. *Pharaoh's People*. Oxford at the University Press, (1984) 1985.
Jordan, Paul. *Egypt: The Black Land*. New York: E. P. Dutton, 1976.
Kamil, Jill. *Luxor: A Guide to Ancient Thebes*. 2nd Edition. London: Longman, (1973) 1980.
Knopf, Alfred A. *Egypt*. New York: Alfred A. Knopf, 1995.
Langenscheidt. *Egypt: Self-Guided*. Maspeth, New York: Langenscheidt Publishers, (1973) 1990.
Lurker, Manfred. *The Gods and Symbols of Ancient Egypt*. London: Thames and Hudson, 1991.
Mann, A. T. *Sacred Architecture*. Rockport, Massachusetts: Element, 1993.
Maspero, Gaston. *History of Egypt, Chaldea, Syria, Babylonia, and Assyria*. XII Volumes. London: The Grolier Society, 1904.
_____. *Manual of Egyptian Archaeology*. New York: G. P. Putnam's Sons, 1926.
McGrath, Nancy. *Egypt: Dollarwise Guide*. New York: Simon and Schuster, (1980) 1982.
Mertz, Barbara. *Temples, Tombs and Hieroglyphs*. New York: Dodd and Mead, (1964) 1978.
Michalowski, Kazimierz. *Art of Ancient Egypt*. New York: Harry N. Abrams, Inc., Publishers, No Date.
Muller, Wolfgang. "Egyptian Art." *Encyclopedia of Art*. (1963: 618-710).
Murnane, William C. *The Penguin Guide to Ancient Egypt*. New York: Penguin Books, 1983.
Murray, Margaret. *The Splendor That Was Egypt*. New York: Philosophical Library, (1949) 1957.
Newberry, Percy E. "An Egyptian Gardener: The Tomb of Nakht." *Scientific American Supplement* No. 1231 (August 5, 1899).

_____. "Ancient Egyptian Gardening." *Scientific American Supplement* No 1256 (January 27, 1900: 20138-39).
Obenga, Theophile. *Ancient Egypt and Black Africa*. London: Karnak House, 1992.
Payne, Elizabeth. *The Pharaohs of Ancient Egypt*. New York: Random House, 1964.
Petrie, W.M.F. *Religious Life in Ancient Egypt*. London: Constable and Co., (1924) 1932.
Pier, Garrett Chatfield. "The Great Temple of Amon-Ra at Karnak." *Art and Architecture* Vol. IV No 2 (August, 1916: 91-100).
Polyglot. *Egypt Travel Guide*. Cairo: Lehnert and Landrock, 1965.
Quirke, Stephen. *Ancient Egyptian Religion*. London: The British Museum, 1992.
Robins, Gay. *Women in Ancient Egypt*. Cambridge, Massachusetts: Cambridge University Press, 1993.
Rohl, David. *Pharaohs and Kings*: *A Biblical Quest*. New York: Crown Publishing, 1995.
Ruffle, John. *The Egyptians*. Ithaca, New York: Cornell University Press, 1977.
Samkange, Stanlake. *African Saga*: *A Brief Introduction to African History*. Nashville, New York: Abingdon Press, 1971.
Sauernon, Serge. "Karnak" in George Posener's *A Dictionary of Egyptian Civilization*. London: Methuen and Co., Ltd. 1962.
Scholz, Piotr O. *Ancient Egypt*: *An Illustrated Historical Overview*. Hauppauge, New York: Barron's Educational Series, Inc., (1996) 1997.
Scientific American Supplement. "The Fallen Columns of Karnak." *Scientific American Supplement* No. 1208. (February 25, 1899: 19359-19364).
_____. "The Destruction of the Hypostyle Hall in Karnak." *Scientific American Supplement* No. 1232. (December 30, 1899: 20064).
Shaw, Ian and Paul Nicholson. *The Dictionary of Ancient Egypt*. London: The British Museum, 1995.
Showker, Kay. *Egypt*: *A Practical and Historical Guide*. New York: Fodor, 1989.
Simpkins. *The Temple of Karnak*. Salt Lake City, Utah: Simpkins, 1982.
Smith, Fay. *Egypt*: *At Cost*. New York: Little Hills Press, 1991.
Smith, W. Stevenson. *The Art and Architecture of Ancient Egypt*. New York: Penguin Books, (1958) 1981.
Spencer, A.J. *Early Egypt*: *The Rise of Civilization in the Nile Valley*. London: The British Museum, 1993.
Time-Life. *What Life Was Like On the Banks of the Nile*? Alexandria, Virginia: Time-Life Books, 1997.
Trigger, B.G., B.J. Kemp, D. O'Connor, and A.B. Lloyd. *Ancient Egypt*: *A Social History*. Cambridge at the University Press, 1989.
Vercoutter, Jean. *The Search for Ancient Egypt*. New York: Discoveries: Harry N. Abrams, Inc., Publishers, (1986) 1992.
Youssef, Hisham and John Rodenbeck. *Egypt*: *Insight Guides*. Hong Kong: APA Publications, Ltd, 1991.
Watterson, Barbara. *The Egyptians*. Cambridge, Mass.: Blackwell, 1997.

QUINTESSENTIAL BOOK "THE HOLY LAND"

Wayne, Scott. *Egypt and the Sudan: A Travel Survival Kit.* Australia: Lonely Planet, 1987.
Weigall, Arthur. *A Guide to the Antiquities of Egypt.* London: Bracken Books, (1910) 1996.
Wilkinson, Alix. *Ancient Egyptian Jewelry.* London: Methuen and Co., Inc., 1971.
Wilkinson, J. Gardner. *The Ancient Egyptians: Their Life and Customs.* Vol. 1 London: Random House, Senate Books, (1994) 1996.
Williams, Chancellor. *The Destruction of Black Civilization.* Chicago: Third World Press, (1987) 1996.
Woldering, Irmgard. *The Art of Egypt: The Time of the Pharaohs.* New York: Greystone Press, 1963.
Wilkinson, Alex. *Ancient Egyptian Jewelry.* London: Methuen and Co., Inc. 1971.

LUXOR TEMPLE
By
Dr. Fred Monderson

The **Temple of Luxor** is a magnificent piece of classical Kemetic architecture. It is also a cultural reservoir and fountain of the wisdom of those early Africans who, in antiquity, created and built systems and schools of thought in theology, science, art, music, and social and moral reverence that migrated to enlighten the world, all thousands of years later, this structure still exudes that esoteric metaphysical spirituality. This significant piece of sacred architecture grew as Amon's second home and came to be regarded significantly because of its structure, its purpose, function, and later influence. So much so, Luxor Temple came to play a tremendously important role in shaping theological, theocratic, educational, religious, spiritual, and scientific belief systems of these early Africans. In this way, this temple influenced the intellectual learning and aspirations in the "Old "World." Clearly, much of that significance has migrated and survives in the modern world's view and consciousness. As such then, Luxor Temple's influence on the world stage is difficult to measure. Today it still radiates the aura of those cultural, artistic, architectural, spiritual and ethical and metaphysical principles, initiated millennia ago.

Built on the water's edge, or cornice, it is a worship or "God Temple." Its orientation towards Karnak temple allowed it to become part of a twin force (the Apts) in worship of the great god Amon at Thebes. Weigall's (1910: 71) commentary on the personal nature of this temple structure built by the XVIIIth dynasty monarch is interesting, for the king says of this work: "'Amenhotep IIIrd,

Ruler of Thebes, is satisfied with the building made for his father Amen-Ra. When the people see it they give praise to His Majesty. It is Amenhotep IIIrd who hath satisfied the heart of his father Amen.'"

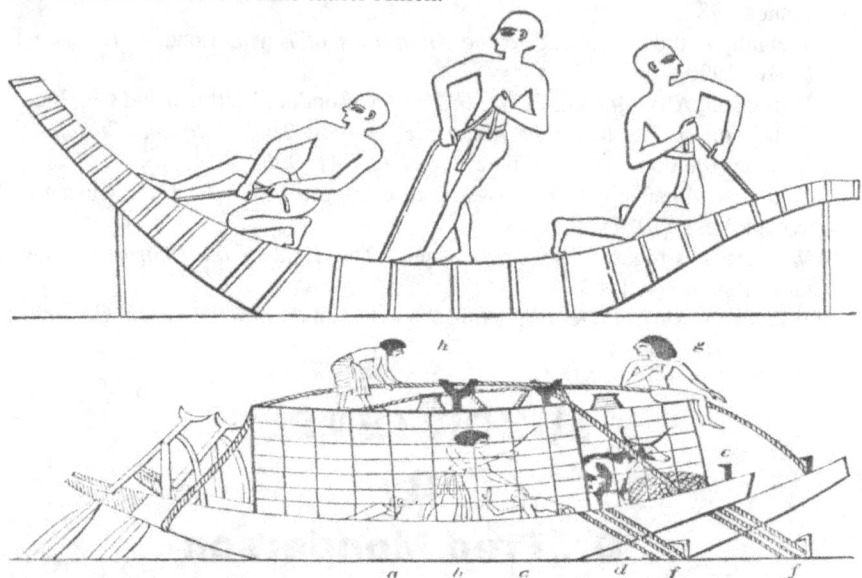

Holy Land Illustration 24. Canoe of papyrus, bound with bands of the same; a boat for carrying cattle and goods on the Nile. Thebes.

The Temple of Luxor is also one of the best preserved of the ancient temples surviving from the time when pharaohs ruled ancient Kemet. As the Temple of Rameses III, in the great court at Karnak, is a single structure and different from the larger temple; so too, the Temple of Luxor, as built by Amenhotep III, during that time of African imperialism and cultural explosion of a "Golden Age," was conceived as a single structure. Still, and though subsequently added to by later kings it was different from its companion at Karnak. More significantly, this temple's conception enjoyed compounded architectural knowledge of Old Kingdom, Middle Kingdom and early New Kingdom temple building practice.

Fedden (1986: 146) espouses the view: "To travel south to Luxor is to move from the Old Kingdom to the imperial phase of Egyptian history (1570-1085), from the pyramid to the rock-hewn tomb, from the chaste simplicity of Sakkara to the grandiose cult and funerary temples of Thebes. New features appear: processional sphinx avenues, massive pylon gateways, and colossal statuary, red granite obelisks. The emphasis is on size, yet the immensely wealthy and impulsive builders of the New Kingdom produced a number of monuments distinguished for their purely architectural qualities. Among such are the forecourt of Amenophis III in the Temple of Ammon at Luxor, Hatshepsut's elegant and revolutionary temple at Deir el-Bahari, the hypostyle hall of the Ramesseum at Thebes, the

QUINTESSENTIAL BOOK "THE HOLY LAND"

temple of Seti I at Abydos, and not least the little temple of Ptah at Karnak (restored in Ptolemaic times) where a single ray of light dramatically illuminates the statue of the goddess Sekhmet."

In fact, Youssef (1991: 189) credits a number of Monarchs with being involved in the construction of the Temple of Luxor. "The major part was built by Amenhotep III (1414 B.C. - 1379 B.C.) with substantial additions by Tutankhamon (1333 - 1323 B.C.), Horemheb (1319 B.C. - 1307 B.C.), Rameses II (1290 B.C. - 1224 B.C.), and Alexander the Great (332 B.C. - 323 B.C.)." By the river's side, it supported crafts of quarrying, facilitated shipbuilding and enabled water transportation of great sized stone from distant regions to aid the construction of this quintessential structure of ancient Kemetic religious worship. Because of its relevance to Amun, Luxor Temple became the "grand lodge" of spiritual, theosophical and epistemological knowledge, practice and experience of ancient Africa. This experience enlightened the world and set standards for the intellectual, scientific and artistic and epistemological phenomena of cultural growth. The lights of tradition shined brightly here! Under Amenhotep III, "the Magnificent," great-grandson of the mighty warrior pharaoh Thutmose III, the empire was intact, vibrant, at the pinnacle of its "Golden Age." Yet, within a decade of Amenhotep III's rule, his son and successor Amenhotep IV, Akhenaten, had ushered in a mighty religious, cultural and artistic revolution that brought great turmoil to the land. Weigall (1910: 71) offers the explanation: "When Akhnaton, the son of Amenhotep IIIrd, came to the throne and renounced the worship of Amen, he ordered that god's name to be erased wherever it occurred; and one may see to this day how it has been chiseled out in all the inscriptions. A shrine of Aton, the new god, was erected within the precincts of Luxor temple. The next king, Tutankhamen, who returned to the worship of Amen, destroyed this shrine; and continued the building of the original temple which Amenhotep IIIrd had left unfinished." This aside, many great achievements in temple construction underscore Amenhotep III's many virtues. However, in addition to the above, Seti I and Rameses II left their names here also.

A great builder, Amenhotep III erected the Third Pylon at Karnak. The massive Processional Way columns, central to the Hypostyle Hall, were his brainchild. This pharaoh constructed the Temple of Mut in Asher, begun by Senmut, Hatshepsut's architect. He placed hundreds of statues of the lion goddess Sekhmet in the Temple of Mut. He also built a sacred lake for its vulture goddess. As the second deity of the Theban Triad, recognition and worship of Mut dates to the Middle Kingdom beginnings of Amon worship, as the "Lord of Karnak" and "Master of the World." Similarly, as much as the temples of Amon and Mut were linked to earlier structures, the Temple of Luxor was erected on an earlier Twelfth Dynasty shrine from where the name of Pharaoh Sobek-Hotep of the XIIIth Dynasty, has been recovered. This Middle Kingdom structure may have been built on even earlier sacred foundations, possibly dating back to the beginnings of pharaonic rule.

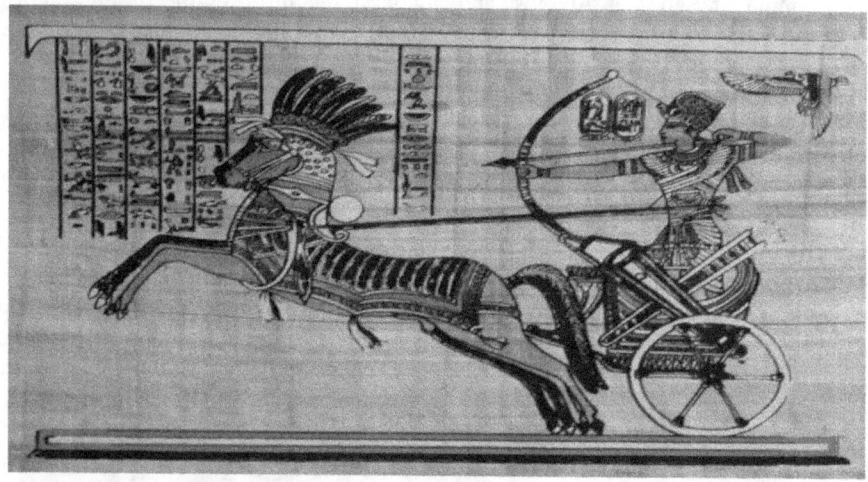

Holy Land Papyrus 8. King out in his chariot firing his arrow while the reins for steering his car are tied to his waist. Notice the protective hawk overhead.

However, evidence indicates, after the war of independence, and founding of the Eighteenth Dynasty and beginning of the New Kingdom, Ahmose had built a temple at Luxor. A later king of the Eighteenth Dynasty, Amenhotep tore this smaller temple down and erected a monumental masterpiece in Kemetic architecture. Kamil (1976: 220) points out: "Though by this time Egyptian military power was past its peak, economic conditions within the capital were sound. Trade was flourishing with wealth pouring in from the distant provinces of the empire, which comprised almost all West Asia including Palestine, Syria, Phoenicia and the western part of the Euphrates, Nubia and Libya. Extravagant caravans brought gold and silver, metal-ware, ivory and timber, spices for the royal taste and strange and exotic animals to roam in private gardens. The temples were bursting with tributes, walls and columns were encrusted with richness and color, feasts and festivals were bountiful, the pace was brisk, the mood content."

Here, and elsewhere, particularly at the Temple of Soleb in Nubia, Amenhotep III experimented with new forms of architecture. Now, this original Temple of Luxor was conceived as a single construction, while Rameses II of the XIXth Dynasty added a court and pylon. This addition provided an axis that more properly oriented this temple with the Precinct of Amon at Karnak and so avoiding the river. Beyond this second axis, was still another. West (1987: 168), quoting Schwaller de Lubicz, wrote, this "curiously skewed complex is strictly aligned

QUINTESSENTIAL BOOK
"THE HOLY LAND"

upon three separate axes. Without exception, every wall, colonnade, hall and sanctuary is rigorously aligned upon one or the other of these axes." West (1987: 168) wrote even further: "The axes are chiseled into the sandstone floor of the Temple and obviously served as a guide for the earliest stage of construction. Thereafter, this floor was covered over in white limestone, but the subsequent construction continued to be rigorously aligned to the invisible axis!" Additionally, and particularly in his researches at Luxor Temple, Schwaller de Lubicz, subscribed to the view, according to West (1987: 197) that "man is not a 'product' of the universe, not a 'scaled model' of it; he is to be regarded as an embodiment, its 'essence' incorporated in physical form." Nevertheless, however we view the juxtaposition of Rameses' addition, on a distinct axis, knowledgeable critics as Maspero (1904, V. 126) could still write: "The whole structure lacks unity, and there is nothing corresponding to it in this respect anywhere else in Egypt. The northern half does not join on to the southern, or the two parts might be regarded as having once formed a single edifice which had become divided by an accident, which the architect had endeavored to unite together again by a line of columns running between two walls."

Notwithstanding, an interesting comment is further made regarding irregularities in Egyptian/Kemetic architecture, particularly at some temples such as Luxor and Philae. In this regard Maspero (1926: 94-95) later wrote: "At Luxor the building progressed methodically under Amenhotep III and Seti I, but when Rameses II wished to add to what had been done by his predecessors, an easterly bend of the river obliged him to deviate in the same direction. His pylon is not parallel with the boundary wall of the last court of Amenhotep III, and his colonnades form a distinct angle with the general axis of the previous work. At Philae the deviation is even greater. Not only is the larger pylon out of line with the smaller one, but the two southern colonnades diverge considerably and naturally do not accord with the plan."

In orientation with the greater Amun temple at Thebes, a Dromos or Processional Way of Sphinxes as well as a canal linked Luxor with Karnak. Bratton (1968: 183) mentions "1400 sphinxes" along the two-mile path, that were "10 feet long, 4 feet high and mounted on 5 feet tall pedestals." Amenhotep III also constructed the palace of Malcata across the river, in western Thebes, for his Queen Tiy. Kamil (1976: 23) states: "His wife, Queen Tiy, was very beautiful and clearly loved by the Pharaoh, as she is depicted in name or person always at his side and far more frequently than was usual for royal wives of earlier rulers." Here they retired while the Aten controversy developed during his son Amenhotep IV's reign. Even further, Kamil (1976: 23) wrote: "Near his palace on the necropolis his enormous artificial lake, over 1,700 meters long and 500 wide, was surrounded by luxuriant foliage." According to Ruffle (1977: 70-71), Malcata was a "huge estate incorporating parade grounds and small chapels, large audience halls, decorated with painted walls, ceilings, and floors, villas for government officials, offices, kitchens, workshops, and huts for the servants."

We know the purpose of Luxor Temple was to celebrate the "Opet Festival." Then again, the origin of this Luxor Temple may be linked to the fact of Karnak being crowded and the pharaoh who had married the beloved Queen Tiy chose this site to represent another light in the constellation of sites of worship to Amun. He had a great repository of knowledge, observations, scientific data and expertise that surrounded the worship at Karnak. After all, this deity had brought great fame and fortune requiring festivals to the nation and the Theban capital. All this, while the south reigned supreme following the expulsion of the Hyksos and great cultural growth during the glorious XVIIIth Dynasty when ancient Kemet became the "light of the world." On the other hand, and reinforcing origins, and purpose, Hobson (1987: 139) mention "a lightly carved relief shows the celebration of the Opet festival, the reason for the existence of the Temple of Luxor." Even further, Hart (1990: 10-11) points to a unique aspect of the Luxor Temple, for like Hatshepsut's Temple at Deir el-Bahari, they "reveal Amon deserting his mysterious confines in the sky for union with the reigning Queen of Egypt, thereby fathering the future monarch." This "divine birth" helped to strengthen the king's claim to the throne of the Sun god. Additionally, during Amenhotep's reign art, architecture, science, medicine, literature, mathematics, mummification, astronomy, and engineering achieved a high level, and the period was rightly called "the Golden Age."

The people of ancient Kemet called the site of Luxor *Waset*. The Greeks considered it a part of *Diospolis Parva* and in Arabic it is called *El Uksor* or *Abou el Haggag*. The name, Luxor, or *El Kosoor*, signifies "the palaces" from the temple there erected by Amenhotep III and Rameses II. In time the name became Luxor, and on a regional basis, it represented both sides of the river. Dr. ben-Jochannan, the noted Egyptologist, likes to say to visitors, regarding this city: "You buy cotton at Aswan, leather at Luxor, and gold in Cairo." Of course, you buy books where you get them! Aboudy bookstore is one of the best in Luxor. No longer in the old location, the bookstore moved around the corner.

David (1993: 83) enumerated in his work, mentions the early travelers and scholars who visited Luxor including: "Norden, Denon, Wilkinson, Burton, Lhote, Champollion, Minutoli and Lepsius." The Scottish artist David Roberts visited the site in 1838. However, even more interesting is the tale told by Fagan (1975: 74) that when Napoleon's troops, sailing up the river, turned the bend at Thebes on January 17, 1799, and they beheld the two temples of Karnak and Luxor: "The division came to a spontaneous halt and burst into applause. 'Without an order being given, the men formed their ranks and presented arms, to the accompaniment of the drums and the band.'"

QUINTESSENTIAL BOOK "THE HOLY LAND"

The modern public approach to the Temple of Luxor was from the west. This has been blocked and the new entrance is from the east on the Abu Haggag Plaza. where the entranceway view is dominated by the monuments of Rameses II. In ancient times, wrote Maspero (1904: V, 68), who cleared this temple in the 1880s: "the naos rose sheer above the waters of the Nile, indeed its cornices projected over the river, and a staircase at the south side allowed the priests and devotees to embark directly from the rear of the building."

In front of two stone towers these now remain one of two standing obelisks, one of four standing statues, and two seated statues of the king before the pylon or gateway. At the bases of these seated statues the Nile gods unite the land, and conquered enemies of Kemet from north and south, are displayed. Lurker (1991: 97) adds: "Originally there were six statues of Rameses II (1304 - 1237 B.C.), before the pylons, one seated and two standing at either side." In fact, Weigall (1910: 71-72) recounts Rameses II's architect, a high priest of Amon named Bakenkhonsu's boast of how he erected the obelisks "where beauty approached heaven," and that he laid out a "garden planted with trees" in front of the pylon. "I made," he continued, "very great double doors of electrum; their beauty met the heavens. I hewed very great flagstaffs, and I erected them in the august court in front of the temple."

The red granite obelisk is covered on four sides with hieroglyphic or *Medu Netcher* inscriptions whose beauty rests in the admirable style of their execution and depth that in many instances exceed two inches. This obelisk measures 84 feet in height. At its base baboons greet the sun god. The other obelisk was given to the French king Louis Philippe in 1831, shipped to Paris and erected in the Place de La Concorde in 1836. That obelisk, also of red granite, is 77 feet tall and rests on a pedestal. Dr. ben-Jochannan (1989: 179) gives a "weight of two hundred and twenty-six [226] tons, approximately." Haag (1987: 200) informs of the French desire for an obelisk after Josephine's brazen request of Napoleon, as he departed for Egypt. "Goodbye!" She said. "If you go to Thebes, do send me a little obelisk!" This admonition motivated Champollion in his work. Haag tells (1987: 201) also of Flaubert, who while standing in front of the Temple of Luxor with its magnificent view in 1850 later remarked: "'the obelisk that is now in Paris was against the right-hand pylon. Perched on its pedestal, how bored it must be in the Place de la Concorde! How it must miss its Nile! What does it think as it watches all the cabs drive by, instead of the chariots it saw at its feet in the old days?'"

FREDERICK MONDERSON

Holy Land Illustration 25. Shawtis, Shabtis, or "Answerers" as they are sometimes called were created to accompany the deceased into the "Afterlife" and supposedly become servants or "Answerers" when a task is required and they are called.

A century later, according to Haag (1987: 200-01) Cocteau wrote: "the plinth of the obelisk removed to Paris 'was surrounded by the low reliefs of dog-faced baboons in erection.' This was not thought to be proper and so the monkey's organs have been cut off." Habachi (1987: 11) has also offered: "On the pedestal of the eastern obelisk, which is still in situ, the king boasted that 'he made a large obelisk [called] Rameses-Beloved-of-Amon [the rising sun].' The western obelisk, which is now in Paris, was named 'Rameses-Beloved-of-Atum [the setting sun].' On the eastern obelisk the king is called 'Beloved of Harakhti [the rising sun].' While on the western one he is styled 'Beloved of Atum.' The names of each obelisk and the epithets on them correspond to the rising of the sun in the east and it's setting in the west.

Today, this decoration of the front elevation to the temple faces the Dromos or partially restored Avenue of Sphinxes of Nectanebo that leads towards Karnak, three miles away. A Chapel of Sarapis and a Chapel of Hathor of the Roman period were within a great enclosure wall enclosing a great court or open area before the pylon and fronting the Avenue of Sphinxes.

QUINTESSENTIAL BOOK "THE HOLY LAND"

When we think of the significance of a Temple as at Luxor, we need examine the cosmological, theological and ethical thought and practice of adherents of the cult of Amon. Portman (1989: 15), in this regard, has described the temple in ancient Kemet as being the "mansion of a living god." He says, it is the: "incomprehensible and mysterious power of creation, embodied in the god, was worshiped with elaborate ritual behind massive stone walls. At the same time the temple was the seat of spiritual authority! The god's wishes were communicated to the world by a priesthood whose position naturally gave them great influence in affairs of state."

The priesthood also had a significant hand in training of the architectural, logistics, labor and administrative hierarchical officials of the state. Most importantly, they erected temples wherein their god resided and these structures reflected the socio-economic and political standing of this deity in the wider landscape of dynastic times. We see even further, Maspero (1926: 54-55) mentions customary practice at the: "building or rebuilding of a temple to place deposits under the foundation consisting of small squares of the building materials and models of the tools employed. Also a number of amulets, which were probably intended to secure by magic the safety of the temple. The foundation deposits are generally found in a layer of clean sand and marvelously fresh and uninjured."

Even more, the French archaeologist and former Curator of the Museum of Antiquities in Cairo, Maspero (1926: 55) explained: "Many of the objects are inscribed with the name of the founder of the temple, and it was by means of its intact foundation deposits that one of the ruined temples to the south of the Ramesseum was identified as that of Queen Tausert of the end of the Nineteenth Dynasty, although all its walls were razed to the ground. Among the glazed objects found in this deposit were scarabs, plaques, and models of offerings, besides many beads. The metal objects include adze, knife, axe-head, hoes, and chisels, made in thin sheet copper. They were also jars and cups, an ebony clamp, and a model corn-grinder."

In a comparative way, the Temple of Hatshepsut can throw light on the question of ceremony at consecration of that structure. It can serve as parallel light to understand such at the construction of Luxor Temple. Deir el Bahari foundation deposits furnished: "numerous models of workmen's tools, including the wooden centerings used in constructing brick vaulting. These were neatly inscribed in blue ink with the cartouche of the foundress Hatshepsut." Therefore, it's believed, the same practice applied at Luxor as at Deir el Bahari. At this temple, across the river, were found, as Maspero (1904, V, 55-56) added further: "Two deposits at the western entrance of this temple afford evidence of a ceremony customary at the foundation of a temple. An animal was slain and the flesh laid on a floor of clean sand over which the blood was allowed to drip; vessels containing unguents and wine were smashed and their contents together with grains of corn, were poured into the cache in addition to the offering of flesh and blood."

Holy Land Photo 13a. Temple of Isis at Philae (Now Agilka) Island. Varied capitals of the Kiosk of Trajan.

Finally, the **Pylon** walls are decorated with reliefs that depict Rameses' campaigns against the Hittites, at the Battle of Kadesh. The court scribe Pentaurt, in 1285 B.C., wrote his account right after the young king ascended the throne. The pylon itself is 79 feet high and 213 feet wide. The scenes on the pylon "were studied," as David (1993: 84) wrote, "by Rosellini and Champollion, Erentz and Breasted. A general account of the temple was published by Gayet in 1894." Polyglot (1965: 40) explains the depiction on the pylon regarding disposition of the campaign, wherein we see: "(left: council of war, the camp, the King battling from his war chariot; right: the King as archer, the flight of the Hittites, the enemy fortress)." The chariots, horses, shields taken from the enemy as well as the holy place that held the ark of the nation in a tent are also represented. This event was retold on major works of Rameses II, such as at Abu Simbel, Beit Wali, his funeral temple the Ramesseum and at Karnak. A parasol shades the king's chariot.

In interpreting this scene, West (1987: 173-74) argued that the representation of this pylon and circumstances surrounding the Battle of Kadesh itself is even more significant in the esoteric message it imparts. "The purpose of this complex relief is the depiction of the battle between the forces of light and darkness. Having vanquished the enemy, the king can enter the temple; to enter the temple, all obstacles in the external world must be overcome. This is why the battle scenes are all on the exterior of the Temple walls."

Youssef and Rodenbeck (1991: 186) show even further that in so many ancient Kemet temples: "In the outer parts of the temple, the reliefs record historical events: The foundation and dedication of the temple itself and details of processions and ceremonies. The pharaoh is very much in evidence leading the activities. He always faces the interior, while the resident god or goddess, often shown together with a consort and attendant gods, faces the outside world." At the

QUINTESSENTIAL BOOK
"THE HOLY LAND"

doorway of the Pylon itself is the name of Shabaka, and on the abacus of the columns beyond, that of Ptolemy Philopator, both added at a later epoch. Interestingly, Richardson and O'Brien (1991: 293) point to flag poles and mention: "The pylon was later embellished by Nubian and Ethiopian kings, as evinced by the relief of Pharaoh Shabaka running the heb [sed] race before Amun-Min, on the left as you walk through."

Min is an interesting ithyphallic god who is also an anthropomorphic form of Amun, the hidden one. Breasted (1923: 46) explores the idea that Min is an archaic god in Kemet/Egypt, in his statement: "The kings frequently record in their annals the draughting of a temple plan, or their superintendence of the ceremonious inauguration of the work when the ground was measured and broken. The great gods were those familiar in later times, which we shall yet have occasion briefly to discuss; we notice particularly Osiris and Set, Horus and Anubis, Thoth, Sokar, Min, and Apis, a form of Ptah; while among the goddesses, Hathor and Neit are very prominent. Several of these were patron gods of prehistoric kingdoms, preceding the kingdoms of the North and South, and thus going back to a very distant age."

In Amun's rise to recognition, Breasted (1923: 248) mentions how: "The triumph of a Theban family had brought with it the supremacy of Amon. He had not been the god of the residence in the Middle Kingdom, and although the rise of a Theban family had then given him some distinction, it was not until now that he became the great god of the state. His essential character and individuality had already been obliterated by the solar theology of the Middle Kingdom, when he had become Amon-Re, and with some attributes borrowed from his ithyphallic neighbor, Min of Coptos, he now rose to a unique and supreme position of unprecedented splendor. He was popular with the people, too, and as a Moslem says, "Inshallah," "If Allah wills," so the Egyptian now added to all his promises "If Amon spares my life."

Holy Land Illustration 26. Chapter XXXIX. Papyrus Musee du Louvre, 93 (left); and Chapter XL. Papyrus, Leyden Museum, No. IV, spearing the serpent (right).

As an attribute therefore of Amun, Min shared in his divinity. In fact, Min is the earlier form of Amon! Even further, Breasted continued, "They called him the 'vizier of the poor,' the people carried to him their wants and wishes, and their hopes for future prosperity were implicitly staked upon his favor. But the fusion of the old gods had not deprived Amon alone of his individuality, for in the general flux almost any god might possess the qualities and functions of the others, although the dominant position was still occupied by the sun-god."

However, Min is not simply colorfully decorated; he is also a controversial figure for his origins have been assigned to distant regions of the country as well as abroad. Whereas, Weigall (1910: 78), in a footnote has argued for possibly an Asiatic origin of Min in the statement: "It may be noted in passing that Min, as god of vegetation and generation, is precisely similar to the North Syrian god Adon, who is again identified with Aton. The son of Amenhotep IIIrd and Queen Thiy renounced the worship of Amen for that of Aton." Interesting, they always associate Egyptian personalities with Syrian parallels as opposed to Syrian with Egyptian.

Scholz (1996: 82), on the other end of the spectrum, has indicated: "Min is one of the archaic ithyphallic gods, thought to be related to the darker skinned Africans. Thus, he was sometimes portrayed as a 'black' god. He symbolized the bull-like potency of the one 'who fertilized his mother [Isis];' thus, he belonged to the circle of the royal gods." Let us not forget, Toby Wilkinson identified Min as the earliest image of a god and locates him in the Eastern Desert of Upper Egypt.

Beyond the Pylon entrance is the Fore-Court of Rameses II, consisting essentially of the "Ramessean Front," the king strategically added in orientation towards Karnak, on this bend of the Nile River.

The **Great Court of Rameses II** measures 190 feet by 170 feet and is surrounded by a Peristyle, according to Jill Kamil (1976: 27) consisting of "smooth-shafted papyrus columns with lotus-bud capitals." Bratton (1968: 183) added that the columns of the Court are as such, but "show the decadence of the Ramesside period." Baines and Malek (1980: 87) describe the columns of this colonnade as: "... arranged in a double row around its sides, and are interrupted by a shrine consisting of three chapels (bark stations) of Amun (center), Mut (left) and Khons (right), built by Hatshepsut and Thutmose III and redecorated by Rameses II. It was the existence of this shrine, which caused the considerable deviation of the axis of the buildings of Rameses II from that of the earlier temple of Amenhotep III."

QUINTESSENTIAL BOOK
"THE HOLY LAND"

In the northeastern corner rests the Mosque of Abu Haggag, the patron saint of Luxor, who came from Syria in the 13th Century A.D., to preach the Islamic religion.

The line of direction no longer continues the same behind this court, the "Ramessean front" having been turned eastward. This was done in order to facilitate its connection with the great temple of Karnak, as well as to avoid the vicinity of the river. In the Southwest of the Court, Kamil (1986: 57) has indicated: "On the right-hand rear wall of the Court is an interesting representation. It shows the facade of the temple of Luxor, with one seated and two standing colossi and one obelisk on each side of the entrance gateway. The flagstaffs are in position and pennants flutter. Approaching (from the right) are some of Rameses II's sons. Behind them are fattened sacrificial animals being led by nobles. Some of the bulls have decorated horns; one has metal tips in the form of hands. Queen Nefertari is shown shaking two Sistra. Behind her are princes and princesses. Rameses II had at least 111 sons and 67 daughters."

Next we move to the **Pillared Portico or Massive Processional Way Colonnade** that has a length of about 170 feet and is part of the temple on its original axis. Names on these massive columns show Amenhotep III, the original builder and Tutankhamon, Seti I, Rameses II, Seti II, and Horemheb, monarchs who did repairs to the structure. The 14 papyrus columns with open capitals stand 52 1/2-feet tall and conceal abaci with the name of Tutankhamon. Fodor (1989: 164) advises: "The best time to visit the temple is in the afternoon. The light of the afternoon sun softens the color of the temple's surface, and the reliefs are more easily distinguished. For photographers too, the colors are deeper and richer. A visit to the colonnades at full moon is also recommended." Equally, a midday visit is additionally recommended as at that time there are hardly any visitors during the hot sun and the place is clear for photography. Regarding the natural beauty of this colonnade, Kamil (1980: 28) has written: "In the early morning and towards the sunset heavy shadows are cast between the seven pairs of columns and the interplay of light has long been exploited by photographers as it slants from heavy architrave to calyx capitals down the slender shaft of this colonnade." Even further, adding to this beauty, Polyglot (1965: 40) explained the reliefs on both sides of the wall, in which the "New Year's Festive procession of the Sacred Barques from Karnak to Luxor and back can be seen were executed by the order of Tutankhamon." The god's journey to the "southern Harim" is depicted on the west wall that shows the procession from Karnak while the east wall shows the return journey.

Wayne (1987: 188) offers the commentary: "The Opet Festival is depicted in great detail with the king, the nobility and the common people joining the triumphal procession of Amon, Mut and Khons from Karnak." This festival occurred during the Nile flood and lasted for "twenty-four days of merry-making." Armour (1989: 146) has provided even more when he explained: "The festival opened with dancing girls who accompanied the priests of Amun as they carried the barge holding the statue of the god to the water's edge." In fact, Weigall (1910: 78-79) has properly instructed: "The visitor should first look at the reliefs at the south end of the west wall; then those on the west wall, north wall; and finally those at the east end of the south wall towards the north."

Kamil (1986: 58) wrote: "The reliefs that give a full picture of this joyous festival are in rather poor condition. The procession begins ... where the white-robed priests bear the sacred barge of Amon out of the gate of Karnak and down to the river's edge. The people clap their hands in unison, acrobats perform; there are priestesses with sistrums (rattles), people dancing and some kneeling in adoration. The procession makes its way upstream; the king's chariot is on a boat, which is towed like the sacred barge of Amon. Finally, there is a sacrifice of slaughtered animals and offerings to Amon, Mut and Khonsu at Luxor temple with great fanfare."

On the opposite wall the return procession is shown; soldiers, standard bearers, dancers and Nubian slaves, lead sacrificial bulls. The barges float downstream, and the final sacrifice and offerings are made to Amon and Mut at Karnak temple.

We now arrive at the **Colonnaded Court of Amenhotep III** that is 167 feet long and 147 feet wide. This splendid work is identified by Pemberton (1992: 94-95) who, in testifying to one of many architects of ancient Kemet's long list of geniuses of architecture, wrote: "The court of Amenhotep III, whose elegant double colonnade of papyrus-bundle columns, testifies to the skill of the royal architect, Amenhotep, son of Hapu." The structure is surrounded by a Peristyle of 12 columns in length and 10 in breadth, for a total of 32. Woldering (1963: 155) believed: "the closely-packed papyri-form columns and subdued light served to remind participants in the procession of the mysterious and solemn purpose of their festivities, and to put them into a proper state of awesome respect for the statues of the gods in the adjoining chapels."

Even further, Woldering (1963: 155) added: "The style of the flowering period of the New Kingdom is characterized by soft and graceful lines and curves and a harmonious symmetry between the various elements." Art as characterized in the temple influenced other building efforts.

"Behind this is a space occupying the whole breadth of the building, divided into chambers of different dimensions, the center one leading to a hall supported by four columns, immediately before the entrance to the isolated sanctuary. On the east of the hall is a chamber containing some curious sculpture, representing the

QUINTESSENTIAL BOOK
"THE HOLY LAND"

accouchement of Queen Maut-m-Shoi, the mother of Amenhotep." This is an interesting phenomenon in the history of ancient Kemet.

Budge (1972: 86) mentions four such oracle experiences, and traces it back to the Fifth Dynasty to a woman named Ruttet, wife of a priest of Ra of Sakhaby. "These children were declared to be the sons of Ra who in human form, had companied with her. The same story is told about Queen Hatshepsut and Amenhotep III, who were held to be begotten by Amen-Ra, and according to the narrative of the *Pseudo-Callisthenes* (Book 1. Chap. 8), Alexander the Great was the son of Amen (Ammon), who took the form of Nectanebus, the last king of Egypt, and begot him by Queen Olympias. In the temple, the original Sanctuary was perhaps destroyed by the Persians; but the present one was rebuilt by Alexander (the son of Alexander, Ptolemy being the Governor of Egypt), and bears his name in the following dedicatory formula: "This work (?) made he, the king of men, lord of the regions, Alexander, for his father Amen-Ra, president of Tape (Thebes); he erected to him the sanctuary, a grand mansion, with repairs of sandstone, hewn, good, and hard stone, in lieu of? (that made by?) his majesty, the king of men, Amenhotep." Even further, Maspero (1904, V, 68) added: "The sanctuary was a single chamber with an opening to its side, but so completely shut out from the daylight by the long dark hall at whose extremity it was placed to be in perpetual obscurity."

Behind the sanctuary are two other sets of apartments of 2 columns each. The larger ones are supported by columns and ornamented with rich sculpture, much of which appears to have been gilded. A second Hypostyle Hall or Great Columnar Hall preceded the Sanctuary. Near the great columnar hall is one of the old chambers, measuring 34 feet 6 inches by 57 feet 1 inch, with a semicircular niche. The walls are covered with Frescoes of late Roman time; and it was evidently a court of law with the usual tribunal, in which are painted three figures larger than life wearing the toga and sandals. The center one holds a staff or scepter (Scipio) in the right hand and a globe in the left; and near him was some object now defaced.

The two other figures have each a scroll in one hand. On the walls to the right and left are the traces of figures, which are interesting from their costume; and on the sidewall to the East are several soldiers with their horses, drawn with great spirit. The colors are much damaged by exposure, and the frescoes can hardly be distinguished. They probably date after the age of Constantine. The costumes are remarkable; and some of the men wear embroidered upper garments, tight hose, and laced boots, or shoes tied over the instep.

The false wainscot, dado, below is richly colored in imitation porphyry and other stones incrusted in patterns, and is better preserved than the frescoes of the upper part, where the old gods of Kemet/Egypt in bas-relief have outlived the paintings that once concealed them. There appears to be traces of a small cross - painted at one side of the tribune, and the figures have a nimbus round their heads, but without any of the character of Christian saints. Nor did the early Christians confine the nimbus to saints.

Behind the temple is a stone Quay, apparently of the late era of the Ptolemies or Caesars, since blocks bearing the sculpture of the former have been used in its construction. Opposite the corner of the temple it takes a more easterly direction, and points out the original course of the river, which continued across the plain now lying between it and the ruins of Karnak, and which may be traced by the descent of the surface of that ground it gradually deserted.

The southern extremity of the quay is of brick (probably a Roman addition), and indicates in like manner the former direction of the stream. When the temple was first built, the river seems to have flowed close under its walls.

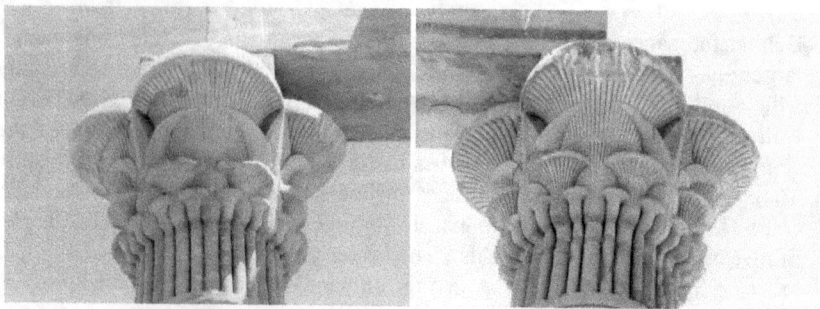

Holy Land Photo 14. Temple of Isis at Philae (Now Agilka) Island. Close up of the varied capitals on the "Kiosk of Trajan" showing its intricate details.

QUINTESSENTIAL BOOK
"THE HOLY LAND"

Holy Land Illustration 27. Shawtis, late XVIIIth Dynasty.

REFERENCE

Armour, Robert A. *Gods and Myths of Ancient Egypt*. Cairo: American University in Cairo Press, (1986) 1989.

ben-Jochannan, Yosef. *From Abu Simbel to Ghizeh*. Baltimore, MD: Black Classics Press, 1989.

Bratton, Fred Gladstone. *A History of Egyptian Archaeology*. New York: Thomas Y. Crowell Company, 1968.

Breasted, James H. *A History of Egypt*. New York: Charles Scribner's Sons, (1905) 1923.

Budge, E.A.W. *Dwellers on the Nile*. New York: Benjamin Bloom, Inc., Publishers, 1972.

David, Rosalie. *Discovering Ancient Egypt*. New York: Facts on File, 1993.

Fagan, Brian. *The Rape of the Nile*. New York: Charles Scribner's Sons, 1975.

Fedden, Robin. *Egypt: Land of the Valley*. London: Michael Haag Limited, (1977) 1986.

Haag, Michael. *Guide to Egypt*. London: Michael Haag, 1987.

Hobson, Christine. *The World of the Pharaohs*. London: Thames and Hudson, 1987.

Kamil, Jill. *Luxor: A Guide to Ancient Thebes*. 2nd Edition. London: Longman, (1973) 1976.

Lurker, Manfred. *The Gods and Symbols of Ancient Egypt*. London: Thames and Hudson, 1987.

FREDERICK MONDERSON

Pemberton, Delia. *Ancient Egypt: Architectural Guide for Travelers*. San Francisco: Chronicle Books, 1992.

Portman, Ian. *Luxor: A Guide to the Temples and Tombs of Ancient Egypt*. Cairo: The American University in Cairo Press, 1989.

Holy Land Photo 14a. Temple of Isis at Philae (Now Agilka) Island. The King makes a presentation to three defaced goddesses, Isis, Nephthys and another (left); and (right) he makes another presentation to enthroned Amon-Ra with Mut at his rear wearing the White Crown.

Richardson, Dan and Karen O'Brien. *Egypt: The Rough Guide*. Luxor: The Rough Riders, 1981,

Ruffle, John. *The Egyptians*. Ithaca, New York: Cornell University Press, 1977.

Scholz, Piotr O. *Ancient Egypt: An Illustrated Historical Overview*. Hauppauge, New York: Barron's Educational Series, 1996.

Showker, Kay. *Fodor's 90: Egypt*. New York: Fodor's Travel Publications, Inc., 1989.

Weigall, Arthur. *A Guide to the Antiquities of Upper Egypt*. London: Methuen and Co., 1910.

West, John Anthony. *Serpent in the Sky*. New York: The Julian Press, (1979) 1987.

Youssef, Hisham and John Rodenbeck. *Insight Guides: Egypt*. Hong Kong: APA Publications, (H K) Ltd., 1991.

Dr. Fred Monderson: Esperanza, please copy and hand out this selection to the group for their evening reading. It contains a selection written over a hundred years ago, but gives a historical and geographical description of the area of Thebes, which I find can be very useful in terms of helping us in orientation of our Knowledge of this important city.

QUINTESSENTIAL BOOK
"THE HOLY LAND"

Holy Land Photo 14b. Temple of Isis at Philae (Now Agilka) Island. In Red and White Double Crown, King presents two jars to enthroned Khnum, God of Elephantine with his wife Anukis at his rear (left); and (right) he again presents two vessels to Isis enthroned as Hathor with accompanying goddess at her rear.

Holy Land Photo 14c. Temple of Isis at Philae (Now Agilka) Island. From the north, view of Hathor Temple with Kiosk of Trajan in its rear.

FREDERICK MONDERSON

Holy Land Photo 14d. Temple of Isis at Philae (Now Agilka) Island. As visitors approach, two lions guard the entrance pylon with the Eastern Colonnade (left) and the Western Colonnade (right).

Holy Land Photo 14e. Temple of Isis at Philae (Now Agilka) Island. Panoramic view of the Eastern Colonnade (left) and the Western Colonnade (right), the "Looking Out" above lions see.

QUINTESSENTIAL BOOK "THE HOLY LAND"

Holy Land Illustration 29a. **1**. View of Ghizeh Pyramids from a makeshift pool; **2**. the Avenue of Sphinxes at Karnak Temple with western hills in the rear; **3**. taking a camel ride in the desert; **4**. watering the camel with the Great Pyramid in the background; **5**. the seated statues of Rameses II at Luxor Temple's entrance with the Processional Colonnade in rear; **6**. Egyptian mosques with their minarets; **7**. entranceway and one half of the Pylon at Edfu Temple with columns of the Peristyle Colonnade in the Court; **8**. and the twin sentinels "Hama and Chama" of Amenhotep III at Thebes.

THE PLAINS OF THEBES

"The Plains of Thebes" *Edinburgh Review* (October 1897: 456-482) is a Review of the following published books.

"ART. VIII.

FREDERICK MONDERSON

1. *Dawn of Civilization*. Second Edition. By G. MASPERO. Edited by A. H. SAYCE, translated by M. L. MCCLURE. London: 1896.
2. *History of Egypt* 2 vols. - By W. M. FLINDERS PETRIE, D.C.L., Professor of Egyptology at University College, London. London: 1894-5.
3. *Egyptian Tales*. 2 vols. By W. M. FLINDERS PETRIE. London: 1895.
4. *Deir-el-Bahari*. By EDOUARD NAVILLE, D.C.L. Parts 1 and II. Egypt Exploration Fund. London: 1895-7.
5. *Pharaohs, Fellahs, and Explorers*. By AMELIA B. EDWARDS. London: 1893.
6. Baedeker's *Upper Egypt*. Leipzig and London: 1892.
7. Murray's *Handbook: Lower and Upper Egypt*. Ninth Edition. London: 1896.

"No one should attempt, at any rate on a first visit to Egypt, to save time by railway traveling. One cannot journey into the past of some four thousand years ago in thirteen hours of noise and dust. Five days on the Nile post boat give a more fitting preparation with their uninterrupted hours on a glassy water, through a landscape monotonous enough, but with a strange incomprehensible fascination of its own - a line of water, a line of mud bank, feathered here and there with palm trees, a narrow strip of cultivation, a line of men and animals - strange misshapen buffaloes and camels - in single file as in a Greek frieze, thrown up against a sky too bright to be blue. And so traveling, one journeys out of the obscure early period into the comparatively modern times of the Middle Empire. For the first day we are in the age of the pyramid builders. One leaves in the morning the sharp-pointed group of the Ghizeh pyramids, showing shadow-like in faint pearly colors of pink and blue behind the palm woods on the bank. At midday one is under the step-pyramid of Sakkarah, earliest of all; the Fifth Dynasty pyramid of Unas; the later Dashur pyramids, where M. de Morgan's engineering skill has been rewarded by the discovery of the finest and most delicate jewelry in the world; and the day closes with sunset light behind the pyramid of Meydum, with its curious irregular-looking stages, the whole effect reminding one of St. Michael's Mount, where the Egyptian meets in death an earlier civilization; for Petrie found two modes of burial in this same pyramid - the mummied Egyptian, full furnished for his journey into immortal life, and the earlier inhabitant of the land, lying on his left side, with knees drawn up.

After Girgeh the scenery changes; the mud banks give way to hills on each side of the Nile. In some places these approach the river so nearly as to rise, a sheer wall, from the water's edge. The wearing of water, or some climatic condition, has graven on these strange marks like lines of hieroglyphics. They are honeycombed with graves; some with squarely made entrances, some mere rough holes where the gray herons sit.

QUINTESSENTIAL BOOK "THE HOLY LAND"

With the memory of the pyramids, surrounded by great cemeteries behind one, in face of these cliffs with their tiers of tombs, one begins to realize the deep irony of the Israelites' taunt, 'Are there no graves in the land of Egypt?'

As one goes further south the coloring becomes more vivid; the hills are no longer tinted with pale pink and purple, but glow at evening with the color and transparency of a sunset cloud, or like snow peaks with their rose light and aerial blue shadows. At last, where the hills, - no longer flat-topped, but with sharp peaks and jagged outline, open out round a fertile plain deep in corn, one comes to Luxor. It is sunset when one arrives by the post-boat, the sky glows behind the Libyan Hills, the water towards the west is a sheet of gold and crimson, the pylons and obelisks of Karnak rise black on the left. Under the hills on the west bank, one can faintly trace the white terraces and colonnades of Deir-el-Bahari; the Colossi are no more than two misty points against the hill; the giant pillars of Luxor stand out against the purple sky where night rushes up from the east; and Thebes is reached.

Of the books mentioned at the head of the article Petrie's history is the latest and most complete yet published; it is of great value, as giving the principal monuments of each reign. The translations of 'Egyptian Tales' also published by Professor Petrie, with explanatory notes, spread over a long period - from the earliest dynasties to Ptolemaic times - and throw much light on the life and thought of the Egyptians. Two articles by the same author give a more detailed account of the results of his Theban excavation. [Pharaoh with the Hard Heart, '*Century Magazine*,' August 1896, Israel in Egypt, '*Contemporary Review*,' May 1896.] Maspero's '*Dawn of Civilization*' combines, with a history of *Egypt up to the end of the Twelfth Dynasty*, the most complete account of the conditions of life - natural, social, political - of customs and beliefs in ancient Egypt. M. Naville's 'Deir-el-Bahari' gives a detailed account of one of the most important temples. In Miss Edwards's '*Pharaohs, Fellahs, and Explorers*,' points of history, of art, of religion, of literature, and of discovery are treated in a popular manner. *Murray's Handbook*, of which a new edition was published last autumn, has been brought up to date, containing results of last year's excavations, with maps and plans. Of these latter *Baedeker's* has also an excellent collection.

Roughly speaking, the city on the west bank is the City of the Dead. The Libyan hills are honeycombed with tombs of royal and private persons, [and] the temples are funerary temples. There, possibly, was the great Lake of the Dead, and the inhabitants were mainly priests, or those occupied in embalming. There were, indeed, two palaces - that of Amenhotep III and that of Rameses III [Unless we are to accept the theory that this was a 'Migdol' (see *Church Quarterly Review*,' July 1897, 'Maspero's *Melees des Peuples and the S.P.C.K.*'). But surely to say that Medinet Habu was a Migdol involves a misunderstanding both of the passage in Maspero and the buildings, which include two funerary temples, one of which is fronted by the tower in question.] - but the dwelling-part of the city was mainly on the east bank; and here were the temples dedicated to the gods, Luxor, and Karnak; with its subsidiary temples where the great triad of Thebes were honored, Amen, the hidden one; Mut, the mother; and their son Khonsu.

Holy Land Papyrus 9. On his papyrus boat, Tutankhamon and his wife Ankh-es-en-Amen hunt birds in the marshes and standing and intimately embracing.

Historically, the interest centers on one of the most fascinating periods of Egyptian history - the Eighteenth and Nineteenth Dynasties - the period which lies between the entrance of the Israelites into Egypt (which took place in the time of the Hyksos between the Fifteenth and the Seventeenth Dynasty) and their exodus, which occurred in the middle of the Nineteenth. There are remains of an earlier time, Sixth Dynasty tombs have been lately discovered by Mr. P. E. Newberry, and there are traces of the work: of the Eleventh, Twelfth, and Thirteenth Dynasties. And there is much building of a later period, notably, temples of the Twentieth Dynasty, interesting records, [and] some lately discovered, of the Ethiopian reigns; much Ptolemaic work.

But the main interest of Thebes centers on the Amenhoteps, Hatasu, the Thothmes; Seti with his son and grandson, Rameses the Great and Merenptah. It is difficult for one who has not visited Thebes to realize the beauty of the natural setting of the temples. The beauty of the country, the exhilarating atmosphere, the 'everlasting wash of air,' all give to one's memories of the place a strange glamour. Thebes, with its golden limestone mountains, the broad flowing river, its deep standing corn, and herds of diverse animals pasturing together; in its morning freshness, with the scent of bean fields on the air; at sunset, when the water glows

QUINTESSENTIAL BOOK
"THE HOLY LAND"

with so metallic a luster that one scarcely believes that the swallows can dip in it, or the pied kingfisher plunge through its surface; by moonlight, when the buildings take that unearthly rose-tint seen only in moonlight in the South-under all its changing aspects, Thebes has always 'the glory and the freshness of a dream.'

Tomb of Rameses IV.   (Musée Guimet, Vol. XV, Plate 40.)

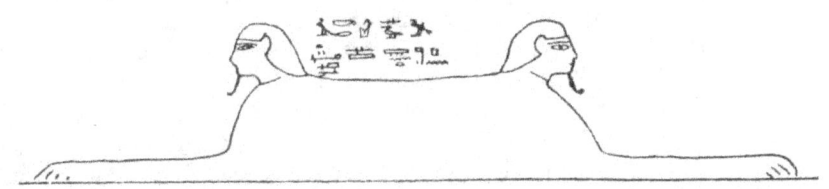

Tomb of Rameses IX.   (Musée Guimet, Vol. XVI, Plate 6.)
Holy Land Illustration 28. Tomb of Rameses IV. (Musee Guimet, Vol. XV, Pl 27) Chapter XV, Book of the Dead.

The best general view of those temples, which are still standing on the west bank, is obtained from a point in front of the Colossi. To the left, which is here the South, is the group formed by the two temples of Medinet Habu and the palace of Rameses III; on the right, where the croplands meet the strip of desert below the Libyan Hills, is the Ramesseum, the ruin of its pylons looking like a heap of tumbled stones. Further to the right the spur runs down to the little temple of Qurneh the "Temple of Millions of Years," built by Seti I. In the angle, which this offshoot makes with the hills, lies Deir-el-Bahari, its white limestone colonnades thrown up against the golden limestone of the hill. There is still one other temple standing - the little **PTOLEMAIC TEMPLE OF Deir-el-Medineh** - out of sight from here in a fold of the hill behind the Ramesseum.

FREDERICK MONDERSON

But what is now standing is only a part of the ancient buildings of Thebes. The Colossi, which appear to be a monument by themselves, were only the great figures by the gateway of a temple; and Professor Petrie's excavations last year were concerned with seven temples demolished down to the foundations, which lie round the Ramesseum in a desert tract, where carved figures and hewn stones lying on the sand indicated the site of some buildings.

The principal excavations on the west bank of late years have been those of the Government, under M. Daressy, at Medinet Habu, in the winters of 1894-95, 1895-96; Professor Petrie, at the Ramesseum in the winter of 1895-96; and that of the Egypt Exploration Fund, begun under M. Naville in 1893, and continued up to the present season, when the work passed, for architectural repair, under the superintendence of Mr. Somers Clarke.

M. Daressy's we might call a restoration of Medinet Habu; Professor Petrie's an excavation for the purposes of research; while M. Naville's work has not only been rewarded by many interesting finds, notably that of a foundation deposit of Hatasu's reign, a beautiful sycamore coffin, and models of boats and houses from an Eleventh Dynasty tomb, but has given back to the world a temple which, though ruined in some parts, - unfinished in others, is, perhaps, the most beautiful, certainly the most original in Egypt, and the earliest of those now standing in the plain of Thebes. 'The general plan is that of a series of three great terraces or platforms, rising one higher than another up the slope of the ground, until the last is backed against the vertical cliffs of the mountain. An axial stairway led from terrace to terrace. Along the front of each terrace the platform was carried on the top of a cloister or colonnade. The upper terrace is headed by a row of chambers, the middle one of which is carried deep into the rock, and lined with sculptured slabs. The chambers, and an altar in a courtyard, lie on either side of the upper terrace.'

This plan, unique among the temples of Egypt, 'to some extent may have been suggested,' to the architect, M. Naville writes, 'by the nature of the site at his disposal, by the huge steps in which the rock of the foundations descends to the plain .... Our excavations have proved that the lowest platform was treated as the garden, or rather the orchard, of the temple, and that the trees planted in it were artificially watered.' [Egypt Exploration Fund Report, 1895-96.]

The stump of a palm tree remains still as witness to this garden of the temple.

A striking feature of the temple, besides its terraced rise, is the Greek-looking colonnade at the north side of the middle platform, for there is one of the chief,

QUINTESSENTIAL BOOK "THE HOLY LAND"

though not the earliest, instances of the proto-Doric column. Those of Beni Hasan are earlier by nearly a thousand years.

These columns are sixteen-sided, and the abacus rests directly on the column without the intervention of a capital. The colonnade was never finished, and had been, the excavators found, divided into compartments for embalmers. Chopped straw for stuffing the mummies, pots of niter, and fragments of papyri were found there.

The excavation of this colonnade, the north-western half of the middle colonnade, the Anubis shrine with its hall and chambers, and the remains of an ebony shrine, interesting inasmuch as only one other wooden shrine has been preserved, form the subject of M. Naville's second volume.

The first volume is concerned with the altar-court and the northwestern hall of offerings. The altar-court is of peculiar interest, as in no other Egyptian temple has the high altar been preserved. This altar is in itself a striking object, made of the same white limestone as the temple, measuring about 16 feet by 13, and standing 5 feet from the ground. A flight of ten steps enabled the priest to ascend, not for the purpose of sacrifice, M. Naville tells us - sacrifice was carried on elsewhere, probably outside the temple - but for placing on it offerings to Ra-Harmachis, the sun god, at his rising, to whom, in conjunction with Amen, this part of the temple was dedicated.

In the walls of this court are several niches, formerly closed by bolted wooden doors of the largest of these, the Thothmes chapel, two very beautiful colored plates are given in the first volume. The object of these niches, which formerly held, in all probability, a portrait statue of Queen Hatshepsut, we can discuss later.

The principle of decoration is the same in all, '... the most important representation is that on the end wall, where a King, or more often the queen in the guise of man, is seen standing in the presence of one or two deities. On the side walls the individual to whom the niche is dedicated is seen seated before an altar, and offerings are presented to him by a priest.'

Apart from their signification, these paintings are also interesting as giving faithful portraits of the family of Hatasu. The figure of the queen herself has been in most cases effaced, but we have in the chapel of Thothmes a portrait of her father, Thothmes I, of her mother, Aahmes, and of her grandmother, Senseneb.

But the great historical interest of the temple, through which it is best known to the world at large, lies in the sculptures of the expedition to Punt. Punt, or

FREDERICK MONDERSON

Somaliland, as it is now supposed to be, was, according to Professor Petrie, in all probability the home of the Egyptian race. They would be thus 'a kindred race to the Phoenicians, or Pun race, whose furthest and latest great colony in the Mediterranean was known as Punic.'

The chief points of the expedition are well known and described at some length in M. Naville's *Introductory Memoir*. The products of the land - its piles of frankincense, the ivory, the ebony from which the shrine was made, the trees in pots for the garden of the temple of Deir-el-Bahari, the monkeys which Hatmu, as Solomon, desired, the long-horned cattle which lasted in Egypt from the time of Hatasu till the present century, when they perished from cattle plague - are all familiar.

Holy Land Papyrus 10. Wearing Blue Crown, Rameses II offers a bouquet of flowers to enthroned goddess Hathor in a crown of horns and disk.

QUINTESSENTIAL BOOK "THE HOLY LAND"

The inhabitants of the land of Punt are no less interesting; the chief with his terribly fat wife, the lady Aty, his sons and daughters. In the 1895-1896 excavation some new carvings belonging to the sculpture were discovered; from these it was found that the Puntites lived in wattled huts much like beehives, raised on piles, and amended by ladders, other stones showed coconut trees on which monkeys are climbing.

The execution of all these sculptures, and indeed of almost all the sculpture of the temple, is wonderfully perfect. The relief is not high; the coloring has lasted unusually well and combines, as only Egyptian artists know how, great brilliancy of color with harmonious effect. The details, the very hieroglyphic signs, have a charming finish; the claws and feathers of the birds are carefully traced, the horned viper has his back neatly dappled. In the Punt sculptures the fish both of the Nile and of the sea are accurately drawn, though proportionate size is hardly more consulted than in the familiar Noah's ark.

The defacement of the temple in various ways has been a matter of speculation. M. Naville attributes it mainly to two subsequent Pharaohs, Thothmes III and Akhenaten. In the first excavation of the temple it was - not indeed at once discovered that Hatshepsut had been the founder of it. In many inscriptions the name of her successor has been substituted for her own. Further observation, however, showed that the personal pronouns in the inscriptions were feminine and that the name of the king was cut in deeper relief than the rest of the writing. Such usurpation is not uncommon among the Egyptian Kings, but it seemed that something more than the desire for fame, some personal animus, must have led to the systematic erasure of the queen's name and figure throughout the temple. The reason will be found in the history of the succession.

Thothmes I, the father of Hatasu, had two wives, Aahmes and Mutnefert; both according to Petrie his half-sisters, daughters of Amenhotep. Such marriages were common among the Egyptians, as sovereignty descended through the female line. Aahmes alone was of royal birth by the mother's side; Hatshepsut was the child of Aahmes, Thothmes II of Mutnefert. Thothmes I, towards the end of his reign, associated Hatasu with himself as co-regent. The reason of this Professor Petrie thus explains - 'This document' (the record of Hatasu's co-regency) 'is almost more than an association of Hatshepsut with the king: it prays Amen to give the sovereignty to the daughter as it had been given to the father, making almost an abdication. This suggests that it must have been at the end of the life of the king, when he felt no longer able to rule. The reason of placing the daughter in power rather than the son is seen in the ages. Hatshepsut was probably twenty-four, and doubtless showed already her vast abilities; while Thothmes II was probably not more than seventeen, and was of no great strength. He was not married to his sister at the time of this inscription. So it appears that on failing health the king placed the power in the hand, of his eldest child, who had the sole right to it by the female inheritance; and then, just a few weeks before his death, married Thutmose II to her, perhaps to insure his receiving some respect for his position if not for his character.'

Thothmes II died early while Thothmes III was still a boy. The exact relationship of Thothmes III to Hatshepsut is not clear. It was at first supposed that he was the son of Thothmes I and therefore the queen's younger brother: but it appears more probable that he was the son of Thothmes II by another wife. In any case it is certain that the mother of Thothmes III was not herself royal, so that he had no claim through her to the throne.

On the other hand Hatasu, whose royal succession was clear, had no son, but only two daughters; Neferu-ra, who died young, and Meryt-ra, whom she eventually married to Thothmes III. This marriage would establish the claim of Thothmes III to the throne, and in the meantime Hatasu associated her nephew with her as co-regent.

Holy Land Photo 15. Kalabsha vicinity with colossal statue of Rameses II and columns of nearby temple.

She did not thereby earn his gratitude; on the contrary he cherished a deep and undying grudge against her. A man of extraordinary energy and power, he bitterly

QUINTESSENTIAL BOOK
"THE HOLY LAND"

resented the division of the sovereignty. He so systematically erased both her face and her name that he nearly succeeded in effacing her memory.

We can well believe that Hatasu's was a character to inspire admiration rather than affection. Thothmes III was in that proximity of position, which dwarfs admiration, and there is spite about his revenge, which makes one believe that he would not be too careful about the justice of his grudge.

The very face of Hatshepsut is hardly womanly; it accords only too well with the beard-case and the dress of a king, which she affected, if not in real life, at any rate in her portraits. The god Amen seems scarcely to have fulfilled his promise that the daughter of Thothmes I should be of an 'appearance above the gods.' One sees that Hatasu must be great, may be admirable, but can hardly be loveable.

But if, like Queen Elizabeth, Hatshepsut was not beloved of her relations, she had the same power of drawing to herself great men. Of such a man, Senmut, the architect of her temple, we have abundant record. He was a man of the people, for 'his ancestors were not found in writing,' and truly his statues give no very highbred features; his is an ugly, capable, complacent face. It is interesting to note the difference between the specialist of today and the glorified jack-of-all-trades of three or four thousand years ago. The many-sidedness of Michelangelo was nothing compared to that of Senmut. The queen's architect, who himself super-intended the quarrying and carving of the queen's obelisks, was tutor to the queen's daughter Neferu-ra, 'that brilliant and beautiful girl,' as Professor Petrie calls her; he was keeper of the temple of Amen; keeper of the granaries of Amen; royal seal-bearer; keeper of the palace; keeper of the heart of the Queen [to which title Petrie compares 'keeper of the king's conscience' or Lord Chancellor]; priest of Aahmes; keeper of the queen's cattle, of which one is called, in a scene at Deir-el-Bahari-it is an interesting and homely touch - 'her great favorite the red.' The Berlin statue of Senmut was the only one known until lately, though there are other records of him; but a small private excavation last year yielded a fine kneeling statue of him, 'presented by favor of the queen,' from which we find that he was architect of other temples besides Deir-el-Bahari, that of Mut among the number; that he was overseer of the fields of Amen, overseer of his garden, chief over his slaves, 'guiding all the handicrafts,' and superintendent of priests.

Great queens make great men, and truly there is an attraction about such greatness as Hatasu's, the greatness of a spirit lifted above the average of humankind.

FREDERICK MONDERSON

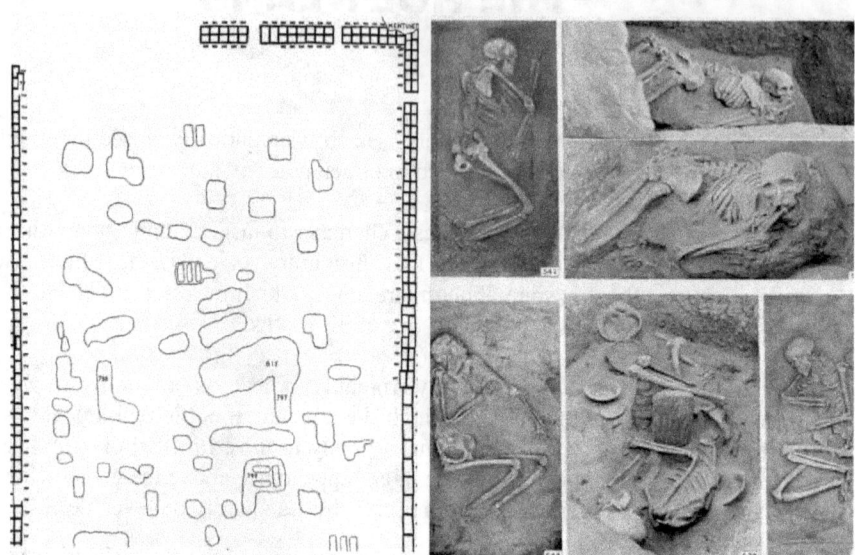

Holy Land Illustration 29. Abydos. Graves of the Courtiers of Zer and Courtiers graves of the Ist Dynasty.

Thus she writes of the great obelisks, her chief memorial at Karnak, one of which is still standing, "'I was sitting in the palace, I was thinking of my Creator, when my heart urged me to make for him two obelisks of electrum whose points reach unto the sky, in the noble hall of columns which is between the two great pylons of the King Aa-Kheper-ka-ra. Behold my heart led me to consider what men would say. Oh, ye who see my monument in the course of years, and converse of what I have done, beware of saying, I know not, I know not, why these things were done. Verily the two great obelisks that my majesty has wrought with electrum, they are for my father Amen, to the end that my name should remain established in this temple forever and ever. They are of a single stone of hard granite without any joining or division in them. My majesty commanded to work for them in the fifteenth year, the first day of Mekhir, till the sixteenth year and the last day of Mesore, making seven months since the ordering of it in the quarry.'"

A relief of the transportation of obelisks is one of the most interesting finds of late years at Deir-el-Bahari. The stones on which it is cut were discovered when the Coptic tower was pulled down in 1895, and Madame Naville traced and arranged the scenes. It is a unique presentation, and we know at last how, the obelisk was transported. Hatasu's were brought down the river from the quarry - probably at high Nile - on a raft-like boat, flat-bottomed, and strong enough to carry the pair lying side by side. This raft was 'towed down by three parallel groups of ten tugs, each group being connected with the barge by a thick cable.'

QUINTESSENTIAL BOOK "THE HOLY LAND"

And the rest of the Acts of Hatasu and the granite chambers that she built have their record written in stone. Can we add that she slept with her fathers? Her tomb is still unknown. Probabilities point, according to Professor Petrie, to it's being in that side valley which runs up close to the cliff behind her temple.

Thothmes III was set free by the death of the queen to begin his independent reign in his thirty-first year. It is perhaps the greatest reign in Egyptian history. Into his campaigns in Palestine and Syria we cannot enter. One unique and beautiful record of them is that part of the temple of Karnak called 'the garden of Thothmes,' where the artist has portrayed in slight relief the flowers and fruits found on the foreign expeditions of the king. It is the prettiest, most artistic production: a clump or two of pomegranates irregularly scattered on the walls, marsh-flowers with water birds walking among them, bushes delicately traced.

But the great feature of the reign of Thothmes is found, not in his monuments, but in the change brought about in Egypt by the introduction of a civilized foreign element. Previous intercourse had taken place between Egypt and less civilized nations, but the wars with Syria now brought the country into contact with a nation more civilized than itself. Petrie mentions the coats of mail, the gilded chariots, the gold and silver vases taken from the Syrians and copied in Egypt; and the multitude of slaves imported many of whom belonged to the higher classes. Hence came the foreign artist and workman, and hence came too that alteration in the Egyptian type of face which is illustrated so strikingly in Professor Petrie's *History of Egypt*, by a comparison of a relief of the face of Usertesen of the Twelfth Dynasty and a photograph of the head of Zey of the Eighteenth.

But the connection of Syria and Egypt was not wholly that of conquered and conqueror. The alliance with Syria through the marriage of Amenhotep III had, as we shall see later, as much effect on the history of Egypt as the new element had on its arts.

Amenhotep III, who followed two Pharaohs of less importance, was a great builder. His funeral temple at Thebes, of which the 'Colossi of the Plain' alone remain, must have been a building of magnificent proportions, 'These stood before the entrance' and far behind them stretched courts and halls, the beauty and size of which we can imagine from the contemporary temple of Luxor. Most brilliant statuary adorned the structure, and an avenue of immense jackals - the sacred animal of the god of the dead - led up to the entrance, like the rams, each guarding a statue of the king, in the avenues of Karnak.'

These Colossi, statues of the 'king with the queen standing at his side' are not indeed the largest monolithic statues known; that at the Ramesseum is said to be larger still, and the statue at Tanis, perhaps, the greatest of all. The Colossi of the

FREDERICK MONDERSON

Plain before they were dis-crowned stood about 70 feet with the pedestal. The statues, that is to say, could just be placed between the floor and the vaulting of Winchester Cathedral. They are so gigantic that it is difficult to conceive that even the destruction of 'Memnon' was a voluntary work. There seems no reason to doubt the often-attested story of the voice at dawn, or to ascribe it to a priestly trick. The explanation now accepted is that the stone, wet with dew, sang when the rays of the sun touched it, much as a basin, whose surface is slightly cracked, sings when hot water is poured on it. The pious rebuilding of the Romans stopped such vibration of the stone, and the plaint of Memnon to his mother Aurora, ceased.

The extraordinary romance of these figures, so majestic in attitude that their complete defacement hardly strikes on one at first, is an old theme, yet can scarcely be comprehended by one who has not seen them looking out towards the east ... like the patriarchs of old ... with their background of the Libyan hills, and the temples of Thebes, and the green corn or the fertilizing flood about their feet.

The marriage of Amenhotep, as we have said, was an event of great importance. Alliances with Syria, had already taken place.

Thothmes III, says Petrie, 'had taken the sons of the chiefs to be educated in Egypt; and as the Egyptian kings married Syrian princesses, it is most probable that the sons of the Syrian chiefs were married to Egyptians at the close of their education.'

And Professor Petrie concludes from a study of the physiognomy of Queen Thy on the one hand, and of her titles on the other, that she was the daughter of a north Syrian prince and an Egyptian princess. Thus, the object of Amenhotep in marrying Thy [Tiy] was probably to secure the right of their son to the throne, and to conclude an important alliance with a Syrian people.

There is an extraordinary attraction about the face of Thy with a curiously prominent chin and slightly receding forehead she cannot, perhaps, be called beautiful; but there is something sweet and wise about the mouth, something at the same time playful and tenacious about the face. One can well imagine that *Thy* would not openly lead, but would influence, that she might be devoted, a fanatic even, but not a politician, and her influence with her husband and her son Akhenaten must have been decisive.

Thy was an Aten-worshipper; she worshipped not the sun god, Ra, but the 'Aten,' the disc of the sun. Professor Petrie gives a most interesting defense of this religion; he calls it a 'more refined and really philosophical worship' than the

QUINTESSENTIAL BOOK
"THE HOLY LAND"

Egyptian; the worship 'of the radiant energy of the sun, of the sun as sustaining all life by his beams.' This cult was not wholly new in Egypt; but at Heliopolis, which alone had received it, it had endured in a somewhat modified form, and it is well known how bitterly it was opposed in Thebes.

Thy had not been married more than a year before her religion had so far affected her husband that he ordered a lake to be made for the 'great royal wife Thy,' and the boat that he sailed on it he called after her god, 'Aten-Neferu' - the beauties of the Aten; but when her son, Akhenaten came to the throne, the influence of the queen was felt in full force. In the fourth year of his reign he married Nefertiti, a Syrian princess. The wife, of the same race and religion as Thy, added her influence to that of the mother, and in the sixth year of his reign, when he was probably about eighteen years old, he became avowedly an Aten-worshipper, and an enemy to the old religion of Egypt. From henceforward his work at Thebes is that of an iconoclast. In the temple of Hatshepsut, in the temple of Luxor, built by his father, indeed wherever he found it he religiously erased the name of Amen.

Thy's character and history form a strange contrast to that of Hatasu; the one, masculine, commanding, carried out great works in her lifetime, and her name is hated, and her memory rooted out by her successor, her nephew, the husband of her daughter. The other, essentially feminine, does little in her own name, but her influence as wife and mother affects through the reigns of her husband and son the destinies of Egypt.

Of the Ramesseum, the funerary temple of that Rameses whom, as Professor Petrie says, 'we take at his own vainglorious estimation and call the Great,' there is little that is new to be said. Recent history reveals his usurpation rather than his acts. The enormous though mutilated statue, the reliefs of the war against the Hittites, including his single-handed combat celebrated in the epic of Pentaurt on the walls of Karnak and the pylons of Luxor, are, all well known. One scene among the reliefs must be mentioned in which Rameses, going, up into the temple, is attended by twenty-three of his hundred sons. Of these the thirteenth is his successor, Merenptah.

It was the temple of Merenptah, which yielded the most interesting result of Professor Petrie's excavation in the spring of 1896. The temple itself, like the Ramesseum, was built out of the materials of former structures. The splendid temple of Amenhotep III was used simply as a quarry. The materials were roughly used, the sphinxes and jackals were broken up and laid head to tail to form a foundation, and it was on the unused side of a stele, polished and engraved by Amenhotep, religiously edited by Akhenaten, re-engraved by Seti I, that the - now famous inscription of Merenptah was found, in which for the first time on Egyptian monuments the - name of Israel is mentioned.

When Merenptah came to the throne, his father, 'sunk in his fatuous pride into a mere despot,' had not only lost his hold on all the foreign conquests of the Eighteenth Dynasty, but had suffered Egypt itself to become the prey of the invader. In the first four years of his reign Merenptah devoted himself to the careful consolidation of his power in Egypt, but in the fifth year, being warned in a dream by Ptah, his patron divinity, he prepared himself against foreign invasion, with such success that an attack attempted in the spring, of the year was repelled with a force which secured the tranquility of Egypt. It is this, which the great tablet celebrates. Most vivid are the touches in which this security is pictured.

'And the people babbled, "Come and walk afar on the road, for there is no fear in the hearts of men."' The garrisoned forts are abandoned; the walls are thrown open; the messengers leap over the battlements of the wall, and cool themselves from the sun until the guards awake; the police lie in slumbers on their beats; the Bedouin of the marshes desire to pasture the herds, abandoning the cattle raids; no marauders cross the flood of the river; there is no shout of the sentinel in the night, "Stop! behold thou one comes, one comes in the name of others (with the wrong watchword); be good enough to go."'

But it is in the last lines of the proclamation that the greatest historical interest is found. The triumphs of Merenptah are enumerated, and the inscription ends, 'the people of Ysiraal is spoiled, it hath no seed.' Professor Petrie decides that the first and most attractive interpretation of this can hardly be the correct one. From the mention of Israel in connection with Syria, and from a comparison of the *Book of Judges* with the date of the last Ramesside invasion under Rameses III it appears that this defeat of Israel must have occurred in Canaan after the Exodus, which Petrie puts also in the reign of Merenptah, but before the entrance of the whole nation into the Promised Land. Thus the theory to which Professor Petrie inclines is that of a divided Israel. That all Israel had not gone down into Egypt, or that some had re-entered Canaan before the close of the forty years' wandering, and were there destroyed by Merenptah, is on the whole the more probable explanation of the inscription.

QUINTESSENTIAL BOOK
"THE HOLY LAND"

Holy Land Papyrus 11. Heavenly it must be, to be sandwiched by two such beauties, especially if you're a king!

To agree with Professor Petrie's judgment of the 'Pharaoh with the hard heart,' archaeological sympathies must be more educated than moral.

'According to his own lights, Merenptah may well claim a high position: he rescued his country from a great danger, and restored its position for a while in its course of decline. 'My country-right or wrong, was his principle, and a far better one than that of most ancient rulers, while he did not, any more than his contemporaries potter about with stray talk of "blood guiltiness." If he found it needful for the State to repress a tribe, he may well have done it without fear of reports being prejudicial to him.'

But much of the same defense might be made for the Sultan of Turkey or the Khalifa 'with any talk of blood guiltiness' when they find it necessary to repress a tribe or a nation. Professor Petrie treats far more seriously his lack of ancestral piety, and consequent destruction of archaeological interest, in which respect he falls below the standard of his race and time.

'The worst blot on his character was his ruthless destruction of the works of his predecessors. No doubt, in such a time of distress, it would be difficult to supply workmen for public monuments; but his utter disregard for everything that went before him outdoes even his orgulous father, and is painfully in contrast to the careful restorations made by his artistic grandfather, Seti 1. Not content with

FREDERICK MONDERSON

taking what he wanted, he further defaced what he could not use, and all over Egypt the statues of the kings may be seen with his name rudely cut over their inscriptions, or battered with a hammer on the exquisitely polished surfaces of the other monarchs.'

Holy Land Illustration 30. Book of the Dead: Chapter XLI, Tomb of Seti I (left); and Book of the Dead: Chapter XLVII *Leyden Papyrus*, No. 16 (right).

But with all his power and his faults it is an interesting personality, and the wonderfully preserved head now in the museum at Gizeh is worth much study. The head is in grey granite, the pupils of the eyes and eyelashes being painted black, the lips and the space between eye and eye-brow colored red, and the wig, necklace, and beard-case decorated in blue and yellow. The head is bent a little forward, the heavy receding brow has something almost animal about it, the lips are thick and the eyes a little prominent; but the nose is fine and aquiline, the molding of chin and jaw strikingly handsome. The Pharaoh of the Exodus has a strange intensity of expression about the face; it is handsome but unpleasing, powerful and unscrupulous.

Important among Professor Petrie's other finds in this locality are foundation deposits of Siptah, the last king of the Nineteenth Dynasty, and Tausert, his hitherto unknown queen. With Rameses III, first king of the Twentieth Dynasty, we pass on to the third great excavation of late years on the west bank of the Nile.

Though personal interest in the founder is more in abeyance than in the temples of Hatasu, Thothmes, and Merenptah, or even in the destructions of Akhenaten, yet from [an] aesthetic point of view the temple of Medinet Habu is perhaps inferior to none; and the French excavation has restored to it much of its ancient impressiveness. Formerly half buried under the ruins of a Coptic village, the leveling of the ground in front of the gateway tower has given it dignity by increased height, and shown up as prominent features the porters' lodges, which

QUINTESSENTIAL BOOK
"THE HOLY LAND"

were hardly noticed before. From this point one looks up through a wonderful vista of gateways and courts. The mounds of earth between the tower and the pylons of the temple itself have been cleared away, discovering on one side the little temple unseen before of Amenardis, wife of Piankhi II, and on the other hand, in all its simplicity and completeness, the small Eighteenth Dynasty temple before mentioned. One's only regret is that the leveling of these mounds has now made it impossible to climb to the chamber over the gateway, where one can study the pastimes of the Egyptian king, as he is portrayed in the reliefs, playing draughts with the ladies of his court.

This clearing has added much to the beauty of the great colonnaded courts, with their Osiride pillars and round campaniform columns. The effects of the deeply incised lines of hieroglyphics and figures on walls and columns, particularly deeply cut here, give to the Egyptian temple that softness of broken line which the stress of climate gives the buildings in other countries. Much coloring, too, is left at Medinet Habu. Sitting in the colonnaded courts one may look up and see, against the intense blue of the sky, the blue of some broken roofing or the lower edge of an architrave, which need be as little ashamed as any earthly blue to show itself against the background of the blue celestial. The uncovering of the small sacred lake, the clearing of the battlemented wall of the precinct, make it possible to realize the Egyptian temple, or group of temples, as an establishment. The excavation has not been unrewarded by the discovery of smaller objects of interest, most important among which was a store of bronze Osiride figures.

In passing from the west to the east bank of the Nile we come to temples with a different object and history. Whereas on the west bank, 'the king began a temple with the intention of completing it himself, and these temples were monuments raised by the king to his own glory and his own memory, the great temples on the right bank of the Nile,' says M. Naville, 'are in the first place buildings erected for the worship of the local deity, and are the work of many generations.' [Introductory Memoir, *Deir-el-Bahari*, by Ed. Naville.]

The setting of the temple of Luxor is very different to that of the temples on the west side.

The temple stands so near the river that on quiet evenings the length of its colonnade, with its fourteen huge campaniform pillars, and the cloistered court of lotiform pillars, are reflected in the Nile. Amenhotep III built the southern end, the sanctuary and its surrounding chambers, the great court and the colonnade. At the further end of the colonnade comes the Court of Rameses II, having a statue of himself between each pair of pillars. The axis of this court is not in the same line as the rest of the temple, but takes a more easterly direction. The reason of this was thought to be that the temple, standing, so near to the Nile, followed the course of the river as it then was; but a more probable explanation has been suggested by M. Daressy, who has excavated there of late years - namely, that the twist was intended to bring the temple into line with the sphinx avenue running from it to the temple of Khonsu at Karnak. In front of the court, again, Rameses built pylons, fronted by a row of colossal statues, and raised two obelisks of red granite, one of which is still in situ, while the other now stands in Paris in the Place de la Concorde. The complete excavation is not yet possible, for a mosque of the patron saint of Luxor, Abu-el-Haggag, stands over one corner of the court.

Holy Land Photo 16. Aswan. Kalabsha area. The "Lotus Memorial" symbol of co-operation between Egypt and Russia (left); and Stela at entrance to the Temple of Kalabsha, home of God Mendulese.

The level of the roadway leading into it is halfway up the pylons. To remove this would make it necessary to rebuild the pylons, which are in a very unsafe condition; but the work would no doubt be rewarding if the Government department possessed sufficient funds for the purpose. M. Daressy's excavation uncovered a very lifelike and complete statue in red granite of Rameses II in the hieratic attitude. With his arms by his side and one foot advanced, he seems to be stepping out into the court from his niche between the columns. An accidental fall of rubbish from the higher ground on which the mosque stands, aided by the parasol of an enterprising lady, has uncovered the face of another statue adjacent and similar to this one, the rest of which is still buried. The front of Luxor temple, seldom visited, as the Arab village hides the way to it, has a wonderful picturesqueness. The western pylon is trenched to the bottom, showing the great statues of the king; those in front of the eastern pylon are still buried to the shoulders. The roadway between the pylons leads to the mosque; over it pass the Arab men to daily prayer, the sheiks to adjudge a quarrel, suspected men to be sworn at the shrine of the saint. Behind cluster the earth-colored houses of sun dried bricks, and beside the obelisk are placed the yellow cane seats of some Arab sellers of sweetmeats. It is a strange mingling of modern with ancient life, and so much does Egyptian tradition still linger, that the ancient procession of the sacred bark pictured on the walls of the temple is still held in Luxor now in honor of Abu-el-Haggag, when once a year a small fishing-boat is carried though the village, and

QUINTESSENTIAL BOOK
"THE HOLY LAND"

charcoal burned on the truck which bears it in place of the incense offered by priest or king.

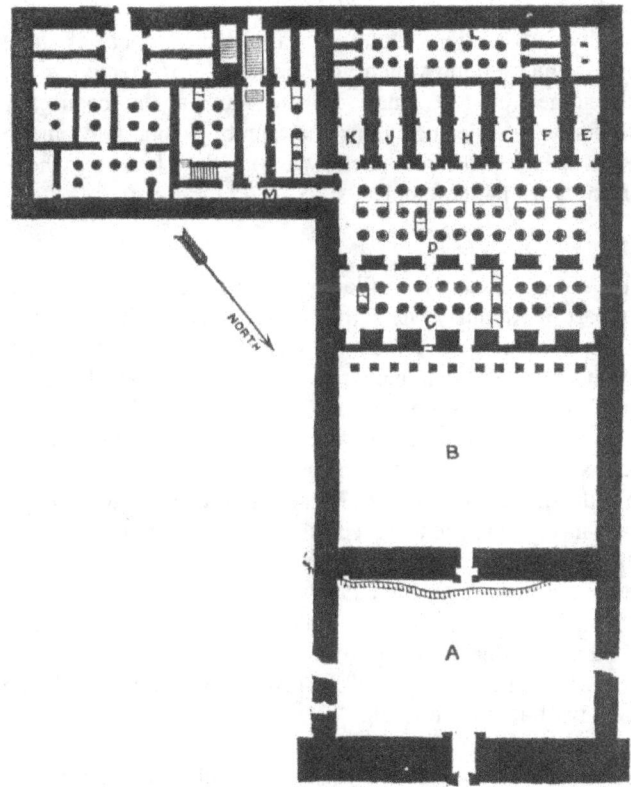

Holy Land – Plan of the Temple of Seti I at Abydos.

The sphinx avenue from Luxor to Karnak has in part moldered away and in part been covered. Where the road emerges from the village a few moldered bases may be seen; and one strike again into the avenue, here in better preservation, on entering the palm groves, which lead to the temple of Karnak. The limits of this paper would not suffice to treat in detail of Karnak, with its multiplicity of courts and pylons, its subsidiary temples and avenues of sphinxes, the history of its building stretching over two thousand years. The whole forms so complicated a study that one has, above all things, need of such a plan as Baedeker supplies.

FREDERICK MONDERSON

The temple of Amen, which itself contains two smaller temples in its great court, stands in a precinct which measures about one-third of a mile each way; the actual building, independent of the detached pylons, is more than a quarter of a mile in length, or about three times the length of Milan Cathedral. Inside this precinct lie also the Sacred Lake, the temple of Khonsu - itself about the size of a small English cathedral - built by Rameses III and against it the Ptolemaic temple of Ap, now used as a storehouse for antiquities, besides other less considerable temples in a more ruinous condition. On the north of this precinct lies another establishment of temples, chief among which was the temple of Mentu, faced by an avenue of sphinxes some 400 feet long. To the south again, connected with the Great Temple first by a series of pylons and then by a sphinx avenue, lies the temple of Mut, encompassed on three sides by a horseshoe lake, on whose banks, are seen the ruins of two smaller temples.

The Government excavation of late years has been directed to the clearance of the western part of Karnak. The soil in the hypostyle hall, built chiefly by Seti I, has been lowered some twelve feet, showing the columns in new and more dignified proportion. The hypostyle ball is in itself a great proof that the Egyptians had no inkling of the true theory of the arch. The number of pillars is immensely greater than is needed to support the roof, too great for architectural dignity: there is no grand transverse view of columns; each way one looks, unless it is straight down a lane of pillars, some six or eight of them block the view. The pylon at the end of this hall has been strengthened. It is a question, however, whether such strengthening will last any length of time, as the stone is much disintegrated from the action of the salts, which the water, rising through the soil at flood time, deposits on it. It was to remedy this that M. de Morgan attempted to drain the Sacred Lake at Karnak, hoping to find its direct communication with the Nile, and through this to let in a supply of fresh water, which should be turned through the temple, to wash it free from salt.

Unfortunately it was not found possible completely to drain the lake; the fact of such an inlet was established as the lake refilled itself, but the inlet could not be found.

Beyond the hypostyle hall the great outer court, with one of its little temples, has been cleared, and some statues, two or three large stela, and several fine sphinxes were found. But the most interesting discovery was of the quay of the temple in front of the great pylon, on which is recorded the rise of the Nile in various reigns.

M. Legrain, Inspector of Antiquities in the district, under whom the excavation has been carried on, has repaired the ram-headed sphinxes. Some might question the advisability, even from an aesthetic point of view, of so thoroughly repairing, almost restoring them; but it is impossible to deny that the quay, with its sloping

QUINTESSENTIAL BOOK
"THE HOLY LAND"

ways on either side, leading down to the ancient level of the water; its obelisks, its rows of closely ranged sphinxes leading up to it; the whole backed by the immense mass of the ruined pylons, is a wonderfully imposing sight.

But far more is learnt of the life and thought of the Egyptian from the tomb than from the temple. The glorification of the king, the highly colored narration of his valor and victories, was, as we have seen, the theme of his temple reliefs. But the tomb gives us the truth of ordinary life and the honest belief of the people.

As we stand opposite the east face of the Libyan cliff, it seems to be pierced with rows of colossal sand-martins' nests. More closely observed; these are seen to be the square doorways of tombs - tombs of private persons. Round a spur of the hill to the south are the Tombs of the Queens and over the ridge of the hill to the north lie the Tombs of the Kings. All the lower slopes of the hills, the ground behind the temple of Qurneh, the sand mounds over which one rides to Deir-el-Bahari, gape with holes, where one may look down and see the carved jamb of a doorway, or fragments of painted and sculptured stone. Many of these were never fine tombs, others are too much defaced for interest; but many of them, both private, and royal, are worth much study. A gate guards some of the finest; but many of the 'eternal habitations' of the Egyptian are now the habitations of the Arab.

However desecrated they have been by the hand of the spoiler; the Tombs of the Kings are at least free from this pressure of modern life into the habitations of the dead. The Kings no longer lie in the sepulchers they had hewn out of the rock. Their mummies, unrolled, so as to show the face with its parched *blackened skin*, are exposed to any irreverent and ignorant sightseer in the Museum at Gizeh, but a visit to their tombs helps one to form some idea of the secrecy and solitude they desired. The road winds for some three-quarters of an hour round the golden limestone buffs of an absolutely arid valley, screened even from the City of the Dead by an offshoot of the hills. At last, under a wall of rock, some mounds are seen, each guarded now by a wooden door. That door opened, one descends, as in a fairy story, down galleries hewn in the solid rock, decorated with strange fantastic pictures, through pillared chambers, and at the last comes a shaft - the mummy pit, at the bottom of which rested the body of the King of Egypt. The tourist, who comes and goes like a flash, 'doing' the regulation three temples and five tombs in a day; the lingering Arab hawker, waiting for his lawful prey at the door of the tomb, his stock-in-trade twisted in his turban, do not seem to disturb the quiet of the place, where there is no other sign of life than the slow-wheeling Egyptian vulture showing black and white against the sky.

Different as the tombs appear, they are in reality only adaptations of the same plan. The Egyptian tomb possesses essentially two parts - the real sepulchral chamber where the mummy rests, and the funeral chapel; these parts may be expanded, multiplied, 'connected by shaft or gallery.'

The inquiry into the reason why these parts are essential leads us to the fundamental question of the Egyptian belief in immortality - to the theory of Egyptian metaphysics without which we can neither understand the arrangement of the tombs, their principle of decoration, nor their prominence in daily life. 'The Egyptian conceived of man as a composite being consisting of at least six parts.' These parts are disunited by death, and immortal life is only attained by their reunion. All alike are not essentially immortal, and during the period preceding this reunion it is necessary that the perishable parts should be preserved.

'The Body,' Miss Edwards says, 'lay inert in the depth of the tomb; the Soul performed a perilous journey through the demon-haunted Valley of Shades; the Intelligence, freed from mortal encumbrance, wandered through space; the Name, the Shadow, and the Heart awaited the arrival of the Soul when its pilgrimage should be accomplished; and the Ka dwelt with the mummy in the sepulcher.' It is with this Ka that we have to deal, for the tomb is constructed not only with reference to the dead body, but also to meet the needs of the Ka. The Ka is the constant dweller in the tomb, the Ba or soul merely an occasional visitor, shown in Egyptian art, flying down the mummy shaft as a bird, human-headed and armed.

But what is the Ka? On this point Egyptologists are not agreed. Miss Edwards would translate it the 'Life,' Wiedemann the 'Personality,' Maspero the 'Double - the living and colored projection of the human figure... reproducing in minutest detail the complete image of the object or person to whom it belonged.'

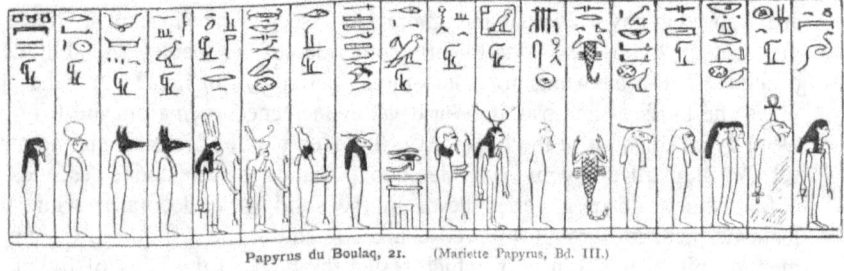

Holy Land Illustration 31. Book of the Dead: *Papyrus du Boulak*; Papyrus of Ani.

QUINTESSENTIAL BOOK
"THE HOLY LAND"

But though its exact meaning is obscure, its needs at any rate are expressed with an admirable clearness,

'Oh ye who live upon the earth!
Ye who come hither slid are servants of the gods!
Oh, say these words.

'Grant thousands of loaves, thousands of jars of wine, thousands of jars of beer, thousands of beeves, thousands of geese, to the Ka of the Royal Friend Pepi-Na, Superintendent of the Royal Household, and Superior of the Priests of the Pyramid of King Pepi!'

So runs a Sixth Dynasty tablet given by Miss Edwards. With such demands for food she connects the beseeching upheld arms and open hands, which is the hieroglyph sign for Ka.

The Ka requires food, and in early times the food provided for it was in part actual material food, for there were animal sacrifices, as among many primitive nations, at the tomb. All pious survivors renewed these periodically, personally or by provision of priests for the purpose, a custom strangely resembling foundations for masses for the dead. Such sacrifices were not mere ritual; food appears to be absolutely necessary to preserve the Ka alive while it exists in separation from the body. The Ka has a right to claim such support; it will revenge itself as a 'revenant' if it is not accorded, and can inflict madness or even death on the impious.

It appears sometimes to exceed its rights in this respect. Maspero gives an amusing instance of an Egyptian who prosecutes at law his wife's Ka, for haunting him without reason. It does not appear how the penalty was to be exacted if he won his case. But the pious survivor must at last die; even foundations for priestly sacrifice may become extinct; how then is the Ka to be insured against starvation? It can be kept alive in two ways - by modeled or painted foods, and by prayers for food. The mere repetition of such a prayer as that quoted above sufficed, Miss Edwards tells us, 'to insure a supply of ideal beeves and geese, ideal jars of wine and beer, ideal onions and cucumbers for the nourishment of the hungry Ka.'

A more simple method was that of painting on the sides of the tombs images of such food as the Ka required, or burying with it such minute models of eatables as Petrie found last year in his excavations round the Ramesseum - blue porcelain images, about an inch long, of the thigh of an ox or the head of a calf.

FREDERICK MONDERSON

But the mysterious Ka who could be fed equally well on thousands of oxen and geese, on prayers, and on blue porcelain, had also other requirements, the first of which was a body.

In the body provided for the Ka, Miss Edwards finds the origin of the portrait sculpture of the Egyptians; for the ideal Ka statue is that in which the Ka would feel most at home - the most faithful possible reproduction of the body in which it dwelt in life. Thus, as Miss Edwards says, 'if the man was ugly the statue must also be ugly; if he had any personal defect, the statue must faithfully reproduce it;' and she instances the Sixth Dynasty statue of Nemhotep, a dwarf, of which an excellent illustration gives us full assurance that the artist has not erred with a view to flattery. In the strange obscurity out of which Egyptian art sprang, full grown and complete, to sink through centuries into gradual decadence, this power of portrait sculpture appears to have been in its perfection. We find no development of art leading up to 'the wooden man of Boulak - a statue too well known to need description, the most realistic kind, evidently a faithful portrait, and so true to type that the Arab workmen who found it pronounced it at once 'the Sheikh of the village.' No less does one feel that the sculptor of the statues of General Rahotep and Princess Nefert, his wife, has seized the very spirit as well as faithfully portrayed the features of his subjects, the one showing the ability of self-made man, the other exhibiting an aristocratic ugliness, the small forehead and the keen eyes showing intelligent perception rather than creative power. The relation of the Ka to these statues must be clearly realized.

'The statues,' says Maspero, 'were not mere images, devoid of consciousness.... When the double of a man was attached to the effigy of his earthly body... a real living person was created and was introduced into the tomb. So strong was this conviction that the belief has lived on through two changes of religion until the present day. The double still haunts the statues with which life was associated in the ... and one can only be protected from him by breaking, at the moment of discovery, the perfect statues which the vault contains.'

For the vault contains more than one statue. Since it is absolutely necessary that the Ka should possess a body, to provide it with one only would be to run a considerable risk. Some accident might occur to a single statue, and the Ka be left bodiless. To provide against such contingencies a number of Ka statues were usually made and walled up in a niche in the tomb. Seventeen such statues of Kaphra, for instance, were found in the wall of the temple of the Sphinx.

Yet this is not the last of the needs of the Ka. The demand for food and for a body only leads to the demand for a dwelling. The home of the Ka is primarily the tomb, which, indeed, is called the 'dwelling house of the Ka;' and more especially the outer chamber or chambers of the tomb, in which the offerings of food were placed - the funerary chapel.

QUINTESSENTIAL BOOK
"THE HOLY LAND"

This part of the tomb, consecrated to the use of the Ka, not the mere receptacle of the body, contains that which Maspero characterizes as 'the essential part of the chapel or tomb' - namely, the stele, which 'perpetuated the name and genealogy of the deceased, and gave him a civil status, without which he could not have preserved his personality in the world beyond; the nameless dead, like a living man without a name, was reckoned as nonexistent.' On the stele, also, were represented pictures of offerings, and prayers for their renewal.

The idea of the tomb as the dwelling-house of the Ka gives us, moreover, a clue as to one of its methods of decoration; as the Ka prefers the body in which it is most at home, so also it prefers to dwell among the scenes which are most familiar.

We shall take as an instance the tomb of Sen-Nefer, in the district known as Abd-el-Qurneh. On entering, a steep and rather winding stair leads downward to the pillared chamber. The roof of the chamber is irregularly hewn out of the solid rock, and all over it creep a vine, painted on the stuccoed surface. On each of the four sides of the four rock-hewn pillars is a painting of Sen-Nefer sitting in an arbor, his wife standing in front of him and offering him food and drink. The Ka of Sen-Nefer might have a worse fate than inhabiting this chamber, with its roof made to resemble as nearly as possible the arbor in which it is evident Sen-Nefer loved to sit. For, as we must remember, to the Ka, which can satisfy its vast appetite on suggestion of food, a painted vine is not merely the representation of, but in the shadow land it is a veritable and substantial vine. These private tombs, with their scenes of private life, are, perhaps, more fascinating, if less instructive, than are those of the greater public officials, or of those of the Pharaohs themselves.

Yet such a tomb as that of the well-known Rekh-ma-ra, 'vizier' of Thothmes III, is interesting, not only because of its historic value - its procession of foreign chiefs with their well-marked racial types and their appropriate offerings - but still more perhaps for its pictures of Egyptian arts and crafts, its sphinx and statue-making, its brick-making and carpentry. Interesting it is, too, to note the arrangement of Rekh-ma-ra's pleasure grounds, with its piece of ornamental water, and the queer perspective of surrounding trees lying out like the fringe of a carpet all round.

In the study of the kings' tombs we must remember that we are dealing with a Ka of a different nature. The divine right of kings has its deepest significance in the Egyptian theory - the king is a son of the gods, and the Ka of the king, as Maspero tells us, is a double of the god Horus - for the gods too have Kas - a divine spark, so to speak, given off from the god. To the king's left alone belongs the distinction of a separate name that enclosed in the 'Ka banner,' as it has been called. In two of the Theban temples we have representations of the royal Ka.

FREDERICK MONDERSON

Hatasu at Deir-el-Bahari, and Amenhotep III at Luxor, carve in their temples scenes celebrating their divine birth and direct descent from Amen.

In one scene at Deir-el-Bahari the god Khnum is seen molding, and Heqt inspiring, not one child but two, exactly resembling each other; and in another the queen mother holding the child in her arms is faced by figures of divine nurses each holding a Ka of Hatshepsut. In one group as many as twelve doubles are represented. No human being, M. Naville tells us, can have more than fourteen.

Holy Land Photo 17. Kalabsha Temple of God Mendulese. In the Court, columns with varied capitals characteristic of the "Late Period" Graeco-Roman times. The netting is to prevent bats from flying into and inhabiting the Temple.

Here we come to the final difficulty in an interpretation of the Ka. To say that Hatshepsut had twelve personalities conveys nothing to us; to say that she had twelve lives has no meaning except in the sense that a cat has nine; and though the conception of the Ka may be allied to that of a 'doppelganger,' the word 'double' is plainly absurd in a case where there are twelve Kas.

Leaving this unsolved question we must return to the tomb. If royalty and divinity are thus conjoined, we must expect to find in the tombs of the kings something more than scenes of earthly life, though these too have their places in most interesting pictures of feasts, of dancing and musical entertainments, and, in the political sphere, of representations of foreign and tributary nations.

QUINTESSENTIAL BOOK "THE HOLY LAND"

In the story of Sanebat, when the death of the king is mentioned, it is said that be 'flew up to heaven and joined the sun's disc, the follower of the god met his maker,' and the message sent to his heir was that a 'hawk had soared with his followers.'

In the Tomb of Seti I, finest of the Tombs of the Kings, a prevailing subject is the journey of Ra and his triumphs over his serpent enemy, the power of darkness; battles and triumphs in which the souls of his faithful followers take part with him. The galleries and stairways leading down to the chambers where the king is portrayed offering to the gods, or Ra receives the homage of the lower world, are decorated with strange reptile forms, huge twining snakes, and serpents walking on human legs.

The connection, fully discussed by Maspero, between this Solar doctrine of immortality and the Osirian doctrines is not capable of a perfectly definite statement; the difficulty here as in all questions of Egyptian religion, being the fundamental one of dealing with a combination of independent religions imperfectly assimilated.

The Egyptian idea of the tomb is, as we have said, that it is the dwelling house of the Ka; but it is in no sense its prison. The Ka is no more confined to its tomb than a person in ordinary life is confined to his dwelling.

Thus in the story of Ahura it is implied of necessity, as Professor Petrie gives it in his restoration of the lost beginning of the story, that the Ka of Ahura, though she is buried at Koptos, dwells in the tomb of her husband, Na-nefer-ka-Ptah, at Memphis.

And as the Ka is not confined to its dwelling house, so, too, it may possess more than one house - not only the tomb with its funerary chapel, but the great funeral temple itself, is its abode.

Thus, then, we come to realize the meaning of much in the plan and history of the Egyptian temple, which has seemed obscure. The great statues of the builder are bodies for the Ka to dwell in. The niches in Hatasu's temple, with their portrait statues and carved tables of offerings, are chambers, bodies, and supplies of food for her Ka and the Kas of her family; and the systematic erasure by Thutmose III of her Ka arms, which form a line of decoration in one of the chapels, we dimly perceive to be the deepest part of his revenge - an attempt not only to blot out the memory of the queen in this world, but to annihilate her very personality in the next. But to follow up the religious questions involved in the arrangement and decoration of the tombs and temples would lead us far beyond the limits of our present subject. We can only here touch upon the impression gained from them of Egyptian life and character.

There is a wonderful double charm about Egyptian life; it has the twofold quality of enduring youth. In spite of the intermixture of race, the type of face and character, the habits, the very implements, of the ancient Egyptian still hold their own in the Egypt of today. Compare the illustration given by Maspero of the head of a Theban mummy and of the fellah of Upper Egypt. Rameses II may any day be seen meekly mopping the decks of a post-boat, or guiding the course of a felucca. The whole prosperity of Upper Egypt depends at this moment on the working of the Shadoof, and paintings of it may be seen on walls of tombs. Mr. Floyer has shown in an interesting paper in the '*Athenaeum*' that the Sakhieh, for all its Persian name, has to this day a special dial of its own to time the watches of the oxen, making them longer or shorter according to the time of year and the depth of the water; and that these working periods are called by pharaonic names. The palm baskets in which boys now carry away earth from an excavation or embankment are like those ancient ones, which Professor Petrie exhibited this year at University College.

Not less enduring is the liability of life and type of character. In the story of the 'Peasant and the Workman,' the peasant, to find cause against his enemy, forces him to ride into his standing corn by covering the path with his clothes. The simple cunning of the device was quaintly paralleled last winter by a fellah who had extended his field of corn over a well-used path, not for the sake of the strip of ground thus gained, but for the more profitable purpose of extorting damages from the passers-by, who must now trample on his crop.

Ceremonies have a strange vitality. The procession of the sacred boat has already been mentioned; and it is difficult not to connect with the sacrifice of the paschal lamb that ceremony of house-warming to which even Europeans in Egypt submit, of smearing the blood of a sheep, killed for this purpose, on the door posts and threshold of the finished house. The very magic elements of the tales are those, which appear in all true fairy stories from India to England. The idea of the child who is shut up in a tower to protect it from a prophesied fate is not original to the 'Sleeping Beauty,' since it appears in the story of the 'Doomed Prince.' Surely there is some connection between the Hathors who prophesy fates at the birth, and the fairy godmother whose gifts are fates. In the same way the king who shuts up his daughter in a tower, and makes her hand the reward of athletic feats, and the stranger who wins her are as much familiar elements of stories as the oppressed younger brother Bata, so superior in character and fortunes to the elder, who reappears in German legend under the name of 'Boots.'

QUINTESSENTIAL BOOK "THE HOLY LAND"

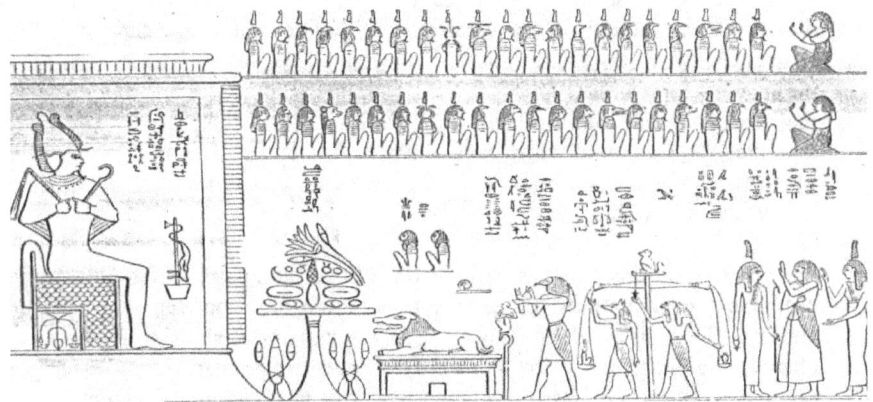

Holy Land Illustration 32. The Judgment Hall of Osiris. Osiris enthroned; 42 judges above; images of Ma'at in feathers encircles the deceased; Anubis and Horus adjust the scales; Thoth does the recording; and Ammit, 'eater of the dead,' waits for lunch, that is, if the deceased is proved unworthy of life.

One is inclined to re-echo the worn-out truism that there is nothing new when one finds that Rameses was manicured; that Egyptian girls played with jointed dolls and doll's furniture; the boys with marbles and tops; and the babies had toy-animals on wheels.

It is in great part the child-element in Egyptian life and character, which keeps it eternally modern. The very conventionality has a freshness about it. The king who excuses his plan of marrying his son and daughter to commoners, children of his officers, on the ground that 'it is often so done in our family;' and who laughs with his daughter, who chaffs him about it, has a boy's feeling of the proprieties. They overlay but do not permeate his human nature. There is a vivid human reality about the characters we come across, typically shown in Na-Nefer-ka-Ptah's speech when he thinks of committing suicide. He is urged thereto, not by his own sorrow for the death of his wife and his child Merab (heart's darling we might translate it), but by the impossibility of presenting himself before his father to say 'I have taken your children to the Thebaid, and killed them, while I remained alive, and I have come to Memphis still alive.'

There is a fullness of life and youth about the Egyptians, which renders even ludicrous the conception of them as a monotonous people under the shadow of the grave. The prominence of the idea of death appears to come rather from the love of life; so intense a desire for life cannot be bounded by the grave; even comedy has its place in the paintings on the walls of the tombs.

FREDERICK MONDERSON

One cannot deny that there is a darker side to the picture. Every picture of the victories of Kings shows a train of captives with their arms tied behind their backs; the sills of Rameses' palace windows at Medinet Habu are supported by such figures. Maspero gives a terrible account of the lives of captives forced to labor on public works or till the Pharaohs' fields; so much did such labor shorten their lives that freemen were impressed by the corvee to fill up their ranks. Well may the Israelites have groaned under such Egyptian bondage. The artisan life, of which Maspero quotes a description, is evidently a life of overpowering labor, in which idleness was penalized.

Yet granting all this darker side, how does Egypt compare among other nations of old time - even nations of modern time? We have not the worst features of slavery. There is no delight in pain, as at gladiatorial shows; the slave is not a chattel, the master not irresponsible. There is an elasticity of spirit in the oppressed, an Irish humor in the men who will not pay their dues until they have been sufficiently beaten. If the lower-classes are oppressed by overmuch labor, there is no justified idleness for the rich; they own the duties of protection, the obligations of the feudal lord; they have a duty and delight in wisdom. Moses, as the son of Pharaoh's daughter, is taught all the wisdom of the Egyptians; Na-nefer-ka-Ptah, priest and king's son, will do 'nothing on earth but read the writings that are in the catacombs of the kings, and the tablets of the House of Life.' The vaunted self-praise of the feudal lord is not so much in riches or honors as in the fact that he was 'the staff of the ages, the foster-father of the children, the counselor of the unfortunate, the refuge in which those who suffer from the cold in Thebes may warm themselves, the bread of the afflicted which never failed in the cities of the south.' In times of scarcity such a man vaunts that he relieves the destitute, and in times of plenty absorbs no unearned increment. 'If there were high Niles, the possessors of lands became rich in all things, for I did not raise the rate of the tax upon the fields.' There are none of the worst and most desperate elements of caste and class distinction. The parents of Senmut, Hatasu's favorite are not 'named in writing.'

Thus, with all its careless cruelty, its hard bondage, its severe discipline, we have still to remember that we are dealing with a nation which upholds a standard of equal justice, and a standard of mercy, which believes in the duty of the rich towards the poor, the helpless, the slave; whose religion teaches that each man must appear before the judgment-seat of a righteous God, and plead not alone that he has performed his duties of divine worship, 'not curtailing the sacred revenue,' but that 'he has not oppressed the poor nor caused the slave to be ill-treated of his master.'

The information shared here is crucial; our people must have it, for it anchors them in their social interactions. They need to know, the Black people of ancient Africa, whose legacy is so contested today, bequeathed a history that Professor John H. Clarke liked to coin as a "rehearsed and full blown civilization" manifestation.

QUINTESSENTIAL BOOK "THE HOLY LAND"

These Blacks, particularly those of Thebes in the Upper Kingdom, whose minds envisioned such a marvel, engineered the thoughts and patterns that are recognized as crucial pillars of civilization.

Thousands of years later, students the world over study and debate this ancient African creative legacy in the art and architectural, religious, scientific, medical and horticultural disciplines. So, we have come to the end of this project."

JOHNSON AND WALES GRADUATION
By
Dr. Fred Monderson

After a lengthy car-ride, I arrived in the State of Rhode Island, in the City of Providence, to attend the graduation of my niece, Kashida Maloney, who received a Master of Business Administration degree from Johnson and Wales University. Sitting in the packed auditorium of the Theater of Performing Arts, I was tremendously impressed by the Keynote Speaker, Dr. Vartan Gregorian, who in his own right received an Honorary Doctorate of Humane Letters for a lifetime of intellectual achievements.

I listened intently as the good doctor sketched the path he traveled after his graduation some forty years ago. The honorary degree came in wake of President Clinton's awarding the National Humanities Medal for intellectual achievement to the former President of Brown University. He was President of the New York Public Library, a Phi Beta Kappa and a Ford Foundation Foreign Area Training Fellow, and Member of the John Simon Guggenheim Foundation and the American Council of Learned Societies. A Fellow of the American Academy of Arts and Sciences, he has been decorated by the French, Italian, Austrian and Portuguese Governments. He received more than 40 honorary degrees from institutions of higher learning. There's no question, this was an outstanding keynote address, and punctuated with humorous anecdotes that made his presentation even more appealing. He told of the Bishop who gave long sermons and his congregation eventually getting up and leaving, and the caretaker remarking "Bishop, here's the key, lock up after you are finished."

Meanwhile, I was impressed with the international flavor of the graduating class of graduate students. There were thirty-eight countries represented in the class of 1999. Nearly forty percent were Asiatic, realized by the sound of the names read as they approached the podium to receive their diplomas. However, the most fascinating revelation was the keynote speaker's praise of the American educational system. He mentioned ancient Alexandria, in Egypt/Kemet, the center

FREDERICK MONDERSON

of literacy in antiquity, where many Mediterranean nations had students in attendance. Further, the Professor recounted how over the last century, following the Civil War and Congress issuing of land grants, the 'American system has transformed and democratized the notion of the medieval university that catered to educating the upper classes. Now it is open to everyone!'

Of course, this was not so for Black people for centuries in America. At one time, young Black children should be constantly reminded today, it was illegal and punishable as a crime, to teach a Black person how to read. Teachers should constantly emphasize the role of the Freedmen Bureau when the Black colleges got started.

Nevertheless, as I struggled to count and identify the few Black students who were receiving their Masters degrees, despite the naysayers, I felt there was still hope for our people. Praise must be given for the yeoman work of Black Colleges transforming young Black minds into professional individuals who are making inroads and uplifting the legacy of our people, once enslaved and illegal to think. Dr. Gregorian spoke of how American Universities transformed the intellectual, political, economic, medical, scientific and technological realms of the American cultural experience. Again, I thought of the inroads our people were making as students, teachers, administrators, even as citizens. Yet, I was mindful of the problems we still face despite the progress so far achieved. As we move further into the 21st Century, a new millennium and end the first decade, such realities as institutional racism, racial-profiling, police brutality, unemployment and discrimination, I'm still encouraged by the possibility of educational achievement, through commitment, dedication and hard work that is still attainable. Yet, as an educator influencing young minds in the trenches of New York City schools I am both pleased and disappointed about that reality.

I am pleased that many young people work hard, respect themselves, their classroom, teachers, and the learning process and are, motivated by this, rightly so, to become achievers. I am pleased to be standing with these young people, despite the difficulties such an undertaking experiences, for one sees it in their eyes, smiles and manners as they reach out to say thanks for what you did for me.

More than 70 percent of the world's college students are in American universities, we were told. Everybody is coming here to be educated! So while American Universities are educating the world's students, future leaders, and decision-makers, Blacks can no longer validly criticize the powers that be in this country, over the issue of education. They will counter such an argument: "Our doors are open. Everybody's coming." Therefore, Brothers and Sisters, we need to get our young people to work harder with a plan and vision of leadership to engage the future.

QUINTESSENTIAL BOOK
"THE HOLY LAND"

Hence, the purpose of this and so much of my writing ventures are to provide my readers with intellectual anchors rooted in African cultural history. Hopefully, this and my other works will aid in this effort and can become important for educating our people. *The Colonnade, Architectural Fragments from Here and There, Reflections on Ancient Kemet, Egypt: Essays on Ancient Kemet, Where are the Kamite Kings?, Karnak: The Majestic Architecture of Ancient Kemet,* and *Research Essays on Ancient Egypt, Hatshepsut's Temple at Deir el Bahari, Medinet Habu: Mortuary Temple of Rameses III, The Ramesseum: Mortuary Temple of Rameses II, Intrigue Through Time, Grassroots View of Ancient Egypt, An Egyptian Resurrection,* and *Barack Obama: Ready, Fit to Lead, Barack Obama: Master of Washington DC* and *Obama: Master and Commander,* as well as *Michael Jackson: The Last Dance, Celebrating Dr. Ben-Jochannan, Ladies in the House, Black Nationalism: Alive and Well, Eternal House: The Egyptian Tomb,* are books that would prepare any student for comprehending the Nile Valley experience. That broadening intellectual experience can become a useful tool in confronting the challenging dynamics of what is happening to our people within the social fabric of this society. Such knowledge can certainly undergird the African-American experience in the African dimension of today's human saga.

Nevertheless, I am disappointed at the level of disrespect our youngsters show their male Black teachers in the public schools. Nobody's talking about it. There is no question that our children respect the White educator, but they should also equally respect the Black educator, for we are just as educated, oftentimes more so than white counterparts.

I remember sometime ago being told about somewhere in the 'Islands' when one day a lad visited his dad, at work, in a bank. The architectural layout of the office with its many desks in wide space manned by clerks and all white, except his father, sticking out like a "fly in buttermilk," filled the boy with awe. In the father and son later recounting of the experience, the elder remarked, "I did not get this job by being as qualified as others, son," he remarked, "I'm here because I have more education than the others. If I had only an equal amount or less, I would not get the job."

Refocusing, the idea of centennials is important, in a number of respects. I always reflect on grandmother Cherise's birthday, January 19, 1895, that day also being an important holy day in ancient Kemet/Egypt. January 19 is also Melinda Melbourne's birthday. It is amazing how modern scientific methods began archaeological excavations with anthropological analyses to unearth evidence that shaped the interpretation of history and 'The Role of Africans' and 'What Role did Africa Play' in shaping pharaonic civilization.

Understanding this experience through familiarity with the literature lends credibility to any effort to navigate today's interpretation with a view to slingshot

FREDERICK MONDERSON

towards the end of the first century in the new millennium, say 2099. Let's not forget, the Afrocentrists have a date, 2027, when they want an accounting of the progress Blacks have made in America. By then we can be well on way with an organized methodology grounded in rigorous inductive and deductive analysis of information, in an age so named.

Archaeology is the science that digs up or unearths evidence of past civilizations, and in this case Kemet/Egypt for familiarity; and anthropology, both physical and cultural, interpret what is found, whether physical, written or artifactual, from temples or tombs. However, the modern 19th century mindset possessed the high culture of rampant global white supremacy, and established European schools of thought that removed Black people from the rich African cultural experience in the Nile Valley of North-East Africa. They created the idea of the "Middle East" with Egypt in it and out of Africa to eliminate the role of Black people in the intellectual, cultural, spiritual and religious experience the River Nile produced in its "gift."

Importantly and moreover, if we could get our people reading *Glory of the Ancestors* and the present work, the information supplied would help prepare them for the next century in those same crucial areas that transformed and shaped this society as, science, medicine, technology and literacy. In reflecting back, W.E.B. DuBois was a champion after his 1896 PHD dissertation *Suppression of the African Slave Trade to America 1638-1870*. Look how many African-American scholars followed him. We have had Marcus Garvey, Duse Mohammed, Dr. Edward Wilmot Blyden, Dr. Alexander Cromwell, Dr. Carter G. Woodson, Dr. J.E. Moorland, Dr. Arthur Schomberg, and Alaine Locke, Kelly Miller, Charles Wesley, John Cromwell, William Pickens, J.E.K. Aggrey, Caseley Hayford, Paul Panda, Dr. Leonard James, John Jackson, Lester Brooks, John Huggins, John H. Clarke, Yosef ben-Jochannan, James Turner, Ivan Van Sertima, Jacob Carruthers, and Cheikh Anta Diop, V.B. Thompson and Theophile Obenga.

QUINTESSENTIAL BOOK
"THE HOLY LAND"

Holy Land Illustration 35. The Shaduf (left); and jar with dated inscription (right).

I will always be inspired by Prof. John H. Clarke's lecture at Aswan in 1991 entitled, *"The Role of the Caribbean Scholarly Identification with Egypt,"* and how this influenced the Black intellectual movement here in the United States. He introduced so many new names that were unfamiliar to me as a scholar and researcher, I had to stand up and mention this to him in my laudatory commentary during the question and answer period. All the teachers taught us to be familiar with the racist pseudo-scientific writers and historians as Henry Fairfield Osborne, Edward Ross-Sociologist; John R. Commons-Psychologist; G. Stanley Hall-Psychologist; James Ford Rhodes-Historian, so too, John W. Burgess, Josiah Nott, and U.B. Philips. There was a Philips School out of Columbia University. Arthur De Gobineau and Lothrop D. Stoddard are famed racists. Samuel Cartwright, the "Banana skinned physician" who wrote *Slavery and Ethnology* and Christian Ministers as Charles B. Calloway, Theodore Debose Stratton, and William Montgomery Brown are no exception. A. Newby wrote *In Defense of Jim Crow* and Thomas Dixon wrote *The Klansman*. Thomas Nelson Page was another racist writer.

Contemporary Racists include William Shockley, Arthur Jensen and Christopher Jenks. In the 1970s, A. Worthy wrote a **Science** article funded by public monies and entitled "The Eyes Have It." He used sports statistics and such personalities as Joe Namath and Pete Rose as leaders in their respective fields and classed them as generals on the field. He created paradigms entitled "self paced" and "reactive." The writer used Joe in the huddle calling the play and executing it in a "self paced," manner. The Black receivers to whom Joe threw the ball were in the "reactive" mode. Then he said, "See, no black has ever won the Super Bowl," and we needed Doug Williams to do it. So too several others.

I'm again reminded of what U.S. House of Representative Major Owens said when he attended one of Caribbean Action Lobby's on-going forums in Brooklyn, on political activity in the city, state and nation in 1999. Candidates for the national assembly in Panama were in attendance to inform the Panamanian Community in New York, Brooklyn, about what was going on. Carlos Russell, creator of Black Solidarity Day celebrations in New York, was in the audience and informed that it was the Panamanian Community in New York that was instrumental in bringing about constructive change in the lives of Blacks in this country. Major Owens got up and pointed out how the African Diaspora is under attack throughout, whether in America, Middle America, South America, and the Caribbean, in Europe and even on the African continent. The Congressman underscored the importance of the vote. He urged our people to get out and vote in every election, keep pressure on their elected officials, be part of the process, be informed and pay attention to what is coming out of Washington. He issued a most convincing comment on praising the work of the Black Caucus in the House of Representatives, when he said: "It is not so much the legislation that we pass but what we stop from getting through. You would be amazed by the frivolous legislation being planned and submitted in the legislative halls of this nation. They are designed to penalize Blacks and the poor. We can only stop so much, so we can't afford not to be there." We must continue to vote and be involved in constructive pursuits is what we must teach the young. However, intellectual pursuits in the library should always be paramount in the minds of all.

We should teach the youth about the socio-economic problems of the non-white community from an inter-disciplinary stance. We should also teach the inmates in prisons, make them aware of this wonderful knowledge. We should help them get a library together. Might I add the great African American activist Sonny Carson wanted to establish a library in every prison across America to get reading about their cultural history especially. We should teach them the application of the principles of critical analysis and how to understand actions, reactions and interactions of the official institutional super-structure toward and with the non-white community.

All people should study the role of historical process and become able to identify and discuss with respect to the psycho-socio-economic manifestations of the history and experience of Black people in the American social ideology. Young and old need to critically scrutinize and learn to analyze the effects of the historical, economic, political and sociological urban-American climate, upon the human element of the non-white community

QUINTESSENTIAL BOOK "THE HOLY LAND"

We need a methodology to accomplish this task and the thoughts and teachings of Dr. Leonard James, Emeritus of New York City Technical College of the City University of New York, are so apropos. Prof. James taught the critical and comparative methodology must be analytic, inductive, systematic and sequential. The students need Criteria for Critical Reading, a Methodological Plan, a Systematic Conceptual Scheme of Analysis, as well as a Historical Perspective that is iconoclastic. They must study, learn and correct distortions and omissions to African history and culture that were systematically implanted by racist Western, European and American historiography. This approach by its nature is part of the method of reconstruction in African historiography, taking place today.

Clearly, if one at random was to ask many people and even college graduates, what is meant by Olduvai Gorge, Imhotep, Menes, Triangular Trade, Types of History, Mansa Musa, Sundiata Keita and Askia Mohammed, Prester John, the Almoravids, Racist pseudo-Scientific Historiography, vis-vis Africa, the Camel, Irrigation, Badarian, Amratian and Gerzean, Cushites, African River Valleys and to describe Sudanese Markets, hardly any would know or be able to give a credible answer to most of these. That is why Black History is so important. No question, our people need to learn the application of principles of critical thought to the historical data interpretations and be able to subject all standard historical and social science postulates and variables to the scrutiny of rational inquiry. And we must accomplish all this from an intellectual stance that is one of detachment.

That historical perspective spoken of must be undulative, dynamic, universal and humanistic. It must reject pernicious pseudo-historical images of African and African-American cultural staticity and deprivation created and maintained by racist historiography, literature and social science. It must affirm that the movement of all human societies is constantly subject to implacable historical, cultural and natural forces. The need to know, the ascent, descent or immobility of any given culture or individual is, therefore, contingent upon their being able to display an ability to subdue the negative forces and cultivate and incorporate the positive forces. In this process, emerges the critical African scholar who must strive to develop a stance from an historical perspective that manifests an affective posture of respect and compassion for the valiant, indestructible spirit of the human family adrift in the cosmos. Last but not least, this transformed scholar must be able to master the Criteria for Critical Reading. In any reading, the student must be able to identify Title, Author, Chronology and Nature of the Source of a book or article. Our hero should be able to identify and understand the Major Thesis, Secondary Thesis and Supporting Arguments and to whom, the Audience, a particular piece is written. Motivation, Intent, Methodology and Documentation are also crucial cornerstones in critical analysis. They must be familiar with the 8 Major Social sciences, viz., Geography, Archaeology, Anthropology, History, Sociology, Political Science, Economics, and Psychology, and be able to apply them critically and constructively in discussion or analysis of any given phenomenon. The operation of the newly created and constructive methodological approach would then be fit to be tested.

Thus, having this knowledge coupled with understandings of the reports, articles, discussions, reviews, and the books of that era, a century ago, and familiarity with the researches, writings, lectures, affiliations, protests, and positions of the mentioned Black scholars and personalities, young and old, can certainly provide grounding for millennia interface. Of course, in addition to readings, one has to as you are doing, visit the Nile Valley, sail the waters of the Nile; experience Cairo, Gizeh, Sakkara, Memphis, Thebes, Abydos, Dendera, Esneh, Edfu, Kom Ombo, and the Temple of Isis of Philae, now on Agilka Island. Even further, in the Aswan area, the optional and challenging Tombs of the Nobles, Mausoleum of Aga Khan, Kitchener Gardens, Unfinished Obelisk, Lotus Memorial, Aswan High Dam, Kalabsha and Beit Wali Temples are all eye and mind opening experiences.

Holy Land Photo 18. Beit Wali Temple of Rameses II. Court entrance to the Temple with its engaged columns; and in good color, Rameses (right) wears the Blue or "War Crown" and presents his name with ankh to enthroned Amun-Ra in feathered plumes holding scepter and ankh.

To the twin temples of Rameses II at Abu Simbel you can add Luxor with the complex of temples to Amen, and the Theban Triad, including Mut and Khonsu, sun, earth and moon gods, at Karnak and Luxor. Together with the mortuary temples and tombs across the river in the west, the land of the dead, Deir el Bahari, Ramesseum, Medinet Habu, you get 3 tombs in the Valley of the Kings and

QUINTESSENTIAL BOOK "THE HOLY LAND"

perhaps 1 or 2 optimal tombs in the Valley of the Queens. When all of this is added to the magnificence of the Cairo Museum of Egyptian Antiquities, that houses remains of most all the sites mentioned, the benefits are enormous.

Then such eras of history from the Prehistoric, Archaic, Old, Middle and New Kingdoms, Late Period and Greek, Roman, Arab, Turkish, French and English periods, will be more meaningful in understanding the creation, excavation, possession, exhibition, and interpretation of ancient African knowledge experienced from the headwaters of the Nile to the Mediterranean Sea.

Inasmuch as Prof. Vartan argues that seventy percent of the world's college students are studying in American Universities, let us challenge eighty percent of Black youth to work towards a college education. Let us not forget, many more jails are being built to contain our people, the Latinos and other minorities. I remember how Malcolm X told of finding himself in prison. But this is too late for some of our young. We need them to find themselves in the first, second, third, fourth, fifth, sixth, seventh, eighth, ninth, tenth, eleventh and twelfth grades. Then we need to get them in college for both undergraduate and graduate degrees. Thus armed we let them loose in society to pursue professional interests. This is how we can put an end to some of the maladies that face our people today. They must constantly strive to function on a high intellectual level and command respect and equality based on display of high professional, scholarly and moral standards of conduct and activities.

FREDERICK MONDERSON

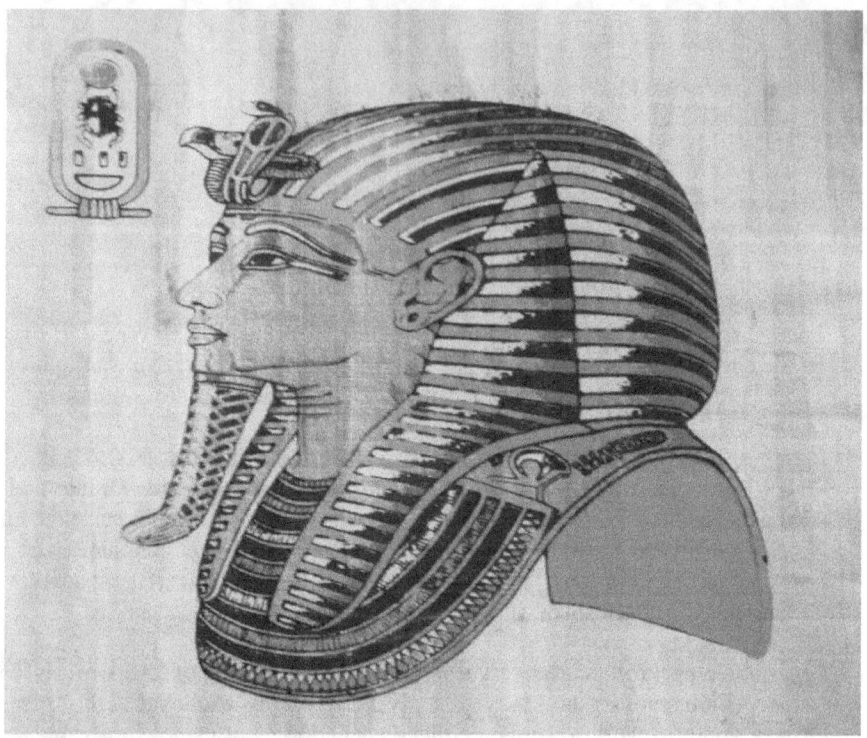

Holy Land Papyrus 12. In a colorful twist, the ever-beautiful Mask of Tutankhamon.

Blacks are not leaving America! Our people on these shores shed an inordinate amount of blood, sweat and tears! Even, Jerry Rawlings, former President of Ghana in West Africa, believed the Black American population in America is the 'African Trojan Horse' in today's complex world, and who can do so much for the continent from over here! Therefore, coordinating and operationalizing an effective plan of cooperation and solidarity in the African Diaspora can assist the continent to then coalesce and be transformed in unity. This is so crucial in these decades of turbulent revolutionary growth that insists, as the world gets more unified, so too must the Africans, those at home with those abroad.

Kwame Nkrumah of Ghana wanted a united Africa under a continental government, but this, to this day, seems elusive. Yet, Europe has implemented a political and economic integration for certainly cultural and political unification. Therefore, Africa and Africans must get their acts together!

QUINTESSENTIAL BOOK
"THE HOLY LAND"

Dr. Alexander Pushkin: Mr. Sinclair, I believe you started us on a discussion and I want to relocate you in the answers you were giving us. Please tell me, what does it mean for something to be centered?

Michael Sinclair: This is a higher-level question. Remember I said you need three aspects to create a framework. These were ethnological location, categorical and functional. Let's say you see something in the newspapers that said George Wallace said something – Blacks will never be able to hold office in the state of Alabama.

Well, Afrocentric scholarship lets us see certain types of detail in language. Categorical, on the other hand, show aspects that deal with certain types of thought. This places women in certain categories. The question is, does it locate women in the right place?

What is meant by function and movement to transform things?

Ethnological means definition and even location of place. European genocide of African people. African genocide of African people. This is using terms. Another is Africans disappeared from the earth without a trace. This is a notion! Hopefully it does not happen! What is important is the idea of how history is presented when Africans are given a peripheral role in European experiences. In this they become adjuncts to European history. We call this marginality. However, Afrocentricity strives to give Africans agency, treat them as subject not object. Thus, Afrocentricity gives subject to Africans while non-Afrocentricity sees Africans as objects. Therefore, allowing Africans to have vision, own opinions, requires discipline in the way we frame ideas, structure arguments, and ask questions. It raises the level of discourse. We can be critical of each other but we should not bash them.

Afrocentricity then is a field of inquiry that allows us to strengthen intellect or to establish a tradition of inquiry.

You have to see where these ideas germinated. They date back to the late 1970s. Today they are a philosophy or philosophic discipline. Hence, Afrocentricity is a rigid discipline, but it is not a grand theory, not a system. It does not answer all questions. We leave this for existentialism. Still, Afrocentricity does answer a particular set of questions having to do with African people. We thus come to re-centering, African people as agents, actors, and subjects. We seek to find what is the most optimal level of performance for the African person; or how we operate in the best interest of African people.

FREDERICK MONDERSON

You see Afrocentricity is a severe discipline. It takes rigid preparation. Still, we do not try to answer all questions. However, we take a philosophical approach to all issues.

Teddy Cubia: I am following you but I need explanation of dislocation.

Michael Sinclair: The problem of agency takes precedence over all issues because fundamentally it is a problem of location. A good example is how the missionaries operated in Africa. They set up schools in Africa. You would say this is a good thing. Sure it is. However, it dislocated the African from his cultural and historical roots. They were forced to do things European. I might add there is always a down side to change. Change makes some things fall apart, yet some change is also good!

Another question we ask is where do you stand? Where you stand lets us see how you think. Let's not forget, some people may be shaky even though they are centered. Where they are going is therefore most important.

Dr. Alexander Pushkin: So, how do you find location and orientation? Well, what do we call you guys?

Michael Sinclair: Let me give you an example. A sociological scholar is a sociologist. A psychological scholar is a psychologist. An economic scholar is an economist and so on. An Afrocentric scholar is an Afrocentrist. So we must be more precise in what we do. Therefore, an Afrocentrist relating to Afrocentricity construction in Afrocentric thought is sound.

Let me explain further. Eurocentrism is only problematic when it becomes a universal idea. The only idea equals abnormal Eurocentrism. This is imposed by force for it takes all the space. That is the problem. Afrocentricity argues for pluralism without hegemony. We argue for co-cultures existing side by side. There is no question of who is in charge. All exist in a co-cultural sense, co-competing metaphors. In a society fueled by racism you only have domination and hegemony.

When Eurocentrism becomes ethnocentric, it equals racism whose intent centers on taking all the space, and as such, the created conflict results in cooption or destruction of African space.

Even further, an example is given when we speak of classical music. We speak of European music, not African classical music. Not African, Zulu, Sotho, not Duke Ellington. In the Eurocentric construction there is only one game in town. This is what we have problems with. That is why point of view is important. In point of view, the person takes an interest in centeredness of XYZ. What am I doing in

QUINTESSENTIAL BOOK
"THE HOLY LAND"

making a center? I am finding value in my own self. Thus point of view has real value. It is the recognition of human knowledge.

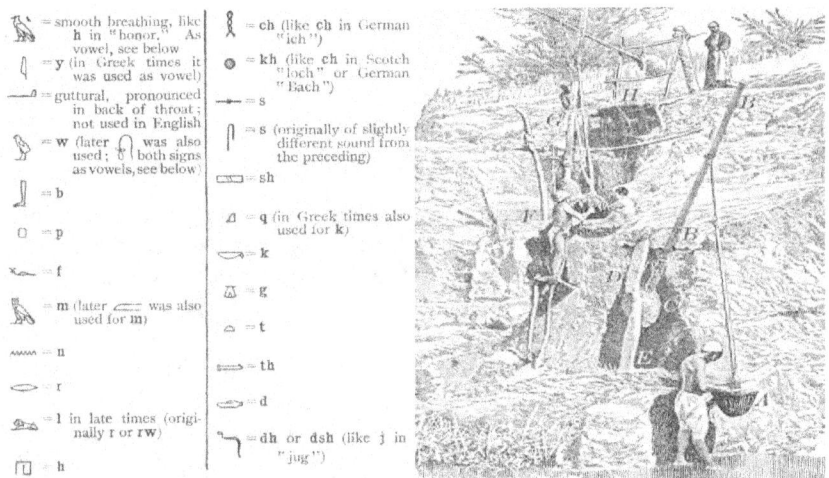

Holy Land Illustration 36. The Egyptian Alphabet (left); and the Shaduf for lifting water to the high ground level (right).

Bus Ride to Luxor Temple

CHARACTERS:

George Washington: On September 11, 1975 we learned African immortality is of two forms. In personal immortality the individual is remembered for 4 or 5 generations. In collective immortality one enters the memory of the group. It is believed in the African consciousness; the unborn can take on the spiritual attributes of the departed. There is a circular concept in which ancestors, the living and unborn are linked in a cycle of time.

Phenomenon – extremely unusual; extraordinary.
Sacred – special, reverence (transcends) beyond.
Phenomenology – a study of religious phenomenon.
Secular – "worldly;" mundane.
Profane – desecrate.
Mind/body
Reason/emotion

FREDERICK MONDERSON

Spirit/matter – feeling, emotion, will. An aspect of existence that is reduced to matter.

Unity – concept of being united in cause or cultural experience.

Harmony – When things appear calm and in unison.

Analysis – The African concept of immortality is twofold, personal and collective. Personal immortality is the state in which the deceased is held for a duration of time up to four to five generations. The time span marks the demise of the last person with whom he was familiar. As if to say that this person will return in this time period and those who are familiar with him by sight or his name will recognize him. Once this last person who can identify him has died then the initial deceased enters the state of:

Collective Immortality – The African at this stage is put in his right historical perspective, particularly if he or she was "righteous;" that is if he had lived for his fellow man.

The African "time" is measured in cyclical form as opposed to the European's lateral view; the ancestors; the living and the unborn. These latter, because of the proximity of the tri - parte; can take on the spiritual attributes of the deceased.

Mind – All of an individual's conscious experience, the thinking and perceiving part of consciousness, intellect or intelligence; the conscious and unconscious together as a unit = psyche.

Reason – Sound thought or judgment; good sense; smart; understanding; (cause and effect).

Spirit – the thinking, motivating, feeling part of man often as distinguished from man; mind.

Michelle Georges – That was very thought provoking. I like it.

QUINTESSENTIAL BOOK "THE HOLY LAND"

Holy Land Photo 18a. Clive Monderson of Guyana, South America, on a visit to the Library of Congress, Jefferson Building, in Washington, DC.

FREDERICK MONDERSON

Regina Hendricks – I could hardly believe you were that thorough in your note taking.
George Washington: Well, you have to be serious about your education. But I think the dynamism of my instructor Dr. Richards was also a factor. You know how a dynamic woman can move a young man.
Regina Hendricks. I know! Believe me!

Return Bus Ride

Mr. John Stewart: Some of the other sayings on the walls of the Library of Congress are that "Ignorance is the curse of God, knowledge the wing where we fly to heaven," "Knowledge comes but wisdom lingers on," and "In books lies the soul of the whole pastime."
Mrs. John Stewart: Honey, how many times have you been there?
Mr. John Stewart: Too many times to mention and, that is why I preach to others the value of books, knowledge, and taking kids on trips. Did you know Swinnock wrote "Knowledge is the Excellency of man, whereby he is usually differenced from a brute?" And even further, "Knowledge without practice is like a glass eye, all for show, and nothing for use."

5. Post-Site Lecture

Mythology is sometimes used to describe the experiences you see on the walls of temples and so forth that the people of ancient Egypt lived for aeons. But, mythology has a historical basis. Myths must be listened to carefully. Fairy tales are for entertainment. This is serious first-time thought-out ideas with no prior prototypes. Mythology takes place in primordial time. Opposing primordial time is chronological time. There are several creation myths in Egypt. In the beginning there was water (Primordial Nun).

If we consider the *Geography of the Gods*, the four centers of popular religious learning teach us Ra was worshipped at Heliopolis, Ptah at Memphis, Osiris at Abydos and Amon at Thebes. Each god is associated with a triad of wife and child. The wife is part of the notion of opposite. The son comes later. There were 8 primordial gods that formed the Ogdoad. There were four pairs of males and females. These were Nun and Nunet, the primordial water of chaos; Huh and Huhet, formlessness; Kuk and Kauket, darkness; and Amun and Amunet hiddenness.

The Ennead – Atum who rose out of the primordial hill and formed the Ennead out of himself. Atum gave birth to Shu (air) and Tefnut (moisture). This gave rise to

QUINTESSENTIAL BOOK "THE HOLY LAND"

Geb (earth), Nut (sky), and this gave rise to Isis and Osiris and Seth and Nephthys. Thus Atum created the nine. Isis and Osiris will have a son, Horus.

Mythology predates writing. Plutarch wrote the most complete version of the myth of Isis and Osiris.

Isis was a goddess of magic. The regenerated eye of Horus was a sign of health.

Plutarch got the myth of Osiris from the oral tradition. It was very important to be complete and to be buried properly. The purpose of mummification was to preserve the body for the resurrection. The "Opening of the Mouth Ceremony" was very important. An adze was used. The boat was the symbol of a long journey.

Shawabti or ushabti statues were "answerers" who would answer and do functions of the deceased if they were called upon to do so. The next world where Osiris presided was in the west. Pyramids, Sakkara and burials are on the west bank of (city of the dead) and the living was on the east bank. The saying: 'He went west' meant he died. The westerners were the deceased. Osiris was the 'foremost of the westerners.'

Three parts of the person were the body, ba and ka. The Ka is shown with a human head and a bird's body. The Ka shows 2 upraised arms and said to be the spiritual double of the body. After the resurrection, the body, the ba and ka unite on the west. You need all three to become a westerner. The ka says nothing. The ba is like a soul. A ka priest made the necessary sacrifices to feed the body with offerings of food. The tomb was a house of eternity to protect the body. Originally there was one priest, the pharaoh. The other priests were stand-ins for the pharaoh. At some time it became more symbolic than figurative.

6. Discussion

Dr. Fred Monderson: Dr. ben-Jochannan, my mentor, has always emphasized certain features we must concentrate on as we enter the temple. He said, press the guide to point out things to you. You must enmesh yourself in the sacred space. The great writer on architecture Rawlinson (1896: 21-22) assessed: "The architecture of Egypt is its great glory. It began early, and it has continued late. But for the great works, strewn thickly over the whole valley of the Nile, the land of Egypt would have obtained but a small share of the world's attention; and it is at least doubtful whether its 'story' would ever have been thought necessary to complete 'The Story of the Nations.'"

FREDERICK MONDERSON

However, let me begin by saying this, Dr. Conrad W. Worrill wrote an article "Egypt: Our Ancient Homeland" in the *Daily Challenge* Tuesday, May 14, 1996 and pointed out the "framework of European hegemony over the history of the world has had a devastating impact on African people and the African mind." He

Holy Land Photo 19. Dr. Marimba Ani and Assistant prepare the "Holy Water" for the Libation at ASCAC's 1999 Conference in New York!

quoted Dr. Jacob Carruthers of *The Association for the Study of Classical African Civilization* (ASCAC) in an earlier paper entitled "Race of the Ancient Egyptians"

QUINTESSENTIAL BOOK "THE HOLY LAND"

who commented on the ideas of Hume and others: "Obviously the emerging doctrine could not gain credibility among those who were familiar with the traditional wisdom among Europeans that the ancient Africans of Egypt had achieved a high level of civilization and had transmitted to the ancient Greeks many of the major ideas considered a part of Greek civilization." Dr. Carruthers also explained: "Several decades after the founding of the concept of white supremacy, George Wilhelm Fredrich Hegel supplied the solution of this latter difficulty when at the beginning of the 19th Century; he asserted that Africa was not a historical part of the world."

Hegel states "Historical movement - in it - that is in the northern part belongs to the Asiatic or European world .... Egypt will be considered in reference to the western phase, but it does not belong to the African spirit."
That the Egyptians were a white or red people or even comparable to ancient whites has never been recognized by ancient commentators. Equally, nowhere is there evidence the ancient Egyptians were painted black for the funerary ceremony. These were all modern creations to support the white Egyptian argument!

Dr. Carruthers put it best: "Thus Hegel took Egypt out of Africa and Africans out of Egypt. He also removed Africans from history."

Of course one has to understand the movement - taking place in Europe and Germany in particular at the turn of the Nineteenth Century. There was much competition throughout that century. The Napoleonic wars were ended; the era of Metternich began with the hundred-year peace, yet still there were conflicts across Europe. The Franco Prussian war of 1870-72, the imperialistic adventures of Europe in Africa that ended with the Berlin Congress, the colonization of the continent, intellectual colonization of Egypt and finally the outbreak of World War I in 1914. There was much chauvinism in Europe at that time. Friedrich Wilhelm Nietzsche (1844-1900) in *Ecce Homo* affirmed: "I believe in French culture and regard everything else in Europe which calls itself 'culture' is a misunderstanding. I do not even take the German kind into consideration." Even further he asserted: "Wherever Germany extends her sway, she ruins culture."

This latter statement thus calls into question Hegel's view of Africa as a part of Historical consciousness.

ARE THERE ANY QUESTIONS?

James Morrison: Who were the ancient Egyptians?
Dr. Fred Monderson: The Afrocentric position holds that the ancient Egyptians were Africans indigenous to the Nile Valley. Albert Churchward held the Masai

FREDERICK MONDERSON

were the original people who formed Egypt. For the most part the dynastic Egyptians were people from the south who dominated the creation of the culture of the Nile Valley. Bauval and Brophy in their *Black Genesis* pointed out the people of Nabta Playa who were Black Africans were in fact the predecessors to the pharaohs. The foreigners who came to the Nile Valley were latecomers and contrary to racist reporting, these people came after the foundations of Egyptian culture were in place!

Michael Montout: What color were they?
Dr. Fred Monderson: It is pretty clear they were Black or even brown. To say they were Caucasian is pretty far out, yet the misguided conception is that they were, according to Wortham, "Caucasian!" In fact, it's been argued that they probably covered the color spectrum as is evident throughout Africa. Consider that much of the knowledge we have of these people is based on no more than 15 to 20 percent of what we should know. Yet, we do know, according to David O'Connor, a respected white Egyptologist out of the Philadelphia Museum: "The Egyptians were not white!" It has taken more than a century for any respectable Egyptologist to admit that the Egyptians were not white. Of course, Black scholars for nearly a century and a half have argued that the Egyptians were Black and not white. Even Arnett in his *Evidence for the Development of Hieroglyphics in Upper Egypt*, affirmed Dr. Diop had dispelled the notion that the Egyptians were white. However, he also claimed Diop had not established they were Black! His argument is that the bones of the excavated remains cannot prove the race of those individuals. Even further, Arnett's contention is not altogether correct for "The Bones of Hen Nekht" seems to show he had Negroid traits, or in fact was Negro! Nonetheless, Diop did provide a litany of evidence to prove the truly African nature of the Ancient Egyptians. Let us also give credence to Albert Churchward's argument that the Egyptians were descended from the Masai of East Africa who were the principal group in the "Forming of Egypt." Because Western, European, and American scholarship is based on white supremacy buttressed through racism particularly at a time, during the 19th Century, when colonialism and imperialism were rampant and as heirs to slave trade and slavery, history has been distorted to show the prominence of whites over blacks in all facets of undertakings. The question therefore is, 'How could two groups look at the same evidence and come to two different conclusions?' Should we believe one group has a vested interest in distorting the results? Such a view is not altogether far-fetched considering it was propounded at a time when Europeans considered themselves superior to all peoples worldwide! We should not forget; the bones of Egypt's remains are 4000-5000 years old, so why can't they tell us anything while million year old fossils tell us much. So too, 250,000-year DNA reconstruction can pinpoint an African woman!

Farouk Ghorab: Really, what evidence is there to show that these people were indeed Black or truly African?

QUINTESSENTIAL BOOK
"THE HOLY LAND"

Dr. Fred Monderson: Not only has insufficient evidence survived the ravages of time, ancient and modern despoilers have destroyed much. Yet still, for a number of reasons some evidence of the blackness of Egypt has survived and so we have had to glean this deduction from the general to the specific. Also, we must remain cognizant of the role of such persons Hegel and Champollion's older brother who very early in the 18th Century distorted the fact and this misconception has remained in effect.

First of all, Dr. Diop has argued that Black Africans who hailed from Thebes in Upper Egypt accomplished the formative years of Egyptian civilization. He identified Narmer, the unifier of Egypt as Theban and therefore, Black. Some scholars have characterized Rameses II as Black. In his mortuary temple the Ramesseum, a scene commemorates Rameses' praise of his Theban ancestors beginning with Menes.

Mindful that later peoples infiltrated Egypt, Diop identified the first significant foreigners as the Hyksos who came after the Middle Kingdom. That is not to say that over the years before this time there were not trickles of people finding their way to Egypt from Southwest Asia. However, by the time of the imperial New Kingdom, many people were captured and brought to Egypt as slaves, traders, settler mercenaries, etc. Of course, in later ages, significant numbers of people infiltrated or came as conquerors and we begin to see morphological change in the color of the people. Let me add another thing about the red color of the Egyptians.

Much has been said about the red color of the Egyptians. Many critical scholars argue that the "black land" meant life and the "red land" meant death or desert. Dr. Ben says the Egyptians used henna which made them red. We know that Amon was Black as well as Blue. He was "so Black he was Blue." The prototype of Amon was Min of Koptos, a Black god whose wooden statues were discovered by Flinders Petrie in that city. Yet, in Hatshepsut's Deir el Bahari he is painted red. Is there any inconsistency here? One last thing, I was recently reading Scholastic magazine in school where I taught in New York City. The article dealt with mummies. It mentioned two statues found in Tut's tomb but showed the king sitting in his chair, where his skin is shown painted red. You tell me whether he was red or Black as the statues? Another important point can also be made of Tutankhamon. At the entrance to the hall with his treasures are two lifelike wooden statues of the king painted Black and covered in gold. Many people downplay this. However, just to the left is another illustration in bronze, showing the king trampling his Nubian enemies. He is the color of bronze and they are painted Black as he is depicted in the two statues. If the Nubians are Black then so is he. Even more significant is the fact that only a painted surface can depict blackness even though the Egyptians are sometimes painted red while the Nubians are oftentimes painted Black. This does indicate there is very little difference between these two peoples. Representations in stone have no relationship to the color of the ancient Egyptians.

Another interesting point can also be made in this respect. In the Cairo Museum on the second floor there is a display case housing small wooden statues of various kings. These statues are painted Black and it is as if they are a sideshow with no relevance. However, juxtaposed there is a panther painted Black alongside one of the kings' statues. Now, if the Black color represents the panther then the Black color of the statues must represent the color of the kings displayed there!

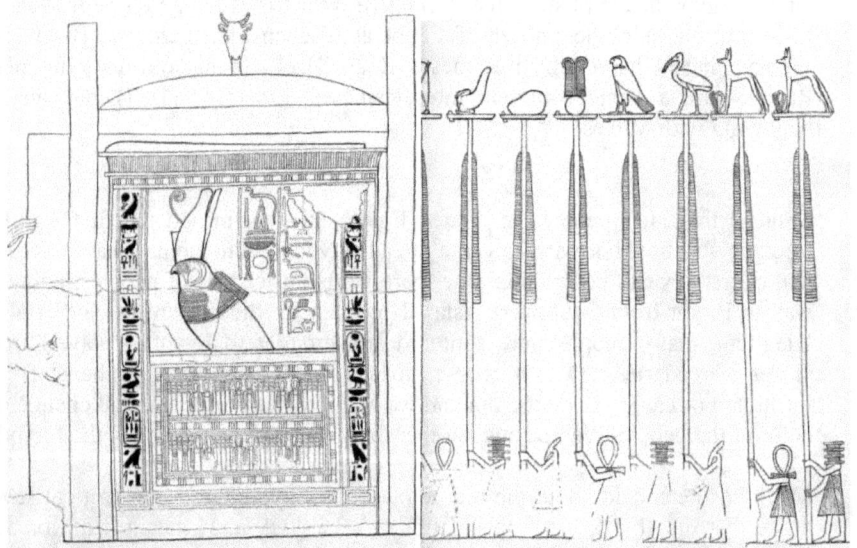

Holy Land Illustration 35. Abydos. Temple of the Kings. Back Hall: Shrine of the Mummified Hawk (left); and Standards at Temple of the Kings.

Let me add even further, in the distorted view projected, they argue Black was for the death ceremony. For example, in 1905 a female guide in the Cairo Museum told this writer Mentuhotep II, whose statue was discovered in his temple at Deir el Bahari, Thebes was so painted for the death ceremony. However, among the princesses buried in the mountain grave adjacent to the temple, one Kemsit painted black was described as black and Negro; yet, Mentuhotep so painted is considered as due to the death ceremony.

John Brown: How much more specific can you be regarding the color of the Egyptians?

Dr. Fred Monderson: Let's begin with the obvious. These have survived the ravages of time and man. Mentuhotep II was Black! Thutmose I was Black. Tutankhamon was Black. Much has been said about his parentage but they could

QUINTESSENTIAL BOOK
"THE HOLY LAND"

not be much different from his color. Aahmes-Nefertari, sister and husband of Aahmes who completed the expulsion of the Hyksos and founder of the Eighteenth Dynasty, was certainly Black and this makes her parents Black. So, her husband and brother must have also been Black. They were Thebans. Consider at this time Upper Egypt was not being visited by whites so there is no way that the rulers of that kingdom could have been white. We should be familiar with Chancellor Williams' argument in *Destruction of Black Civilization* concerning falsification of history that the important Eighteenth Dynasty began Black and ended white, particularly through the "marriage route."

Mrs. John Brown: I have to press you on this issue, but beyond Tutankhamon and Aahmes-Nefertari, is there any other evidence of blackness among the rulers of Egypt?

Dr. Fred Monderson: The Predynastic demographic foundations were essentially African and black. The bones of Hen Nekht of the Second Dynasty indicate he was Negro. The Middle Kingdom pharaohs whose tombs have not been found seem very Negroid from their statues. As Thebans we presume they were black. We know that Thutmose I was black and he was the grandson of the queen. These people were in direct descent from the Middle Kingdom pharaohs who were themselves black. That is how we get the likes of the fore parents of Thutmose I. Even Hatshepsut when she was challenged expressed the view of her lineage with Aahmes-Nefertari. Every Black image has been explained away but no Egyptian whites have been found. Thus, Red Egyptians, White Egyptians, Brown Egyptians, are only fiction of modern racist imagination.

Frank James: I don't recall any modern books that indicate Thutmose I was black.

Dr. Fred Monderson: That is precisely the reason we take the position omissions and distortions must be exposed. Let me give a more focused explanation. During the 19th Century Europe colonized Africa politically, economically and militarily. Once Europe had secured Africa she began its systematic exploration to determine the geographical, mineralogical and agricultural potential of the respective colonies now in its sphere. In fact, the colonizers were also interested in the art and music aspects of the African culture. I read at Oxford University's Bodleian Library the English had a questionnaire of 105 questions on music that was part of a given package to every English traveler who went abroad. This is one way important data was collected. Professor John Clarke liked to say: "The people who preached racism, colonized history." In addition he said, "When Europe colonized the world, she colonized the world's knowledge." More importantly, Europe unleashed what was later called intellectual imperialism particularly as it was aimed at Egypt. If a musical questionnaire, it stands to reason there were others.

FREDERICK MONDERSON

As England, France and several other European nations gained access to Egypt in the 19th Century, individuals began systematically traversing Egypt looking for evidence of the ancient culture. This form of exploration became a cottage industry. A.H. Sayce, traveled up and down the Nile River and discovered an ancient tomb at Thebes where an official was shown worshiping Thutmose I who was painted Black. This was printed in the emerging 'penny press' but got lost in the systematic exclusion of information that threatened the false notion that the Egyptians were white. Let us also add the great gods of Egypt were Black. Are we to suppose, if the Egyptians were white, then they worshipped Black gods? We know Min was Black and so too Amon. Amon was both black and blue, and these are synonymous colors. Green is a form of black! Amon's counterpart Min was Black. Hathor came out of Nubia. Osiris also came out of Africa, and he was called the Great Black! So we must suppose also his sister and wife Isis was Black. So too, their son Horus. Then the other gods of that circle, Seth, Osiris, Mendulese, Nephthys, etc., must be associated with Africa and thus be black. Ptah, great god of the artisans, maker of everything was a bald-headed Pygmy. Where did they come from? Let us not forget Hunefer, the 19th Dynasty nobleman and priest of Seti I reminded regarding their origins: "We came from the beginning of the Nile at the foothills of the Mountains of the Moon, where God Hapi dwells." This area is in Kenya, East Africa, in the plains. Let me add finally again, since Amon was black and blue as the sky, don't be confused when you see him painted red or brown or even green! Again, green is a form of black as in blue. Further, Hatshepsut's expedition to Punt in East Africa brought back lots of tropical products from "God's land." This is as credible as any evidence that could be propounded. Conversely, the seated statue of the Louvre scribe is said to have blue eyes and he retains a prominent position in that museum. The average visitor would easily say, 'See the Egyptians had blue eyes!" First, their craftsmen did employ inlaid eyes in their statues. Second, the statue does not represent a real person but a contrived idea. But still, in the modern mindset, this statue holds more credibility than Hunefer's statement.

Now, if we were to assume the ancient Egyptians came from someplace in Asia and migrated to Africa, why then is East-Central Africa considered "God's land." Should not God's land be somewhere in Europe or Asia where the Egyptians were thought to come from and Egypt simply a colony??

Stephaniea McCall: What are the most credible sources of our knowledge of who were the true Egyptians?

Dr. Fred Monderson: We need to begin with the ancients who were for the most part eyewitnesses. First there was Herodotus, the 'father of history.' He observed and claimed the Egyptians, Ethiopians and Colchians were black or "Burnt of skin." Diodorus Siculus also observed and wrote on Egypt with its connection to Ethiopia. One of the strategies European writers use is to claim a misinterpretation

QUINTESSENTIAL BOOK
"THE HOLY LAND"

of what Herodotus said when he described the Egyptians as Black. But Aristotle and many other classical writers also reported the same observation. Let us not forget, the great philosopher Aristotle wrote, "The Ethiopians and Egyptians are cowards because they are Black!" Naturally, he was both wrong and right!

Carmelitiea Shabazz: How did we get to this debacle of claiming the Egyptians were white?

Dr. Fred Monderson: In modern times, around 1750 the English philosopher David Hume asserted, "I am apt to suspect the Negroes to be naturally inferior to the whites." On the other hand, during the Slave Trade, Baron Montesquieu in his work *Spirit of the Laws* was concerned to write that: "It is impossible for us to suppose these creatures to be men, because allowing them to be men, a suspicion would follow that we ourselves are not Christian." This was picked up by Hegel at the start of the 19th Century as he sought to exclude Africans from Egypt and so the distortion took on a life of its own as the institutions of slave trade and slavery further dehumanized, debased and attempted to destroy the humanity of the African spirit. In his *Medu Netcher: Divine Speech*, Dr. Jacob Carruthers specifically addresses this.

Star Jackson: Who was Isis?

Dr. Fred Monderson: Isis was the wife of Osiris. She was the great lady of magic and enchantment. She is the quintessential goddess of Egypt. She is seen everywhere and in the transposition of the Black Madonna and Child, this is Isis nursing Horus. There are many manifestations of Isis, even as Hathor.

Jack Bender: Luxor, it has been said, is the world's first university. How did it get this designation or is there a more ancient school of learning?

Dr: Fred Monderson: There is indeed a more ancient school of learning that fueled the thoughts, practices and ideas of the Middle Kingdom and New Kingdom when the great flowering of Egyptian civilization took place.

Myers (1900: 293-295) in discussing the four editions of the *Book of the Dead* mentions this first university where the first edition was compiled. He says the *Books of the Dead* can be divided into four editions for convenience. The first was: "I. That edition was made by the priests of the High School or University at *An* or *Annu*, the *On* of the Old Testament, the *Heliopolis* or City of the Sun, of Greek writers. The original texts of this edition are lost; but there is proof that they passed through editions and revisions as early as the Vth dynasty (circa 3721-3503 B.C.) This edition, as far as known, was always written in hieroglyphs. It may for convenience of reference be termed the Heliopolitan version. It is now known only through five copies found by MM. Mariette and Maspero, 1880-1884, inscribed on the walls of the passages and chambers inside of the Pyramid Tombs of the Pharaohs Unas, Teta, Pepi I, Mentu-em-sa-f, or Mirinri, and Pepi II, at Sakkara."

Then Myers gives particulars about the world's first intellectual center in Africa and the world. "This priestly University of the land of Mizraim, at *An or Annu,* the *On* of *Genesis* (XLI, 45, 50; xlvi, 20), the Aven of *Ezekiel* (XXX, 17), the Beth-Shemesh of *Jeremiah* (XLIII, 13), and *Samuel* (1 Sam., VI, 14, 18); the Heliopolis or City of the Sun of Strabo, Diodorus, Herodotus, Plutarch, Josephus, etc., as far we now know, formulated the earliest authorized version of the Books, which were afterwards put together for the use of the dead. The sacred Egyptian name of the city was Ha-Ra, the abode of the risen-sun, and of the deity Atum or Tum, the setting-sun, or sun of the other world: the abode of darkness or chaos proceeded, according to the archaic belief of that people, light. Here was also worshipped Shu, the deity of the Energy of Light, who was thought of as the son of Atum, Tum or Tmu; and Tefnut, the goddess of Humidity, his daughter; Nut, the sky; Seb, the earth; Set, Nephthys, Osiris, Isis also the Bennu-bird, according to Manetho, the Phoenix; and here the light-colored bull Mnevis, sacred to Atum, was worshipped as early as Kalechos or Ka-kau, II dynasty (circa 4515-4212 B.C.). This seat of learning appears to have been a power even in the reign of Mena, king of the Ist dynasty, assuming that he existed. It was a town famous for its learning and it was there, under the teaching of its priests, that Moses most likely obtained his learning and religious training; it was there Jeremiah wrote his *Lamentations*; it was a daughter of one of the priests whom Joseph married .... was taught the true length of the month and year; and there Aristotle, Plato, Solon, Pythagoras and Thales, sat at the feet of the *Hir seshta* and obtained knowledge which later, they expanded, idealized, formulated and glorified, as Greek wisdom, philosophy and learning. Its priests from the most remote period, were the great dignitaries of Ancient Egyptian theology, philosophy, mysticism and historic learning; its dogmas were accepted by the priesthood throughout the entire Egyptian Empire as correct, and its political importance was so great that, though never a large town, it furnished ten deputies, one third of the entire number of the Great Council which assisted the king, in the administration of justice throughout the entire kingdom. Here, Mer-en-Theuti, i.e., beloved by Thoth, called also Manetho; its chief priest, collected from its archives, at the command of Ptolemy II, Philadelphus, his history of the kings of Ancient Egypt. The inscriptions in the ancient Pyramids of Unas and Pepi show the veneration for and power in their time, of this great seat of archaic Egyptian thought and learning. Even the abode of the blest had its heavenly Annu, and in the heavenly Annu, the souls of the pious and wise were united to their glorified Ka and live face to face with the deity forever. The heavenly Annu was considered the source of all instruction coming from the divinity of man. This Annu of the Books of the Dead had not, however, a geographical position, but was purely an ideal creation like the heavenly Jerusalem."

QUINTESSENTIAL BOOK
"THE HOLY LAND"

"The religion of the University at Annu controlled largely that later expounded at Thebes, and that of the latter, was mostly copied from that anciently existing in the Northern kingdom."

Even further Myers (1900: 296-97) added: "I. Of the Ancient Recensions of Annu, or Heliopolis. On the walls of the corridors and in the tomb chamber, inside the Pyramid tomb of king Unas, fifth king of the Vth dynasty (circa 3536-3503 B.C.), near the Great Step-Pyramid of Sakkara, are hundreds of lines of texts of the most archaic books of the dead of the Recension of Annu. One of these reads: 'The bone and flesh are miserable which have not the writings: Behold, the writings of Unas are sealed with the great seal … Unas goes toward heaven, his spirits upon him, his books on his two sides, his talisman under his feet.' The inscriptions on the inside walls of the Pyramid of Pepi I, read: 'The Khus (1.9), come unto thee paying homage (unto thee), and they bow down, even to the ground at thy feet by reason of thy book, O Pepi (l. 20), in the cities of the *Saa* (i.e., the Sahu)… Hail, Pepi (l.21), thy book it is which worketh upon their hearts and thy name liveth upon earth…. (l.160). The heaven speak and the earth walketh by reason of thy book, O Osiris.' Also, 'The uraeus of this Pepi is upon his forehead, there is a magical writing on each side of this Pepi, the talisman of this Pepi is at his feet,' and so arrayed he enters heaven."

Frederick Maloney: What are the other three editions of the Book of the Dead?
Dr. Fred Monderson: According to Myers (1900: 295-96) these were: "II. The Theban Version: This was usually written on papyri in hieroglyphics, and was composed of really distinct books, each having its separate title, but no fixed position in the entire content, except as follows: certain collections appear to have been frequently grouped together, the first fifteen books appear to be distinct and were usually grouped together; to them Dr. Lepsius incorrectly attached a sixteenth, which is only a vignette; they have not, however, been discovered on any very ancient coffins or sarcophagi, but seem to be of more recent date than the other principal collections, but are more ancient than the additions from CXXIV to CLXV. Books XVII to LXII usually go together; also LXIV to CXXIV. After these come later additions, of which CXXV is the most ancient and important. The most ancient are, the XVIIth, which is complete in itself, the LXIV, the XXXB and the CXXXth."

FREDERICK MONDERSON

Holy Land Papyrus 13. Birds in a tree in all their beautiful splendor.

"Books XLII employ words which are in Book CVIII and some of those which are in Book CLIX. Some of the texts and divisions of Book CXXV appear to be of more modern date than others. Book XV is old, but subsequent to the reunion of the country under one monarch. It shows the sun crowned with the diadems of the North and the South. This version was much in vogue from the XVIIIth to the XXth dynasty (circa 1587-1200 B.C.) Although called, to distinguish it from No. I, the Theban Version, it is really the original composition of the priests and scribes of Annu, which was copied in subsequent dynasties. Amon-Ra, the great deity of Thebes, however, is not mentioned in it, except in supplementary books added after Book numbered CLXI, which Book likely ended the Canonical writing

QUINTESSENTIAL BOOK
"THE HOLY LAND"

of the collection, the Theban priests adding others, in some cases copies of old forms, and putting in the name of Amon-Ra, deity of Thebes."

"III. A Version not yet named, but somewhat familiar to the Theban written on papyri, and in the hieratic character, and also in hieroglyphs. This version was in vogue about the XXth dynasty. The arrangement of the Books has not, in it, as yet become definite."

"IV. The Saitic Version – In this, which was made likely before or during the XXVIth dynasty (circa 666-528 B.C.), the Books (Chapters) were arranged in a definite order. The copies are written sometimes in hieroglyphs, at other times in hieratic script. It was certainly in vogue from the XXVth dynasty to the end of the Ptolemaic era and later. The *Papyrus of Turin*, hereafter mentioned, is of about this epoch. See *Ante*, pp. 284, 287, 291."

Michael Sinclair: The sky is very clear. How did this aid science?
Dr. Fred Monderson: This is a very complex question for it involves not just astronomy but astrology as well. Herein lies the foundation of astrology as well as aiding the foundation of other branches of science.

Myers (1900: 445-447) has written: "We learn from Macrobius that in ancient times, and this most likely can be applied to Ancient Egypt, this time of happening of the Summer Solstice in the constellation of Cancer was called: 'The Gate of Men,' and new souls were considered as coming down into the sphere of our earth, from the upper treasury of souls, through it. The souls of human beings were considered to be in a spiritual and eternal stage of existence, before they were born in-closed in flesh, on this earth; and were assumed to be, in such prior condition, at first attached to the disk of the Sun. They were thought to proceed downward through the spheres of the different planets to that of the earth, getting certain qualities in the sphere of each planet. This idea is the foundation of Astrology and is very ancient. Joseph de Voisin says: "Souls are said to descend through cancer and to ascend through Capricorn. And this, some interpret thus: the souls descend through Cancer, because Cancer is the abode of the Moon, which is destined for generation (for the Moon rendered stronger in cancer, exerts her power to the greatest degree). They ascend through Capricorn, because Capricorn is the house of Saturn, and of contemplation, by which the soul is raised to heaven. Moreover they descend through Cancer because by Cancer's retrograde motion is signified a departure from perfection and a lapse to destruction."

"The happening of the Winter Solstice in the Sothic year, in the same year when the Summer Solstice was in Cancer, was in the zodiacal constellation Capricorn (i.e., the He-Goat) and the winter solstice was called "The gate of the gods." The spirits which had been in the human body ascended through it to the Psychostasia or Judgment, and if found pure, at this judgment, by Osiris and the Forty-two assisting judges, the spirits were asserted to proceed on the ascent to the Egyptian heaven, likely the assumed abode of Ra, the deity of Light. This last day of the month Mekhir, of the Book of the Dead No. CXXV was most probably considered as the day of the entrance of the spirit of the dead, on the journey to the Day of Judgment, when it is said, 'the Eye is full in Annu.'"

Holy Land Illustration 36. Abydos. Temple of the Kings. The King kneels before emblems of Osiris (left); and the Ibis on a standard (right).

"The last day of Mekhir, which was the Month of Harvest of the sacred Egyptian Sothic year, the 30th day of this month, was the last day of the VIth month of that year. In the Julian year it began December 17. The Egyptian therefore likely considered the last day of the Month of gathering the Harvest, as the Great Day of Rendering the Account, before Osiris and the Forty-two judges, of the good or evil works, done by the Ba of the mortals when in the flesh."

Cherise Maloney: How did the society in general respond to authority?
Dr. Fred Monderson: Authority was well respected in Ancient Egypt. This was a society with social, religious, administrative and labor hierarchies. So one would imagine adherence to authority. However, it also had a moral maxim attached to obeying authority. The Book of Ptah-Hotep insists on obeying authority. It asks

QUINTESSENTIAL BOOK
"THE HOLY LAND"

to "Show deference to a superior. Do not be annoyed because an authority is above thee." Like any other society, then, the Egyptians believed in respecting authority and cooperating in any task that is directed by one in authority.

Henrietta Potter: Can you further clarify differences between the Ba and the Ka?

Dr. Fred Monderson: The Ka was considered a double of the physical body that was embalmed and placed in the tomb. Myers (1900: 268-69) writes: "The Soul was called *Ba* or *Bai*; plur. *Baiu*. The word really means something like "sublime" or "noble," but has been usually translated by Egyptologists as "soul." This was the eternal part of the spiritual, which was thought to contain the elements necessary for the world-life of a man, such as judgment, conscience, etc., yet it was not considered as absolutely incorporeal. It was supposed to inhabit man's heart. The idea of it seems to be similar to that termed psyche by the Greeks. This Ba performed a pilgrimage in the netherworld, and was judged for the conduct of the man it inhabited in this world, by Osiris and the Forty-two judges. It was usually represented as a bird, especially as a human-headed sparrow hawk. It fluttered to and fro between this world and the next, and could pass into heaven and dwell with the perfected souls therein, also, sometimes visiting and conversing with the spiritual of the body or mummy, in its tomb .... It was believed to enjoy an eternal existence in heaven in a condition of glory. On the death of a man it left him so as to fly to the gods, with whom it abode when not united to the other spiritual parts of man, but it cannot be thought of, as having been separated absolutely from the Ka of the man in whose body it existed during his life, until it was decided at the Psychostasia before Osiris and the Forty-two judges, that the Ka should not be united to its Ba, and there are representations of the Ba waiting for the results of the weighing at the Psychostasia."

Bryce Menkheperre: Who is Goddess Ma'at and what is her symbol?

Dr. Fred Monderson: The symbol of Ma'at was the shape of the foundation of the Shrine of Osiris. The symbol of or crown of Ma'at was a feather. She is one of the Maati Goddesses and shares the name of a Hall in the place of judgment. In a note, Myers (1900: 287) explains: "Some Egyptologists deem 'The Hall of the Two Truths' to be that of Truth and Righteousness. It may be that the reference is to the prototypic Harmony or Real Truth of the Upper Celestial World, and to its lower copy, the Harmony or Phenomenal Truth of Our World. Maut, Maat has the meaning of the Harmony of everything; it is the beautiful, good and true, the Law and Order by which the entire universe exists." In a further note Myers (1900: 12-13) writes: "The Ma (or Maat) was the sacred emanation of, 'He who conceals His Name and who lives and sustains Himself by His Eye.' The Ma (Mat) says to one of the Ptolemies: 'I associate Myself with thy Majesty in all places in which thou art, and none separate Me from thee.'" "Truth" (or, Ma) was considered as "the daughter of the sun, attendant of Ammon, Eye of the Sun.' It is said of Osiris:

FREDERICK MONDERSON

'Truth, i.e., the Ma, is established for thee against thy enemies. Thoth has given it to thee. *Comp. Le Pantheon Egyptien*, by Paul Pierret, Paris, 1881, pp. 18 et seq. 104. The Ma, however, has a more elevated meaning than Truth as we usually understand the latter; it comprehends the entire and absolute, true harmony, law, and order, of the universe by which the latter exists; and it may have something to do with the pure and true prototypes or ideals of Egyptian metaphysics, and have the meaning of the True or Real in contrast to the Phenomenal."

George Washington: How then did these ancient Africans of Egypt view the possession of knowledge?

Dr. Fred Monderson: The ancient Africans of Egypt treasured knowledge! It was something to strive for. It was well respected, the method of how it was acquired was respected, and the whole philosophy of knowledge goes to the fiber of the society. Myers (1900: 30) says, according to the *Prisse Papyrus*: "To appear with honor before posterity, one should have reverence for knowledge, wisdom and moderation, and try to inspire love and not fear. God forbids us to terrify the feeble. The great man should always remember that he is only the dispenser of gifts from God" Ptah-Hotep says: "Be not haughty because of thy knowledge, none having perfection in Wisdom or artistic knowledge." Ptah-Hotep also says further: "If thou art powerful give thy respect to knowledge and calmness of speech. Command only so as to direct; not to be absolute (unnecessarily?) is to run into evil. Let not thy thoughts be haughty, that they (the subordinates) be not cast down. Make thy orders heard and thy replies penetrate; but speak without heat; let thy countenance be stern (serious?). As for the vivacity of an ardent heart, temper it; the man who is gentle overcomes obstacles. He who is agitated the entire day does not have a good moment, and he who amuses himself all day does not keep his fortune. Aim at the unconditional as (do) the pilots; (at one) time (one) is seated, and another works and applies himself to obey the commands."

Peter Monderson: Why have temples survived the ravages of time while other structures have not?
Dr. Fred Monderson: The temple was the house of the god which was to be a permanent structure. In its evolution, finally it was built of the most durable material which was stone. Domestic structures were for temporary sojourn so they were built with less costly and more readily accessible material which in this case was mud made into brick. While the stone resisted the ravages of time, mud brick was easily dissolvable. This is the same for the tomb in later, Middle and New Kingdom times. We must understand, however, mud brick was a formidable material and its uses in palaces, civic structures, temple enclosure walls and even fortresses attests to its usefulness.

Joshua Monderson: What was the philosophic purpose of the tomb?
Dr. Fred Monderson: Naturally the primary purpose of the tomb was to dispose of the dead. That is to house the physical body of the deceased. In time the style and

structure changed so that the body was housed in a simple hole in the ground in predynastic times and so remained for the poorest of the lower classes; these evolved into the more structured Abydos and Sakkara tombs for the Kings of the First and Second Dynasties, the Pyramids and Mastaba tombs of the Old Kingdom and to the more elaborate and decorated tombs in the Valley of the Kings, Valley of the Queens, Valley of the Nobles and Valley of the Artisans by the time of the New Kingdom.

Cherise Maloney: How would you characterize the purpose of the Abydos and Sakkara tombs of the Kings?
Dr. Fred Monderson: For the longest time a debate waged as to whether the Abydos or Sakkara royal tombs were the actual or a cenotaph or dummy tomb. Walter Emery excavated the Sakkara tombs and posited the view they were the actual ones and the Abydos the cenotaph. This has confused scholars for some time. However, "most people in the know" argued the Abydos tombs were the actual ones.

One of the fundamental problems regarding ancient Egypt, the eyewitness accounts of the ancients are disregarded and conveniently dismissed in some respects while other modern deductions are affirmed. The descriptions of Herodotus regarding the ancient Egyptians, as well as his observations on mummification are good examples. Other classical writers have expressed the same view but moderns conveniently dismiss them. Since the king was sovereign over the north and south it stands to reason he would have a second tomb but his real and actual tomb has to be at Abydos. Seti's temple at Abydos was oriented towards and dedicated to the kings buried at Abydos. This is as good an example as to determine those kings were actually buried there. There were temples there from the beginning of the First Dynasty and this may be associated with the sacred nature of these burials. Osiris does not become god of Abydos until after the Archaic Period, the first and second dynasties. As such we must believe Abydos held the bodies and Sakkara, cemetery of Memphis, the capital, contained cenotaphs or symbolic tombs.

That is enough for today. The field is wide open. Remember, if you go to the market or anywhere outside of the hotel, please try to travel in pairs at least and stay together. Have things done and return as soon as possible.

7.   Free Time

FREDERICK MONDERSON

Holy Land Photo 20. Kalabsha Temple of God Mendulese. In the Court, varied capitals and a winged disk with uraei. Notice how the abacus or die is centered and in turn centers the pieces of the architrave from one to the other, providing the bridge across the void in the Court, affording a better view of the varied capitals, architrave and winged disk with uraei.

8. Dinner

Joy Brown: Mr. Stewart, that was some recollection, you had today on the bus. Washington is such an exciting place to visit. Do many people who live in District of Columbia go to see the monuments?
Mr. John Stewart: Not sufficient. I don't think teachers do enough trips with kids. Most of them wait until practically the end of the school year and then do a few trips to keep the kids in line busy but I think tripping should begin very early in the school year.
Joy Brown: How many years did you teach public school?
Mr. John Stewart: Thirty years and loved every minute. Over the years I have had a few run-ins with some parents but the children were very pleasant. I don't remember meeting any of my former students and having them say anything negative to me.
Joy Brown: I guess you did a good job.
Mr. John Stewart: Yes, it's been said: "Science is organized knowledge."

QUINTESSENTIAL BOOK "THE HOLY LAND"

Mrs. John Stewart: After such an enlightening day, I will have a big dinner. Asantewaa, would you like to get a few people and let us do a little night shopping?
Joy Brown: Good idea. I will talk to a few of the ladies, only wish there were some guys who could go with us.
Mr. John Stewart: My stomach is not feeling well, but you ladies do be careful.
Star Jackson: Mr. Stewart, that first comment you made, had me thinking of a brother in New York, his name is Michael Hooper and he is with *Roots Revisited*. He takes kids to Africa, along the *Underground Railroad* trail and also to college campuses. He believes we wait too late to take children to Black College campuses and this has an effect on their educational development. He takes kids to college campuses as early as the sixth grade!
Mr. John Stewart: I say more power to Mr. Michael Hooper! That is very good what he is doing with the children. I only wish more educators would take that bold step.

Mrs. Marilyn James: Well Leonard, what do you think of today's temple visits?
Dr. Leonard James: I think it was excellent. That wonderful experience I have taught about all these years, finally I am able to visually experience both Karnak and Luxor temples.
Mr. Walter Brown: You know Leonard, I admire your wife. That many years of marriage and you two seems to have worked out your system so well, you act like a pair of well-oiled machines. Of course, my wife and I are well on our way to that level of wisdom and understanding in our relationship.
Mrs. Juliet Brown: That does not mean we don't have our differences. I stay on his case, whether it's about the house, children, myself or even his own habits and practices. I guess by doing that, I mean paying that much attention to him, that has held us together.
Dr. Leonard James: That I can see. As for Marilyn, what can I say or perhaps as the *Apocrypha* puts it: "The light that cometh from her wisdom never goeth out."

9. Lounge Discussion

Dr. Alexander Pushkin: Hi Michael. Glad you could join us. Can I get you something? Teddy and I are having a beer.
Michael Sinclair: A coke is good enough for me. I drank so much water and Kakadee (sorrel) today; I don't feel like drinking any other liquids. However, the coke will do.
Dr. Alexander Pushkin: Good. Waiter, can I have a coca-cola for my friend. So, let us continue this interesting education you are giving us. What is Africology?

FREDERICK MONDERSON

Michael Sinclair: Africology is the Afrocentric approach to the study of Black people. In Africa there are no Black people. There are Shona, Yoruba, etc. Only in the west do we have Black people. Also, only in the west do we have white people. In Europe we have English, French, Italian, and so on. However, where there may be whites, it's not the same as in Europe. In fact, a non-European white is probably not on the same level with those of Europe. For example, in Europe the Portuguese are considered white, albeit on the lower end of the spectrum. However, in places as Guyana and Trinidad, etc., they are not considered white but Portuguese. Consider colonialism restructured everything, particularly ethnological classification and this emanated from Europe. So you see African people cannot participate in a European mission to Africa and remain neutral. This has been the strategy of Europeans in Africa and it has undermined and destroyed that ancient tradition and culture. As such then, Afrocentricity is a self-conscious philosophy. Africanity, whose time has certainly come, and Afrocentric confrontation is what we do best. We take all comers! Afrocentric scholarship is global. It's in Nova Scotia, Ethiopia, Tanzania, Zaire and Ghana as well as the West Indies. Thus there is a global community of Afrocentric scholars even in a Eurocentric structure.

Teddy Cubia: You mean they are carrying the battle flag of racial intellectualism across the globe.

Michael Sinclair. Yes, that is true. It's like the Trinidadians are doing with Steel Pan music and Carnival, only they are doing it in a cultural context. Their intent is that everybody should celebrate carnival and the whole world should be dancing and listening to pan music!

Teddy Cubia: I think this is an appropriate time for me to give you a poem that I wrote in the early 1970s reflecting the struggles. It's called *Battle Cry*.

"Battle Cry"
By
Teddy Cubia

Black is Beautiful. This indeed is a revelation.
But beauty is not enough
For this new generation
For beauty alone
Will not achieve power
For the masses of Black men
Dying slowly every hour.
Men stripped of dignity, culture and name
Who now realize just who is to blame
For all the tribulations
Ever cast on us Blacks
Now my Brothers, now my Sisters
It's the time to Attack.

QUINTESSENTIAL BOOK "THE HOLY LAND"

Teddy Cubia: Let me say, I define attack as any effort that is designed to consciously raise the intellectual curiosity and cultural and historical awareness and sophistication of our people. All this can be extended to political and economic as well as educational empowerment, providing our people are all pulled up by their bootstraps, wherever they are.

Michael Sinclair: That was wonderful Mr. Cubia.

Teddy Cubia: I find this culture to be fascinating. I only wish I came here earlier in my life. Perhaps things would have been even better. That is not to say I am not happy with the way things turned out, but having this cultural understanding earlier, then my children and grandchildren would have benefited from it. I agree with you. But you know our people, and people in general, don't always have the money to travel extensively. That brings us to Dr. ben-Jochannan, who, very early in his career, in his own way, began exposing this rich culture to our people.

I know he suffered for this. But that is the breaks. He felt happy doing what he did, praising African culture and exposing Black people to its wonders. He saw African culture equal to all others and preached this, much to his detriment. However, no matter what, his people love Dr. Ben for what he did for them. That is all that matters.

Well, he did teach, as Thomas Carlyle (1795-1881) believed: "The great law of culture is: Let each become all that he was created capable of being." Of course, different people define culture differently. Jose Ortega y Gasset (1883-1955) extolled: "The choice of a point of view is the initial act of culture," and "Culture is not life in its entirety, but just the moment of security, strength and clarity."

Matthew Arnold (1822-1888) added: "The men of culture are the true apostles of equality." Further he argued: "Culture is then properly described not as having its origin in curiosity, but as having its origin in the love of perfection; it is a study of perfection."

May I just add, Charles Darwin (1809-1882) in his *Descent of Man* (1871) believed: "The highest possible stage in moral culture is when we recognize that we ought to control our thoughts." That must be my clue. I must turn in. Tomorrow will be a long day. I wish you good folks good night.

10. Hotel Room

Regina Hendricks: Michelliea, George promised to come by our room to further share some of his notes with us. He would certainly enjoy the view of our wonderful sunset across the Nile. We should have some form of refreshments to entertain him.

FREDERICK MONDERSON

Michelliea Georges: I think that would be nice. Perhaps we could order some drinks from the hotel. There is the doorbell. It may be he. Let me check. Hello George.
George Washington: Hi. How are you sisters doing this wonderful evening?
Regina Hendricks: Very well, thank you. While you are here, you can enjoy the wonderful view of the sun going down in the west.
George Washington: Why thank you. I have heard so much of this sunset I am sure to enjoy all the amenities of this evening. Nevertheless, let's get down to the note taking first of all. On September 11, 1975, I noted Demotic was a parallel to Hieroglyphic. Champollion (1790-1832) was one of the geniuses who worked to decipher Hieroglyphics. He discovered the cartouche of Cleopatra using hermophony, use of one sign for two or more letters. On September 14, 1822 he cracked the code. He realized Coptic is a derivative of Hieroglyphic. Assyriology is the study of Mesopotamia.

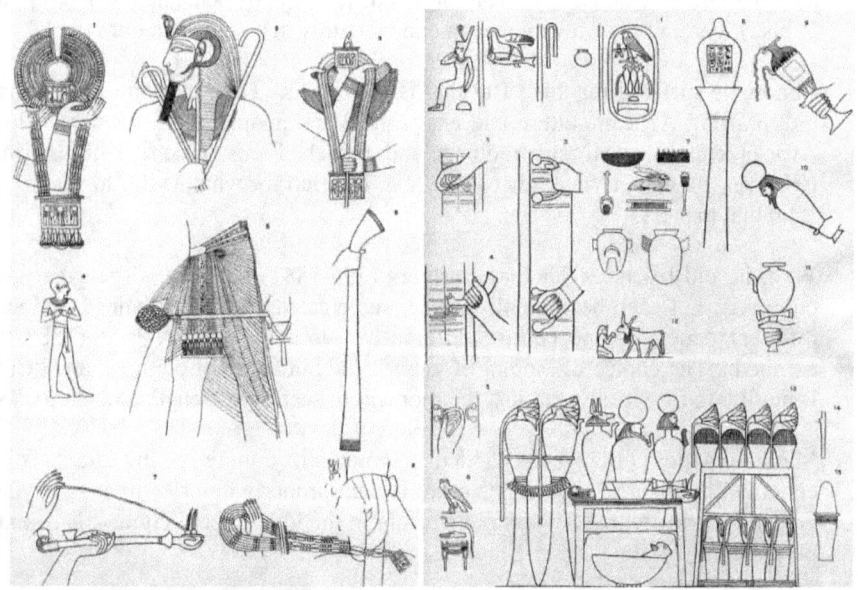

Holy Land Illustration 37. Abydos. Temple of the Kings. Clothing and Selected vases.

Meso-Potamos (Mesopotamia) is the land between the rivers, Tigris and Euphrates. There were no floods after the pre-dynastic period and this posed a problem for the people. The people had two rivers to contend with. With the floods, cities would be flooded. Without the floods no silt was washed down and fertilized the land. The people faced serious problems. By 2400 B.C. wheat comprised 16 percent of the harvest. By 2100 B.C. wheat was reduced to 2 percent of the harvest. By 200 B.C. no mention is made of wheat. Here's another

QUINTESSENTIAL BOOK "THE HOLY LAND"

way of looking at it. By 2400 B.C. there were 28 bushels of wheat; 2100 B.C., 1500 bushels of wheat; and 200 B.C., 10 bushels of wheat. Then I read about the Egyptian and Mesopotamian landscape in *Britannica*.

I was interested and disturbed when I read two statements by the historian Arnold Toynbee who said: "Geography has a profound effect upon the rise of a high culture." "An environment has a stimulus, and when people overcome that stimulus, civilization is produced." Then he said the most disturbing thing: "The Black race has never contributed anything to civilization." My analysis for that day is as follows: Champollion (1790-1832) can be looked upon as the man who most dramatically revolutionized the study of Egyptology for on September 14, 1822, he cracked the Code Hieroglyphic that had until then retarded any intensive Egyptological study. He studied the newly discovered Rosetta Stone and later discovered the cartouche of Cleopatra which he deciphered after extensive use of what was Hermophony, use of two or more letters for one sign.

It's getting late so I'll have that refreshment and tomorrow I will give you the other part, the **African Religious Thought Systems**, notes.
Regina Hendricks: That is wonderful. How can we ever thank you?
Michelliea Georges: You are not only handsome but very intelligent. I have a very cold drink for you. Are you sure you are not married.
George Washington: I was married but now I am single. But, I don't mind meeting a nice woman who knows how to treat a man well.
Regina Hendricks: Wow. You go, girl.
Michelliea Georges: Well, I will keep that in mind. See you tomorrow.
George Washington: Good night, ladies.

Day 4. VALLEY OF THE KINGS, DEIR EL BAHARI AND RAMESSEUM

1. Wake up

Esperanza Rodriguez. Good Morning, Mi Amor. Your schedule today takes you across the river to the Valley of the Kings, Hatshepsut's temple at Deir el Bahari and the Ramesseum, mortuary temple of Rameses II. I have reproduced your selection for the group and passed it out as they came down to Breakfast.

Dr. Fred Monderson: Thank you, my dear. I feel we will work very well together.

FREDERICK MONDERSON

Holy Land Photo 21. Native Egyptian Guide Showgi Abd Rady, "The Black," relaxes aboard a launch returning from the Temple of Isis (left) and Rocks in the River at Aswan.

"THE RAMESSEUM"

The Ramesseum or Mortuary Temple of Rameses II represents a splendid culmination of the building efforts of one of the greatest pharaohs to sit on the throne of ancient Egypt/Ta-Meri/Kemet. This wonderful architectural masterpiece, one of the largest temples of Egypt, is considered a classical representation of ancient Nile Valley building practice. It has been a subject of visitors' commentary and fascination for centuries and is equally a major attraction for modern tourists at Thebes. The mortuary temple was significant to the pharaoh for though he built to the gods, in this structure he built to himself, as a deity. In addition to the mortuary temple there were worship temples such as at Karnak and Luxor on the East Bank of the River at Thebes or Luxor. Nevertheless, the mortuary temple became such an essential feature of the pharaoh's next life; nearly every king, in the New Kingdom, built a mortuary temple. Seeking cosmological answers to human situations, the Egyptian looked to the heavens. In explaining this cosmic view, Maspero (1926: 111-112) wrote: "At the Ramesseum, at Edfu, Philae, Denderah, Ombos, and Esneh, the very depths of the firmament appeared to open, and reveal their inhabitants to the eyes of the faithful. There the celestial ocean displayed its waters, over which sailed the sun and moon, escorted by the planets, the constellations and decani, while the genii of months and of days marched in interminable succession. During the Ptolemaic period, signs of the zodiac, copied from the Greek, are found among astronomical figures of purely Egyptian origin."

QUINTESSENTIAL BOOK
"THE HOLY LAND"

Holy Land Photo 22. View of the Tombs of the Nobles from the Oberoi Hotel at Aswan (left); and view of the Oberoi Hotel from the Tombs of the Nobles across the river.

Hoefer, Youssef and Rodenbeck (1991) said of the Mortuary Temples of the West Bank at Thebes: "The innovative pharaohs of the 18th Dynasty broke with the pyramid tradition and began to have their tombs tunneled deep into the mountainside, hoping that they would thus avoid the depredations of tomb robbers. On the edge of the valley, at some distance from their final resting places, each one built his individual mortuary temple. Those of Hatshepsut, Seti I, Rameses II, and Rameses III still stand. Two colossi in the fields by the side of the road are all that remain of the Temple of Amenhotep III, the famous Memnon."

The architecture and decoration of these mortuary temples follows essentially the same lines as those of the temples already described, except that in the sanctuary area there is a false door through which the ka or spirit of the deceased king could pass freely back and forth to enjoy the offerings and ceremonies in his honor, as he became a deity at his death.

In fact, Bonechi (1994: 88) identifies mortuary temples in the Necropolis of Thebes as including those built by: "Seti I, Mentuhotep I, Thutmosis III, Hatshepsut, Ramses VI, Mentuhotep II, Amenophis II, Rameses II, Thutmosis IV, Merneptah, Ptolemaic period, and Rameses III, Thutmosis I, Amenhotep III, and Thutmosis II."

The Ramesseum is indeed a special and magnificent temple designed to convey to the world how great its builder really was. In explaining its makeup, Kamil (1980: 87) supplied the following: "The entire structure of the Ramesseum within the girdle-wall measures approximately 275 meters by 168 meters, though a large portion consisted of subsidiary buildings and storerooms." Regarding building methods, Maspero (1926: 54) provides an interesting contrast on the depth of the foundation of both east and west bank temples at Thebes. "At Karnak the foundation of the walls, columns, and obelisks are barely 7 to 10 feet in depth; at

Luxor, on the side close to the river, the walls rest on a gigantic substructure of three courses of masonry, each to them about 2 1/2 feet in height. At the Ramesseum the course of dried brick, which supports the colonnade, does not appear to measure more than 7 feet. These depths are very insignificant, but the experience of ages has proved them to be sufficient." Now, according to Pemberton (1992: 105) regarding this funerary structure, the Ramesseum: "Built on the conventional temple plan, it comprises two pylons, two colonnaded courts, a hypostyle hall, a series of antechambers and subsidiary rooms, a bark shrine and a sanctuary. In addition, there was a modest palace on the south of the first court, which connected with the court by means of a Window of Appearances. A small temple to Rameses' mother, Muttuya, adjoined the north side of the hypostyle hall." Seti I is also associated with this temple.

Several features of the Ramesseum lend to an understanding of the great glory of Egyptian architecture, and to its mighty warrior king. This ingenuity is particularly evident in such aspects as the use of the colonnade, the processional way and the clerestory, a library, school and statuary.

However, Bratton (1968: 189) believed: "The glory of the Ramesseum is the Hypostyle Hall. This reminds visitors of Karnak with its stately nave of great papyrus columns and clerestory windows. The pillars are profusely decorated with battle scenes. Three smaller hypostyle halls follow in succession on a straight axis, each one having eight pillars. The first of the three halls has a roof which is decorated with a map of the sky showing the position of the various constellations at the time of Rameses' coronation." Wayne (1990: 230) offered the following comparison regarding the buildings of Rameses II: "Many of his other works were rather crudely constructed but in this, his mortuary temple, he demanded perfection in the workmanship so that it would stand as an eternal testimony to his greatness."

Smith (1991: 167) pointedly states: "The Ramesseum was built by that indefatigable builder Rameses II to prove to the people of his day, and those of generations to the end of time, that this warrior king was the greatest that ever lived." Richardson and O'Brien (1991: 336) added: "The Ramesseum or mortuary temple of Rameses II was built to awe the pharaoh's subjects, perpetuate his existence in the afterlife and forever link him to Amun-United-With-Eternity. Had it remained intact, the Ramesseum would doubtless match his great sun temple of Abu Simbel for monumental grandeur and unabashed self-glorification." Campbell (1996: 85) also adds: "The Osiride colossi which punctuate the facade of the Ramesseum are an indication of the funerary nature of the Temple of Rameses II." Even further, Campbell (1996: 432) continued: "It was started at the beginning of his reign and took twenty years to complete." Again, Campbell (1996: 451) could add: "Three thousand workers toiled to provide stone for the

QUINTESSENTIAL BOOK "THE HOLY LAND"

Ramesseum." Langenscheidt (1993: 174-75) explained: "It also included a kind of temple school in which scribes and painters were trained."

"In the *Second Antechamber*, once the temple library, only four of the original eight columns have survived. The remains of relief on the walls depict the worship of various gods and the king making offerings to Ptah and Re."

Holy Land Photo 23. Aswan. The Nile as viewed from the balcony of the Old Cataract Hotel.

Erman (1995: 186) informed of a book entitled *Papyrus Hood* and also another papyrus in Moscow concurs in his statement: "It must have been also used in the above-mentioned school attached to the Ramesseum, and its title at least occurs on the verso of a papyrus in Cairo."

Even further, according to Erman (1995: 186-187) in assessing educational practice by which the young were schooled in ancient Egypt/Kemet: "When the schoolboy had finished with this elementary course of instruction, and was entered as 'scribe' in some administration, he received there also yet further instruction, and that at the hands of an older official, possibly his immediate superior. While undergoing this higher education, the pupil has still to write out model compositions, though not, as heretofore, a few lines a day only, but larger portions, in one case three pages a day. What the pupil thus wrote out his teacher corrected in the margin of the papyrus, unfortunately but seldom paying attention to the nonsense which the pupil had written, but so much the more to the shape of his characters; we might really think that we are merely concerned with an exercise in calligraphy. Of course it was not that alone, and the contents of most of these 'school manuscripts' clearly show what objects were actually had in view: education on one side, and training in commercial style and in orthography on the other. The orthography was no light matter, for scarcely any system of writing provides so many possibilities for mistake as the hieroglyphic. How the writing of the individual word was imparted to the schoolboys can still be seen in a book which must have been much used in the schools, and which 'the scribe of the God's Book in the House of Life, Amenemope, son of Amenemope, devised.'"

Holy Land Photo 24. View of the surrounding terrain from the Old Cataract at Aswan (left); and view of the rocks in the river that makes much of this area impassable at Aswan. Notice the little boat with people in the center of the right picture.

This notion of copying was not limited to instruction of pupils for it was also done by adults, in fact, kings. Rameses III so loved his namesake Rameses II that he imitated him in his name and works, particularly his mortuary temple. As a matter of fact, McGrath (1982: 182) wrote regarding the Ramesseum: "This is the monument on which Rameses III based his Medinet Habu temple, but it hasn't withstood the trials of time as well as its copy. There are just some bits of the walls and pylons, and lots of columns still standing."

According to McGrath (1982: 192) who wrote further: "The temple's two pylons are mostly ruined; you enter the temple from the north side, behind the second one. If you turn to the left into the remains of the first courtyard, you'll see strewn across a large area the rocks that once have been over 50 feet tall, so it didn't quite match up to the 65-foot height of his statues at Abu Simbel. Behind the second courtyard, through which you entered the temple, there's the usual array of hypostyle hall, offering rooms, and sanctuary. Again, most of these are in ruins. But all around the temple are structures, which made this place unusual. It was not just a funeral temple with an attached palace like Medinet Habu, but also a center for craftsmen and artisans of all types. Around the main temple buildings are the

QUINTESSENTIAL BOOK "THE HOLY LAND"

remains of brick structures which served as workshops, storerooms, and maybe even residences for the workers."

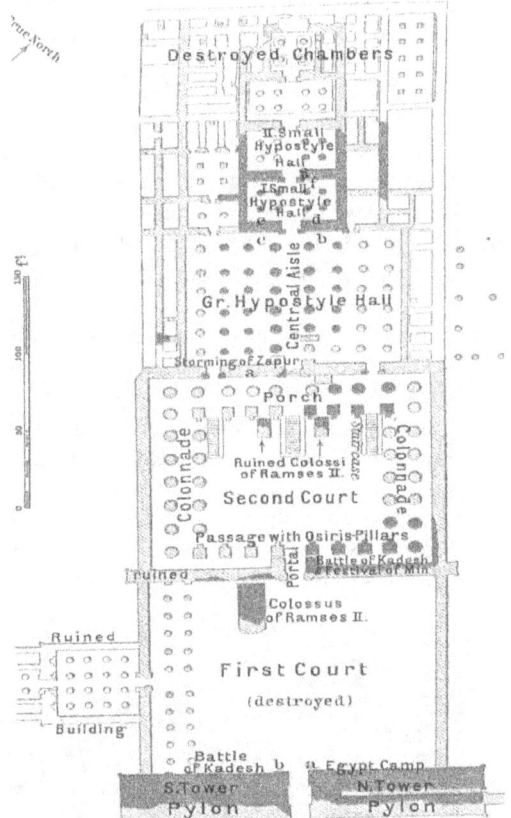

Holy Land – Plan of the Ramesseum, Mortuary Temple of Rameses II, Thebes.

Yoyote (1963: 238-239) instructs the visitor: "Two well-known features at this site should be noted: the torso and broken parts of the red granite colossus which showed 'Rameses, Son of Sovereigns' 58 ft high and weighed 1,000 tons, and the very well preserved temple storehouses, the brick vaultings which are in line with the back of the enclosure." Richardson and O'Brien (1991: 336) inform us again: "Nineteenth-century writers knew the ruins as the Memnonium. The present name only caught on late last century, by which time the Ramesseum had been plundered for statuary - not least the seven-ton head of one of its fallen colossi, now in the British Museum. Yet its devastation lends romance to the conventional

FREDERICK MONDERSON

architecture, infusing it with the pathos that moved Harriet Martineau to muse how 'violence inconceivable to us has been used to destroy what art inconceivable to us had erected.'" Yoyote (1963: 238) pointed out in the statement: "The 'Mansion of Millions of Years of the king Usi-ma-R,' 'chosen of Re,' 'who is united at Thebes, in the domain of Amun on the west of Thebes,' was called more simply 'The Ramesseum' by XIXth century scholars."

Michael Haag (1987: 244-245) mentions the workmen's strike at the Ramesseum that is probably the first such work stoppage in history. "The area was filled with vaulted brick storehouses, now entirely ruinous, which were once invaded, as is known from an extant papyrus, by desperate tomb workers who had not been paid for two months: 'We have reached this place because of hunger, because of thirst, without clothing, without oil, without fish, without vegetables! Tell Pharaoh, our good lord, about it, and tell the vizier, our superior, to act so that we may live.'"

Of course, as all temples associated with this pharaoh, his famous encounter with the Hittites in the Battle of Kadesh is represented here as at such places as Luxor, Karnak, Abu Simbel, Beit Wali, etc. Eames (1992: 233) puts it this way when he wrote regarding Rameses II: "His favorite theme was his famous alliance with the Kings of the Hittites, as depicted on the great pylon that forms the eastern entrance to the Ramesseum. Another series of reliefs concern the festival of Min. The pharaoh was borne on a richly-decorated carrying-chair, led by priests and soldiers, and followed by his sons and courtiers, to witness sacrifices and to watch the release of four birds to fly to the corners of the earth to carry the royal tidings."

Holy Land Illustration 40. Meydum Geese, one of the earliest paintings from the Old Kingdom; and Winged Sun-Disk, Symbol of the Sun-God (below).

QUINTESSENTIAL BOOK
"THE HOLY LAND"

Kamil (1996: 79) provided an interesting summary of the famous encounter. "The history of the battle may be summarized as follows: Rameses II's objective was to capture the Hittite stronghold at Kadesh on the Orontes River in Syria. He encountered little resistance until he approached the Northwest of Kadesh, when his intelligence brought two prisoners of war (who were in fact, spies). They told Rameses that the Hittite King Mutwallis had retreated in fear of the advancing Egyptian army, and Rameses II was delighted to hear this. Without taking even the most elementary precautions, he pitched camp, making ready for his march on Kadesh the next day. But the Hittite army lay hidden beyond the crest of a hill. They took Rameses completely by surprise and, in fact, his first brigade was completely cut off from the rest of his forces. It was fortunate for Rameses that the Hittite army was not as well organized as the Egyptian. After several chariot charges, and timely arrival of his other battalions, the tables were turned, allowing Rameses to drive the enemy back. Although, he did not achieve his objective, Kadesh, neither did he suffer a defeat."

However, though parts of the Ramesseum have not withstood the ravages of time, the essential features of the temple are intact and enable the visitor to grasp some of the grandeur of this structure and the great builder. Woldering (1963: 189) believed: "The remains that have survived of the pylon, hypostyle hall and massive Osiride pillars still evoke an impression of the monumental effect this magnificent building must have had upon contemporaries." Even more, rivaling Thutmose III and Amenhotep III, prolific builders themselves, Rameses left specimens of his architectural imprint all over the land from and beyond Aswan towards Luxor and Cairo. White (1970: 177) explained: "Rameses II (1298-1232), Seti's son, has always bulked large in accounts of ancient Egypt. Early Egyptologists bestowed on him the title of 'the Great,' for he bequeathed to posterity a series of monuments executed on a staggering scale. Among them were his rock temples in the Sudan, the Ramesseum, at Thebes, the completed hypostyle hall at Karnak, extensive additions to Luxor and the reconstruction of the buildings of his forerunners and an untiring fabricator of obelisks and colossal statues. His prenomen and nomen, Usermaatra-Ramses, were corrupted by Greek writers into Ozymandias. 'Look on my works, ye mighty, and despair!'"

Rameses II, son of Seti I and grandson of Rameses I ruled during the Nineteenth Dynasty, New Kingdom. Comprising the second longest reign in Nile Valley history, Rameses II had been ruler, warrior, general, builder, father, husband, high priest, and divinity, patron of the arts and sciences who littered the landscape of his glorious country with a mighty array of wonderful civil, military, religious and mortuary structures that still baffles the imagination. Ruffle (1977: 86) comments on the relationship between the early Ramesside kings and their cooperative nature in the statement: "Seti and his father Rameses I shared a temple near the approach to the Valley of the Kings at Gurneh, but Seti and Rameses II also built important temples at Abydos." White (1980: 15) said this about the young monarch:

"Here is a description of the solemn moment when King Seti I decided to adopt the Crown Prince, who was about 15-years-old at the time, as his co-ruler: 'The Universal lord himself [i.e. King Seti] magnified me whilst I was a child until I became ruler. He gave me the land while I was in the egg, the great ones smelling the earth before my face. Then I was inducted as eldest son to be Hereditary Prince upon the throne of Geb [the earth-god] and I reported the state of the Two Lands as captain of the infantry and the chariotry. Then when my father appeared in glory before the people, I being a babe in his lap, he said concerning me: 'Crown him as king that I may see his beauty whilst I am alive.' And he called to the chamberlains to fasten the crowns upon my forehead. 'Give him the Great One [the uraeus-serpent] upon his head,' said he concerning me.'"

Where he did not build for self, he repaired or improved the work of others and he is also credited with appropriating the work of still more. Maspero (1926: 57) shows how despite the time of the entire great artistic and architectural flowering there were imperfections in building practice: "The architect did not give sufficient attention to superintending the working or the laying of the blocks and would allow the vertical joints to come immediately over each other for two or three courses. When utilizing materials from ruined edifices he would not trouble to work them into shape; round shafts of older columns were thus mixed with rectangular blocks in the walls of the Ramesseum."

Nevertheless, the monarch and his workers, his superintendents and craftsmen and their architectural achievements have certainly added to their names and his name as universally household words relating to the ancient African holy land, Tawi/Egypt/Ta-Meri/Kemet, along the Nile River in North East Africa.

After the stupendous accomplishments of the Eighteenth Dynasty, the Nineteenth or first Ramesside Dynasty, attended to the lingering problems facing the society. Moving beyond the chaos at the end of the religious conflict that had wreaked such havoc, particularly at Thebes and throughout the empire, the Ramessides restored much of the glory of the past and contributed their share of magnificence that further embellished the fame and fortune of ancient Tawi/Kemet/Ta-Meri/Egypt.

Nevertheless, Chancellor Williams (1996: 112) points out: "Our references to dynasties formed by alliances between two groups against a third could be misleading to those who failed to grasp what had been said about the changing ethnic character of the dynasties over many centuries. From Fifth and Sixth Dynasties on, we have pointed out; Asian penetration through the 'royal marriage

QUINTESSENTIAL BOOK
"THE HOLY LAND"

route' caused the succeeding dynasties with few exceptions to become increasingly mixed. Often they were only predominantly Asian or Egyptian (Afro-Asian). The founders of the Eighteenth Dynasty, like many similar instances, illustrate the reality of the process. For it is well known that the famous Queen Nefertari was "all-black," while her equally great husband, Ahmose I was mulatto (Egyptian). So that the Eighteenth, like the great Nineteenth Dynasty of the Ramses, was predominantly black, not all-black."

So much has been written about the art and architecture of the Ramesside times. The colonnade played an important role in this period, and nowhere is it more elegantly displayed than at the Ramesseum. Base, shaft, capital, abacus, architrave all found full employment in this structure. The bell shaped capital is also known as campaniform, and these so splendidly adorn the great halls at the Ramesseum.

Holy Land Photo 25. Aswan. The Old Cataract Hotel as seen from the Nile.

In this regard, Maspero (1926: 65) has supplied a description in the following: "Round the neck of the bell-shaped capital is a row of leaves similar to those at the base, and from these spring stems of lotus and papyrus in flower and bud. The height of the capital and its projection vary according to the taste of the architect. At Luxor the campaniform capitals measure 11 ½ feet in diameter at the base, 17¼ feet at the top, and 11½ in height. At Karnak in the hypostyle hall the height is 12½ feet, and the greatest diameter 21 feet. A square die surmounts the whole. This is fairly low, and almost completely masked by the curve of the capital. In rare instances, as in the small temple of Dendera, the die is higher, and on each face is sculptured in relief a figure of the god Bes. This column with campaniform

FREDERICK MONDERSON

capital is most usually employed in the central aisles of hypostyle halls, as at Karnak, the Ramesseum and Luxor; but it is not confined to that purpose, and it is to be seen in the porticoes of the Fifth Dynasty valley temples at Abusir, and those of Medinet Habu, Edfu, and Philae."

Today, their artifacts are scattered across the globe and in this way, these great Africans can be considered to have achieved the immortality they set out to create.

Breasted (1923: 443-444) commented on the architectural proliferation that characterized the exploits of this warrior pharaoh whose fortunes enabled his building efforts in praise of mighty Amun-Ra, king of the gods. "Of his buildings at Heliopolis nothing remains, and only the scantiest fragments of his temples at Memphis have survived. We have already noticed his extensive building

Holy Land Photo 25a. Sign indicating the aerial panorama of the complex of Karnak's temples - @ 2001.

QUINTESSENTIAL BOOK
"THE HOLY LAND"

operations at Abydos, in the completion of his father's mortuary temple, another beautiful sanctuary for his own mortuary service, known to all visitors at Thebes as the Ramesseum; a large court and pylon in enlargement of the Luxor temple; while, surpassing in size all buildings of the ancient or modern world, his architects completed the colossal colonnaded hall of the Karnak temple, already begun under the first Rameses, the Pharaoh's grand-father. Few of the great temples of Egypt have not some chamber, hall, colonnade or pylon which bears his name, in perpetuating which the king stopped at no desecration or destruction of the ancient monuments of the country. A building of king Teti of the Sixth Dynasty furnished material for Rameses' temple at Memphis; he ransacked the pyramid of Sesostris II at Illahun, tore up the pavement around it and smashed its beautiful monuments to obtain materials for his own neighboring temple at Heracleopolis. In the Delta he was equally unscrupulous in the use of Middle Kingdom monuments, while to make room for his enlargement of the Luxor temple he razed an exquisite granite chapel of Thutmose III, reusing the materials, with the name of Thutmose thereon turned inward. Numberless were the monuments of his ancestors on which he placed his own name. But in spite of these facts, his own legitimate building was on a scale quite surpassing in size and extent anything that his ancestors had ever accomplished."

Holy Land Tourist Day Extravaganza Art 1. The stage background decoration for the "2012 World Tourist Day Festival" at the Luxor Theater, Saturday September 30, 2012.

FREDERICK MONDERSON

Holy Land Tourist Day Extravaganza Art 2. The Maestro instructs the band; and the troupe begins their workout on stage.

Breasted (1923: 460-461) further painted a lively picture of Rameses that lets the observer look into the nature of the man called "Rameses the Great."

"The young Pharaoh under whom these momentous transitions were slowly taking place in dealing with them for us to discover the manner of man he was. For his records are almost all of sacerdotal origin, and in them all the priestly adulation of the time, with its endless reiteration of conventional flattery, prevails so largely, or we may say often so exclusively that we can discern little individuality through the mass of meaningful verbiage. His superb statue in Turin is proven by his surviving body to be a faithful portrait, showing us at least the outward man as he was. In person he was tall and handsome, with features of dreamy and almost effeminate beauty, in no wise suggestive of the manly traits, which he certainly possessed. For the incident at Kadesh showed him unquestionably a man of fine courage with ability to rise to a supreme crisis; while the indomitable spirit evident there is again exhibited in the tenacity with which he pushed the war against the great Hittite empire and carried his conquests, even if not lasting, far into northern Syria. After his nearly fifteen years of campaigning, in which he more than redeemed the almost fatal blunder at Kadesh, he was quite ready to enjoy the well-earned peace. He was inordinately vain and made far more ostentatious display of his wars on his monuments than was ever done by Thutmose III. He loved ease and pleasure and gave himself up without restraint to voluptuous enjoyments. He had an enormous harem, and as the years passed his children multiplied rapidly. He left over a hundred sons and at least half as many daughters, several of whom he himself married."

QUINTESSENTIAL BOOK
"THE HOLY LAND"

Holy Land Tourist Day Extravaganza Art 3. Two different scenes of six and eight men in the presentation of part of a wonderful evening of entertainment.

"He thus left a family so numerous that they became a Ramesside class of nobles whom we still find over four hundred years later bearing among their titles the name Ramses, not as a patronymic, but as the designation of a class or rank. Unable, perhaps, to find suitable wives of rank and wealth for his army of sons, one of them, as we have seen, received the daughter of a Syrian ship-captain. Ramses took great pride in his enormous family and often ordered his sculptors to depict his sons and daughters in long rows upon the walls of his temples. The sons of his youth accompanied him in his wars, and according to Diodorus one of them was in command of each of the divisions of his army. His favorite among them was Khamwese, whom he made High Priest of Ptah at Memphis. But his affection included them all, and his favorite wives and daughters appear with noticeable frequency upon his monuments."

Holy Land Tourist Day Extravaganza Art 4. The male dancers are joined by a female and now the program gets more interesting.

Maspero (1904, V: 236-239) has written: "Rameses, having completed the funerary chapel of Seti at Qurneh upon the left bank of the river, then began to think of preparing the edifice destined for the cult of his 'double' - that Ramesseum whose majestic ruins still stand at a short distance to the north of the

FREDERICK MONDERSON

giants of Amenhotep. Did these colossal statues stimulate his spirit of emulation to do something yet more marvelous? He erected here, at any rate, a small more colossal figure. The earthquake, which shattered Memnon, brought it to the ground and fragments of it still strew the soil where they fell some nineteen centuries ago. There are so many of them that the spectator would think of himself in the middle of a granite quarry. The portions forming the breast, arms, and thighs are in detached pieces, but they are still recognizable where they lie to each other."

Holy Land Tourist Day Extravaganza Art 5. A one man extravaganza of dazzling showmanship, one has to wonder how this "Spinning Man" does not lose his balance.

"The head has lost nothing of its characteristic expression, and its proportions are so enormous, that a man could sleep crouched up in the hollow of one of its ears as if on a sofa. Behind the court overlooked by this colossal statue lay a second court, surrounded by a row of square pillars, each having a figure of Osiris attached to it. The god is represented as a mummy, the swathings throwing the body and limbs into relief. His hands are freed from the bandages and are crossed on the breast, and hold respectively the flail and crook; the smiling face is surmounted by an enormous headdress. The sanctuary without the buildings attached to it has perished, but enormous brick structures extend round the ruins, forming an enclosure of storehouses. Here the priests of the 'double' were accustomed to dwell with their wives and slaves, and here they stored up the products of their domains - meats, vegetables, corn, fowls dried or preserved in fat, and wines procured from all the vineyards of Egypt."

QUINTESSENTIAL BOOK
"THE HOLY LAND"

Holy Land Tourist Day Extravaganza Art 6. In full effect; and finished and satiated, the hero prepares to receive his well-deserved applause.

Holy Land Tourist Day Extravaganza Art 7. The "Stick Dance" is a fascination thing to behold for it begs the question, "How is it with that much pounding the stick does not crack or splinter?" and then it the Ladies turn to get in the act.

Holy Land Tourist Day Extravaganza Art 8. Everyone having participated, it is time to stand together and be inundated with applause for an outstanding performance.

FREDERICK MONDERSON

Holy Land Photo 26. Aswan. Egyptian deities as represented in the Dining Hall of the Oberoi Hotel.

QUINTESSENTIAL BOOK "THE HOLY LAND"

Holy Land Tourist Day Extravaganza Art 9.
Entertainment over, the Governor (center) and other dignitaries join Native Guide Showgi Abd el Rady and American author Dr. Fred Monderson for picture taking; and, Dr. Monderson poses with three of the musicians who supplied the exquisite musical accompaniment to the performance honoring World Tourist Day celebrations.

Rameses I, *Nile Year* 2937-2939 (Murnane c. 1293-1291 B.C.), was the founder of the XIX Dynasty after the confusion of the Amarna Heresy. The Ramesside Kings of this era were successful in adding luster to the golden age. They restored the primacy of Amun of Thebes, continued the imperialist policies of the past and relished in prosperity. Extensive and meaningful building projects were undertaken. After this time, however, the world began to change significantly. Whereas in the past, Pharaonic troops carried the sword to the world, the legacy could not be continued by their successors. The later Ramesside kings could not hold back the inevitable hordes that had scores to settle with the Ta-Meri (Egypt). The weak kings of this era could not stem this tide and the nation entered into a relative, though not inevitable, decline that lasted for another thousand years.

REFERENCES

Bonechi. *Art and History of Egypt.* Florence, Italy: Casa Editrice Bonechi, 1994.
Bratton, Fred Gladstone. *A History of Egyptian Archaeology.* New York: Thomas Y. Crowell, 1968.
Breasted, James H. *A History of Egypt: From the Earliest Times to the Persian Conquest.* New York: Charles Scribner's Sons, (1905) 1923.
Budge, E. A. Wallace. *A Book of the Kings of Egypt.* London: 1903.
Campbell, David. *Egypt. Everyman's Guide.* London: David Campbell Publishers, Ltd., (1995) 1996.
Cottrell, Leonard. *Egypt.* New York: Oxford University Press, 1966.
Eames, Andrew. *Insight Guides: The Nile.* Hong Kong: APA Publications, 1992.
Erman, Adolf. *Ancient Egyptian Poetry and Prose.* New York: Dover Publications, Inc., (1923) 1995.

Haag, Michael. *Guide To Egypt*. London: Michael Haag, 1987.
Kamil, Jill. *Luxor: A Guide to Ancient Thebes*. New York: Longman, (1973) 1980.

_____. *Upper Egypt and Nubia*. Cairo: Egyptian International Publishing Company, Longman, (1983) 1996.

Holy Land Photo 27. Colorful Feluccas docked at the wharf at the Oberoi Hotel.

Langenscheidt. *Self-Guided Egypt*. New York: Langenscheidt Publishers, (1973) 1990.
Maspero, Gaston. *A Manual of Egyptian Archaeology*. New York: Putnam's Sons, 1926.

_____. *History of Egypt, Chaldea, Syria, Babylonia, and Assyria*. XII Volumes. London: Grollier Society, 1904.
McGrath, Nancy. *Frommer's Dollarwise Guide to Egypt*. New York: Simon and Schuster, (1980) 1982.
Murnane, William C. *The Penguin Guide to Ancient Egypt*. New York: Penguin Books, 1983.
"The Osireion." *American Journal of Archaeology* XVII (1913: 98-99).
Pemberton, Delia. *Ancient Egypt: Architectural Guide for Travelers*. San Francisco: Chronicle Books, 1992.
Petrie, William Matthew Flinders. *A History of Egypt*. 3 Volumes. London, 1905.
Richardson, Dan and Karen O'Brien. *Egypt: The Rough Guide*. London: Harrap Columbus, Ltd., 1991.
Ruffle, John. *The Egyptians*. Ithaca, New York: Cornell University Press, 1977.
Smith, Fay. *Egypt At Cost*. New York: Little Hill Press, 1991.
Wayne, Scott. *Egypt and the Sudan*. Berkeley, Calif.: Lonely Planet, (1987) 1990.

QUINTESSENTIAL BOOK
"THE HOLY LAND"

White, J. E. Manchip. *Ancient Egypt: Its Culture and History.* New York: Dover Publications, (1952) 1970.

_____. *Everyday Life in Ancient Egypt.* New York: Perigee Books, (1963) 1980.

Williams, Chancellor. *The Destruction of Black Civilization.* Chicago: Third World Press, (1987) 1996.

Woldering, Irmgard. *The Art of Egypt: The Time of the Pharaohs.* New York: Greystone Press, 1963.

Yoyote, Jean in Georges Posener's *A Dictionary of Egyptian Civilization.* London: Methuen and Co., Ltd., 1959.

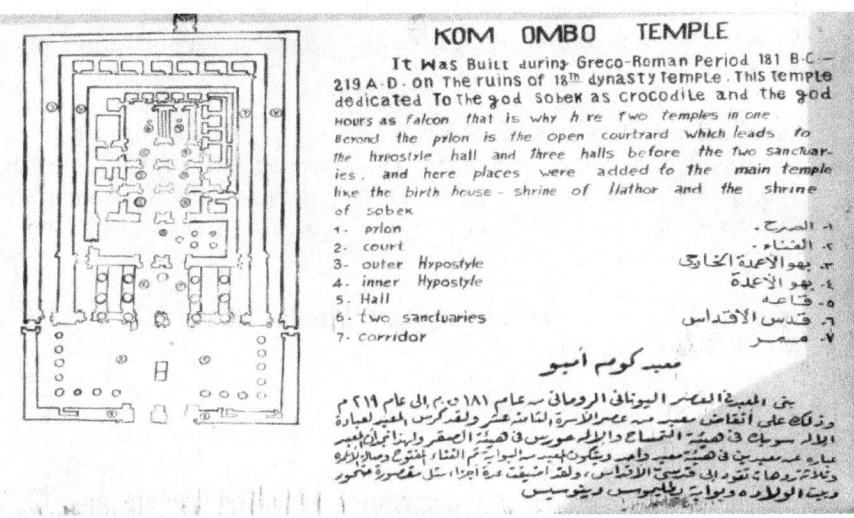

Holy Land Photo 28. Plan of Kom Ombo Temple of Elder Horus (Haroeis) and Sobek the Crocodile. Illustrated are a Pylon, Court, Outer and Inner Hypostyles, Hall, two Sanctuaries and corridors.

2. Breakfast

Dr. Alexander Pushkin: How are you good people this wonderful day? Today we make our way to the Valley of the Kings to behold the majestic history of those great African Egyptian men and women who were such significant players on the world stage way back then.

Mrs. Alexander Pushkin: My sweet, I am with you but my stomach is not feeling so good. How are you this morning, Teddy?

FREDERICK MONDERSON

Teddy Cubia: I am fine, my sister. Today I feel like eating a very big breakfast. I am having peaches, oranges, watermelon, and cocktail. Two eggs scrambled in an omelet with toast, apple juice and coffee. Also, waiter, may I have a bottle of water for the road. Thanks.

Michael Sinclair: At a lecture on November 3, 1992, Dr. Asante spoke about how the Afrocentric idea forced others to stand up and take notice. He argued that Afrocentrists have been reinterpreting the intellectual history of Egypt. They have argued that Nubia is "Egypt's rival in Africa." The origin of civilization may be somewhere in Zaire, Central Africa.

He asked the question: 'Why did DuBois organize a Pan African Congress in Manchester, England?'
Then he answered. Manchester was the heart of the cotton industry. It was also the heart of the labor movement. Engel was at Manchester. This made it the center of British Marxism. The Guardian, England's most progressive newspaper was also here.

Again, did capitalism produce racism?
The answer was: Marx was a racist. The American economy was based on slave labor, reproduction of a knowledge pattern. Thoughts based on people's culture dictate their actions. Marxist analysis is a subject of 15th century white supremacy. Marx's analysis of capital is excellent.

Race, culture, class are equally significant. In the US the principal problem for W.E.B. DuBois, was race.

We should support the Irish struggle based not on race, but on economics.

He was asked: Why do the Irish not support Black liberation in the US?
Ans. In Ireland it's economic. As a third world country, the Irish support all third world nations in their economic struggles. However, in the US the issue changes to one of race first then economics, because of the principal position of race in this culture.

All scholarship has an explicit or implicit theoretical foundation.
All writing has a point but the sharper the point the more definite.

Defend only the defensible. Malcolm said 'Never defend the indefensible.' You must have a fallback position.

All intellectual work must have humanity in mind. First help Africans. Second, help other oppressed persons. Third, help all humanity. Naturally, the disabled, widows, orphans, etc., come in for their share of help.

African people must have information as agents of history.

QUINTESSENTIAL BOOK "THE HOLY LAND"

Anticipate your enemies.

The Melanin issue is problematic.

Afrocentrists do not believe in the melanin theory. We have melanin. This is not defensible.

Don't defend another person's paper or research. Don't be put in a position to defend an indefensible position.

Afrocentricity and Afrocentrists cannot argue the biological question. Still, in a way you can say there are many closet melaninists.

Diopian analysis is multidisciplinary, thus, it is simply a method. Afrocentrists search out political, social, economic and historical issues that can be discussed precisely.

Walter Brown: How're you folks doing this morning? How is today's writing coming, Dr. James?
Dr. Leonard James: Well! From the earliest times scholars and travelers have been fascinated with the study of Egyptian culture, the esoteric symbolism of the hieroglyphics and the wonderful majesty of the experience. Evidence indicates New Kingdom visitors from Thebes were in Memphis and Sakkara shining an intrinsic appreciation for the culture. Even Abu Simbel has inscriptional evidence of its visitors during ancient times.

Nearly fifteen hundred years after the last Egyptian inscriptions were written on the Island of Philae, interest in this antique culture was again jolted by discovery of the Rosetta Stone in 1799. During that age of antiquarian inquiry several scholars began attempts at decipherment of the tri-lingual inscription. The principals were De Sacy, Young and Champollion. The latter was most successful and by 1822 he had deciphered the ancient script. He began working feverishly but within ten years he was dead in 1832. After this many took up the study and for the next half century the field of Egyptology began to take shape. Garner Wilkinson, Bunson, Birch, Chabas, all began to study the history, culture and apply their linguistic skill in translating the language and writing books to move the study along. To reiterate, early Egyptologists were motivated by establishing connections between Egypt and Biblical history.

FREDERICK MONDERSON

 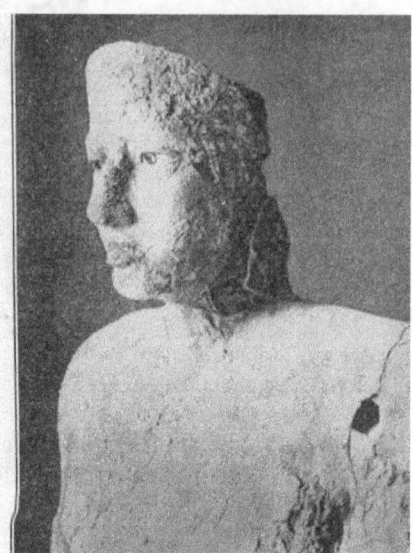

Holy Land Illustration 39. Portrait of King Khafre, builder of the second Pyramid of Ghizeh; and head of royal statue of bronze in the Pyramid Age.

In the next half century from 1880 to 1930, a new generation of scholars emerged, and they were certainly aided by Europe's dominance in Egypt and elsewhere in Africa. These scholars now lent the study of Egyptology the disciplines of history, archaeology and anthropology. The field was further helped by even more new disciplines as anthropometry, biometrics, photography, architecture, medicine, and art. The French led the field followed by the Germans, the British and Swiss. Later Americans became involved but America emerged as a potent force.

Auguste Mariette worked tirelessly to excavate, help restore some of the existing structure in Egypt and to build the Cairo Museum. Gaston Maspero, who excavated and became a prolific writer on Egyptian culture, followed him, in this post of Antiquities Curator. He inscribed many of the inscriptions in the display cases at the Cairo Museum. He was succeeded by De Morgan and later Le Grain who particularly did restoration work at Karnak where he discovered the "Cachette Court" with its thousands of statuettes of numerous pharaohs spanning the entire history of Egypt. By the end of this second period, the discipline had been set on firm footing, and practically everything written after were analyses and interpretations of the data. There was still scaled down excavations being conducted by museums and through the Second World War and into the sixties as scholars scrambled to reassess their knowledge of Egypt. Along and parallel this path is that taken by the Black intellectual awakening from the slavery experience that still plagues us today. Martin Delaney, Henry Highland Garnett, W.E.B. DuBois, Marcus Garvey, Carter G. Woodson, J.A. Rogers, Yosef ben Jochannan,

QUINTESSENTIAL BOOK
"THE HOLY LAND"

John Henrik Clarke, John Jackson, G.M. James, Ivan Van Sertima, Jacob Carruthers, Na'im Akbar, Maulana Karenga, Molefi Asante, etc., have all sought to involve our people in the consciousness of Egypt and the challenge to correct the distortions and omissions of its historiography.

Our scholars, who informed the history has been distorted to denigrate and ostracize Africans from participation in the wonderful experience that is Egypt, have lighted this process.

Teddy Cubia: Very good Doc. I see you touch all the bases. That is good. Well, I look forward to the others as the trip unfolds.
Dr. Leonard James: I'll do my best.
Mrs. Marilyn James: Mrs. Brown, perhaps we could do a little shopping this evening after dinner just across the street in the mall there.
Mrs. Brown: That would be a wonderful idea. I look forward to it.

George Washington: Good Morning, ladies. Good to see you. What are you having for breakfast?
Regina Hendricks: I am having an omelet, croissant, and fruit with juice.
Michelliea Georges: I am having scrambled eggs, falafel and juice. Let me ask you this George. What books did you use in your course on *African Religious Thought Systems* taught by Dr. Donna Richards?
George Washington: Willie Abraham, *The Mind of Africa*; Leonard Barrett, *Soul Force*; Jomo Kenyatta, *Facing Mount Kenya*; Camara Laye, *The Dark Child*; and John S. Mbiti, *African Religions and Philosophies*. From these sources our Course Leader explained by virtue of the communal nature of the society, mind produces unity and harmony in a spiritual whole.

Sacred – is interrelated with religion. A cultural society, which is sacredly based, is more humane. Continuously sacred-based society is more "democratic."
Secular – non-religious based society.
Desacralized – when spirituality is continuously denied.
Profane – ordinary, everyday, man made.
Experience – something one has lived through and gained some knowledge from.

Sacred   Profane

Sacred	Profane
Special	Ordinary
Extra-ordinary	Everyday
Not limited	Desacralized

FREDERICK MONDERSON

Religion is experiencing the sacred.

Sacred goes beyond boundaries of ordinary existence. An experience of the "ordinary" is manifested in the sacred and is made "extraordinary." Regarding childbirth, a hospital becoming "factories" reflects the culture of the society.

The analysis shows the culture of a society is reflected in its social institutions. In most experiences, from an African-centric viewpoint, an ordinary profane everyday occurrence is manifested in a sacred way and made extraordinary or divine. For example, the birth of a baby, which in some cultures may be an ordinary experience, to the African, this continuation is such an emotional-sacred happening that, no matter how many times it happens, the emotional experience, each succeeding time takes on a more joyous atmosphere than the time before.

By virtue of the communal nature of the society, mind produces unity and harmony in a spiritual whole. Societies can be either interrelated with religion in which it is sacredly based or secular in which it is non-religiously based. In this latter a form of desacralization of spirituality is constant as opposed to the former in which the religiosity is continuous.

3.   Bus Ride

Dr. Alexander Pushkin: Teddy that was a great poem you read last night. Have you published any of your work?
Teddy Cubia: No. When I was young, I was very black-conscious and my wife and me would sit down and have these long discussions after we had marched in every protest there was. I seem to remember those poems, discussions and marches, as if the civil rights movement was only yesterday.
Michael Sinclair: In a way there was an east coast and a west coast civil rights movement. Let me give you some insight on the civil rights developments on the West Coast as told in class by Dr. Molefi Asante.

Maulana Karenga was part of the 1965 uprising in South Central Los Angeles. It was significant as the first major eruption in a western progressive city. It led to the growth of African-American organizations (A City of Integrated Organizations). In 1966 Karenga organized the "US" organization. Since the 1965 uprising it was necessary to reconstruct the cultural values of African-Americans. He was geared toward structure. No other theorist was as clear as Karenga on structure. His is the only political system articulated by an African-American thinker. The Black Panthers in the US can be traced back to Malcolm X. He also got his ideas from the church.

QUINTESSENTIAL BOOK "THE HOLY LAND"

Using customs and tradition, Maulana Karenga created the Kawaida Theory. This called for reconstruction of cultural values. Therefore, the language he chose was Kiswahili. This is the least ethnic language in Africa. Kawaida Theory was the most direct precursor to Afrocentricity.

Asante, whose real name was Arthur Smith, got his Ph.D. in August, 1968 and began teaching in September at Perdue University. At UCLA he was the compromise candidate for the Center for African-American Studies. The shootout in Los Angeles between the Black Panthers and "US" left two brothers dead. They were Black Panthers. "US" argued "You have to win the minds of the people before you can win a military struggle." So Karenga created the **Kawaida Theory,** the **Nguzo Saba** and **Kwanza**. The struggle must be waged intellectually, first.

There are 5 core issues of the **Kawaida Theory**. These are:

1. There is a cultural crisis among Black American people. Our identity is confused. We are off-centered.
2. Any real analysis of our problem must be Afrocentric.
3. All social change begins with redefinition.
4. All good thoughts about African reconstruction have to draw from the best Nationalist, Pan Africanist, Socialist thought.
5. All critique must be followed by corrective action.

There is a need for social responsibility. Our mission is to humanize the world.

Once you make a critique, there are 8 ways to look at it.

1. Myth – Mythology is like religion. Who are you, where in the world are you?
2. History - You must have a sense of history, a coherent body of history.
3. Motif – Subject - Emblems of the African people Red/Black/Green.
4. Art/artifact – Destruction of the cultural values.
5. Ethos – How are you presented to the world outside?
6. Political Organization.
7. Social Organization.
8. Economic organization.

People who criticize Afrocentricity never give the position of Afrocentricity. When you criticize you must give the other side, along with your side.

FREDERICK MONDERSON

KAWAIDA argued that the new value system must be based on tradition and reason. Asante believed 'Religion was a very viable part of African tradition; while Maulana Karenga's theoretical construction is based on reason. He is creating for conscious purpose. He created Kwanzaa out of reason for African people though it's not traditionally an African holiday.'

The **NGUZU SABA** has 7 principles. These are Umoja, Kujichagulia, Ujima, Ujamaa, Nia – Purpose; Kuumba – Creativity; Imani – faith.

If we look at the 7 Corinthians' **Faith**, **Hope** and **Charity**, these all came from reason.

These were the principles African people needed to observe. Value system must be based on tradition and reason. Tradition cannot be adapted as it were; it must be adapted based on reason and according to our needs.

Dr. Alexander Pushkin: Nicely put young man but the East Coast protest movement was also significant. Not enough emphasis has been placed on the work of Dr. W.E.B. DuBois (1868-1963) the man who single-handedly carried the mantle of Black protest for the greatest part of the twentieth century. Very early this "Father of Pan Africanism" pointed to the question of race in America. In fact, he coined the issue of the twentieth century as the question of color. In his *Souls of Black Folk* (1903) he wrote: "Herein lies the tragedy of the age: not that men are poor - all men know something of poverty; not that all men are wicked - who is good? Not those men are ignorant - what is truth? Nay, but that, men know so little of men." Even further he wrestled with the question of what to call the Black man in America for he found it was an anomaly. He wrote: "It is a peculation sensation, this double consciousness, this sense of always looking at one's self through the eyes of others …. One feels this two-ness - An American, a Negro; two souls, two thoughts, two un-reconciled strivings; two warring ideals in one dark body, whose dogged strength alone keeps it from being torn asunder." So we too know struggle, young man.

Michael Sinclair: Trust me Sir, I respect my elders. Had you not been there, I would not be here!

QUINTESSENTIAL BOOK "THE HOLY LAND"

Holy Land Photo 28a. Clive Monderson of Guyana, South America, while visiting the Library of Congress, Jefferson Building, stands before the mythical Greek god, presiding over his water kingdom.

Asantewaa Harris: Mr. Stewart, why do you think the Library of Congress is considered so important in the intellectual life of our country?
Mr. John Stewart: Simply put, my dear, the Library of Congress is the intellectual repository of the nation. It is also the hearth that motivates people to create literary and other artistic productions. After all, it registers, safeguards and protects intellectual property. It's as is said on its walls: "The history of the world is the biography of great men" and that "Books will speak plain when counselors blanch."

FREDERICK MONDERSON

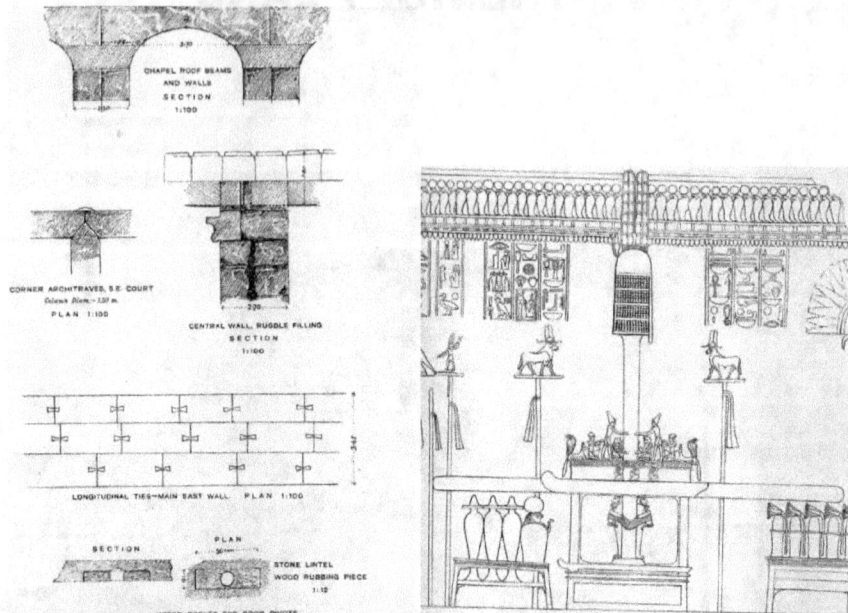

Holy Land Illustration 40. Abydos. Temple of the Kings Architectural features. Chapel roof beams and walls; and upper socket for door pivots and Shrine of Osiris.

John Singleton: Dr. Benjamin, how would you define civilization? I was having a discussion with a friend in the lounge last night and we seem to differ on the meaning or definition of civilization. So I promised I would ask you.
Dr. Benjamin: Well, civilization is simply a high culture. It depends on the defining entity. Some people like to intertwine the emergence of civilization with the emergence of writing. But the definition keeps changing. How would you define it, John?
Dr. John Africa: James Baldwin in *Nobody Knows My Name* argued, "Civilization lies first in the mind." Richard Wright in *12 Million Black Voices* (1941) wrote: "We had our own civilization in Africa before we were captured and carried off to this land. We smelted iron, danced, made music and folk poems; we sculpted, worked in glass, spun cotton and wool, and wove baskets and cloth. We invented a medium of exchange, mined silver and gold, made pottery and cutlery, we fashioned tools and utensils of brass, bronze, ivory, quartz, and granite. We had our own literature, our own systems of law, religion, medicine, science and education." In addition, Joseph Danquah, who wrote *Africa at the Bar of Nations* also tells us in *Akan Law and Customs* (1928), where he made an interesting note: "By the time Alexander the Great was sweeping the civilized world with conquest after conquest from Chaeronicia to Gaza, from Babylon to Cabal, by the time the first Aryan conquerors were learning the rudiments of war and government at the

QUINTESSENTIAL BOOK "THE HOLY LAND"

feet of Aristotle, and by the time Athens was laying down the foundations of European civilization, the earliest and greatest Ethiopian culture had already flourished and dominated the civilized world for four centuries and a half. Imperial Ethiopia had conquered Egypt and founded the XXVth Dynasty." William Wells Brown (1877) also tells us: "Civilization is handed from one people to another, its great foundation source, God, our Father." So, as Richard Barthe said in 1939: "When I look at the world, I wonder if Africa is not more civilized."

John Singleton: Thank you, Sir.

Dr. Benjamin: May I also add, young man, "Cheikh Anta Diop in *Civilization or Barbarism*: *The Legacy of Cheikh Anta Diop*" published in the *Journal of African Civilizations* in November 1982 noted: "Mankind's prohibition against incest marked a starting point toward civilization." Even further, Patrice Lumumba in *Congo, My Country* (161) argued: "When you civilize a man, you only civilize an individual, but when you civilize a woman, you civilize a whole people." Of course, Chevalier de St. Georges, an African in Europe wrote "Civilization, like an immense stream, is carrying in its current – science, power and wealth, and any effort to oppose it must be utterly defeated." While Mrs. Balfour defined Civilization as "Mankind's struggle upwards, in which millions are trampled to death, that thousands may mount on their bodies;" Edmund Burke added: "Our manners, our civilization, and all the good things connected with manners and civilization, have, in this world of ours, depended for ages upon two principles – I mean the spirit of a gentleman, and the spirit of religion."

Holy Land Illustration 41. The Great Sphinx of Ghizeh and the Pyramid of Khafre inundated in the desert sand. Notice the Bedouin and their camel on the Sphinx's paws.

Michelliea Georges: So what do we have on ancient history?
Regina Hendricks: What was the reading assignment for that day?

FREDERICK MONDERSON

George Washington: On September 17, 1975, the reading assignment was Moscati Chapter 2 and *Britannica* - Mesopotamia, Prehistory.

Mesopotamia – (1) Floods have covered the valley with rich alluvial deposits; (2) not really protected by the deserts. The military grew.

Marduk was the God of War.

Wood and stones, metal resources had to be gotten from an external source. The society did not develop in a vacuum. Mesopotamia was always in contact with outsiders.

Egypt was the Gift of the Nile. While Herodotus is credited with saying this, it has been traced back to Hecataeus of Abdera. There, an entire population existed on a narrow strip uplift of land. The name Kemet has been termed the Black land though some scholars say it meant the color of the people.

If the flood was off by one foot then famine occurred. If the river was too high it meant destruction of villages and therefore problems arose. In the "Inundation of the Nile," the river rose as much as twenty feet. In the formative years the military was non-existent.

Greek time was linear development while Egyptian time was cyclical. This circular pattern as opposed to a linear measurement is similar to the African concept of immortality viewed from the circular pattern. They believed: "As seeds are planted, come up and die, so surely man must be born, develop, die, and be reborn." Isis was viewed in all aspects of femininity.

Circa 300 B.C., the Phoenicians were sea traders. Jews and Arabs conducted caravan trades. Jerusalem, by its location, exacted heavy tolls on trade that passed through its territory. Owing to the diversity of its topography in the Levant, cities developed individually until conquests by foreign kingdoms. Anatolia was very rich in obsidian. Analysis of the day's work shows: Mesopotamia, owing to its geographical location, faced both good and bad times. Rains in the Assyrian highlands had a profound impact on the valley below, on the land, which the Greeks named *Mesos Potamos* (land between the rivers Tigris and Euphrates). When the rains were too heavy the floods would destroy villages in the valley, but, in passing, a thick black alluvial fertilizer was deposited, similar with the deposit after the Inundation of the Nile. When floods never came, agricultural produce was badly affected.

In this location, the valley, even though it was somewhat surrounded by desert, was hardly protected from nomadic and unscrupulous forces that would plunder the small kingdoms that grew up. Owing to this, the military grew intensively, but still to no avail. Marduk the God of War was constantly called upon by his

QUINTESSENTIAL BOOK
"THE HOLY LAND"

worshippers to save his patron cities but to no avail. Much of the commodities and resources needed for this society had to be gotten from external sources such as Mesopotamia, which, from its location was in constant contact with most people owing to its geographical location which straddled some of the major caravan routes. Some of the imports were wood, stones, metals, and flints. This society did not develop in a vacuum like Egypt did.

Egypt was the gift of the Nile. Owing to the inundation, a geological phenomenon called "uplifting of the land" occurred. Almost the entire population existed on a narrow strip of the land. This land, owing to its blackness was called Kemet. Generally, the inundated Nile rose by 20 feet, and this produced a prosperous harvest. When the overflow was as much as one foot off, famine resulted.

Again, in explaining the time cycle of man, the analogy of a seed was used. The seed was planted, shot-up, and died, so surely man must be born, develop, die and be reborn, ad continuum. Isis, the divinity was seen in all aspects of femininity, baby, young virgin, girl, and mother. Well, so much for now.

Regina Hendricks: Thanks, we will have to treat you after dinner.
Michelliea Georges: I think you are doing an excellent job. Keep it up.
George Washington: Why, thank you ladies. See you later.

4.   Site
        Deir El Bahari
        Valley of the Kings
        Ramesseum
5.   Post-site Lecture

Dr. Fred Monderson: Let me give you some dates to begin our understanding of the emergence of human consciousness along the Nile Valley and elsewhere. Generally the dates given are Early Paleolithic at 500,000 B.C.; Early Middle Palaeolithic 70,000-43,000 B.C.; Late Middle Palaeolithic 43,000-30,000 B.C. (Neanderthal); Late Palaeolithic 30,000-10,000 B.C. (Homo Sapiens); Mesolithic 10,000-5000 B.C.; Neolithic 5000-3100 B.C.; Historic 3100 B.C.

FREDERICK MONDERSON

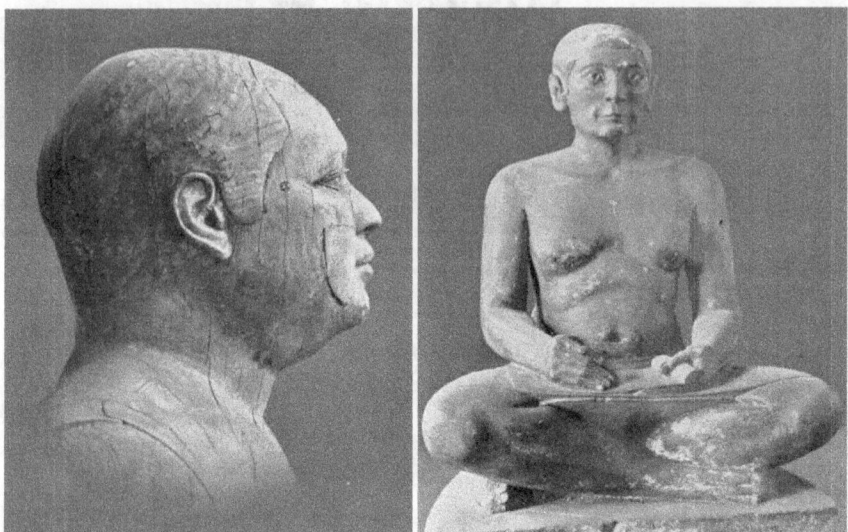

Holy Land Illustration 42. Bust of Old Kingdom figure, the "Sheikh of Beled" so named by the natives upon its discovery; and the Louvre "Scribe," thought to be a bust but not of an actual person.

The Neolithic Period corresponds with the Badarian, Amratian and Gerzean or Naqada I and Naqada II periods. The Badarians first began use of copper and their repertoire particularly in pottery began to expand. By 5000 B.C. these early Africans and primitive peoples elsewhere such as Asia and the Americas, were using stone pottery, stoneware, and clay pottery. Some scholars believe Sudan had pottery before Egypt and that the earliest beliefs for a life after death come from about 10,000 B.C. In this period pottery became important for dating. Sir Flinders Petrie made Egyptology scientific. He made broken pottery become archaeologically significant with his sequence dating. Nevertheless, by the end of this Neolithic period, "all the trappings" of Egyptian civilization were in place.

By the time Narmer marshaled his Theban military machine and marched north and unified Upper and Lower Egypt, there were already in place two well-developed forms of centralized government. Very evidently he did not conquer chaos but an established viable political and economic entity. Nevertheless, it's very probable that the concept of central government and even writing may have been developed as early as 4000 B.C., or earlier. The Eastern and Western Deserts of Upper Egypt produced a wonderful dynamic of cultural evolution in the millennia of these two periods.

Because there is so much dynamics evolving in the prehistoric or predynastic period, 3100 B.C. is accepted as an artificial starting point, but even more because it provides a framework to view the three thousand years of history, government and culture.

QUINTESSENTIAL BOOK
"THE HOLY LAND"

The Egyptians counted their years by the length of a pharaoh's reign. For example, we have day 5, month 4, year 15 of Ramses II. Then there is day 8, month 3, year 5 of Merenptah. Nevertheless, they were accurate in their chronology. They developed a calendar of 3 seasons of 4 months each of 30 days. The first season was called "Inundation," then "Emergence," then "Summer" when there was no water. Theirs was a lunar calendar, which is more important than the sun, and a solar calendar. Diop dates the Egyptian Calendar to 4241 B.C.

We can probably and safely say the Archaic Period of Dynasties 1 and 2 lasted more than 400 years. The Old Kingdom of Dynasties 3-6 lasted from 2664-2184 B.C. when political boundaries were set up and the conventions of the society were laid down. This age of the pyramids created much that sustained later civilizations. Alas, the age could not support strong leadership and everything slipped into chaos of the First Intermediate Period of Dynasties 7-10. Intefs and Mentuhoteps of the Middle Kingdom united the country from 2134–1870 B.C. before the Second Intermediate Period of Dynasties 14-16. This was followed by the 17th Dynasty followed by vigorous leaders of the 18-20th Dynasties of the New Kingdom.

Egypt declined after the New Kingdom. The Assyrians threatened and the Ethiopians invaded and then came the Persians, Greeks and Romans. Then came the Arabs and Islam, and the Turks.

Holy Land Photo 29. Kom Ombo Double Temple to Horus and Sobek. On a back wall in the outer corridor, a colossal figure pours a libation to a "Table of Offerings."

FREDERICK MONDERSON

6. Discussion

Dr. Fred Monderson: In the examination of history and search for knowledge and truth, we must remember the age in which the modern history of Egypt was recorded. It was the 19th and 20th centuries of our era. This was an age of western intellectual as well as economic and political imperialism after the "Dark Age" centuries, the Medieval Renaissance and Reformation ages. It was an age of the expansion and the glorification of Europe; therefore, the slant was to propel Europeans as progenitors of all that was good in Europe; in fact, in the world, it is only after a century of relentless denial of the role of Asia and Europe in Egypt that some people have relented. The paltry admissions notwithstanding, most of the new books and even in discussion scholars omit the role of Africans in Egypt. The question then is why? It is probably because, western scholars argue, the Egyptians were a mixed people, whose culture was influenced by Europeans from Asia. In schools they teach man originated in Africa, but that Africa stultified and Europe emerged and later influenced World History. Naturally civilization was progressing concurrently in Asia but not predating Egypt!

Nevertheless, in most discussions, many argue we are not dealing with race but culture. However, they do seem to praise Europe even though, on the one hand, the argument is made that Greece is the foundation of European civilization. Still, we know Greece never emerged until after the Ethiopian era in Egypt and Alexander and the Greeks did not rule until after 332 B.C. The Hellenistic world exploded after Greece's expansion in the Mediterranean and contacts with Egypt.

Are there any questions?

Calif. Lady: Can you give us some insights into what we saw at Deir el Bahari today?
Dr. Fred Monderson: What you visited today was the XVIIIth Dynasty Temple of Queen Hatshepsut built by her architect Senmut. Thutmose III's zealots destroyed much of the Temple which was patterned after Mentuhotep II's Middle Kingdom structure nearby. The Valley Temple is long gone. So too is the Avenue of Sphinxes. Naturally the First Pylon is also destroyed. You did notice the two holes for the trees that were planted at the front of the pylon. When we get to Sakkara you will see the first enclosure wall that was introduced by Imhotep for Zoser. At Deir el Bahari part of the enclosure wall to the south is still intact. The hills to the north served as the northern wall beyond the 16 remaining columns of the Northern Colonnade beside Anubis' Chapel with its columns. See how the paint in Anubis' Chapel is well preserved. Besides this Northern Colonnade there are the Lower, Middle and Upper Colonnades. Two Ramps along the center of the temple reach these and divide north from south. The Lower Colonnade as the

QUINTESSENTIAL BOOK "THE HOLY LAND"

Obelisk Colonnade to the north and the southern part is decorated with fishes and birds being caught in nets. The Birth Colonnade is to the north near the Anubis Shrine and the Punt Colonnade is to the south of the Middle Colonnade. The Punt Colonnade abuts the Hathor Chapel that has pillars and columns and Hathor Headed Capitals.

The Second Ramp leads to the Upper Terrace and Upper Platform or Colonnade where the Altar and Amon Sanctuary are located amidst the Hypostyle Hall in the Upper Court. Fronting this Upper Terrace on the Upper Platform are Osiride Statues of Queen Hatshepsut. Thutmose III's people destroyed most after he had deposed the Queen. However, the temple was not utterly destroyed simply because it was dedicated to Amon. That would have been sacrilege.

At the "Feast of the Valley," when the god visited the temple, the Procession began at the Valley Temple located at the river's edge. There were fights between two opposing groups of priests. As the procession of the god's barque approached the temple one of these groups' functions was to stop the procession while the other was to move it along. This is basically a part of the ritual.

Food was an important part of the ritual of the temple. The relationship between the king and the god was crucial because the divinities had to crown the monarch. Heliopolis played an important role in this; otherwise the king was not fully consecrated. In the story of her virgin birth, Hatshepsut tells how all the gods came to her.

For more than two centuries explorers visited Deir el Bahari but it was not until the 1890s that the Swiss Egyptologist Eduardo Naville, under the auspices of the Egypt Exploration Fund, began the excavation of the temple and finally clearing it after three or so seasons of meticulous excavation. These were recorded in the English journal *The Academy*. Of course after each season there were lectures and exhibitions in London at the Egypt Exploration Fund's hall. For many years a Polish group of scholars restored the Court of the Upper Platform and this has now allowed visitors to that part of the temple previously closed to the public.

Regina Singleton: How did the architect Senmut get so close to the queen considering her divine nature?
Dr. Fred Monderson: You must read the written handouts. Senmut was a commoner who rose to prominence because of his abilities and talents. However, even though he was a commoner this did not prevent his aspirations from being realized. Also, he was a general in the queen's father Thutmose I's army. One thing could be said of this culture, as with the imperial Chinese civil service, people with skills and abilities and those who were loyal to the monarch could rise to prominence in the society. Senmut headed a political party and he also undertook many projects to legitimize the queen's rule. She showered him with

FREDERICK MONDERSON

more than 40 titles including Master of the Royal Bedroom. Of course he did build many things for her, but was later replaced by another architect, Amenhotep. Perhaps Senmut had too many assignments. However, when Hatshepsut was deposed Thutmose's people also took after him. Some scholars believe there was a love relationship going on.

Sylvester Singleton: Can you explain the emergence of Amon and the difference between Amon and Amon-Ra?
Dr. Fred Monderson: These are two good and difficult questions. I will take the first one first.

Holy Land Photo 29a. The expressive power and potency of African womanhood, especially intelligent, as they communicate with the "spirit world" through Libation, to help empower the 1999 ASCAC Conference in New York and attendees with clear-sightedness and good intent in the struggle against *Isfet*.

Amon as we know him was a minor deity at the beginning of dynastic rule. Consider that Narmer was a Theban who unified the nation and only showed Hathor on his Palette and apron. He founded the worship of Ptah at Memphis as well as incorporated the worship of Ra at Heliopolis. Yet, nothing is said of Amon at this time, even though he is mentioned in the Pyramid Texts of the Old Kingdom. However in the emergence of the Middle Kingdom Amon rose to prominence as the national god. Then following the expulsion of the Hyksos at the end of the Second Intermediate Period, the 18th Dynasty kings again credited Amon with giving them victory. So his fortunes skyrocketed and he became the recipient of much of the imperial plunder acquired in Asia and Nubia.

QUINTESSENTIAL BOOK
"THE HOLY LAND"

Interestingly enough, however, Amon had to share Thebes with Sokaris. A stela shows the two gods sharing Thebes. Amon ruled the east bank; land of the living; and Sokaris ruled the west bank, land of the dead. Then came the Amarna heresy that challenged Amon's position and with the overthrow of the Aten cult Amon re-emerged supreme.

To commemorate the end of that era at the end of the 18th Dynasty, the Ramesside kings of the 19th Dynasty fused Amon with Ra as the supreme deity of the land. Some scholars have argued that the fusion took place during the Middle Kingdom, even more that it was done during the age of Hatshepsut. After this Amon reigned supreme as the Theban and national god of that imperial age. Of course, his wife Mut and son Khonsu, the earth and moon gods then comprised the Theban Triad in the central and southern groups at Karnak.

Let us not forget, in the syncretism of Amon with Ra, Amon's prototype was Min an archaic and Black god who was of the earliest royal circle of gods.

Juliet Brown: A lot's been said of the origins of writing. Is hieroglyphics a foreign importation in Egypt?
Dr. Fred Monderson: The origins of Egyptian writing like the origins of its mythology are found in the landscape of its natural environment in its distant past. Cheikh Anta Diop and William Arnett have traced the beginnings of Egyptian writing to the southern part of the country where many of its flora and fauna were found. They argue for the independent and exclusive development of Egyptian writing from an indigenous base. Equally too, other theories suggest that the middle eastern trade routes introduced concepts of writing, with letters of credit and other commercial instruments. While trade generally spreads culture in the interaction, it is extremely unlikely that writing could have been an importation into another culture. We know by the time of Narmer's unification they were counting in the millions and certainly writing; yet, most other cultures were still in hibernation for such accomplishments.

Glenda Stewart: What do we know of libraries in ancient Egypt?
Dr. Fred Monderson: There was a library in every temple. A people with a love of knowledge as the Egyptians were, would probably have had libraries in the homes of the well-to-do as well. However, very little evidence of this has survived. Myers (1900: 20-21) explained: "In one of the tombs of Gizeh, a great functionary of the first part of the VIth dynasty (circa 3503-3335 B.C.) takes the title of 'Governor of the House of Books.' This simple mention, thrown incidentally between two more elevated titles, would be sufficient, in default of others, to show us the extraordinary development at that time of Egyptian civilization. Not only had they a literature, but that literature was also large enough to fill libraries, and its importance was so great, that to one of the functionaries of the court was especially attached to the preservation of the royal library. He had, without doubt,

to keep with the contemporary works, the books written during the first dynasties, the books dating from Mena, and perhaps the kings anterior to Mena. The foundation of that library would be composed of the religious books, the Chapters of the Book of the Dead, copied after authentic texts preserved in the temples; scientific treatises upon geometry, medicine and astronomy; historical books in which were preserved the sayings and doings of the ancient kings, with the years of their lives and the exact duration of their reigns; manuals of philosophy and practical ethics; also, probably, some romances. All these, if we had them, would form a library which would be much more precious for us than that of Alexandria; but, unhappily, we possess of all these riches only the fragments of a philosophic collection."

"In the opinion of most Egyptologists, the greatest portion of Egyptian history had been enacted (before 2100 B.C.) The Ancient and Middle Kingdoms of the sons of Ham had then already fallen; Egypt had reached its point of culmination, and its most flourishing epoch was already left behind. The religious literature of the Hebrews, venerable as it is for its antiquity, does not begin before Moses; but we possess a Manuscript from Thebes in hieratic characters, written several centuries before the time of the Hebrew lawgiver, under the XIth Egyptian dynasty."

The *Murray Papyrus*, Brit. Mus., 10,010 and *Malcolm Papyrus*, Brit., Mus., 10,081, contain rubrics that mention: "one part of the original text was discovered written on a roll of leather in the Library of the Temple of Osiris, at Abydos, in the time of Thotmes III, of the XVIIIth dynasty (circa 1414-1383 B.C.) These texts were in existence certainly 1000 years and likely 2000 years, before either of these kings; there is, therefore, nothing unlikely in the account of the find of them in the XVIIIth dynasty. The Temple of Osiris was renovated about that time."

For every library it stands to reason there was a librarian. Myers (1900: 308-309) tells of the world's first librarian. "Shepses'ka'f, sometimes called Shopsiskaf, (circa 3759-3737 B.C.), was the 6th king of the IV dynasty. Most of our knowledge of him comes from the tomb of his son-in-law Ptah'shepses who married Ma'at-Kha, the king's eldest daughter. M. de Rouge' evidently refers to this king when he says: "Ases-ka-f was the immediate successor of Men-kau-Ra. Under this king appears an important personage Ases-kaf-anx, he was vested with the priesthood commemorative of Soupis." His tomb is at Gizeh. He also possessed the title of Mur-per-ha-Taa per sesa, i.e., 'Governor of the great dwelling,' that is to say, undoubtedly, of the palace, and he also had charge, "of the house of writings,' the library. This person Ases-kaf-anx was also 'Superintendent of the houses of the young princes.' Ases-kaf-anx was undoubtedly our Ptah-shepses with a different rendering of his name; Manetho names Shepses'ka'f, king Bikheris. Ptah'shepses was therefore the first librarian in the world whose name and period we know. Others undoubtedly preceded him."

QUINTESSENTIAL BOOK "THE HOLY LAND"

Dr. Mc Flair: Did the Ancient Egyptians view life as we do?
Dr. Fred Monderson: They lived life to full enjoyment but also with an aim to gain the second birth. They sought immortality through morality in their social relations and chose to stand proud at the Judgment. That is to say, they lived an exemplary ethical life to stand confidently before their god at the Judgment. Thus, they provisioned their tombs with the necessities to make that afterlife as enjoyable as this one.

Esperanza Rodriguez: Like every society, love is an issue, how did the ancient Egyptians view and experience love?
Dr. Fred Monderson: We could begin with the love of Isis for Osiris and what she did to ensure his name. But there are different kinds of love. There is love for the god, a mother, father or siblings, relative, a woman, and so on. There can be love of knowledge, literature, and spirituality. Love your wife. Be careful of the danger of love affairs. The love a people holds for their chief. Live for love, love of festival, love of fellow man. Ptah-Hotep says: "No one is to cause fear to men, this is the will of God." I would venture to say, love did not dictate marriage. For the longest and earliest time, marriage was generally a financial, political or social affair and love bloomed or developed from the interaction. That is not to say, people like Senmut did not love Hatshepsut, Amenhotep III did not love Queen Tiy nor Rameses II did not love Nefertari!

Charles Palms: Can you define Ma'ati?
Dr. Fred Monderson: Ma'at or Ma'ati is the principle of equilibrium, justice, equality, balance, etc. There is a Hall of the two Maati Goddesses. This is the name of the hall named for the Two Maati goddesses, Ma-at and Isis. It is where the Judgment takes place. We get an example of this drama in the *Per-em-hru*, regarding Paheri, 'Prince of Nekheb.' Paheri is shown making an offering to Osiris in which he says: "'Hail to thee, O noble god, lord of earth, great (one) of the Nome of This, mighty in Abydos: I have come to thee, my lord, in peace, give me peace: there are for thee peace offerings, hear thou my call, grant thou my words: I am one of those who adore thee.'" Myers (1900: 347) says further: "Paheri subsequently addresses prayers to Amen (Amon-Ra), lord of the thrones of the two lands, king of eternity, lord of everlasting, the prince possessing the great double plume, sole one in the presence, heir .... men and gods, living flame issuing from Nu (i.e., the firmament), light (?) of mortals. He addresses Nekhebt, Osiris, Hathor, Ptah-Sokaris and Anubis, respectively, that they may give food to his ka: 'Oxen and wild fowl, (the enjoyment of) offering of provisions by the thousand; gifts of flowers and of everything that grows upon the face (literal, "back,") of the earth by the thousand; the reception of food that has appeared in the Presence and milk that has appeared upon the altar," etc.

FREDERICK MONDERSON

Maat was a goddess who represented righteousness and whose symbolism and ethical principles guided the society in harmony and well-behavior. Without strict adherence to Ma'at principles, Paheri could not receive what he asked for.

Holy Land Illustration 43. Abydos. Temple of the Kings. Divine barques.

Michael Palmer: How important is Manetho?
Dr. Fred Monderson: Manetho is important in that he was a high priest in Graeco-Egypt and had access to secret documents. His *History of Egypt*, though now lost, informs of events of great antiquity when gods and Demi-gods ruled before the pharaohs. He supplied many names that have been collaborated by later research. His most significant contribution is the arrangement into dynasties or houses of rule that modern scholarship has accepted. Thus for the most part, Manetho is "trustworthy." Despite his work being lost we know of him through commentary made on his history by classical scholars whose fragments are still useful.

James Morrison: How would you evaluate the manners of the Ancient Egyptians?
Dr. Fred Monderson: Well, the Egyptians always praised good manners. Certain types of behaviors were prescribed with certain kinds of situations and in all this was the insistence on a certain type of decorum, which we call good manners. Good manners were an ideal for every type of relationship and it was a boasting point at the Judgment for having acted with this form of behavior. A good example of a maxim about good behavior or manners is found in the *Papyrus of the Scribe Ani* who says: "Young man, be not seated whilst a man more aged than thyself remain standing, (even when thou art more elevated than he is in his employment)." Myers (1900: 158) says equally: "This Maxim of politeness is one which many, so-called, well-mannered, refined and educated people among us, do not live up to to-day. It shows the elevated thoughts and good manners of the gentlemen of Ancient Egypt, and might yet be followed with benefit to themselves, by the well-bred and educated people of today. Indeed, the Maxims of Ptah-Hotep and Ani show that the manners and refinement of the Egyptian gentlemen of thousands of years before Christianity can compare very favorably with those of *men who claim to be gentle-mannered to-day.*"

QUINTESSENTIAL BOOK
"THE HOLY LAND"

Leonard James: What do we know of the Books of Thoth?
Dr. Fred Monderson: The Egyptians attributed many books to Thoth, the "Hermes of the Greeks." Clement of Alexandria ascribes 42 books to Thoth, while Iamblichus says 20,000 and Manetho said they were 36,525. Clearly since Thoth was the author of writing, music, wisdom, and chronographer, lawyer and librarian of the Gods, we expect he would have a great many books attributed to him. Hence, an answer of no precise number of books attributable to Thoth is also plausible.

Marilyn James: How important was marriage to the Ancient Egyptians?
Dr. Fred Monderson: There are many maxims extolling the young man to marry whilst a young man, have a son to perform those ceremonies important to his father when dead and in this others will praise you when young. Myers (1900: 116) tells further: "To this day it is customary in Egypt for the authentic descendants of the Ancient Egyptians, which is the Fellahs and Copts, to have their children married when they are very young. The young scholar appears to have married early, Rameses II, at the age of ten or twelve years had a harem given to him by his father Seti I. There appears to have been anciently, among the wealthy and higher classes of Egypt only one wife to a man, but there were also a number of concubines allowed him." In Egypt today marriage is a big affair celebrated with much festivity.

Erik Joel: What are Mastabas?
Dr. Fred Monderson: The most archaic monumental tombs of the Ancient Egyptians are in the form known as the mastaba, a "bench like structure," derived from the Arabic word for a *Bench.* All these ancient tombs have a grand simplicity. The Mastabas were likely constructed before the Pyramid tombs. One of the Pyramids of Sakkara is older than those of Gizeh; so are some of the Mastabas of Sakkara.

In the Old Kingdom, officials built these gigantic structures nearby within the vicinity of the pharaoh's pyramid so that his divine and august presence can bless their resting place. The erection of mastabas and funeral and religious monuments increased in the Vth dynasty, which signaled religious maturity on the part of the ancient peoples of the Old Kingdom. The mastabas were elaborately decorated and contained much food, drink and earthly accoutrements to make the deceased happy in the next life.

James Madison: How did Maxims aid society?
Dr. Fred Monderson: Maxims were tremendous aids to the society because of the moral ideas they installed in the youth, family and community. The two principal books with Maxims are the *Papyrus of the Scribe Ani* and the *Maxims of Ptah-Hotep.* Whether they were aimed at a family member, son, or the society in

FREDERICK MONDERSON

general, maxims carried a strong moral and ethical message that everyone subsequently tried to aspire to.

Frank James: Seems like every society emphasizes interest in weights and measures. Did the Egyptians have protections or provisions for measurement?

Dr. Fred Monderson: To jump ahead, I remember Askia Mohammed, upon coming to power in Songhai during the Western Sudanic golden age, restructured the state and paid particular attention to weights and measures. This was probably the same approach to the issue the Egyptians took. The deceased in the *Negative Confessions* asserts he did not shorten the measuring devices so it must have been considered important. In fact, perhaps many people did it and that is why there is a proscription against it. Even today, there is such a proscription, and officials of the government to prevent cheating the customer perennially inspect merchants.

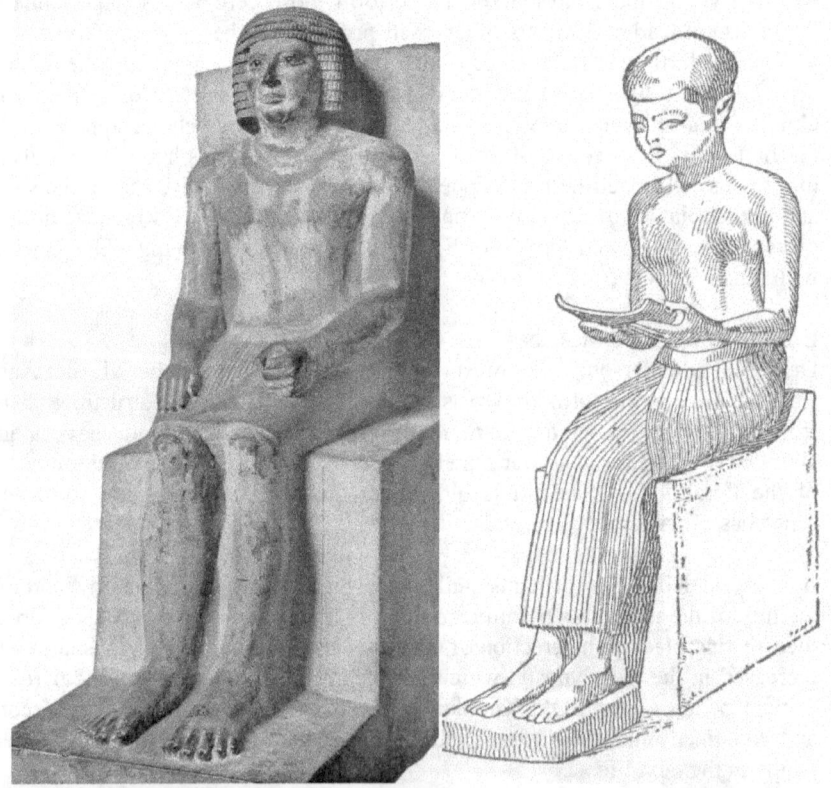

Holy Land Illustration 44. Hemset sits enthroned (left); and "Imhotep the Wise," the earliest Architect of stone buildings (Nearly 3000 B.C.)

Walter Brown: What is the role of the messenger in Ancient Egypt?

QUINTESSENTIAL BOOK
"THE HOLY LAND"

Dr. Fred Monderson: The role of the messenger in Ancient Egypt is to deliver the message without any alteration. The *Maxims of Ptah-Hotep* says "The Messenger must deliver the message in exactly the words it was given to him. Perversion of it is detestable. 'If thou are one of those, who carry messages from one great (man) to another great (man), conform thyself exactly, to what he (the sender) has entrusted thee with; perform for him the commission as he hath enjoined thee. Beware of altering, when speaking, the disagreeable things that one great (man) addresses to another great (man). He who perverts the truthfulness of his message, so as to repeat only what may be pleasing of the words of any man, great or small, is a detestable person."

Teddy Cubia: How would you say Unas' pyramid differed from the others?
Dr. Fred Monderson: For one thing, Unas' fifth dynasty pyramid was served by a Valley and Worship temple containing a Causeway or roadway. His Causeway contained low-relief decoration on it walls and the ceiling is adorned with stars. His pyramid temple extensively used granite for many of its important features such as doorways, flooring and palm capitals on monolithic columns. Even more important, Unas' pyramid was the first to inscribe religious writings on its walls; moderns have termed "Pyramid Texts."

Cherise Maloney: Why is Mentuhotep's temple at Deir el Bahari significant?
Dr. Fred Monderson: Mentuhotep II's of the XIth Dynasty built the first of three mortuary temples at Deir el Bahari. The others are Hatshepsut's and Thutmose III. Mentuhotep's temple is considered transitional from the Old to the New Kingdom in terms of its architectural features. It is the oldest temple at Thebes and the best preserved of the Middle Kingdom structures. It was cleared by Edouard Naville who discovered it in 1903 after he had cleared Queen Hatshepsut's structure in the mid 1890s. Many had wondered about Hatshepsut's temple layout but after Mentuhotep's discovery it was shown Hatshepsut's temple was patterned after the older one. Both temples used the space between the Valley Temple beside at the river's edge to the pylon for decoration of courts lined with sphinxes and trees. Early on scholars theorized there was a pyramid at the center of this structure but that has changed. Beyond the Pylon there is an Open Court, pillared ambulatories and a hypostyle hall containing nearly 100 pillared columns. There were princesses and priestesses buried in the cliff tomb. The king was thought to be buried there but his body has not been found.

The temple was thought built for his Heb Sed Festival ceremony where six statues were found. One in the Cairo Museum depicts the king wearing the Red Crown of Lower Egypt. The one in best condition and housed in the Museum shows the king having "Black flesh!" Some of the princesses are colored red while Kemsit is colored Black. It is interesting that she is recognized as being black but the king is though, wrongfully, to be colored black for the death ceremony or because he was dead. Keep in mind this is a praise temple for a rejuvenation festival. But this is how they mislead on Egypt.

Joshua Monderson: Why did Thutmose I choose to be buried in the Valley of the Kings at Thebes?
Dr. Fred Monderson: Old Kingdom tombs were enormous structures that were easy prey to tomb robbers. Middle Kingdom tombs have not been discovered, for the most part. Thutmose I chose to be buried in the limestone hills of the Valley of the Kings as a way to thwart and prevent tomb robbery. He was followed there by kings of the 18th, 19th, and 20th Dynasties. Archaeology has revealed the beauty of some of these tombs and those of the queens, nobles and artisans. They were elaborate and were remarkably decorated, generally providing the occupants with the easy life they led on earth.

Dr. Alexander Pushkin: How were royal tombs different from private tombs?
Dr. Fred Monderson: In the Old Kingdom, the nobles built their private tombs in the vicinity of the pharaoh's pyramid hoping they would share in his immortality. The large mastaba tombs do show the growing independence of the nobility from the royal centralized authority. By the time of the New Kingdom, the private tombs were assigned their own valley while the royal tombs, king and queens were buried in their own special place, Valley of the Kings and Valley of the Queens. The private tombs were decorated, perhaps not as elaborately as the royal tombs and they were somewhat smaller.

Dr. Leonard James: Why were noble tombs called mastabas and what was their significance?
Dr. Fred Monderson: Workers digging for Auguste Mariette named these rectangular structures Mastabas because they looked like benches on which the Arabs sat. Their significance is indicated by their size which indicated independence from royal control. Some of the really large tombs were those of Khabausokar and Hesire; Ptah-shepses and Ti; Akhethetep and Ptahhotep and Mereruka. In the case of Mereruka, a vizier of the Sixth Dynasty during Teti's reign, he had 21 rooms for himself, 6 for his wife and 5 for his son. Away from the Sakkara burial ground, Nobles buried at Beni Hasan in Middle Egypt and Thebes in Upper Egypt chose to be buried in rock tombs cut in the hills. In their layout and pictorial decorations, the tomb provides ample evidence of the state of the culture allowing scholars to fill in gaps in their understanding of the history of the Nile Valley Experience.

Ok. That is all for today. Remember Dinner is at 7:00 PM. Have a good afternoon.

7. Free Time

QUINTESSENTIAL BOOK
"THE HOLY LAND"

Some people chose to go shopping, lounge around the pool or even engage in discussions in the hotel lounge. Still others relax in their hotel rooms, repairing their camera equipment and preparing their plan for the next day's outing.

8. Dinner

Teddy Cubia: I must admit Dr. Pushkin, Mr. Sinclair has been exemplary in his presentation of some of what he learned at Temple University under Molefi Asante. I think he deserves recognition for the perspicacious manner in which he has defended Afrocentricity. Won't you agree?

Dr. Alexander Pushkin: Well, I must admit he has been very pertinacious in his defense of his school, teacher and philosophy.

Mrs. Alexander Pushkin: However, one question I have for you Mr. Sinclair is this: What does a course of study consist of at Temple University's Afrocentric Institute headed by Dr. Asante?

Michael Sinclair: Well, a course of study can be very intensive with courses being offered at the 400, 500, 600, 700 and 800 levels. Each one is at a different level of complication as it relates to African history and research. For example, I will give you a description of the Graduate Course List so as to get a feel of the complexity of the work.

400 - Proseminar in Graduate work in African-American Studies is an introduction to the intellectual and professional foundations of the field. Examines the historical origins of African-American Studies in the United States and Africa, as well as the context and contents of classics, creative, analytic, and autobiographical works. Students will write papers on selected aspects of the development of African-American studies.

447 - The Afrocentric Idea is an intensive critique of African studies within the context of evolving theoretical and methodological issues. Topics include boundaries of particularism, frames of reference, etymology, historical cleavages, and the idea of the African voice. Students will write major papers analyzing the various perspectives advanced by scholars within the field of African studies.

667 – Seminar in African Aesthetics. Examines the philosophical foundation of African aesthetics by concentrating on the cosmology, ritual, religions, oral traditions, and proverbs of African people. Examines the question of what is beauty, or art, or good, or culture.

Teddy Cubia: I must hand it to our young man who is exceptionally sharp as usual.

Dr. Alexander Pushkin: I am convinced that Temple Afrocentric Institute has a wide scope of interest in its outreach. Considering the dimensions of problems Mr. Sinclair has identified, the school is doing a terrific job in addressing those issues.

FREDERICK MONDERSON

Mrs. John Stewart: Stephaniea, my husband will join us in a few. He is recovering from this hectic day. How do you like the trip so far?

Stephaniea McCall: Stupendous. I never dreamed it would be like this. The temples and tombs are really mind blowing. The architecture and art are certainly inspiring. I must bring my son here next year.

Mrs. John Stewart: How old is he?

Asantewaa Harris: He is fifteen and in the 10th Grade in high school. I have been working with him from the first day. I now realize I should have brought him to Egypt even sooner, but the finances, you know.

Mrs. John Stewart: I understand. Here comes my husband now. Hi John, feeling better?

Asantewaa Harris: Good morning, Mr. Stewart. Hope you are over the discomfort and raring to go.

Mr. John Stewart: Feeling much better. I will order a lemon squeeze and two slices of lemon. Dr. Monderson told me to chew the lemon with the rind, skin and all. I say this: "Only the actions of the just smell sweet and blossom in the dust." Therefore we must aspire to higher things, study hard, do research and spend our money on things like this trip and buy books. "The true university of these days is a collection of books."

9.   Lounge Discussion

Dr. Alexander Pushkin: Teddy, give us one of your poems and I will spring for the refreshments. I am having a local Stella beer because it's cold. What would you have?

Teddy Cubia: I will have the same. Lemon squeeze for you, Michael, or do you want the hard stuff, Stella? Ha. Ha.

Michael Sinclair: I will have the lemon squeeze if you read us the poem.

Teddy Cubia: This is an interesting poem, written in one of those discussions with my lady. It's called *Black Love*.

QUINTESSENTIAL BOOK "THE HOLY LAND"

Holy Land Photo 30. Kom Ombo Double Temple of Horus and Sobek. From the Hypostyle Hall view into the deep recesses of the Temple towards the Sanctuary.

"Black Love"
By
Teddy Cubia

The conception of Black Love has never really been defined.
It has always been clouded or distorted by a white man's movie,
Or a White man's book, in a white man's fantasy world.

In a Black man's love there are no roses to buy for a Black man cannot afford roses.
There are no violins playing because a Black woman cannot dig this music.
There are no fairy tale happy endings or sweet lullabies.
Because love is living every day together and a Black man's life is seldom made up of fantasy and sweet music.
A Black woman knows her man must struggle hard
To survive in this White man's world
She knows that loving him is to cook for him, to clean for him, and to bear for him sons to carry his name.
She knows that love is comforting him and letting him know he is still a man.
In a world where a Black male has had his manhood stripped

FREDERICK MONDERSON

Every day the Black man works in his hustle.
His purpose is not to be rich and live happily ever after
But to survive
In this fine world of Whites
He assures her that one - day all will be better
He'll get that job – that one big break
That will make everything easier
And with all of these hang-ups
I can only say
Black love is the most beautiful thing happening today!

Dr. Alexander Pushkin: Well done Teddy. It's a pity you did not have it written down for I would read it to my wife when I get to our room.
Michael Sinclair: Perhaps you should buy Teddy another beer, Dr. Pushkin?

Mr. Stewart: Hello Dr. Pushkin, Mr. Cubia and Mr. Sinclair, so this is where you guys meet after dinner. This is the watering hole! What's up?
Dr. Alexander Pushkin: Mr. Sinclair here is giving us a lesson on Afrocentricity. He has studied Afrocentric philosophy under Dr. Molefi Asante and has written his thoughts down and he writes very well. He is the future.
Mr. Stewart: How nice. The Library of Congress teaches that "Reading maketh a full man, conference a ready man, and writing an exact man," and "Words are also actions and actions a kind of words."
Dr. Alexander Pushkin: I think those words reflect well on this young scholar coming out of Temple's Afrocentric Institute.

Holy Land Illustration 45. View of the Ghizeh pyramid group from the desert.

QUINTESSENTIAL BOOK "THE HOLY LAND"

10. Hotel Room

Michelliea Georges: So my friend, what do you have for us this evening?

Regina Hendricks: It would be nice, this beautiful evening, if you could give us both history and religious notes. Perhaps we could even go to the Hotel Lounge for a glass of lemon squeezes.

George Washington: I could go for that. Let's see what I have. On September 18, 1975 we began with the reading of Moscati Chapter 2 on the emergence of Civilization in Mesopotamia. The Stone Age was divided into Palaeo, Meso and Neolithic or Old, Middle and New Stone Ages. In this region, the climate has not changed much since 10,000 B.C. Recent archaeological discoveries have found at least three pre-agricultural societies. These are Chayanu Huyuk, Shanindar, and Zawi Chemi, and these were farming communities without planting. They only reaped wild grains and fruits. Chatal Huyuk (6500 B.C.) in Asia Minor on a plateau. (10,000 to 6500 B.C. was a period of transition to agriculture). Within 32 acres, Chatal Huyuk had a population of approximately 32,000. Obsidian, when chipped, can be used for shaving. Burial of the dead shows some belief in an afterlife. Sprinkling of red ocher (dust) on the deceased. This is called substitute magic.

By 7000 B.C. the male deity had to do with the hunt. Male god's standard was a wild bull. Female goddess was similar to the Grimaldi woman, 'Venus of Willendorf,' with large breasts and large fatty buttocks. Around 4000 B.C. when hunting became less important and agriculture predominated, the male god's role decreased. Seasons had a profound effect on the lives of the people. Specialization of labor occurred with the birth of civilization with settlements of large groups of people. With this we have a population increase. Continuous childbirth and malnutrition caused women to probably die by 30 years. Real estate took on a value in a sedentary society.

That represents the history notes. Now let me move along and provide the **African Religion** notes.

Later that day, the discussions centered around religion as a systematic set of beliefs shared by a group of people. It is therefore closely associated with culture; *all* religion is "culture-bound" in this sense.

Culture is necessarily generalizing group behavior based on traditions, customs, art, language, living together and so on. Values are cultural values. Belief systems have rationale. In a sacred society, religion has a tremendous effect, for it is a connecting link for the people. Worldview, ideology, and cultural philosophy are parts of the glue that holds things together. Aesthetic is a concept of beauty.

FREDERICK MONDERSON

This is just one of the many units which culminate in "cultural refinement." Art is life! Art is isolated as opposed to communally based. Therefore it is sacred.

Ideology – A commitment to the study of ideas, their nature and source; the theory that all ideas arise from sensations; thinking or theorizing of an idealistic, abstract, or impractical nature; fanciful speculation; the doctrines, opinions, or ways of thinking of an individual or a class of people.

Culture – The concepts, habits, skills, arts, instruments, institutions, etc., of a given people in a given period; civilization; the training and refining of the mind, emotions, manners, tastes, etc.

Worldview – The way some people view the secular life and interests as distinguished from the religious or spiritual life of others; people primarily concerned with the affairs and pursuits of the present life.

Aesthetics – Sensitive to art or beauty; the study or philosophy of beauty; theory of the fine arts and of people's response to them.

George Washington: That is all for now.
Michelliea Georges: Thank you, George.
Regina Hendricks: With all that I am learning on this trip, and what you are supplying, this is a fantastic experience.

Day 5.   Day Off – Medinet Habu

1.   Wake Up

Esperanza Rodriguez. Good Morning, Mi Amor. Your schedule for today is a little off the hectic pace. It's a day-off but you gave permission for some to hire a boat and cross the river to see Medinet Habu Temple of Rameses III. Yes my sweet, but the guide tells me it would be easier to go across the bridge by bus.
Dr. Fred Monderson: Thank you, my dear.

"A TRIBUTE TO BLACK WOMANHOOD"
By Frederick Monderson *Daily Challenge*

As we celebrate Women's History Month in March this year, some comments and praises are due to Black women who have given so much, from the earliest times up to now.

QUINTESSENTIAL BOOK "THE HOLY LAND"

Science, utilizing a method of DNA reconstruction, has demonstrated that the earliest surviving progenitor of the human race has been a woman who roamed the plains of East Africa over two hundred and fifty thousand years ago. Earlier, a Palaeo-anthropologist named Johansson discovered the most complete human fossil. It was of a woman found in the Hadar region of Ethiopia, who was subsequently, nicknamed "Lucy," and dated to more than two million years old. Dr. ben-Jochannan said her name is actually *Denk Nesh*. The next great flowering of African womanhood occurred in the Nile Valley.

As a result, the role of women in ancient Egypt/Kemet has been essential, appreciated, respected and necessary. From the earliest times the indispensable position of Egyptian women has been depicted in the graves of the prehistoric period and in the tombs of deceased nobles. Their roles as goddesses, queens, princesses, mothers, and plain old folks, were demonstrated and the impact on numerous pharaohs as well as Egyptian society has been recounted.

Many women have ruled as queens of Egypt, but Hatshepsut of the Eighteenth Dynasty has been the only woman bold enough to substantially rule as King or Pharaoh of this ancient land. A queen, perhaps Nitocris, did reign at the end of the Old Kingdom.

Holy Land Illustration 46. Restoration of the Great Pyramid and other tomb monuments in the ancient cemetery of Egypt (After Hoelscher) in (Breasted 1926); and Relief scene from the chapel of a Nobles' tomb in the Pyramid Age.

The female principle in Egypt, as in Africa, is divine in nature. In Egyptian cosmogony and religious beliefs, female divinities have played important roles. They have featured prominently in triads, and in a number of instances females were a part of pharaonic triads.

FREDERICK MONDERSON

The goddess Nuit or Nut was from the earliest times a water goddess who formed part of a divine company of eight. The males were Nu, Hehu, Keku and Kerh. The females were Kerhet, Keruit, Hehut and Nut. Not much is known about the other goddesses, but in the New Empire, Nut was represented as a woman and as a cow.

According to the *Book of the Dead* or the Hieratic Transcript of the *Papyrus of Ani*, translated by E.A. Wallis Budge, there were a number of female deities in the Egyptian religious drama. The male Shu and the female Tefnut were children of Ra, the Sun God. Tefnut formed the third member of the company of gods of Anu. Tefnut is sometimes shown as moisture and at other times as sunlight. This goddess originated in the Nubian Desert. She had a lion head and wore a disk or uraeus or both. She drank her enemies' blood and had fire in her eyes.

The next female divinity of importance was Isis or Auset. She was the seventh member of the company of Anu, wife of Osiris and mother of Horus. She is usually depicted as a woman with a headdress in the shape of a seat or throne. Her principal temple is located at Philae, now Agilka Island. Some early names ascribed to her are "the great goddess, the divine mother, the mistress of words of power and enchantment." In later times she is called mother of the gods and the living one. Isis is sometimes shown as a cow and has a solar disk between her horns with a throne or seat, and she also has plumes or feathers. Her most famous depiction is as the mother suckling her child Horus. One could consider the original Madonna and Child concept is based on this depiction.

Nephthys was Isis' sister and wife of the evil god Seth. "When the sun rose at the creation of the primeval waters Nephthys occupied a place in his boat with Isis and other deities; as a nature goddess she either represents day before sunrise or after sunset, but not associated with night. Her hieroglyphic name means "lady of the house." Plutarch tells of a legend that said she was the mother of Anubis by Osiris, who later became judge of the dead. She is shown as the companion of Isis and was grieved during Osiris' murder.

The next female divinity of significance was Ma'at, the counterpart of Thoth. The Heliopolitan tradition makes her a daughter of Ra. She was the wife of Thoth, the god of writing. A feather symbolizes her name and she also holds a scepter in one hand and an ankh in another. The name Ma'at means straight, upright, genuine, righteous, just, real, truth, balance, order, steadfast, unalterable, etc.

Hathor, the "House of Horus," was the goddess of the sun where the sun god rose and set. Hathor is depicted as a woman with a disk and horns on her head. She is also shown as a cow with a disk between her horns. Budge says that as a "Cow-goddess she is probably of Sudani origin." That is Africa proper, to the south of

QUINTESSENTIAL BOOK
"THE HOLY LAND"

Egypt. It is interesting that the Africans of Nabta Playa originated the "Cow Goddess worship" and Hathor is shown on Narmer's Palette at Unification.

Neith has been called "the divine mother, the lady of heaven, the mistress of the gods." She is mentioned in the *Pyramid Texts* as the mother of Sobek, the crocodile god. Neith was believed to be self-produced and an ancient Saite tradition made her to be the mother of Ra, the Sun God. She is depicted in the form of a woman, having upon her head the shuttle or arrows, or she wears the Red Crown and holds arrows, a bow and a scepter in her left hand.

Sekhmet was the wife of Ptah, and the mother of Nefer-Temu and of I-Em-hetep. She personified the terrible heat of the desert. "When Ra determined to punish mankind with death, because they scoffed at him, he sent Sekhmet, his 'Eye' to perform the work of vengeance; illustrative of this aspect of her is a figure wherein she is depicted with the sun's eye for a head." Bast was a sort of opposite to Sekhmet. She personified the gently and fructifying heat of the sun. She is usually pictured as cat-headed.

Nekheb-ka is the name of a goddess represented by a serpent. Uatchit and Nekhebt were very special goddesses. They personified Upper and Lower Egypt and comprised the Pharaoh's "Two Ladies" name. Uatchit, a form of Hathor, is depicted as a woman with the crown of the north and a scepter. Nekhebt was the vulture goddess, tutelary deity of Upper Egypt from the city of Nekhen. Mut the earth goddess was wife of Amon-Ra the Sun god and mother of Khonsu the moon god. She was an essential part of the Theban triad, of Amon-Ra, Mut and Khonsu. She too is sometimes shown as a vulture.

As a result, female roles in the divine cosmogony and religious drama of the Egyptians gave them a special place in the social fabric of the society. Whether, wife, mother or sister, females were respected, cared for, and had equal status before the law. They could inherit property, become literate and were able to conduct business. Diop lauds their matriarchal role in the society.

The graves of the Badarian and Naqada I burials show much evidence of some association between the dead and women. What we call female paraphernalia can be found in many graves of the time. These include combs, rings, bracelets, and studs for the nose, jewelry of shells, carnelian and coral around the neck. There, earrings and dresses are also included. These early Africans utilized dyes with green malachite and castor oil for cleansing and softening the skin.

By the time of the Gerzean culture or Naqada II, figurines of the fertility goddess are found in graves. Carved bone and ivory figurines of women are also found in graves. They were designed to accompany deceased men into eternity.

FREDERICK MONDERSON

Female jewelry was made from a wide variety of materials including amethyst, button-pearl, amber, agate, onyx, and glass. The jewelry included necklaces, girdles, bracelets, and a circlet or diadem for the head. Therefore, in the pre-dynastic time, before 3200 B.C., the role of women was considered important enough to receive the attention indicated in such graves.

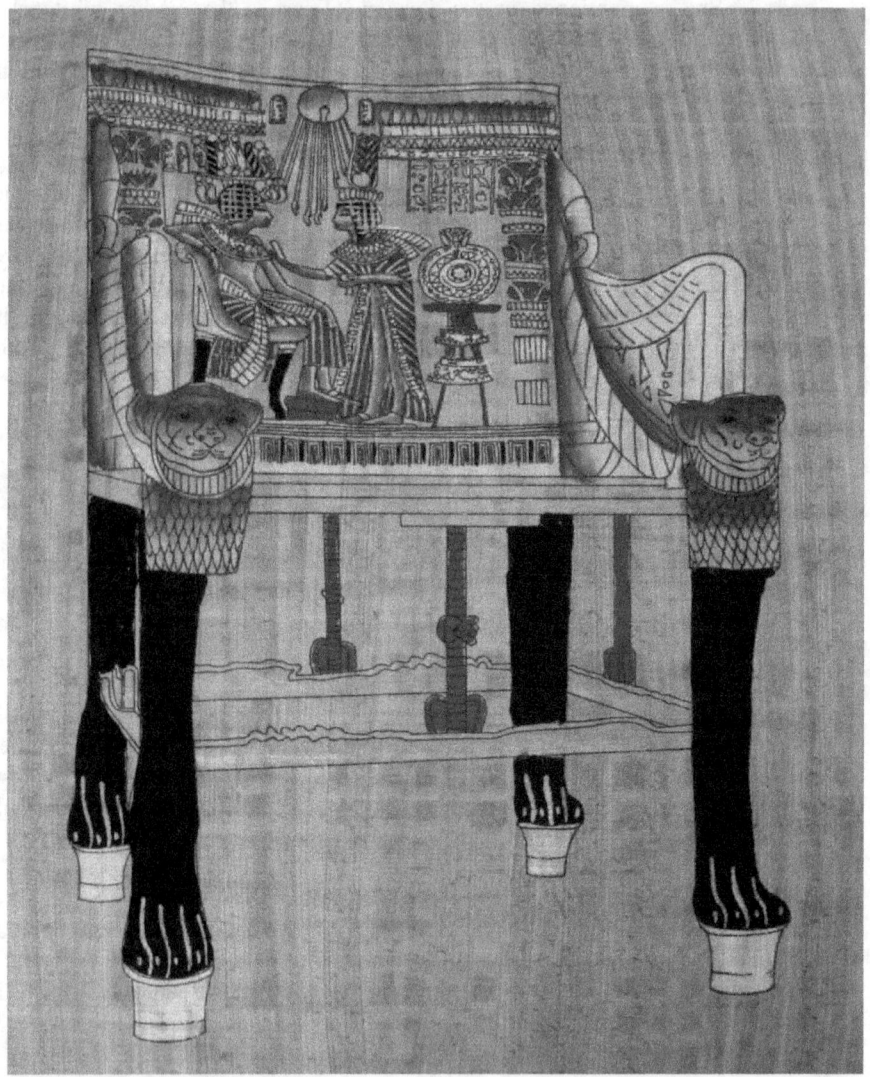

Holy Land Papyrus 14. The famous chair of Tutankhamon with its decorated back showing the enthroned monarch, his beautiful wife and the Aten shining its rays on them both.

QUINTESSENTIAL BOOK "THE HOLY LAND"

From the time of the First Dynasty, c. 3200 B.C. onwards, the position of women seems advanced and appreciated. On the Narmer Macehead the king is shown under a pavilion. His wife, Queen Neithhotep, is shown also seated and facing him. Some feel this is probably a marriage ceremony. However, it clearly shows an elevated position for his wife. They had a son named Aha, who succeeded his father to the throne. Equally too, Hathor is shown on the Narmer Palette, is the first imaged female divinity.

While Narmer was buried in a regular sized mastaba tomb at Abydos, Aha built an elaborate tomb for his mother, Queen Neithhotep. The indications of this are that the husband and son, in ancient Egypt, loved and respected the wife and mother. The same care and concern could be found for the daughter and for the sister.

In this respect, the basis for the love, respect and proper consideration of women or females in Egypt is clear. This treatment is evidenced by the roles of and respect for the goddesses, queens, mothers and princesses. It stands to reason that the ordinary woman also enjoyed some of this special attention. However, it must also be pointed out, there were women who held positions as household help and slaves, as in many societies in the modern and ancient world.

The significance of women in Egypt is further indicated by their status before the law. The Supreme Court, according to an inscription on the walls of a tomb at Sakkara, upheld a certain woman's right to inheritance. Schafik Allam's *Everyday Life in Ancient Egypt*, has argued women could "inherit moveable things, house and landed property."

Even more, women were held accountable for their actions in the society. Still, they could also engage in business or represent their husbands in business transactions. They could receive loans, mediate between two parties and were allowed to bear witness in many judicial proceedings. Women also had the legal right to conduct legal affairs without the prior authorization of their husbands.

The inscription at Sakkara tells of a woman named Ornero, who was "designated by the courts as representative for a group of heirs and who consequently had to administer on trust all the property in question." Women could also sue in court. Many wives of officials were "responsible for regulating their husbands' affairs and looking after their husbands' interests." Many were authorized to act in the husband's absence. Therefore, it's clear that a number of dynamic Egyptian, African, women have impacted on three thousand years of socio-political-religious cultural expression in dynastic Egypt.

The Third Dynasty began the first "golden age" in Egypt. It also began the Old Empire or Old Kingdom.

FREDERICK MONDERSON

The accomplishments of the preceding Pre-dynastic and Archaic periods set the stage for the new era. The Step-Pyramids and the great mastaba tombs became prototype for the true pyramids of the Fourth and Fifth Dynasties.

The pharaohs who dominated the Fourth Dynasty were Snefru, Khufu, Khafre and Menkaure. The first built two pyramids at Dashur and Meydum. The other three built the famous Giza group. What is significant, however, is the role Queen Hetep-Heres played in influencing these four great Egyptian kings. Queen Hetep-Heres was the wife of Pharaoh Snefru, mother of Khufu, grandmother of Khafre and great-grandmother of Menkaure. What a progeny! She must have been a powerful African woman.

In 1925, excavators in an expedition from Harvard University worked at Giza. Behind the pyramid of Khufu, they discovered the "only intact tomb chamber from the Old Kingdom" found up to that time. According to J.E. Manchip White's *Ancient Egypt: Its Culture and History*, a "wonderful collection was unearthed."

There, archaeologists found: "... there was a canopy, a bed, two chairs and a carrying chair, all sheeted in gold. There were alabaster vessels, a copper and gold manicure instrument. There was a toilet box with cosmetics contained in eight little alabaster pots, and a jewel case with twenty silver anklets inlaid with lapis lazuli, carnelian and malachite. Inlaid gold hieroglyphs on the ebony panels of the carrying chair carried the fourfold inscription: "'Mother of the King of Upper and Lower Egypt, follower of Horus, guide of the Ruler, favorite whose every command is carried out for her, daughter of the god (born) of his body Hetepheres.'"

In the tradition of powerful African women, Hetepheres was one of the greatest. The bust of Pharaoh Khufu is so African with his broad nose and thick lips; one can only wonder what his mother and father looked like. At the start of the Middle Kingdom, a conflict between Intef and Mentuhotep, Queen Aam and Intef's mother played an important role in mediating their differences.

However, who's better than the greatest? The answer is Teti-Sheri!

The Eighteenth Dynasty was the most remarkable of all others. This was so because of the females who provided the progeny and inspiration for this greatest golden period. Teti-Sheri was the wife of Sekenenra Tao I. In *Temples, Tombs and Hieroglyphs*, Barbara Mertz wrote: "Teti-Sheri survived him; she lived to see her daughter [Ahotep] marries her own brother, Sekenen-re the Brave. Her granddaughter Aahmose-Nefertari also married her brother, Ahmose .... Ahmose's queen was a lovely woman, and a great lady, who was deified in later times."

QUINTESSENTIAL BOOK "THE HOLY LAND"

Sekenen-re was killed with an axe-blow to the head in the war of liberation against the Hyksos, or Asiatic invaders.

The family relationship of Teti-Sheri's progeny is important for it clearly establishes the Blackness of the Eighteenth Dynasty. In *The Splendor That Was Egypt* Margaret Murray describes Ahmose, the founder of the dynasty as a: "strongly built man, broad-shouldered, and with curly brown hair; he was not good-looking for he had projecting front teeth, and his portraiture suggests an admixture of Negro blood."

From her portrait in the British Museum the beautiful Ahmes-Nefertari leaves no doubt about her Black Ethiopian origin. Her granddaughter Queen Hatshepsut had to contend with the fact of her "Ethiopian blood" as the heiress to the throne after her father Thutmose I's death. She also indicted her relationship to the people of the land of Punt where she sent an expedition, of historical and anthropological significance. This equally remarkable woman challenged male dominance and ruled for two decades. Senmut, her favorite and architect who built the magnificent Deir el-Bahari temple at Thebes, headed her personal circle.

Senmut also quarried and erected two obelisks for the queen. Another architect, Amenhotep, erected two others. Two have disappeared and one still stands at Karnak, while the zenith of another remains beside the Sacred Lake. The standing obelisk measures 105 feet and is the tallest in Egypt. This queen who described her-self as: "beautiful to look at above all things; her voice was that of a god; her frame that of a god; her spirit was like a god" maintained the prosperity of her nation but succumbed to male rage and dominance. Her name still ranks as one of the most beautiful and powerful of female heroes.

Queen Tiye was the wife of Amenhotep III and the mother of Amenhotep IV. Her husband ruled Egypt at the height of the New Kingdom's "Golden Age." She played a prominent role in events of her time. Amenhotep III built a palace called Malcata for his beautiful Nubian Queen Tiye. She had a significant impact on her son Amenhotep IV. He changed his name to Akhenaten and ushered in a new religious movement. Also, the art of the time was probably influenced by his ideas. Critics have credited her with influencing the rebellion her son introduced.

Nefertiti, Dushrata's daughter Thadukippa, was a Mitanni princess who came to Egypt and married Queen Tiye's son Akhenaton or Ikhnaton. She came into a powerful family and played a significant role in her husband's rule. She bore him five daughters and visibly displayed her love for him in a number of representations.

In the Nineteenth Dynasty Rameses II, the great builder and warrior Pharaoh built the Abu Simbel temple in Nubia. He married Nefertari, a Nubian princess and built her a temple next to his at Abu Simbel. This was the supreme test of love, which clearly indicates the power of this African woman.

This selection seeks to highlight the majesty, power, beauty and everlasting testimony of the greatness of African and African-American womanhood. Clearly, no nation on earth can boast such a splendid line of outstanding women as Egypt who have influenced their states and the world. They remain to be admired and serve as role models of integrity and accomplishment for an entire race of people. These were indeed great African women and they set powerful examples for progeny of the African race.

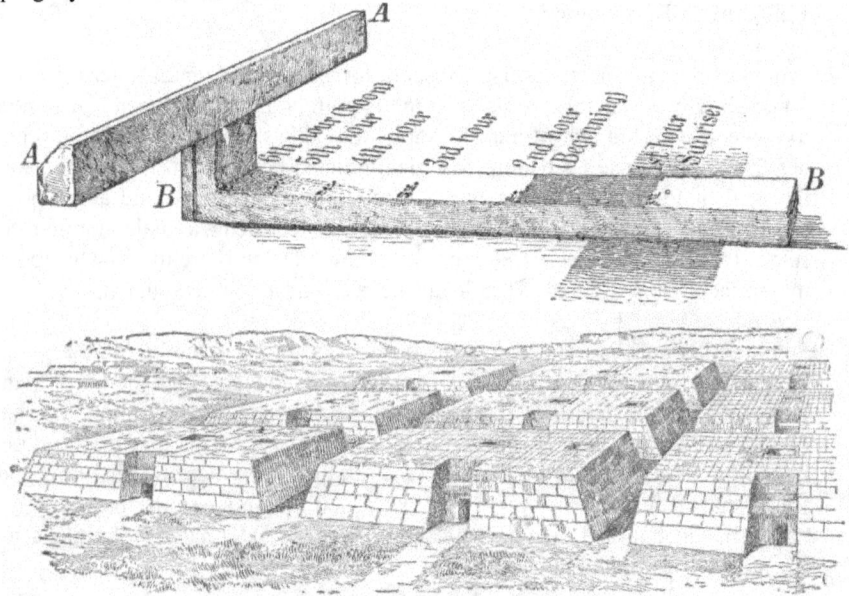

Holy Land Illustration 47. The oldest clock in the world – An Egyptian Shadow Clock; and Restoration of a group of Tombs of the Nobles in the Pyramid Age.

Queen Amenardis, sister of Piankhy of the Twenty Fifth Dynasty was a beautiful woman who became "God's wife" to Amon-Ra at Thebes following the Ethiopian conquest of Egypt.

Ethiopia later produced a strong line of queens called Candace who were warrior Queens and represented their nation and people with distinction. These followed in the tradition of Queen of Sheba, who while not a warrior, was Ethiopian and founded a dynasty with her child from Solomon. Queen Cleopatra, of the Ptolemies, was beautiful and had to contend with the changing realities thrust upon her nation and she rose to the occasion

QUINTESSENTIAL BOOK "THE HOLY LAND"

In West Africa the role of Queen and Queen Mother was very significant contributing much to that culture cluster of the Ghana, Mali and Songhay empires. The descendants of these women were dragged off to be slaves in the New World. One of the first of those was Angela who disembarked from the Dutch Man O' War in 1619 and Isabela who in 1624 gave birth to the first black African child born in the New World. Tonya Bolden, in *The Book of African-American Women*, mentions some 150 crusaders, creators and up - lifters of black men in America. These women were in every walk of life, from slave to plantation owner. Some were entrepreneurs, preachers, abolitionists, activist-lecturers, thinkers, conductors of the Underground Railroad, writers, singers, mothers, nurses, spies, real estate investors, playwrights, cooks, poets, journalists, educators, civil rights activists, doctors, pharmacists, aviators, army officers, judges, lawyers, anthropologists, historians, dancers, psychologists, politicians, athletes, mathematicians and even more. Some were lynched and there were the "four little girls," victims in a Birmingham Church bombing.

In looking at James Allen's exhibit on "Lynching across America," a grandmother in the line said: "I must get my grandchild to come over to look at this," as she viewed the Black woman Laura Nelson who was lynched in Oklahoma in 1911. That day both mother and son were lynched! Interestingly enough, there is no question that in the more than one hundred slave rebellions Herbert Aptheker chronicled in this hemisphere, women played a significant role, and we can add to this the revolutionaries Angela Davis and Assata Shakur.

Recognition is due the dignity and accomplishments of the ancient "sheroes" mirrored in the struggles and untiring efforts of many modern women. Today, Queen Mother Moore, Joyce Dinkins, Adelaide Sanford, Winnie Mandela, Coretta Scott King, and Mrs. Jessie L. Jackson stand for the same principles of African achievement. We should also not forget Phyllis Wheatley, Harriet Tubman, Sojourner Truth, and Mrs. David Walker, Mrs. Henry Highland Garnet, Mrs. Frederick Douglass, Mrs. Booker T. Washington, Mrs. W.E.B. DuBois, Mrs. Marcus Garvey, Carmen Rodriguez Alcantara Monderson, Priscilla Dunjee, Mrs. Carter G. Woodson, Mary McLeod Bethune, Fannie Lou Hamer, Septima Poingette Clarke, Gemma Grigsby and Anna Arnold Hedgemon. Miriam Wright Edelman founded the Children's Defense Fund. Let's also mention the great Dorothy Height, Barbara Jordan, Patricia Harris, Cybil Holmes, Haidee Idelfonsa Galan, Juliet Plummer Cobb, biologist, Alice Walker, and Zora Neal Hurston; writers, Johnnetta Cole, educator and Rev. Elizabeth Lott, mother and member of the C.M.E. Church. Then there is Jean Leon, Marjorie Matthews, Kathie Rones, Mrs. Benjamin, Jacqueline Lennon, Kadiatou Diallo, Audrey Phillips-Caesar, Mrs. Steil, Mrs. Parris, Mrs. Benjamin, Gloria Thomas, Jeromane Berger-Gaskin, and the Auxiliary Ladies at Kings County Hospital Center, Angela Cooper at DSSM, and Betsy Youman, Katie Harrell, Renee Morgan, Deborah Souvenir-Tyndale,

FREDERICK MONDERSON

Mrs. Mock, Josephine Braithwaite, Renee Smoke, Marilyn Washington, Ruth Green and Carmen Rudder.

Betty Dopson, Ella Fitzgerald, Carmen McRae, Vonetta Price, Bessie Smith, my aunts Edith Maude Graham and Mavis Hill, then Aretha Franklin, and Philippa Duke Schuyler, Bessie Smith, and Sybil Williams Clarke and Gertrude ben-Jochannan, Shirley Chisholm, Una Clarke and Diane Choyice Robinson, are only some of the names.

Then there's "Moms Mabley;" "Me Moms" Mitta Monderson, "Me grand-Moms" Cherise Preville, "Me Sisters" Cherise Monderson-Maloney and Megan Monderson and Bridget Duncan, "Me Aunts" Enid Graham and Mavis Hill and we could add Keisha Monderson and Queen-Tiy Monderson, Bridget Monderson, Kashida Maloney, as well as contemporary woman educators, Rhonda Hurdle-Taylor, Charissa Wright and Ms. Danzi, Mrs. Purdie, Hyacinth Rowe, Lucille Lang, Mrs. Ilene Loncke of New York, Prof. Joycelynne Loncke, the French teacher in Guyana, and her sister, Yvonne Loncke-Waithe holding it down as Pan African Philosophy stalwarts, as well as Hessel Woolcock, Mrs. Harper, Mrs. Elizabeth Buckman Jones, Suhail Monderson, Mrs. Virginia Jackson, Mrs. Jane Roberts, Estelle, Valma and Lorna Browne, Rhonda Mormon Harris, Merimba Ani Richards, Yvette Monderson, Mrs. Winna Allette, the ladies at American Airlines Mrs. Delores Green, Yvonne Robinson, Adowa Benjamin, Gillian Stewart, Lydia Oliveri, Mrs. Delores Greene, and Sandra Fillippone who do such a wonderful job; then there are Sophie Williams, Sue Ellen Luton of Caribbean Airlines, Ethel Foy, Melinda Melbourne, Mrs. Murray, Bernice Wiley, Evelyn Castro, Debra Braithwaite, Mrs. Angela Jitu Weusi, and so many more. We must remember Yonette Heyligar, Manager of Customs, Cheddi Jagan International Airport in Guyana, as well as Customs Officers Elita Chapman and Claire Brotherson, also at Cheddi Jagan Airport. Ms. Blackmon and Camille Elcock, hold it down at Home Affairs Ministry in Georgetown, Guyana.

Even more, we can't forget Kiatdou Diallo, Agnes Green, Mrs. Haggler, Linda Bascombe, Osela McCarty, philanthropist, Sarah J. Hale, humanitarian, Annette Robinson and Mary Pinkett, City Councilwomen, Andre Pennix Smith, Lois and Ruth Goring and Gwendolyn Harmon community minded. Marcia Melbourne, Toni Morrison, Lori Sharpe, Madame C. J. Walker, Mary Church Terrell, Lory Howell, Registered Nurse at New York University Hospital in Manhattan and Tamani Wooley, Photographic, Professional Reporter for New York 1 TV Station, Lorraine Geneva Title at American Airlines, Mrs. Estelle Brown, Ava Stagger, Carmen Alcantara Rodriguez, Pura Belpre, writer, Bessie Coleman, Aviator, and other women in music, Pearl Bailey, Marian Anderson, Marlon Williams, Sarah Vaughn, and Lena Horne, Rosetta Dunning, Veronica Corbett, Doris Alexander and Priscilla Maddox, Bernice Green and Viola Sanders, a wonderful friend Holly Fuchs Ferguson and all the School Nurses.

QUINTESSENTIAL BOOK
"THE HOLY LAND"

Condoleezza Rice, Michelle Obama, Susan Rice, Valerie Jarrett, Melody Barnes, Lisa Jackson and Cassandra Butts, all beautiful and effective political administrators, vibrant, wise and worth emulating.

The African-American male is therefore fortunate to have such powerful women to stand with, beside and behind him to help guide his endeavors. This tribute to these women is well deserved. There are conduits in the tradition of strong black women bequeathing the strong yet tender and ferocious African womanism in the American experience. Black men, make your women proud!

Holy Land Photo 31. Kom Ombo Double Temple of Horus and Sobek. Pass the uraei wall in the Court, the upper reaches of the massive columns with varied capitals at the double entrance to the Temple with twin winged disks with uraei.

MIDDLE SCHOOL TRANSFORMATION

On March 4, 2000 Community School District 17 in Brooklyn, sponsored its First Middle School Conference entitled: "Engaging the Community for Middle School Transformation - A Conference to Empower Middle School Students." In this effort, Students, Parents and Educators came together to dialogue and plan strategies for the task ahead, echoing Mychal Wynn's belief: "The Greatest quest

FREDERICK MONDERSON

in life is to reach one's potential." Equally too was emphasized, Helen Keller's dictum: "We can do anything we want to do if we stick to it long enough."

David A. Hamburg, President of the Carnegie Corporation of New York tells that: "The problems of adolescence deal with deep and moving human experiences. They center on a fateful time in the life course when poorly informed decisions can have lifelong consequences. The tortuous passage from childhood to adulthood requires our highest attention, our understanding, and a new level of thoughtful commitment."

Gladstone Atwell Middle School 61 was host for the conference and its Principal Rhonda Hurdle rolled out the welcome mat. After breakfast and registration, in the morning session a number of workshops were scheduled, before the Plenary Session in the auditorium. And after, lunch in the cafeteria with drawing for prizes, capped a special and successful effort on the part of all concerned.

The Workshop Schedule read as follows: "Using the Internet to Access African-American Resources" by Presenter Mr. Amoye Neblett and Wilbur Johnson, Technology Staff Developers; "Read Together - Parents as Reading Partners" by Presenter Ms. Omiyinka Barton, CSD 17 Literacy Coordinator; "Using Oral Tradition as a Bridge to Literacy for the English Language Learner" by Presenter Ms. Christine Damas, Bilingual Language Instructional Specialist; "The Middle School Years" by Presenter Ms. Estelle Brown, Guidance Counselor MS 61; "The Adolescent Learner: Helping the Middle School Student Meet the English Language Arts Standards" by Presenters Ms. Lorna Brown, Literary Specialist, MS 61 and Ms. Norma Palmer, Literacy Specialist MS 61; "Building A Bridge from Middle School to College Entrance Exams (SATs)" by Presenter Mr. Joe Habib, Teacher PS 161; "Getting Together to Learn: Cooperative Learning in Action" by Presenter Mr. Gary Newman, Teacher Center Staff, CSD 17; "High School Articulation" by Presenter Patricia Ramseur, Executive Assistant to the Superintendent; "Helping Students Develop a Positive Self Image" by Presenter, Ms. Kathleen Burgess, Supervisor of Early Childhood; "Introducing the New Science Standards" by Presenter Mr. Dan Forbes, Science Coordinator; "The Academic Social and Spiritual Development of the Inner City Student" by Presenter Mr. Carlos Walton, Math Teacher, MS 61; "Parents, Pupils and Puffy" by Presenter Ms. Phyllis Bynum; "Empowering Ourselves Through Defining A Clear Sense of Purpose" by Presenter Dr. Brenda Boyd-Bell, Consultant; and Dr. Fred Monderson offered a "Slide Presentation on Ancient Egypt."

The Mistress of Ceremonies, Ms. Debra Braithwaite was "very happy that students are a part of this conference. Everyone here has undertaken the task to build understanding of the fascinating experience before us. The basic human needs must be addressed." She expressed the view, "Students must find ways to earn respect. They must become involved in peaceful ways to manage conflict as well

QUINTESSENTIAL BOOK
"THE HOLY LAND"

as espouse the highest standards of ethical behavior. They must use social support systems and acquire a positive view of themselves, their parents, teachers and community. We stand here on the prayers of our ancestors who were kings and queens and continue in the vein of their aspirations to uplift the children and improve education."

Dr. Jacqueline P. Davis introduced Principal Rhonda Hurdle-Taylor, of MS 61, one of the youngest in the school system.

Ms. Hurdle spoke of "a sense of urgency in the will to excellence. The teachers are here to release the full potential of our students." She spoke of 5 challenges before young and old people. These are: "Intellectual reference, good citizenship, caring ethical behavior, healthy lifestyles and a will to excellence to transform Middle School students." Ms. Hurdle said further: "We're here for young people. What you see here in the auditorium are not students but young adults and leaders of our future. I see future doctors, teachers, and lawyers in the audience. We thank you for the food to nourish our lives, souls and spirits."

The poem "Don't Quit" was utilized to send a message to young people. The first stanza read as follows: "When people pull you down, as they often will, When the battle you're fighting is all uphill, When the funds are low and the debts are high, When you're laughing, although you'd rather cry, When you discover yourself slowing down a bit, Stop and take a deep breath, but don't you quit."

Equally too, Sarah Rosen, 16, wrote: "I think that being a kid is the most important stage of your life. It's a time when you start to develop a personality. It's when you start to learn about who you are, and what you want to do with yourself. And it's a time when you develop trust. It's a time when you learn how to be a person in society.

Unfortunately a lot of kids don't have that. If you don't grow up learning how to be a productive person, then you're going to have a problem once you grow up."

Dr. Evelyn W. Castro, Superintendent of Community School District 17, as customary, gave the greeting in Spanish, Buenos Dios, in French, Bon Jour, and in English Africa they say, "How are the children? If the children are doing all right, we will all be fine," she echoed.

She informed: "there are 27,000 children in Community School District 17. Of this amount, there are 9,000 in the Middle Schools. There has consistently been talk of transformation. Over the last 3 years there has been a 15% improvement in reading and almost 50% in math. The nation is worried about the Middle School crisis. We are here to serve, to show love, to transform our schools and give information to parents, teachers and students."

Holy Land Illustration 48. Abydos. Temple of the Kings. The Barque of Osiris (left); and the Barque of Ra-Harakhti (right).

She spoke of the singer Isaac Hayes who was at Middle School 2 as part of the District's Black History Month's celebration. His father had died. He was picking cotton by the time he was in Middle School. His clothes were shabby and he was not going to school regularly. School or not he picked cotton. There was an airfield nearby. He would look up at the planes flying overhead and say, 'Someday I will be on one of those planes.' "So don't let anyone tell you what you can't do. However, while basketball has helped some people, out of every 1000 applicants only 50 get selected. You must get your graduate degree. Michael Jordan has a college Education Doctorate. We must transform our Middle Schools."

"How many of our ancestors came through the Middle Passage? Many did not make it. But we did because of their sacrifices. Students here must succeed. They can succeed. Don't let your friends choose you. You pick your friends. Pick those who are going someplace. Young people you must have a vision of who you are and what you want to do." She was emphatic that "Only people who take notes and carry books are the people I trust."

QUINTESSENTIAL BOOK
"THE HOLY LAND"

Ms. Debra Braithwaite, Deputy Superintendent for Curriculum and Instruction, introduced the Keynote Speaker, Dr. Molefi K. Asante of Temple University and author of the increasingly popular social and educational philosophy, Afrocentricity. She mentioned that Dr. Asante had authored some 42 books and written many articles. She explained: "He has emphasized that each centered person becomes an owner not a renter of knowledge so young and old African people in America and worldwide must center themselves. He is one of the ten most cited African-American authors. He has appeared on Nightline, 60-Minutes, Talk Back, Black Entertainment Television, and a host of other programs."

Molefi Asante is the author of *Afrocentricity*, *The Afrocentric Idea*, and *Kemet, Afrocentricity and Knowledge*. His newest works are *Scream as Blood, Ancient Egyptian Philosophers, The African-American Atlas* and *Malcolm X as Cultural Hero*.

Dr. Asante thanked Ms. Hurdle for hosting this conference. He thanked the community leaders, teachers and Superintendent and Assistant Superintendent. Turning to the audience he pointed out faces that had become so familiar because of his many trips to Africa. "You look so handsome," he said. "You look like a Mandinka King. You look like a Yoruba Princess. The greatness and traditions of Africa I see in front of me today. You are an Ibo lady. I have seen African faces in the West Indies, the Caribbean, and South America. We have contributed to the universe. Science says Africa is the home of all humanity. We are all products of the African mother who roamed east Africa 250,000 years ago. The 6 billion people on the face of the earth are descended from her." Some of the students in the audience included Jomo Bartholomew, Patrick Whittaker, Renroy Chase, Devron Monroe, Kevens Jean-Jacques, Robenson Pualena, and Sarana Purcell.

"I don't believe Middle School students are an endangered species" he remarked. "You are the great gift we can give to the world. I can see Senegal. I can see all the power we have. I know our scores can be higher."

Dr. Asante admonished students to: "Read more school books each week. Read 30 minutes more per week. Some of you can do 30 minutes a day but do 30 minutes per week. We are a people with an enormous capacity for life. African culture always has had a great responsibility for life. We find truth and hope. We find life, joy and dignity. Read 30 minutes more. There are two things you need to know. These are, "love your ancestors" and "love Ma'at," he implored.

FREDERICK MONDERSON

"First, the ancestors! You need to know who you are. In Brooklyn many African people have powerful Nubian faces. Not only do I know who I am but, I know to whom I am connected. In this country they broke our connection," he emphasized.

"How many people know who are Rodinga, Dead Brass, Khnum?" he asked. "I met with these groups. I told them you can't use the N-word and the B-word. We can't use those words. They say that the N or B words are words of endearment. Do you know what they meant when they called us Niggers?" he asked. "What scares me is when a 7-year old kid calls his friend Nigger. Only people who hate themselves call each other Niggers."

He supplied some historical examples of the experiences of our people here in America.

"The Black Community in Tulsa Oklahoma in 1910 was a well-to-do community. They had 200 stores. They were a progressive community. A white girl on an elevator said a Black man made a pass at her and 10,000 whites rioted and burned down the town."

"In Rosewood, Florida, in 1927, the white community burned down Rosewood. They said they were Niggers. This is to destroy memory. They did not bring slaves to Trinidad, Cuba, America. They brought farmers, blacksmiths, musicians, priests, and members of royal families. They made slaves. You destroy the memory of a people and you make slaves out of them." This is why he believes people must know their history and the African-American especially must know the history of Africa and of the African-American in America.

"The word Nigger is kept in existence for a purpose. No African got off the boat saying I am Andrew Jackson. They had African names like Murtala, Obasanjo, Nkrumah, Lumumba. If you destroy the name you destroy the memory. That's why education is so important because it enables one to remember his history, ancestors and experiences."

"Ethics is important. Ma'at is important. Ma'at is the earliest word in history that tells you how to maintain discipline. Ma'at is powerful. It is beautiful," he confessed.

"I will give you 7 categories to which Ma'at applies" he remarked.

"1. *Harmony*. Search for relationships with my peers and teachers. I want harmony to reduce anger and hostility.
2. *Order*. Keeping things straight. Know where you are all the time.
3. *Justice*. Fairness.

QUINTESSENTIAL BOOK
"THE HOLY LAND"

4. *Balance.* In Africa they did not believe you could work for perfection; you needed balance.
5. *Truth.* Truth may hurt, but tell the truth. Peers put pressure on you but remember the truth is always good.

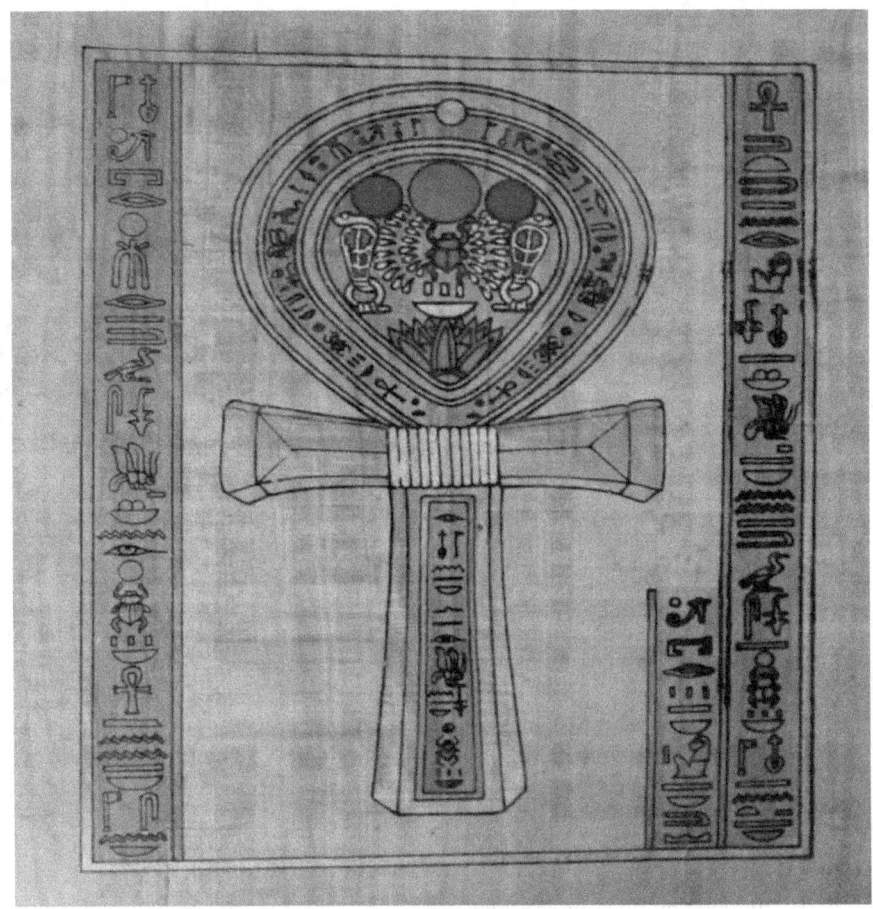

Holy Land Papyrus 15. The Ankh, in color, symbolizing **LIFE**!

6. *Righteousness.* Have an attitude towards all things that are good. Help other people. Help in social upliftment. Help to make sure that other people are ok.
7. *Reciprocity.* The Bible says: Do unto others as you would have them do unto you."

FREDERICK MONDERSON

"In life if you want things to be good for you, work for other people. Reciprocity helps us to keep Ma'at. These were the fundamental bases of ethics."

Regarding American history: "It should not be taught as American history with Africans in it; but American history with African-Americans as agents. Historical. Live. Consciously." "Harriet Tubman was the greatest person that I know who lived in the United States. I don't know of anyone else. In her 20s she did not want to be a slave. As a slave, you can't get up, have sneakers, and eat when you want. Someone had control of your time, body and mind. She ran away, yet went back to get her father, brother, sister. She went 19 times to the south. It shows an incredible amount of patience, energy. She brought 300 people to freedom. No one ever risked his or her life like that. You should read about Harriet Tubman. No person in American History did that."

"You must start doing that now; you must have a plan in your head."

"I was in West Africa, Burkina Faso, Ouagadougou, Middle High School. I walked in and all students rose to their feet. There were 60 students in a classroom. These were Black children in West Africa. There are Black children in Philadelphia, but they have no control. The thing that happened to Black people was America.

Part of my mission with Middle School children is to help them understand America."

"I recommend that young people do three things. The first is do 30 minutes of studying. The second thing is learn to listen. If you listen well and you read more you will destroy all common images of African people."

"I went to the prison to visit some people there. A young man came to me and said: 'On the outside I did not listen, I did not read. Since I have been in prison I have read, I have been listening to people.' Listening creates for you an advantage of what is possible."

"The things you must do are love your ancestors, read 30 minutes more, listen to people and to yourself, do Ma'at."

On April 6, a show on TNT at 8 PM. "The faces of Evil." It's about the slave trade and the killing of a Black man in Jasper Texas.

On Mummia Al Jamal: "We're trying to get another hearing in the U.S. Supreme Court. There are many others. You have your own situation in New York. The

QUINTESSENTIAL BOOK "THE HOLY LAND"

police in Louisville, Kentucky shot a young man 19 times. They gave him a medal."

"Don't lose your memory. Don't let people steal your history. The only history book written for African people is the one I wrote."

In the Question and Answer Period he was asked: "How do you feel about the Diallo Case?" "Initially I was stunned. After I thought about it, I realized this is America. In a race-based society you get race-based judgments." "In 1914, Monroe Trotter of Boston wrote President Woodrow Wilson complaining he had re-segregated Washington, D.C. A delegation of blacks walked and sang. They refused to meet if Monroe Trotter was not with them. Monroe Trotter was not trying to embarrass the President. The first 12 presidents were slaveholders. The society they put in place for free men, property owners, was mainly to benefit white people."

Fred Monderson, a student at Temple University for one year, made four unsuccessful attempts to matriculate there, and received four denial letters. Still, he got up and expressed the following sentiment: "I want to publicly thank Dr. Asante for teaching me when I studied with him at Temple University: 'Never let a historical situation pass you by without writing about it.'" Dr. Asante replied: "It was a case of the student knowing more than the teacher!" Dr. Lindamichellebaron, a Columbia University Graduate and former New York City Public School teacher is a poet with a message. She believes that: "Being black don't mean being stupid." She is the author of *The Sun is On*; *Rhythm and Dues: Poetry and Idea Book*; *Love for the Love of Life*; and *Grady Grasshopper* and *Anthony Ant*. The new editions of these books provide opportunities for self-development through written reflections. The idea books suggest goal attainment strategies and methodologies consistent with Lindamichellebaron's innovative and expanding educational enrichment program *Driving the Dream: Language Driven Believing and Achieving*. She is also co-author of *The Write Direction*, an instructional writing book.

FREDERICK MONDERSON

Holy Land Illustrations 49. Ploughing and sowing in the Pyramid Age; and Potter's wheel and furnaces.

In a **Biographical Note**, Dr. Adelaide Sanford, New York State Regents has said of Lindamichellebaron's book *The Sun is On*: *Poetry and Idea Book*: "Lindamichellebaron's intellectual light burst like a sunbeam flashing into unlit places. She brought vigor, energy, hope, and joy to children whose school experiences had been devoid of color, brightness or cultural relevance. She lit their 'unlit lamps.' Until today, she persists in this sacred mission." In this work the author invites all to achieve, to grow, to resolve conflicts, to love themselves and to love each other. Her idea books support her creative messages and provide self-reflective activities as a "how to" guide for life and learning, even as they resonate with the author's extensive background as a writing process consultant and author.

"Why me? You are a Black man and we need you.
You have to hear yourself. He did not love himself.
You talking to me, you're the man
You're the man, even if you're a woman.
Good to be the man"

"Don't have any children, don't have any women who you won't respect" is what she told the young men.
"Not just about me, it's about we, We be the man."

"Hey, come here!
He like potato chips. He won't even treat me like the whole bag
I don't have to live here."

QUINTESSENTIAL BOOK "THE HOLY LAND"

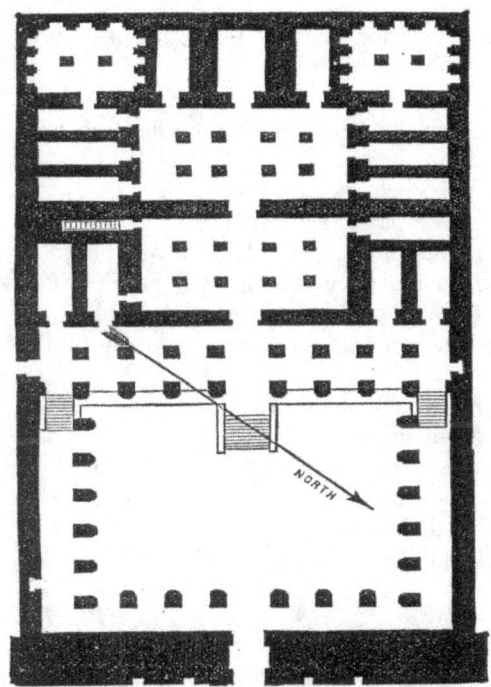

Holy Land – Plan of the Rameses II at Abydos.

"I'm in charge
I'm in charge, I know where I stand
I have a plan
I'm the man
Stand
Demand
I made a decision to elevate my position
It's about me. It's a higher authority
I'm doing this for your own good."

"People don't respect you if you don't respect yourself."
She tells of the hot date on the night of the High School Prom.
And she coined a poem:

"I'll do my thing when I get my ring"

FREDERICK MONDERSON

Walking him to my door, she repeated: "I'll do my thing when
I get my ring."

"If I want to be a doctor, I have to learn something now, Go to college I must get
my knowledge."

"Some young men who treat their sneakers better than their bodies
Can I get a Hello?
I'm only doing this because I love you
By any means necessary to get you to hear it
Don't let everybody put their naked feet in your blues
Be happy and thankful to be in company of people who love you
Love yourself and get a piece of the sky
Sex, drugs, jail are not rites of passage but wrongs of life."

"We need you to step up to the plate
And carry forward our message
Act like you want to be somebody and you will be like you act
Go and do it, Got to do it
Knowing our history, knowing ourselves
Thanks to Ms. Hurdle for having us."

Holy Land Photo 32. Kom Ombo Double Temple of Horus and Sobek. On a Pylon depiction, the King adores Sobek with Hathor to his rear. The King and Gods are all on the same plane. Notice the crocodiles in center.

Afterwards, in the lobby of the school an elderly gentleman who was in the audience offered to speak with this reporter. He indicated that he listened to Dr. Asante intently and was pleased with much of what he said. He noted Dr.

QUINTESSENTIAL BOOK
"THE HOLY LAND"

Asante's praise of Fred Monderson as a "student who knew more than his teacher." However, he reminded of a letter he had read some years ago in the *New York Times*. It told of a teacher who retired after 30 years teaching. The teacher told how the kids were sometimes unruly and difficult to teach. Nervous that at times he appeared to be unable to control the behavior of his students and whenever he saw the Principal coming down the hall he would close his door, hoping that he would not be too wise to what was going on. One day, the Principal who was sympathetic came to him and said: "You are not teaching Math. You are teaching kids." He felt that was so important, and though it seems things do get tough in there, keep doing your best. This agrees well with Dr. Asante's belief that "Middle School students are not really an endangered species."

TECHNOLOGY IN A GLOBAL COMMUNITY
By
Frederick Monderson

Community School District 17, under the leadership of Dr. Evelyn Castro and her Deputy Superintendent Debra Braithwaite, sponsored the Second Annual Technology Conference in a Global Community at Middle School 2 in Brooklyn, on Saturday December 11, 1999. After breakfast and registration, a number of workshops were conducted including the following: "How to Purchase a Computer; Claris Works;" "Digital Photography;" "Mpower;" "How to Evaluate Educational Software for your Children;" "How to use District 17's Web Site, www.district 17.org, as a Learning Center;" "How to Use the Internet;" "How to Use the Internet for Resources on Science;" and "Technology for the New Millennium Apple."

In the Plenary Session, Debra Braithwaite in charge of District Curriculum and Instruction was the Mistress of Ceremonies. She introduced Councilwoman Una Clarke, State Senator Marty Markowitz, and School Board Members Ms. Youngblood and Jesse Hamilton. Dr. Castro made the opening remarks, thanking Una Clarke for $4 million dollars she was able to secure for the district's needs. Community Board Member Agnes Green presented the Keynote Speaker, Mr. Alfred Edmond, V.P. and Executive Editor for Black Enterprise Magazine.

Assistant Superintendent Mr. Harold Wilson held drawings for 2 Mac Computers and a number of other software prizes.

FREDERICK MONDERSON

Dr. Castro began by categorically stating: "None of us can ignore what the future brings. Parents must try to keep up with Computers. Parents must keep up with the use of computers. They must be aware of what their children are doing on line. But you must be educated and not be afraid of computers. District 17 is, Thank God, on the cutting edge of this."

Marty Markowitz admonished that despite all the advances: "We should not lose touch with people. Nothing will ever replace people working and being in touch with each other."

Jesse Hamilton, First Vice-President of the Community School Board remarked: "Our children are the brightest in the world. Nothing can hold us back. The parents in the community put together a community technology program in the summer. This is the gold rush time. It is the only profession where you don't need a college education. This is a time of opportunity. We must start with the parents. Don't buy the $150.00 sneakers; put that money into computers."

Debra Braithwaite thanked Shirley Patterson and Gwen Youngblood as well as the students in T-shirts who were learning the principles of learning-apprenticeship. She thanked the supervisors, teachers, parents and staff who put the conference together.

Linda Barnett, MS 2 Principal, thanked the PTA President, Margaret Smith, parents, students, staff and well wishers and explained she "was pleased to be the person whose school was selected to host this conference." She boasted, "the school now had 4 computers and 1 television in each room, a media studio and all this was thanks to Una Clarke. They had all the equipment in the TV studio. This building does not need to be in Long Island. It can be here in Crown Heights. The school, parents, students, all should be making a difference in the lives of our children. We cannot afford to see our children fail. I have a passion for children. I want to see children grow. All our children need is guidance and direction. Children, your dream can be fulfilled. If you keep your eyes on the prize."

When Dr. Castro followed, she remarked: "Isn't it inspirational when you love children and you hear people praise them. Keep working for the best of the children." She then gave greetings in Spanish, Creole, and said that among the Masai in East Africa the greeting is "How are the children. How are the children doing?" If the children are doing all right, then we have a chance.

"Ms. Green pushed us to get technology. The children must have access to technology. There is an issue where people are being brought from outside of the country to fill technology jobs. We must teach our kids technology." She gave an example that a "Black family making $50,000.00 a year is less likely to have a computer than a white family making $35,000.00 a year." Children are growing

QUINTESSENTIAL BOOK "THE HOLY LAND"

up into the technology. Harold Wilson, Mike Handy, Wilbur Johnson, and Mr. Vanzani are all to be thanked for making this possible. Bob Schwaber, Marcia McFadden, Everton McIntyre, Keith Chisholm, Kamzat Mair, Robert Raymond, Arcilia Garcia, and Amoye Neblett all did workshop presentations. Kathleen Burgess Coordinator Early Childhood Programs; Jacqueline Burton Coordinator of Staff Development; Phyllis Bynum, Coordinator of Literacy Initiatives; Omyinka Barton, Coordinator of Literacy Middle Schools and Joyce Anderson, Pre-K Specialist, were very helpful to this conference."

Dr. Castro remarked that we have to work hard to close the digital divide. "For $20.00 a month we spend more than that on nails. We must keep up the war on technology ignorance."

Ms Agnes Green is the chairman of the technology committee. She thanked everyone for coming. "District 17 is not just starting; it is well up the technology ladder. This is fabulous. Take a personal look at what needs to be done. Make life real. Be accountable by working for the success of the children. We can be successful without someone else doing it for us."

Margaret Smith, PTA President, reminded those in attendance that just like the conference held in December, it was the same month a year ago when her daughter died in MS 2. She thanked all parents who took time to come out. She asked for "a moment of silence for Mrs. Francis Haggler whose husband recently passed away. Ms. Haggler has been a mountain of concern and a gadfly in service to the district's parents and children. We all thank Mrs. Haggler." Mrs. Smith also mentioned Luann Dyer and Doris Edwards. However, Mrs. Smith was very thoughtful and insightful in her advice to parents. She stated: "If your child comes home and told you the teacher did him or her something, don't just rush up to the school to fight the teacher. Stories have 3 sides. There's your child's side, the teacher's side and the truth. Come up to the school in a calm manner and investigate. If there is something wrong there is a way to handle it. If you come up to the school in an abusive manner word gets around to the teachers 'that parent is a fighter.' Then teachers won't want to come near your child for fear of you. The end result the child suffers."

FREDERICK MONDERSON

Holy Land Photo 33. Kom Ombo Double Temple of Horus and Sobek. The King wearing the Osiris Crown with horns, triple feathers and disks, is embraced by all the Gods - Thoth, Hathor, Sekhmet and the Elder and Younger Horuses as they lay hands on him.

Dr. Sims explained that District 17 was the only district to put on a massive technology conference. "We are leaders not followers."

Mr. Wilson offered a big, big thanks to Debra Braithwaite.

Alfred Edmond marked the 30th anniversary of his magazine's entrepreneurial adventure. He mentioned a declaration of financial empowerment and leadership in technology for empowerment of African-Americans. He talked of redlining in cyber space that businesses were responding slower in minority communities. We must work to close the digital divide. "We must start right here in our communities, in our schools, in our homes. Get a computer for your family and it will open new vistas. It does not matter if you get on the main entry of the super highway or a side street. Just get on. We must be aggressive because the doors will be closed soon. He mentioned a few tips on what you can do in your homes and churches. Things you should do:

Help form a technology community at your kid's school. Do home work, business, and talk monthly.

Create a technology plan and use the school technology. Help foster relationships between business and your school. Tell them give us something we could use.

QUINTESSENTIAL BOOK
"THE HOLY LAND"

Think of what benefits your bottom line. Volunteer your time. Information is the real currency. The air you breathe changes when you have access to resources.

Work with your churches and community groups. You have to do this as part of your own home. Shift priorities. Don't buy Tommy Hilfiger, buy computers.

Holy Land Illustration 50. Abydos, Temple. Pottery and inscriptions of the First Dynasty and King Khufu, builder of the Great Pyramid; and objects of other monarchs.

2.   Breakfast

Dr. Leonard James: Good Morning, Mr. Brown, would you and Mrs. Brown join Marilyn and me?
Walter Brown: Of course, Dr. James. We people from Atlanta should always stick together. Where are we going today?
Dr. Leonard James: You know, at that hectic pace we have followed, the day off is welcome. Some people are going to Medinet Habu Temple of Rameses III of the Twentieth Dynasty. I hear it's a well-preserved temple and well worth the effort. I am not sure if they are going to cross the river by boat or use the bridge. Whichever, I am always reminded of John Milton (1608-1674) who said: "To know that which before us lies in daily life is the prime wisdom."

FREDERICK MONDERSON

Walter Brown: I have to hand it to you; even though you are retired you seem to retain a sharp mind about some of the things you taught.

Dr. Leonard James: Well, it's my wife Marilyn, my better half, who over the years has helped me to stay focused and retain my sharpness. There is nothing like a good wife, partner, who supports your every effort. We have been married for 38 years and love every one of them.

Walter Brown: Mrs. Brown and I have been married for over 28 years and have agreed to work out differences to stay married. We have two wonderful sons and a very stable relationship, very respectful. This is so important for the children, who in their own right were taught to respect marriage and all that it entails. This is why I was a bit disturbed when I heard someone in the lounge last night quoting another and said "Marriage is a desperate thing."

Dr. Leonard James: If that is so, then both of us have beaten those odds for the longevity of our marriage proves that is not an accurate statement.

Michelliea Georges: An interesting lecture I attended was with Professor Rene Parker in the Chair, Ms. Sandra Millner as Rapporteur, as Dr. Kariamu Welsh Asante of Temple University discussed "Afrocentricity and Aesthetic." She mentioned connections between the academy and community. What is a beautiful, tall, slender, light skin Black woman with long hair? Marla Friedman killed her lover in Philly.

What constitutes beauty in the African community? This is wrong. When we see Black dolls they are referred to as "Voodoo dolls." We must have young people doing African dances in class. The project must be more encompassing and more inclusive. Naturally, there is nothing wrong with ballet, tap or ballroom dancing.

MOVE had a different lifestyle. Kids among those killed – Surname Africa. No matter how noble MOVE's cause – Ramona Africa equating wearing locks and eating raw food as being African is wrong. Afrocentricity says locate yourself, center yourself, study - we were not born in Africa. We must move beyond what is Afrocentricity and find out what is real. We must find ourselves. We must go to the bus, but I will continue this on the bus.

Regina Hendricks: Good Morning George. Join us. How are you today? Are you ready for the challenges of this day? What are you having for breakfast? That was wonderful what you did last night covering both history and religion in one session. What do you have for us today?

George Washington: I am fine, sister. Ready. I guess more of the same. On September 22, 1975, we began doing comparative chronology between Egypt and Mesopotamia. The dates are B.C.

QUINTESSENTIAL BOOK
"THE HOLY LAND"

Egypt   Mesopotamia

	Egypt	Mesopotamia
1.	Predynastic	Proto-literate
2.	Archaic (Dyns 1-2)	Early dynastic
		2900-2300 (Age of Sumer City States)
3.	Old Kingdom (Dyns 3-8) 2685-2180	Akadian Sargon - 2300
4.	First Intermediate Period 2180-2040	
5.	Middle Kingdom (Dyns 12-13) Period of several dynasties. (Classic period) 2040-1630	Isin/Larsa/Mari/Assyria 2000-1850
6.	Second Intermediate Period (14-17)	Babylon 1800-1600 Hammurabi
7.	New Kingdom a. Empire (18)	Dark Ages 1600 (Sealands, Kassites) Mitanni/Babylon/Assyria

8.	Ramesside Period I
	  b. Empire (19) 1300-1200
	  c. Ramesside Period II (20)	

Wilson, Chapter 2 "Out of the Mud"

Writing developed to record economic transactions and all records were found in temples. Theocracy predominated. En-male consort of female deity.

Ziggurat – A temple on high ground (mountain). Early dynastic period marks coming of age of city-states. Great flood (Ur) 2900 B.C. at each city flood at a different period. Early dynastic period was after the flood.

The concept of the great flood is very widespread in most cultures. Kingship comes back after the flood and first appears in city of Kish.

The Golden Age - Early Dynastic I - 2900-2700 B.C. Period dominated by city of Kish. Dynastic succession not yet hereditary. Kingship elected. King owing religious strength by being consort to female deity. No palaces found. King lived in temples? Semites gradually granted power and came to dominate.

FREDERICK MONDERSON

Early Dynastic II – 2700-2500 B.C. Age of heroes. Hero Gilgamesh. Royal tombs of Ur were wealth-dominated. Kings servants slaughtered at his death.

Damuzi hero. Dynasties now appear. Hereditary succession established. Kish no more dominant city. Fortification walls are thickest in UR. City on Persian Gulf – Port town trade with Magan (Arabian coast) copper imported.

Dilmun – Island in Persian Gulf. Large trade city. Meluhha – location unknown. Possibly Egypt or Asia.

Early Dynastic III – 2500-2300 B.C. Secularization of Mesopotamia. This is first sign of conflict with church and state. Lugal – military leader. Ensi – Secretary of Agriculture. He decided which areas would plant what crops.

Urukagina – King of Lugal. Set up reforms, which abolished private ownership of land and returned same to temple. Palace must stop using temple personnel for secular purposes. Polyandry is outlawed. Cylinder seal used to mark a person's personal possession, analogous to the cattle branding out west.

Holy Land Papyrus 16. The Register enables a multiplicity of themes to be depicted around preparation of the mummy for burial.

In Egypt the Nile River flows from south to north. Early pre-dynastic – Badarian, Tasian Periods most pots were very open at the top; figurines were developed as well. The Amratian Period occurred circa 4000 B.C. The Gerzean Period was the last stage of pre-dynastic Egypt, which saw continuity in forms of pottery as well as decoration of ware. A painted tomb was discovered at Hierakonpolis.

So much for now. Perhaps we could continue this on the bus.

QUINTESSENTIAL BOOK "THE HOLY LAND"

Mr. Sylvester Singleton: What would you gentlemen consider the greatest contribution of Africa?

Dr. Benjamin: There are so many things that could be considered. Man himself. Architecture, religion, trade, science, and navigation, these are some of Africa's greatest contributions. These are the developments that have had the most far-reaching impact on all subsequent peoples, nations and civilizations.

Dr. John Africa: It's a good question. First I would like to say we must promote the life and work of W.E.B. DuBois. He was one of the greatest minds of the 20th Century. I mean he was on par with the great minds of the world. In *The African Roots of War*, 1915, the same year he wrote *The Negro*, he stated: "Always Africa is giving us something new. Out of its black bosom arose one of the earliest, if not the earliest, of self-protecting civilizations and grew so mighty that it still furnishes superlatives to thinking and speaking man. Out of its darker and more remote forest fastness, came the first welding of iron - we know that agriculture and trade flourished when Europe was a wilderness. Nearly every empire that has arisen in the world, material and spiritual, has found some of its greatest crises in Africa."

Dr. Benjamin: Finally I would say Malcolm X in his famous "The Ballot or Bullet" speech at Cory Methodist Church, in Cleveland Ohio on April 3, 1965, put it best: "This is our contribution - our blood. Not only did we give of our free labor, we gave of our blood. Every time [we] had a call to arms; we were the first ones in uniform. We died on every battlefield the white man had. We have made a greater sacrifice than anybody who's standing up in America today."

Teddy Cubia: How is your wife today, Dr. Pushkin?
Dr. Alexander Pushkin: She will join us shortly. Michael, Is Afrocentricity a new philosophy or did it borrow from earlier movements?
Michael Sinclair: In a way Afrocentricity is a synthesis of prior African-centered scholarship and the stalwarts of early African national identity. This certainly numbers such individuals as Marcus Garvey, W.E.B. DuBois, Cheikh Anta Diop, Maulana Karenga, Theophile Obenga, and Gonzales who paved the way. Many others contributed to this philosophy including Wole Soyinka, Walter Rodney, David Walker in his *Appeal*, Abida dos Nasciemento, Amilkar Cabral, Mko Abiola, and Naomi Nhiwatiwe who argued the essential unity of African culture. This is what Diop affirmed in his *Cultural Unity of Black Africa*.

Let me refer you to two sources, "Afrocentricity and the Human Future" by Molefi Kete Asante in *Black Books Bulletin* Vol. 8 (1991: 137-140) and the "Afrocentric Idea in Education" by Molefi Kete Asante, from Temple University, in *Journal of Negro Education* Vol. 60, No. 2 (Spring 1991: 170-178). These are points of departure for studying the discipline of Afrocentricity.

FREDERICK MONDERSON

Dr. Alexander Pushkin: Come on, young man, you know I won't be able to get to those sources. Tell you what; since you are so smart and I know you read those sources, I will let you tell Mr. Cubia and me here, what the articles are all about. If you do, then I will buy you a cold lemon squeeze at dinner.

Michael Sinclair: OK. Let me begin with the *Journal of Negro Education* article. This is "The Afrocentric Idea in Education" by Molefi Asante. He said in essence:

"Carter G. Woodson's classic *The Mis-education of the Negro* (1933) reveals the fundamental problems pertaining to the education of the African person in America."

"African-Americans have been educated away from their own culture and traditions and attached to the fringes of European culture; thus dislocated from themselves, Woodson asserts, African-Americans often valorize European culture to the detriment of their own heritage."

"Woodson – assuming African-Americans hold the same position as European Americans *vis-à-vis* the realities of America, would lead to the psychological and cultural death of the African-American population. Furthermore, if education is to ever be substantive and meaningful within the context of American society, Woodson argues, it must first address the African's historical experiences, both in Africa and America. That is why he places on education and particularly on the traditionally African-American colleges, the burden of teaching the African-American to be responsible to the long traditions and history of Africa as well as America."

"Woodson's alert recognition, more than 50 years ago, that something is severely wrong with the way African-Americans are educated provides the principal impetus for the Afrocentric approach to American education."

In this article, Asante seeks to: "examine the nature and scope of this approach, establish its necessity, and suggest ways to develop and disseminate it throughout all levels of education. Two propositions hang in the background of the theoretical and philosophical issues Asante presented. These ideas represented the core presuppositions on which he based most of his work in the field of education and they suggest the direction of his own thinking about what education is capable of doing to and for an already politically and economically marginalized people - African-Americans."

"1. Education is fundamentally a social phenomenon whose ultimate purpose is to socialize the learner; to send a child to school is to prepare that child to become part of a social group."

QUINTESSENTIAL BOOK
"THE HOLY LAND"

"Schools are reflective of the societies that develop them (i.e., a white supremacist dominated society will develop a white supremacist educational system)."

"In education, Centricity refers to a perspective that involves locating students within the context of their own cultural references so that they can relate socially and psychologically to other cultural perspectives."

"Centricity is a concept that can be applied to any culture. The centrist paradigm is supported by research showing that the most productive method of teaching any student is to place his or her group within the center of the context of knowledge." (Asante 1990)

"American education is not centric, it is Eurocentric. Consequently, non-white students are also made to see themselves and their groups as the 'acted upon.'"

"Discussions on the slave trade concentrate on the activities of whites rather than on the resistance efforts of Africans. A person educated in a truly centric fashion comes to view all groups' contributions as significant and useful. Even a white person educated in such a system does not assume superiority based upon racist notions. Thus, a truly centric education is different from a Eurocentric, racist (that is, white supremacist) education."

"Afrocentricity is a frame of reference, wherein phenomena are viewed from the perspective of the African person. The Afrocentric approach seeks in every situation the appropriate centrality of the African person (Asante 1987). In education, this means that teachers provide students the opportunity to study the world and its people, concepts, and history from an African worldview. In most classrooms, whatever the subject, whites are located in the center perspective position."

"The little African-American child who sits in a classroom and is taught to accept as heroes and heroines individuals who defame African people is being actively de-centered, dislocated and made into a non-person, one whose aim in life might be to one day shed that 'badge of inferiority: his or her blackness.'"

"In Afrocentric educational settings, however, teachers do not marginalize African-American children by causing them to question their own self-worth because their people's story is seldom told to see themselves as the subjects rather than the objects of education or medicine. Be the discipline biology, medicine, literature, or social studies - African-American students come to see themselves not merely seekers of knowledge but participants in it. Because all content areas are adaptable to an Afrocentric approach, African-American students can be made to see themselves as centered in the reality of any discipline."

FREDERICK MONDERSON

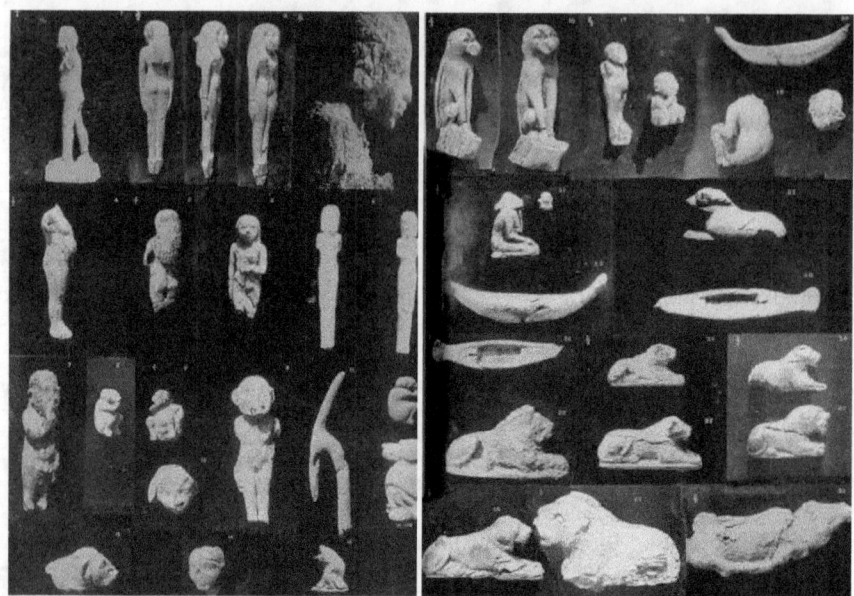

Holy Land Illustration 51. Abydos. Temple. Ivory Figurines of the First Dynasty; and more Ivory Figurines of the First Dynasty.

"Afrocentricity is not a black version of Eurocentricity (Asante 1987). Eurocentricity is based on white supremacist notions whose purposes are to protect white privilege and advantage by degrading other groups' perspectives. Moreover, Eurocentricity presents the particular historical reality of Europeans as the sum total of the human experience. (Asante 1987). It imposes Eurocentric realities as "universal;" that which is white is represented as applying to the human condition in general, while that which is non-white is viewed as group, specific and therefore not 'human.' This explains why some scholars and artists of African descent rush to deny their blackness; they believe that to exist as a black person is not to exist as a universal being."

"The person of African descent should be in his or her historical experience as an African, but Eurocentric curricula produce such aberrations of perspective among persons of color."

"Multi-culturalism in education is a non-hierarchical approach that respects and celebrates a variety of cultural perspectives on world phenomena. The multi-cultural approach holds that although European culture is the majority culture in the United States, which is not sufficient reason for it to be imposed on diverse student populations as "universal." Multiculturalists assert that education, to have integrity, must begin with the proposition all humans have contributed to world

QUINTESSENTIAL BOOK "THE HOLY LAND"

development and the flow of knowledge and information and that most human achievements are the result of mutually interactive international effort."

Without a multicultural education students remain essentially ignorant of the contributions of a major portion of the world's people.

THE REVOLUTIONARY CHALLENGE

"Because it centers African-American students inside history, culture, science, and so forth rather than outside these subjects, the Afrocentric idea presents the most revolutionary challenge to the ideology of white supremacy in education during the past decade [of the article]."

It questions the imposition of the white supremacist view as universal and or classical (Asante, 1990).

It demonstrates the indefensibility of racist theories that assault multiculturalism and pluralism.

It projects a humanistic and pluralistic viewpoint by articulating Afrocentricity as a valid, non-hegemonic perspective.

FREDERICK MONDERSON

Holy Land Photo 34. Edfu Temple of Horus. The massive entrance Pylon depicting the King and Gods in ritual display. Notice two hawks at the entrance.

SUPPRESSION AND DISTORTION: SYMBOLS OF RESISTANCE

The forces of resistance to the Afrocentric, multicultural transformation of the curriculum and teaching practice began to assemble their wagons as quickly as word got out about the need for equality in education (Ravitch, 1990).

This is a paradoxical development because only lies, untruths, and inaccurate information need defending.

The Committee for the Defense of History is nothing but a futile attempt to buttress the crumbling pillars of a white supremacist system that conceals its true motives behind the cloak of "American liberalism."

Afrocentricity says: "The acceptance of Africa is central to African people."

Ravitch (1990), who gives two types of multiculturalism – pluralist multi-culturalism and particular multi-culturalism - is the leader of those professors whom Asante calls 'resisters' or opponents of Afrocentrism.

QUINTESSENTIAL BOOK "THE HOLY LAND"

It is "inevitable that the introduction of the Afrocentric idea would open up the discussion of the American school curricula in a profound way."

"What is revolutionary about the movement from the idea (conceptual stage) to its implementation in practice is when we begin to teach teachers how to put African-American youth at the center of instruction."

"African-American children learn to interpret and center phenomena in the context of African heritage while white students are taught to see that their own centers are not threatened by the presence or contributions of African-Americans and others."

THE CONDITION OF EUROCENTRIC EDUCATION

In the United States a "whites-only" orientation has predominated in education.

THE TRAGEDY OF IGNORANCE

"The vast majority of white Americans are likewise ignorant about the reservoirs of African and African-American history, culture and contributions. For example, few Americans of any color have heard the names of Cheikh Anta Diop, Anna Julia Cooper, C.L.R. James or J.A. Rogers; all were historians who contributed greatly to our understanding of the black world. Indeed, very few teachers have taken a course in African-American studies; therefore, most are unable to appreciate the contributions of African-Americans, and thus, to provide systematic information about African-Americans."

AFROCENTRICITY AND HISTORY

"Most of America's teaching forces are themselves victims of the same system that victimizes today's young. Thus, American children are to be taught the names of the African ethnic groups from which the majority of the African-American population are derived. Few are taught the names of any of the sacred sites in Africa. Few teachers can discuss with their students the significance of the Middle Passage or describe what it means to be African. Little mention is made in American classrooms of either the brutality of slavery or the ex-slave's celebration of freedom."

FREDERICK MONDERSON

"Americans have little or no understanding of the nature of the capture, transport, and enslavement of Africans. Few have been taught the true horrors of being taken, shipped naked across 25 days of ocean, broken by abuse and indignities of all kinds, and dehumanized into a beast of burden, a thing without a name. If our students only knew the truth, if they were taught the Afrocentric perspective on the great enslavement, and if they knew the full story about the events since slavery that have served to constantly dislocate African-Americans, their behavior would probably be different. Among these events are: the infamous constitutional compromise of 1787, which decreed that enslaved African-Americans were, by law, the equivalent of but three-fifths of a person (See Franklin, 1974); the 1857 Dred Scott decision in which the Supreme Court avowed that an African-American had no right which whites were obliged to respect (Howard, 1857); the complete dismissal on a non-enforcement of Section 2 of the Fourteenth Amendment of the Constitution (This amendment passed in 1868, stipulated as one of its provisions a penalty against any state that denied African-Americans the right to vote, and called for the reduction of a state's delegates to the House of Representatives in proportion to the number of disenfranchised African-American males therein; and the much-mentioned as-yet-unreceived, 40 acres and a mule, reparation for enslavement, promised to each African-American family after the Civil War by Union General William T. Sherman and Secretary of War Edwin Stanton).

Holy Land World Tourist Day Extravaganza 10. The Band supporting Kena dancers at 2012 World Tourist Day celebration in Luxor.

If the curriculum were enhanced to include readings from the slave narratives, the diaries of slave ship captains, the journals of slave owners; the abolitionist newspapers; then knowledge and understanding would be different. The comfortable teachings that art and philosophy originated in Greece then becomes

QUINTESSENTIAL BOOK
"THE HOLY LAND"

questionable, if one learns that the Greeks themselves taught that the study of these subjects originated in Africa, specifically ancient Kemet. (Herodotus, 1987).

The first philosophers were the Egyptians Kagemni, Khun-Anup, Ptahhotep, Kete and Seti; but Eurocentric education is so disjointed that students have no way of discovering this and other knowledge of the organic relationship of Africa to the rest of human history. Not only did Africa contribute to human history, African civilization predates all other civilizations.

Holy Land Photo 35. Edfu Temple of Horus. In the Great Court, panoramic view of the entrance hall with its screened engaged columns, Peristyle colonnade (left and right) with roofed ambulatory, two hawks, one fallen and the other erect.

Two other notions should be refuted. There are those who say that African-American history should begin with the arrival of slaves in 1619 but it has been shown that Africans visited and inhabited North and South America long before European settlers "discovered" the "new world." (Van Sertima, 1976). Secondly, although America became something of a home for those Africans who survived the horrors of the Middle Passage, their experiences on the slave ships and during slavery resulted in their having an entirely different (and often tainted) perspective about America from that of the European and others who came for the most part of their own free will seeking opportunities not available to them in their native lands. Afrocentricity therefore seeks to recognize this divergence in perspective and create centeredness for African-American students."

FREDERICK MONDERSON

CONCLUSIONS

"The reigning initiative for curriculum change is the movement being proposed and led by Africans namely, the Afrocentric idea.

Whites are accustomed to being in charge of the major ideas circulating in the American academy. Deconstructionism, Gestalt psychology, Marxism, structuralism, Piagetian theory, and so forth have all been developed, articulated and elaborated upon at length, generally by a plethora of mainly white scholars. On the other hand, Afrocentricity is the product of scholars mainly black, such as Nobles (1986), Hillard (1978), Karenga (1986), Keto (1990), Richards (1991), and Myers (1989).

Afrocentricity provides all Americans an opportunity to examine the perspective of the African person in this society and the world. The resisters claim that Afrocentricity is anti-white; yet, if (Afrocentricity) as a theory is against anything it is against racism, ignorance, and monoethnic hegemony in the curricula. Afrocentricity is not anti-white; it is, however, pro-human. Further, the aim of the Afrocentric curriculum is not to divide America; it is to make America, as it ought to, flourish.

By virtue of the protection provided by society and reinforced by the Eurocentric curriculum, the white child is already ahead of the African child by the first grade. Our efforts thus must concentrate on giving the African-American child greater opportunities for learning at the kindergarten level.

The American educational system does not need a tune-up, but an overhaul. Black children have been maligned by the system. Black history has been maligned. Africa has been maligned."

"Two truisms can be stated about education in America. First, some teachers can and do effectively teach African-American children. Secondly, if some teachers can do it, others can, too.

"Afrocentric education along with a significant reorientation of the American educational enterprise, seeks to respond to the African persons' psychological and cultural dislocation. By providing philosophical and theoretical guidelines and criteria that are centered in an African perception of reality and by placing the African-American child in his or her proper historical context and setting, Afrocentricity may be just the "escape hatch" African-Americans so desperately need to facilitate academic success and "steal away" from the "cycle of mis-education and dislocation."

QUINTESSENTIAL BOOK "THE HOLY LAND"

Dr. Alexander Pushkin: Very well put young man. Mr. Cubia don't you think this young man did a superb job with Dr. Asante's article?
Teddy Cubia. Without a doubt. Clearly he is a student who listened well and did excellent research and took copious notes. In this young man I am reminded of a saying of old, "two ears will outlast one hundred lips."
Dr. Alexander: Mr. Sinclair, how are you able to recall Asante's words so well?
Michael Sinclair: I studied the man and his writings. He insisted on two things: (1) "Never let historical situations pass you by without writing about it." (2) "Research every subject to the last detail and take copious notes both in research and in class."

He always wanted to see that you reached out for that last reference to make your paper stronger because you never knew who would read it. I did take copious notes and later was able to go back to my notebooks whenever I needed to go over the issues we discussed and analyzed in class. That is how I am able to remember those ideas as if they were yesterday even though I graduated a decade ago.
Teddy Cubia: Well Doc, looks like the lemon squeezes are on you tonight.
Dr. Alexander Pushkin: Yes, but that is only one of the two articles he promised.
Teddy Cubia: I suppose in time he will give us that too. Be careful, you may have to buy more lemon squeezes.

Dr. Alexander Pushkin: Good Morning, my sweet. Honey, this young man has been giving us a history lesson on the topic of Afrocentricity. Let us welcome him and probe his very active mind. Teddy will join us shortly. He went for seconds. Here he comes now.
Mrs. Alexander Pushkin: Hello young man. How are you this morning? Sorry I could not be in the discussion earlier but this diarrhea has kept me indoors for a few days.

Michael Sinclair: Sorry to hear that Ma'am. It's recommended eating a piece of lime to help combat that virus. Of course, don't eat too much for you will go from one extreme to the other and nothing will come out.

FREDERICK MONDERSON

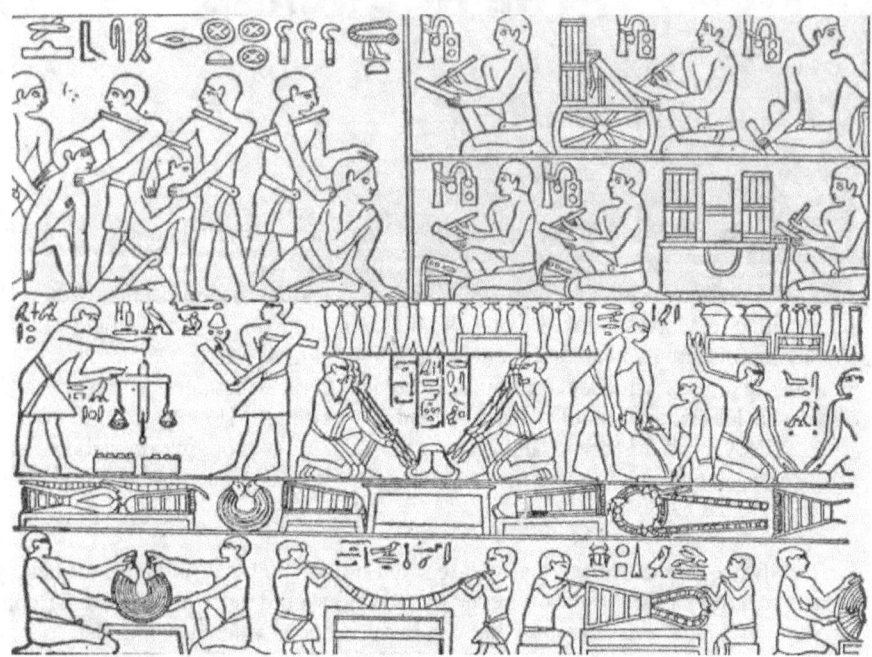

Holy Land Illustration 52. Collection of taxes by local treasury officials in the Pyramid Age (top); and Goldsmith's workshop in the Pyramid Age.

Mrs. Alexander Pushkin: So, what have I missed?
Alexander Pushkin: You missed his definitions of paradigms and Afrocentricity.

Michael Sinclair: Dr. Keto of Temple University reminded us of a South African proverb. "If you don't know where you have been, you don't know where you are and if you don't know where you are, you can't know where you are going, and if so, any road will take you there."

Fact is we have no quarrel with the Eurocentric view of the world. We have a problem when the Eurocentric view becomes the only view, when it accepts all the space. If the Eurocentric view takes all the space then there is no space for the Afrocentric view. That is where the trouble starts.

Mrs. Alexander Pushkin: So these paradigms raise questions about knowledge.
Michael Sinclair: Yes. Centrism can be viewed from a number of perspectives. Let's take for example, Eurocentric, Asian, American, or African. These are centrisms or paradigms.

The "Middle East" is a term viewed from a Eurocentric reference point. So too is New Jersey, New York and so on.

QUINTESSENTIAL BOOK
"THE HOLY LAND"

We must remember, an African got on the boat in Africa, and a slave, a Negro, disembarked. Europeans got in the boat in Europe and when they got to America they were still Europeans, whether French, English, Italian, German or whatever. An Asian got on the boat in Asia and remained so in America. Even when they got to Africa in Rhodesia, Portugal, South Africa these people remained Europeans. Therefore, the African needs to know knowledge from various centers of thought.

We need to examine a paradigm that explains the American Dream. Europeans left Europe with nothing; came to America, got land, position, economics, and leisure. Then, your son becomes President. At the bill signing, they were singing, "When the Irish are smiling." Kennedy was also singing. A Kennedy woman was appointed Ambassador to Ireland. Therefore, multi-cultural education should be multi-centered education. You can't just add something for Blacks. We don't want additives.

Teddy Cubia: I seem to remember the image from the photo in the newspapers.
Dr. Alexander Pushkin: What were some geopolitical aspects of how Europeans came to be so powerful and dominate?

Michael Sinclair: Let me say firstly, there is no Third World. This is a European or if you will, an economic term. You see, after World War II the world became divided between developed America and the West who were capitalists. They faced a threat from the Communist world led by Russia or USSR. These then became the First and Second Worlds. Now, many nations, starting with Yugoslavia led by Marshal Tito did not want to be in any camp so they started this concept of the Third World. The Third World then was a collection of developing nations. Soon it was realized there were rich and poor nations in the Third World. Those nations who had such resources as oil formed OPEC, Organization of Petroleum Exporting Countries, and they benefited from having this resource asset. Still, there were the very poor countries in the Third World who had no such resources. I mean such nations as Bangladesh, Mali, Haiti and so on. Economists then placed the OPEC nations in the Fourth World and the others in the Fifth World. Of course, there is only one world. Just like the Middle East. This was a European concoction in 1948. It should be a place between Asia in the East and Europe in the West. So we got the Middle East.

Mrs. Alexander Pushkin: So I see.
Michael Sinclair: Most important we much have a methodology of Afrocentric geopolitics linkage for our very survival. We can only challenge European dominance as an African people globally. We must create an Afrocentric global re-dedication or we can call it Afrocentrification. There was no African Slave Trade. We must see this crime to humanity from an Afrocentric worldview. In

that phenomenon which Donna Richards (Marimba Ani) calls the *Maafa* or great enslavement, Europe operated as subject and Africa as object. When we understand all this, inclusion becomes empowerment.

Dr. Alexander Pushkin: How then do you characterize the Eurocentric worldview?
Michael Sinclair: For the Africans, the Eurocentric worldview has been one of domination, inhuman and vicious, destruction and death to African people. This needs to be replaced by an Afrocentric outlook that is human, caring, cooperative and collectivist. The Eurocentric worldview is racist, divisive and ahistorical. Cultural diversity has to become a functional reality because of the geopolitical racist reality of the New World order. We must also be careful with the view of multi-culturalism for they will create a hierarchical system with European culture at the top or center.

Dr. Alexander Pushkin: So you want a form of measured multi-culturalism?
Michael Sinclair: Yes. We want cultural specificity. Multi-culturalism is a stepping-stone of Afrocentricity not the other way around. All cultures are distinct; none is superior or inferior to the other. You can't disrespect my culture, history, and then turn around and respect me.

Mrs. Alexander Pushkin: What then is the answer?
Michael Sinclair: We must work on the African mindset. We have to de-Europeanize him, detoxify, de-mystify and de-brainwash our minds from Eurocentric global consciousness. Remember we have been exposed to 500 years of Eurocentric dominance. We have become disunited, powerless, self-destructive, and homeless. If you look at our children's textbooks, are they studying Pythagoras or Imhotep?
Mrs. Alexander Pushkin: Pythagoras.
Michael Sinclair. Exactly. It's psychological warfare. It is ahistorical, racist, and dysfunctional. Afrocentricity is about feeling good and respecting African culture. Afrocentricity helps to relocate our African minds. It takes us back to Mother Africa and not Father Europe. Like we do when we come here to Egypt to look at the work of the ancestors. Therefore, Afrocentricity is a state of mind, a particular subconscious mindset rooted in African principles, philosophies, history and culture.
Mrs. Alexander Pushkin: How then would you define culture?
Michael Sinclair: Frances Cress Welsing in *The Isis Papers* (1991) explained: "Culture is a quilt of intricate geometrical design in which all of the many colored pieces, their shapes and stitching flow into one another, and constitutes the whole." However, we must not forget the old African proverb: "A man without culture is like a grasshopper without wings" and Franz Fanon in *Wretched of the Earth* (1963) wrote: "Destroy the culture and you destroy the people." Leopold Senghor, in a speech given at the *First World Festival of Negro Arts*, Dakar, Senegal, 1966, said: "Culture is the first requisite and the final objective of all development."

QUINTESSENTIAL BOOK "THE HOLY LAND"

Teddy Cubia: Wow. The young brother is amazing. He learned well at Temple's Afrocentric Institute under Dr. Asante. Doc. You do have the lemon squeezes.

Holy Land World Tourist Day Extravaganza 11. Male and female dancers in the Kena Troupe.

2. Bus Trip

Michelliea Georges: There are many Afrocentric aesthetics out there. Many contradict and cancel each other out. Does this negate being? An Afrocentric Scholar studies the visualization, articulation, gesticulation, materialization, and imagination of a particular African culture. Among the Kikuyu a woman with a gap in her teeth is prized. The Wolof prefer a woman with no gap in her teeth.

As a global, encompassing, inclusive, very large task, it must be very general so as not to lose people.

We don't want the woman in Zimbabwe or America to go beyond herself into Europe to be located. Many people have a romanticized notion of what Africa is. Ramona Africa was a very naïve young woman who was no match for the Eurocentric imperialists. Or, African-American naiveté of what African aesthetics is about. Clothing is important. How you walk. How you greet people. It is not a lineal, hierarchical mandate. African aesthetic is polyrhythmic.
Regina Hendricks: George, what can you add to that, whether history or African religious or philosophic beliefs?
George Washington: First, let me say that in Egypt, boats were used by the Pharaohs to sail across the heavens in the transition from this world to the next. Decorated vases were never found in cities, only in temples. Farmers only saw the

gods when they had reaped their harvests. Slate Palettes, the longest are of an earlier period. As slate palettes progressed they became more and more decorated. Egyptian deities can and did have more than one function. Hathor as a dual divinity. Egyptian religion presented the gods here as opposed to western religion, which makes god transcendental. Most dynastic temples have not survived for they, for the most part, were made of perishable material. Palettes show three distinct peoples living in Egypt.

Pay particular attention to the palette of Narmer for the hair of the pharaoh is frizzy as opposed to the enemy whose hair is long. With that we were given a Map Quiz Study Guide. Following are the terms as I defined them from various sources.

Persepolis – City to the east of the Persian Gulf located along a very important caravan trade route.
Persia – Area of present day Iran, home of Darius and Ashurbanipal, conquerors of Egypt.
Media – An area of northern Persia to the east of the Zargos Mountains.
Zargos Mountains – Located to the east of Elam. Also separating Persia from Elam.
Elam – An area around Susa, to the north of the Persian Gulf.
Ur – Southern Mesopotamia along trade route from Persian Gulf. Change in course of Euphrates on which it stands caused its decline.
Urus – On eastern bank of Euphrates to the south of Babylonia, to the north of the city of Ur.
Kish – City to the east of the Euphrates, probably a day or two's march from Babylon.
Babylon – A city in the Akad region of Mesopotamia, on the eastern bank of the Euphrates.
Sumer – Southern region of the Mesopotamia Basin that emptied in Persian Gulf, site of early civilization.
Agad – Area in Babylonia between Babylon to the south and Sippar to the north.
Babylonia – The area of King Hammurabi's (c. 1700 B.C.) empire, to the northwest of the Persian Gulf.
Tigris – Eastern of the two rivers that bordered the region of Mesopotamia.
Euphrates – Western of the two rivers that bordered the region of Mesopotamia.
Nineveh – City on the Tigris.
Assyria – Great military power in Mesopotamia, east of Tigris, between 1900-1700 B.C. in the northern region of Mesopotamia.
Mitanni – A tribe defeated by the Hittites (c. 1350 B.C.) who lived in an area to the north of Mesopotamia.
Hittites – Indo-European peoples who inhabited the region of present-day Turkey.
Kassites – Indo-European tribe of uncertain origin who pillaged Mesopotamia area between 1600 and 1200 B.C.

QUINTESSENTIAL BOOK
"THE HOLY LAND"

Urartu – Up in the highland region of northern Mesopotamia, between Lake Van and the Caucasus.
Kadesh – City on the eastern coast of the Mediterranean, along the trade route on the Orontes River.
Byblos – Coastal city along the eastern Mediterranean, full of natural harbors, lively sea trade and between Posidium and Sidon.
Jerusalem – On the banks of the Jordan River; no natural harbors.
Megiddo – On the eastern Mediterranean.
Memphis – Large city in Lower Egypt on the Nile River.
Nile River – The gift of Egypt, inundated annually and was mainly responsible for fertilizing deposits on the land.
Giza – To the west of the Delta, home of the Great Pyramids.
Thebes – a major city to the south and one time capital of Egypt, below the First Cataract.
Karnak – Northern half of the ruins of Thebes; site of the three great temples.
Aswan-Elephantine – On the east bank of the Nile. A city on the first of six cataracts. Actually, this should be the last of six cataracts since the river flows north from its source in inner Africa.
Anatolia – Asian territory of Turkey also known as Asia-Minor.

Now, let me give you a bit on the **African Religious Thought Systems**. On September 22, 1975, the focus was:

Cosmology – The science that deals with the origin and structure of the universe, including the parts of nature and how they interrelate.
Ontology – Thoughts and concepts about the nature of reality; nature of being; what goes beyond to give meaning to things that are right here.
Epistemology – Theory of knowledge; the origin, nature and limits of knowledge; involves the process of knowing; concepts of truth.

In Africa science and religion are merged as opposed to European society in which science and religion are in occasional conflict and are separate disciplines.

Order – produces the processes of value and meaning.
Worldview – How you define the world around you. How you see things in other societies and how they relate to "you." A way of relating the self to the world. Every culture has a worldview at its base. This "worldview" concept is very critical to understanding African religious thought. What is the African "concept of time?"

"Concept of self?" Read Laing "Self and Others." This will help to clearly distinguish how I "see" things. Behavior is related to worldview.

FREDERICK MONDERSON

Ideology – A statement of goals, a commitment based on culture and worldview. Ontology then comes to give meaning to things, events and people. Metaphysics then participates in a reality which transcends, because of its meaning. This in turn becomes spiritual.

Transcends – Surpass; surpassing others in excellence.

Chaos – Has no meaning as opposed to cosmos, which in itself shows order.

Mind – The conscious and unconscious functioning together – psyche.

Ethos – the characteristic genius, emotional fiber, spirit of a people, institution or system. Barrett has argued that African ethos is spiritual in nature. Worldview helps to determine ethos. Self-image; self-concept; Aesthetic – idea or concept of benefit; behavior – ethics.

African concept of being – "becoming" concept of time only one aspect of African concept of being.

"Idea of progress" - change towards what???

That then represents both history and religion.

Regina Hendricks: This is great.

Michelliea Georges: You are being so helpful. This helps our understanding of not just Egypt, but its relation to the ancient world as well as how the Africans thought religiously.

George Washington: I am happy to share with you sisters. After all, this is an educational trip and Dr. Monderson asked that we talk to each other and share information. I too am growing from this exchange for I have not reviewed this information in two decades.

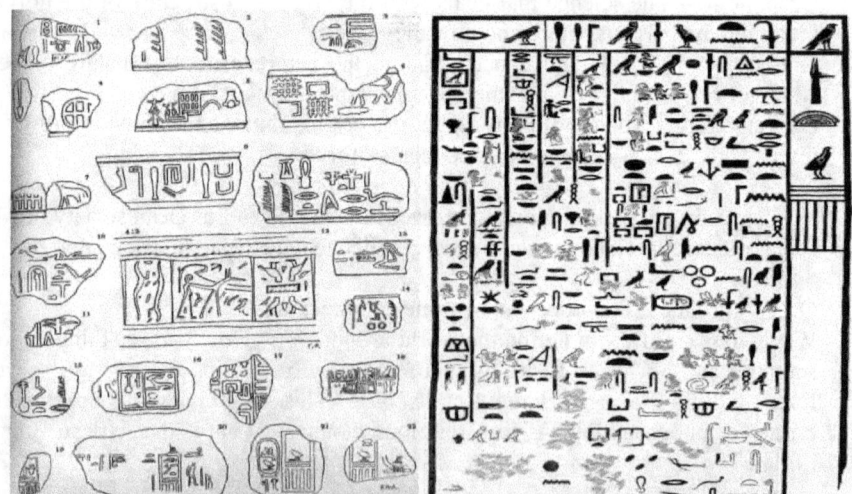

Holy Land Illustration 53. Abydos, Temple. Sealings of the First through Fifth Dynasties (left); and Decree of Neferkara, Fifth Dynasty (right).

QUINTESSENTIAL BOOK "THE HOLY LAND"

Asantewaa Harris: Ra is in all his glory in his morning sunrise. What a beautiful day this promises to be. Imagine seeing this everyday for years. No wonder the ancient Egyptians were so creative in their philosophic, artistic and religious expressions and practice.
Mr. John Stewart: "Well, all are but parts of one stupendous whole whose body nature is and god the soul."
Asantewaa Harris: That is so beautiful, as the rising sun on the horizon. I am so fortunate to be on this trip and with such wonderful and enlightened people.

Hattie Jones: Honey, isn't this a wonderful day?
Jerome Smith: My dear, I cannot refrain from being grateful for the opportunity of being in Egypt with you. I feel my love complete and hope we will be together forever.
Hattie Jones: Publius Syrus of the first century explained: "Speech is a mirror of the soul; as a man speaks, so is he." Therefore, you should be prepared to marry me when we get back to California. Even though there is a minister on this trip, I will still not call your hole card and insist that you do it here but give you enough time to make up your mind when we get home.
Jerome Smith: I appreciate the consideration. Thanks.

Mrs. Alexander Pushkin: Let me tell you how proud I am that a young man can articulate so well despite the antagonisms from old fools like my husband and Teddy here.
Teddy Cubia: Well, we are just probing the parameters of the discussion so the young man can show us how well he is prepared based on his training under Asante.
Michael Sinclair: Dr. Asante taught us to "Be firm on your own principles and the truth," and that "Your position must be one of honor."
Dr. Alexander Pushkin: Got to hand it to you Mr. Sinclair, you did an excellent job.
Michael Sinclair: I must thank you and Mr. Cubia for you bring out the best in me.

4.   Site:

MEDINET HABU: MORTUARY TEMPLE OF RAMESES III

Holy Land Photo 36. Edfu Temple of Horus. In the rear corridor, plan of the Temple with hawk emblem of Horus presiding.

After the glorious achievements of the Eighteenth Dynasty, and that of the Nineteenth Ramesside Dynasty, the Twentieth Dynasty, *Nile Year* 3045-3160 (c. 1185-1070 B.C.), continued the tradition of civil and religious architectural construction, and maintaining and defending the empire. However, the nation now faced a changing geo-political reality in the ancient world. Having dominated the ancient world stage and been the principal imperialist nation, Ta-merry/Kemet, today's Egypt, now faced the combined wrath of a confederation of her traditional

QUINTESSENTIAL BOOK "THE HOLY LAND"

enemies. Struggle as the nation did to hold back the inevitable historical changes; it was only a matter of time before external enemies overcame the Nile River country, as she grew weaker internally. Unable to produce strong pharaonic leadership, emerging nations now chose to settle scores with the Northeast African State.

5. Post Site Lecture

Dr. Fred Monderson: Today was certainly a wonderful experience. I noticed some of you examining Rameses' bathroom. Yes, they did wash in those days. You saw the alternation of pillars and columns and how deep the hieroglyphs were. In some places, the paint was still fresh. George William Curtis (1824-1892) in the *Call of Freedom* said: "While we read history we make history" and being here we are making history! Equally too, Francis Parkman (1823-1893) insisted on: "Faithfulness to the truth of history" so we must be accurate and work vigilantly for the reconstruction of African historiography, for that is the only way the historical record will be corrected. After all, Dr. Arnold thought "History may be defined as the biography of nations" and Colton wrote "To cite the examples of history, in order to animate us to virtue, or to arm us with fortitude, this it is to call up the illustrious dead to inspire and improve the living." Even further, Dr. Fuller offered "History makes a young man to be old without either wrinkles or grey hairs, privileging him with the experience of age without either the infirmities or inconveniences thereof." Oliver Wendell Holmes (1841-1935) the great American Supreme Court Justice, on interpreting the law, once offered: "Upon this point a page of history is worth a volume of logic." This temple is the history of the reign of Rameses III. However, within the last few years of the reign, especially after the assassination attempt on his life, not much has survived.

That aside, some scholars argue for the 18th Dynasty and others for the 19th Dynasty and which pharaoh can be considered the greatest. While some may give that nudge to the megalomaniac Rameses II others argue that the greatest pharaoh of all Egypt was Thutmose III. He was an imperial pharaoh, great military strategist who stood almost 5 feet tall. Imagine!

The first thing he did upon ascending the throne was to march north and engage adversaries in the Battle of Megiddo. This was his first and probably most impressive campaign for he surprised his adversaries and was victorious. He conducted 14 military campaigns in regnal years 26-33. He made 17 altogether in that region, not counting those he waged in Nubia.

He had a long reign, counting the years when Hatshepsut denied him for a total of some 54 years. He left many records of his campaigns both in Asia where he went

FREDERICK MONDERSON

as far as the Euphrates and in Nubia as far as the 4th Cataract. He was well liked and so no one dismantled his monuments. He had at least 6 wives. Three had foreign names. Many of his marriages were for the sake of political alliances. When he died in 1433 he left Egypt strong. His tomb in the Valley of the Kings is in a unique position, way in the back and about 100 feet high up in the rocks. The tomb is unusual, non-rectangular and in the shape of a cartouche as is the sarcophagus.

The paintings in his tomb were unique. They had scenes from the *Book of the Dead* with cursive forms of hieroglyphics as if written on a papyrus. He was succeeded by Amenhotep II and then Thutmose IV whose son Amenhotep III followed. Remember Thutmose IV did not follow Thutmose III nor did Amenhotep III follow Amenhotep II. Nor was Amenhotep III the son of Thutmose III. Thutmose III's son was Amenhotep II. Amenhotep II's son was Thutmose IV. Thutmose IV's son was Amenhotep III.

So Thutmose III's great-grandson was Amenhotep III, the "magnificent." Amenhotep III's son was Amenhotep IV. However, to understand the latter, you have to understand his genealogy. Amenhotep IV's parents were Amenhotep III and Queen Tiy. Amenhotep III's parents were Thutmose IV and Mutemwia. Queen Tiy, on the other hand, was a commoner. Her parents were Yuya and Tuya. Some have tried to attribute Syrian parentage to her but she was Nubian, and therefore Black. Some believe she exerted a great deal of influence over her husband and son.

Holy Land Photo 37. Edfu Temple of Horus. Scenes from the war between Horus and Seth.

Amenhotep III was the first to use commemorative scarabs to tell about particular events of his reign. He commemorated his marriage to Queen Tiy (the marriage scarab). He made a lake for his queen to sail on and he created the Great Scarab (beside the Sacred Lake at Karnak). His lion hunts were recorded on scarabs. He made scarabs for his second marriage even though he was still married to Queen

QUINTESSENTIAL BOOK
"THE HOLY LAND"

Tiy. Amenhotep III built his queen a palace on the west bank of the river and carved a lake for her to sail on. He gave the name of "Aten gleams" to Queen Tiy's boat. There is no question she was instrumental in his rule. Nevertheless, he elected his son Amenhotep IV as his co-regent.

Some theories have been offered as to why he chose his son as co-regent. Some scholars argue that he was becoming feeble and had to groom his successor. Queen-Tiy may have started the worship of the Aten. She may have become a power broker during the co-regency or even earlier as her influence with her husband grew. Their sons were Amenhotep IV, Tutankhaten and Smenkare.

In the sixth year of his reign, Amenhotep IV changed his name to Akhenaten. Realizing that the influence of Amon was too strong at Karnak he decided on moving his capital to Amarna in Middle Egypt. He had boundary stelae set up marking out his territory. The city was on both sides of the Nile. Along with the religion and capital, the art also changed. He introduced many new concepts that were scientific. The people saw him as he was not some idealized notion of what a vigorous youthful pharaoh looked like.

He married Nefertiti who had come to marry his father in a political alliance. In fact, her name was Thadukippa, daughter of Dushrata. The Egyptians changed her name to Nefertiti "the fair one cometh." They had several daughters, Meritaten, Neferneferu, Meketaten, Baketaten, Neferneferatentasherit, and Ankhesenpaaten, and so on. Dr. ben-Jochannan says her name is "the beautiful one cometh." However, he also says of Aahmes-Nefertari, the "Black Goddess" "the most beautiful one cometh."

As his character was attacked by modern scholarship he was derided as being deformed. Some call his "illness" Freulich's Syndrome, claiming it was a pituitary problem. Apparently this problem is associated with sterility. So therefore, they questioned whether the children were his. Seems the problems of Black men are not new.

Smenkhare served as co-regent with Akhenaten. He married Meritaten and they left Tel el Amarna. This may be a sign of pressures from the priests of Thebes.

Nefertiti moved to the northern palace together with her daughter Ankhesenpaaten who married Tutankhaten. Akhenaten probably had another wife called Kia. There is a possibility that Tutankhaten is the son of Akhenaten and Kia.

Despite what is said, Akhenaten was not a pacifist for he engaged in military campaigns during his reign. This is generally kept low key. An old lady digging for bricks found the Amarna letters written to the king from Assyria. There are 150 royal archival tablets. Akhenaten was either killed or died naturally, though there is no record of his death.

When Tutankhaten succeeded Smenkhare he changed his name back to Tutankhamon and returned to Thebes. After Tutankhamon's return to Thebes, Amon re-emerged as paramount. The 19th Dynasty Ramesside kings restored much of the glory of Amon. Following Rameses II, Merenptah his 13th son followed him to the throne. He was the last vigorous pharaoh of this dynasty.

After Merenptah, Setnakht seized power and founded the 20th Dynasty. Not much is known about him though he reigned for only 2 years. His wife was probably Tausert who had a tomb in the Valley of the Kings. She ruled as the last pharaoh of the 19th Dynasty. Of course, this was unheard of, even though Hatshepsut also had a tomb in the Valley of the Kings.

Holy Land Photo 38. Edfu Temple of Horus. In the Peristyle Court looking back at the Entrance, columns left and columns (left); and the throngs of people who visit this and other temples on the tourist route (right).

His son Rameses III succeeded Setnakht. Setnakht had no royal blood, though his son Rameses did. Rameses III reigned from 1182-1151 for 31 years. His most famous monument was Medinet Habu, which is a record of his many wars against the Libyans and Peoples of the Sea. Three functions have been identified for the Temple of Medinet Habu. First it was the king's mortuary temple and used by priests for religious ceremonies in his honor. It also had a palace attached to it as well as a fort, which some called a Migdol. Some see both a palace for mortuary rituals and a permanent palace at Medinet Habu.

During the last 15 years of his reign, his rule began to weaken and records are missing. However, there is one important thing that happened when workers building his temple went on strike. The workmen had not been paid in 2 weeks, so they went on strike. They were generally paid in kind and this had not been met.

QUINTESSENTIAL BOOK
"THE HOLY LAND"

Most workers lived in the workmen's village at Deir el Medina.

In the last years of his life there was a harem conspiracy that tried to kill Rameses III. An extant letter tells of the plan to kill the king. Apparently there was a belief that you could kill people by using wax figures. A posited theory is that the king became physically and mentally incapacitated and that is when the attempt was made on his life.

Rameses III was succeeded by Rameses IV, V, VI, VII, VIII, IX, X, and XI. They ruled 6, 4, 7, 1, 1, 17, 3 and 27 years respectively. Rameses XI was probably the strongest of this lot. His succession was the culmination of a succession of weakened Ramesside king. In the shade, however, lurked the priesthood who began to develop designs on the throne. Herihor, a Theban high priest, wanted to take over as pharaoh. By this time the priesthood grew enormously because every pharaoh wanted to be favored by the gods and the priesthood held the key.

Holy Land Illustration 54. Cabinetmakers in the Pyramid Age (top); and a page from the story of the "Shipwrecked Sailor," the earliest Sinbad, as read to the boys and girls of Egypt four thousand years ago, (One third the size of original).

FREDERICK MONDERSON

At the end of the XIXth Dynasty priests of Amon-ra owned $1/4^{th}$ of the land in Egypt. There were over 81,000 priests by the end of Rameses II's reign. In the 19th year of his reign Rameses XI built a chapel at Karnak, which was unusual because not much building was being undertaken. The king's challenger Herihor wrote his name in cartouche at Karnak. He had both the nomen and prenomen. So the 20th Dynasty ended with two claimants to the throne, Rameses XI and Herihor, High Priest of Amon at Thebes. No one has found Herihor's tomb or body.

Therefore there were two ruling families claiming the throne in the XXIst Dynasty. The descendants of Herihor ruled Upper Egypt but do not claim to be pharaohs but high priests. In the north, Pinudjem put his name in a cartouche. These pharaohs ruled in the Delta at Tanis, a rather strange city with no buildings but lots of statues. The XXIst Dynasty lasted form 1087-935. There were many king including Smendes, Psusennes I, Nephescheres, Amenophis, Osorkon, Psinaches Amun and Psusennes II. Their reigns were 26, 46, 4, 9, 6, 17, 9 and 14 years respectively. These kings chose to be buried in the north and not in the Valley of the Kings. Psusennes I's tomb has been found. Since the high priests of Dynasty XXI do not call themselves pharaohs they were not buried in the Valley of the Kings.

Tomb robberies were rampant during the time of the XXIst Dynasty so the priests hid the mummies of many important pharaohs. In 1881, a cache of mummies was discovered at Deir el Bahari. Apparently the Rasul family was looting this site for years until they were caught and told to confess. The high priests of the XXIst Dynasty had huge coffins and wives of the pharaohs of the dynasty adopted names of earlier women.

Holy Land Photo 39. Edfu Temple of Horus. In the rear "Corridor of Victory" two Gods baptize the King with streams of Ankhs (left); and the Goddesses Isis (left) and Nephthys (right) sit enthroned.

QUINTESSENTIAL BOOK "THE HOLY LAND"

Holy Land Photo 39a. Beauty, joy and the power of the intellect contained in the wonderful smile of Professor Merimba Ani.

6. Discussion

Alfred Lord Tennyson (1809-1892) in *Sir Galahad* affirmed: "My strength is as the strength of ten, because my heart is pure" and also in *The Two Voices*: "Self-reverence, self-knowledge, self-control, these three alone lead life to sovereign power." Such sayings as these encourage us to seek knowledge for herein lies our salvation and the future of our progeny. Sir Francis Bacon (1561-1626) in *The Advancement of Learning* expressed the idea that: "Knowledge is a rich storehouse for the glory of the creator and the relief of man's estate." Herein then is our mandate in search of the wisdom of the ancestors. He continued that: "An exact knowledge of the past helps in interpreting the future." In the *Life of Samuel Johnson* (1709-1784), Boswell's statement held: "Knowledge is of two kinds. We know a subject ourselves, or we know where we can find information upon it."

Are there any questions?

Cosmo Palmer: Who was Nefertiti?
Dr. Fred Monderson: Nefertiti was a Mitanni princess who came to marry Amenhotep III in a political marriage, but ended up marrying his son, Amenhotep

FREDERICK MONDERSON

IV who led the Amarna revolution against Amon at Thebes in favor of the Aten. It failed religiously but triumphed historically and intellectually. She gave him five children and ended up having tremendous power in her husband's kingdom. Some say she ruled for a short while after he died and was succeeded by Tutankhamon.

Michelliea Georges: Perhaps you can explain the difference between the two Nefertaris and Nefertiti.
Dr. Fred Monderson: Glad to. These three women lived hundreds of years apart but their forcefulness, charm and their intelligence influenced, as Dr. John Clarke would say, "Men and Movements."

Aahmes-Nefertari is pictured Black in a British Museum portrait wearing red, white and blue, 1500 years before the Christian era. She is the ancestress or founder of the 18th Dynasty. She married her brother Ahmose who expelled the Hyksos. These were high living Blacks. Both she and her son Amenhotep I, father of Thutmose I, were deified, or became gods of the Theban necropolis, having their own temple for worship. That is, they were worshipped as Divinities.

Nefertiti, as I just said, came at the end of the 18th Dynasty in her marriage to Amenhotep IV, Ikhnaton, or Akhenaten. Nefertari, on the other hand, was the favorite wife of Rameses II of the 19th Dynasty, for whom he built a temple at Abu Simbel in Hathor's honor. Her tomb is in the Valley of the Queens.

Dr. Leonard James: Where does the Divine Lineage of the kings begin?
Dr. Fred Monderson: The Religious Character of the King is very complex yet rooted in tradition. There is an exclusive religious or divine origin of the various elements of the Egyptian definition of monarchy. Theirs is a conception of monarchy, which is composed of purely theological elements and based solely on the assimilation of the king to the gods who are the makers of the world and the mythical founders of Egyptian society. The Divine Lineage of the King begins in the formation of Egyptian society. The lineage begins in pre-dynastic times and culminates in the Pyramid Texts of the Old Kingdom, with force of tradition molding the society.

Frederick Maloney: What is the oldest name we have of the King?
Dr. Fred Monderson: The earliest names of the king date to the Thinite or Archaic Period and are sometimes called the Horus or Standard name. The Two Horuses represents the union of earth and sky or heaven and earth. The King is also the successor to Horus, son of Osiris and Isis. The King is not a representative or interpreter of the Supreme God, but is either a god himself, manifest on earth in a human body in which is incarnate one of the souls of the god, or he is the god's own son. This is traceable to Menes, the unifier of the two kingdoms at the beginning of the dynastic period. Before this the king traced his lineage through

QUINTESSENTIAL BOOK "THE HOLY LAND"

the mythical period of Horus and before that Osiris and Isis.

An article on "The King" in *Encyclopedia of Religion and Ethics* Volume 7, (1914) gives three examples of divine intervention in the birth of the pharaoh. Deir el Bahari records Hatshepsut's divine birth; Luxor Temple records Amenhotep III's divine birth; and Erment records Alexander the Great's divine birth in Egypt. At these places the texts record all the details of the union with the child's mother, magic involved in the process and activities of the presiding divinities.

"Underscoring the power of the priesthood, they insisted that the king have connection with all the principal gods and goddesses as a form of legitimizing his reign and heritage. He or she is thus adopted by all and becomes son of the gods or receives milk from the goddesses as a form of succor. Yet still, for the king to be truly or theologically accepted as pharaoh he had to receive at Heliopolis all the magico-religious consecration which transform him into a living incarnation of Ra, the sun-god, creator of the world. The sources for this knowledge, according to the article are: (1) the historical inscriptions, such as that of the celebrated Ethiopian conqueror Piankhi, (2) the ritual published in the Pyramid texts, (3) the bas-reliefs and special enactments of the solar temples of Abusir, (4) the extracts from anointing and coronation scenes sculptured in the great temples, chiefly at Thebes, (5) the statues and statuettes commemorating coronations (notably at Karnak), and (6) the descriptive scenes telling of the 'jubilee' feasts of *habsadu*. Finally, the Thinite monuments discovered at Abydos provide evidence that the whole of this ceremonial was already established, in its essential elements, at the Thinite period. Even under the 1st dynasty there appeared scenes of that distant epoch similar to those found in the Greek period upon the walls of the temple of Edfu or other sanctuaries built in Egypt by the Ptolemies."

It is believed that parents gave their children a secret name at birth. It is believed reincarnation of the dead in newly born children, shows that cultural practice possibly existed very early in man's consciousness along the Nile River in Northeast Africa.

FREDERICK MONDERSON

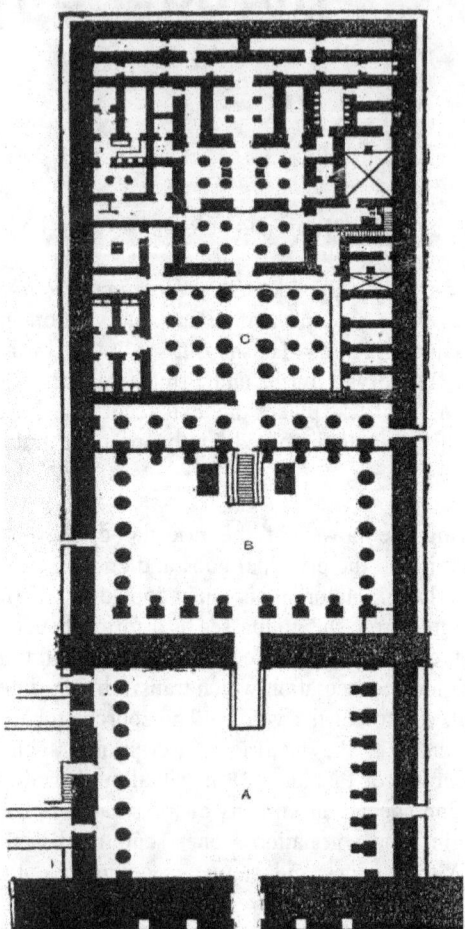

Holy Land – Plan of Medinet Habu, Mortuary Temple of Rameses III, Thebes.

Carmelita Shabazz: How many names did the King have and can you explain some of them?
Dr. Fred Monderson: By the time of the great flowering of the Egyptian culture, the king was known to possess five names. The first is his birth name. Second is his coronation name. Third is the hawk name. Fourth is the vulture and uraeus name. Fifth is the golden hawk name. These are generally also given as the *Horus, Golden Horus, Two Ladies, Suten-Bat and Son of Ra*. Dr. ben-Jochannan gives nine names. Quite frankly, I don't remember the other names, they are someplace in one of my books. I know one is "the Good God." Other names are when he is at the head of the army in some military engagement; another is when

QUINTESSENTIAL BOOK
"THE HOLY LAND"

he officiates at the temple, and so on.

George Washington: How would you define the relationship between the King and the gods?

Dr. Fred Monderson: We can probably say the king's person contained all the essential qualities of the human personality as well as elements of the god's divine persona, which meant he had more souls, doubles and shadows than ordinary men. Foucart's explanation in *Religion and Ethics* Vol. 7 is that the king "is in every function an earthly image of the various gods, and performs their legendary activity on the earth."

Regina Hendricks: So you are saying the name is a powerful part of the personality. Would you say it is the most powerful part of the personality?

Dr. Fred Monderson: I won't say it is the most powerful part of the personality. I would say, the article on "Names" tells us: "All the texts, ritual, and magic of Egypt rest essentially on the fact that the name, thus understood, constitutes a material soul, and it is his very reason for living. The name is therefore the ego. It exists by itself. It is the subtlest of the various souls of the individual. It is the last term in the series of active principles; gradually increasing in airiness and 'evocability,' result from the combination of body and bone with the blood, the ghost, the shade, etc., to form the life par excellence."

Star Jackson: When does the Egyptian chronology begin?

Dr. Fred Monderson: It's difficult to say. This question gets into "long chronology" and "short chronology" dynamics. Prominent scholars differ from c. 3100-5700. One argues for 6200 B.C. for the first dynasty, depending on who did the work. The year 3100 B.C. is more manageable. The Old Kingdom dates are approximation. You can't know anything certain before 1875-2000 B.C. Some have even said 3100 B.C. is more political because it makes it contemporary with Mesopotamian history, particularly for those who wish to give that area primacy. Conversely, Petrie gives 5700 B.C. as the date of the First Dynasty. Maulana Karenga gives 6200 B.C. as the start of the First Dynasty.

FREDERICK MONDERSON

Holy Land Photo 40. Karnak Temple of Amun. Between the columns, emblematic unity pillars depicting the Lotus of Upper Egypt and the Papyrus of Lower Egypt, placed here by Thutmose III; and looking west, a visitor passes through the ruins of the Processional Colonnade while to the left stands Thutmose I's remaining standing obelisk.

Frank James: What is meant by the earliest fixed date in history?
Dr. Fred Monderson: James Henry Breasted coined the phrase and set it up in 1915. It is 4241 B.C., thought to be the date the Egyptians invented the calendar. Some scholars think the date should be extended one more Sothic cycle to 5701 B.C. This coincides with Petrie's First Dynasty date based on the "Long Chronology." Later Diopian scholars oriented 4241 as *Nile Year* 1 in their struggle.

James Madison: What is the Palermo Stone and what evidence does it contain?
Dr. Fred Monderson: The Palermo Stone is a black basalt slab, now in Palermo Italy, that lists the names of rulers from the mythical period down to the Fifth Dynasty. It gives the king's names and biennial year listings.

Walter Brown: how would you define some other sources of Egyptian history?
Dr. Fred Monderson: In addition to the Palermo Stone, there are "day-lists" in

QUINTESSENTIAL BOOK
"THE HOLY LAND"

temples, "annals" and "king lists" such as the *Sakkara Tablet* found in the tomb of Tjunery or Tenroy; the *Karnak Tablet* of Thutmose III; and the *Abydos Tablets* of Seti I and Rameses II.

The Palermo Stone lists Lower Egyptian rulers down to Horus who was succeeded by Menes. It consists of a series of regnal years listing significant events of the different kings. It records cult ceremonies, tax records, sculptures, buildings and warfare.

Then there are the works of Manetho, his *History of Egypt, Aegyptiaca*, and Herodotus, Strabo, Diodorus Siculus, and many others who made commentaries in antiquity. The archaeological and anthropological records in Egypt's recovery during the 19th and 20th Centuries are equally significant for the foundations of modern interpretations. Except for commentaries on each other's works, particularly Black scholars have made no critical or serious analyses way back then. With the serious critiques of such people as DuBois and later Diop, not to discount the work of ben-Jochannan and other black writers, the racists began to cry foul. Only when a white writer is bold enough to comment on the race of the Egyptians do we get some concession. It's like Frederick Douglass used to say: "Power concedes nothing without a struggle." Yet still, we must remember these latter sources are important. Equally too, Dr. ben-Jochannan insisted we get the earliest or oldest of these sources and do critical analysis because despite some prejudice in reporting, they are still tremendously important.

Kashmoney Malone: Perhaps you could be more specific with these sources of kingly representation?
Dr. Fred Monderson: Sure. The *Sakkara Tablet* was found in the tomb of an Old Kingdom nobleman, Tanjeri or Tenroy; The *Karnak Tablet* was recognized and removed by Prisse D'Avennes to Paris sometime around 1864. It gives the names of predecessors of Thutmose III, kings who benefitted Karnak. They list 62 kings but when found, only 48 were legible. The *Abydos Tablet* or *Tablet of Kings* is in a corridor and contains seventy-six kings from Narmer to Seti I. It is still in the Abydos temple. There was another *Abydos Tablet* found in the Temple of Rameses II at Abydos with 50 kings and this one was removed and is now housed in the British Museum. Of course, as a priest in second century Graeco-Egypt, Manetho had access to important records and this makes his work equally important. However, it has not survived complete and what we know is based on commentaries of ancient writers. There is a translation of Manetho in the Loeb Classic series.

Melvin Escobar: What did the word Milky Way mean to the Ancient Egyptians?
Dr. Fred Monderson: Something is said about the souls of human being considered to be spiritual and in an eternal state of existence and their descent from and ascent through the Milky Way. Myers (1900: 448) explained: "As soon as at the

FREDERICK MONDERSON

happening of the Winter Solstice, the bark of the gun-god appeared at the last bend of the Celestial Nile, the instructed Kau seized the occasion to secure recognition and their reception on board to it, and the Osiris – (i.e., the Ka of the dead one), started towards the Hall of the double Maati, to participate in the trial of his accountable spiritual parts before Osiris and the Forty-two judges. From here also, some said, was extended the Ladder, or staircase reaching to Heaven, mentioned in the Books of the Dead. The spirits were supposed to ascend and descend from Heaven upon the stairway at the proper times. The Stairway may have been a conventional idea applied to the vast mass of stars called by the astronomers of our day, the Milky Way. The Milky Way embraces in such a manner the Zodiac, that it cuts it into two opposite points, one being in Cancer and the other being in Capricorn. These were in general both called, 'Gates of the Sun,' because each, at the solstitial points, seem to man, to limit the course of the sun and it, apparently to the inhabitants of our earth, appeared to go no further, but always returned from one solstice to the other, over its path in the ecliptic and never got beyond them; the solstitial points were therefore thought by the ancients to wall in and keep the sun within its proper bounds." We are told further of Neb-qed in the hall of Double Maati: "Alongside of him is the ladder or stairway to Heaven, upon the top of which is an uraeus defending it. In a Hall having such a Stairway at each end, are the Forty-two assisting judges, standing up and enveloped as mummies, each coifed with a wig and the feather of Ma'at, and each having a beard. In the center of the frieze of our picture, are the symbolic Eyes of the Double Maati."

Robert Matthews: Where does the name Moses come from? Or, Who was Moses? Dr. Fred Monderson: Certainly not Charleston Heston who played in *The Ten Commandments*. This is Hollywood's version, shot principally in Arizona. This question also goes to the other question of whether there was an Exodus. Freud, in *Moses and Monotheism* denied the Moses we are fed on was a real person and Jewish theologians meeting in Canada denied there was an exodus saying this was a rallying cry of the people in that early age of nationalism. Myers (1900: X) says: "Some dispute exists as to the exact date of, and the Pharaoh under whom, the Exodus of the Hebrews occurred. Dr. Hommel thinks it must have taken place either in the closing years of Rameses II, the Great (circa 1348-1281 B.C.), or more likely in the fifth year of his successor, Merneptah II (1277 B.C.). The Egyptians, as appears from an inscription found by Professor Petrie, of the fifth year of Merneptah II, at that time knew of the Hebrews as Isri'il, and likely by the Egyptian name of Epri and Epriu (the plural), the Hebrews were meant."

QUINTESSENTIAL BOOK
"THE HOLY LAND"

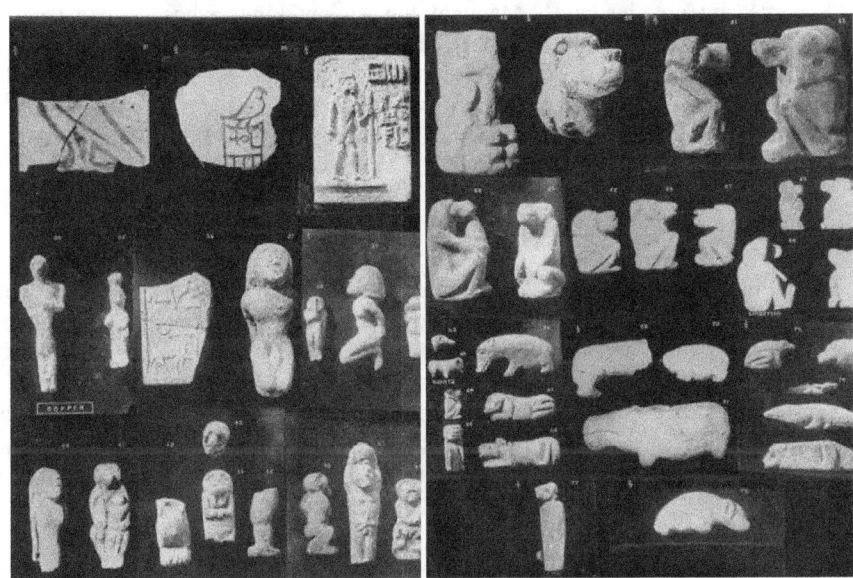

Holy Land Illustration 55. Abydos, Temple. Glazed figures of the First Dynasty; and more glazed figures of the First Dynasty.

We do know Moses or Moshe along with many of the religious personalities and intellectuals of that age, were taught at the University of Annu or Heliopolis. It been said: "Moses was learned in all the wisdom of the Egyptians." In his time the wisdom of Egypt was housed in the University of Annu. Of course, some of it was also housed in the Temple of Luxor, which had also grown as a University. Myers says: "The name of Moses was probably *Theuti-mose* or *Thutmosis,* from *Theuti,* or Thoth, and mose. He was named after the kings of the XVIIIth Dynasty (circa 1587-1414 B.C), Thutmose I, II, and III." Again, Dr. ben-Jochannan has reminded us the Temple of Ptah at Memphis was also an important theological and intellectual center. Remember the temple was founded by Menes at the beginning of the First Dynasty when he also ushered in the worship of Ptah.

Joshua Monderson: Could you perhaps paint a picture of what have the monuments told us about the people and culture of the ancient Egyptians?
Dr. Fred Monderson: The monuments tell us much about the people and culture of ancient Egypt. They tell us about the foods they ate, the jobs they did, the gods they worshipped, types of building they erected, types of stone and other building materials they used, their science, astronomy, metaphysics and moral and ethical behaviors. We know some had the physical and racial features of black people until much later when hordes of people infiltrated, were brought in as slaves or simply came as conquerors. We know they were not painted black because they

were dead, the term "Black Land," according to Prof. Obenga, referred to the people and not the land. Many of the ancient kings whose remains we have showed distinct Negroid or Black features. One thing is certain; you won't find Black people in the Egyptian displays in museums in the western world and America. When you do see them, it is because they played a significant role in the society and their remains "survived" the ravages of time and man at their discovery!

Teddy Cubia: As a musician myself, I am curious as to what do we know of ancient Egyptian music?
Dr. Fred Monderson: Music was an essential part of the society. The Egyptians were a people who made merry. Music was played at banquets, in temples, on boat excursions, and taught in schools, etc. Tombs in the Valley of the Kings show harpers playing music. Therefore, music was a feature of all walks of life. Myers (1900: 245) recounts from the *Papyrus of Sayings*: "One needs the voice (i.e., in intoning, singing, oratory, etc.,) when the voice is ceasing, (i.e., from old age); (but) in the years when the voice is possessed, the voice is not used (i.e., cultivated).'

"This means to say; when a person's voice is strong and good, as in youth, it is not an educated voice; but when it has been educated, life has advanced and the strength and vigor of it are not of long duration. The Egyptian priests used a great deal of chanting, intoning, etc., in their temple worship, and the correct religious intonation was of the greatest importance in all religious matters, and an error in it destroyed the mystic effect. They are said to have made great mystical use of the vowel sounds. Hymns and litanies to be chanted or sung are amongst the most examples of Egyptian sacred literature."

Peter Monderson: How would you say private tombs differed from noble tombs during the Old and New Kingdom?
Dr. Fred Monderson: In the Old Kingdom, Not every king built a pyramid. So, king, private and noble tombs were essentially mastaba type, large and small and built of stone. Their many rooms allowed for extensive decoration depicting their lives on earth as mirror expectations for life in the afterlife. That meant their work, sport, recreation, family relationships, social status and much more were depicted either on the tomb walls or recounted on stela detailing their accomplishments and letting the world know of the lives they lived with expectations of a favorable judgment in the afterlife. In the New Kingdom, noble or private as well as kings' tombs were cut into the rock with elaborate extensive mural decorations, again detailing their accomplishments and expectations. The structures were somewhat different with more space for decorating, compartments and roof often depicting heavenly drama.

That's all folks. Don't forget dinner is at 7:00 tonight.

QUINTESSENTIAL BOOK "THE HOLY LAND"

7.   Free Time

8.   Dinner

Michelliea Georges: There are 5 major components in Afrocentric paradigm. These are:

1. Njuri Model: Beautiful equals good. Philosophy. Pretty is as pretty does, ugly to the bone. Criticize what constitutes beauty. It does dichotomize beauty. A mass murderer cannot be beautiful. You cannot say: "This woman is gorgeous even though she mistreats her children."

2. Equivalency and parallelism: People saying Jewish Holocaust. We must not let anyone equate their particularity with our own Middle Passage, what Donna Richards termed *The Maafa* or Great Enslavement, must not be equated with others' experiences.

There can be parallelism but not equivalency. Commonality, oppression, pain, victory. Their struggle was not our struggle. The motifs, icons, etc of their struggle are not ours.

3. Seven Senses: dance, music, and theater. We must use and investigate these disciplines.

4. Process and Response. We have an interaction between the dance and audience; the speaker and receiver; actor and audience.

5. Transformation and Synthesis: Change and bringing together of Africans who were lumped together. We have both particular and general here. The categories of Afrocentric paradigm - space, location, and place are very important in Afrocentricity.

Women are taken for granted. All Black people have rhythm! Rhythm is everything. Modulating of voice, the way we walk, wearing of Kente cloth, etc. Rhythm is linked to cosmological attitude of all African people. The African being is in-tuned to the cosmos. Rhythm is the connection between the practical and spiritual worlds. An old African proverb is 'you may leave a log in water 5, 10, 20 years, but it may never become a crocodile."

FREDERICK MONDERSON

Holy Land World Tourist Day Extravaganza 11.
Another routine of the dancers.

Regina Hendricks: Heavy. How do you remember all that stuff?
Michelliea Georges: I take good notes. Besides, one of the insistences of The Afrocentric Institute is that we be copious in our note taking and prolific and precise in our documenting data. Professor Asante wanted us to write down everything!
George Washington: My professors were just as demanding of their students. Dr. Clarke wanted his students to read 15 books on every subject we reported on. Dr. Richards had several books and there were also many assignments to insure that we really learned what was being taught. That is why my information is so copious. That brings us to the issues I intend to discuss with you sisters this evening. In fact, maybe we should meet in the lounge after dinner rather than in your hotel room. If we are not able to finish then perhaps we could visit your place for the nightcap. Nothing personal I'm sure you understand.
Regina Hendricks: It's ok with me. How about you Michelliea?
Michelliea Georges: I am willing to meet anywhere to enhance the knowledge I am receiving on this important trip.
George Washington: Ok then, I'll see you sisters in the lounge after dinner.

Teddy Cubia: So what do you have for us today Michael?
Dr. Alexander Pushkin: I know Asante and Afrocentricity have been criticized but has anyone had anything good to say about the philosophy?

Mrs. Alexander Pushkin: Honey, I think we need to be a bit gentler with our young

QUINTESSENTIAL BOOK
"THE HOLY LAND"

friend. After all, in addition to what we are getting on this trip, Mr. Sinclair is doing a wonderful job and this is a terrific bonus.

Michael Sinclair: In all modesty, I agree and am really pleased to be in such intellectual and experienced company and given this opportunity to be a teacher in my own right. I think you are doing me a great service by letting me tell you what I have learnt in my studies at Temple University's Afrocentric Institute studying under Dr. Molefi Asante. In "African Studies and the Afrocentric Paradigm: A Critique" written by Bayo Oye Bade of Temple University and published in *Journal of Black Studies* December 1990: 233-238 the author stated: "The study of peoples from an African-centered prism has been referred to as Afrocentricity. This paradigm of studying Africa, which has its theoretical foundation in the works of contemporary scholars in the United States, is, to be sure, not an entirely new perspective in African intellectual thought. Africa centered historiography, in fact dates back to the closing years of colonial rule in Africa. In the early 1960s, the approach found increased expression in the works of African scholars who consciously grounded their research in African methodology. However, the development of an Africa-centered approach as a theory and philosophy is a product of the 1980s and of Diasporian-African writings. The theoretical conceptualization of an African-centered Approach is the handiwork of Afrocentric scholars such as Molefi Asante, Tchelone Keto, Maulana Karenga, and a host of others based in the United States."

"The subject matter of the Afrocentric paradigm is its placement of Africa at the center of any analysis of African history and culture, including the African-American experience."

"Keto (1989) says 'The Africa-centered perspective of history rests on the premise that it is valid to posit Africa as a geographical and cultural starting point in the study of peoples of African descent. The need to create an Africa centered perspective that takes Africa as a point of departure for African studies stems from the nature of the Eurocentric paradigm, which has been used in many African studies. In the history of intellectual thought, the Eurocentric paradigm has often assumed a hegemonic universal character, and European structure has placed itself at the center of the social structure, becoming the reference point, or the yardstick, by which every culture is defined. For instance, the western definition of civilization has become the standard of what constitutes a civilization. The Eurocentric worldview has become so dominant in the contemporary world that it has overshadowed other worldviews. The Afrocentric perspective seeks to liberate African studies from the Eurocentric morphology on scholarship and thus assert a valid worldview through which Africa can be studied objectively.'"

"Afrocentric scholars hasten to add that an African perspective does not aim to replace Eurocentricity as a universal perspective. Indeed, Afrocentricity recognizes the validity of other non-hegemonic perspectives. Asian-centered,

FREDERICK MONDERSON

America-centered, and Europe-centered in its non-hegemonic form. It is the totality of these non-ego-boosting perspectives that constitutes what Keto calls a 'Pluriversal' perspective. This possibility of looking at the world from different centers rather than a single angle is necessary if we are to have a better understanding of this diversified and multicultural universe."

METHODOLOGY

"Since Afrocentricity adopts Africa as a take-off point in any discussion of African civilization, it is Diopian in methodology. Indeed, the Diopian school of Afrocentric though insists that the ancient Kemetic (Egyptian) civilization should be the classical reference point for the study of African civilization, as the Greek civilization is for analysis of European civilization."

"Cheikh Anta Diop's (1974) *The African Origin of Civilization* to Martin Bernal's (1987) *Black Athena: The Afro-Asiatic Roots of Classical Civilization*, have confirmed beyond any reasonable doubt the African origin of the Kemetic civilization."

"Kemet seems to have resolved most of the issues that contemporary civilization faces today – justice, government, interpersonal relations, and racial harmony. This near perfection of the Kemetic civilization is the basis of its adoption by Afrocentrists as a classical reference in which studies of African civilization should be anchored."

Holy Land Illustration 56. Part of the contents of the Tomb of Tutankhamon; and Cliff tomb of an Egyptian noble of the Feudal Age.

"The African scholar Saburi Biobaku (1971), in the early 1960s propounded a theory linking the origin of the Yoruba of West Africa to the Nile Region. Before

QUINTESSENTIAL BOOK
"THE HOLY LAND"

him, Olumide Lucas (1948) had speculated on the Egyptian origin of the Yorubas. However, the present trend in Afrocentric scholarship is that researchers are consciously making Egypt the point of departure in the study of African culture."

"Afrocentricity sees African-American experience as a dimension of African history and culture. Afrocentricity therefore insists that African-American experience be considered as a dimension of African history and culture. Afrocentricity therefore insists that African-American studies should be Africa-centered. It does not see any dichotomy between the African past and the African-American history. Afrocentricity rather sees African-American history as an integral part of African history. This presupposes that Afrocentricity is incompatible with any perspective that tends to see the beginning of African history in the Emancipation Declaration.

The weakness from which initial African-American history has been approached is that it is ahistorical in that it tended to block out African-American historical experience prior to freedom. Such a perspective fails to recognize the antiquity of history and is therefore incompatible with Afrocentricity."

"For Afrocentricity, any perceived discontinuity of African-American history at any given point in time is a myth. To be valid any study of African-American experience must be rooted in African culture."

"What Asante calls *Nommo*, the power of the spoken word is well articulated among African-Americans. But this rhetorical power in speech, song and myth is a carryover of the ancestral practice. When enslaved Africans arrived in America, they carried with them the African power of oral expression in which they expressed in drumming, storytelling, and praise singing. Nommo was an effective communication power used by the enslaved Africans to protest their incarceration. The pioneers of the Civil Rights movement also used the power of the spoken word thorough sermons, lectures, raps, gospel songs, and poetry. Thus to ignore linkage with Africa in treating African-American history and culture is to miss an essential part of the study."

FREDERICK MONDERSON

Holy Land Photo 41. Karnak Temple of Amun. Brother Kabibi, son of Brother Abdul, stands majestically with the obelisks and ruins of the Hypostyle Hall in rear.

Holy Land Illustration 57. Vases of Pepy, Sixth Dynasty and Temple Inscription of the Eleventh and Twelfth Dynasties.

CONCLUSION

QUINTESSENTIAL BOOK
"THE HOLY LAND"

"Afrocentricity as a theory of Africology is undoubtedly still in the process of evolving." "Afrocentric scholars are not yet agreed on whether Marxism has a role to play in Afrocentric discourse." Asante (1987) holds "Marxism is not helpful in developing Afrocentric concepts and methods because it, too, is a product of a Eurocentric consciousness that eludes the historical and cultural perspective of Africa." (p. 8). Keto (1989) holds an opposing view: "The relationship between an African-centered perspective and Marxist theory can be either mutually exclusive or symbiotic. One is inclined to believe that Marxist theories can be compatible with Afrocentricity when they are used for example to analyze Africa's political economy in relation to the exploited global economy dominated by the capitalist west."

"The array of scholarship on the question of slavery, colonialism and neocolonialism – those authors who engage in Marxist analysis seem to provide the best understanding of these themes. But whatever methodology of research and analysis is adopted by the Afrocentric scholar, Afrocentricity insists that investigation of African phenomena, be it language, history or gender studies must be subjected to proper research. For those who confuse Afrocentricity with Negritude, those who tend to see it as a reincarnation of Negritude, this insistence on meticulous research distinguishes it. Afrocentricity it is true, is similar to Negritude in its ideological orientation, but it deviates from Negritude at the point where the latter adorns itself with a romantic garb. To the extent that Afrocentricity rejects undue glorification of Africa, it goes beyond Negritude."

"Afrocentricity is also particular on a proper language of discourse. For too long Eurocentric writers have used derogatory language to qualify Africa and Africans. Unfortunately, even African scholars have helped to perpetuate this historiography. They still, for insistence, use terms like "tribes" and "Third World" when they are discussing Africa. These are terms defined by others to deny African civilization. This is why the definition of Africa must be Africa-centered."

"Afrocentricity expresses the need to change hegemonic cultural expression through research and writing from the African perspective. But it aims beyond this. Apart from asserting a valid perspective from which Africa will be objectively studied, it aims at the humanization of the universe by the Black man. Afrocentricity is thus a search for those values that will make man to relate to man in a humanistic way and not in an imperialist or exploitative way."

9. Lounge Discussion

FREDERICK MONDERSON

Mrs. Alexander Pushkin: Teddy how about reading one of your poems for us tonight. It's such a wonderful star-filled sky and your voice is so melodic for the occasion.

Dr. Alexander Pushkin: Don't worry. I have the drinks tonight. Waiter, a round of the usual for everyone. Ms. Georges, what are you having?

Michelliea Georges: What everyone is having!

Michael Sinclair: Mr. Cubia, you said you marched with Dr. King and met Malcolm X and Stokely Carmichael?

Teddy Cubia: Yes. Stokely changed his name to Kwame Ture. My poem is entitled Red, Black and Green.

"Red, Black and Green"
By
Teddy Cubia

That old generation – going, going, gone
Makes room for the new generation to come on strong.
And that old power structure that stood so long
Is like that old generation - soon to be gone.

And like the greatest pain stood by the great Black mass
In these nature covered hills, greener than all grass
The blood, sweat and tears of our ancestors will soon be past

Dr. Pushkin: Very good Teddy. It's a pity you did not publish some of your writings, we would have it today.

Teddy Cubia: I am planning to pass some of my writings to my nephew who is Black conscious and should be on this trip. Interestingly, when I look at all the people who come to Egypt, I am at a loss why so many of our people are not here for the enlightenment.

Dr. Alexander Pushkin: Some of them are coming awake. Perhaps they will follow Dr. Monderson and come here for the enlightenment from this intellectual growth and pictographic adventure.

QUINTESSENTIAL BOOK
"THE HOLY LAND"

Holy Land World Tourist Day Extravaganza 11.
Important people came to greet the Governor of Luxor Governorate who was also in attendance.

Regina Hendricks: Michelliea lets hurry, I'm sure the brother is on point waiting for us. I could use a nice beverage when I get to the lounge.
Michelliea Georges: Ok. I am almost ready. Let's go.
George Washington: Hello, sisters. Good to see you. Can I order you something to drink? I am having lemon squeeze.
Regina Hendricks: We'll both have the same.
George Washington: Good. Now let's begin. Tonight we will start with African Metaphysics or concept of being. Nature has religious values. In African metaphysics nature goes beyond, so it is super-nature. The cosmos has a sacred nature. The universe emerges as a spiritual whole for it is a sacred creation because "God created it." The spirit, the divine presented the world to man.

The African has the ability to discover the many aspects of the sacred in the world; therefore, he is discovering "reality" and "being."

Fecundity – fruitfulness; fertility of invention.

In terms of this system chaos becomes cosmos which is representative of order.
Natural things can reveal phenomena which transcends.
The sky equals infinite distance, transcends the divine, creator, spirits.
Nature, order, harmony and permanence which is the earth that is symbolic of "mother" or "nurse."

Conflict is a basic western concept. Its man versus man; man versus nature. Therefore, "conquer" and "control."

FREDERICK MONDERSON

Nature becomes a symbolization of the sacred. The rhythms of nature (seasons) become manifestation of cosmic order. The cosmos becomes at one time mystical. Harmony underlines the cosmos also unity.

Principles that underlie African religiosity are harmony, unity and spirituality. As such, then, the universe is seen as a spiritual whole. Things are perceived and conceived as a unified totality and affects the African epistemology. "Knowing" causes the African to interact with the cosmos. Thought, experience, life, belief, becomes one, thus producing a unity between fact and faith. Medical theory and religion are one, for the mind and body is one. What is contradictory and irreconcilable to the European is not so with the African. Ambiguity in African religion lends flexibility to the dogma as opposed to rigidity in the western dogma.

The categories of being as indicated in Alexis Kagame's *Theory of Ontological Being* are as follows:

I. Muntu – "man," "human beingness," plural Bantu

II. Kintu – "thing," plural Bintu

III. Hantu – Place and time; Zamani, Sasa Kuntu – Modality, manner of presentation

Ntu – Universal force. The first four are parts of the last. Spirit is a part of the living.

There is a connection between the ancestral spirits, the yet unborn and us.

Now, let me turn to ancient history. Wilson, Chapter 3, related to continuity of sequences. There were differences in Lower and Upper Egypt.

From 3000 B.C. to 4000 B.C. the following is how specialists would find the culture on an archaeological expedition. The last is the oldest:

Dynasty I, Proto-dynasty, Dynasty 0; Gerzean, Amratian and Badarian.

The University of Texas expedition to Egypt found flints dating back to 13,000 B.C. The Mesolithic period did exist in Egypt. The existence of man in the Nile Valley dates back to 1 million years. Before 4000 B.C. there is discerned a split in Upper and Lower Egyptian history. Dialects were so different that confusion for travelers was shown in papyri. Pottery was different. There were also different crowns used by Lower and Upper Egyptian kings.

QUINTESSENTIAL BOOK "THE HOLY LAND"

Holy Land World Tourist Day Extravaganza 12. Mr. Sayeed (left) and Mr. Rady pose for this picture after the festival ceremony.

Helck proposed a theory that argued 2 aspects of kingship. (1) There were hunting nomadic elements in the Gerzean (or Naqada I and Naqada II). (2) A settled agricultural element in the Amratian. In the Amratian period warlike implements are absent. In the Gerzean they are deadly. Animals on crowns are very deadly. Den, 4th king of the 1st Dynasty introduced the *Heb Sed* festival, which marked 30 years of reign of the king in which he would go out, and hunt and then be rejuvenated. At the beginning of the agricultural season the king opens the waters. He also appears at the harvesting. Use of an agricultural pavilion is evident. The *Atef Crown* is pastoral in nature. While the king is alive he is Horus, when he dies he is Osiris, king of the netherworld. The Amratian people were peaceful, the Gerzean were more warlike.

Kaiser's Theory argued that all king lists tend to show work of pre-dynastic times. There were 10 to 12 kings in pre-dynastic times. There were 12-19 kings of a unified Egypt before Dynasty I.

At the Abydos cemetery millions of cowrie shells were found. This shows inner Africa's presence for cowrie shells were used for economic purposes. Some of the early king identified here included Ka, Hor Ra (?), Narmer and Hor Aha.

FREDERICK MONDERSON

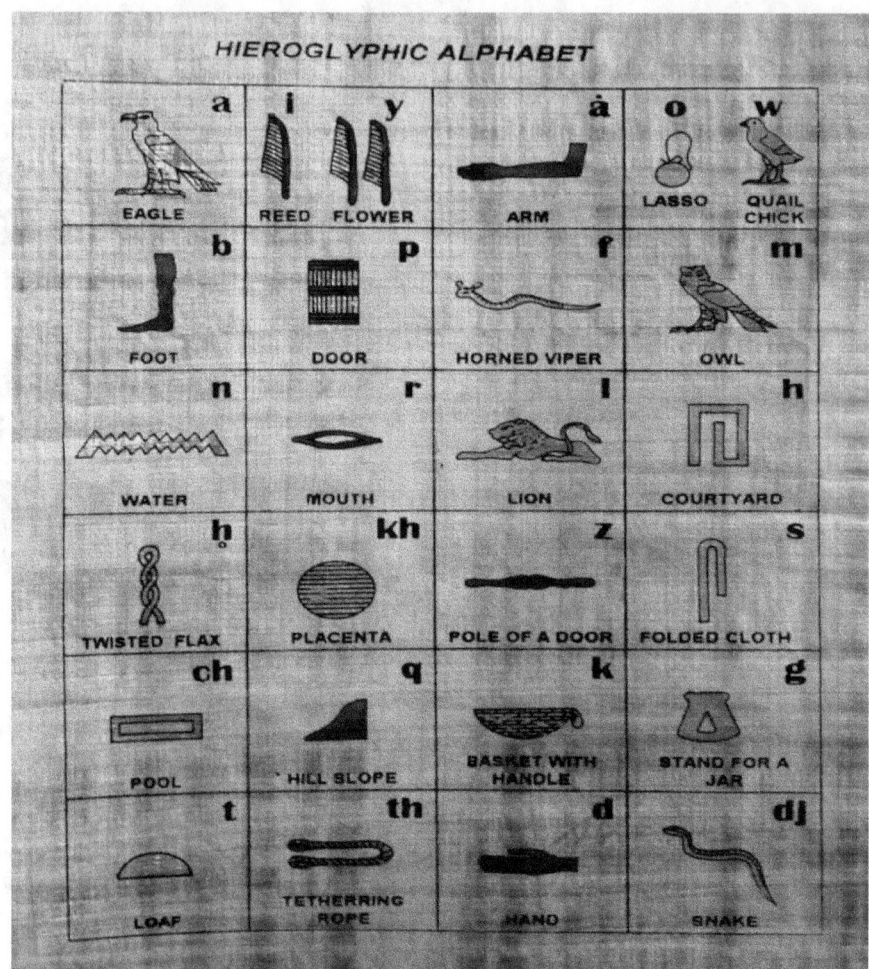

Holy Land Papyrus 18. The Egyptian Alphabet.

At the Tura cemetery at Memphis the northern half was used. There are names of kings 150 years before Narmer. Hierakonpolis is possibly the place of pre-dynastic kings whose tombs remain undiscovered.

The Amratian was a period of intensive agriculture, while the Gerzean was a period of intensive warfare. Dynasty 0 is dated to 3250 B.C. Tura kings' names were found in the Delta. Curly haired people were indigenous to the Delta. The unification of Egypt was a process rather than an event and happened over a period of years. The Professor argued that by 2000 B.C. "The Bible in this time was already in oral form."

QUINTESSENTIAL BOOK
"THE HOLY LAND"

10.   Hotel Room

ABYDOS AND DENDERA
Day 6.   Abydos and Dendera

1.   Wake Up

Esperanza Rodriguez: Good Morning, Mi Amor. Your schedule for today takes you on a lengthy bus ride to Abydos and Dendera. There will be a military escort to these outlying temples. I have prepared your selection for today and have distributed them to the group.

Dr. Fred Monderson: Thank you so very much Esperanza, my dear. You are so helpful. Thanks. Again!

AFRICAN ART
By
Frederick Monderson

African Art is older than man for man himself is art from Africa. Importantly, however, African man, in conscious domestication of himself after long thought and experimentation with early tools, envisioned the forest, savanna, hillsides, mountains, valleys, rivers and animal and vegetative forms of life, along with man, littering the African landscape as themes for artistic representation. From such juxtapositioning with nature man was able to create some of the earliest art themes and motifs generally using the walls of caves as early canvases. From the Sahara "Tassili Frescoes" in the north, Stone Age art of Tanzania and the so-called Bushman Art of South Africa, Art of the Nile Valley, together with Nok Art and later Art of the Western Sudan, Africa today boasts the earliest and most extensive historical artistic landscape on the face of the earth. Here artists, canvases, materials and nature, as models, came to reflect and represent the great mysteries and conceptions; art expressing a number of cosmological representations and practical applications to life's many experiences.

Holy Land Illustration 58. Bas-Relief from the Tomb of Ra-hotep at Medum and Sepulchral stele in the form of a door, of Sennu, an Inspector of Agriculture (British Museum); and Ptolemy II, Philadelphus and Queen Arsinoe adoring Menu, Harpocrates and Uatchit, c. B.C. 260.

Henry Lhote (1987: 181) in "Oasis of Art in the Sahara" tells of a time when the "Sahara was green, millennia ago, man hunted buffalo and drove cattle over grasslands where giraffes browsed and hippos wallowed in lakes." Here he mentions, among a multitude of artworks of that era, an "archer stands poised in sandstone at Tassili-n-Ajjer." From this collection, over 4,000 paintings in the Algerian remote massif, "plateau of the rivers," were dated near 12,000 years ago. Lhote, collected some 8,000 colored prints of this spectacular gallery, and considers these artifacts "the world's greatest collection of prehistoric art."

The author's Tassili time-line suggests four major styles that "dominate the numerous artistic traditions of successive cultures." The *Round Head* style began before 6,000 B.C. or 1760 *Before Nile Year* 1 beginning at 4240 B.C. The Round Heads depict "Featureless faces and rounded heads" that characterize a period of stylized painting and may have lasted some 2,000 years. Figures vary in size, some reaching more than 15 feet in height.

The *Pastoral* frescoes appear ca. 5000 B.C. (760 *Before Nile Year* 1). Here, Lhote's (1987: 183) reproductions introduce "Herders of unknown origin" who developed a: "naturalistic style depicting scenes from everyday life. Compared with the Round Head, these works show greater concern for detail and composition."

QUINTESSENTIAL BOOK
"THE HOLY LAND"

Holy Land World Tourist Day Extravaganza 13. Both Mr. Sayeed (left) and Mr. Rady (right) seem exceedingly pleased because of the wonderful festival extravaganza they just witnessed.

Holy Land World Tourist Day Extravaganza 14. Important people as Mr. Rady must constantly check their cell-phone for breaking issues, while the other gentlemen seem more relaxed.

The *Horse* period began about 1200 B.C. (*Nile Year* 3040) and, according to Lhote: "Horse-drawn chariots reflect contact with cultures from the eastern Mediterranean." *Camel* period begins around 100 B.C. (*Nile Year* 4140) for "As the Sahara became more arid, the camel - more suited to the climate - replaced the horse." As to the Pastoral period, Lhote (1987: 182) continued, the "features of the archer painted during the Pastoral period, suggest to me the presence of Black peoples."

FREDERICK MONDERSON

Modern art lovers often wonder what type of materials these earliest artists used. Lhote (1987: 182) again indicated the Tassili painters "favored shades of yellow, red, and brown, made by mixing ocher with a liquid, and applied with feathers or animal-hair brushes." Lhote (1987: 187) tells of a figure wearing a mask in a: "deep recess that may have been a sanctuary. Dating from the Round Head period, the figure covers the white image of a woman whose legs are still seen. Measuring about five feet high, the masked figure sprouts plants from its arms and thighs. Created about 7,000 years ago, this Tassili painting is perhaps the oldest record of the cult of the mask, still practiced in the ceremonies of sub-Saharan tribes."

On one particular canvas with giraffe head and horns of wild sheep and other figures, the "expedition discovered 12 superimposed layers painted during a period of perhaps 2,000 years." To this revelation, Lhote (1987: 191) reasoned: "It is not known why different artists used the same locations. Some sites may have offered a better painting surface than others or held special religious importance. Perhaps the act of painting filled a ceremonial function more important than the artwork itself."

Elsewhere, in East Africa, the anthropologist Mary Leakey and her husband Louis, between 1935-1951 (*Nile Year* 6175-6191) discovered and catalogued 186 rock-painting sites. This extensive gallery supplied 1,600 individual scenes, over a 500 square mile area in Tanzania. Through Mary Leakey's (1983: 86) "Tanzania's Stone Age Art," we are helped in understanding an archaeological study of man's distant past that brings to us the startling conclusion: "Those long-ago works of art tell us, for example, that Stone Age man in Africa wore clothing, had a variety of hairstyles, hunted, danced, sang, played musical instruments, and may even have known the secret of fermenting spirits."

For these early East African painters, in many respects similar to those of the Tassili artists, painting materials were of principal concern. Their choice of colors is interesting for: "the predominant red was made from ocher, which is derived from iron ore. Black probably came from manganese, and bird droppings may have provided the basis for the white."

From these early and humble beginnings, Leakey (1983: 92) says: "The beauty and delicacy of some of the paintings are extraordinary, particularly when one considers that those ancient artists did not erase or correct their work as modern painters do. There is no blurring strokes or abrasion of rock surfaces that would have resulted from rubbing or scraping out of lines. Perhaps the artists sketched in rough shapes first with charcoal or some other medium that has not survived."

These prehistoric artists were obviously hunter-gatherers rather than a pastoral

QUINTESSENTIAL BOOK
"THE HOLY LAND"

people. Leakey (1983: 92) informs: "Stone Age painters took certain artistic license. They often exaggerated the salient features of various animals. For example, snakes are shown with more loops than they normally have. The kudu, an antelope with horns that always have fewer than three complete spirals, is sometimes depicted with as many as eleven spirals. Roan antelopes with their characteristically large ears are drawn with that feature greatly exaggerated."

Holy Land Photo 41a. Karnak Temple of Amun. Hypostyle Hall. Decorated columns and other features in the hall with intricacies; and other line arrangements of the columns of this hall.

Stone Age artists tended to be selective of subjects on the basis of size. Small creatures as hydraxes, hares, and little antelope are rarely depicted. Though, they are known from heaps of bones left after the hunter's meals. In contrast, Leakey (1983: 99) commenting on choice of larger themes remarked: "the artists concentrated instead on large animals such as elephants, giraffes, rhinos, and the carnivores. Plainly, the killing of a large animal, which would provide food for many people, was considered of greater significance than an average small kill. Thus the number of elephants painted probably does not reflect the number killed, but rather importance of such events."

FREDERICK MONDERSON

Alfred Friendly has spent a great deal of time chronicling: "Africa's Bushman Art Treasures." From Cape Town in South Africa to just below Lake Victoria, the author discovered more than 2,000 sites where these more recent Stone Age artists left depictions of the African fauna known to them, including: "elephants, giraffes, felines, serpents, birds, fish, and the Bushman's principal diet - rhebok, eland, springbok, hartebeest." Friendly (1963: 849) wrote, this background and models created a "gallery filled with thousands upon thousands of exhibits, each one a gem or a collection of gems, displayed against a natural backdrop of mountain, valley, or broad savanna." He further remarked: "Such is the gallery of Bushman paintings in Africa, fabulous and infinitely rewarding to the observer, whether art lover, naturalist, archeologist, or mere sightseer."

Combining these surviving ancient art expressions we can help construct a more complete view of African man creating art in his many habitations and circumstances as he pictured and represented nature throughout the continent.

Interestingly enough, Friendly's (1963: 854) interpretation regarding the representations left by these early artists, allows a glimpse back into times when scant records exist for much of this. "In all respects, the early Bushman was the classic Old Stone Age man. He was a hunter and food gatherer; he had no agriculture whatsoever. As a hunter, he had no fixed abode, being obliged to follow the game on its migrations. Accordingly, he had only the fewest and lightest possessions: stone, bone, and wooden weapons and tools; a weighted stick to dig edible roots and tubers; a few skins for clothing or for the rigging of a windscreen when he was encamped away from his beloved rocks. He spun no cotton, made almost no pottery, and domesticated no animals. His vessels were gourds and shells of ostrich eggs, the source of his jewelry as well." Friendly (1963: 854) tells further, the "essence of the Bushman's world," was represented in his art work, where he left: "illustrations of the most central aspects of his life, his times and his temperament, examples of the basic techniques of his artistry; revelations of his arsenal, his religion, his economics - even of his disposition."

Finally, Friendly (1963: 857), quoting Malan who recalled what Dr. W.H. Bleek, the classic authority on "San" or "Bushman Lore" had written: "... these animal headed Bushmen represented sorcerers; he found them somewhat reminiscent of the Egyptian mythological representations in which animal heads were placed on human bodies. Bleek added: This fact of Bushman paintings illustrating Bushman mythology gives at once to Bushman art a higher character and teaches us to look upon its products not as the mere daubings of figures for idle pastime, but as a truly artistic conception of the ideas which most deeply moved the Bushman mind and filled it with religious feelings."

QUINTESSENTIAL BOOK
"THE HOLY LAND"

Holy Land Photo 41b. Karnak Temple of Amun. Hatshepsut's standing Obelisk (left); and a close-up of one of its sides.

These graphic examples can serve as vivid reminders of the nature and purpose of African art and sculpture, being careful observations of nature as the mind evolved through the countless centuries upon centuries of inquiries and experimentation. Therefore, early man's pristine and subsequent creations of art to express his religious concerns, questions about nature, philosophic speculations, conceptions of beauty, etc., became important aesthetic mediums employed in Africa to portray art-science fusion with their metaphysical implications and dynamics. So, with the aid of scientific consciousness, art and sculpture came to be viewed as beautiful and timeless works of artistry that have expressed cosmological and social themes in the life history of various African peoples.

These rhythmic vibrations in the undulative evolutionary history of Africa teach us that thousands of years ago man first domesticated himself. Later, art and philosophy were his next additions. His first technology, the hand-axe, was a work of art that became more sophisticated with further application of the brain to experiment and create craft. At night, he sat around the campfire after a day of success in hunt and feast. Here tools were repaired and the next day's hunt planned. As far back in the Old Stone Age, man began to philosophize about life's

FREDERICK MONDERSON

hopes and challenges, its mysticism and science.

Early man first asked questions about death and the sky. He thought of the moon and planets as sources of wondrous creativity. In man's primitive state animals were painted on walls of caves. This belief, in his superstitions, sought favor and success in the next day's hunt. His technology or tools were an early artistic creation. Then painting aided in creating more lasting impressions of an ethical and moral nature and beauty to be preserved for posterity.

In idleness he may have whittled bone or stone against wood. Another time he may have needed a wooden tool for some utility. This led down the road to woodworking, and later industry in bone, ivory and stone. On these art foundations science, sculpture and architecture blended to construct some of the most lasting testaments to early man's creation of monumental art. Of its most important contributions, art in Africa was significantly revolutionized in ancient Kemet, today's Egypt. It served practical, philosophic, religious and social purposes. Art and sculpture created a message. Using nature themes these ancient Africans first mentally thought out religious, philosophical and spiritual concepts and their processes. Then they erected and decorated temples as places of worship and adoration of their gods, in veneration for favorable gifts in return.

Such emblems as hawk, lion, scorpion, jackal, or pelican were the earliest forms of the anthropomorphic quintessence of theosophical creation, which was splendidly thought out by the earliest and ancient African theologians along the banks of the Nile River in Northeast, Africa. Petrie's "Egyptian Art" in Volume I of Hastings *Encyclopedia of Religion and Ethics* (1909: 862) explains how the Divine Forms were represented:

QUINTESSENTIAL BOOK
"THE HOLY LAND"

Holy Land Illustration 59. Sepulchral stele in the form of a door, of Sennu, an Inspector of Agriculture.

"The compound theology of sacred animals and deities resulted in a variety of strange combinations. The animal element is always the head, placed upon a human body for a deity; a human head upon an animal body is used only for a sphinx, emblem of a king, and for the ba-bird, emblem of a soul. The combination of animal heads on human bodies is found in the second dynasty (Set, on seals of Perabsen) and the fourth dynasty (Thoth, on scene of Khufu); and it became very unusual in later times."

Dress was an important aspect of the deity, for as Petrie mentions: "The gods are usually clad in the oldest form of close-fitting waist-cloth; it is always older forms of dress that are thought appropriate for religious or artistic purposes, and in Babylonia the oldest figures of worshipers are entirely nude. The gods never wear the projecting peaked waistcloth common in the Old and Middle Kingdoms."

Petrie indicated further: "Another primitive piece of costume was the animal's tail, hung at the back from the belt. This is shown as a bushy tail, like a fox's, on the archaic hunters, carved on a slate palette. It appears on all kings from the first dynasty onward (... figure of Rameses IV .... the kneeling Hatshepsut, where it is brought forward). And it gradually becomes almost universal for gods after the early ages It can be seen on the figures of Horus and Thoth, in the long form, and thinner than usual." Four principal ceremonies depicted in illustrations are Sacrifice, Offering, Laying on of Hands, and Purification. Again, as depicted in some of the first forms of art, we see that illustration in: "early sculptured tombs the sons of the deceased are shown as trapping birds, and sacrificing the ox, for the festival in their father's honor. It is rare to find representations of sacrifice later, such as this example of the nineteenth dynasty. Burnt-sacrifice was a foreign importation, and is only known in pictures at Tell el-Amarna (eighteenth dynasty), and in a description at the Ramesseum (nineteenth dynasty)."

This idea of the offering is very significant for we see the pharaoh in many attitudes of communing with deity. Whether making an incense, liquid, or food offering, the king represents the people in expressing their religiosity. This form of private and royal art came to portray the profound philosophic tenets ancient Africans were privileged to create as they established the axioms of human progress measured by the arts, sciences, technology, and ethical behaviors.

QUINTESSENTIAL BOOK "THE HOLY LAND"

Holy Land Ceramic Art 3. The Ram of Amon in ceramic decoration.

An interesting commentary can be interjected here, for as Petrie has indicated in "Egyptian Art" Volume I, Hastings *Encyclopedia of Religion and Ethics* (1909: 863) where he noted: "The Egyptian never burnt incense on an altar, but always in a metal censer held in the hand. It was a long metal rod, with hand holding a cup for the burning incense at one end, and a hawk's head at the other end; in the middle of the length was a pan or box in which the pellets of incense were kept ready for burning. The heat requisite to light it was obtained by using a hot saucer of pottery placed in a cup, on which the resin fused. When the incense was burnt, the saucer was removed and thrown away, and thus no cleaning was required for the metal cup."

The art of the incense holder is interesting and significant. To recall, Bruce Williams discovered at Qustul in Nubia, the "World's Earliest Form of Monarchy." He commented on displayed illustrations depicting the enthroned monarch, with white crown, palace facade, royal barge, incense burner, etc. This form of religious expression is therefore directly linked to Africa before ancient Kemet/Egypt certainly came into being. It indicated a creative African man, whose art has left representation of his expression, depicting connections with a

FREDERICK MONDERSON

higher form of metaphysical, spiritual, theological and theosophical consciousness.

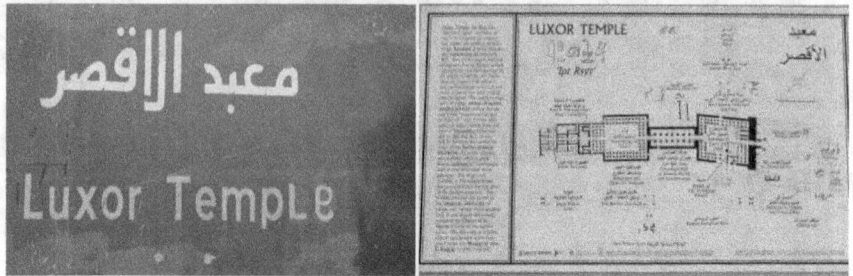

Holy Land Photos 42. Temple of Luxor. Sign; and plan of the Temple with inscriptions and modern description.

"Laying on of the hands," wrote Petrie in *Religion and Ethics* "was represented as being done by the gods, in order to impart the Sa. This was a divine essence which the gods drank from the heavenly 'lake of the Sa,' and which the earthly images of the gods could impart to beings and to priests who knelt before them. The benefit was not ceaseless, but required renewal from time to time. The same form of laying on of hands was used, as in our illustration, for conferring the kingship as in the case of Hatshepsut; the inscription reads, 'giving of the kingship of both banks of the river, the complete office, to his daughter, Maat-ka-ra' (Hatshepsut).

Purification was the last and most significant ceremony performed by the priests or pharaoh. Petrie repeats the old adage: "Personal cleanliness was strictly observed by the priests; and the purifying of the king was performed symbolically by the gods .... Each god holds a vase from which he pours out a stream over the king. It is stated that Ramessu 'is purified with life and power.'"

Gold was an essential metal to represent things religious, spiritual, and the early craftsmen of the Old Kingdom set some of the highest standards for early African art. Petrie notes further the: "Egyptian often describes large objects as covered with gold, which was usually of considerable thickness. The reliefs were usually worked in hard stucco and then thickly gilded and burnished. The art of high burnishing upon a stucco base was kept up till Roman times. The sets of vases for the purification ceremonies and further libations of wine were kept on wooden stands.... A stand with water jars, covered with lotus flowers, and with bunches of grapes placed below it. On another stand at the extreme left is a figure of the king kneeling, offering a large ankh, or sign of life; this is crowned with flowers, and has convolvulus and vine growing up beneath it. Another stand at the extreme right has a figure of the king offering a large bouquet of flowers. A main part of the religious art was spent on these statuettes of the king making a great variety of

QUINTESSENTIAL BOOK
"THE HOLY LAND"

offerings. Unhappily all this wealth of figures has perished, and only a few fragments remain to give reality to the innumerable pictures of the temple riches shown upon the walls.

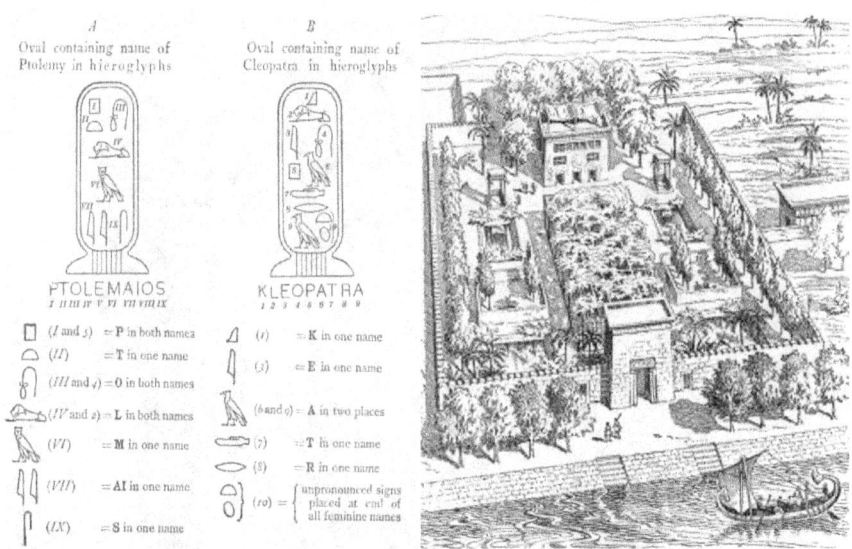

Holy Land Illustration 60. Diagram showing the first steps in Champollion's decipherment of Egyptian Hieroglyphics (Breasted); and Villa and Garden of an Egyptian Noble of the Old Kingdom. (After Perrot and Chipiez) Breasted's *History of Egypt*.

In addition, the ancient Africans of Kemet further expanded their technological or artistic repertoire by building tombs, temples, pyramids, and palaces. Housing, villages or settlements, towns and even fortresses reflected their art, some of a permanent nature, some as fleeting structures. Architecture and monumental portrait sculpture are best examples of Egyptian art. Ceramics is also a significant art medium that exhibits much artistry and contains purposeful historical evidence.

In regards to painting and sculpture, the first artists were not tied to an arbitrary canon of proportions, but were desirous of representing what they saw as exactly possible. The oldest Egyptian painting yet found is that of a flock of geese pasturing, and now in the Cairo Museum. It comes from a tomb at Meydum. Also discovered from this earliest time were two statues from another tomb also at Meydum, and dated to the reign of Snefru.

FREDERICK MONDERSON

Holy Land Papyrus 19. Young Rameses II, *Usr-Ma'at-Ra* greets the Goddess Hathor wearing horns and disk.

Murray (1888) also indicated: "In the goldsmith's art the excellence of every work is remarkable, though the mechanical finish is sometimes inferior to the design and execution of the more ornamental portions. The jewelry of Queen Aahotep, in the Boulak Museum, shows more taste in color and design than actual skill in workmanship. Metal work was much developed under the pharaohs of the Middle

QUINTESSENTIAL BOOK
"THE HOLY LAND"

Empire and retained its vitality to a late period. Bronze statuettes of great beauty were made even down to Roman times. Pottery was another manufacture in which the ancient Egyptians excelled at all periods; the finest examples occurring under the XIXth Dynasty. They were also acquainted with glass from an early time."

The crafts, that created these majestic works of art then, were parents of art. Their masterpieces were created in workshops. Precious and semi-precious metals were worked. They yielded much beautiful jewelry and wooden works. Stone was used in architecture. Together, these accomplishments can tell a great deal about the art and aesthetics of the people. Hence, works of quality are associated as timeless art produced in ancient African artistry, in Nile Valley cultural flowering that came to impress and fascinate people of both the ancient and modern worlds. Therefore, through the art medium, Africa could be considered the Mother of Invention. An interesting interjection made here can underscore this view of Mother Africa.

The *American Journal of Archaeology* published "Tools and Weapons" about Professor Flinders Petrie's book of the same name. Here Petrie under-girds the view of Africa's role in technological developments that came to have such a tremendous impact on later civilizations. Imagine what influence the following throws upon the social, cultural, architectural, and military development upon subsequent cultures, particularly in those areas of the world as America and Europe where much of Africa's artifacts are held in captivity.

The *American Journal of Archaeology* XXII (1918: 441-42) has indicated: "Professor Flinders Petrie has published under the auspices of the British School of Archaeology in Egypt and Egyptian Research Account a work entitled Tools and Weapons. It is concerned particularly with implements from Egypt although many illustrations are drawn from other parts of the world. He discusses in turn the plain blade axe, the socketed axe, the double axe, adzes and picks, the adze and hoe, the lug adze, the hoe, the chisel, the knife, the symmetric knife, the sword, the dagger, the spear-head, the arrow, the throwing-stick, slings and bullets, harpoons, fish-hooks, scale armor, rasps and scrapers, artisans' tools. Builders' tools, the saw, the sickle, the pruning-hook, shears, razors, leather cutters, tweezers, borers, pins and needles, implements for spinning and weaving, agricultural tools, the horse-bit, the spur, stamps for branding, fire-hooks, manacles, fish-spears, flesh-hooks, shovels, ladles, spoons, mortars and pestles, fire-drills, stirgils, the bolt, lock and key, pulleys, compasses, chains, and tools used in casting."

These ancient African craftsmen therefore, worked in a variety of mediums of metal and stone including limestone, grey granite, basalt, alabaster, and syenite. They also worked bronze, copper, lead, bronze and lead-electrum, slate, serpentine, steatite, quartz crystal, and hematite. Such materials as black quartz, sandstone, malachite, blue glass, white glass, and burnt syenite helped expand the repertoire of African art. Not mentioned here is cobalt, which was early used by the people of ancient Kemet.

A. Wiedemann (Jan 10, 1893: 113) informs about a small quadrangular Egyptian amulet, which from the: "description of Lepsius appears to date from the later time of the New Empire, turned out to be a dark blue opaque glassy flux, painted with cobalt. An oblong dark blue glass-bead was painted likewise with cobalt; the quantitative analysis gave 2.86 per cent oxide of cobalt; and another glass bead contained 0.95 per cent oxide of cobalt."

Even further Wiedemann (1893: 114) tells, the "blue frits of the time of Rameses III, at Tell el Yehudiyeh were painted often with cobalt. The mineral was therefore used by the Egyptians though the blue color was usually obtained from copper."

Beautiful rock-cut Tombs of the Nobles line the hills near Elephantine Island at Aswan. These wondrous works of mortuary art retain early links with interior Africa. Since background and canvas is important in creating and viewing works of art, the high view with Aswan below is nature's art. The magnificent panoramic view from these hills is art in choice to build art here.

Art in many of the tombs, on the high cliffs, portray African beliefs in the afterlife. They adorn the tradition of Egypt as African and retain visible links to Kemet's early past. It is also a challenge to the modern visitor, brave enough to scale the hundred plus steps to the summit that must be scaled before 9:00 AM. Here the intense heat of the desert has preserved beautiful and realistic African art. Recent studies show the Egyptians got many materials and ideas from their southern neighbors. In reality we must look to Central Africa, where human life seems to have originated, thousands of years prior. These early cultural dynamics call attention to art as reflective of science and religious beliefs.

African art and science, we now know pioneered metallurgy, mining, and smelting processes. The chemistry of working in gold, copper, electrum, silver, iron, tin and lead is a wonderful experience. However, the drawbacks are intense heat, callused hands and an offensive smell. Yet, these minor impediments are a small price to create such beautiful art.

With their primitive smelting technology African craftsmen built bowl furnaces. They improved the bowl furnace and created a sophisticated shaft furnace. This was far more effective in providing heat. Such a technological improvement was art to create art.

QUINTESSENTIAL BOOK
"THE HOLY LAND"

In innovation, today respected for its timelessness and ingenuity, these early and ancient African metallurgists decreased the top of the bowl. According to Bernd Scheel in *Egyptian Metalworking and Tools* (1989: 11-34), they then shaped the inside. This change developed more Lome in the structure. The bellows passed through the mud bricks. Then it stroked the charge through the Lome to smelt the metal. The hot liquid would then exit through the tap hole and into the slag pit.

These ancient metallurgists worked gold into sheets. This was also the way they prepared copper. They made sandals and other precious jewelry that now adorn fine museums in Brooklyn, New York, London, Paris, Berlin, etc.

Early art in ancient Kemet retained its propaganda nature. The earliest forms of such representations are on slate palettes. The most famous of these is the *Narmer Palette*. Here the king is shown wearing the White Crown of Upper Kemet/Egypt and the Red Crown of Lower Kemet/Egypt. Scholars reason that this pharaoh is responsible for uniting the two lands and choosing the united red and white Double Crown as a symbol of unification. The significance of this artifact is the propaganda role it played in establishing conventions in art and social customs that were key aspects of the culture.

However, the most important art innovation introduced during this time was the register. It became the dividing line between pre-dynastic disorder and dynastic order in art and society. The *Narmer Palette*, in raised relief, shows the king as monumental in scale to his subjects. This depiction of the king in a convention of social classes remained in much of pre-dynastic and dynastic art. Other early artistic portrayals of the pharaoh show him engaged in agricultural ceremonials, ritual worship, smiting Egypt's/Kemet's enemies and dancing before the Gods. These attitudes were symbolic and also helped to serve propaganda purposes. Nevertheless, it was the artist who rendered the images for us. Public art, on the facades of enclosure walls and other public places were introduced for the common use. But, other art, in tombs, particularly, was never meant to be seen by anyone after the internment. That is why we must decry the irreverence of some modern visitors who seem, in their dress and attitudes, to desecrate these holy places and the philosophic and religious intent of their creators.

Conventions of such beginnings set the stage, order, stability and unchanging reality of Kemetic and African art. Together with the canon, or set of rules, for representing the human figure, art changed yet remained traditional and timeless. Classical art, certainly dating to the Old Kingdom, remained the ideal well past the New Kingdom and into the Late Period. It was the quintessential imitative style that represented the permanence of the society bequeathed by the gods. The influence of the Greeks after Alexander's conquest in 332 B.C. brought new innovation that still looked to the African past for inspiration. Nevertheless, an interesting observation can be made at the Graeco-Roman double Temple of Kom Ombo, dedicated to the gods Sobek and Haroeis, the Older Horus. Here, in many friezes, the Queen can be seen with one of her upper female anatomical parts exposed.

Still, from the earliest times, the human body was represented in a particular manner based on order. The artists used a Canon of Proportion to represent the human body. This changed slightly from period to period. In the Old Kingdom or Pyramid Age, 2680-2240 B.C. (*Nile Year* 1560-2000), they used 13 divisions for the height of a man. Petrie (1940: 54-55) notes, these included "2 for the head, 1 to the armpit, 4 to the fork, 2 to the knee, 4 to the ground." For the position of the figure during the Dynastic Period, 3000-30 B.C. (*Nile Year* 1240-4210) they used a rule that "a vertical line must pass the edge of the wig, or center of the head, the middle of the waist, equidistant between the knees and between the heels."

Holy Land Photo 42a. Temple of Luxor. From the left, frontal view of the entrance Pylon with seated statues; and remaining standing obelisk.

The New Kingdom began at the expulsion of the Hyksos, Asiatic nomads, who essentially overran Kemet and ruled for a century, from their stronghold in the Delta. With today's hindsight, an interesting aside can be interjected here. We know very much about Upper and Lower Egypt, Northern and Southern Egypt. So, from this time, can we also begin to speak of native and foreign Egypt? In the wake of the resulting Kemetic imperialism, the wealth, glamour and opulence of the New Empire, built its art upon those earlier developments of the Old and Middle Kingdoms.

The "Canon of Proportion" emerged as a rigid yet accurate mechanism that further highlighted the artistic contributions of these Africans along the ancient Nile. During the New Kingdom, the Canon of Proportion for the human body changed. Now, the height of a standing figure was divided into 19 units. Petrie (1940: 54) further explained the: "head down to the top of the shoulders is 3 units, divided at the top of the forehead and base of the nose. From the shoulders, 4 units to the waist, then 6 to the knees, and thence 6 to the ground."

QUINTESSENTIAL BOOK "THE HOLY LAND"

There was some difference for seated figures. These seated figures were, Petrie (1940) wrote "15 squares high. Thus assigning 19-15 = 4 units to the thighbone. The seat is 5 units over the ground."

As the civilization entered its decline by the XXVIth Dynasty, the artists adopted a third canon. Here again, Petrie (1940) has informed, the: "figure became 22 1/2 or 22 1/3 units high; of this increase 1/3 unit is in the head, 2 units in trunk and 1 unit in the lower leg."

While the Kemetic artists had Canons of Proportions for the human figure, these were mainly for standing or seated models. In addition, there were many examples of figures in motion. Petrie (1940: 55) again continued, the "long rows of wrestlers at Beni Hasan in the XII Dynasty," dancers, acrobats, and "field workers in action in the XVIII Dynasty" show movement. These representations show how readily the "instantaneous positions were grouped and reproduced." Significantly, however, as early as the XIth Dynasty, in the mortuary temple of Mentuhotep at Deir el Bahari, the artist Mertisen was first to boast of "being able to depict people in motion." With this innovation the artist blended color in further experimentation and thus enhanced the quality and texture of painting.

The life of artists was challenging, pleasing yet austere. They made funerary art that was timeless yet designed to never be seen by the human eye. They specialized in various crafts, but generally speaking, they were exposed to intense heat, developed callused hands, and often exuded an offensive smell. This aside, the strict division of labor aided the creation of beautiful works of art that defied time while exhibiting the greatest of finished artifacts, so adored by modern art lovers.

FREDERICK MONDERSON

 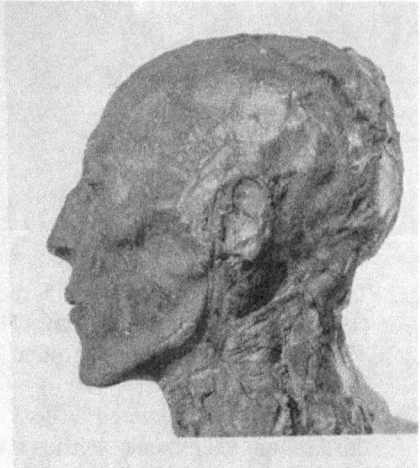

Holy Land Illustration 61. Remarkable limestone head of Ikhnaton, the earliest Monotheist (left); and head of the mummy of Seti I, father of Rameses II, now in the Cairo Museum (right).

These foundations of art developed in guilds controlled by the palace or wealthy nobles as well as by the priesthood. In such highly organized arrangements, Michalowski (No Date) informs: "one specialist made the designs, another worked in plaster, and others specialized in stone cutting in relief sculpture, in carving statues, in finishing and polishing them, in decorating temple walls, and so on. The jeweler's art also had specialist categories; workers, who washed the gold, did enamel work, and there was even a category of bead stringer."

He argued, in theory, no single workman did an entire piece. Those equated with our "foreman" or "overseer" inspected the work of the artist. "Black was used for outline, while alongside, red was used to indicate corrections."

The ruling class that comprised the Gods, Pharaoh, and high dignitaries represented the official portrait. Their formal poses were shown in painting, sunk, raised and painted relief and statuary, as shown in temples, palaces, on public monuments, in quarries and in tombs. They were shown striding or seated. However, the artist was bound to observe the rules of the canon when portraying this upper crust of society. Nevertheless, Ostraca, sometimes pottery bits or chips of stone were used as "sketch pads." Here, sometimes, the artist deviated from the established norm and created caricatures that would not be associated with the "official standards" for art.

The pharaoh especially was shown in an official portrait. Generally depicted with all kingly panoply, any defects or shortcomings he had were concealed by an

QUINTESSENTIAL BOOK
"THE HOLY LAND"

elaborate costume. Michalowski (ND) again tells, the king "was a god, a living Horus, and as a divinity his body had always to be represented as timelessly youthful."

The administrative bureaucracy was the second class of artistic models. Because of their closeness with the local people the artist did not adhere strictly to the convention that bound the first more formal portraits. These latter presented "only the most obvious facial characteristics." Whereas, the governors or mayors were shown with "sagging flesh, prominent bellies, and thick legs, but in a dignified posture carrying a staff."

Artistically, the main difference between the way the top two classes, the nobility and the administrative bureaucracy, were represented was in the modeling of the body. Michalowski (No Date: 188) believes the "conventions of timeless youth was obligatory for the first group, whereas dignitaries were shown more realistically."

Holy Land Photo 42b. Temple of Luxor. From along the "Avenue of Sphinxes" looking at the Entrance Pylon (left); and from before the Pylon, looking down the "Avenue of Sphinxes" (right).

The third group of the society comprised a vast array of workers. In the mastaba tombs of the Vth and VIth Dynasties as represented, Michalowski (No Date: 188) mentions: "reliefs of laborers, harvesters, herdsmen, and artisans at work in warehouses, fields, pastures, and workshops. There are also fishermen and boat builders, musicians and dancers." In representing this group, the artist was free to deviate from the canon and represented this group more as they were. This may be because, for Michalowski (No Date: 189) believed "realistic scenes of common people possess great expressive power."

Scribes were generally shown either in the standing or seated position. A wooden relief figure of the famous third dynasty scribe Hesire, found at Sakkara, is now at the Cairo Museum. It stands 44 7/8 inches. He is shown holding his working tools and the **SEKHEM** rod, emblem of executive officials. In this as in so many examples, the diagram of canon for this Old Kingdom masterpiece of realistic art required, notes Michalowski (No Date: 174), a different canon. He shows this to be: "18 rows of squares, as follows: 'from the top of forehead to base of neck, 2 rows; from neck to knees, 10 rows; from knees to soles of feet, 6 rows. An additional row for the hair above the forehead was not included in the total of 18 rows.'" The other posture of the scribe was the seated position. The finest known statue of a scribe comes from the Vth Dynasty and is housed in the Louvre, Paris.

Here the subject is shown, as Michalowski (ND) notes: "Wearing a loin cloth, he is seated with legs crossed, an open roll of papyrus on his knees, and a reed pen in his right hand. It is made of painted limestone and stands 20-7/8 inches. At a much later time the scribe was represented in a more obscure way simply as a block statue, with face and writings on the block."

Holy Land Ceramic Art 4. Kheper splendidly depicted in a full array of ceramic colors, doing its job of moving the sun along its journey.

The question is always asked whether there was realism in ancient Kemetic/Egyptian Art. If the term realism is defined in broad concepts as denoting: "the effort to represent a given phenomenon in its most typical form, and

QUINTESSENTIAL BOOK "THE HOLY LAND"

the fact recorded by the artist has thus a general significance that every viewer can grasp. In this sense, Egyptian art was certainly realistic." How else would the artisans record such profound religious and social testimony to their life and culture? This is particularly evident, when these early artists, as civilization trailblazers, were engraving the *Tabula Rasa* of human progress in so many fields of artistic and science fusion.

Nevertheless, Kemetic/Egyptian painting and sculpture of the Old Kingdom can be summed up as follows, as Michalowski (ND: 190-91) outlines them:

"1. the canon was a unique historical phenomenon and has a peculiar indigenous character.

2. It was the result of a lengthy process of observation and experimentation, which culminated in an art, based on the most typical forms of nature; as such, the canon was formulated in terms of certain constant proportions.

3. The aim of the canon was to record phenomenon in the most legible and understandable manner, to reflect reality in both its visual and its social aspects.

4. The canon performed an important function in the ideological superstructure, serving the ruling class by perpetuating the conviction that the existing social function was by glorifying the gods and the Pharaohs.

5. The canon was essential to the maintenance of artistic quality and standards of workmanship."

The resulting quality of Kemetic art can be found in Cairo, Luxor, Aswan, and other museums worldwide. Here the art-science fusion notion is seen in artifacts of wood, papyrus, metal and stone. Much of these glorified the culture, or adorned temples and noble people. Today they are far from home, a "culture in captivity," highlighting foreign institutions. Nevertheless, such pieces provide important evidence of daily life and sacred festivals celebrated by Africans along the Nile in Northeast Africa. If we include Charles Finch's revelations regarding archaeological work at Katanda and the Ishango bone with "mathematical markings;" African Art extends for many millennia.

Much cultural evidence of ancient Africa is contained in the tombs of pharaohs and nobles. These are found mainly in the Valley of the Kings, at Thebes. Many other sites in Egypt have yielded their beautiful troves of wealth. Thebes, however, has given and preserves much cultural wealth and history, more than anywhere else on earth. The majesty of Kemetic/Egyptian, African, art, in

FREDERICK MONDERSON

painting, sculpture and architecture is here represented in its greatest glory.

The site of Thebes in Southern Egypt attracts thousands of visitors each year. They all remain in awe at the artistic and cultural accomplishments of these ancient Africans. Elsewhere in Africa, the same art quality can be imagined. However, throughout the continent, much art has not survived because of environmental factors. Moreover, throughout the artistic landscape, from Egypt to South Africa, art served a particular purpose, whether religious, military, economic, social or agricultural. It was not like art appreciation in Europe, where art is generally made to hang on museum walls, to be viewed by art lovers and the curious.

Moving right along, the art of the Western Sudan is traceable to the Nok discoveries at Jos, Nigeria. To complement this, numerous other sites in the Sahara hold evidence of early African art in the form of paintings depicting plant, animal and human life experiences.

Holy Land Photo 42c. Temple of Luxor. The Roman Shrine beyond the Pylon to the north west, with its enclosing colonnade as seen from a frontal and side view.

Bernard Fage's *History of West Africa* included interesting insights into the early history of this region. He showed fragments of coal were found at Nok sites that dated "greater than 39,000 years." Whether such sites were continuously occupied is uncertain. What is certain, by inference, is that many thousands of years ago, the entire continent seemed inhabited and producing art, though much of it has not survived. To underscore, Freeman-Granville (1976: 6) gives these dates for other occupational sites in North Africa, Hawa Fata c. 38,750 to 2,910 B.C.; Malewa Gorge 31,000 B.C.; for Matjes in Southern Africa he gives dates at Pomongwe 33,570-19,700 B.C.; Florisbad c. 39,000 to 17,000 B.C., and Mufo in the Congo at c. 12,5000 B.C. Conjecture would let us believe these early Africans had thought out some of the fundamental human questions regarding nature and science. If they did, then their art may have shown it. However, not much has survived. Again, Freeman-Grenville (1976: 4) calls attention to sites at Kanyatsi along the

QUINTESSENTIAL BOOK
"THE HOLY LAND"

Upper Nile, having relationship to Olduvai, and Yayo in Chad. At Ain Hamech, Algeria; at the Atlas Mountains near Casablanca and at Makapan, Sterkfontein and Taung in South Africa, all dated approximately c. 1,800,000 B.C. After 500,000 B.C. many sites were in early occupation. Lochad in Zimbabwe, Broken Hill and Victoria Falls in Zambia, Ismailia and Kalambo Falls, Kharga Oasis in Kemet, Khodaine, Tachengitin, Algeria and Sidi Zin in Tunisia round out Early Stone Age culture in Africa.

The Later Stone Age boasted sites of occupation as follows as given by Freeman-Grenville (1976: 6) who gave: "Kalambo Falls, 41,000-7,500 B.C.; Pomongwe, North of the Limpopo 33,570-19,700 B.C.; Florisbad, 39,000-17,000 B.C.; Matteo River 10,800-6,500 B.C.; Malewa Gorge near Lake Victoria, 31,000 B.C.; Mufo in the Congo at 12,500 B.C.; Fashi, near Chad, at 19,350-9,750 B.C.; El Daba on the Libyan Mediterranean coast at 38,750-2910 B.C." For sure, as indicated, the illustrious African historical and cultural heritage has had ample time to experiment and create foundations for art.

Nevertheless, following the 6,000 B.C. Round Head style of the Tassili painters, Nok revealed stratification showing occupations at 3500 B.C. (*Nile Year* 740), 2000 B.C. (*Nile Year* 2240), 900 B.C. (*Nile Year* 3340), and 200 A.D. (*Nile Year* 4440). Therefore, tools from this society let scholars consider Nok a "transitional" culture, from stone to metal workings. These early African artists at Nok also worked tin and iron.

In their excavations of these sites, archaeologists at Nok discovered, wrote Bernard Fage, a "couple of human heads" in pottery. They also found parts of a human head and foot. Fage tells us Nok produced "well fashioned pottery."

Clearly, it can be argued that Africans in this area must have developed other crafts. Their craftsmen can be considered pioneers in working the various mediums. From North Africa through the Saharan and Nok sites, the East and South Africa regions show evidence of sensitive and fresh African art. The analogy of "Bushman art" in the essence of his world as depicted can be applied to all those ancient areas of habitations where no art has remained to portray their early lifestyles and beliefs.

FREDERICK MONDERSON

Holy Land Photo 43. Temple of Luxor. West of the Temple, "talatat" pieces recovered therein; and stored for display and later research.

Such descriptions can only help strengthen the view of an early African culture with great antiquity. More importantly, this early cultural ethos laid the foundations for other areas such as the Western Sudan where art came to play an important role.

Thousands of years later, from the 11th through the 16th centuries, Islamic scholars recount the history of the Western Sudan. They provide primary sources for this period. Here is recounted the growth and expansion of Medieval African states. Successes of these empires were attributed to trade, good government and strong armies. Islam also played a pivotal role. The new religion helped, yet destroyed, Ghana, aided Mali, and was also a factor in Songhai's growth and also destruction.

Under Islamic influence, in higher education we see literacy flourish and produce works of intellectual art in academic manuscripts. Philosophy, law, astronomy, mathematics and medicine were taught at the Universities of Sankore, Djenne and Timbuktu, in West Africa. The *Tarikh es-Sudan* and *Tarikh al-Fattah* are sources of Western Sudan literary art. These chronicles recount the history of *Bilal es-Sudan*, "land of the Blacks." They speak of the art of the period that was primarily supported by the state. Royalty was a supporter of art that blended African conventions and social needs with Islamic beliefs and building practices. Here also a cultural infusion created new innovations in African architecture.

Despite the importance of the large states, the Western Sudan still had no uniform art style. Economic factors influenced art from this region. Agricultural practices supported sedentary hoe farming, with millet, maize and rice as staples of their society.

To support farming activity craftsmen demonstrated African creativity in the tools they produced. Their crafts were grouped into two classes, blacksmiths and professionals.

QUINTESSENTIAL BOOK
"THE HOLY LAND"

Blacksmiths made metal tools for farming, domestic purposes and military uses. They also did some gold work. These blacksmiths also served as a theosophical-religious medium between this and the African spirit world. Professionals on the other hand utilized gold in various forms of jewelry. In a land where gold was found in great abundance, goldsmiths flourished. The gold of the Western Sudan became legendary. E.W. Bovill's *The Golden Trade of the Moors* (1970) mentions gold production was large as late as the start of the sixteenth century. Much of the gold-trade by that time had been diverted to the Atlantic coast. This rerouting of trade came after the destruction of Songhay by the forces of the Islamic Moroccan al-Mansur, and his mercenaries with their guns.

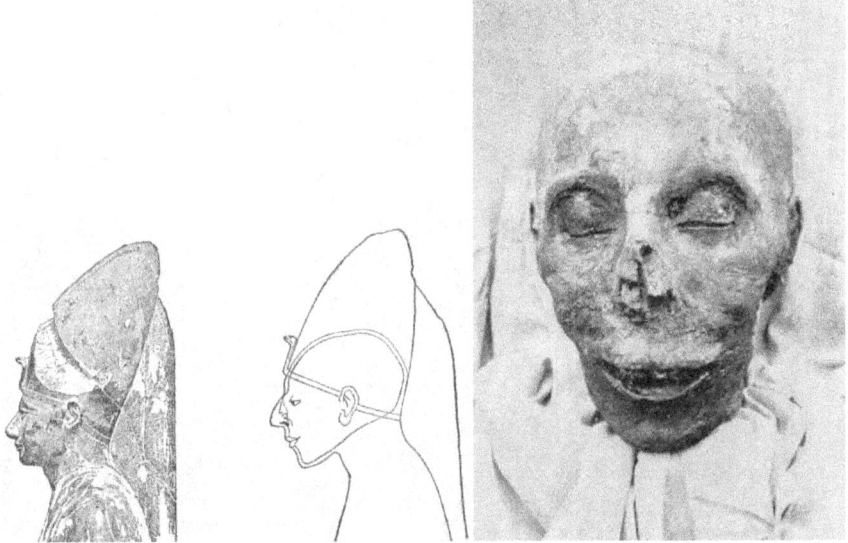

Holy Land Illustration 62. Portrait of Thutmose III, the "Napoleon of far antiquity" (left); compared with the mummy (right).

Bovill (1970) informs, "gold from the Gold Coast was accounting for an amount that has been estimated at about one-tenth of the total world supply at that time. This was an immense total from one small region. Mining gold and supporting industries helped the development of other crafts in wood and metals, creating a wide array of implements to foster commercial exchange and to undergird cultural, social and religious practice. International, regional and local markets developed as a result, from the Trans-Saharan trade. Here could be found a wonderful array of crafts that expressed African art designed for the commercial markets. In these markets one could find cloths, thread, straw hats, mats and calabash bowls. Much of these had geometric and other forms of decorative patterns. Craftsmen worked in glass beads, did leather work and made iron hoes. Gold, therefore, characterized the 'Golden Age of West Africa.'"

From the time of ancient Ghana, the Trans-Saharan trade exported some 9 tons of gold annually. Much of this was in the form of well-worked jewelry. The state supported coins of gold. Goldsmiths worked with twisted thread and ingots, using a variety of art mediums. Craftsmen produced weapons of iron and copper. Those who worked for the king made royal weapons of gold. Goldsmiths made bracelets, rings and necklaces. For bravery, the state awarded "toe rings" of gold. These are reminiscent of Kemetic pharaohs awarding the "Gold of Valor" for similar activity.

Holy Land Photo 43a. Temple of Luxor. The "Open Air Museum" housing thousands of "talatat" blocks rescued; and preserved for later research and possible refitting.

The sword scabbard worn by the royal interpreter and instruments played by musicians of the king, were made of gold, attesting to a craftsmanship unsurpassed. Ceremonial sabers, and lances and arrow quivers were made of gold. Also, the trappings of horses as well as such utensils as royal dinner plates were made of gold. Royal dogs were leashed in gold. Therefore, African artists can be credited with working in fertile fields to produce some of the most profound forms of social and religious ceremonial expressions of art in praise of deity, and the

QUINTESSENTIAL BOOK "THE HOLY LAND"

growth, development and advancement of society.

2. Breakfast

Dr. Leonard James: "Egypt as Black History should be celebrated every day, 365 days per year. Naturally this flies in the face of the falsity taught by those imperialists who colonized the intellectual and artifactual history of ancient Egypt." As you know, Dr. John H. Clarke reminded us "the people who preached racism, colonized history." To that end, the true history of Egypt might best be taught from the perspectives of both standard (largely European) and Afrocentric (largely African-American scholarship). The standard perspective teaches the intrinsic beauty of the art underscored by the wonderful architecture, science, and mythology of Egypt which is further demonstrated by the equally wonderful artifactual displays contained in museums and private collections in cities across Europe and America. Interestingly enough the displays are highlighted under wonderful lighting that obfuscates their true metaphysical and ethnological origin as the general racial origin is thought to be Indo-European. This is not so with the Black version that seeks to emphasize African spirituality and mustici9sm rather than the reality of a "culture in captivity."

Holy Land Illustration 63. Sepulchral stele of Anpu-hetep, with scenes representing the worship of the deceased by his family; and Sepulchral stele of Ath who died in the fourteenth year of the reign of Usertesen I of the XIIth Dynasty (British Museum).

FREDERICK MONDERSON

Afrocentrists believe that the standard Egyptian culture themes are a fabrication began more than two centuries ago when European nationalism and wars, as well as education was underway. To this can be added the proliferation of scholarly societies, journals, and tabloid newspapers. This was when Africa and Africans were prostrate in chains and all forms of justification were used to deny the humanity of black Africans. In that "age of naked imperialism" the "clash of empires" led to a discovery of ancient Egypt. Napoleon's soldiers and savants found the Rosetta Stone and began the systematic study of ancient Egypt, and this lead to Champollion's decipherment of hieroglyphics. In those early beginnings the African connection to Egypt was evident but Professor Clarke's Afrocentric observation emerged in a divergent strand of scholarship. Just then the "true history" became distorted through the writings and pronouncements of individuals as Hegel, Samuel Cartwright in *Slavery and Ethnology*, Dr. Hunt, and theories as the "Hamitic Hypothesis." The movement to remove Africans from Egypt and Egypt from Africa began at that time.

Yet still, there were credible European scholars who decried the emerging falsification of the historical record, such as Baron Vivant Denon; Godfrey Higgins in *Anacalypsis* (1936) and later the Frenchman Lenormant. Unfortunately it was a terrible time for Africa and Africans who were victims of the piranha mentality of the age paradoxically, when men of Europe and America spoke of freedom, justice, humanity, brotherhood. But truth crushed to earth shall rise and from mid-19th century onwards Blacks particularly from the New World, became involved in the intellectual fray regarding Egypt. First Edward Wilmot Blyden, the West Indian who went to West Africa began arguing of a Black Egypt from the perspective of Biblical sources. Then Martin Delaney and other religious Blacks, with very scant sources available to them, began to question the incorrect portrayal of the ancient Blacks of Egypt. In the wider world, however, from mid-century onward a new impetus on Egypt emerged. Concomitant with the "whitening of Egypt" the search for antiquities for private and museum collections unleashed a "Rape of the Nile." This was all masked under the umbrella of ensuing "grand tour" adventurism and "enlightened imperialism" of the last half of the nineteenth century. Under this banner, intellectual imperialism unleashed a multitude of botanical, ethnological, and archaeological studies to determine the whereabouts of everything. That brings us to 'who possesses what' today in museums and private collections across the globe in Brooklyn, New York, Chicago, Philadelphia, Detroit, London, Paris, Brussels, all over.

Walter Brown: Very good, Dr. James.

Michelliea Georges: What Dr. Abu Abarry of Temple University told us in his lecture on "Orality and Literature in African Theory" is simply this:

QUINTESSENTIAL BOOK
"THE HOLY LAND"

"Conventional and literary theorists have been weak in interpreting African literary theory. Conservative literary theorists demand too much of Africa. Prof. John Clarke stated, 'When Europe colonized the world they also colonized the world's knowledge.' Also, Professor John Clarke reminded us: 'The people who preached racism colonized history.'

Holy Land Photo 44. Temple of Luxor. From the west beyond the Temple, columns of the Peristyle Court in the Ramessean Front, the Processional Colonnade; and the Court of Amenhotep III. In the foreground are pitifully small columns of the Graeco-Roman Period; and again from the external western view, papyrus bundle columns with bud capitals with two bands of the Court of Amenhotep III.

"Europeans believe they are the highest point in the human scale. This is an unfair and unreasonable imposition of European particularism as universal."

"Values and artistic criteria differ between European and African scholars. Centrality of African history, drama, world view, anchors our analysis in African phenomena."

"We look for, in an Afrocentric literature, certain stylistic values, differences, etc."

"When it comes to Afrocentric aesthetics we cannot pontificate in the same western perspective. Values, criteria, perspective are based on historical and social experiences."

"Harmony has repetition, balance, continuity."

"There is a set of particular values, meaning, ethnos, motifs, form. Goodness is transcendental. There is no purpose of art for art sake."

"A formulation of groups, aesthetics, artistic. Harlem Renaissance, Negritude, Pan

FREDERICK MONDERSON

Africanism. Literature is essentially the key."

"To embark on an Afrocentric critique you must examine cosmological – creation; epistemological – knowledge; aesthetical – notions of beauty; axiological. There is a rigorous learning on an ongoing process, not restricted to Africans but to anyone who is interested in getting to truth."

"There should be critical thinking but not destruction and self-hatred."

"Metaphor of location is important. We have to locate the writer on how she or he uses language. We cannot have characters engaged in activities in someone else's community. That way there is less stress on the spiritual and more on marginality."

Holy Land Papyrus 20. There's that ubiquitous and beautiful couple, Tutankhamon and his lovely wife, Ankh-es-en-pa-Aten (Ankh-es-en-pa-Amon) in another intimate mood.

"Relocating in the traditions, culture, and art must be seen in relationship to other

QUINTESSENTIAL BOOK
"THE HOLY LAND"

components of existence, literature, history, politics, sociology."

"Our act has to speak to our particular situation. Our art must move us to our optimum vision of the future. Afrocentric critique is a humanistic exercise demanding humanism. We have visions of an interracial, intercultural, as well as multicultural approach to knowledge and problem solving. We have not yet arrived at Afrocentricity. It is a transitional phenomenon."

"There are communicative styles that link us. We can tell if certain behaviors or actions are Afrocentric. Afrocentricity is the language, metaphors. There is no manual. There is a process. We know of "Custer's Last Stand" from an American perspective. How did the Indians feel about it? The Native Americans are not Indians. They got the name from early European explorers, adventurers, seeking a water-route to India. The battle was not reported from their perspective. Afrocentricity is not imperialistic or racist."

Holy Land Photo 45. Temple of Luxor. Bases and shafts of Calyx columns colonnade of the Court of Amenhotep III; and more column bases.

Regina Hendricks: I feel for a big breakfast. Today should be an important day. What do you have for us today George?
George Washington: Well, we know there were pre-dynastic kings. The unification of Egypt was a gradual process rather than an event. Narmer smiting the Semites on his Palette underscores the warlike nature of the time. Narmer was the last king of pre-dynastic Egypt. His son Hor Aha or Menes, first king of dynastic Egypt, founded Memphis as his new capital. Sakkara was the first cemetery, but when this was filled up, Giza or Ghizeh, the place of the great pyramids, was used.

Hor Aha – The first king of the first dynasty was born in Upper Egypt. This is in keeping with Cheikh Anta Diop's view that Narmer was a Theban. Hor Aha

FREDERICK MONDERSON

married a princess from the Delta. At least one temple was built in the Delta.

Mr. Sylvester Singleton: Are there any real differences among religion?
Michael Montout: I don't think so.
James Morrison: It depends on the religion you practice. African people are particularly religious. We practice Judaism, Christianity and Islam.
Dr. McFlair: I know but we are principally Christian. Most of the Africans in America are Christians. Essentially all the religions believe in one god who preaches love thy neighbor and do well for people.

Henrietta Potter: Good morning, Mr. Stewart. What a beautiful day it is. How beautiful the rising sun seems against the eastern horizon. I'm reminded of one of St. Thomas Aquinas' arguments for belief in God that he made nature and all living things that are so beautiful.
Mr. John Stewart: Yes my dear, "Nature is the art of God" and this is one of the wise sayings that decorate the walls of the Library of Congress.
Henrietta Potter: Now I seem to see the intent of their quotations. Clearly art is powerful and is reflected in statements of very powerful people. Lucius Armaeus Seneca (8 B.C. – 65 A.D.) also expressed "All art is but imitation of nature." Richard Frenck (1624-1728) explained "Art imitates nature and necessity is the mother of invention." Equally, Victor Cousin (1792-1867) opined "We need religion for religion's sake, morality for morality's sake, art for art's sake."

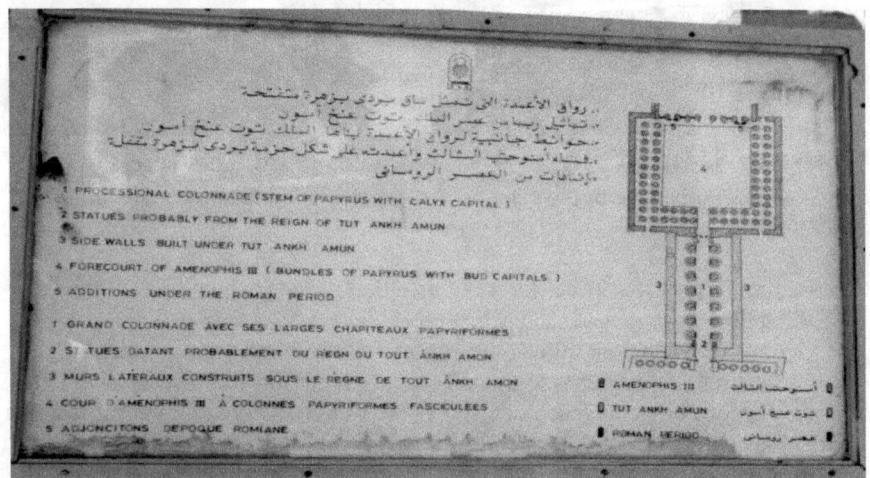

Holy Land Photo 46. Temple of Luxor. Plan of the Court of Amenhotep III with the Processional Colonnade.

QUINTESSENTIAL BOOK
"THE HOLY LAND"

Teddy Cubia: Today I am not eating so much as previously. I am having fruit and juices for breakfast this morning. Last night was not so good.

Dr. Alexander Pushkin: I am going for the big breakfast today. I'm having pancakes, with scrambled eggs, bacon, juice, coffee and fruit.

Mrs. Alexander Pushkin: Honey, take it slowly. I hear you could eat a lot and still lose weight on this trip. However, I don't want you to become too sick and not be able to challenge Mr. Cubia and Mr. Sinclair and still hold your own in the discussion.

Dr. Alexander Pushkin: Don't worry, honey; I'll be all right.

Michael Sinclair: Perhaps we could continue the discussion on the bus. Looks like they want us to go now.

3. Bus Ride

Mrs. John Stewart: My dearest, you seem so pensive, are you all right? You seem so alone. This is an important temple we are off to see, and I want you to be in the best frame of mind when we get there.

Mr. John Stewart: Not to worry, my sweet. "They are never alone that are accompanied with noble thoughts." I am just thinking of the wonderful experiences we have had so far on this trip to Egypt. Those written hand-outs of Dr. Monderson, his lectures, the temples, tombs, scenery, food, ambiance, excellent discussions at breakfast, lunch, after the lectures, in the lounge and even on the bus have been very enlightening. We have come so far on this trip. Still, there is so much more to see, the experience seems to be calling us back for a return trip.

Mrs. John Stewart: Well, perhaps we can make a return trip if we cancel that trip to Alaska we were planning for next year.

Mr. John Stewart: Alaska can wait. If that is the choice, I choose Egypt.

Mrs. John Stewart: Well said, and it's still early, but we must wait and hopefully we can return to see what we have missed.

Teddy Cubia: Dr. Pushkin, won't you agree, if the young Afrocentric scholar should present his next article by Dr. Asante with the same amount of clarity and straightforwardness then you should pay for his lemon squeeze at dinner this evening.

Dr. Alexander Pushkin: Well, I suppose so. Honey, what do you think?

Mrs. Alexander Pushkin: Fair is fair.

Michael Sinclair: In that case, Let me explain it this way then. In his "Afrocentricity and the Human Future" in *Black Books Bulletin* Vol. 8, (1991: 137-140) Molefi Kete Asante believed: "with the loss of terms comes the confusion of the people; so much so that some of us argue for the enemies of Africa and believe sincerely that we are making a case for rationality. Such 'mentacide,' the destruction of our minds, becomes the only principal preoccupation for which there is no limit."

Holy Land Photo 46a. Temple of Luxor. Ladies face off in the "Open Air Museum." Clearly the one on the right seems to have had her nails done recently.

"In the year 2027, let it be said that Africans represent the new hope of the human race because of integrity, excellence, historical correctness, and commitment to economic self-reliance. This means that we cannot be a beggar people. Beggars, moved off their economic and political terms by others, are too often servants in the cause of others.

"With a commitment to an Afrocentric future it will become increasingly possible for us to turn the situation in favor of African development.

What is necessary!

"The situation calls for drastic action. It must be a critical action, exposing everywhere and in every place the aim of the European world supremacy to establish hegemony over African and Asian peoples. We must debate the racists and their defenders who come in the guise of capitalists and socialists, and reclaim

QUINTESSENTIAL BOOK
"THE HOLY LAND"

for the struggle those Africans who have become drunk from an orgy of Marxist phrase-making or capitalist reactionary conservatism... the victims have often assumed the rhetoric of their Eurocentric godfathers and have cheapened the need for a practical solution to our own problems.

"They are blinded by the pernicious forms of what Carlos Moore has called 'western rationalism.'

"Our economic, political and cultural motifs must remain African; otherwise we are moved off of our strengths. In the new century we must refute the critics of our ancestors and say that while we do not want to follow everything done in the past, we do want to build upon the positive foundations the past provides.

"To remain African is not to be "primitive," "backward," or "heathen," but to be correct, positive, sane and intelligent. We must see ancient Kemet as having as much relevance for us as Greece and Rome have for the Europeans wherever they happen to live in the world.

"Despite the bitter antagonism against the culture of our ancestors, we must seek to interpret contemporary developments in every sector and every field in light of our own terms.

"The 21st Century of this era cannot be an era of African disarray. It must be an age of reclamation and reconstruction based upon the regaining of our centers. There is no more correct place for any human being than centrality, particularly in regards to explanation, interpretation and analysis.

FREDERICK MONDERSON

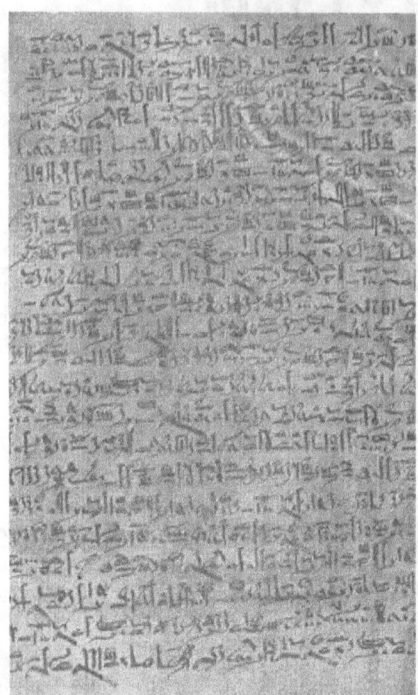 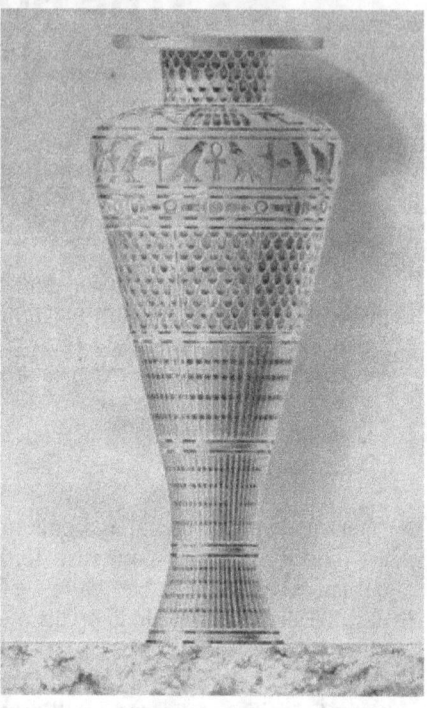

Holy Land Illustration 64. Column from the Edwin Smith Papyrus, an Egyptian Medical Book of the seventeenth century B.C., the oldest known scientific treatise; and Restoration of an Egyptian vase of the Pyramid Age (After Burckhardt).

"We must see ourselves as the masters of our own destiny.

"To master our destinies means that we must internalize an African centered consciousness in everything we do or think. This position should not be reactive but rather the natural, organic way for the African person.

"Rendezvous in Ouagadougou, Burkina Faso in April 1990. Institute of the Black Peoples in Ouagadougou, Burkina Faso:

"Established an ambitious set of strategies to reclaim the African mind and provide material direction toward reconstruction. From the various African communities throughout the world these parties met to discuss our future. The occasion was solemnly determined, committed and proactive. The US delegation headed by Abiyi Ford and Sheila Walker included Elliot Skinner, Earl Shimhoster, James Turner, David Roberson, Locksley Edmonson, Howard Dodson, Leonard Jeffries and Molefi Kete Asante.

Asante said: "Our commitment was to the Black World."

QUINTESSENTIAL BOOK
"THE HOLY LAND"

"The Institute presents for the first time, an international forum where all people of African descent can meet to share ideas in the spirit of solidarity.

THE COMMITMENT

"African nations as the principal repositories of material means must commit their energies that uplift the people through self-reliance. The African world is in need of education, buildings, fertilizers, scientists, scholars, teachers, road builders, pilots and economists.

"The legacy of the past is one in which enslaved Africans were considered incapable of self-government, education and thought. Of course, this racist ideology was responsible for the maligning of our cultures and civilizations for five hundred years by Europeans. Prior to that we suffered immensely at the hands of the Arabs. On both sides of the continent, in different eras and under different conditions, others have victimized African contributions. We can no longer accommodate the wishes of others against ourselves. This means that language, which is a pre-eminent carrier of visions and myths, must reflect a new African person emerging from the 20th Century.

"Let the Afrocentric spirit multiply, let us compete in every arena, let us demonstrate our wills, let us contest indifference and let us win the struggle."

Teddy Cubia: That was good timing young-blood. That brought us to the Temple of Abydos. Very good. Dr. Pushkin, now let me ask your wife, Mrs. Pushkin, Do you think the young man did as good a job as he did earlier when he presented Dr. Asante's article on Afrocentricity?
Mrs. Pushkin: I think he certainly did. Like I said fair is fair.
Teddy Cubia: Looks like you're buying the lemon squeezes this evening, Doc.
Dr. Alexander Pushkin: I guess you got me.
Michael Sinclair: If you brothers will keep the lemon squeezes coming, I may even let you read my first paper draft submitted to Dr. Asante entitled "Development of the Field through expansion of ideas." The second was entitled "An Essay to distinguish Africology from another Discipline – History." They were not regular papers just my thoughts in brief for the assignment.
Dr. Alexander Pushkin: I would like to see how your thoughts have developed since that time to now. It is good to see how you started.

FREDERICK MONDERSON

Holy Land Photo 47. Temple of Luxor. The Processional Colonnade of Amenhotep III viewed from the west, showing Roman columns in the foreground.

Holy Land Photo 47a. Temple of Luxor. View of the Processional Colonnade of Amenhotep III from within the Court of Amenhotep III. Column bases of the Court are in the forefront and the Entrance Pylon and Minaret of Mosque of Abu al Haggag at the rear.

QUINTESSENTIAL BOOK "THE HOLY LAND"

4. Site ABYDOS

Abydos is the highlight of the tour. When you consider Sakkara, Giza, Abu Simbel, Edfu, Kom Ombo, Philae, Rock Tombs of the Nobles, Valley of the Kings, Hatshepsut, Rameses, Tutankhamon, Karnak Temple, Luxor Temple, and now Abydos and Dendera, we begin to wonder about the nature of the men and women of ancient Africa who thought out and constructed those wonderful testaments to man's intellect, religiosity and tenacity.

Abydos is the "Holy Land!" Here is where the theosophical philosophies began. Here you get information on a basis of moral turpitude, trust, rules and regulations. This information must be interpreted.

ABYDOS: HOME OF OSIRIS

Abydos, "where it all began," is a site of extremely important political, economic, historical, mortuary, theological and artistic significance. Lying between Assuit and Thebes, in Upper Egypt, it is the only place in that land of ancient Kemet, where can still be observed the "Tet" or "backbone of the God Osiris," that was set up on January 19th, an extremely important holy day. During these festivals, great rejoicings accompany every activity. Yoyotte (1962: 2) informs, "during the 'mysteries' conducted by a representative of the king, the statue of Osiris, richly adorned, was borne on the shoulders of his priests towards the tomb. A mime of the victory of Osiris over evil was performed and funeral lamentations were sung while a mummiform image was interred according to a secret ritual." As a result, it can be argued, from the first dynasties, Abydos has commanded great awe and reverence as the world's earliest place of pilgrimage. So, while eschewing moral, ethical, religious and philosophic tenets that molded social belief systems throughout dynastic rule, this "holy city" of Abydos competed with other centers of religion for worshiping and ritualizing the ancient African divinities. Consequently, and because of that importance throughout 3000 years of history, and into the modern world, Abydos has attracted those in search of spiritual upliftment, cultural roots, as well as a cadre of tourists and the essential workings of archaeologists and the scientific disciplines that flow from their works. Together these interests, efforts, and realization of scientific, theosophical and epistemological truths have enlightened the world to the genesis of this early African creativity, along the banks of the Nile River in North-east Africa.

FREDERICK MONDERSON

Holy Land Photo 48. Temple of Luxor. Two of the fat cows in Procession to the Temple of Luxor as depicted on the south-west wall of the Ramessean Front, Court of Rameses II.

TEMPLE OF DENDERA

Located 30 miles north of Luxor and across from the city of Kena, the Temple of Dendera takes its name from *Tentyris* or *Tentyra*, in Coptic *Tentore* or *Nikentore*. It has its origins in that of the goddess Hathor, the cow. Tentyra is probably taken from *Tei-n-Athor*, the abode of Athor or Hathor. Hoefer, Youssef, Rodenbeck and Buatti (1995: 196) have pointed to the following regarding the existing structures: "The Temple of Dendera like those of Esna, Edfu, Kom Ombo and Philae, and others further south that have been lost under Lake Nasser, is approximately a thousand years younger than the New Kingdom temples, and its construction was initiated by the Ptolemies." Though evidence indicate earlier constructions at this particular site, Kamil (1983; 158) offers: "Evidence of actual temple building at Dendera dates to the Middle Kingdom, and some restoration was carried out in the New Kingdom, when Thutmose III revived the greatly popular ancient 'Voyage of Hathor." Complete reconstruction, however, was started under the later Ptolemies and was finished some 158 years later under the Roman emperor Tiberius, with the names of other first-century A.D. Emperors appearing on the entrance gateway. It is, therefore, of pure Graeco-Roman style."

It should be added, however, that all these temples were accomplished under Egyptian and Nubian craftsmanship, as had been going on for millennia. Maspero (1926: 272-273) tells accordingly: "Thebes had been destroyed by a[n] earthquake in the year 22 B.C. and it was now no more than a place of pilgrimage where devotees came at daybreak to listen to the voice of Memnon, but at Denderah and Ombos the decoration of the temples was completed by Tiberius and Claudius. Caligula worked at Koptos, and the Antonines at Philae and Esneh. The workmen employed had sufficient knowledge to execute thousands of bas-reliefs according to the ancient rules. The work done by them is feeble, ungraceful, and absurd, inspired merely by routine, but nevertheless it is founded on ancient tradition,

QUINTESSENTIAL BOOK
"THE HOLY LAND"

enfeebled and degenerate, but still living and capable of being invigorated with new life. The changes that occurred in the middle of the third century, the incursions of the European and Asian barbarians, and the progress and triumph of Christianity led to the abandonment of the work and the dispersion of the workmen. With them died all that yet survived of the national art."

Holy Land Photo 49. Temple of Hatshepsut at Deir el Bahari. Visitors leave on the Second Ramp with the Middle Colonnade and Upper Colonnade and Terrace in the rear as author and photographer Dr. Fred Monderson raises his arms in adoration; and right, the true "Northern Colonnade" and Anubis Shrine (left).

Paying further attention to this decline in art and craftsmanship, Murray's *Handbook for Egypt* (1888: 440) tells us even further: "Egyptian sculpture had long been on the decline before the erection of the present temple of Denderah; and the Egyptian antiquary looks with little satisfaction on the graceless style of the figures, and the crowded profusion of ill-adjusted hieroglyphics, that cover the walls of this as of other Ptolemaic or Roman monuments. But architecture still retained the grandeur of an earlier period, and though the capitals of the columns were frequently overcharged with ornament, the general effect of the porticoes erected under the Ptolemies and Caesars is grand and imposing, and frequently not destitute of elegance and taste."

On the west bank of the Nile and oriented south to north or facing north, the present Temple of Dendera was begun in the reign of the XIth Ptolemy, completed in that of the Emperor Tiberius, though sculptures and decoration were not finished till the time of Nero. It took 250 years to build this temple. Equally too, it contained a unique feature, religious decoration of the ceiling utilizing Gods, boats, animals, fruits and flowers that blended well with the cosmological significance of the architecture of this and so many other temples. Maspero (1892) has argued how: "At the Ramesseum, at Edfu, at Philae, at Denderah, at Ombos, at Esneh, the depths of the firmament seemed to open to the eyes of the faithful, revealing the dwellers therein. There the celestial ocean poured forth its floods, navigated by the sun and moon, with their attendant escorts of planets, constellations and decans, and there also the genii of the months and days, marched in long procession."

Thus, this well-preserved temple of Dendera is a picturesque representation of esoteric knowledge of those ancient Africans, along the Nile River. It too had its characteristic triad of gods. Chalaby (1989: 57) informs: "Dendera, the Greek name of the city of Tentris, is a city made holy by the presence of three different sanctuaries, that of Ihy, the sistrum-playing son of Horus, that of Horus himself and that of Hathor."

Holy Land Photo 50. Temple of Hatshepsut at Deir el Bahari. On the Upper Terrace, head of broken Osiride Figure of the Queen (left); and in the Upper Court visitor mills around before the Portico to the Sanctuary with niches in the wall containing Osiride statues of the Queen. Two headless statues remain in the center.

The Open Panel: To Discuss the Influence of Egypt

Moderator: Brother Sabuba.

Dr. Alexander Pushkin
Rev. McNair
Sister Stephaniea
Bryce Menkheperre - Youngster who won the prize
Sister Carmelitiea
John Brown
Jack Bender
California Lady

QUINTESSENTIAL BOOK
"THE HOLY LAND"

Holy Land Photo 50a. Seriousness contained in the intellect of a beautiful sister, Dr. Merimba Ani, who has influenced untold minds over decades.

Q. WHAT DID EGYPT DO FOR ME SINCE I DISEMBARKED?

Ans.
John Brown:
     Personally and collectively

Personally: This trip has given me a certain bond with the land of Kemet, Kemet-nu. It will bring me closer to my soul mate for the rest of my life. It helped me become more disciplined and forces me to give honor to the ancestors.

FREDERICK MONDERSON

Collectively: African-American ancestors have a great culture. We must not only educate the young but also the adults. We must retain the educational values of Egypt. I hope to return to Los Angeles and do something constructive with what I learned here.

Dr. Alexander Pushkin: There is a fundamental issue each time I visit Egypt. Egypt or Nile Valley requires us to identify and acknowledge our human ancestors at a very high level – the motherhood of mankind.

What Egypt means from the master. Fundamental. The Master Teacher is Doctor Benjamin. Equally I would equate that designation to Dr. Yosef A. A. ben-Jochannan. It forces us to acknowledge where knowledge originates. Dr. ben-Jochannan is probably the only real master teacher outside of this that I know.

I acknowledge that all the knowledge I know comes from many masters. Woe be unto me if I do not learn.

Holy Land Photo 51. Temple of Hatshepsut at Deir el Bahari. In the Upper Court. Opening at the top right leads to Court of Ra-Horakhty with eastern and northern walls of the Upper Court and showing remains of the double line of Peristyle Colonnade that characterized this inner region of the Temple. Opening to the right is an exit (left); and (right) Anubis, in good color, stands in his Shrine.

QUINTESSENTIAL BOOK "THE HOLY LAND"

Jack Bender: This trip to Kemet has helped me to learn more about the ways my ancestors lived every day.

Sister Stephaniea: It is an honor to be here with our ancestors. This is a confirming time for me. It can be a lonely and difficult road to travel. Dr. Benjamin has helped me to know what the ancestors did and how great we are. I can say the same for Dr. ben-Jochannan. The struggle must continue. We as a people will never die. Our extended family has helped us to prepare to live as long as man is on earth. The human spirit is that living breath.

Holy Land Photo 52. Temple of Hatshepsut at Deir el Bahari. Shrine of Anubis. Anubis sits enthroned before a "Table of Offerings" (left); and Amon-Ra also sits enthroned before a "Table of Offerings" (right).

Sister Carmelitiea: First honors to the ancestors and to the elders. This is not my first trip. It is, however, a time for rededication. The hope is that we do something positive with what we have learnt. There is lots of work to be done. Our people may be resurrected with the knowledge of these ancestors.

Rev. McNair: This is my first experience. It is rich and rewarding. I have learned

FREDERICK MONDERSON

so much from seeing the people I know of long ago.

Q2.   Bro. Sabuba:

What was your high point in Egypt?

Ans.

John Brown: The XVIII-XIX Dynasties was most fascinating.

Rev. Alexander Pushkin: The image of Heru nursing from Auset's breast.

Q3.   **How has your image, your perception of an African man/woman changed?**

Ans.

Dr. Alexander Pushkin: Isis was a loving and faithful wife; she manifested all the significant values I look for in a Black woman.

Q4.   **To the ministers on the panel.**

There is no historical evidence of the Christ!

Dr. Alexander Pushkin: I agree. The idea of Christ is traceable back to Osiris, the first crucified savior.

Rev McFlair: I must admit there is much history of my Bible in this culture. While I cannot tell my people there is no god, I can only show them where god comes from!

Sister Stephaniea: The Black Madonna of Mary nursing Jesus could very well be Isis nursing Horus!

QUINTESSENTIAL BOOK
"THE HOLY LAND"

Q5. **There are many fundamental contradictions. How do we recognize or reconcile what we have seen?**
Ans.

Dr. Alexander Pushkin: There are 18 branches of the African educational system and 42 Negative Confessions in the ancient Egyptian philosophy. 10 Commandments – Some of these have been distorted.

The Curse of Ham is imbedded in the psyche.

Sister Carmelitiea: We must deprogram and then reprogram.

Sister Stephaniea: We must network extensively.

Dr. Alexander Pushkin: Men wrote the book. In a manner of speaking, one could argue that the Bible is a kind of political document to inspire a people to control others. We Know Ra.

Jack Bender: We have the Book of the Dead, use it.

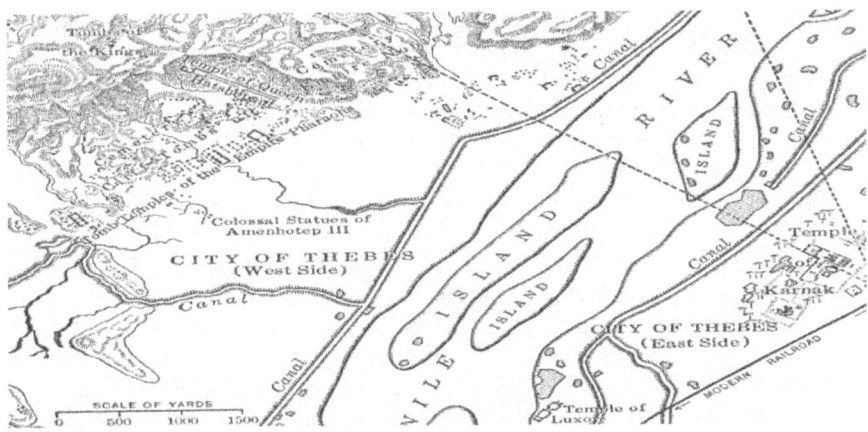

Holy Land Illustration 65. Map of Egyptian Thebes.

FREDERICK MONDERSON

Holy Land Photo 53. Ramesseum Temple of Rameses II. Osiride and Columned Porch before the Hypostyle Hall with its massive columns and clerestory windows.

5. Post site Lecture

Dr. Fred Monderson: Tomorrow we begin the bus trip to Aswan where the principal feature is the Temple of Isis of Philae Island, now relocated to Agilka Island. However, before that I would like to give some background on the Ethiopians who ruled before the later invasions. Nevertheless, what we saw today at Abydos and Dendera represents high and low points but useful developments in Egyptian art. Let us not forget that Egyptian art, according to Petrie and Diop achieved its highest plateau by the time of the Old Kingdom after untold centuries of evolution. The later developments were attempts at imitation and sustaining. Thousands of years later, by the time of the Greeks and Romans, however, art had retrograded but the temples were now replete with inscriptions complementing the art. Even though the art was not the highest quality, it was still beautiful. Henry Wadsworth Longfellow (1807-1882) wrote: "Great is the art of beginning, but greater the art of ending; many a poem is marred by a superfluous verse" and "art is long, time is fleeting." Hippocrates (c. 460-400 B.C.) believed: "Life is short, the art long, timing is exact, experience treacherous, judgment difficult." While Varro (116-27) explained "Divine nature gave the fields, human art built the cities" and Ezra Pound (1885-1972) in the *Spirit of Romance* (1910) wrote, "The history of an art is the history of masterwork, not of failures, or of mediocrity." Last but not least, John Fitzgerald Kennedy in an address at Amherst College October 26, 1963 stated: "When power leads man towards arrogance, poetry reminds him of his limitations. When power narrows the area of man's concern, poetry reminds him of the richness and diversity of his existence, when power corrupts, poetry cleanses, for art establishes the basic truths which must serve as the touchstone of our judgment."

QUINTESSENTIAL BOOK "THE HOLY LAND"

Holy Land Photo 54. Ramesseum Temple of Rameses II. Osiride and columnar inner face of the Porch entrancing the Hypostyle Hall.

As if that is not enough insight on that wonderful craft which we see at Abydos and Dendera, one of the highlights of any Egyptian trip, Walter Pater (1839-1894) reminded us: "Art comes to you proposing frankly to give nothing but the highest quality to your moments as they pass" and that "Art constantly aspires to music." Ivan Krylov (1769-1844) argued that people such as the ancient Egyptians could "charm creation with their art." Henry James (1843-1916) in a letter to H.G. Wells on July 10, 1915 explained: "It is art that makes life, makes interest, makes importance, for our consideration and application and of these things, and I know of no substitute whatever for the force and beauty of its process."

Now to the Ethiopians. We know of Khasta who preceded Piankhi. Piankhi ruled Egypt 730-711; Shabaka 711-697; Shebitku 697-689; Taharka 689-667; Tanutemon 665-663. These dates correspond with Tiglath-Pileser III 745-727; Shalmaneser V, 726-721; Sargon II, 721-705; Sennacherib, 705-681; Esarhaddon, 680-669, and Ashurbanipal 669. By 730 B.C. internal Egypt was in chaos. Assyria invaded Egypt. There was no strong centralized authority with a strong standing army.

FREDERICK MONDERSON

The Nubians or Ethiopians under Khasta then Piankhi headed north and defeated the Delta king Tefnakht. He united Egypt again and removed the threat of Assyria to Egypt. The Ethiopians spoke Middle Egyptian. They were ahead of Egypt with their pottery. They also spoke Meroitic. They had a theocratic monarchical system. Their artistic culture was advanced. The Nubian statues have a double uraeus. The new Nubian Museum at Aswan presents an outstanding outline of the long duration of life beyond Egypt's border to the south.

Hezekiah of Judea asked for help against Sennacherib.

The Shabaka Stone in the British Museum is very important. It maintains "Shabaka found the writings of the ancients in disrepair and re-established them better than before."

The Taharka Column in the Great Court is one of ten. This surviving Taharka Column stands pretty close to 60 feet and was restored early in the twentieth century. However, some authorities such as Mariette who illustrated the plan, believes there were 16 such columns surrounding an inner structure with four entrances to the north, south, east and west. While DuBois and Petrie mention this structure, they do not give a number of columns. Sir Benjamin Bannister gives the number 12.

Taharka built a temple beside the Sacred Lake on the North-South Axis. He also built the Treasury north of the *Akh Menu* as well as a building east of the *Akh Menu* of Thutmose III.

The Egyptians erected forts at Semneh and Kumnah near the Second Cataract during the Middle Kingdom. These were for protection of trade routes with the hinterland. Semneh is on the west and Kumnah on the east. This was a very inhospitable region. Budge visited here in 1905 and Reisner excavated there in the mid-1920s. The walls of the forts were 30 feet thick, 40 feet high and made of mud brick. The term *Glacis* came to define the defensive military fortifications found in Nubia. There were three cemeteries with graves of 240, 60 and 40 each.

Kush was important to the Egyptians mainly for gold. An estimated 30,000 ounces of gold a year came from one mine in Nubia. Kush was a border territory under military jurisdiction. Much Kushite culture was influenced by Egypt.

The 25th Dynasty defended Egypt from foreign invaders. After their defeat by Assyrians the capital was moved to Napata. Three cataracts separate Napata from Aswan. The capital was then moved to Meroe in the 4th Century B.C.

QUINTESSENTIAL BOOK
"THE HOLY LAND"

Meroitic offering tables have Egyptian inscriptions around the edges. This is same as Egyptian offering styles.

Holy Land Photo 55. Ramesseum Temple of Rameses II. View of the rear of the Temple from the bus.

There were 4 major cemeteries at Napata and 1 at Meroe. These are of the 25th Dynasty and later. A Harvard Team led by Dr. Reisner excavated the site.

The Meroitic kings used truncated pyramids. The Taharka Pyramid was built in 2 stages. First, it's made of smooth sandstone, 75 feet high. Next to it is a chapel with 51 steps going down. The burial was below ground in the substructure. The portion of the building above ground is the structure and the portion above this the superstructure, whereas the portion below ground is the substructure.

The second stage of the Taharka Pyramid had an outer enclosure above the smaller structure which became its superstructure. The final height almost doubled to 150 feet. Sandstone is again used. This was not a huge pyramid, but about the height of a 15-story building. Smaller pyramids were built for queens. The culture became more and more African with its move into Africa's bosom.

Two reasons have been given for the move from Napata to Meroe. First, there was an abundance of iron ore deposits. There were trees for wood as well as the occurrence of stone for building. It is not known when the Meroitic Pyramids were robbed. Some believe the area was ransacked during the Coptic period. There were 66 Kushite kings traced in succession from cemeteries at Napata and

Meroe.

Budge, and then Petrie believed the Kushites reverted to prehistoric decapitations of the body. Petrie seems to follow Budge, in some strange belief about the Egyptians. Decapitated burials were found at Naqada and Ballas.

Leaning forward about 2000 years, in the 1950's, the High Dam created Lake Nasser that's 500 miles long. The new lake created accumulated water. The end result of this man-made lake; built to control the flow of water is that it created hydroelectric potential for much of Egypt. This has helped tremendously in the economic revitalization and vitality of many places in the south. However, the drawback was the need to manufacture fertilizer, which, unfortunately was naturally deposited over the land with the inundation. Salt also created a problem for the monuments. Finally, the problem of siltation at the dam requires constant cleaning.

Holy Land Photo 56. Ramesseum Temple of Rameses II. Another view of the massive columns and Osiride Figures of the Porch.

6. Discussion

Dr. Fed Monderson: Art is such a wonderful experience it can be considered the quintessential creation of man, perhaps outside of childbirth. Oscar Fingal O'Flahertie Willis Wilde (1854-1900) in *The Critic as Artist* wrote: "It is through art, and through only art, that we can realize our perfection; through art and art only that we can shield ourselves from the sordid perils of actual existence." Philippe Nericault-Destouches (1680-1754) put is simply: "Criticism is easy, art is difficult."

QUINTESSENTIAL BOOK
"THE HOLY LAND"

Are there any Questions?

James Morrison: When you speak of art are you simply referring to painting?
Dr. Fred Monderson: My goodness, no! All creation is art. If you recall, my article on African Art begins by saying "African Art is older than man for man himself is art from Africa." The pyramids, architecture, the temples, tombs, military equipment, household utensils, farming equipment, boats, shoes, anything man makes is art. Sir Max Beerbohm (1872-1956) believed "The past is a work of art." He concluded everything about man's existence can be considered art. We can say nature is art and art sometimes tries to reflect nature. Sir Thomas Browne (1605-1682) argued "All things are artificial, for nature is the art of God." Equally too, John Dryden (1631-1700) wrote, "By viewing nature, nature's handmaid art, makes mighty things from small beginnings grow." Speaking of early man who viewed his surroundings and experimented with its gifts, continued Dryden "He was naturally learned; he needed not the spectacle of books to read nature; he looked inward and found her there." William James (1842-1910) perhaps put it best in the statement "The art of being wise is knowing what to overlook."

Holy Land Photo 57. Valley of the Kings. From on high, panoramic view of the Valley and entrance to some of the tombs.

Michael Montout: How many temples are at Deir el Bahari?

FREDERICK MONDERSON

Dr. Fred Monderson: There are three temples at Deir el Bahari. This was indicated before. These belong to Mentuhotep II of the 11th Dynasty; Hatshepsut of the 18th Dynasty; and Thutmose III, also of the 18th Dynasty. His temple is between the other two. We can probably argue that he wanted to put a wedge between Mentuhotep and Hatshepsut or that because the place was sacred from earlier times he wanted to share in its aura and majesty. He simply squeezed his between the two, since there was no other space in the cirque.

James Madison: Did Hatshepsut ever visit Punt?
Dr. Fred Monderson: Not to my knowledge. She sent emissaries but never visited Punt. Nehesi, her Chancellor was put in charge of the expedition that also included Senmut and another. This voyage to Punt was not the first for an earlier one dates to the Middle Kingdom when pharaoh sent ships to the East African country. However, Hatshepsut's is the most graphic, considered an anthropological study of an alien culture.

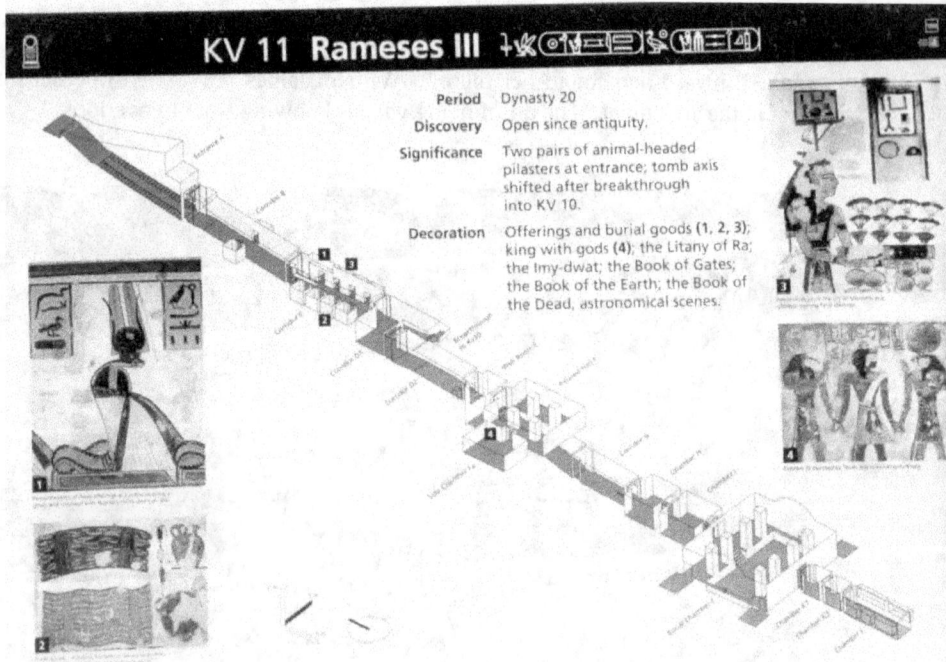

Holy Land Photo 58. Valley of the Kings. Tomb of Rameses III. Significance: Two pairs of animal-headed pilasters at entrance and tomb axis shifted after breakthrough into KV 10. Decoration: Offerings and burial goods, King with Gods, the *Litany of Ra*, the *Imy-dwat*, the *Book of Gates*, the *Book of the Earth*, the *Book of the Dead* and astronomical scenes.

QUINTESSENTIAL BOOK
"THE HOLY LAND"

Frederick Maloney: What is the proper name for Abydos?
Dr. Fred Monderson: The ancients call Abydos *Abtu* or *Abt*. It is in the 8th Nome the Greeks called *Tini, This* or *Thinite*. It was capital of the southern kingdom and one of the earliest capitals of Egypt. The Arabs called Abydos *Harabat el-Madfuneh*.

Teddy Cubia: Why is Abydos so special?
Dr. Fred Monderson: Archaic kings of Dynasty I and II were buried at Abydos. Evidence remains of enclosure walls of forts dating to this period. Petrie discovered ten levels of temples at Abydos. Menes and Khufu built here. Narmer, though Theban, is thought to have begun his armada here as he sailed north to conquer. There was a temple of Osiris at Abydos from the earliest times. His head is thought to be buried there. However he did not become the principal god of Abydos until the Old Kingdom when he displaced Khenti-Amenti as god of the dead.

Holy Land Ceramic Art 5. The "Great Cackler," a goose, often a form of Amon-Ra, is decked out in colorful ceramic pieces.

Petrie discovered a small figure of Khufu, builder of the Great Pyramid at Abydos. It is of excellent workmanship. Nevertheless, because of these features, this meant like the god, the city remained prominent throughout dynastic times. Plutarch says that men of distinction frequently selected Abydos for their place of final repose so that their bodies might be near the head of Osiris buried there. In many tomb decorations, the deceased is shown making the pilgrimage to Abydos. So if one could not be buried there or erect a stele there, because of the value of this real estate, one just got there and then returned to their true place of burial.

Holy Land Photo 59. Valley of the Kings. Tomb of Thutmose III. Significance: Depiction of all the deities in the *Imy-dwat* receiving offerings, first occurrence of the *Litany of Ra*, first complete example of the Imy-dwat, unique depictions of King and family and cartouche-shaped burial chamber. Decoration: *Litany of Ra* and the complete *Imy-dwat*.

Under the XIth and XIIth Dynasties Abydos attained its highest splendor. Then under the XVIIIth and XIXth Dynasties Abydos was held in especial honor. The XIXth Dynasty particularly promoted Abydos. Today, the outstanding temple of Seti I of the XIXth Dynasty displays some of the finest art surviving in Egypt.

QUINTESSENTIAL BOOK "THE HOLY LAND"

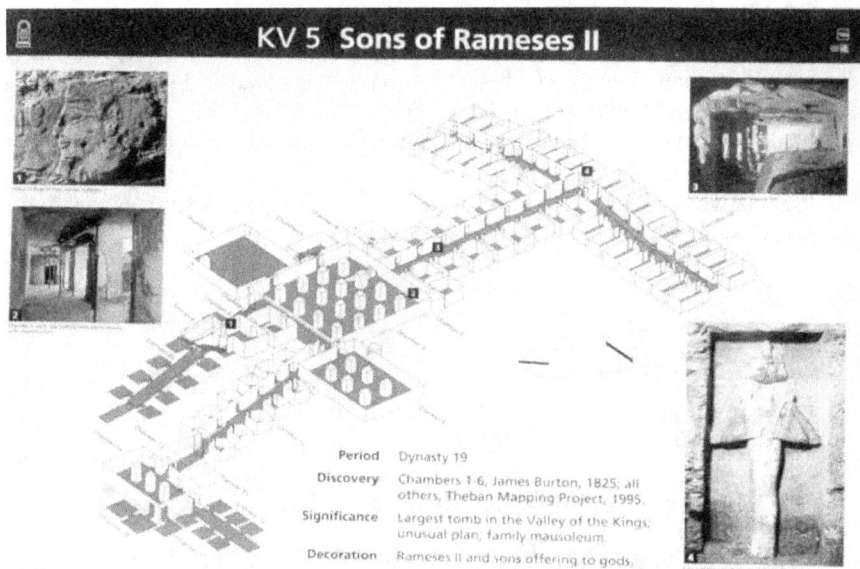

Holy Land Photo 60. Valley of the Kings. KV 5, Tomb of Sons of Rameses II. Mapping Project, 1995. Significance: Largest tomb in the Valley of the Kings, unusual plan and family mausoleum. Decoration: Rameses II and sons offering to Gods.

Cherise Maloney: What would you consider the most important festival in Egypt? Dr. Fred Monderson: There were several festivals depending on the time of year. We could easily say the New Year Festival because it begins a new year. There were the Opet Festival, Feast of the Valley Festival, Nile Festival and a whole host of others. The Opet Festival is well celebrated for this is when Amon left Karnak to travel to Luxor by boat along the river amidst great fanfare. Then there is the return voyage back to Karnak along the canal connecting these two temples about three miles apart. Both journeys are depicted on the walls surrounding the Processional Colonnade at Luxor, thought to be placed there by Tutankhamon and Horemhab.

Myers in the *Oldest Books in the World* (1900: 448-450) wrote: "The period of sadness on earth culminated with the Winter Solstice and the sun apparently born anew after the happening of that event, caused in Egypt, a period following which was that of the Festival of the New Year, in which mirthfulness and joy ruled the land; this opened in Ancient Egypt about the 9th of January, therefore the fathers of the Church after the establishment of Christianity in Egypt, which was easily accepted by the Copts, had no difficulty in fixing the time after the happening of the Winter Solstice for the celebration of the birth of Christ. Till the time of Chrysostom (*circa* 347-407 A.D.) Christmas was always celebrated in the Eastern Church in conjunction with the Festival of Epiphany, on January 6th. Julius I (337-352 A.D.) transferred it to December 25th. There were other celebrations in the early Christian Church which seem to have originated in Egypt. There was the Festival of All Souls. Tertullian mentions that annual offerings (oblations) were made for the souls of the dead, likely on the anniversary of the death, and they were especially the business of the surviving husband or wife, if married, and of the relatives of the dead. Chrysostom (Hom. 29. in *Acta Apost.*), and Augustine, (*De Cure pro Mortunis* ch. 4.), speak of this."

Holy Land Photo 61. Valley of the Kings. Alabaster Factory. Great repertoire of artifacts made by the local craftsmen and available for sale to tourists.

In the most ancient Christian Liturgies is a prayer that, "Christ will, through the intercession of His holy martyrs grant to our dear ones, who sleep in Him, refreshment in the abode of the living." Another says, "That the prayers of the blessed martyrs will so commend us to Christ, which He will grant eternal refreshment to our dear ones who sleep in Him."

"Tertullian calls these anniversaries, birthdays, and the offerings birthday honors. That is the 'Second birth' or 're-birth,' of the spirit of man. Another celebration was Candelas-day or the Day of the Lights. This is the Epiphany as a distinct Festival, celebrated in the Western Church on January 6th, the 12th day after Dec. 25th and hence called, Twelfth day. With the Ancient Egyptians it was a festival at which they ate sugared cakes. Herodotus mentions a Feast of Candles held in his time at Sais in honor of the Egyptian sky-goddess Neith. It was also an old Roman custom to burn candles to the goddess Februa, mother of Mars, to scare off evil

QUINTESSENTIAL BOOK
"THE HOLY LAND"

spirits. This was always done on February 15th until the time of Justinian, but in 541 or 542 A.D., he made it happen February 2 and a Christian Festival in honor of the Purification of the Virgin. Wilkinson says the Egyptians had a Festival just after the Vernal Equinox, which would be about the time of the Hebrew Passover and our Easter."

Holy Land Photo 62. Valley of the Kings. Alabaster Factory. More of the repertoire of artifacts made by the local craftsmen.

Hattie Jones: What are some names of important Papyri?
Dr. Fred Monderson: There is the ancient name given by the Egyptians or that of the owner. Then there is the name of the individual who discovered it, who purchased or acquired it, who translated it or where it is located. Some popular names were *Abbott Papyrus* with scenes of the Psychostasia and *Amen-neb* – weighing of the heart. There were others such as *Papyrus of Ani* the Scribe, then *Papyrus of Hunefer*, *Wilbour*, *Petrie*, and *Berlin*, *Moscow*, *Turin*, and so on.

Contrary to the many arguments for the origins of the Egyptians, the *Papyrus of Hunefer* states, according to Dr. ben-Jochannan: "We came from the foothills of the mountains of the moon where the god Hapi dwells." The foothills of the mountains of the moon are the plains before Kilimanjaro and Mount Ruwenzori in East Africa and the God Hapi is a manifestation of Osiris.

FREDERICK MONDERSON

Holy Land Photo 63. Valley of the Kings. Alabaster Factory. Even more of the colorful stones, carved and offered for sale to visitors.

Jerome Smith: What type of actions or behaviors did the Egyptians frown on or detested?
Dr. Fred Monderson: Those things called abominable. More or less the same things we frown on. Avarice, greed, deceit, murder, adultery, arrogance, stealing, lying, bullying, cheating, boasting, covetousness, cursing, disputatious behavior, were all held in abomination. These were things the deceased denied as part of the *Negative Confessions*. Maulana Karenga said the Egyptian was concerned about "how he stood before his god," so this reality molded his social and religious behavior. Rev. Dr. Jones spoke at the funeral for Mary Pinkett, the first Black woman elected to the New York City Council, and re-elected for almost 30 years. He mentioned Louis XIV, king of France. When he died and lay in Notre Dame Cathedral the place was packed and the bishop spoke. He simply said: "You are what you are before God. Titles and accolades aside, you are what you are before God." I guess this is how the Egyptian felt so he lived his life with that in mind.

QUINTESSENTIAL BOOK
"THE HOLY LAND"

Holy Land Photo 64. Abydos Temple of Osiris. A second set of stairs past a destroyed Pylon leading to the Court before the entrance with its pillars and one entrance. The second set of stairs elevates the Temple further.

Holy Land Photo 65. Abydos Temple of Osiris. Right side of the decorated entrance pillars against the entrance wall.

Henrietta Potter: How did these ancient Africans view death?
Dr. Fred Monderson: Depending on how you lived, death was either good or bad. You prepared for death during life. This meant living the good life and erecting a

secure site as your body's final resting place. Everyone was afraid of the second death for this occurred when you failed the judgment and was punished by the devourer.

Juliet Brown: How was adultery viewed? Was equal treatment or contempt for men the same as for women?
Dr. Fred Monderson: Adultery was a serious crime, so a severe penalty was meted out to him and her.

The *Oldest Books in the World* informs the *Papyrus of the Scribe Ani* also called *Papyrus of Bulak No. IV* admonished: "Keep thyself from a woman whom thou wouldest have outside, even when that would not be known in her city."

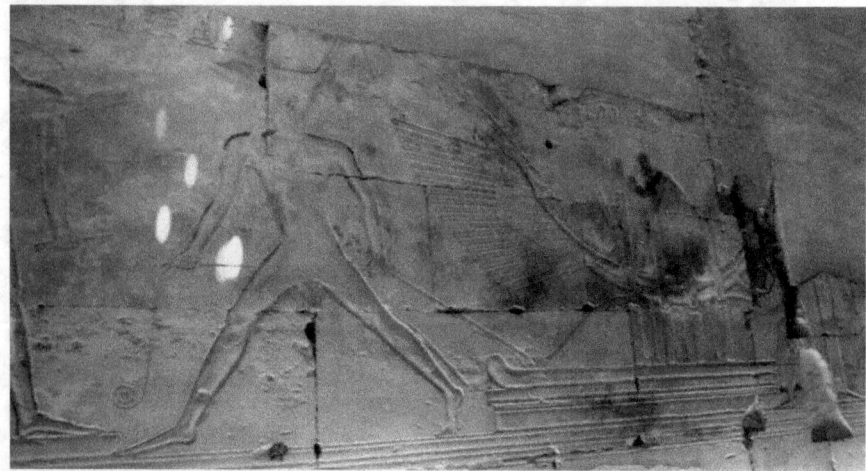

Holy Land Photo 66. Abydos Temple of Osiris. Seti I drags a sled with the Barque of Osiris before Thoth, one of the guardians of the dead God.

There was the Danger of Seduction by Evil Women. "Keep thyself from a woman whom thou wouldest have outside, even when that would not be known in her city. Do not incline towards her like her similars (equals); do not know her or fill thy heart with her; she is a deep water, and one does not know its windings. If a woman whose husband is afar (sends thee) writings, if she speaks to thee each day without witnesses and holds herself to throw the snare, it is a crime worthy of death through following it, if people hear of it, even when she has not accomplished her designs in reality. Men will commit all crimes solely for this (pleasure)."

QUINTESSENTIAL BOOK
"THE HOLY LAND"

Holy Land Papyrus 20. Horakhty sits enthroned alongside his consort, Amentet, a version of Hathor.

"The laws against adultery were very severe in Ancient Egypt, as this Maxim tends to show, being in touch with the later statements of the Greek writer, Diodorus Siculus, who says: 'The laws concerning women were very severe. He who was convicted of violating a free woman had his genitals cut off; because they considered that this crime comprehended three very evil things: the insult, corruption of morals, and confusion of children. For adultery committed without violence, a man was condemned to receive a thousand strokes of the rod and the female to have her nose cut.'"

Chabas mentions the "strange woman" from Hebrew sacred writings who is "not known in her city." The penalties accord with the warnings in our Maxim, and the

FREDERICK MONDERSON

dangerous nature of the crimes mentioned, under the law of Ancient Egypt.

Walter Brown: How did the ancient Egyptians view and deal with murder?
Dr. Fred Monderson: Murder in any society is a crime. The Egyptians abhorred murder for this form of action is how Seth killed his brother Osiris, the good god. The *Papyrus of Sayings* mentions a Pharaonic decree against murder: "The Protector (Pharaoh or Shepherd) sends the command through the land to all men: 'He, who at any time kills his brother, is accursed. I will fulfill my word upon the disturber. The familiar Mosaic Law against murder follows the Egyptian from which Moses got his training."

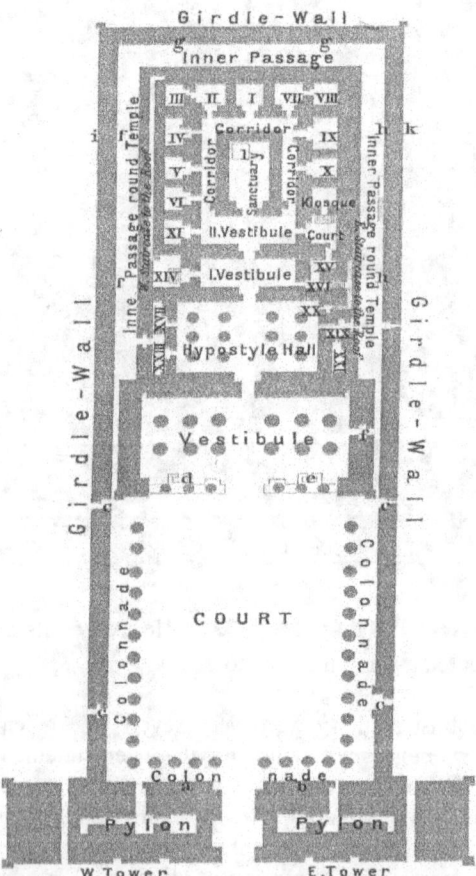

Holy Land – Plan of the Temple of Horus at Edfu.

The prescription against murder insisted no one commit this hideous act. In fact, the deceased in the *Negative Confessions* denied having committed murder while on earth. Hence murder was condemned in the Egyptian society. The Stele of

QUINTESSENTIAL BOOK
"THE HOLY LAND"

Taharka, the Ethiopian of the XXVth Dynasty, tells of a prescription against men who plotted a murder in the temple. This is why, according to Dr. ben-Jochannan, you must be very careful when you visit the temple. Dress properly, do not speak evil there, do not desecrate the holy site, do not enter the Holy of Holies, and so forth.

Mrs. McNair: What is the relationship between mother and child?
Dr. Fred Monderson: Like that of all societies the mother held a strong bond of affection and attachment to the child. The child is told very early to love the mother and father. "Injure not the feeling of thy mother." He is admonished to act in a manner that both mother and father can be proud of his actions. Hence, there was praise for a mother or father when a child did something worthy and was recognized by the society. Conversely there was grief on the part of the mother when the son had done something terrible. The child also had an obligation to perform certain ceremonies for the deceased parent.

Holy Land Illustration 66. Earliest representation of a sea-going ship (Twenty-Eighth Century B.C.) (above); and Part of the fleet of Queen Hatshepsut loading in the land of Punt (below).

Leonard James: How did the Egyptians view the Inundation?
Dr. Fred Monderson: The Inundation was a gift of nature that was anxiously awaited yet it was feared if it was too much. Hence expectation and anxiety. If the river's volume was too little it meant food shortages for the whole society. If the river was too voluminous it brought flooding and destruction. Thus, the

FREDERICK MONDERSON

Egyptians very early learned how to study the river and how to exploit and control it. This studious approach to the river gave birth to mathematics, geometry, as well as several other disciplines for it also coincided with heavenly activity. Thus we have early astronomy and astrology.

Nilometers were erected at different key positions along the Nile to measure its volume. There was one at Abu Simbel, and most significant temples along the way with two at Philae, one at Elephantine Island, Kom Ombo, Edfu had two and so on all the way to Memphis. There was naturally one at Luxor. This enabled engineers and surveyors to survey the land after the inundation and put the people back to work. The deceased confessed he did not divert the waters of the inundation.

Rev. Mc Flair: What types of offerings were made and to whom?
Dr. Fred Monderson: Unquestionably there were a number of ceremonies with prescribed rituals and prescribed offerings. The god had to be lustrated and fed every day. Flowers had to be placed on the altar and incense had to be burned. However, incense was never burned on an altar. It was either held in a vessel in the hand or in an incense burner on the ground in a corner.

In an imperial society such as the Middle and New Kingdoms, booty of slaves and wealth were given to Amon who brought his adherents victories and successes in their endeavors. The great girdle wall of Rameses II at Karnak like so many other places shows the king in different attitudes when he makes presentations to the gods. Most times these are made in front of a "Table of Offerings." In most cases, he has something in his hand that is presented to the god. This could range from flowers, to the feather of Ma'at, and from jars of ointment to sphinxes, even obelisks. The field of offerings was very wide.

George Washington: What is the symbolism of Tomb Paintings?
Dr. Fred Monderson: Well, there were different meanings. Perhaps they were meant to come alive when certain magical words were uttered, perhaps by the deceased or even those who passed by the grave or those who did honors to the individual. However, Myers (1900: VII) informs: "The mural paintings on the walls in Ancient Egyptian tombs are not for decoration, they are symbolic and mystic and the figures thereon are intended for a spiritual purpose." They also helped to depict how the individual lived in society.

Charles Palmer: How did the ancient Egyptians regard resurrection?
Dr. Fred Monderson: The people of ancient Egypt believed in "resurrection" and this was a strong moral imperative in how they lived their lives and related to others on earth. Myers (1900: 265-66) explained further: "Life on this earth, to the people of Egypt, certainly under the Theban dynasty, and most likely long before,

QUINTESSENTIAL BOOK
"THE HOLY LAND"

was only "to become" (khopir or kheper) in the content of many "to becomes" (khopiru) which had preceded and would follow it. It had an infinity of duration, a pre-existence before birth in this world, it would have an infinity of duration after such birth, and the soul would pass through all this content, guarding its own identity."

Regarding the soul, "Before its birth in this world it had been born and died in many other worlds. The life after death could also die, and in the Nether world were persons termed the 'Twice dead,' and the doctrine of spiritual annihilation of the living-dead is to be found in the *Per-em-hru*. The usual idea of immortality in Christianity is, that it is the result of one death of the human being born into this world-life, which is to continue forever without change of condition, but there is also even in it the idea of a 'second death.' Now, in order to die a second time, it would be necessary to be alive after the first death. From the foregoing and other authorities, we are sure that the Ancient Egyptians, at a very early period, believed in an eternal condition of the soul, pre-existing forever before its entrance into its earthly life, and having an existence forever after it; subject, however, to the decrees of the authorities of the Nether-world, which might cause its annihilation and 'the second death.' The idea of the immortal existence of the soul previous to its imprisonment in the human body may be found in the books attributed to Hermes Trismegistus, and in Plato. It is a curious coincidence that the statement of the fall of souls from the Treasury of Souls, in the division of the books of Hermes, called, the Virgin of the World, should be exactly paralleled by an account in the Sepher ha-Zohar of the Hebrew Qabbalah, as to the creation of soul and of the Treasury of Souls, before the creation of the universe, and the descent of these souls from that Treasury into the human body, and their objections to doing so."

Michael Palmer: What is the Ka?
Dr. Fred Monderson: N.W. Thomas answered that question in *Journal of Egyptian Archaeology* VI, October 1920: 265-73, "Regarding the Ka." He wrote: "It is most commonly represented as a double or a genius, or the image of a genius; but it has also been regarded as an image, or funerary statue of a deceased person, as the embodiment of a life principle or as a totem."

Michelle Georges: What is the Ba?
Dr. Fred Monderson: The Ba is the soul of the person.

Michael Montout: Allow me to return to Luxor Temple. What makes Luxor temple so different to other similar worship temples?
Dr. Fred Monderson: Several things. We could start by saying it was built by two monarchs and that several kings left their names there including Amenhotep III, Horemhab, Tutankhamon, Seti I, Rameses I and Alexander the Great. Second, for

the most part it is very well preserved. Third, it is the only place where the Opet Festival is depicted. Most important is the purpose for which the temple was built which is to celebrate the Opet Festival in which Amon and his wife after traveling from Karnak spend some 24 days secluded therein while his adherents party to the fullest. He came by sea in a flotilla and returned by land in a procession. Even further, Luxor had a more esoteric, spiritual, mystical nature as the "Grand Lodge" where learning and mysticism were special practices. Last and finally, Amenhotep IV wreaked havoc on the structure even though it was his father's temple. This was because Luxor was the most visible place of the manifestation of Amon and so he obliterated his name everywhere it was found. Seti I and Rameses did restore the names, though somewhat clumsily following the Restoration begun by Tutankhamon. This temple actually had three axes. That is an invisible axis beneath the floor, the one above along the temple's contours and the one added by Rameses II.

Mr. Jesse James: How would you describe the essential components of the Mortuary Temple?
Dr. Fred Monderson: While the worship temple was essentially a God temple, the mortuary temple was a King temple, designed to propitiate and worship the king during his lifetime and when he died and became a real god. All the important 18th, 19th and some 20th Dynasty kings built mortuary temples on the west bank at Thebes. These New Kingdom mortuary temples, while dedicated to the king also praised Amon-Ra as the King's father. Thus, whether it is Deir el Bahari, Ramesseum, Medinet Habu or the temple of Merenptah or Seti I at Kurneh, the temple showcased some facet of the King's life and its decoration depicted his aspirations for the next life. Naturally, he was shown worshipping Amon as "King of the Gods."

Mrs. Jesse James: Now, how would you describe the essential components of the worship temple?
Dr. Fred Monderson: The essential components of the worship temple comprised, an enormous Enclosure Wall with an equally large Entrance Pylon that entranced into an Open or Great Court. Here could be found statues, shrines, Kiosks, altars, sphinxes, porticos and much more. Beyond the Court lay the Hypostyle Hall, sometimes a second and even a third Hypostyle Hall (Ramesseum, Dendera, Medinet Habu), all possessing columns of an enormous state, decorated. The walls are decorated with aspects of the temple ritual with the king in a prominent position. Just as on the temple's exterior walls he is shown battling Egypt's enemies, natural, divine or cosmological; on the Hypostyle Hall walls he is shown worshipping and ritualizing his god.

That's all folks. Now, let me now share with you a lecture I attended, given by James Allen, Associate Curator in the Department of Egyptian Art at the Metropolitan Museum of Art on Friday March 6, 1992 in the Conference Center of Urus Hall at the Metropolitan Museum of Art on Fifth Avenue and 81st Street. It

QUINTESSENTIAL BOOK
"THE HOLY LAND"

was a three part Lecture Series. In fact I will include the other two sessions based on my notes taken there. The second lecture took place on March 13, 1992, and was entitled "The Egyptian Universe." That will be included in tomorrow's discussion.

"The Egyptian Mind"

Getting through the images of Egyptian texts and art. How the Egyptian thought and their logic differed from ours.

Major Egyptian texts – Read and analyze.

Creation Accounts

What the Egyptians thought the universe was like. This is not based on actual evidence but on inference, deduction, and reason.

The ancient Egyptians existed before the timeline of the transcription of the Book of Genesis, which suggests that mankind evolved or was created about 4000 years ago.

The process of scientific speculation did not begin with the Greeks. It is rather the literature of the Greeks that survived and so that is what we learn.

Prehistoric man had many of the same notions about the sky, stars, etc., as we do.

TWO DIFFICULTIES ARE PRESENTED

a. The language and images;
b. The cultural context the language fits into.

> The decipherment of hieroglyphics resulted in there being little lost wisdom from the ancient Egyptian ages.

1. Primitive superstition – the least innocuous.
2. If we did not find the lost wisdom we did not translate hieroglyphics. It is possible that, if there is lost wisdom, it is because somewhere there are hieroglyphics that have not been translated, or where is wisdom from a primitive culture that was either oral and lost, or written in a permanent fashion that has not yet been found.

FREDERICK MONDERSON

Holy Land Photo 67. Abydos Temple of Osiris. Seti I leads four bulls before Ra-Horakhty.

Adolf Erman was the first modern man who completely understood the hieroglyphics. We can read the words but don't always get the meaning of the words. To translate the texts did not mean you understood the concepts behind the symbols. Sometimes you have to divorce yourself from the concepts.

Cultural Contexts

"Science" versus "religion"

The ancient Greeks were perhaps the first to separate science from religion.

2 Modes of perception

1. **Objective** – science – tries to find external proofs of what a thing is. People want objective looks at things.

2. **Subjective** – Religions worship beings. Looks for people and its criteria are internal; no religion can demonstrate its objectivity, beliefs. One has to believe in God.

I. **OBJECTIVE**: They look for mechanical factors and objective forces for which something happened.

QUINTESSENTIAL BOOK
"THE HOLY LAND"

II.   **SUBJECTIVE**: Who - looks for whom or a being as responsible for something?

A simple question is: Who made the Nile rise?
Ans. God.

Subjective thought looks at objective in the universe.

Falcon is important.

People are a part of nature in subjective thought. No concentration on creation of people. No difference between animate and inanimate. Animate nature with a will - people; animal nature with no will - plant.

Everything has its own personality. There was a personality behind the thing.

OBJECTIVE THOUGHT

We explain nature in physical terms. In a subjective world everything has a source. We call them gods. People thought of offering to gods at temples to win the god's affection. The gods were higher officials who made the world work. They had big houses and servants (priests).

Priest = Personal servant of the god. Their houses were temples. The gods were in the forces and things in the universe. The god was not controlling the sky or sun. The god was in the sun or forces in the universe.

III.   **IMMANENT**

Their gods were part of nature. In ancient Egypt science was religion. There was no difference. An attempt was made to interact with the gods. Their textbooks were stories of the actions of the gods.

IV.   **MYTHS** are real scientific attempts to explain something.
        Egyptian - mythopoeia
        Modern man – scientific writing.

        Logic of exclusion – modern man; Logic of Inclusion – ancient Egyptians.

FREDERICK MONDERSON

SUN GOD

Re or Ra was the Sun God. He was Khepra in the morning sun; Ra Horakhti – Son of Horizon at midday; Atum – sun at sunset. There were many names but one being. This is the logic of inclusion.

V.　SYNCRETISM

Ra-Horakhti-Atum. Each aspect of a thing is similar to the whole thing.

Horus was the child, husband of Hathor. Not contradictory but complementary. Dreams as same as reality. Image as same as reality. The name is as real as the person or thing.

Kingship is eternal. The individual king was a man. The kingship was an eternal force of nature.

VI.　SPACE

In temples there was a space with dirt that was the primeval hill.

VII.　TIME

Each new day was a separate creation. Each New Year was a new beginning in creation. They spoke of "the first occasion" when the pattern began. For man, to deserve creation is the original purpose of life. The past is the model for the present and future.

Ancient Egyptian texts (hymns, prayers, etc.) are not speculation about how creation came about. Ancient Egyptian creation accounts are centered in the major centers of thought.

QUINTESSENTIAL BOOK "THE HOLY LAND"

Holy Land Papyrus 21. Hathor holds the hands and leads Nefertari, wife of Rameses II.

FREDERICK MONDERSON

1. Heliopolis – Re or Ra

2. Memphis - Ptah

3. Hermopolis – (Ogdoad) Group of 8 with Thoth

4. Thebes – Amon

These centers all had different creation accounts.

Remnants of ancient Egyptian thought possibly inspired by an even more ancient people lost in the midst of time, shows incredible, complex, images of thought. They had a really remarkable and consistent view of creation. The various texts are not contradictory but complimentary.

Holy Land Photo 67a. Imagine the power and intellectual creativity contained in the expressiveness of this great Egyptological scholar, Dr. Theophile Obenga.

So here then is the ancestral heritage, culture, history, religion and spirituality. Seize the opportunity to drink in the culture, to ponder its origins, and to go forth from here. Edmund Burke (1729-1797) in his *Reflections on the Revolution in France* reminded us: "People will not look forward to posterity who do not look backward to their ancestors." Junius, in 18th Century England, offers rather appropriate insights in the statement: "We owe to our ancestors to preserve entire

QUINTESSENTIAL BOOK "THE HOLY LAND"

their rights, which they have delivered to our care: we owe it to our posterity not to suffer their dearest inheritance to be destroyed." If that is not sufficient, then Marcus Tullius Cicero 106-43 B.C. added: "History is the witness that testifies to the passing of time; it illumines reality, vitalizes memory, provides guidance to daily life, and brings us tidings of antiquity."

Dr. Leonard James: We hear so much about Egyptian temples, how about Nubian temples?
Dr. Fred Monderson: *Encyclopedia Britannica* (11th Edition, 1911) pointed out, in Nubia there were: The temple of Daboud, the temple and quarries of Kertassi, the temples of Kalabsha, Beit el Wali, Dendur, Gerf Hussein, Dakka, Merikare, Es Sebu'a, Amada and Derr, the Grottos of Elles Ya, the tombs of Aniba, the Temple of Ibrim, the great rock-temples of Abu Simbel, the temples at Jebel Adda and Wadi Halfa, the forts and temples of Semnah, the temple of Amara (Meroitic) and Soleb. Beyond are the Ethiopian temples and pyramids of Jebel Barkal and other pyramids of Napata at Tangassi, etc., the still larger pyramids of Meroe at Begerawa, and the temples of Mesauwarat and Naga, reaching to within 50 miles of Khartoum.

Any further questions?
Hearing none. Dinner this evening is at 7:00 PM.

7.   Free Time
8.   Dinner

Dr. Leonard James: Mr. Brown, after a long day, you do seem to have a hearty appetite.
Walter Brown: With that, I agree Dr. James. I am having everything this evening. I am sure you are quite aware that Edward Robert Bulwer-Lytton in *Lucile* offered wisdom of the ages: "We may live without poetry, music and art; we may live without conscience, and live without heart; we may live without friends; we may live without books; but civilized man cannot live without cooks." He also reminded us: "Beneath the tred of mighty armies, the pen is mightier than the sword."
Dr. Leonard James: I cannot argue with such logic. After all, where would we be if cooks did not play such an important role even in our primitive lives?

Michelliea Georges: Well, I am looking forward to hearing from our brother this evening. I think he has done a wonderful service of sharing with and enlightening us with his knowledge.

FREDERICK MONDERSON

Regina Hendricks: I cannot dis-agree with you at all. Here he is now. Hello, sir. How are you this evening? Let me say how much we appreciate what you are doing.

George Washington: Why thank you, kind and beautiful sisters. I think you will like this evening's presentation for the esoteric nature of its contents

During the Vth Dynasty the solar cult predominated. Re was worshipped as sun god at Heliopolis, city of the sun, and Thoth was known as the god of wisdom. The *Westcar Papyrus* is an interesting document of this age. According to the *Westcar Papyrus*, a woman was pregnant with triplets and was told that her children would be three kings of Egypt and their father was the sun god. It was a sort of immaculate conception. An early King List, the *Palermo Stone* shows huge tracts of land and monuments being erected in honor of the sun god. In Dynasty V, more and more temple lands became tax-exempt, thus becoming a rising tax burden on the peasants. In addition, most kings in this dynasty, besides building a pyramid, also built a sun temple. The kings of the V Dynasty included User-Khaf, Sahu-re, Neferkare, Niusen-re, Izezi and Unis. The last two kings did not build solar temples.

Holy Land Illustration 67. Sepulchral stele of Khenti-em-Semti, a builder and architect who flourished in the reign of Amen-em-hat II (left); Painted sepulchral stele of Usertesen, a high official of the XIIth Dynasty (right).

QUINTESSENTIAL BOOK
"THE HOLY LAND"

Osiris surfaces in the V Dynasty. Since they were state and private gods, Osiris was considered a private god. First, the original local administration of provinces was religious in nature. Abydos was the city of the cult of Osiris.

The bureaucracy of the V Dynasty had so greatly increased that royal family members were notable for occupying all posts as in the IV Dynasty. This shortfall caused private citizens to get jobs as civil servants. In the economy, trade greatly increased. Sahu-re's pyramid shows pictures of ships going out to the Levant, namely Byblos, for trade.

Regarding **African Religious Thought Systems**, the laws of opposites signifies complimentarity while the spiral motion symbolizes continuity. Ozu Tonolo signifies complimentarity: a pair of opposites supports each other in equilibrium.

The Infinite extension of the universe is expressed by the continual progression of matter along a spiral path. This is conceived as taking place in an egg-like form.

Aduno Tal is the egg of the world. The germs of things exist in the Aduno Tal. The potential of life is embodied in an "egg." Because of the spiral movement, germs develop in seven segments of increasing lengths. They symbolize seven fundamental seeds of cultivation found in the human body. Seven segments along with Kize Uzi make up "the divine 8," Ogdoad, which is basic to Dogon cosmology and mythology. The organization of the cosmos, society and man are all symbolized in the "divine 8" (Dogon). Man is prefigured in the egg of the world, the Aduno Tal. The seventh vibration is where energy breaks out of the sheath of Kize Uzi. This seventh segment is a symbol of "the seed," Emme Ya or female sorghum. Emme Ya represents life and the ideal food. It cannot be made impure or Desacralized.

Creative process takes place on the seventh vibration (breaks thru the sheath); life emerges and follows a pre-determined, predestined movement of being.

The central core inside the first seed is an oblong plate (ovoid plate) divided into four sectors each of which has 22 categories. In this creation process, categories are distributed. Movement of creation is rotary, turns on itself and flings categories on the things they represent. Prior to this there was only potential being; now it is given reality. Universal force touches potential force and being given reality and place into its category. Cosmos gives order and universe comes to life. Dogon relate the infinitely small to the immeasurable vastness of the universe.

FREDERICK MONDERSON

Order of the Heavens. An infinite expanded conception phenomenon, which occurred in the infinitely small (Kize Uze = seed). This is a microcosm of the universal order.

Creation of the heavens – star O smallest and heaviest (smallest star = smallest seed).

Smallest star contains seed of all things. Smallest star moves around Sirius axis on own that movement upholds all creations and its orbit determines the calendar. In the Astral Plain – Seven seeds comes out of the smallest seed (Kize Uzi). This equals "8" Divine of Dogon. Amma – God the Creator was the first personality.

Aduno Tal is an enormous egg. All previous phenomena take place in Aduno Tal, which is a model of creation.

Nommo is the son of Amma.

Two placentas. Each is divided into two. Each placenta contains a pair of "Nommo," direct emanations "son of Amma" pre-figurations of man. Twin beings are fundamentals of the principle of twin-ness. Each human being equipped with two spiritual principles of opposite sex. Each helps in determination of society and the family. This equals cosmology and conceptual structure of the universe.

Holy Land Photo 68. Abydos Temple of Osiris. Between the columns of the Second Hypostyle Hall. Notice the rise in the flooring moving into the Temple (left); and, Seti presents an offering, assists Isis to set up the Tet or backbone of Osiris and the Tet set up (right).

Given Humanness "Peopling of the Universe"

Mythology – In one placenta of egg was formed Yurugu, the male person. He did not wait for full period of gestation (9 months), period that was ordered by 'Amma.' He emerged from the egg and took a fragment and brought it down to earth. He brought Kize Uzi. He intended to create his own earth, but this was not

QUINTESSENTIAL BOOK "THE HOLY LAND"

according to Amma's plan. Earth at this point had a male soul only since the maker's creation was (imperfect) incomplete. This is disharmony. Yurugu returned to the heaven to find his twin female soul. Amma handed over his twin soul to the other pair in the placenta making it three. Yurugu could not get back his twin soul and since then has engaged in an endless search for her. Yurugu then returned to the earth now totally dark and totally dry, and found many single incomplete beings. He procreated his own placenta into the earth, his symbolic mother, this was an incestuous act.

Since this, Amma sent the Nommo of the other placenta to the heavens and this created the firmaments. They came down in an enormous ark. Nommo is the twin of life (blacksmiths).

10-22-1975

Earth in this point of the mythology, was in total darkness. At four cardinal points of Ark are other Nommos. These are manifested incarnations and are first ancestors of man. The four ancestors who began procreation of Dogon are Amma, Seru; Lebe, Seru; Bini, Seru; Dyongu, Seru.

Ark constituted a new undefiled earth as descent takes place, light comes to the earth and water in the form of rain (fertility) in new undefiled earth "divine 8" seeds are sown in the form of animals, Humans, 8 gives birth to twelve, this gives birth to 22 (10 females, and 12 males).

With the help of Nommo social organization was created. Ark of Nommo denotes dehumanization of space and the movement of time and seasons. Year is linked with earth rotation to the sun. As day alternates with nights, seasons follow. It took 22 years for creation to be finished. All systems were established. First 4 years correspond to first 4 "seed times." This is symbolized by priest's ritual. This symbolizes planting, re-enactment of creation, and helps to insure the continual or perennial procreation of the (Dogon) human beings. From the 5th sowing on, ritual (Bulu) indicates the idea of purpose (to make alive again). The dry, uncultivated earth belongs to Yuguru; the day of light, cultivated habitable earth belongs to Nommo. Death signifies infertility.

MAN

Man is the seed of the universe in that man is prefigured in Kize Uzi. Kize Uzi is a conception of the creative process. The vibrations and extensions present the creation of man. First movements of creation were also first pre-figuration of man.

FREDERICK MONDERSON

And man was the being around which everything surrounded man in his own person. Seven segments of vibrations represent seven seeds plus Kize Uze and this represents "divine 8." This symbolizes man's substance. He is the image of first being of creation and the image of the universe. Man is the image. He is the beginning of creation and existing order. He is the life of the world. The egg of Aduno Tal is filled with germinating cells. The head, neck, body, right arm, left arm, right leg and left leg represent microcosmic man and heaven and earthly placentas. Joining of heaven to earth by twinness, with each being possessing two souls. This represents the person's identity with creation. Man is thought, like the process of creation, to possess two souls.

Holy Land Ceramic 6. The Khepre beetle, doing its work of pushing the sun along its path, disguised as a ceramic version of this important creature.

The seed represents the four pairs of twins, equaling "8." All man's actions and activities are interconnected with the functioning of all beings. "The seeds" symbolize the food of mankind. They are important in the life of the cultivator for they depend on them for his food. It also symbolizes renewal of life. The way in which a seed unfolds and generates human life is the sign of the universal order.

Disorder among the seeds results from the breaking of the rules of life from one generation to another. The function of ritual is to reproduce a state of harmony.

QUINTESSENTIAL BOOK "THE HOLY LAND"

DOGON: Behind the Mask on the Niger River in West Africa.

Sculptors make visible the invisible. The Dogon scorn the much more modern religious belief systems but strive to imitate the natural! Greeting is by ritual. Outside influences such as Islam and Christianity have hardly encroached upon their metaphysics. Many shrines are built in the villages. Ritual is nourished by millet and blood. They delight in capturing vivid impressions of the world around them. European art simply echoes Africa.

Sculptors portray, not the visible but the unseen. The highest quality sculptures mostly represent gods. They are highly prized by outsiders.

The village priest is always the keeper of treasured sculptures in hiding, a place, known to him and few others. The first Dogon came down from heaven, feet extremely hot, and had to wear special sandals in order not to scorch the earth. In ancient statues with hands raised to the sky, the people say a prayer for rain. The Dogon, who today grow many onions, harvest them during February and March. Then you pound them into pulp. Millet is a main staple among them.

Intermediate between the people and the gods is the blacksmith, one who cannot own land or riches. He forges a wedge between god and man.

There is a profession or trade hierarchy.

Young children prepare themselves for circumcision by learning initiation songs. Ceremony performed in cave high in hills. Hieroglyphic impressions are "burned" into the minds of the young. They now join AWA. The dance is very important in ceremonial ritual. Masks are brought from hiding places to be used in ceremonies in the village. The Bao Bab tree is used for making masks, but only blacksmiths can make masks. No woman or child can see a mask before the time. No one is so shameless to sneak a look.

A statue is made of an old woman who died and will be worn on the head of the chief mourner in the ceremony. The mask represented the woman in her younger days with firm pointed breasts. This was how her family wanted to remember her. Holes are pierced for string to attach the mask to the mourner's head. Art with a capital "A" has no meaning to the Dogon; it has to be seen in its proper context. Masks vary in sizes and styles. After the ceremony masks are discarded in the mountains, for they then have no meaning. The mother of masks is 20 feet tall, and used in village funerals. Sounds of guns are tears for a lost companion. The mother of masks leaves her cave to give a final benediction on the village. Their ceremonies are picturesque. In the blackness of the night men become heroes as

FREDERICK MONDERSON

masks become spirits of the dark. The old man has sculptures of first primordial couple of children of Amma in his hut. Many other pieces depict many mythological figures. These sculptures are priceless in Europe. The Frederick Douglass Museum of African Art in Washington, D.C. is an important repository of African art.

Regina Hendricks: Oh, my goodness! Oh, my goodness!!!

Michelliea Georges: Mr. Stewart, what do you think of the wonderful art of the Abydos Temple of Seti I?
Mr. John Stewart: Superb. It's the only place in Egypt where there are seven deities in one temple and the art is so well preserved. I am reminded, "Art is long and time fleeting." It's a pity we had to leave so quickly.
Michelliea Georges: It is a long way off and we had to do the other temple at Dendera. What I found interesting is the four star general who came out with the police escort.
Mr. John Stewart: Well that is part of the Antiquities Police contingent. They do provide the best security for tours such as ours. Tourists are well protected in Egypt because they contribute so much to the local economy. Really, they don't want visitors to feel uncomfortable when they visit Egypt and that is why so many precautions are taken to make things run as smoothly as they do.

Dr. Alexander Pushkin: What's that on your plate, Teddy?
Teddy Cubia: Food. Lettuce, black olives, tomatoes, peas, and peaches on the side. Dressing is made of vinegar with lemon juice. But don't worry about what's on my plate; order the young man's lemon squeeze and one for me as well.
Mrs. Alexander Pushkin: Waiter. Make that 4 lemon squeezes. They are on my husband.
Dr. Alexander Pushkin: Well, ok. I've got the lemon squeezes.
Michael Sinclair: Keep it up, Doc. I will show you an early sample of my writing when I first attended Temple's Afrocentric Institute. Please don't laugh.
Mrs. Pushkin: No matter what young man, it's not where you were but how far you have come.
Dr. Pushkin: Perhaps I will meet you at the old watering hole in the lounge later this evening. Seems it's one place where you can get something cold to drink.

QUINTESSENTIAL BOOK
"THE HOLY LAND"

Holy Land Illustration 68. Group statue of two women and a boy.

Holy Land Photo 69. Abydos Temple of Osiris. In Double Crown, Seti stands before Anubis in the Temple Shrine as evidenced by the overhead uraei wearing feathers and disks.

9.   Lounge Discussion

Michelliea Georges: Let us invite the brother to our room and watch the sunset in all its splendor.
Regina Hendricks: I think it's a wonderful and intelligent suggestion. Ok brother, come with us. That was some explanation you gave earlier. It boggles the imagination.
George Washington: Gladly, ladies. Please let me savor this cold beer before I join you. I too am fascinated with how beautiful the sun is as it changes its color

QUINTESSENTIAL BOOK "THE HOLY LAND"

when making its descent behind the mountain overlooking Deir el Bahari.

The **Ancient History** mid-term set for November 3, 1975 and the readings are Wilson, chapters 1-5; Moscati, chapters 1-4; *Before Philosophy*, Chapter I, Part II; Gardiner, *Egypt of the Pharaohs*.

October 16, 1975

Dynasty VI consisted of Teti, Pepi I, Mern-re, and Pepi II. This was a very good time indeed, very prosperous. During this dynasty, tranquility, farming and anti-belligerency are Egyptian characteristics. The cult of Ra was very significant during this dynasty. We see the rise of the priestly status in the society. Teti supported the religion of Osiris. The Nomarch was the highest administrative office in the province. He was the governor of these "states."

Abydos, the city of the cult of Osiris became very important. Pepi I married 2 women from this city, daughters of a Nomarch. His sons were Meren-re and Pepi II. During the reign of the last three pharaohs Pepi I, Meren-Re, Pepi II, there is evidence of military expeditions to the north and south, but primarily to keep the trade routes open. The Germans called this period *Volkwanderungen* or "Great Migrations."

Harkhuf was a noble adventurer who led expeditions to Nubia for spices, animals and also secured a dwarf that fascinated Pepi II. His voyage is recorded on the doorway of this tomb at Aswan.

The pyramid texts are found in dynasties V and VI in royal pyramids. Here is also found the first poem entitled 'The dead king hunts and eats the gods.' This is sometimes known as the "Cannibal Hymn."

During Dynasty VI trade routes were being threatened. Due to the lack of rain in the Levant and Asia Minor, many people were forced into Egypt.

Pepi II reigned for 94 years. He decreed great lands to the temples and to the monarchs to win their allegiance. Taxes on the farmers increased during this period. In addition, pyramids were built during the inundation when farmers were unproductive. Equally too, extreme famine forced mothers to abandon babies. Drought in Asia and Arabia affected Paunit and Central Africa, vastly affecting the annual inundation of the Nile, and this resulted in extreme famine in Egypt.

Nitocris was Pepi II's daughter. She followed him to the throne. With the internal decay and decline of the state, Nomarchs began to administer for their provinces and control of the central bureaucracy was lost. At this time the temples owned between 40 to 60 percent of all lands. By reducing taxation on them, revenue was greatly reduced. Famine caused many people to encroach upon Egyptian territory and this helped to gradually erode and destroy the Old Kingdom.

The Semites in ancient times were the Babylonians, Assyrians, Aramaeans, Canaanites and Phoenicians.

Holy Land Illustration 69. Transportation of Queen Hatshepsut's 350-ton obelisks down the Nile (Fifteenth Century B.C.).

Strabo wrote the "Egyptians settled Ethiopia and Colchis." Diodorus Siculus also noted, the Ethiopians claimed that "Egypt was a colony of theirs." Herodotus reports, the "Egyptians, Ethiopians and Colchians have thick lips, wooly hair and are burnt of skin," meaning black.

Webster's dictionary defines the word Negro as Black, Black person (Latin, Niger, black). A member of the dominant black race of Africa living chiefly in the Congo and Sudan region; a member of any of the Black races of Africa, as a Bantu, Hottentot, etc.; any person with some Negro ancestors.

October 27, 1975 Mbiti, p. 97

Things in life symbolize the invisible, which is really very significant. A people's worldview is the way they see the origin of their culture. Sky reveals infinite distance; nature represents harmony, order, rebirth; earth is the mother and a sign of permanence.

The worldview is patterned thought systems while culture is patterned behavior.

QUINTESSENTIAL BOOK
"THE HOLY LAND"

Contained in all this is foundation, frame of reference, definition of concept of self and concept of human nature. Ideology is an underlying principle, belief, and philosophy. Religion answers certain kinds of questions, relating to metaphysics, value, meaning.

The next time I will show you how I prepared for the midterm.

Michelliea Georges: Well, it's still early and since you have your laptop, why not do it in our room. Let's continue there. We've got the lemon squeezes and it's still early.
Regina Hendricks: Good idea. Let's go.

Holy Land Papyrus 22. It's an all ladies blue affair!

10. Hotel Room

George Washington: I prepared written definitions for all terms from the different authors, then I reviewed and reviewed.

Laye

The religious and metaphysical significance of the snake in Laye's family was that it represented the departed ancestors' links with his father. It was the guiding spirit of his people. It was the interconnected medium of the physical and spiritual

FREDERICK MONDERSON

worlds.

The relationship between Laye's father and the snake was of a highly religious nature. The snake, besides being the guiding spirit of the people, was his messenger from the spirit world. One that foretold him of events that were of significance to his people and also instructed him in the manner in which he should proceed in all situations that were important to his people.

It indicates the African's world view and belief in the phenomenon of ancestor communion and the way in which they see the departed ancestors keeping in touch with the physical world.

The act of melting and fashioning gold takes on a religious significance in African life and thought, not only in the sense that the blacksmith is the mediator between the spiritual and physical world but that gold is a substance that could not be made impure.

Ritual is a prerequisite to any act or function. It physically and psychologically expresses the motivations of the unconscious and brings out innate manifestations in its totality. This helps to express the inward feelings fully.

The Douga is a chant, somewhat, synonymous to the hymns of the Christians, for it gives more meaning to the understanding and is a sacred song.

The praise singer's function is twofold. He somewhat influences how a person would react to any task and psychologically influences his performance, in that he motivates or reaches into the inner man as he performs his function.

The philosophical implications involved are that he is a medium between the spiritual and physical worlds for he invokes the air of spirituality that must exist in any function of importance.

BARNETT

The traditional African worldview is seen as an interacting force between animate (God, man) and inanimate things. This is clearly defined in the relationship of the ancestors, the living and the unborn, all-interacting in one state of harmony. That is to say the relationship between the ultimate who passes on the moral and ethical values to the ancestors who passes this on to the oldest living being who in turn pass this interacting harmony to the young and they to the later born.

To Barrett the significance of traditional African religion for New World Blacks is for them to become familiar with the interacting harmony of the religious paraphernalia and use this as a means to overcome the disharmonizing influences

QUINTESSENTIAL BOOK "THE HOLY LAND"

that they are constantly being exposed to.

THE AKAN OF GHANA

The concept of god is innate. Nyame and his lesser deities (saints) exist for the Akan. Nyame is removed from contact with the world. Nyankopon, a lesser deity is present in the daily lives of men and can be called upon for succor and strength and Asase Yaa, the god of earth who gives succor to man.

Nyame possesses all the attributes of god. The deity's representatives on earth inhabit certain rivers and trees and priests are mediums between them and the people. Their places of habitation are also sacred.

THE YORUBA OF NIGERIA

Olodumare is the supreme deity. He can be covenanted with man at any place or time. His attributes are all absolute and he rules heaven and earth. He is surrounded by some four hundred Demi-gods. He is so removed that he does not concern himself with man's affairs and leaves this to his Demi gods called Orishas. Four Orishas of importance are Orunmila, god of wisdom and knowledge; Ogun, god of iron and steel; Shango, god of lightning and thunder; and Esu, the trickster god.

Holy Land Photo 70. Abydos Temple of Rameses II. Native Guide Showgi Abd Rady, "The Black," points to Rameses before a Goddess (left); and (right) the Cartouche of Rameses, *Usr-Maat-Ra, Seten en Ra*.

THE FON OF DAHOMEY

Nana Buluku is the highest god, perhaps equivalent to the one god. He is somewhat removed and delegates Mawa and Lisa to represent him. Mawa is male and represents the moon and symbolizes coolness, wisdom and mystery and is like the aged. Lisa represents the sun, symbol of energy. Together they represent the laws of opposites functioning in equilibrium. The interaction of Mawa and Lisa is like a force or power and symbolizes the serpent.

MBITI

The five ontological categories are:

Muntu – man

Kintu – thing

Hantu – place or time

Kuntu – modality

Ntu – universal force. The four are parts of the fifth interacting.

Time is two-dimensional. It has a long past, a present and no future (Sasa, Zamani).

The relationship between the Sasa and Zamani are that they interlock.

Sasa – represents two to six months from now down to yesterday.
Zamani – is an hour or two ago back into the remote past. The Sasa represent potential time, that is, time between yesterday and up to six months from now. The Zamani represents a few hours ago way back into the remote past.

The term phenomenal calendars represent period between two significant events, for example, from conception to birth of a baby.

Spiritual implications of forgetting the ancestors are very bad, for the ancestors who are supposed to protect the group, become annoyed when forgotten and can bring harm to all.

Day 7. ESNEH, EDFU AND KOM OMBO

QUINTESSENTIAL BOOK "THE HOLY LAND"

1. Wake Up

Esperanza Rodriguez: Good Morning, Mi Amor. Your schedule for today involves a bus ride through Esneh, Edfu and Kom Ombo on way to Aswan.

I have copied and handed today's selection to the group.

Dr. Fred Monderson: Thank you, my dear.

Holy Land Photo 71. Valley of the Nobles. Tomb of Sennufer. Cat Goddess vanquishes the Serpent at the Persea Tree.

"The Dance, Music, and Musical Instruments"
By
Frederick Monderson

Music and dance are cultural and aesthetic creative expressions that fundamentally express the greatest intellectual and spiritual creativity of the African mind. While it's a given that music was created in Africa it is also the best example of African

FREDERICK MONDERSON

high culture or civilization. It's generally believed that in Africa music and dance enables African spirituality to be in contact with the universe. All the great African musicians, particularly African-Americans, Dizzy Gillespie, Max Roach, Charlie Byrd Parker, Hassan Roland Kirk, Miles Davis, all not simply loved and respected music but indicated musical expressions enhanced their spirituality. Many also allowed that high state of consciousness to awaken and express their discontent with social, economic and political conditions in their homeland. As such they paid a price! Perhaps we should honor those who sacrificed to tell the truth with their music!

The dance, accompanied by some form of music, is one of the oldest, aesthetic expressions in Africa. Gods, kings, nobles, and just plain folks enjoyed the dance. Whether for social relaxation, banquet festivities, in religious functions, on military expeditions, an accompaniment to working or simply when boating down the Nile River, music was always pleasing to the soul, and a wonderful form of enjoyment. When we consider the enormous strides humanity has made in musical expression and its assistance in developing language and other social conventions, the significance of music becomes even more apparent. Budge I (Osiris: 243) quoting Sir H. H. Johnston in *The Uganda Protectorate II*, mentions five dances performed in Black Africa. These were: "(1) The dance to celebrate the birth of twins; it is danced by men and women, and the gestures are obscene; (2) the death dance, which is danced by both sexes; (3) the dance of the sexual initiation ceremony, which is danced by both men and women; (4) the wedding dance in which only women join; (5) the dance which takes place in seasons of drought to propitiate the good spirit and bring down rain."

It is not certain if these specific dances were done in Kemet/Egypt. However, Budge II (Osiris: 253) further commented that: "the chief African peoples regard ceremonial dancing before a god as an act of worship .... 'the dance of the god,' the 'god' being presumably, Osiris, and we are justified in assuming that this 'god' had his special dance, which was not generally known in Egypt." This suggests an "other" African source. In Kemet, the "black land," it appears that the king danced on religious and ceremonial occasions and probably did at any number of palace banquets to celebrate marriage, accessions, victories in war or at any of the numerous festivals including the Heb-Sed, and Opet, Feast of the Valley, New Year, etc., celebrated throughout the united lands. More so, it is again shown by Budge I (Osiris: 233), "Egyptian bas-reliefs of all periods contain many illustrations of kings dancing before Osiris and other gods."

The earliest representation of such a ritual as the king dancing before a god that we know of involved Semti (Hesepti) of the First Dynasty so depicted on an ebony tablet in the British Museum. Displayed in the Third Egyptian Room in table case L, No. 123, this plaque also records several events in the reign of this king. Here Budge (1885/1972) recounts, minimally clothed: "The king is seen wearing the crowns of the north and south and in his right hand he holds his whip and in his

QUINTESSENTIAL BOOK
"THE HOLY LAND"

left a paddle." Elsewhere, Budge I (Osiris: 33) again describes other features of the illustration of Semti. There he notes: "on each side of him are three signs, which represent objects that were associated with dancing. The king, I believe, is dancing, though his back is turned to the god, and this representation appears to be the prototype of all the scenes, down to the Ptolemaic Period, in which the king dances before his god."

Indeed this notion of dancing was a ritual enjoyed throughout dynastic rule. On the great Mace-head of King Narmer, uniter of Upper and Lower Kemet/Egypt, three men are seen dancing. Elsewhere, on a limestone relief from the Zoser temple complex at Sakkara, the king, according to Woldering (1963: 78) is, "... shown performing a ritual dance. Wearing the crown of Upper Egypt/Kemet and carrying a ceremonial whisk, he is shown in the ritual dance, as part of the festivities connected with the jubilee of his accession to the throne. In another representation from this early period the king is shown involved in an agricultural pursuit, where the dance is ritually performed to ensure prosperity in the endeavor."

Holy Land Photo 72. Valley of the Nobles. Tomb of Sennufer. Sennufer sailing in the Solar Barque with Isis (right), Thoth, Ra and another God.

The next depiction of royal involvement with the dance occurs in the Fourth Dynasty, dating to the reign of King Assa. Budge I (Osiris: 232-233) mentions a high official called Ba-ur-tet who "... brought from Punt a tenk (Twa/Pygmy), who knew how to dance 'the dance of the god'... and was said to come from the land of the spirits."

FREDERICK MONDERSON

Pepi I ruled as king in the VIth Dynasty. In a text of his pyramid, Budge I (Osiris: 232-233) distinctly mentions the "Pygmy dancers of the …. " It reads: "Come northward to the court immediately; thou shalt bring this dwarf with thee, which thou bringest living, prosperous and healthy from the land of the spirits, for the dances of the god, to rejoice and (gladden) the heart of the king of Upper and Lower Egypt, Neferkere, who lives forever. When he goes down with thee into the vessel, appoint excellent people, who shall be beside him on each side of the vessel; take care lest he fall into the water. When (he) sleeps at night appoint excellent people, who shall sleep beside him in his tent; inspect ten times a night. My majesty desires to see this dwarf more than the gifts of Sinai and of Punt …."

Breasted (1923: 140) says the boy king promised "Harkhuf a greater reward than king Isesi had given to his 'treasurer of the God,' Burded, when he brought home a dwarf from Punt." On another abstract, Budge I (1904: 233) provides a clear indication of the sacredness and high regard for these dancers of the Twa people that a king of Kemet: "considered it an honor to him in the other world, if he could dance like a pygmy before Osiris, and proves clearly that the object of the dance was to comfort, cheer and strengthen the deity whose special dance he danced."

In *Osiris and the Egyptian Resurrection*, Budge I (234-235) provides an enlightening description recorded in *Albert Nyanza* by Sir Samuel Baker, who made a visit to Katchiba, King of Obbo. The quotation is a bit lengthy, but it characterizes the intensity, drama and significance of the dance.

"The king determined upon a grand dance, and soon the nogras (drums) were beaten, pipes and flutes were soon heard gathering from all quarters, horns brayed, and men and women formed a circle. Each man held in his left hand a small cup-shaped drum, formed of hollowed wood, one end only being perforated, and this was covered with the skin of the elephant's ear. The dance commenced by all singing remarkably well a wild but agreeable tune in chorus, the big drum directing the time, and all the little drums striking at certain periods, with such admirable precision, that the effect was that of a single instrument. The dancing was most vigorous ... the figures varying continuously, and ending with a 'grand gallop' in double circles at a tremendous pace, the inner ring revolving in a contrary direction to the outer; the effect of this was excellent. Although the men wear a skin slung across their shoulders and loins, the women are almost naked, and instead of wearing the leather apron and tail of the Latukas, they are contented with a slight fringe of leather shreds, about four inches long by two broad, suspended from a belt. The unmarried girls are entirely naked, or wear three or four strings of small white beads, about three inches in length, as a covering. The old ladies wear a string round the waist, in which is struck a bunch of green leaves, the stalk uppermost. Here we have a complete parallel with King Pepi, whose earnest desire was to dance before the god."

QUINTESSENTIAL BOOK
"THE HOLY LAND"

Holy Land Illustration 70. The obelisks of Queen Hatshepsut (right) and that of her father Thutmose I (left) at Karnak.

Religion was central to life in ancient Kemet/Egypt as well as among other African peoples. This important parallel with the peoples south of Egypt finds support in the *Papyrus of Hunefer*, a nobleman of the XIXth Dynasty, which states inter alia, regarding 'Origin of the Egyptians,' that "We came from the foothills of the

FREDERICK MONDERSON

Mountains of the Moon where the God Hapi dwells."

King Sesostris I reigned in the XIIth Dynasty. On the detail of a limestone pillar, the king is shown, Woldering (1963: 120) wrote, "performing a ritual dance before the god Min at Coptos, and also a relief on a pillar depicting the god Ptah embracing the king."

Another example of the king dancing before a divinity comes from the New Kingdom. Here, in *Dwellers on the Nile* (1972: 132) Budge explained Thutmose III of the XVIIIth Dynasty is shown "... wearing the Khnum headdress, with ankh and *waz* scepter in right hand and offers a bird while dancing before the goddess Hathor."

At a much later time, the god Bes is shown dancing on a column in the small Hathor chapel at the Temple of Isis. Throughout, these examples show the significance of the dance to the king and the gods. That meant as Budge (1972: 31) believed "... the person who knew how to dance the dance of the gods was an honored and respected person." It is interesting, the "God's land," "Land of the Spirits" and those who inhabit, particularly "Those who knew the dance of the Gods" were so special and important in the scheme of things.

Art in the form of sculpture, architecture and pictorial decoration, particularly in tombs, depict musicians, singers and dancers that paint a lively picture of daily life in ancient Kemet with bustling preparations for the afterlife.

In the Mastaba of Ptahhotep, who was a high official of a king of the Fifth Dynasty, is an excellent collection of wall decorations. This form of sepulcher and later tombs became a prototypal place where scenes of dancing, musical scenes, particularly at banquets, with musicians and their instruments were represented and have come down to us.

Polyglot's *Egypt Travel Guide* (1965: 32) describes the Mastaba of Ptahhotep, where: "Nearly all the walls, corridors, chambers, and rooms are decorated with reliefs, which illustrate Ptahhotep life - with his servants, dogs and monkeys, with singers, harpists and dwarfs; Ptahhotep sacrificing or taking a meal, on a tour of inspection of the provinces, busy with state affairs."

The creation and enjoyment of music as aesthetics, was an early part of the consciousness of Nile Valley man who ushered in civilization. Music as a cultural mode of expression is traceable from the mythical traditions and the people of ancient Kemet believed their God Asar/Osiris was a patron of music. Further, they believed, this deity had his scribe the God Tehuti (Thoth) invent music and as well as some other instruments. Thoth is also credited with inventing writing, arithmetic, sculpture and a system of astronomy. Among the 42 "priestly books"

QUINTESSENTIAL BOOK "THE HOLY LAND"

attributed to Thoth, there were two books of the singer. Anthropologically speaking, the God Bes represented music, dancing and food. Among his other attributes during Roman times was as god of wine (Bacchus, thus bacchanal) and protector of women at childbirth. Though dating to remote antiquity among the gods, Bes is seen preserved playing a tambourine in a decoration of the small temple of Hathor at the Temple of Isis. The statue of him in the Court of Dendera, Dr. ben-Jochannan tells, is shown wearing a necklace whose "beads" really consists of 42 penises. Today at Aswan, in southern Kemet/Egypt traditional Nubians dance, sing and play instruments similar to those of antiquity. Some aspects of ancient Kemet dance forms are thus preserved and can be observed on any properly orchestrated trip to Egypt.

Holy Land Ceramic Art 7. Still another version of the Khepre beetle, doing the same work, this time in a different ceramic color scheme.

During pharaonic times music was played at annual festivals and parties or banquets. In Ancient Egyptian society, there were titles such as 'the superintendent of the singing,' 'superintendents of the royal singing,' and 'superintendent of the singers of Pharaoh,' and 'superintendent of the singers of all the gods.' Temples and palaces had orchestras that played vocal and instrumental music. Instrumental music was played at funerals and this soothed the saddened condition of the mourners. Soldiers used drums along with flag signals in wars. Boatmen sang and played varied instruments in their sometimes serene and sometimes exhilarating voyages up and down the Nile. Baikie IX (1917: 34) affirmed: "The singers seem at all periods to have marked the rhythm by clapping the hands - in fact, this simple method of marking time is so inseparable in the Egyptian mind from the idea of music that the word 'to song' is written in all periods by the hieroglyph of a hand. Blind performers were not unknown - a representation from tell el-Amarna show a blind harpist accompanying several blind choristers who mark the rhythm with the clapping of hands." The tomb of Rameses III is called the "Tomb of the Harpists" because two such individuals are shown playing harps, and one or both are blind.

Dance, instruments and musical praxis in a dynamic and enduring civilization as Kemet, raised the fine art of manufacturing the delicate and balanced musical instruments to the level of an "industry." Therefore, it can be argued that dance, music and instruments were among early Nile Valley cultural gifts as part of universal aesthetics.

This essay examines a variety of themes and artifactual survivals in dance, music and musical instruments from ancient Kemet.

Beethoven, the musical genius, it was argued, had "Moorish" blood implying he was Negro, African or had what we would call African-American features. Authorities differ on the "racial Origin" of this musical great. Writing in *Sex and Race* Vol. III, J.A. Rogers (1944: 306) supplies *Notes on Beethoven* showing "Beethoven was German and because his portraits are usually shown with a white tone and abundant hair nearly every one thinks of him as white." Rogers' beliefs on Beethoven's color are based on commentary supplied by the musical genius' biographers that are included here as follows. Fanny Giannatasio del Rio says "mulatto;" May Byron "swarthy;" Alexander Wheelock Thayer "negroid;" Frederick Hertz "negroid;" Brunold Springer "negroid;" Brunold Springer "negro;" Emil Ludwig "dark." Well, you go figure!

On Beethoven's writing-table Naumann (1882: 36) mentions a framed copy of an inscription from the Temple of Sais, which ran thus: "I am all that is, that was and that will be; no mortal has lifted my veil." It's believed that the veil belonged to Auset/Isis, the goddess to whom Kemet man and woman also attributed the origin of music.

Naumann (1882: 34) further tells that on an island of the Upper Nile, the German Egyptologist Brugsch found the following inscription supposed to date from the fifteenth dynasty. "Epra-He, the great, Prince of Kusch, and singer to his Lord Amon." These examples are only added to support the indication of the proximity

QUINTESSENTIAL BOOK "THE HOLY LAND"

of Egyptian/Kemet deities to music in early Northeast Africa and elsewhere in Africa.

The philosopher Plato is quoted as saying (Gnomon, 1882: 37) of the Egyptians/people of ancient Kemet: "In their possession are songs having the power to exalt and enable mankind, and these could only emanate from gods or god-like men." This early accolade of early African cultural and aesthetic creativity is indeed noble.

A number of classical authors have commented on Kemet/Egyptian dance, music and musical instruments. The first such commentator was Herodotus of Halicarnassus who traveled the Nile around 450 B.C. and wrote *Euterpe*, Book II of his *Histories*. This History of Egypt provides some interesting eyewitness accounts of Nile Valley culture that is a constant source of debate among scholars of early civilization. Baikie (1917: 33) says: "Herodotus (ii. 79) speaks of his surprise at finding that the song called Maneros by the Egyptians, a dirge said to have been named after the son of the first king of Egypt, was similar to the Cyprian dirge Linor or Alinios."

In *The History of Music*, Chappell (1874: 50-51) makes an interesting observation regarding early African origin of the musical scale and how it had close proximity to the Greek "origin" of musical systems. The author's statement is quoted in its entirety below. He states, "Nichomachus, quoting Pythagoras and Plato, tell us that the Egyptians ascribed twenty-eight sounds to the universe, calling it 'twenty-eight soundings.' So the Egyptians must have had twenty-eight sounds, i.e., twenty-eight notes in their scale. That is the precise total number of Greek notes, in their greater and lesser perfect systems combined, and including all their scales - Diatonic, Chromatic, and Enharmonic, neither in Egypt or in Greece was there an actual limit to twenty-eight sounds, because all scales were transposable, but only twenty-eight notes could be defined starting from any given pitch. Euclid, Nichomachus, Aristides, Quintilianus, and others enumerate the Greek scales and their notes, and all authors are agreed as to the number being precisely twenty-eight. This most remarkable coincidence between Egypt and Greece seems nevertheless to have escaped the observation of historians of music. If it stood alone it would almost suffice to prove the origin of Greek music. The number is too peculiar to have arrived at by accident, within a compass of only two octaves."

FREDERICK MONDERSON

Holy Land Photo 73. Valley of the Nobles. Tomb of Sennufer. Sennufer before the great bird, the Horus falcon.

Diodorus Siculus flourished around 60 B.C. and wrote on Egyptian/Kemet music. Baikie (1917: 33) made the following commentary. He tells about "... ancient Egyptian music from the writings of the classical authors. They confine themselves to general observations, none of which carry us very far, and some of which are demonstrably inaccurate." Diodorus (I. 80), indeed, is responsible for an observation on the subject, which led, for a time. "It is unfortunately impossible to derive much information with regard to the mistaken idea that the Egyptians were an unmusical race. 'It was not customary,' he says, 'for the Egyptians to practice music, because they considered it effeminate and undesirable.' On what grounds his statement is based it would be difficult to say, and he himself admits that the Greek poets and musicians visited Egypt in order to improve their art."

Another avid commentator on Kemet, he is credited with preserving the view that the Ethiopians founded Egypt as a colony. Strabo, who lived during the time of Christ also, commented on Egyptian music. According to Baikie IX (1917: 33) Strabo has indicated: "Plato ascribes a very high antiquity and a very noble character to the sacred music of the Egyptians, whose rules concerning it were, according to him, most rigid, only certain things being allowed by Government. This is confirmed by Strabo (XVII, 1), who says: 'the children of the Egyptians were taught letters, the songs appointed by law, and a certain kind of music, established by government, to the exclusion of every other;' and, further, that vocal and instrumental music was usually admitted in the worship of the gods, especially at the commencement of the services, except in the temple of Osiris, where neither singers nor players on the flute or the lyre were allowed to perform."

QUINTESSENTIAL BOOK "THE HOLY LAND"

Two other classical writers who commented on Egyptian music were Dion Cassius and Clemens Alexandrinus who both lived around 200 A.D.

While clapping of the hands may have been the first employment of musical instruments, the tambourine is probably the first instrument and the earliest form of the drum. There were two types of tambourines, a square or sometimes oblong and a round one. Women most usually played this instrument, found in temples and used at funerals and other ceremonies. A round tambourine is shown being played by the god Bes in the chapel of Hathor at the Temple of Isis/Auset, formerly on Philae but now on Aguilkiya (Agilka) Island.

The drum proper was both long and short types. There were three kinds of drums. The first was a small hand-drum, 2 or 3 feet long, covered with parchment at both ends, and braced by cords.

The second type of drum was 1½ ft. high and 2 ft. broad. There was a double drum variation of this one that's found as part of a decoration of Horemheb, XIXth Dynasty. The large drums were beaten with sticks. Some sticks were padded. A third type of drum is identical to the Darabukker, a closed vessel with parchment over the mouth that the modern Egyptian plays.

The sistrum was a form of rattle. Its *Medu Netcher*/hieroglyphics name is *seshesh*. Mainly employed at religious ceremonies, it was principally used by females to drive away evil spirits. Naumann (1882: 52) held that the people of Kemet/Egypt "attributed to the sistrum the power over evil spirits and believed at its sound the evil Typhon fled."

FREDERICK MONDERSON

Holy Land Photo 74. Valley of the Nobles. Tomb of Sennufer. Thoth wearing the "Khnemu Crown," Ra-Horakhty and other Gods sail in the Solar Barque with "Eyes of Horus" at fore and aft.

In *Wisdom of the Egyptians* Petrie (1940: 57) mentions the sistrum as being two distinct objects. "There is the emblem of Hat-Hor, with a face bearing horns, and a building placed over it, thus reading Hat-Her; and there is also a rattle placed over a head of Hathor and lotus flower. The first is seen carried by Hathor, the queen as priestess of Amenhotep III at Thebes and in the Amarna period. Rameses II is shown carrying a sistrum while adoring Hathor. These are not instruments of sound but purely emblematic and appear in religious scenes."

Petrie (1940: 57) notes the sounding Sistrum first appears at Beni Hasan, in the XIIth Dynasty where it is borne by a servant and in this instance has no religious significance. Still, by the time of the XVIIIth to XXth Dynasties there were five variations of this musical instrument. Petrie further shows (1940: 57) they were carried by a servant to the Vizier Rekh-ma-ra, held by Amarna princesses, by all daughters of Rameses II at Sabua, Derr, and Abu Simbel, and Queen Nefertari at the Ramesseum. Significant to the expropriation and export of African art and cultural motifs, Petrie (1940: 58) adds more: "Actual sistra of bronze are in the British Museum, Berlin, and at University College, with bust of Horus on the top, of Roman age. Also at U.C. is the blue glazed head of a sistrum of Amenhotep II and late fragments of Apries, Aahmes, and Nekhtnebef."

Naumann (1882) says the sistrum: " ... consisted of a frame of bronze or brass, crossed with three or four metal bars and was furnished with an ornamented handle; at the end of these bars were moveable pieces of metal for the purpose of

QUINTESSENTIAL BOOK
"THE HOLY LAND"

producing a jingling noise when the instrument was struck with a metal clapper."

Trumpets, generally made of wood, were used for civil and military purposes. There were two types. There was a long conical type with an open end. Then there was a shorter form.

The flute is one of the few instruments that have survived from the Old Kingdom. In the earliest times they were originally made of bone and rested on the ground. The number of finger holes numbered six or seven.

Pipes were of two varieties, the single and double type. The single pipe was generally made of reed with four-finger holes. Sometimes they had three, five or more holes. Both single and double pipes were played with a vibrating reed held within the mouth. The mouthpiece was made of ivory.

The lute had a long straight stem. This instrument varied in shape and the number of strings. Petrie (1940: 59) explained the lute looked similar to the Nefer sign and has supplied three facts to prove the separate nature of the figures.

(1) The marks on the body of the Nefer are never found on a lute, and the stem of the lute crossing the body is never seen on a Nefer.

(2) The lute has pegs only on one side; the Nefer has projections on both sides.

(3) The Nefer was figured as early as the Ist dynasty, on the black cylinders; the lute does not appear till the XVIIIth dynasty. The real source of the Nefer sign, meaning "good," is echoed in the tradition in Horapollo that states, "a man's heart hung from the windpipe means the mouth of a good man."

FREDERICK MONDERSON

Holy Land Photo 75. Valley of the Nobles. Tomb of Sennufer. Sennufer stands before the Gods and the enormous snake that spans "the chasm."

Dancers also played the lute. Engel (1864) noticed one in the Berlin Museum that appears to have 13 strings instead of 10. He noted a similar but smaller one was in the Leiden Museum.

The sancho had a bowl body and a curved neck. It is somewhere between the lute and harp. Naumann (1882) writes the Temple of Dakkeh contains "… a picture representing the fire-god Ptah playing a harp."

The harp is a musical instrument indigenous to the Nile Valley. Representations show different sizes and shapes with varied numbers of strings. While all had strings, only some had tuning pegs. Some harps had stands and could be played standing, sitting or kneeling. The harp had a long snout, slightly curved beam with various strings. It sometimes expanded at the waist. Some harps had double strings. Interestingly, Petrie (1940: 61) adds: "The representations often show only half of the strings, which were in double row; and of 63 harps there are 8 in which there are many more sets than strings, often double the number, and there are two instances of the two sets of strings crossing each other, proving the double set. Thus about one in six was double-strung. There is no evidence of three rows of strings, as in some Welsh harps."

In the Twelfth Dynasty, according to Naumann (1882: 50), the "… base of the harp increased in size and it served as a large resonance body; and in the New Empire the bowl form and bent outline of the harp disappeared entirely and was

QUINTESSENTIAL BOOK "THE HOLY LAND"

succeeded by the triangular shape."

The harp became a favored royal instrument during the Ramesside years. Baikie IX (1917: 34) mentions this in his writing in that: "... the greatest elaboration of the harp is reached in the time of dynasties XIX and XX. The representations of priests playing the harp in the tomb of Ramessu III show instruments which are not only distinguished by the number of their strings, but are also very elaborately decorated, the framework being carved and inlaid with gold, ivory, tortoise-shell, and mother-of-pearl, and ornamented with various figures." Wherein, Gnomon (1882: 50-51) could add regarding expansion of its strings employing more elaborate decoration. "During the period of its greatest perfection it had thirteen, eighteen, twenty-one, and even twenty-six strings, and was most probably played only by priests and kings, which may in some degree account for its elaborate ornamentation. The framework was carved in the richest and most elegant manner inlaid with gold, ivory, tortoise-shell, and mother of pearl; and is further ornamented with mythical figurines, or with the heads of gods, goddesses, sphinxes, and animals. It was sometimes decorated with colors, the edges covered with Morocco velvet, imparting to it a bright and cheerful appearance."

The *Medu Netcher*/hieroglyphs name of this instrument was *bunion beni*. The harpist was described as *Seb an ben* "scraper of the horn."

The trigonon is a triangular form of the harp that looks more like a lyre. It had a wooden frame that was sometimes covered with leather. As many as 20 strings could be mounted on this instrument. "It had no tuning pegs," Engel (1864) wrote, "but the strings were affixed to the upper part of the frame and were tuned by being wound round a rod which was inserted into the lower part of the frame."

The lyre first appears in the XIIth Dynasty and had sometimes six, seven or eight strings. The tamboura is a lute like a modern guitar. The gong was made of metal and designed to give a gong sound to exit.

Crotola are clappers or castanets mentioned by Naumann (1882: 38) who describes a scene on the walls of a catacomb dating from the time of the seventeenth dynasty. Here, he wrote: "... the departed master and his consort are represented as listening to the performance of female singers accompanied by two harps and one flute, while a little girl is beating time with the well-known Egyptian wooden clappers." Two pairs of Egyptian Cymbals are on display in the British Museum.

FREDERICK MONDERSON

Holy Land Illustration 71. Sepulchral stele of Ankh-ren, an overseer of the department of the Treasury of the XIIth Dynasty (left); and Stele set up by Sehetep-ab to the memory of his father Khensu-user and his mother Nekhta-ankh of the XIth or XIIth Dynasty and now resides in the British Museum.

Bells have for long been a part of religious and civil ceremonies. Bells are on display in the British Museum. It can be conjectured that bells played a musical part in Egyptian/Kemetic architecture. When pharaonic builders employed the bell motif capitals instead of papyrus, lily or lotus, and even Hathor headed types, they probably intended this instrument to resonate its sacred vibes on sacred and civil occasions.

It could be added here, this writer found at the Bodlian Library, Oxford University, a questionnaire with 105 questions. Apparently, particularly during the 19th Century, every English traveler abroad was given one of these questionnaires. The intent was to gather every bit of information about the music of the peoples of their destination. It stands to reason there were other similar questionnaires designed to gather information in every other cultural walk of like so as to enhance the knowledge base of the British Museum.

QUINTESSENTIAL BOOK "THE HOLY LAND"

Holy Land Photo 76. Valley of the Nobles. Tomb of Rekhmire. Busy as a beehive, craftsmen and workmen doing the jobs of their professions.

REFERENCES

Baikie, James. "Egyptian Music." *Hastings Encyclopedia of Religion and Ethics.* Vol. IX (1917: 33-36).
Breasted, James H. *A History of Egypt.* New York: Charles Scribner's Sons, (1905) 1923.
Budge, E. A. Wallis. *Dwellers on the Nile.* New York: Benjamin Bloom, Inc., Publishers, (1885) 1972.
_____. *Osiris and the Egyptian Resurrection.* 2 Vol. New York: Dover Publications, (1911) 1973.
Chappell. *The History of Music.* 1874.
Davidson, Basil. *African Civilization Revisited.* Trenton, New Jersey: Africa World Press, 1991.
Engel. *History of Music.* 1864.
Naumann. *History of Music* 2 vol. 1882-1882.
Petrie, W. M. Flinders. *The Wisdom of the Egyptians.* London: Methuen and Co., 1940.
Rogers, J.A. *Sex and Race.* 3 Vols. New York: Helga Rogers, 1944.
Woldering, Irmgard. *The Art of Egypt: The Time of the Pharaohs.* New York: Greystone Press, (1962) 1963.

FREDERICK MONDERSON

THE PRIESTHOOD
By
Frederick Monderson

In ancient Kemet, now Egypt, along the banks of the Nile River, one of the earliest professional organizations came into being. This body, the Priesthood, combined a number of functions - religious, political, scientific, educational, administrative, economic, artistic - and came to exercise tremendous power for the duration of dynastic rule. In times of unity and division, prosperity and stagnation, this organization transmitted the ancient Egyptian, African, Nile Valley culture - synthesizing, preserving and creating ideas and civil and politico-religious structures for the propagation of the gods. Out of the religiosity of these ancient Africans, order in society emerged and helped to bequeath mankind a tremendous legacy of achievement in social civility, art, construction, government, and science.

The land of Kemet is very dry, mysterious, cultural, and full of history. It is artistic, philosophical, spiritual and religious. Boasting the earliest sense of theological consciousness, these ancient Africans created a religious system and attendant intellectual, mortuary, spiritual and festive dynamics that helped to enshrine practices to influence peoples and cultures, far and wide, then and even now. Owing to the significance of religion in the theocratic state, a bureaucracy very early grew up around kingly and divine worship at their principal centers of theology in Memphis, Heliopolis, Thebes, Hermopolis, Abydos, and in the Mortuary cults at Giza, Sakkara, Abu Sir, etc. This involvement earned these practitioners the professional designation of Priesthood. So much so, Kamil (1984: 36) could write: "... the fabric of ancient Egyptian mythological tradition, which survived in embellished or mutilated form for thousands of years, was woven and rewoven, time and again, to justify new conditions to explain political trends; it was sometimes even entangled to promote a cause."

The Priesthood was thus a significant institution from the earliest times. During the archaic first and second dynasties, institutions of religion were established and essentially the major precepts of justice, honor, work, and art were practiced and prevailed until very late in Kemetic history.

By the beginning of the Old Kingdom, with the king considered a god and theocracy the form of government, this "elaborate officialdom bureaucracy" helped fuse civil and ecclesiastical offices in the Pharaoh and his high officials. Throughout this period of great intellectual growth, artistic innovation, enshrined religious beliefs and practices, remarkable accomplishments were thus achieved in architecture, astronomy, engineering, and medicine.

QUINTESSENTIAL BOOK
"THE HOLY LAND"

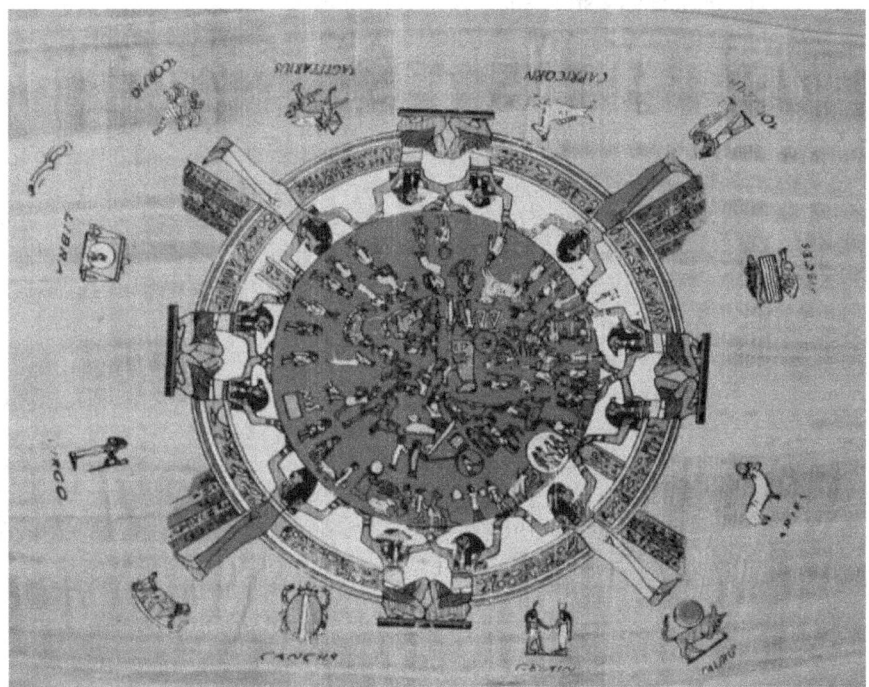

Holy Land Papyrus 23. The Egyptian Horoscope showing all signs of the Zodiac.

Growth in the wealth and political power of the nobles, led them to rival the monarch in elaborate funerary preparations to reflect their newly acquired social status. Later, during the New Kingdom, according to Wilson (1959: 171) regarding the principal administrators of the state: "The highest officials of the land under the Pharaoh were the High Priest of Amon at Karnak, the Vizier for Upper Egypt, the Vizier for Lower Egypt, and the 'King's Son of Kush' or Viceroy of Ethiopia. The last named position included three responsibilities; the delegated rule of the African Empire; the responsibility for gold mines of Nubia; and the command of the army in Africa, pharaoh having the responsible leadership for pushing the Empire in Asia. This viceroyship was often a training ground for the Crown Prince."

Within the dynamics of constructive growth under strong leadership, the state went to great lengths to propagate cultural, architectural, and artistic innovations, and the Priesthood was generally avant-garde in this effort. Still, while their earliest beginnings may be shrouded in the mysteries of time; it is safe to argue, the accepted date of invention of the calendar at 4241 B.C. This scientific innovation then places the Priesthood there, and speculation as to how many thousands of years earlier, may be still valid.

Their growing positions of power notwithstanding, the Pharaoh as the principal religiant in the land, assigned the religious organization responsibility for worshipping and ritualizing the gods and himself as a son of god on earth. In this role, the Priesthood became a powerful body and the king endowed them with lands, free from taxation. As a result, they became self reliant and in symbiotic harmony as a community were able to perpetuate the religious, spiritual and political symbolism the king represented, to bring order, justice and harmony to the state.

Two of the earliest centers of religious and cultural rivalry were Memphis and Heliopolis. Near the borderline between the two lands we now have evidence of political rivalry. Heliopolis was situated on the eastern bank of the Nile about 9 miles west of Cairo and Memphis on the western bank some 16 miles further south. Such proximity enabled two theologies, the Heliopolitan Ennead and the Memphite Doctrine, to share many similarities.

Compare these with two other centers of Abydos, and the earliest dates for mention of Karnak, which may very well extend to the earliest period, though presently the latter holds remains from the Middle Kingdom.

Very early, priests in ancient Kemet were concerned about education and became "teachers and exponents of religious and moral duty." Significantly, and additionally, as a powerfully organized body, they practiced hereditary succession creating their own systems of loyalty and practice. In this, the eldest son succeeded his father. That being the case, Wilson (1959: 171) writes: "The retention of position within a few trusted families and the interlocking of the highest offices may be illustrated with two or three examples, albeit "Late." Hatshepsut's Vizier for Upper Egypt, Hapu-Seneb, had been preceded in that office by his grandfather; but Hapu-Seneb was also High Priest of Amon, as his great grandfather in that office. A certain Thutmose held the Vizierate for Lower Egypt, and his son Ptah-mose became High Priest of Ptah at Memphis." Nevertheless, writes Sauernon (1962: 224) though lacking the powerful social or family connections a man could equally-well become a priest by co-option, without priestly forebears, either by buying his office or by royal favor. In this latter the King was able to keep a check on the sometimes-alarming power of the Priesthood. This "power of the priesthood" is recognized in Wilson (1959: 272) where the effective grip of the High Priest of Amon upon the civil affairs and finances of the state, may be shown by the distribution of offices within one

QUINTESSENTIAL BOOK
"THE HOLY LAND"

family. "Ramses-Nakht was the High Priest of Amon under Ramses IV. His father Meri-Barset had been Chief Tax-Master and Ramses-Nakht's sons were to hold two of the most potent offices in the land: Nes-Amon and Amen-hotep successively as High Priest of Amon, and User-Maat-Re-Nakht as Chief Tax-Master and Manager of Pharaoh's Lands. Thus the priesthood of Amon could manage the finances of the state for its own benefit and withhold resources from the pharaoh as it desired."

Wilson (1959: 273) has tried to illustrate the power of this priestly head in that Rameses-Nakht, while not commander of the army, had acquired tremendous authority, resources and power concentrated in Upper Egypt making him someone to reckon with.

"His son Amen-hotep, who held the High Priesthood of Amon from Rameses IV to Rameses XI, dared to sweep aside part of the pretense and violate one of the oldest canons of Egyptian art. The pharaoh had always been depicted in colossal size in proportion to all other Egyptians, who were only human and not divine as he was. In a scene in the Temple of Amon at Karnak, we see Ramses IX recognizing the services of the High Priest Amen-hotep with decorations. Pharaoh is shown in his customary heroic size in proportion to the two bustling little officials who carry out his instructions, but Amen-hotep had the arrogance to have his figure carved in the same scale as the king. Furthermore, the composition makes him the focus of attention instead of pharaoh. Nothing could illustrate more clearly that reality which the texts piously ignored: that the king was only an instrument of a ruling oligarchy."

Thus we see, the Priesthood dramatically involved in the crucial arteries of the society, viz., politics, economics, art, transmitting from generation to generation, the skills and ideas necessary to serve the society, do justice, do Ma'at, and learn in the process. This represented social stability from a moral responsibility of their religiosity.

The weather and climate has not changed significantly since ancient times. Dryness, humidity, ennui from the heat of the sun caused great concern about purification of the body, echoing an old admonition "cleanliness is next to godliness." The priests shaved their heads. They also shaved the entire body every third day. Strict rules of purity also dictated that priests be circumcised and abstain from sexual contact during time of service in the temples. They should also observe taboos of local gods. Sauernon (1962: 224) wrote, "dress only in fine linen, wearing no wool nor leather which had been taken from a living animal."

Therefore, they wore linen clothing and papyrus shoes. Gold and silver shoes

FREDERICK MONDERSON

were used in religious ceremonies. Each priest had at least six pairs of papyrus and at least one pair of gold or silver shoes. They took baths in cold water twice per day and twice per night. Most priests abstained or did not use wine and animal foods. However, some did drink wine while the onion and pig were prohibited in their diets.

In the prehistoric period origins are difficult to trace. Still, in *Egyptian Religion*, Flinders Petrie has argued: "the office of the priest was more often developed from civil than from religious functions." As such, the emergence and function of the priestly bureaucracy, representing millennia of cultural continuity, is reflected in the names or titles they bore. In prehistoric times they were the "Servant of the Crown." Later, they became professionals and blended priestly and civil functions as "Great One of Medicine," "Chief, Commander of Workmen," and "Inundation Man." In Defense, they were "Splendid," "General," "Warrior," and "Guardian who leads the *Mesniu* Troops of Horus." In religion, they were "Tongue of the God," "Lord of True Speech," "Opener of the Gates of Management," "Hider of Sins," "Servant of the Cow" (The Lady Isis), and "Guardian of the Guardian of the Pig." Many of these titles and even more honorific ones persisted throughout dynastic history.

Duration of service was easily worked out for the priestly institution. Accordingly, Sauernon (1962: 225) mentions times of service in the temples varied. "Each priesthood was divided into four classes of identical composition (the four *phyles*), which took turns to be in charge of the temple, its possessions and its ritual for a month. The same group would not be on duty again for another three months. During this time the priests returned to their villages to continue their lives as ordinary citizens."

Clearly, the civil experience of priests enabled them to become enmeshed in the social, economic, religious, political, cultural and intellectual lifeblood of the state, the essential prerequisites for the growth of civilization Africans can take pride in today. This institution's contributions are thus seminal as "think tanks." Positions as "Chief of the Palace," "Secretary," and "Chief of the Architects," "Keeper of Granaries," "Keeper of the Treasury," "Chief Justice and Keeper of the Armory," are additional examples of their civic power.

From the time of the Old Kingdom onwards, first Memphis then Heliopolis competed for primacy in politics and religion and in this rivalry, the intellectual wheels of ancient African civilization unfolded.

QUINTESSENTIAL BOOK
"THE HOLY LAND"

Holy Land Photo 77. Valley of the Nobles. Tomb of Rekhmire. More workmen at their tasks.

FREDERICK MONDERSON

Holy Land Photo 77a. Valley of the Nobles. Tomb of Nakht. Nakht sits enthroned beside his wife who embraces him (left shoulder) before a "Table of Offerings" as assistants mill around.

QUINTESSENTIAL BOOK
"THE HOLY LAND"

Holy Land Photo 77b. Valley of the Nobles. Tomb of Nakht. Nakht and family hunt birds in the marshes.

At Memphis, writes Kamil (1984: 37) the High Priest of Ptah, who was also the Chief artist, promoted his deity as the inspiration behind the metal-worker, carpenter and sculptor. However, in the areas surrounding Memphis, two other deities were revered, these being: "Sekhmet the lion goddess and Nefertum a lotus god. As Memphis expanded it drew those into its orbit. The problem of having three deities in a single area was early resolved by explaining Ptah as chief deity, Sekhmet as his consort and Nefertum as his son. United they formed the Memphite Triad. Later, Imhotep would be adopted and the triad would then consist of Ptah, Sekhmet and Imhotep, their son. This then shows the Priesthood as theorists and as well as patrons of the arts. The end result was the enormous rise in the wealth and power of this thrifty and creative priestly body. By the Middle and New Kingdoms, their wealth increased from tribute and plunder of surrounding lands such as Nubia, Syria and Palestine. Pharaohs made generous contributions and endowments in their worship and mortuary temples. In addition, tributes from foreign conquests that funded extensive architectural constructions were all part of the glorification of their father Amon, later Amon-Ra. In this they also sponsored and supported art and music.

Endowments, tribute, and produce from priestly lands increased the wealth of the priestly body. This enabled them to play an active role in non-religious matters, providing teachers and technicians as in the military and in furthering astronomy, learning, building, mummification, farming, exploiting the Nile for irrigation, practicing mathematics, and utilizing transport of quarried stone for greater building of secular and religious structures.

Sauernon (1962: 224) explained, in addition to the priests who were administrators of the economic organization of the sanctuaries; there were specialists who lived in these "Houses of Life." Here, he (1962: 224) has written: "They could, at the king's summons, represent the priests in a given temple. Among these specialists mention must be made of the 'Scribes of the House of Life,' the 'Sages,' the 'Lector priests,' the 'Hour watchers' (astronomer priests, who decided when ceremonies should be performed) and astrologer priests, learned in hematology, who knew how to determine the lucky or unlucky character of the days of the year."

Having this skilled auxiliary at their disposal further increased priesthood power since their people were involved in management of the lands of the god, control over collection of revenues, provisions for altars and for priests (who lived on the offerings placed on the altars) and negotiations with associated temples and with the royal administration.

The lowest of these was *Uab*, "the washed" or purified man. He had to examine the animals for sacrifice and perform the routine of the temple. Next was the *Kher Heb* or reciter of liturgy and spells. Then came the *Her*, who was over the temple. Above him was the *Kherp* or director of the temples. There was also the *Sem* priest who conducted the feasts and worship of the king. Above these was the High Priest or Chief Divine Servant or *Neter Hemtep*. This individual was actually the pharaoh.

There were also priestesses, women, in the temples. There was the *Neter Hemt*, or Divine Wife of Amen and High Priestess of Thebes. Next was *Urt Kheneru Ne Amen*, Great One of the Harem of Amen. Then the *Abyt* priestess, of various gods or goddesses. The *Sesheshet*, sistrum player and lastly, *Shemoyt*, musician of various gods, round out this lot. The role of the women, however, was limited even though they outnumbered the male priests in the temples. Still, on the level of the gods, females perennially accompanied the gods in triads or associations just as Isis and Nephthys accompanied Osiris.

Herodotus is considered the "father of history" who visited Egypt in 450 B.C. and wrote the Histories. Book II, *Euterpe* is devoted to Egypt. In this important

QUINTESSENTIAL BOOK
"THE HOLY LAND"

historical and anthropological study, Herodotus recorded the thoughts of an Egyptian priest who had remained studying underground in a temple for many decades. Such devotion shows the great respect the people of ancient Kemet had for learning, "for its own sake and the respect it gave." The society crafted a practical and philosophical view of life that insisted students love learning like a mother. "Learn to write," admonished a wise sage, "there is no profession that is not governed. It is only the learned man who rules his-self." This seems an earlier version of an idea, Aristotle, the Greek philosopher (384-322 B.C.) called *entelechy*. In this, he believed that knowledge should be pursued for its own sake and not for some practical purpose. *Entelechy* can thus become the reasoned mechanism that transforms the individual into a knowledgeable and useful member of society.

Education was high priority among the Priesthood. The priests of ancient Kemet taught justice and morals. They believed that justice should be the same for all. They also taught self-righteousness for the individual, self-restraint in one's doings and love and respect for the family. Equally too, the pharaoh, as the supreme father and judge, acted according to the philosophical beliefs of Ma'at, the goddess of justice, equality, balance, order, goodness. The monarch feared judgment in the afterlife if he did not adhere to fairness. So as an example, in legal matters he often admonished judges to be strictly balanced in their actions and not show any partiality to the rich. Treat them as you would treat the poor, he said. Thus, "leaning to one side in a cause is abomination to the gods," and this tenet became a philosophic pharaonic admonition.

Holy Land Illustration 72. Gigantic portrait statues of Amenhotep III, at Thebes which the natives call "Hama and Chama" (1400 B.C.).

FREDERICK MONDERSON

The priests taught self-righteousness is sinful and mankind should seek to avoid it. Further, they believed persons should have honorable dealings with god and men. As a way of life, violence should be avoided and one should remember one's religious obligations. The strong should show respect for the rights of the weak. Merchants should practice commercial honesty and try not to hinder the affairs of others. They also taught the ancient Kemetic ideal was a man who should be strong, steadfast, and self-respecting. He should be active and straight-forward, and quiet and discreet. He should also avoid covetousness and presumption.

Holy Land Photo 78. Dr. Obenga lectures on Hieroglyphics with emphasis on the meaning and significance of "the black land" which he determines means the "black country" not the "black land" since the determinative points to the former not the latter.

Then, in a number of ways, Senmut can be considered an "Ideal man." For, according to Wilson (1959: 172), rising from humble beginnings, this nobleman achieved social status and titles as: "Hereditary Prince and Count, Seal-bearer of the King of Lower Egypt, Sole Companion, Steward of Amon; Overseer of the Fields, the Garden, the Cows, the Serfs, the Peasant Farmers, and the Granaries of Amon; Prophet of Amon; Prophet of Amon's Sacred Barque; Chief Prophet of Montu in Hermonthis."

Other titles of Senmut included, "Spokesman of the Shrine of Geb; Headman in the House of the White Crown; Controller of the Board Hall in the House of the Official; Steward of the King; Overseer of the Royal Residence; Controller of Every Divine Craft; Steward of the Princess Nefru-Re; Great Father-Tutor of the Princess Nefru-Re; Controller of All Construction Work of the King in Karnak, Hermonthis, Deir el-Bahari, the Temple of Mut at Karnak, and Luxor; and 'a

QUINTESSENTIAL BOOK "THE HOLY LAND"

superior of superiors, an overseer of overseers of construction works.'" Significantly, Senmut could not have achieved such social prominence had he not been a member of some priesthood.

In family relations, priests taught that a man should not be rude to a woman in her house. In this ancient African Nile Valley culture of North-east Africa, the house belonged to the woman. That's even if the husband built or purchased it. She was the "Lady of the House" or "Mistress of the House." There was no "Master" of the house.

Though there was an occasional divorce, "marriage" or "unions" seems to always have been for life. "Children are sweet," is what they believed and taught. As such, the father did what he could for a dutiful son, who "should be regarded a true incarnation of the family spirit or Ka and treated with sympathy." The son, therefore, was taught "not to forget his mother and to remember all she had done for him." The daughter, however, was considered the heiress with property and lineage being passed down in the female line.

General associations with ancient Kemetic (Egyptian) culture emphasize pyramids, temples, tombs, religion, art and mummification, as part of the effort to explain trans-human metaphysical existence. Mummification and the climate had an important role in this process, and it not only helped to preserve the remains of the wealthy and famous, but also became the catalyst for experimentation in science, anatomy, medicine and surgery. With overseas expansion and migration, preservation of the body spread far and wide, as Kemetic culture diffused, so that many of their secrets are being used today in morticians' never ending work.

The priests were responsible for the mummification of the dead before burial for which a fee was paid. Herodotus mentions three types of mummification for the Pharaohs and nobles, middle class and the poor. While the wealthy was often entombed through elaborate preparation, fanfare and sepulchral structures, the dryness of the soil has helped to preserve some bodies of the poor in shallow graves. Still, the earliest mummified body using this process is now recognized as that of the Queen of King Zer of the first dynasty. However, the earliest fully resined body comes from Meydum in the third dynasty. Now, according to Herodotus, in preparing the body, it was opened by a long slit, usually on the left side from the hip to the ribs. The intestines were then removed and the body was washed with palm oil, aromatic spices, resin and perfume. It was then sewn up again. Next, it was soaked for up to 70 days in natron and then studded with jewelry and magical charms under the bandaged linen. The "Opening of the Mouth Ceremony" was performed and the body placed in its coffin and sarcophagus for burial. As if linking dynastic craft with prehistoric beliefs, the

FREDERICK MONDERSON

gods in the afterlife, used an adze to perform the opening of the mouth ceremony. In Tutankhamon's tomb, the High Priest Ayi is seen performing this function with adze and all. Generally made of iron, this tool's early existence poses important questions for the origins of iron. Therefore, throughout dynastic rule, the Priesthood providing an important service and so played a significant role in the development and practice of the pharaonic system.

Holy Land Photo 79. Ghizeh Plateau. Visitors admiring the Sphinx and Great Pyramid of Ghizeh.

REFERENCES

Bierbrier, M. L. "Hrere, Wife of the High Priest Painkh." *Journal of Near Eastern Studies*, (July 1973, 32: 311).
"Egyptian Tomb Endowments." *American Journal of Archaeology*, VIL (1942: 342).
Herodotus. *The Histories*. Baltimore, MD: Penguin Books, (1954) 1973.
Kamil, J. *The Ancient Egyptians*. Cairo: The American University in Cairo Press, (1976) 1984.
Maspero, G. *Manual of Egyptian Archaeology*. New York: G.P. Putnam's Sons, 1926.
Mertz, B. *Black Land, Red Land*. New York: Dodd, Mead and Co., (1966) 1978.
"Occult Sciences in the Temples of Ancient Egypt." *Scientific American* I: 470, 496.
Oswald, M. "Egyptian Tomb Endowments." *American Journal of Archaeology* 44 (July 1940: 364).

QUINTESSENTIAL BOOK "THE HOLY LAND"

Petrie, W.M.F. *Egyptian Religion*. London: Constable, 1923.
Piccine, P.A. "In Search of the Meaning of Senet." *Archaeology* 33 (July-August 1980: 55-58).
Posner, Georges with Serge Sauernon and Jean Yoyotte. *A Dictionary of Egyptian Civilization*. London: Methuen and Co., Ltd., (1959) 1962.
"Priest Amidst Birds found in City of Dead." *Science News Letter* 36 (October 7, 1939: 231).

2. Breakfast

Dr. Leonard James: **The Wisdom of Ancient Egypt**. The wisdom of ancient Egypt is renowned for its originality and long lasting influence over time and geographic regions. From religious beginnings, through architectural and artistic experimentation, astronomy and other scientific observations and practices, medical applications, creative literary recording and agricultural and navigational practices, the wisdom of the ancient peoples of Africa manifest through the Nile Valley region, has propelled humanity along the undulative march of civilization.

Applying geographic, botanical and zoological themes to literary expression ushered in the earliest recorded writings. Exploiting the Nile River for agricultural and transportation methods and techniques, provided food, solved the problems of movement and allowed military strategy to support stable government, religious expression and patronizing of the arts. Thus, the wisdom of the ancient Egyptians can also be seen in the realms of social love songs, wisdom sayings and educational teachings as well as in art and architectural constructions. Such wisdom can be observed in the divinely inspired religious ritual and royal and noble testimonials associated with their funerary practices.

Politically centralized administration rested upon monarchical pronouncements, judicial rulings and traditional bureaucratic and social practices. Military daring spread cultural expression and adherence to civil order, imperialist accumulation of wealth with patronage of the arts funding to fullest expression in statuary, painting and civil and religious architecture. So much more can be said for the renown of the wisdom of the Ancient Egyptians. These Black men and women of ancient Africa who inhabited the Nile Valley spread their wisdom and influence down and up and beyond the majestic Nile River in North-east Africa. Millennia later, we celebrate their brilliance, wisdom and influence in all facets of knowledge, viz., building, science, religion, arts, medicine, astronomy, literacy, transportation, measurement, and agricultural and funerary practice. Truly, the wisdom of these ancient Blacks of Africa is unparalleled.

FREDERICK MONDERSON

Walter Brown: This is an interesting piece, my friend.

Michelle Georges: What do you have for us today, Brother?
Regina Hendricks: How can we ever repay you?
George Washington: I think you sisters have done a great deal by gracing me with your wonderful company. On 10-23-1975 in **Ancient History**, we discussed:

THE FIRST INTERMEDIATE PERIOD

In the first part, Egypt is not unified in this period. Dynasties VII and VIII produced weak kings. The eastern delta was lost to Semitic speaking peoples. Nomarchs gained greater power. The two most important Nomarchs were at Hieracleopolis and Thebes.

The second half was much more stable than the first. Heracleopolis conquered Lower Egypt to Abydos. Thebes held everything from Thebes to Elephantine. Absence of Ma'at (what should be), the cause of chaos, is what most Egyptians thought. Manetho records there were "70 kings ruling for 70 days" is an exaggeration. Dynasties VII and VIII were at Memphis. Dynasties IX and X were at Hieracleopolis and Dynasty XI was at Thebes.

Science shows their greatest invention was agriculture and many of their techniques are still in use today. Medicine was greatly advanced in this age. Religion, showed god was a power and anything powerful was a god.

African Religious Thought Systems

October 29, 1975

The profane is not special. The experience of the sacred is something extraordinary. Western metaphysics is a mechanical description of the universe. There is no cosmology, thus no spirituality and spiritual whole.

Ontology is an investigation of the nature of being and reality beyond the structure of the present world. Spiritual forces are primary.

Cosmology is a systematic attempt at explaining the origin and structure of the

QUINTESSENTIAL BOOK "THE HOLY LAND"

world.

Epistemology is the theory of knowledge.

Holy Land Ceramic Art 8. A beautiful bird in a kaleidoscope of colors in ceramic construction.

African religion allows people to transcend to a level of meaning. Again, the five categories of beings are: Muntu, man; Kingu, thing; Hantu, place or thing; Kuntu, modality; and Ntu, universal force. The first four are parts of the fifth and they all interact.

Abase Ya is the Akan god of earth who gives succor to man. Nyankopon is a lesser deity who is present in the daily lives of many and can be called upon for succor and strength.

FREDERICK MONDERSON

Holy Land Photo 79a. Ghizeh Plateau. View from the rear of the Sphinx.

Michael Montout: Mr. Morrison, you promised to answer a few questions I had about religion and philosophy but we have been so busy, I didn't have a chance to get with you.
Dr. McFlair: It's been such a wonderful experience so far. All that we have seen in the temples, tombs, and there is much more to go. Perhaps you should answer some of his questions about both religion and philosophy.
Mr. Morrison: Well, I'll be glad to lend my expertise to this discussion.
Mr. Sylvester Singleton: Well, let me get the first question in then. Did the Egyptians practice philosophy?

Mr. Morrison: Of course the Egyptians practiced philosophy. The ancient Greeks thought highly of the Egyptians. Socrates said: 'The wisest of all people were the Egyptians.' Plato remarked: 'The greatest philosophers were the priests at Thebes.' Diodorus wrote: 'The Egyptians were more skilled in ethics than all people.' Herodotus reported: 'The Egyptians were extreme in their wisdom.'

No philosophical papyri have survived.

Plato remarked 'No priest of Thebes would write down his philosophy.'

There is a treatise or book called 'The Report of a Dispute between a man and his Ba.' This is a philosophic debate!

QUINTESSENTIAL BOOK
"THE HOLY LAND"

There is another text called 'The Philosophy of a Memphite Priest.'
Mr. John Stewart: Well, let me add, "How charming is divine philosophy." As I listen I am pleased to know that the Egyptians did practice philosophy. After all, philosophy is at the base of all knowledge, in its findings and explanation and exposition.

Dr. Alexander Pushkin: Mr. Sinclair, Have there been any serious challenges to Afrocentricity?
Michael Sinclair: Of course, all the time. Some good and some bad. For example. Deborah Atwater Hunter wrote "The Rhetorical Challenge of Afro-Centricity" in *Western Journal of Black Studies* Vol. 7, No. 4, (1983: 239-243).

In her introduction she states: "Blacks must have a strong sense of identity, history, and culture in order to survive in the next century. The concept of Afro-centricity advanced by Molefi K. Asante and others may be one way in which blacks might acquire a strong sense of social awareness and racial identity in order for them to persevere during the years ahead."

The purpose is: "Not an attack on Asante, it is an expression of the misapplication of Afro-centricity in some of his efforts to influence and affect culturally the social destiny of peoples of African descent; definition of Afrocentricity as a social movement. The persuasion process in Afrocentricity; and Methods and Channels of Dissemination."
Teddy Cubia: Again, I think the brother is on point. Don't you think so Doc?
Dr. Alexander Pushkin: I must agree you are both right.

Michael Sinclair: Simons, Cathcart and Griffin have argued: "A revolutionary movement loosely defined seeks the total replacement of existing norms, values, and power distributions with new ones. Rhetoric refers to the process by which a social movement seeks through the manipulation of verbal and nonverbal symbols to affect the perceptions of target audiences and thus bring about changes in their ways of thinking, feeling, and acting."

"Social movements are a sort of collective behavior organized to produce a change."

"A social movement usually includes a shared value system, a sense of community, norms for action and an organizational structure. It seeks to influence the social order and is oriented toward definite goals. These goals must be conveyed to a group of individuals and the message of togetherness is conveyed by rhetoric."

Griffin assumes that "all movements are essentially political, concerned with governance or dominion, the wielding and obeying authority; that politics above all is drama; and that drama requires a conflict .... all movements are essentially moral strivings for salvation, perfection, the good. To study a movement is to study drama, which is an act of transformation, an act that ends in transcendence, the ultimate achievement of salvation. Truth is situationally created through the interaction of the speaker, and his symbolic strategies with the audience and its particular circumstances. Afrocentricity involves the process of self transformation in its target audience who are blacks in Diaspora."

Holy Land Illustration 73. Restoration of the Great Hall at Karnak, ancient Thebes – Largest building of the Egyptian Empire (above); and the dead Osiris embalmed with trees sprouting from his body (below).

"The primary rhetorical test is of the leader. Afrocentricity is a revolutionary social movement. All movements are essentially moral strivings for salvation, perfection and good. Afrocentricity is no different."

QUINTESSENTIAL BOOK "THE HOLY LAND"

"The motivational appeal is simply Afro-centricity's own force of truth."

Mrs. Alexander Pushkin: I like this young man. He is so forceful with his facts and not afraid to take a stance. I think that is the face of true leadership in education. Won't you agree Teddy?

Teddy Cubia: I certainly agree. I must admit, Dr. Asante was certainly stern in his insistence that his students be comprehensively thorough in their learning and note taking. I will try to match him in my simple way by reading a poem on the bus.

Dr. Alexander Pushkin: I look forward to your poems Teddy. They seem to throw much light on the civil rights struggle and the awareness of black people of those years.

Michael Sinclair: There is a uniqueness about your poems Mr. Cubia because not only do they come out of the civil rights movement, they tell and give the philosophic flair of such feelings. Might I add, Dr. Asante taught us to write down everything, every note, every source to be most knowledgeable on the discipline we were writing about.

3. Bus Trip

Henrietta Potter: That issue Dr. Monderson raised about philosophy in Egypt, it puzzles me. How could these people not be able to understand and practice philosophy, when they could erect such great buildings and done so much in the fields of knowledge?

Michelliea Georges: In one of our classes at Temple University, Dr. Asante dealt with the same issue as to whether the Egyptians were philosophers. In fact, I think he has written a book on Egyptian philosophers, since my class. However, he taught us that 'philosophy is the most supreme of all knowledge.' He disagreed with the idea that there is a Greek beginning of every form of knowledge.

Philo Lover; Sophia, wisdom, the wise person is a lover of wisdom. In the tomb of Antef I there is an inscription of Seba the Wise.

Seba – Sebo – Sophia – Sufi, *mdu neter* – neb-Het = Nephthys.

The word Seba may be very old. Homer's *Iliad* is probably about 800 B.C. We must remember the first Greek philosophers were no earlier than Thales 600 B.C. Pre-Socratic philosophers were Thales, Isocrates, and then Socrates. Plutarch *Lives* are no earlier than 100 B.C. Cheikh Anta Diop has argued; if Homer did exist he must have done so during the time of Ethiopian conquest of Egypt c. 750 B.C. If you recall, both the Ramesseum and Medinet Habu Temples of the 19th and 20th Dynasties have illustrations/inscriptions on their walls that mirror events in Homer's *Iliad* and this makes you wonder whether he got his ideas from there.

FREDERICK MONDERSON

Holy Land Photo 80. Ghizeh Plateau. Pillars used as the earliest form of support.

Regina Hendricks: I agree on both counts.
George Washington: I do know that Marcilio Ficcino was sent by Cosimo de Medici to bring back books to Florence, Italy. Besides the *Republic*, he brought the *Corpus Hermeticum* or *The Hermetic Texts*, the book of Thoth, Hermes or Djehuti. This African book was the first book translated for the Renaissance. In 1321 Leonardo Fibbonacci was the first person to bring Hindu knowledge to Europe. Clearly it seems Europeans cannot allow Egypt to be African because it makes Europe appear normal.

In **Ancient History** on October 27, 1975, the topic dealt with:

GOD	CONSORT	CITY
An		
Enlil	Ninhl	Nippur
Enki	Ninki	Eridu
Nannak		
Utu		
Innana	Ishtar	Uruk

QUINTESSENTIAL BOOK "THE HOLY LAND"

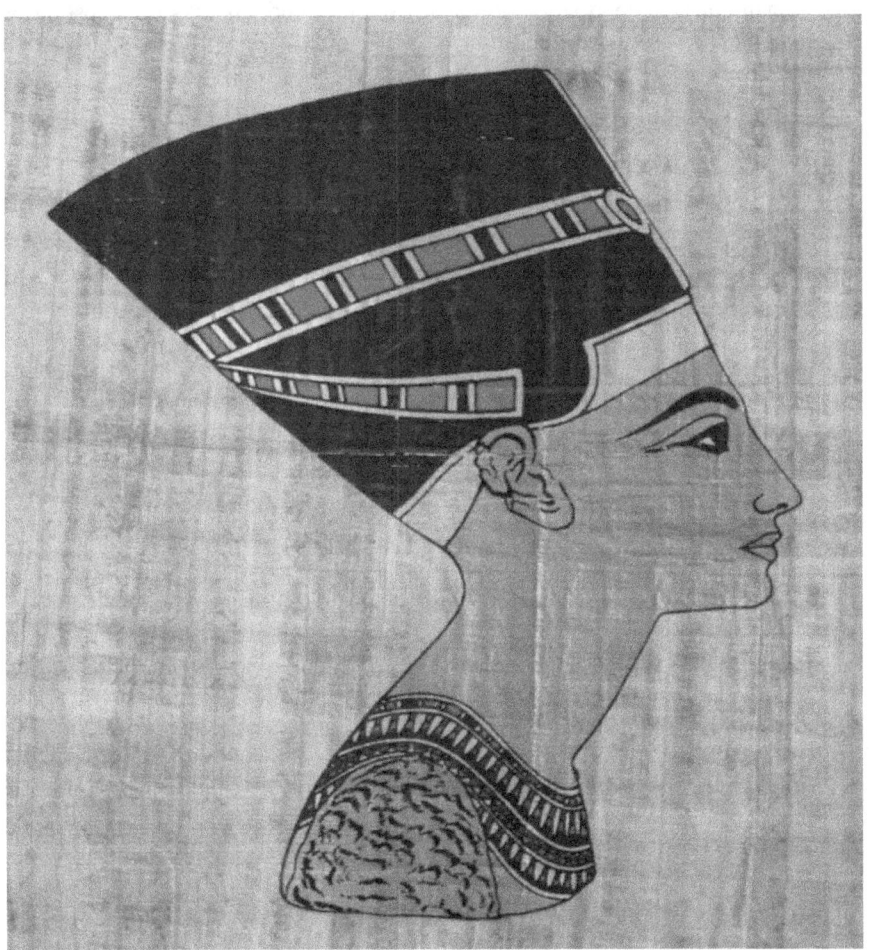

Holy Land Papyrus 24. The famous Nefertiti portrait from an original in Berlin.

Sumerian contribution included any measurement that had a multiple of 6 such as the hour, minute, day.

An is the sky god, father of the gods. Enlil is the god of air. He brought air to the world. Enki is the god of water. Nanar is the moon god.

Damuzzi and equally Osiris are both gods of vegetation who both rise after death.

FREDERICK MONDERSON

Most literature comes from the IIIrd period.

There is didactic literature, epics, poems and prayers from this period. The Epic of Gilgamesh is a flood story similar to Noah's flood. It asks the question of why man must die. It is written in the 4th Millennium B.C., at least 1,000 years before the Bible.

Enkiduis is a friend and Utnapishtim is the same as Noah.

Last class December 22, 1975.

In **African Religious Thought Systems**: African religion is an ontological phenomenon. The ideology of progress is one universal.

MBITI

DAHOMEAN THOLOGY AND COSMOLOGY

Vodun (Vodu) is equivalent to the divine beings, spirits, and gods.

Pantheon – "Family" or grouping of gods. Study will include genealogy, nature, origins and their characteristic attributes. It is important to know what pleases and displeases the pantheon.

FON - A world created by one divine being who is bi-sexual, Nana Buluku who is their creator being. Twins are special to some people.

Nana Buluku created Mawu and Lisa and gave them the responsibility of looking over the welfare of the earth and its inhabitants.

Mawu was the female principle and was given charge of the night and Lisa the male was given charge of day. Mawu represents night, the moon and the west. Lisa represents day, the sun and east. Twins had no children when given dominion over the world but later procreated and started the genealogy. A festival is held annually to honor Nana Buluku in which portions of the offerings are taken to the Dume in Abomey.

Priests who enter Dume are well purified and after can speak in 100 tongues in medium.

Mawu is associated with Vudun and represents mother, woman, gentle, forgiving.

QUINTESSENTIAL BOOK
"THE HOLY LAND"

Lisa is male, younger, and robust and represents ruthlessness. He is all complementing.

Jerome Smith: I was looking at CNN this morning and they spoke about Democracy being an issue for many third world nations at this time. Why is this?

Mr. John Stewart: Democracy is credited to the Greeks but that concept may be thousands of years older. Consider people wanting to work out the situations of their times and they may have worked that out. Americans did not bring democracy to the New World. They found it there, being practiced by the native peoples.

Teddy Cubia: I am going to read a poem entitled "Now's the time to kill the swine."

"Now's the Time to Kill the Swine"
By
Teddy Cubia.

Once upon a time near a shack down home
Stood an old Black farmer, whose name is not known
That old Black cat didn't have nothing big
Just an ol' sterile chicken and 2 white pigs

That farmer needed money and he needed it fast
Cause grocery man Sam was on his ass
Had to pay that bill and pay it today
Or wasn't no more food gonna come his way
So old Black farmer – he decided to find
A likable person to buy his swine.

There's a man down the road and he's as Black as the night
Farmer thinks: That's a brother looks like he's all right.
He walks up and offers a deal on his swine
Brother says: "Old man, are you out of your mind?"
The pig is darker than the rats in hell.
They're ugly, they're poison, and man do they smell.
Listen old man; I'll teach you something new

FREDERICK MONDERSON

Swine ain't what's happening, for me and for you

Now the farmer rears back, then he scratched his head
"Boy, all my life I eat pork – and I ain't dead."
"Yeah, you ain't dead – but, you damn sure is close
If your pressure gets higher, in hell you gon' roast,
If swine don't get your pressure, your sugar gon' rise
Your heart gon' get sick and your kidneys gon' die.
And if you still breathing after all this takes place
Then, old man, you are definitely in the wrong race
You should be colored white – instead of all Black.
Cause you're a natural pig and that's a fact.

They're the only ones living consider that slap
For you are what you eat – that's why they can't slap

You, and me we're all Black, not part White, not part hog.
So clear your head brother, come out of that pig

Now the old man's been listening, he's been listening fine

Ok. Little brother let's get rid of this swine
I'll run down and give him to Grocery Sam
He's white, he loves pork, and my bills in a jam
No more pig for me – no more of that meat

Its beef, veal and lamb – that's all I'm gonna eat
The young brother smiles; pats the old farmer's back
I love you old man – for you're now truly Black.

Dr. Alexander Pushkin: Very good, Teddy. Well said.
Mrs. Alexander Pushkin: Teddy, you are indeed a poet. Reminds me when we were young and attended those lectures of Dr. John Henrik Clarke and Dr. ben-Jochannan in Harlem, New York. We were so fired up then. I see shades in our young friend Michael Sinclair. This tells me all is not lost. We may suffer some setbacks, but our people will move ahead, if the likes of Michael Sinclair has anything to say or do about it.
Michael Sinclair: Thank you, Ma'am. I feel so delighted and thankful to be on this trip and in your company. Both your husband and Teddy have been an inspiration to me.

QUINTESSENTIAL BOOK "THE HOLY LAND"

Holy Land Photo 81. Ghizeh Plateau. More columns used as support and decoration.

4. Site

ESNEH TEMPLE OF GOD KHNUM

EDFU TEMPLE OF GOD HORUS

KOM OMBO TEMPLE OF ELDER HORUS AND SOBEK

The next and interesting stop in this southern tour is the Temple of Edfu. It is the best preserved of all ancient Kemetic temples, particularly among those erected during the time of Greek rule. Again, it should be restated, these temples, though called "Greek Temples," utilized indigenous building and decorative techniques. Egyptian and Nubian workmen, plans and practices built them, during rule by the Greeks but they also added innovations.

Also on the west bank of the Nile, and 60 miles south of Esna, and 90 miles south of Luxor, the Temple of Horus at Edfu is now approached from the South before the still intact Enclosure Wall, as you get off the bus or carriages to the south of the center of the city. Within the last few years, the direction has been changed and visitors approach the temple from a new area that entrances from in front of the pylon. Oriented north to south, or facing south, the visitor walks up from the south, towards the temple entrance. Interestingly enough, the temples of Dendera and Edfu face each other and this may be because of the festivals linking the two temples.

Walking past the Mammisi one gets a panoramic view of the entrance pylon split by the gate. The gods are incised in sunk-relief across the entrance. Off to the left, the king, in traditional pose, grasps the enemies of Kemet/Egypt and strikes them with his mace. Nevertheless, while the upper "register" exhibits continuity of theme, the lower left side duplicates the lower right side in representation.

Magi's (1990: 13) commentary is well made that: "Not even the temple of Karnak, the only one larger than Edfu, is so well preserved. All of 137 meters long and with a pylon measuring 79 meters on the front and 36 meters high, the plan is extremely homogeneous."

This temple was covered by debris with only the Propylon visible, until a century ago. The terraces and roofs were amidst the mud huts of the nearby-village. The indefatigable Mariette began clearing the temple, after he was appointed *Conservator of Monuments*. He was also *Director of Excavations* conducting researches throughout the land. Mariette was an extremely busy man, for as Brian Fagan (1975: 278) explained: "At one point men was digging under his direction at thirty-seven different locations simultaneously from the Delta to the First Cataract."

The Temple of Horus at Edfu, (*Apollinopolis Magna*) was begun, according to Woldering (1963: 222) by Ptolemy III Euergetes in *Nile Year* 3803 (237 B.C.), and completed *Nile Year* 4183 (57 B.C.). It was dedicated to Horus, the Falcon headed son of Osiris, who according to the myth, slew his father's killer on the same spot on which the temple was built. Scott Wayne (1994: 310) believed: "In conception and design it follows the traditions of authentic Pharaonic architecture, with the general plan, scale and ornamentation, right down to the 'Egyptian' attire worn by the Greek kings depicted in the temple's reliefs."

QUINTESSENTIAL BOOK "THE HOLY LAND"

This important temple has its original Enclosure Wall intact, and a massive Pylon gives entrance to a great forecourt with a Peristyle consisting of thirty-two columns on three sides. There were two falcon statues before the pylon and two others before the Pronaos or hypostyle hall. In this latter, only one now remains. West (1995: 414) offers a philosophical explanation of the awe conjured up in seeking an understanding of the cosmological and metaphysical significance of this entry into the temple. At the end of this Peristyle Forecourt one enters the temple proper, and the First Hypostyle Hall. Once inside one passes the Morning House or Hall of Consecrations on the left. The Library is on the right, and Wayne (1994: 312) wrote, the illustration "features a list of books and a relief of Seshat, the goddess of writing." Evidence of the artist's paint palette rests above the entrance to the Library.

The First Hypostyle Hall has a horizontal colonnade of three rows of six columns each divided by the aisle of the axis. The Second Hypostyle Hall has a colonnade of three rows of four each, similarly disposed. To the left of this first lay the "Chamber of Solid Offerings" and ahead lay the workroom. To the right lay the "Chamber of Liquid Offerings." Further into the temple, one encounters the "Offering Chamber" then the "Dentral Hall." To the left of the "Dentral Hall," we find the "Chapel of the God Min" then ahead the "Sacrarium" or "Holy of Holies." A number of rooms for various purposes surround this inner enclosure of the temple, as well as a "Clothing Cella." West (1995: 415) has indicated: "The sanctuary is encircled by a corridor and ten chapels. Ten is commonly associated with Hathor. A corridor and eleven chapels surround the Dendera sanctuary, architecturally very similar. Eleven is often associated with Hathor (e.g., the eleven-columned colonnades at Deir el-Bahari). The corner chapels have undecorated crypts beneath them."

There is a stairway with 242 steps leading to the roof beyond these rooms on the western side of the temple. To the west and east of the temple is found the illustrated "Passage of Victory" showing where and how Horus avenged his father. On the opposite or eastern side of the temple was found a Nilometer. Some scholars believe an older Nilometer was located to the southeast of the entrance pylon, though this was away from the Nile.

FREDERICK MONDERSON

Holy Land Illustration 74. Psychostasia. Judgment scene. The heart being weighed against the feather of truth, Ma'at.

As a people of long-standing celestial observation, the myths were solar and this certainly influenced the evolution of the religion and nation. In this regard, Maspero (1904, I: 285-291) sketched a graphic picture of the legendary history of ancient Kemet, by which the solar developments blended with earthly and architectural evolution that influenced how these ancient Africans worshiped and practiced their belief systems. "The connection, always increasingly intimate between Osiris and Ra, gradually brought a blending of the previously separate myths and beliefs concerning each. The friends and enemies of the one became the friends and enemies of the other, and from a mixture of the original conceptions of the two deities, arose new personalities, in which contradictory elements were blended together, often without true fusion. The celestial Horuses one by one were identified with Horus, son of Isis, and their attributes were given to him, as his in the same way became theirs. Apophi and the monsters - the hippopotamus, the crocodile, the wild boar, - which lay in wait for Ra as he sailed the heavenly ocean, became one with Set and his accomplices. Set still possessed his half of Egypt, and his primitive brotherly relation to the celestial Horus remained unbroken, either on account of their sharing one temple, as at Nubit, or because they were worshiped as one in two neighboring nomes, as, for example, at Oxyrhynchus and at Heracleopolis Magna. The repulsion with which the slayer of Osiris was regarded did not everywhere dissociate these two cults: certain small districts persisted in this double worship down to the latest times of paganism."

"It was, after all, a mark of fidelity to the oldest traditions of the race, but the bulk of the Egyptians, who had forgotten these, invented reasons taken from the history of the divine dynasties to explain the fact. The judgment of Thoth or of Sibu had not put an end to the machinations of Sit: as soon as Horus had left the earth, Sit resumed them, and pursued them, with varying fortune, under the divine kings of the second Ennead. Now, in the year 363 of Harmakhis, the Typhonians reopened the campaign. Beaten at first near Edfu, they retreated precipitately northwards,

QUINTESSENTIAL BOOK "THE HOLY LAND"

stopping to give battle wherever their partisans dominated, - at Zatmit in the Theban nome, at Khaitntrit to the northeast of Denderah, and at Hibonu in the principality of the Gazelle. Several bloody combats, which took place between Oxyrhynchus and Heracleopolis Magna, were the means of driving them finally out of the Nile Valley; they rallied for the last time in the eastern provinces of the Delta, were beaten at Zalu, and giving up all hope of success on land, they embarked at the head of the Gulf of Suez, in order to return to the Nubian Desert, their habitual refuge in times of distress. The sea was the special element of Typhon, and upon it they believed themselves secure. Horus, however, followed them, overtook them near Shashirit, routed them, and on his return to Edfu, celebrated his victory by a solemn festival. By degrees, as he made himself master of those localities which owed allegiance to Sit, he took energetic measures to establish in them the authority of Osiris and of the solar cycle. In all of them he built, side by side with the sanctuary of the Typhonian divinities, a temple to himself, in which he was enthroned under the particular form he was obliged to assume in order to vanquish his enemies. Metamorphosed into a hawk at the battle of Hibonu, we next see him springing up to the back of Sit under the guise of a hippopotamus; in his shrine at Hibonu he is represented as a hawk perching on the back of a gazelle, emblem of the nome where the struggle took place. Near to Zalu he became incarnate as a human-headed lion, crowned with the triple diadem, and having feet armed with claws which cut like a knife; it was under the form, too, of a lion that he was worshiped in the temple at Zalu. The correlation of Sit and the celestial Horus was not, therefore, for these Egyptians of more recent times a primitive religious fact; it was the consequence, and so to speak the sanction, of the old hostility between the two gods. Horus had treated his enemy in the same fashion that a victorious Pharaoh treated the barbarians he conquered by his arms: he had constructed a fortress to keep his foe in check, and his priests formed a sort of garrison as a precaution against the revolt of the rival priesthood and the followers of a rival deity. In this manner the battles of the gods were changed into struggles, in which, more than once, Egypt was deluged with blood. The hatred of the followers of Osiris to those of Typhon was perpetuated with such implacability that the nomes which had persisted in adhering to the worship of Sit, became odious to the rest of the population: the image of their master on the monument was mutilated, their names were effaced from the geographical lists, they were assailed with insulting epithets, and to pursue and slay their sacred animal was reckoned a pious act. Thus originated those skirmishes, which developed into actual civil wars, and were continued down to Roman times. The adherents of Typhon only became more confined in their veneration for the accursed god; Christianity alone overcame their obstinate fidelity to him. The history of the world for Egypt was therefore only the history of the struggle between the adherents of Osiris and the followers of Sit; an interminable warfare in which sometimes one and sometimes the other of the rival parties obtained a passing advantage, without ever gaining a decisive victory till the end of time. The divine kings of the second and third Ennead devoted most of the years of their earthly

FREDERICK MONDERSON

reign to this end; they were portrayed under the form of the great warrior Pharaohs, who, from the eighteenth to the twelfth century before our era, extended their rule from the plains of the Euphrates to the marshes of Ethiopia. A few peaceful sovereigns are met with here and there in this line of conquerors - a few sages or legislators, of whom the most famous was styled Thoth, the doubly great, ruler of Hermopolis and of the Hermopolitan Ennead. A legend of recent origin made him the prime minister of Horus, son of Isis; a still more ancient tradition would identify him with the second king of the second dynasty, the immediate successor of the divine Horuses, and attributes to him a reign of 3226 years. He brought to the throne that inventive spirit and that creative power which had characterized him from the time when he was only a feudal deity. Astronomy, divination, magic, medicine, writing, drawing - in fine, all the arts and sciences emanated from him as from their first source. He had taught mankind the methodical observation of the heavens and of the changes that took place in them, the slow revolutions of the sun, the rapid phases of the moon, the intersecting movements of the five planets, and the shapes and limits of the constellations which each night were lit up in the sky."

Holy Land Photo 82. Ghizeh Plateau. The Khufu "Solar Boat Museum" as seen between the two Great Pyramids.

KOM OMBO TEMPLE OF SOBEK AND HAROEIS

TEMPLE OF KOM OMBO

QUINTESSENTIAL BOOK
"THE HOLY LAND"

Kom Ombo is the last temple stop before Aswan, on the scenic bus tour from Luxor. Leaving the much earlier Middle Kingdom and New Kingdom cultural presence we head into the Graeco-Roman domain. Kom Ombo is on the right or east bank of the Nile.

Kom Ombo, oriented east to west and 30 miles south of Edfu and 120 miles south of Luxor, was dedicated to the twin deities Haroeris and Sobek. This temple is largely dismantled. The left side of the temple was dedicated to Haroeris, Horus the Elder, and the right side to Sobek, the crocodile-headed deity. In this unusual temple, Scott Wayne (1994: 314) wrote: "Everything is doubled and perfectly symmetrical along the main axis of the temple. There are twin entrances, twin courts, twin colonnades, twin hypostyle halls, twin sanctuaries and, in keeping with the dual nature of the temple, there was probably a twin priesthood."

In identifying the builders of this temple, Scott Wayne (1994: 314) continued: "The Greco-Roman structure faces the Nile. The entrance pylon, the outer enclosure-wall and part of the court, all built by Augustus after 30 B.C., have been either mostly destroyed by pilfering stonemasons or eroded by the river. The temple proper was actually begun by Ptolemy VI Philometer in the early 2nd century B.C.; Ptolemy XIII (also known as Neos Dionysus) built the vestibule and hypostyle hall; and other Ptolemies and, after them, Romans contributed to the relief decoration."

To the right of the entranceway stood a small Chapel of Hathor that today exhibits evidence of mummified crocodiles, replicas of Sobek and some Stone Coffins, dug from the cemeteries in which they were buried.

Entering through the largely disappeared first pylon, one enters the court through two entrances, where Magi (1990: 43) notes accordingly "sixteen painted columns" stood in the "courtyard on three sides." An altar was located in the center of this court. The pylon dividing the court from the first hypostyle hall is decorated with reliefs. On the court's side of the pylon, reliefs depict Horus and Thoth with Sobek on the right and Horus and Thoth with Haroeris on the left. Next is the first hypostyle hall, with a colonnade horizontal to the two axes, that contains three rows of five each columns. The same pylon side of the first hypostyle hall with its massive columns contains reliefs of King Neos Dionysus with Haroeris, Isis, Nut and Thoth, off to the left. To the right, the king is blessed by the protective Goddess and Neos Dionysus is shown making offerings to four fabulous beasts. At the other end of this Vestibule of first hypostyle hall, various offering scenes are represented to the right and to the left; Philometer and Cleopatra are show before Khons. The second hypostyle Hall is similarly colonnaded but this time with two rows of five columns each, before which stands

FREDERICK MONDERSON

the sacred crocodile, Sobek of Kom Ombo. Three sections of vestibules or chambers follow leading to the double Sanctuary of Haroeris on the left and the sanctuary of Sobek on the right. Besides an inner passage and an outer passage and beyond these sacred places, depictions on the rear wall represent a number of interesting friezes or pictures of sculpture relating to medicine and other secrets of the temples. To the right of the court, lay the Mammisi or birth house.

The back of the outer corridor of the Temple contains a number of important raised and sunk relief friezes. Here could be found the remains of two large sunk-relief statues of Imhotep. In the center of the temple's inside wall, ears and eyes mark the place where visitors made supplications in the temple. On the opposite wall of the same corridor, medical instruments are displayed including an alabaster "basin" for washing the physician's hands before and after the medical procedure. Some controversy surrounds the true determination as to whether these are in fact medical instruments.

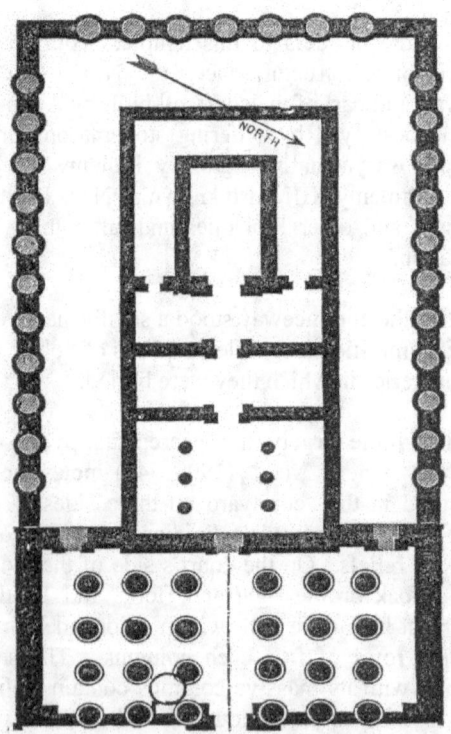

Holy Land – Plan of the Temple of Esneh.

QUINTESSENTIAL BOOK "THE HOLY LAND"

West (1995: 423) argues to the contrary, in that: "Ghalouig, notwithstanding, doctors and nurses looking at this inscription easily identify the medical nature of practically every instrument shown: curettes, forceps, surgical saws, droppers, a birthing stool, pharmaceutical scales, etc." Nearby the pregnant Isis sits in the birth chair. Back to the front and off to north of the second hypostyle hall, there is a Nilometer. South of this hall there is a well-preserved calendar of feast days.

ARRIVAL AT ASWAN

CHECK IN AT OBEROI HOTEL

LIST OF TRAVELERS.

TAKE PASSPORTS FOR SAFE-KEEPING

5. Post site lecture

"Alexander the Great" from Macedonia conquered Egypt in 332 B.C. after he had practically conquered the known world. He died in 323 B.C. and his Egyptian Empire went to his general Soter who became Ptolemy I. Alexander was a great general whose skill was military strategy. He moved quickly. Sometimes his moving army comprised 60,000 men. He was always on the move. Nevertheless, Alexander revered Egyptian culture.

The City of Alexandria was founded to commemorate him. However, in previously ancient times this city was called *Racotis*. It was an early planned city with eleven streets running east to west and seven streets running north to south. These streets were cut so as to take advantage of the winds. He only stayed in Egypt for summer. He died in Babylon.

FREDERICK MONDERSON

Holy Land Papyrus 25. Nefertari, wife of Rameses II, is another of those frequently portrayed beautiful Egyptian Queens.

The famous Library of Alexandria was his brainchild but he never saw the Library. It was probably built by Soter I (Soter = Savior). No one knows where the library was when it was built or when it was destroyed. Strabo saw it in 43 B.C. The library had 500,000 manuscripts. It is unique and very important. Western civilization knowledge was patterned on the Alexandrian Library. This was the first place of centralized learning.

The word Museum (place of the muses) comes from the library.

QUINTESSENTIAL BOOK
"THE HOLY LAND"

70 Hebrew scholars wrote the Septuagint in Alexandria. The Dead Sea Scrolls were written in the First Century.

The later Ptolemies became debased. They reduced Egypt to a colony and heavily taxed the people. There was a peasant revolt in 173 B.C., which was put down.

Another comment can be made regarding the priesthood. It essentially controlled the country. The pharaoh ruled but they were afraid of the priesthood and so seeking the fortune and protection of the gods they built temples and donated gold, land, slaves and other precious objects to the god's domain. By the time of Rameses III of the 20th Dynasty, there were over 50,000 priests in Egypt. There were Osiris plays that were recited. The walls of the Temple of Edfu are replete with the Drama of the struggles of Horus against Set for his actions against Osiris.

At first there was only 1 priest. He was the pharaoh and a bureaucracy developed in propagating the gods, standing in for the pharaohs and taking their places.

Each temple had its own high priest. The High Priest wore the leopard skin as a sign of his stature. On Narmer's Palette, the sandal bearer is wearing a leopard skin.

Priests were not necessarily religious. It was a job they did. They did a minimum of 3 months service each year. The *uab* or *wab* priest was of the lowest rank. There were 16 or 17 hierarchies of priests. One thing that can be said about the priests is that they were clean.

Priests had to be purified. They had to make a statement of being pure before they entered the temple. You had to declare you had not eaten fish. Fish does not appear on offering tables. The prohibition against eating fish was because fish were good things and should not be eaten. Priests were also prohibited from eating fish caught by a hook. Chastity was the rule they had to follow. There was a basin of water placed outside the temple for priest to wash before they entered. Almost everyone shaved to prevent lice. Priests wore white linen. Weavers of white linen were located in the Temple of Medinet Habu.

It can be said even further, the practice of medicine in Egypt may have begun in treatment of wounds suffered in building these magnificent projects to dead pharaohs. While we know Athothis or even Aha had medical knowledge, there are principally three major sources on Egyptian Medicine. These are the *Edwin Smith Surgical Papyrus*, the *Ebers Papyrus* and the *London-Leyden Magical Papyrus*.

The Edwin Smith Surgical Papyrus is unique in its clinical approach to medicine.

FREDERICK MONDERSON

It is based on knowledge of the causes of the ailment.

Forty-eight cases or injuries are discussed from the head downwards. For each the surgeon is told of the illness. "This is an ailment, which I will treat." "This is an ailment with which I will contend." "This is an ailment: This is an ailment I may cure; will possibly treat; there is no treatment." The preceding formulation is based on physician's contention and is found in the *Edwin Smith Surgical Papyrus*. It has no magic.

Edwin Smith's treatments are sultrices, splints, and poultices. These are not radically different from today's methods. The date is c. 1700 B.C., based on the language, but the medical treatments are from a much older period. Most of these ailments seem to be from accidents in pyramid building, injuries from construction. Therefore, some certainty may be attributable to Imhotep.

Horus is the sign of healing. So too is Isis. The Eye of Horus has healing potency.

There were three classes of physicians. The first group is mostly priests. Priest physicians. Most physicians are priests of Sekhmet. There are priests of Isis. There were also women physicians. There were also women priestesses. The second group was lay physicians. Perhaps they were attached to the military as medics. The third group is magicians. Other side *of Edwin Smith Surgical Papyrus*. There are 8 illnesses mentioned.

The *Ebers Papyrus* was found at Thebes around the US Civil War (1860-65). It is mainly magical. This has been called the necessary art. "The heart is important." Sekhmet priest are associated with it. Dendera was a hospital. Deir el Bahari was also associated with healing in the late period.

The *London-Leyden Magical Papyrus* is associated with magic. It's written in Demotic and Greek in the Third Century A.D. Anastasi bought it.

Part of the Beard of the Sphinx is in the British Museum.

Thoth was the god of writing. Clemens of Alexandria refers to the "42 Books of Thoth." More than 36 were on general knowledge and philosophy. One treated of the eye, one of women, one of fevers and one of remedies. Thoth was associated with Hermes. Thus, the Hermetic Books.

The three temples you visited on way to Aswan are Edfu, Temple of God Horus; Esneh Temple of God Khnum; and Kom Ombo, Temple of Gods Elder Horus and Sobek the Crocodile; were all built and decorated during Graeco-Roman occupation on principles of ancient building practices. Utilizing Egyptian and

QUINTESSENTIAL BOOK "THE HOLY LAND"

Nubian craftsmen, these occupiers added a few innovative features such as inundating the temples with the formulas of the ritual and a few artistic additions. This latter, particularly, has helped preserve much of the ritual practice not exhibited especially in New Kingdom temples.

Holy Land Photo 83. Parts of the surrounding landscape at Deir el Medina, Valley of the Nobles.

6.   Discussion

Are there any questions

Joshua Monderson: What types of sacrifice were practiced, if any, in ancient Egypt?
Dr. Fred Monderson: In the earliest times, the ancient Egyptians practiced human sacrifice but this was soon discontinued. After all, most primitive societies viewed their leader as a bringer of good fortune to the group and when he got old and could not do so anymore, they killed him. This is until some wise ruler came up with an alternative, which we called the Heb Sed Festival. With that settled, in the Archaic Period, human sacrifices were practiced in a few instances. Narmer and perhaps another king had retainers buried near their tombs. This was subsequently discontinued. However, other forms of sacrifice were continued.

The Papyrus of the Scribe Ani says: "Give thyself to God, keep thyself each day for God, and let to-morrow be like today. Sacrifice: God sees him who sacrifices. He neglects him who is negligent." Myers says one should serve God constantly and it is "necessary not to fail in performing the sacrifices, because He desires to see deference and worship paid Him by His creatures, and punishes those who do not follow His *culte* but rewards those who do. How far the self-interest of the worshipper enters into religious worship now or in the past, this is not the place to discuss."

Holy Land Ceramic Art 9. Another bird colorfully depicted, this time a falcon, an important bird in the Egyptian religious pantheon.

"The conception of the highest divinity in our Maxim is probably not the most elevated. He is considered as a Deity to be bribed by sacrifices, presents and gifts made, and worship paid to Him in the world, which are to be rewarded by Him to the worshipper in the next. How can one give the Supreme Deity gifts? He who owns and has owned everything from eternity and gives to man always? He regards with anger, says the text, those who neglect his cult, who do not sacrifice to him. The idea of the Supreme above All, and His rewards to His worshippers, is however elevated, as we sometimes find it set forth in some of the Hebrew Holy Writings and even in parts of the New Testament."

"The Maxim within itself, however, contains a very elevated morality. The Egyptian sacrifice was frequently only of bread, wine, incense, or water."

"The sacrifices in Egypt were not so bloody as the Jewish; they were mostly of fruit, flowers, bread, water, and wine, but sometimes and rarely of oxen, or geese. Some of the Festivals of Egypt may be found in the Christian Church to-day for instance, All Souls Day, a Festival of the Dead of the 29th day of Paophi, the early part of November. There were also in Ancient Egypt, feasts celebrated about the time of the Vernal Equinox, and a festival at the Summer Solstice to celebrate the

QUINTESSENTIAL BOOK
"THE HOLY LAND"

rising of the Nile, which parallels the celebration of the Festival of St. John, the Baptizer, by the Christian Church to-day."

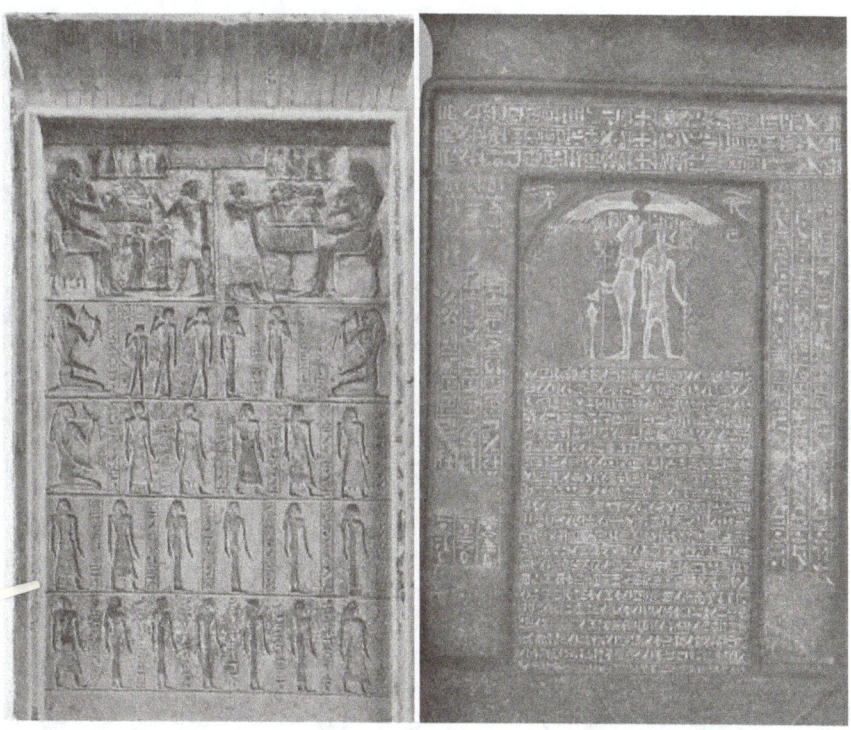

Holy Land Illustration 74a. Sepulchral stele of Aqer-ur, sculptured with figures of his three wives, and his sons and daughters of the XIth or XIIth Dynasty (left); and Stele of the twin brethren Heru and Sutui, overseers of the works at Thebes of the XIIth Dynasty, now in the British Museum(right).

"The ancient Egyptians had an absolute faith in the intervention of the Deity in the events of their daily life, and without cessation they implored Him to give them assistance and protection. Their vast pantheon contained not only symbols, or personifications, of the good influences whom they asked the aid of, but they also did not cease to conjure the personifications of evil and malign influences, to stay the hand of injury or punishment as to them, both in this world and the next. This is shown by the formulas, litanies, prayers, hymns, amulets, talismans, symbols, and especially by the content of the Per-em-hru, the so-called Book of the Dead, which have reached our day. In all periods of which we have knowledge, they used these, reciting them, wearing, or hoarding them, in their houses. The Hebrew appears to have used similar things, e.g., amulets, earrings, phylacteries or frontlets, fringes, mezuzoth, and talismanic writings."

FREDERICK MONDERSON

Flowers were a part of the daily ritual sacrifice. Actually, it was nearly sacrilege for one to interfere with the sacrifices to the gods and this was condemned. In fact, the deceased, in his *Negative Confessions* declared: "I have not troubled the sacrifices of the gods."

I suppose you could probably add Jesus' saying: "Give unto Caesar and to god what is his due!"

Marilyn James: What type of behavior would be considered sacrilege?
Dr. Fred Monderson: Sacrilege would be considered any behavior that is committed against the god or the temple of the god. Myers (1900: 254) tells: "Sacrilegious thieves do not respect the religious rules set up in the Temples. 'When the robber (of the Temple) has to appear before the Circle of the Nine gods; (i.e., the very ancient Eight Cosmic deities, and Thoth); then is revealed the well-known character of the court (judges?)' This is the same as to say - The robber of the Temple may escape punishment here on earth, but he will not escape punishment in the hereafter by the gods, and through his punishment the characteristics of the severity of the tribunal of the dead will be revealed. Dr. Lauth's note is: "I think this shows that the idea of retribution in the next existence for sins committed in this was a popular Egyptian idea at the time of the writing of our Papyrus."

Farouk Ghorab: Have any famous ancient Egyptian sayings come down to us?
Dr. Fred Monderson: Certainly. There have been many beginning with Imhotep who said: "Eat, drink, be merry, for tomorrow we die." Of course there were books such as *The Ancient Sayings*, *Papyrus of Sayings* and *The Good Sayings*. Still, the most famous is probably The *Book of Ptah-Hotep*.

It is interesting how he arranges his wise sayings as for instance: "Be not haughty because of Thy Knowledge, none having perfection in Wisdom or Artistic Knowledge." He says: "The beginning of the arrangement of the Good Sayings, spoken by the noble lord, the divine father, loved by God, the son of the king, the first-born (eldest) of his race, the prefect (and feudal lord) Ptah-Hotep, as a means for instructing the ignorant in a knowledge of the estimation of the Good Sayings. It is profitable for who shall hear them; it is a loss to who shall transgress them."

QUINTESSENTIAL BOOK
"THE HOLY LAND"

Holy Land Photo 84. Sakkara - Home of the Step Pyramid. Mr. Jackson prepares to enter the gate of the Enclosure Wall.

He says to his son - "Be not haughty because of thy knowledge; converse thou with the ignorant as with the scholar; for the barriers of art are never closed, no artist ever possessing that perfection to which he should aspire. (But) wisdom is more difficult to find than the emerald, because as to the latter, it is by slaves that it is discovered among the rocks of pegmatite."

Even further Ptah-Hotep says. "Do not lose your temper when disputing; be calm and silent if the other person loses his."

"If thou has to do with a disputer whilst he is in his heat and he is thy superior in ability, lower the hands, bend the back, do not get into a passion with him. As he will not permit thee to destroy (his) speech; it is a great error to interrupt him that proclaims that thou art not capable of being tranquil when contradicted."

FREDERICK MONDERSON

Holy Land Photo 84a. Sakkara - Home of the Step Pyramid. The Step- Pyramid built by Imhotep for Pharaoh Zoser, Third Dynasty, c. 2600 B.C.

"If thou have to do with a disputant when he is hot, act as one who cannot be moved. Thou (then) have the advantage over him, if only in keeping silent, when he is using evil speech. He who refrains is of greater worth, say the hearers, and thou art right in the opinion of the great."

John Brown: I saw the famous Scarab at the Sacred Lake in Karnak Temple. Who built it and for what purpose?
Dr. Fred Monderson: The Scarab beside the Sacred Lake at Karnak was placed there by Amenhotep III, the "magnificent." This beauty came from his mortuary temple across the river later destroyed by an earthquake. It was in commemoration of his marriage to Queen Tiy. In fact, this king began a practice of using scarabs on a wide scale in presenting many of his rulings. However, from the earliest times the scarab had a symbolism connected to the weighing of the heart of the deceased in the Hall of Judgment. This aspect of the *Psychostasia* is connected with Book XXXB of the *Book of the Dead*. Myers (1900: 322) says: "The oldest copy of it on a scarab now known, is of the period of king Sebak-em-saf, of the XIIIth dynasty, and is now in the British Museum, No. 7,876. The heart considered as the source of life, the place of conscience, and of good and evil conduct in man's world-life, was symbolized by the scarab and also by Khepra, the scarabaeus deity. Book LXIV, one of the oldest of all the Books of the Dead, uses similar language as to the heart as that found in XXXB. The doctrine of the 'Sacred Heart' of Horus, to the Ancient Egyptian was a great mystery. To-day it is

QUINTESSENTIAL BOOK
"THE HOLY LAND"

cherished with reverence by both Christians and Mahometans, in Egypt, as a symbol of life. In ancient times, it was the pip of the fruit of the Persea tree, which was looked on with veneration as its symbol, indeed that entire tree and its fruit, was considered sacred. The fruit is sometimes placed on the heart of Isis, cut open to show the pip."

Rev. Dr. Mc Nair: How did one experience the "second birth?"
Dr. Fred Monderson: The "Second Birth" was experienced after one survived the judgment in the next life. However, in order to experience this one had to have lived an exemplary life here on earth.

It's been said, the *Papyrus of Ani* is the best example of the Psychostasia wherein the Ka of Ani and that of his wife Thutu are pictured in the Judgment. Myers (1900: 45-426) explained: "She is wearing a Menat and is carrying a vine branch and a sistrum in her hands, the last evidencing that she held a position in one of the Temple at Thebes. They appear wearing the white robes and clothing of righteousness, black wigs, necklaces, etc., similar most likely those worn by them when alive. They are entering the Hall of the Two Truths or Hall of the Double Maati i.e., of Righteousness and Truth. In front of them to the right are the goddesses of the birth-chamber and early childhood, named Renenet and Meskhet (or Meskhenet) just in front and above them is the Ba, i.e. Soul, of Ani, represented as a human-headed bird likely a hawk, it is standing upon a pylon; then comes the left arm and scale-pan of the Balance, it contains the vase in which is Ani's heart, the symbol of his conscience, the content of his good and bad conduct when alive. Beyond this is a representation of Ranen, his destiny or fate, and over it is the head of his Meskhen, the "cubit with the human head," the representation of his embryo or new birth. Seated on the top of the standard of the Balance is the Cynocephalus ape consecrated to Thoth, it is an emblem of the equilibrium and adorer of the rising-sun. Anubis, deity of the dead, is testing the index of the Balance, and behind him is its right arm and scale-pan containing, in this picture, the ostrich feather representing Maat."

Leonard James: What role does Thoth play in the Judgment?
Dr. Fred Monderson: Thoth is a pivotal figure in the Judgment. As the emblem of the highest intellectuality and maintainer of the harmony of the universe, he is shown "holding in his right hand a reed-pen and in his left, an ink-palette and a sheet of papyrus, upon which to subscribe the results of his weighing." Myers (1900: 427) added further: "Watching the result is Aman, the devourer, also called Ammit, the accuser, punisher, eater and destroyer of the wicked dead; other names of this demon are Baba and Babai. This composite demon as given on this and other papyri is comprised of the head of a crocodile, the fore part of the trunk and the front feet of a lion, and the posteriors and hind feet of a hippopotamus. He may parallel the Satan of the Old Testament, who was one who opposed, the adversary, the accuser. Beginning in this same compartment, to the extreme left

but in the upper register, are shown representations of the assisting judges of Osiris who judge the earthly conduct of the deceased, and to whom he makes the many Negative Confessions of Book CXXV. They are all facing Osiris and an altar of sacrifice, and are seated, holding in their hands the Cucupha-head or Uas scepter (shaped like a feather, the symbol of Maat)." Many scholars believe Ammit, the eater of the dead, is a woman.

Mrs. Mc Flair: Who were the other judges in the Hall?
Dr. Fred Monderson: In this Papyrus, only twelve assisting judges of the dead are shown, they bear the names of well-known deities; these are beginning at the right respectively: "(1) Ra-Harmakhis, the personification of each day renewed and reborn rising sun (he is also called Horus and Haremkhu), at the moment its light has triumphed over its enemy, darkness. Darkness was also called Set or Sut; he was the demon opposed to light. Horus, by his new birth of To-day, has avenged the death of his father, Osiris, the dead sun of Yesterday. (2) Temu, Tm, Atum or Tum, the daily setting-sun. He was called "Father of the gods." Chaos and darkness, according to the Ancient Egyptian cosmogony, at the making of the universe, having preceded the creation of light. (3) Shu, deity representing the producing or generating, radiant energy of the sun. (4) Tefnut, lady of heaven, daughter of the sun, with the head of a lion (perhaps a lioness) personifying the force of the eyes of the sun, the moisture. The life of whomever sees her is affected. The goddess of vegetable growth. Goddess of moisture and associate of Shu. (5) Seb, deity of our earth. (6) Nut, a goddess, the personification of the sky, the mother of the gods, and the vault of heaven portrayed as a female, paralleled by Neith. (7) Isis, sister and wife of Osiris. (8) Nephthys, sister of Osiris. (9) Horus, the sun god, said to be by some Egyptologists, not Horus, the son of Isis. (10) Hathor, the space of the nocturnal heaven, lady of Amenti, the concealed region or under-world. Goddess of the land of the West, the Nether world, and of the true in speech, or those of the dead having the intonation of the righteous. She was also the golden goddess of the sky, of the setting-sun and the rising-sun, the goddess both beautiful and good. She gave birth to all the gods. (11) Hu, deity of the Nome Nefer-Ament in Lower Egypt. (12) Sa, of this deity we have not much knowledge. It may be that this name is an abbreviation of the name of the deity Sati."

Cherise Maloney: What happens next for the couple, Ani and his wife, Thutu?
Dr. Fred Monderson: Having passed the test, they are granted everlasting life. Myers (1900: 428-429) explained further: "Ani's earthly conduct is now to be weighed through the symbolism of the weighing of the heart, emblem of his conscience, against the norm of Ma'at or Righteousness, Ma'at personification of the rule of all moral rectitude and good behavior. Before the weighing, upon his entrance to the Hall of the Double Maati, the Ka of Ani pronounces the introductory hymns and praises to Ra and Osiris ... before the weighing of his heart, repeats the contents of Book XXXV of the Per-em-hru relating to the heart."

QUINTESSENTIAL BOOK
"THE HOLY LAND"

"The weighing having been accomplished by Anubis, and the heart, conscience, and soul of Ani, found pure and free from all sin; the Cynocephalus ape seated on the standard of the Balance so reports to Thoth, who is the Register of Righteousness and Truth of the great company of the gods who are in the presence of Osiris; and Thoth announces the same, saying, "Hear ye this judgment. The heart of Osiris the scribe Ani has in every truth been weighed, and his soul has stood as a witness for him; and it hath been found true by the Trial in the Great Balance. There hath not been found any wickedness in him; he hath not wasted the offerings in the temples; he hath not done harm by his deeds, he hath not uttered any evil reports whiles he was upon earth." The great company of the gods then says in reply to Thoth: "That which cometh forth from his mouth (O Thoth!) is declared true, Osiris the scribe Ani *ma kheru*, is holy and righteous. He hath not sinned neither hath he done evil against us. It shall not be allowed to the devourer Amamet that it prevails over him. Meat-offerings and an entrance into the presence of the god Osiris shall be granted unto him, together with a homestead (mansion?) forever in Sekhet-hetepu as (is granted) unto the followers of Horus."

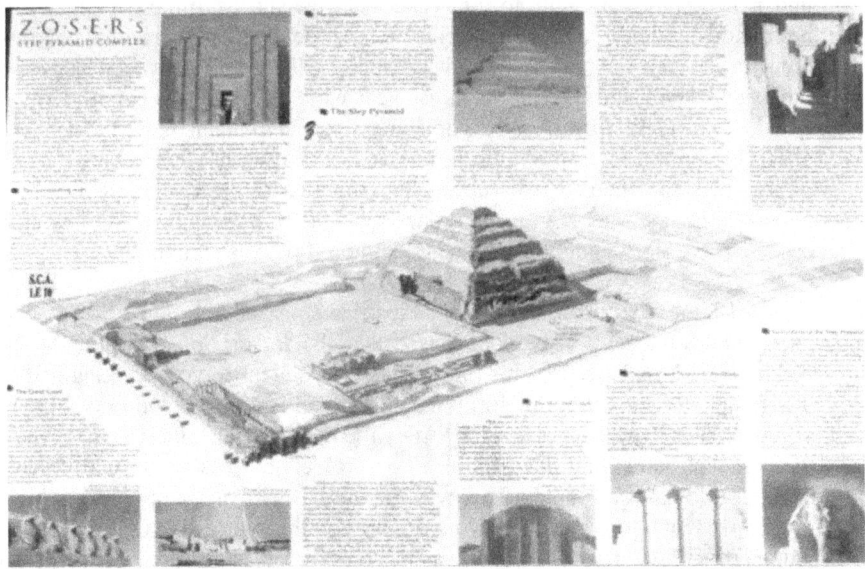

Holy Land Photo 85. Sakkara - Home of the Step Pyramid. Illustration of the Step Pyramid Complex with its constituent parts.

Michael Sinclair: What role has the serpent played in ancient Egypt?
Dr. Fred Monderson: A very important role. The serpent can be considered both a good and bad omen in ancient Egypt. In the Judgment where the twelve gods

assisted Osiris, Apap or Apophis the great serpent was among those present. This representative of darkness as opposed to light was also called Set or Sut, also the demon opposed to light. He was the evil serpent and this had an astronomical connection as previously stated. However, in the medical profession, the serpent, which is on the symbol of prescriptions, was shown on every temple as well as a uraeus that protected the brow of the pharaoh. It was thought to spit fire. Hence the notion of good and bad.

Jack Bender: How did the ancient Egyptian view of the notion of silence?
Dr. Fred Monderson: We know "silence is golden" and could appreciate this action as positive on the part of the Egyptians. It's been said; "In dangerous times wise men say nothing or remain silent." When one spoke in the Council it was wise to weigh one's own words. Otherwise, one should remain silent and ponder one's opponent. Then there were certain things one may observe from one's house regarding one's neighbor and silence should be the rule. However, if one witnessed a crime or injury to another then intervention would be the rule to assist the injured party. If intervention is not possible for a positive outcome, then denouncing the criminals become obligatory. This point is made more clearly by Myers (1900: 124) in that: "An Egyptian who witnessed an act of violence ought, under the penalty of death, to intervene and give succor to the person assailed; if he found it impossible to give succor, he must denounce the criminals and expose them to the tribunals. The non-observance of that legal provision was severely punished. The fact of living in a house near which a crime was committed was not deemed sufficient for arrest or punishment, the defendant must have been seen observing or hearing, or exhibiting knowledge that he had heard and stated some of the facts to others; it was necessary that this be positively proved, he came under the laws of our Maxim is at once evident from this law. The law as to the crime of accessory under the English Common Law was similar."

Leonard James: How did the ancient Egyptian construct the soul?
Dr. Fred Monderson: The soul was called the *Ba* or *Bai*. The human-headed sparrow hawk really represents the soul as the Ancient Egyptians imagined it, and it is frequently shown in this form in sculpture and paintings and drawings. Myers (1900: 268-269) wrote: "The soul was called Ba or Bai; plural Baiu. The word really means something like "sublime" or "noble," but has been usually translated by Egyptologists as "soul." This was the eternal part of the spiritual, which was thought to contain the elements necessary for the world-life of a man, such as judgment, conscience, etc., yet it was not considered as absolutely incorporeal. It was supposed to inhabit man's heart. The idea of it seems to be similar to that termed *psuke* or *psyche* by the Greeks. This *Ba* performed a pilgrimage in the Nether world, and was judged for the conduct of the man it inhabited in this world, by Osiris and the Forty-two judges. It was usually represented as a bird, especially as a human-headed sparrow hawk. It fluttered to and fro between this world and the next and cold pass into heaven and dwell with the perfected souls therein, also, sometimes visiting and conversing with the spirit of the body or mummy, in its

QUINTESSENTIAL BOOK
"THE HOLY LAND"

tomb. It was sometimes symbolically represented as a ram-headed scarabaeus, or a crane, at others as a lapwing. The Rua'h of the Hebrew Qabbalah parallels it. It was considered to have both form and substance; the latter was very subtle and refined. It was believed to enjoy an eternal existence in heaven in a condition of glory. On the death of a man it left him so as to fly to the gods, with whom it abode when not united to the other spiritual parts of man, but it cannot be thought of, as having been separated absolutely from the Ka of the man in whose body it existed during his life, until it was decided at the Psychostasia before Osiris and the Forty-two judges, that the Ka should not be united to its Ba, and there are representations of the *Ba* waiting for the result of the weighing at the *Psychostasia*. Therefore, the possession of the formula set forth in Chapter CXLVIII of the Per-em-hru, was to insure funeral food to the Ba of the dead one, which it partook of with the Ka. From the XVth to the XIth century B.C., it is usually represented as the ram-headed scarabaeus, which was its hieroglyphic symbol. The phonetic value of the ram is Ba, and of the scarabaeus *Kheper* – i.e., *to be,* or *to become*; this composite representation could be read "He who has become a soul."

James Madison: Could you get away with slander or were there laws against slander? Or more precisely, was slander considered a form of injustice and were there laws against it?
Dr. Fred Monderson: The ancient Egyptians had proscriptions against the use of slander advising use of discretion in speaking of others and insisting one not circulate injurious reports of others. According to the *Papyrus of Ani*, "Do not make thy thoughts known to a man with an evil tongue, so as to give him an occasion for abusing (thee) with his mouth. A disclosure going out of thy mouth circulates quickly; through the repetition of it thou createst enemies. The fall of a man is through his tongue; guard thyself from procuring thy ruin."

Stephanie McCall: What were the pros and cons of ancient Egyptian view of speech?
Dr. Fred Monderson: The Egyptians praised proper speech at the proper time. They also praised gentleness in speech. The *Book of Ptah-Hotep* advises: "Use great care as to what thou sayest in the Council, and the reasons for this. If thou art a wise man, sitting in the Council of thy lord, direct thy thoughts towards what is wise. Impose silence upon thyself rather than pour out thy words. When thou speakest, know what they (thy opponents) can object against thee. It is an art to speak in the Council, and speech is criticized more than all (other) work; it is contradiction which puts it to proof." In addition, they advised to be discreet in speech. The Ka of the deceased denied using noisy speech when alive and they denied use of exaggeration in speech.

FREDERICK MONDERSON

Holy Land Illustration 75. Sepulchral stele of Thuthmose, Captain of the Gate of Memphis, XVIIIth Dynasty (left); and Sepulchral stele of Heru-em-heb, a Prince, scribe, and Commander-in-Chief of the XVIIIth Dynasty (right).

Kashmoney Malone: Where do you think the ancient Egyptians got their ideas for the religious ritual in the Book of the Dead?
Dr. Fred Monderson: Undoubtedly the ancients got much of their ideas, moral, spiritual, geographic and linguistic from the cultural ethos and geographic, zoological and botanical environs of inner Africa. The ideas were very old, difficult to assess how old and one can only wonder at how early man formulated such pioneering ideas. Myers (1900: VIII) tells us: "There is not any question, that the ideas from which the content of these writings were formulated, were traditional and of a very much earlier time than when written, but when and where they originated, and from whom they first came, we shall likely never know, unless we accept that the content of these writings were original ideas from the minds of the men whose names are attached to them, which we think far from certain. One may be sure, however, that a people having in vogue such ideas, had advanced far beyond a condition of primitives or barbarism, and, indeed, the

QUINTESSENTIAL BOOK
"THE HOLY LAND"

earliest historic knowledge we have of the people of Ancient Egypt shows an acquaintance with a perfect language and writing, a religious priesthood and ritual and a belief in a resurrection of the spirit of the dead, and as to such resurrected spirit, its continuance in a future eternal life, subject to punishment in the spiritual life, for evil conduct committed whilst in this world imprisoned in the flesh." Therefore, reason dictates these events in sum, occurred before the coming of the whites!

Teddy Cubia: Can you explain the "Osiris Myth?"
Dr. Fred Monderson: Certainly. Osiris was a wise and beneficent king who reclaimed the Egyptians from savagery, gave them laws and taught them handicrafts. The prosperous reign of Osiris was brought to a premature close by the machinations of his wicked and jealous brother Seth, who with seventy-two fellow-conspirators invited Osiris to a banquet, induced him to enter a cunningly-wrought coffin made exactly to his body measurements, tricked him into sitting in it and then shut down the lid and cast the chest into the Nile. Isis, the faithful and loving wife of Osiris, set forth in search of her dead husband's body, and after long and adventure-fraught wanderings, succeeded in recovering it and bringing it back to Egypt. Then while she was absent visiting her son Horus in the city of Buto, Seth once more gained possession of the corpse, cut it into fourteen pieces, and scattered them all over Egypt. But Isis collected the fragment, and wherever one was found, buried it with due honor; or, according to a different account, she joined the limbs together by virtue of her magical powers, and the slain Osiris, thus resurrected, henceforth reigned as king of the dead in the nether world. When Horus grew up he set out to avenge his father's murder, and after terrible struggles finally conquered and dispossessed his wicked uncle; or, as another version relates, the combatants were separated by Thoth, and Egypt divided between them, the northern part falling to Horus and the southern to Seth. Such is the story as told by Plutarch, with certain additions and modifications from older native sources. There existed, however, a very ancient tradition according to which Horus and Seth were hostile brothers, not nephew and uncle; and many considerations may be urged in support of the thesis which regards their struggles as reminiscent of wars between two prominent tribes, one of which worshipped the falcon Horus while the other had the Okapi Seth as its patron and champion. The Horus tribes were the victors, and it was from them that the dynastic line sprang; hence the Pharaoh always bore the name of Horus, and represented in his own hallowed person the ancient tribal deity.

Carmelita McCall: Who was the supreme deity in ancient Egypt?
Dr. Fred Monderson: The supreme deity in ancient Egypt depended on the time or period, the royal family and the favored deity. Clearly it was Ra the sun god who originated in Heliopolis or Annu. When Narmer moved his capital to Memphis he recognized and emphasized the importance of Ptah, architect of the universe. By the Middle and New Kingdoms, it was Amon and later Amon-Ra who became the

supreme deity. Nevertheless, throughout Osiris was a deity of equal standing as opposed to being favored by time and circumstances. He was unique in that he had a mortal and divine nature having lived, died and resurrected to become the judge of the dead in the underworld.

Holy Land Ceramic Art 10. Talk about the Penguin being decked out in tails, how about this bird in a similar fancy suit?

Walter Brown: How significant was the Amarna revolution?
Dr. Fred Monderson: The Amarna Revolution, coming as it did at the end of the XVIIIth Dynasty, was a significant movement that failed purely because of the cruelty of its adherents and the vigor with which they pursued and sought to obliterate Amon's influence. The influence of Amenhotep IV, Akhenaten, was not simply in religion and politics but art, architecture and building as well. Myers (1900: 356-357) relates: "The great find of baked terra-cotta tablets written in the cuneiform text, at Tell el-Amarna in Egypt, is composed of political and other important letters and correspondence, carried on during the XVIIIth Dynasty. This was also the period of Amen-Hotep IV, afterwards known as Akhen-aten, who changed his devotion from Amon-Ra the great deity of Thebes and of all Egypt, to that of the worship of the more abstract qualities of Ma'at, the harmony of the universe, the true; and of the radiant energy of the sun; the sun creating, energizing

QUINTESSENTIAL BOOK
"THE HOLY LAND"

and sustaining all earthly existence by means of its rays: very scientific and philosophical ideas, the truth of which has only been discovered within the past fifty years by great modern scientists. It was likely during this dynasty, if not earlier, under which king we do not know, were fully formulated in writing, the ethical truths set forth in the Book now called Chapter CXXXV, of the Book of the Dead.

Holy Land Photo 86. Sakkara - Home of the Step Pyramid. From the Great Court, view of the Colonnade that entrances or exits the structure through the Enclosure Wall.

Peter Monderson: Despite its futuristic view, generally speaking, why did Akhenaten's religious movement fail?
Dr. Fred Monderson: Akhenaten's religious movement failed principally for one important reason. His concepts, ideas and innovations in art, science, architecture and even governance were great! However, he used violence and this strategy did not go well with prevailing religious beliefs. He reasoned there was corruption in the practices of the Amon Priesthood. After all, their wealth had blossomed and their power commensurate with such wealth threatened the monarchical system. He sought to change this and so attacked Amon's priestly administration, beliefs, and his image, wherever it was found he chiseled it out. Strange he did not attack Amon's wife, the goddess Mut who represented mother.

Some have argued you could kill a man's family and anything so serious and he would eventually forgive you; but steal his money and he never forgets. Akhenaten's attacks on the wealth and privilege of the Priesthood generated a reaction that ultimately led to his downfall. Even more important, however, besides his violent actions against Amon, this move forced people to change their belief system. He did find himself uncomfortable in visiting the national temple at Karnak where Amon's worship was extremely visible. Thus, he moved to Amarna and founded a new city and capital while he executed his proscription against Amon and Thebes. Maspero has argued, every town or city in ancient Egypt has had a founding god and what essentially Akhenaten wanted to do was force the people to renounce Amon who was the founding god of Thebes.

Now let me turn you over to "**The Egyptian Universe**" by James Allen, delivered in that series in 1992.

An illustration of the world shows an arching figure on the horizon from east to west.

Shu = dry, empty

Nut is known, Geb is not known.

Ceiling of Cenotaph of Seti I, father of Rameses II, located at Abydos, burial place.

Rameses IV, papyri from Fayum 200 A.D.

Uniform doctrine [Direction]. This is an area from which the bird comes. Rear is east. Facing west, feet in east.

A good question is: Why do birds come to Egypt?
Ans. Birds in Europe take Egypt in migration path to Africa. The soul is a bird with human head. Birds from the north identified with people who have died and live in the Duat.

The upper part of the sky is in darkness and there is no light; the Sun does not shine there. This is the universe outside of the world.

Beyond the sky there was nothing, a vast endless ocean because the sun was beneath the sky. This vast nothingness was NUN.

The known world was finite. The ocean outside the dark was infinite and of uniform darkness.

Akh is form without a body after death.

QUINTESSENTIAL BOOK
"THE HOLY LAND"

Ba = soul
Akh = ghost.

Outside the sky there is an endless ocean. Nut is the watery one. Nut is the surface of the vast universal ocean. The point where the atmosphere and the universal ocean meet is what Nut represents.

The Duat is a part of the world that is not sky or the world.

The netherworld underneath the world. It's the Duat. Naunet is the watery one, the under-sky. Tefnut is the atmosphere.

Holy Land Photo 86a. Sakkara - Home of the Step Pyramid. From within the ruins of the "Heb Sed Court," at a distance, a side view of the previous colonnade and roofing.

Where the sun goes is where the dead people go.
The Coffin Text has spells to not walk upside down.

The Book of Gates – The sun is presented by primeval god to Nut at the beginning of the day.

The sun went into the goddess Nut at night. Nut is the coffin, sarcophagus containing the dead. Another idea of Nut – Nut as a cosmic embryonic sac. The coffin is a solidified embryonic sac.

Winged disk at the mouth of Nuit.

The sun is inside the body of Nut, in the night, pregnant and will be born in the

FREDERICK MONDERSON

morning. The sun really enters the Duat in the second hour of the night. In the middle of the night, the sun rests on Osiris in the Duat. The two of them merge. The ram headed god says this is Ra in Osiris, Osiris in Ra.

The sun gets new life, resurrected through Osiris. Osiris, once dead, lives again in the resurrected person of the sun.

Another question is: Why is the sky red after the sun is born?
Ans. This is the afterbirth. The sun is born 1 hour before it comes up on the horizon. Akhet, the place where the sun is born, "slapped" him, cleansed him and sent him on his way. The mummy is a person's Osiris.

Baboons – as sun worshippers, are chattering at dawn, welcoming the sun.

Sunrise in the morning is the same as creation.

Every sunrise is creation repeated.

Sunrise is beginning of the second hour of the day. The sun was born one hour before. He is Khepra, the sun coming into existence.

Universal Ocean of water

Bubble of air.

That was the second lecture in the series by James Allen.

Holy Land Photo 87. Sakkara - Home of the Step Pyramid. From the Great Court, stairs to the left and uraei atop the retaining wall.

Frederick Maloney: We saw the Calendar at Kom Ombo. Were there others? And

QUINTESSENTIAL BOOK "THE HOLY LAND"

how old were these?
Dr. Fred Monderson: There were certainly others. That one has survived. Another is visible at Esneh. We are told the only calendars in Egypt are of Greco-Roman origin. However, any argument from the absence of monumental evidence is risky. Nevertheless, today Egypt is the only country that practices four calendars, the old Egyptian farming, European (Gregorian), Coptic religious and Islamic religious.

Myers (1900: 444-445) explained: "The ancient Egyptians had different calendars. They had (I). The vague or civil year. It consisted of 365 days, and was divided into twelve months of thirty days each; to this five intercalary days were added at the end. (II) The Sothic or Canicular year of 365¼ days. The first year of a Sothic period began with the helical rising of Sirius or Sothis also called the Dog star; and continued to the next helical rising of this star. The first helical rising in June, at the Summer Solstice, agreed with about the time of the beginning of the Inundation of the Nile. The first appearance of the Inundation may be noticed in the early part of June at the cataracts, beginning, after it has decreased in this month, to its lowest level. (III) The Solar year. This was ¼ of a day shorter than the Sothic year and consisted of 365 days, an error which corrected itself in 1461 common years or 1460 Sothic or Julian years. The true year was estimated from the conjunction of the rising Sun with Sirius, that would be about June 21."

"The Egyptian Sothic year began at a very ancient time with the Sun in the zodiacal sign Cancer (i.e., the Crab), when that was the zodiacal constellation at the happening of the Summer Solstice, about our June 21, and at the time of the helical rising of Sothis or Sirius, which was also about the time of the more evident beginning of the Inundation of the Nile; and Cancer, it has been said, was considered by the priests, to have presided at the hour when the world itself came into existence. The Egyptians also began one of their years about the time of the happening of the Winter Solstice, say December 21, when the light of the day was shortest, which after that day increases, ending with the coming again in the same period, as a new commencement of another year. The zodiacal constellation of the Winter Solstice was at one time the He-Goat, Capricorn. Dr. Brugsch says: 'that as early as 2,500 B.C., the Ancient Egyptians had in use four different forms of the year. The constellation of Cancer, the Crab, was consecrated to Anubis, god of the dead; and that of Capricorn, the He-Goat, to Mendes. They each refer to the apparent retrogression of the sun at the time of the solstices. The Balance (then most probably included in the zodiacal constellation Scorpio) would have been at that time, that of the Vernal Equinox, and the Ram that of the Autumnal. This would be about 8712 B.C. The Bull was at the constellation of the Vernal Equinox about 4400 B.C. Scorpio would at that time have been that of the Autumnal Equinox, which would perhaps account for the archaic Egyptian antipathy to one for the serpent; texts in the Pyramid of the king Unas (circa 3536-3503 B.C.) show this aversion was in his period very great. Aquarius would be then, the zodiacal

FREDERICK MONDERSON

constellation of the Summer Solstice and Leo that of the Winter Solstice."

Holy Land Photo 87a. Sakkara - Home of the Step Pyramid. Ruins in the "Heb Sed Court;" and repairs being done to the Step Pyramid.

Joshua Monderson: Where would you say are located the most significant collection of Egyptian antiquities?
Dr. Fred Monderson: I presume you mean outside of Egypt, for the most part, but let me say this. In 1881 while Maspero was Director of Antiquities, discovery of the Deir el Bahari cache revealed the great mummies of the New Kingdom and their enormous treasures. This discovery of mummies brought the Egyptian Museum on par with the Museum of Turin. The second discovery in the tomb of Amenhotep II in 1898 enhanced the museum's standing. Just to show how lucrative the Turin Museum was as early as the 1880s, *Encyclopedia Britannica* (Ninth Edition, 1911) states: "Of the collections of Egyptian antiquities in public museums those of the British Museum, Leiden, Berlin, the Louvre, Turin were already very important in the first half of the 19th century, also in a less degree those of Florence, Bologna, and the Vatican. Most of these have since been greatly increased and many others have been created. By far the largest collection in the world is that at Cairo. In America the museums and universities of Boston, Chicago, Philadelphia, San Francisco and New York have collections of greater or less interest. Beside these the museums of Edinburgh, Liverpool, Manchester and Oxford are noteworthy in Great Britain for the Egyptian antiquities, as are those of St. Petersburg, Vienna, Marseilles, Munich, Copenhagen, Palermo and Athens; they are also collections in most of the British Colonies. The numbers of private collection are too numerous to mention. That is all for today. See you at dinner at 7:00 PM.

7. Free Time

8. Dinner

QUINTESSENTIAL BOOK
"THE HOLY LAND"

Dr. Leonard James: Brother Brown, I hear the ladies are going shopping to the Sook right after dinner. Do you want to come with us? I hear you can get good bargains on cotton cloths.
Walter Brown: Ok, Dr. James. I will try to get Juliet to go with me. We need some things such as table cloths, and perhaps some gifts for our neighbors. Ok, I will meet you in the lobby after dinner.
Dr. Leonard James: Good idea.

Ms. Malone: How about us ladies do a little shopping after dinner?
Stephaniea McCall: I think it's a wonderful idea. Are you coming Carmelitiea?
Carmelitiea Shabazz: I think I will. Will you get any of the other ladies?
Ms. Malone: I will round up as many of the ladies who want to go. Are you coming, Esperanza?
Esperanza Rodriguez: Yes, I am.

Holy Land Papyrus 26. Strange that the King shoots from the seating position as the Queen points to a possible target for his arrow.

George Washington: I thought I would come over early before dinner to discuss the events of November 12, 1975

Michelliea Georges: Good idea. What do you think, Regina?
Regina Hendricks: Does that mean, Brother Washington, that we would get a second piece after dinner?
George Washington: I'm not sure. I hear some people are going to the Sook to do a little shopping. It depends on how I feel this evening. I think I'm coming down

FREDERICK MONDERSON

with the "Scourge of Egypt." But let's see. So, in **African Religious Thought Systems** on that day we discussed:

Gikuyu society is determined by 3 governing principles.

The family group (mbari or nuomba), both nuclear and extended.
Clan (moherega), which comprises many family, groups or mbaris.
The age-grading system (riika), which unites and solidifies the whole tribes in all its activities as opposed to the other two, which can be independent.

Holy Land Photo 88. Sakkara - Home of the Step Pyramid. A better view of some of the ruins of the complex and roof to the Colonnade from the side.

DAHOMEAN THEOLOGY AND COSMOLOGY: DIVINE GENEALOGY OF THE SKY FAMILY

Nana Bukulu and Mawu and Lisa were worshipped at Abomey with the main shrine at Jena.
Gu represented iron and was charged with making the earth habitable.
Age was a hunter, Vodun of forest, all animals under his control.
Dji was the sixth child.
Wete and Alawe were two sons who were keepers of the treasures of Lisa.
Aziza and Akazu were two daughters who kept the treasures of Mawu.
Loko has care of trees and Adjak Pa looks over water or life.
Mawu (female) and Lisa (male) were principles. Lisa symbolized heat.

Mawu is female, mother, older, elder, representing gentleness and forgiving. Lisa was male, younger, robust, ruthless, reigns in day, men condemned to toil and

QUINTESSENTIAL BOOK "THE HOLY LAND"

Holy Land Illustration 76. Tutankhamon and his Queen in a palace chamber (left); and a corner of the Gilded Burial Shrine of Tutankhamon's tomb (right). Note the two black statues of the boy king!

suffering in the hot sun, in anger and feverishness. Mawu reigns at night when it is cool, resting, rest is necessary. The whole structure is divinely inspired. Pleasures of life are pursued including lovemaking. When Lisa punishes Mawu pardons or forgives.

Coolness symbolizes wisdom, Mawu becomes concentrated wisdom of the people; and wisdom comes with age. Young men are physically strong but old men have wisdom. The principal shrine to Mawu is in Abomey at Djena. Mawu-Lisa is the most royal of divinities. All spirits have different specialties, likes and dislikes.

Mawu and Lisa gave birth to three principles. These are thunder, earth and sea.

Gu is very important with all people who work with metals. He represents the special deity of all ironworkers who are protected by him. Gu was charged with making the earth a habitable place for man. His body is made of stone and his head is made of iron. He is a god of metal and war. The blacksmith himself is the spirit of Gu. A shrine was built to him with an open roof (top) to let smoke out and avoid burning the roof as smith constantly works there.

Age is a hunter, Vodun of the forest and all animals are under his control. Papa Bois of Trinidad also called the "old man of the forest."

Dji is the sixth child of Mawu and Lisa. He is represented by the rainbow and brings thunder pantheon to earth and sea. Wete and Alaw are keepers of all valuables and supplies, which Lisa has power to give to man. Loko has care of

FREDERICK MONDERSON

trees. His younger brother Medje assists him.

Spiritual power equals western magic and associated with healing. Aziza becomes the principle of medicine in forest that transfers power. Loco is related to spirits of ancestors. Trees and leaves are very important in Dahomean medical practice.

Now for the **Ancient History** part as done October 29, 1975.

Sargon established the first Mesopotamian empire. He destroyed all fortifications of Sumerian city-states. These fortified city-states were almost impregnable. He appointed his sons and friends as governors in the various city-states in his empire. His daughters were made high priestesses in the lands. He established military garrisons throughout the empire. Trade became a state monopoly. This dynasty lasted from 2340-2150 B.C., that is 190 years.

Sargon's son Rimush succeeded him. Just then several Sumerian city-states rebelled, testing the new king's strength.

Naramsin, Sargon's grandson, put down all Sumerian city states rebellions and consolidated his empire. He also decreed that he was a god, husband of Ishtar (Venus), God of Akkad. A divine monarchy was formed afterwards. At this time the Mesopotamian population was 50 percent Semitic. Paternal descent and patriarchal descent became the order of the day in that culture.

C. 2150 B.C. droughts were very instrumental in bringing about the empire's collapse. Gutians, Elamites and Hurrians came from the mountainous regions and pillaged the lands and destroyed irrigation canals. Naramsin allowed his invading forces to sack the city of Nippur, home of the God Enlil.

In 2135 B.C. the City of Ur conquered the area and established stability. This lasted for about 100 years. Ur-ammu established the Third Dynasty of Ur. This dynasty was contemporary with the Egyptian XIth Dynasty. A library was established with many clay tablets.

Diodorus Siculus was a first century B.C. Greek historian and author of Historical Library with 40 books of which only books I-V and XI-XX are extant. Strabo lived 63 B.C. to 24 A.D. He was a Greek geographer, born at Amasya in Pontus, and settled in Rome c. 20 B.C. He traveled widely and wrote geography describing Europe, Asia, Egypt and Libya.

Plutarch lived 46-120 A.D. He was a Greek biographer who wrote Parallel Lives and taught in Rome. He also wrote the Myth of Isis and Osiris.

QUINTESSENTIAL BOOK "THE HOLY LAND"

Manetho was an Egyptian priest and historian of the 3rd Century B.C. He was the author of a History of Egypt, written in Greek. He also recorded the first dynastic listing of 30 dynasties.

George Washington: I decided to make this short so we can all go shopping with the gang.

Michelliea Georges: Good idea. Are you coming, Regina?
Regina Hendricks: Yes, I need to get some things for my little brother.

George Washington: First Intermediate Period was studied after the Mid Term on November 5, 1975.

There was some stability in the second half of the period. There were two camps established at Heracleopolis from the 6th to the 10th Dynasty and the 11th Dynasty at Thebes. Art schools were discontinued and the quality of art declined. Thebes revived the quality of art. Nebhepetre Mentuhotep was the first of the 11th Dynasty kings from Thebes. Creation of magnificent literature in the north – (Meri Kare). There are signs of monotheism and signs of religious drama. Egypt was reunited in two camps with both showing economic stability.

VISIT TO THE METROPOLITAN MUSEUM OF ART November 22, 1975 at 10:00 AM.

First Intermediate Period continued.

11th Dynasty – Mentuhotep (the God is satisfied) ruled about 1820 B.C.? Nebhepetre Mentuhotep extended Theban influence to Abydos; and Heracleopolis influence from Abydos to the North. In the 14th year, Meri Kare led Abydos in rebellion against Thebes. Thebes nevertheless prevailed and the unification took some 50 years. A Nubian kingdom to the south was hostile to Thebes and allied to the north. Mentuhotep was king of all Egypt with the unification. There was significant population decrease in the First Intermediate Period. The population now stood at 3 million. Coptic was a derivative of Middle Egyptian. In the last 2 years of last 11th dynasty king, an inscription at Wadi Hammamat tells of an antelope that gave birth on the inscription stone.

12th Dynasty Amenemhet ruled c. 1991 B.C. He was not of royal blood. His mother was from Elephantine, perhaps Nubian. A great deal of propaganda literature was associated with this period.

New texts were made mandatory in schools. The *Prophecy of Neferti* and

FREDERICK MONDERSON

Instruction of Amenemhat were important literary works. The eastern delta was economically important for fishing, cattle breeding and agriculture. Now, 50 percent of the population lived in the delta.

The *Prophecy of Neferti* is set in the 4th dynasty. Great calamities will befall Egypt, Ma'at will leave. A great man from the south will restore Ma'at to Egypt. This was Amenemhat. He established the Temple of Karnak. It is the greatest temple ever built for god Amon-Re.

Holy Land Photo 89. Sakkara - Home of the Step Pyramid. Noble with his staff and a small female figure before him (left); and Tomb of Ptahhotep. Colossal size of the Nobleman Ptahhotep with staff in one and ankh in his other hand (right).

Teddy Cubia: I will read another of my poems. This is a short one entitled "What is a Brother?"
Dr. Alexander Pushkin: Go ahead Teddy. As is customary, I have the lemon squeezes.
Mrs. Alexander Pushkin: Honey. I think they deserve it. You are so fortunate to be paired with these two intelligent and outspoken artistic young men.
Dr. Alexander Pushkin: Teddy is not so young. He is retired.
Mrs. Alexander Pushkin: Retired. How old are you Teddy? You don't look a day over thirty-five.
Teddy Cubia: Nice complement Mrs. Pushkin. I am fifty-five. Work hard and

QUINTESSENTIAL BOOK
"THE HOLY LAND"

sleep early. That is my motto.

"What is a Brother?"
By
Teddy Cubia

> A brother is
> A special blend
> Of pal and pest
> Of foe and friend
>
> He teases a lot
> Makes fun of you, too
> But if you're in a pinch
> He'll stand up for you
>
> He can't be fluttered
> (He's much too bright)
> but he can be bribed
> if the offer is right!
>
> He's tough on the clutch
> He won't fall apart
> And he'd never admit
> That he has a soft heart!
>
> You can't help loving him
> He's as great as can be
> And you're proud to be part
> Of the same family!!

"Deborah Stokely wrote this for me on July 7, 1977. I remember it well for that person spoken of was my brother." (Teddy Cubia)

Michael Sinclair: My hat's off to you Mr. Cubia. Your poetry is about the people. You know, the man in the Street. It appeals to all people across the spectrum. Pity you didn't publish your writings.
Teddy Cubia: Well, I am in the process of organizing my writings and considering some kind of publication.
Dr. Alexander Pushkin: Teddy, here's your lemon squeeze and a cold beer to go with it. Your poems bring back memories of the struggle we waged for respect

FREDERICK MONDERSON

and rights in America. We need more young people like Mr. Sinclair to take our people to the next level. Remember what Frederick Douglass said, "Without struggle, there is no progress."

Day 8.   ASWAN: ABU SIMBEL
1.   Wake Up

Esperanza Rodriguez: Good Morning, Mi Amor. Your schedule today calls for a bus trip to the Aswan Airport for a flight to Abu Simbel. There will be a return flight and lecture this afternoon.

Dr. Monderson: How are you this lovely morning, my dear?

Esperanza Rodriguez: Very well sir.

Holy Land Photo 90. Sakkara - Home of the Step Pyramid. Butchers at work!

QUINTESSENTIAL BOOK
"THE HOLY LAND"

"The Nile Valley in Antiquity History"
By
Frederick Monderson

The ancient Nile Valley civilization of Kemet, modern Egypt, was an African and by today's standards, Black culture, first of its kind to become conscious of its intellectual, philosophical, artistic and spiritual creativity. The Black people of Ancient Kemet along the Nile enlightened the world! So argued the great African intellect Cheikh Anta Diop in systematic, inter-disciplinary, erudite, irrefutable and well thought-out scholarship entitled, *The African Origin of Civilization*: *Myth or Reality*. A number of dedicated writers including Martin Delaney, W.E.B. DuBois, Carter G. Woodson, George G.M. James, John Jackson, Yosef ben-Jochannan, Ben Carruthers, John H. Clarke, Theophile Obenga, Molefi Asante, and Ivan Van Sertima among these, after many years of research and teaching, have asserted the exact idea. This then, is the idea to advocate! For, if our scholars and heroes tell us after their long years of research, teaching, lectures, writings, intellectual disappointments, etc., that the historical record has been falsified to show prominence of Europe and degradation of Africa, who are we to believe?

The great achievement and gift of this Northeast African culture was its theosophical, religious, architectural and moral genius embodied in the ancient Egyptian or Kemetic temple. This creation, unlike the Jewish synagogue, Greek or Roman Temple, Muslim Mosque, or Christian Cathedral, was unique and still evokes and exudes profound theological and cosmological spiritualism, posing thoughtful questions for scholars still seeking to define it. Here, no public worship was performed, the faithful did not congregate for public prayer, and no one was admitted inside the deeper echelons of the temple except the priests. Still, wrote Maspero, the "temple was built as an image of the world, as the Egyptians imagined it to be."

The architecture seemed divinely inspired and with space for the principal gods, the buildings became complex with small rooms for secondary gods, statues, dim lights, maze of halls, and arrangement of trick doors, as well as stairs to the roof. There were also side rooms for keeping garments, jewelry, and cult objects for the religious ceremonies on altars. Libraries were an essential part of any temple, for scholars congregated in temples that were considered "Colleges." Some temples had a well, Nilometer, granaries and dwellings for the temple staff. To meet needs of the daily rituals, gardens provided fresh flowers for the temple service and food for the staff. Granaries and storehouses were filled with staff produce, looked-over by large contingents of scribes, overseers and managers in charge of administration. Temples were frequently provided with allocations of prisoners-of-wars for work on temple lands. They were also recipients of kingly and noble endowments for mortuary cults, and they enjoyed tax-free status. The library was also an essential part of every temple for the daily ritual, as well as functioning as universities for training other priests, government bureaucrats, nobles and physicians. Thus, it's easier to speak about the ancient Kemet/Egyptian temple, rather than say what it really is, since it meant many things.

Principally, however, Marriet-Bey wrote: "Egyptian temples are always dedicated to three gods. It is what Champollion calls the triad. The first is the male principle, the second is the female principle, and the third is the offspring of the other two. But these three deities are blended into one. The father engenders himself in the womb of the mother and thus become at once his own father and his own son. Thereby are expressed the un-created-ness and the eternity of the being who has had no beginning and who shall have no end."

So, to help understand the temple of the nation of ancient Kemet, it can also be viewed within the context of the principle of sculptural decoration. Pictures are arranged symmetrically side by side. Several series of pictures are disposed in tiers one above the other and cover the walls of chambers from top to bottom. The role of the king is thus key as he "presents an offering (a table laden with victuals, flowers, fruits, and emblems) and solicits a favor from the god. In his answer the god grants the gift that is prayed for." Thus, decoration of the temple consists of nothing more than an act of adoration from the king. As such, a temple can be both a primordial hill and the "exclusive personal monument of the king by whom it was founded or decorated." In foundation deposits, founders' emblems, tools, food and blood from sacrificial animals were deposited to ensure blessings to the temple.

The king is generally shown in the pictures on one side and on one or more divinities on the other.

The worship consists of prayers, recited within the temple in the name of the king, and above all, of processions. In these processions which the king is supposed to head, are carried the insignia of the gods, the coffers in which their statues are enclosed, and also the sacred barks which later are generally deposited in the temple, to be brought out on fete days. In the middle, concealed under a veil, stands the coffer within which lies the emblem that none must see. The processions are commonly held within the temple. They generally ascend the terraces and sometimes spread themselves inside the enclosure away from the profane gaze. On rare occasions, the processions may be seen leaving the city and

QUINTESSENTIAL BOOK
"THE HOLY LAND"

winding their way, either along the Nile or along a canal called the Sacred Canal, toward some other city more or less distant. Close to every temple is a lake. In all probability the lake played an important part in the processions and the sacred barks were deposited there, at least while the fete lasted.

These early Africans were the genesis of their own genius who thought out the fundamental principles of religion and its significance for salvation of their people. These "houses of life," for whom were crafted the cosmological creation of the particular cult, grew from simple beginnings into huge and complex structures of stone. As such then, the temple can be seen as a: "royal proscynem, or ex voto that is a token of piety from the king who erected it in order to deserve the favor of the gods. It is a kind of royal oratory and nothing more."

Some two hundred years ago in the aftermath of the American and French Revolutions, Napoleon invaded Egypt in "carrying the war to Britain." Whatever the intent, he helped to unleash intensive European scholarship interests after his men found the Rosetta Stone. Dispersed throughout the land his savants studied temples as Kom Ombo, Edfu, Dendera, Karnak, Esneh, and a host of other wonderfully enlightening educational sites producing a monumental photographic *Description of Egypt*. Their efforts culminated in academic revivals in ancient studies and with Champollion's decipherment of Hieroglyphics, began the discipline of Egyptology. A century later, anthropology and archaeology in the Nile Valley, capitalized on opportunities presented in the dynamics of European imperial intrigue and designs of the Berlin Congress of 1884.

By 1900, the British and French, still in Egypt since the days of Napoleon, were joined by the Germans, Americans, Swiss, Turks, Belgians and Italians. Together they unleashed extensive and systematic expeditions to excavate and map the ancient land. They unearthed much buried treasures, which were later dispersed to adorn museums throughout Europe and America. However, a derivative benefit was unearthing, clearance and reconstruction of Egyptian/Kemetic architectural history enabling scholars to trace the evolution of the temple.

Briefly, it's agreed that pharaonic civilization from the first dynasty to the Greco-Roman experience was divided into the Old Kingdom, the Middle Kingdom and the New Kingdom. The Late Period included the Ethiopian conquest, and that of the Persians, Assyrians, Greeks and then Romans.

FREDERICK MONDERSON

Holy Land Illustration 77. Sepulchral stele of Kha-Bekhnet, with scenes representing the deceased worshipping Ra and Hathor, XIXth Dynasty (left); and Sepulchral stele of Naia, a king's messenger of the XIXth Dynasty (right).

The Old Kingdom is associated with achievements of the Pyramid Age, while the Middle Kingdom ushered in salvation, reorganization and literary and linguistic flowering. The Middle Kingdom also provided the transition from Old to New Kingdom, whether in language, literature or architecture. The New Kingdom in turn, represented a grander flowering of culture, imperial expansion, reformulation of religious beliefs, democratization of the afterlife, new forms of art, quarrying and transportation of stone and construction of monumental architectural projects.

After the decline of the New Kingdom, the Ethiopian conquerors of Kemet/Egypt founded the Twenty-Fifth Dynasty. Headed by Piankhy, Shabaka, Shabataka and Taharka, they restored some of the old greatness to a culture exposed to the changing geo-political dynamics of a world now awake and aroused to the possibilities of the human spirit. The Persians, Assyrians, again Persians and Greeks and Romans sacked Egypt. However, while the former two more visibly destroyed, the latter two nations sought to imitate, placate and inculcate the culture. In this process they initiated great rebuilding efforts helping to preserve much that we know today. After this juxtapositioning, Greek and Roman culture

QUINTESSENTIAL BOOK "THE HOLY LAND"

would now set western tradition in vogue. These conquerors built extensively, using Kamite/Egyptian technology, craftsmanship and knowledge. They erected many temples that are today called Greco-Roman, such as Edfu, Kom Ombo, and Esneh.

The walls, columns and ceilings of these structures, were inundated with sculptures. These later temples were modeled after more ancient ones and built on sites already consecrated as holy, dating to the earliest times of their history. Their greatest contribution was to inundate the temple with illustrations and graphic depictions of the temple's history and ritual. This helped to preserve much that mirrored the most ancient beliefs and practice. Thus, just as King Zoser's Step Pyramid of the third dynasty was, according to John Lundquest in *The Temple*, an "architectural realization of the primordial hill," the Graeco-Roman temple building was later modified into depicting "aspects of the origins, growth, and construction" of the most ancient Egyptian or ancient Kemetic houses of the gods.

In the Pre-Dynastic Period before 3100 B.C., there were 42 mini states later called Nomes and headed by Nomarchs or minor kings. This number 42 was also symbolical of the 42 Negative Confessions and 42 Books of Thoth. Wars of religious animosity, competition for trade and early geo-political dynamics before the emergence of a strong Nile Valley leadership made life unsafe. Still, as the local deity emerged to prominence in the nomes, their temples became the center of the community. Here pilgrims came, feasts were held and the finest art could be found. Still, because of prevailing conditions, the enclosure wall emerged as an essential feature of the temple.

Petrie's *Religious Life in Ancient Egypt* tells, in the earliest times, the "great wall which surrounded each temple formed a fortress, which was the last refuge in case of invasion." Even so, temple origins in pre-dynastic times were patterned after the simplest huts made of reeds or maize stalks. Such early temple buildings had projecting roofs for shade as well as rope in front to keep out stray cattle.

Admittedly a product of the Pyramid Age, and located at Giza, the Temple of the Sphinx is an early surviving religious building. Constructed of blocks of red granite transported from Aswan, it also had blocks of beautiful alabaster. Consisting of a descending passage, leading to an open area, it's divided into three aisles by columns and lintels. A short passage leads to a second transept where were found statues of Khafra, builder of the second largest pyramid on the Giza plateau. Also found in this spot were cynocephali apes in hard green stone. In this chamber granite blocks measure 18 feet in length and 7 feet in height. In the SW corner of the transept was a mortuary chamber with six niches for mummies. This temple is connected with the temple of the second pyramid by a causeway cut in the rock, about a quarter of a mile in length. The upper temple is also constructed of massive blocks of granite and alabaster.

FREDERICK MONDERSON

Petrie's chronological sequence explains: "First, the pyramid of Khafra; secondly, the temple built symmetrically in front of that pyramid; third, the causeway, leading askew from that temple down a ridge of rock; fourth, the granite temple at the foot of the causeway." This puts the Temple of the Sphinx in great company and served as prototype of the physical structure and its theological and philosophical implications.

Holy Land Ceramic Art 11. Still another bird, this time a goose, a form of Amon-Ra, equally decked out in ceramic coloration.

During the First and Second Dynasties (Archaic Period 3100 B.C. - 2780 B.C.), the earliest temple shrine had three chambers as at Abydos. In the Pyramid temples of the IVth and Vth Dynasties the temple chambers were increased to five. While the three and five chambers appear in temples of the XIXth and XXth Dynasties, the XIXth Dynasty Temple of Seti I at Abydos was increased to seven chambers, each dedicated to a separate deity. From right to left, these deities in their respective chapels were Horus, Isis and Osiris of the Osirian cycle; Amun, Re-Horakhte and Ptah, the great gods of the Egyptian Empire; and Seti I, the deified king.

With site plans plotted, archaeologists further informed of differences between temples whether mortuary, prayer or processional. The first of these was the Mortuary Temple dating to the Pyramid Age; Mentuhotep's, Hatshepsut's and Thutmose's at Deir el Bahari; Rameses II's Ramesseum; and Rameses III's

QUINTESSENTIAL BOOK
"THE HOLY LAND"

Medinet Habu. In fact, Carpiceci (1994: 88) shows how in a three mile area, the Theban Necropolis houses: "Mortuary Temples of Seti I, Mentuhotep, Thutmosis III, Hatshepsut, Rameses VI, Mentuhotep II, Amenophis II, Ramses II, Thutmosis IV, Merneptah, Ptolemaic, that of Amenophis III with the nearby "Colossi of Memnon," Rameses III, Thutmosis I, Amenhotep and Thutmosis II." Baines and Malek (1980: 95) tell about the Mortuary Temple. "Their main function was to maintain the cult of the deceased kings buried in their tombs cut in the cliffs further to the west, though gods also were worshiped there, particularly Amun and Re'-Horakhty. The most important of these temples are those of Deir-el-Bahari, the Ramesseum and Medinet Habu. The mortuary temple of Sethos I stands at Qurna, with only huge seated statues, while the 'Memnon Colossi,' and other fragmentary sculptures mark the site of the temple of Amenophis III. Several of the temples of the West Bank were not mortuary, such as the temples of Hathor (Deir-el-Medina), Thoth (Qasr el-'Aguz) and Isis (Deir el-Sheltwt), all of the Greco-Roman Period."

All mortuary temples were generally constructed on the West Bank, the land of the dead. Worship temples as Luxor, Karnak, Esneh, Edfu, Dendera, Kom Ombo and Abu Simbel were generally on the east bank, land of the living. The third type was the processional temple, a sort of "halfway house" where the Ark or image of the god was housed when being transported from one temple to another on festivals or other solemn occasions. These were generally on the east bank.

It's further recognized that the Pyramid Age (Dynasties III-VI 2780-2240 B.C.) came to an end when Pepi II became old and weak after a reign of 94 years. During his later years, nobles increased their power and influence. With the collapse of strong centralized government the social order broke down and ushered in the First Intermediate Period, Dynasties VII-X (2240-2100 B.C.).

The XIth Dynasty under the Intefs and Mentuhoteps reunited the states of Upper and Lower Egypt/Kemet, and founded the Middle Kingdom. They conquered the warring Nomarchs, curtailed their power, restored centralization and reorganized the society and consolidated their power. These kings ushered in a period of prosperity, heralded by artistic, literary, religious, linguistic and architectural accomplishments that in turn set standards for the greater legacy of the New Kingdom. They credited Amon for being the "wind beneath their sails."

The Middle Kingdom is tremendously significant and provides a transition from the Old to New Kingdom cultural and building practices. Modern archaeology lets us identify Mentuhotep's XIth Dynasty Mortuary Temple at Deir el Bahari as an important bridge in transition from 2240 to 1600 B.C.

FREDERICK MONDERSON

Mentuhotep's temple was profound architecturally, artistically and philosophically. It served as inspiring prototype and model for Hatshepsut, female ruler, 500 years later. Juxtaposed at Deir el Bahari, the architect Senmut built an enlarged mortuary temple, for his beloved Pharaoh Hatshepsut. She hoped to connect it by tunnel to her tomb in the Valley of the Kings, an unheard of yet revolutionary proposition for a woman.

The next famous ruler to build extensively was Thutmose III. He erected several buildings in the religious complex at Karnak. His fabulous Festival Hall or Jubilee Temple of columns and pillars is exceptional. In addition, he added a smaller temple at Deir el Bahari, against the cliffs and between the earlier Mentuhotep and Hatshepsut temples.

Amenhotep III was a prolific builder as his great-grandfather, Thutmose III. He began the Hypostyle Hall at Karnak Temple, with a dozen center columns, the *Processional Colonnade*, as part of the 134 of this hall, made famous by Seti I and Rameses II. Amenhotep built his renowned Luxor Temple, at the time Egypt/Kemet reached a "golden age." With successive Pharaohs doing repair work here, the names of Tutankhamen, Smenkare, Horemheb, Seti I, Rameses II and even Alexander the Great are credited with adding restoration. Hatshepsut built an early shrine to three Theban deities in the later Court of Rameses. Thutmose III usurped it and inscribed his name, like he did in so many places, in his vendetta against the queen. Still, evidence links her work here. Rameses II did repairs to it. Her cartouche was also found at Edfu and is now in the Cairo Museum.

The Temple of Seti I at Abydos is a masterpiece of temple architecture. Strabo mistakenly called this building the Memnonium but also mentions a well here. The temple's foundations belong to one of ten successive temples Petrie discovered at Abydos, that date back to the first dynasty. The plan is irregular. Sculptures show Rameses receiving blessings from Thoth, Anubis, Osiris, and Horus.

In this temple the king is shown as a young man and as an adult pharaoh. The building is littered with massive columns all decorated with figures and the royal cartouche. Some authorities tend to link the oval with the Phoenix, the mythical bird that rises from the ashes.

The corridor of Kings is located to the south end of the second hall. This area is singularly important having ceilings and sides covered with sculptures, stars and ovals of the kings. Also, an inscription here commemorates the dedication of the temple. "On the left or east wall are four scenes. The first, second, and fourth represent offerings made to Amon, Horus, and Osiris. In the third Sethi and his son Rameses are represented standing in front of a table on which are engraved the names of 130 divinities, which texts call 'the great and the small cycle of the

QUINTESSENTIAL BOOK
"THE HOLY LAND"

divinities of the sacred places of the north and the south.'"

Significantly, the opposite west wall is divided into four scenes similar to the one on the left. The famous *Tablet of Abydos* is here with Sethi I and Rameses II offering homage to 76 predecessor kings. The list of kings begins with Menes, founder of the First Dynasty and ends with Sethi I, father of Rameses II. Five ovals are left without names. These belong to the heretic Akhnaton and Tutankhamen, Aye, and Smenkare, all associated with the Amarna heresy. Hatshepsut is also excluded because she ruled as King, constructed a tomb in the Valley of the Kings, wore a beard and built the Deir el Bahari structure greater than her predecessor Mentuhotep II, uniter of the land. Beyond the Temple of Seti I, is the Temple of Osiris, where Amelineau is thought to have found the divinity's body lying in his bed.

The *Tablet of Abydos*, discovered by Mariette in 1865, was conjectured to be the original of the fragmentary one found in a Temple of Rameses II, off to the side, at Abydos. This is now in the British Museum. This tablet is similar in substance to a king list engraved by Thothmes III in what is called the "Hall of Ancestors" of Karnak and now in Paris. Inscribed are names of kings who particularly benefited Karnak. The *Palermo Stone* is a similar, though earlier, king list, from the First through Sixth Dynasty.

Holy Land Photo 90a. Sakkara - Home of the Step Pyramid. Deep within the reaches of the Step Pyramid Complex, further ruins of the "Heb Sed Festival Court (left);" and doorway into some place of secrets (right).

FREDERICK MONDERSON

Holy Land Photo 90b. Sakkara - Home of the Step Pyramid. Illustrated false door (left); and enthroned, defaced monarch with the vulture symbolic of Goddess Mut on hand (left).

Rameses II was a builder of exceptional note, who added a Court at Luxor, completed and partially decorated the Hypostyle Hall at Karnak, and also built a magnificent rock tomb at Abu Simbel, in Nubia. Juxtaposed to his Abu Simbel temple for worship, he built a second temple for his Nubian wife Queen Nefertari. This Pharaoh also built the splendid Ramesseum, his mortuary temple. The statue at Memphis Museum was being shipped abroad by Belzoni, but this effort was abandoned at that site.

The Temple of Rameses III at Medinet Habu is considered the last major New Kingdom building project. The classical writer Diodorus Siculus is thought to have mentioned Medinet Habu as one of four temples he wrote about. The others were Karnak, Luxor and the Ramesseum.

The Temple of Philae is dedicated to the Goddess Isis. In Egyptian the island was called *Pilak* or *Ailak*, and *Ma-ne-lek* "the place of the Frontier." The Arabs call it

QUINTESSENTIAL BOOK
"THE HOLY LAND"

Anas el Wogood, or more generally *Gezeeret el-Beerbeh*.

This Temple of Isis is the principal building in its new home, the Island of Agilquiyyah or Agilka. Ptolemy II Philadelphus and Arsinoe commenced it. Succeeding monarchs built here including Euergetes I, Philometer, his brother, Euergetes II, the two Cleopatras, and Ptolemy, the elder son of Auletes, whose name is found in the area and on the pylon. Many sculptures on the exterior are of the later epoch of Roman emperors Augustus Tiberius, Claudius, Domitian, Nerva, and Trajan.

Nowhere has the mania of the Egyptians for irregularity been carried to such an extent as here. J. Ferguson, the 19th Century authority on architecture is quoted in Murray's *Handbook for Egypt* (1888) as follows: 'No Gothic architect in his wildest moments ever played so freely with his lines and dimensions, and none, it must be added, ever produced anything so picturesque as this. It contains all the play of light and shade, all the variety of Gothic art, with the massiveness and grandeur of the Egyptian style; and as it is still tolerably entire, and retains much of its color, there is no building out of Thebes that gives so favorable an impression of Egyptian art as this. It is true it is far less sublime than many, but hardly one can be quoted as more beautiful.'"

The Temple of Dendera takes its name from *Tentyris* or *Tentyra*, in *Coptic Tentore* or *Nikentore*. It has its origin in that of the goddess Hathor, the cow. *Tentyra* is probable taken from *Tei-n-Athor*, the abode of Athor or Hathor. It is in a superior state of preservation. The portico is considered a noble specimen of architecture. The temple, begun in the reign of the 11th Ptolemy, was completed in that of the Emperor Tiberius, though the sculptures and decoration were not finished till the time of Nero. In the Portico, the names of many Caesars are inscribed including that of Tiberius, Caligula, Claudius, and Nero. The oldest names here are of Ptolemy Caesarian, or Neo-Caesar, son of Cleopatra and Julius Caesar. The portrait of Cleopatra and her son are on the exterior back wall.

The Temple of Edfu is a perfect specimen of the complete Egyptian temple. It is the best preserved of all temples in Egypt. It is similar in planning and in preservation compared to Dendera. However, Edfu also has uniquely preserved the Propylon towers and the enclosure wall. Ptolemy Philopator, who built the sanctuary, founded Edfu and the chambers round it. He also built all the back part of the temple. The name of Ptolemy Philometer is found in the center halls, and their decoration is probably due to him. Ptolemy Philometer and Euergetes II; the latter of whom also built part of the enclosure wall, the other part being the work of Ptolemy Alexander I, who constructed the portico. The pylon, or Propylon, was either built or decorated by Ptolemy Dionysius.

FREDERICK MONDERSON

Holy Land Illustration 78. Market scenes in time of the Old Kingdom.

The Temple of Kalabsha was dedicated to the Nubian God Mendulese, brother of Osiris. It was relocated on the present site by a German archaeological team who cut the temple into 16,000 pieces before reassembling it. It appears to have been built in the reign of Augustus and though other Caesars, particularly Caligula, Trajan, and Severus made considerable additions to the sculptures, it was left unfinished. On the quay before the entrance a granite statue bears the name of Thothmes III during whose time it was in existence.

REFERENCES

ben-Jochannan, Yosef. *Abu Simbel to Ghizeh*: *A Guidebook and Manual*. Baltimore, MD.: Black Classics Press, 1987.
Badawy, A. *A History of Egyptian Architecture* II. Berkeley, California: University of California Press, 1966.
Clarke, Sommers and R. Engelbach. *Ancient Egyptian Construction and Architecture*. New York: Dover Publications, (1930) 1990.
Erman, Adolf. *Life in Ancient Egypt*. Trans H.M. Tirard. With a New Introduction by Jon Manchip White. New York: Dover Publications, (1894) 1971.
Haag, Michael. *Guide to Egypt*. London: Michael Haag, Limited, 1987.

QUINTESSENTIAL BOOK "THE HOLY LAND"

Lundquist, John M. *The Temple*. New York: Thames and Hudson, 1993.
Maspero, Gaston. *Manual of Egyptian Archaeology*. New York: G. Putnam's Sons, 1926.
Murray's *Handbook for Egypt*. London: John Murray, 1888.
Wayne, Scott. *Egypt and the Sudan: A Travel Survival Kit*. Berkeley, California: Lonely Planet Publishers, 1987.

2. Breakfast

Dr. Leonard James: Thebes in Upper Egypt is a city with an illustrious past unrivaled by any other. The fifth nome of the Upper Egyptian Kingdom, Thebes experienced its greatest flowering in the middle and new kingdoms. Thebes' history however dates to the beginnings of Egyptian history. When Narmer mobilized his forces in the Upper Kingdom Capital and marched and sailed north to conquer and unify the land, he nevertheless for administrative reasons, established the new capital located at Memphis. However, Thebes retained more than a nominal role in the nations developing relationship, particularly in the developments, First Intermediate Period and evolving Middle Kingdom.

With the triumph of the Middle Kingdom, Thebes became the national capital of the Kingdom of Upper and Lower Egypt. As with all national capitals a number of architectural constructions were undertaken to expand and beautify the city. Amon had triumphed in aiding these kings in the struggle of unification. He emerged supreme and at that time was fused with Ra into Amon-Ra. By the time of the New Kingdom, Egypt entered full-blown into an age of Imperial expansion and development from which great wealth flowed into the capital. With this largesse, Amon's city was glorified, and temples, tombs, and other civic and social projects undertaken.

Karnak, home of the Theban Triad, Amon, Mut and Khonsu, was enormously enlarged during the eighteenth, nineteenth, and twentieth dynasties. The west bank boasted the Valley of the Kings, Valley of the Queens, Valley of the Nobles and Valley of the Artisans as well as a tremendous display of mortuary temples across the western landscape. This and more was Thebes.

Walter Brown: Well done Dr. James. I think you have done well in summarizing these developments with a wonderful clarity and brevity. You're getting better.

George Washington: Ladies, since my class on **African Religious**

FREDERICK MONDERSON

Thought Systems taught by Prof. Donna Richards I have developed a fascination for African religions. On November 13, 1975, subject matter dealt with:

Read *Black Exodus* by E.S. Redkey.

An old saying is "If you know everything there is to know about the leaves, you will know everything about Dahomean religion."

Adjakpa looks over water, which is associated with life.

Ayaba is the younger sister of Adjakpa who takes care of the hearth, associated with cooking food. When wood is burning and sparks fly it is thought that Ayaba is present.

Legba is the youngest son of Mawu and Lisa and associated with Fa, the destiny of man. He is a divine trickster with a mischievous personality. He protects people against evil and tests the faith of all people. He represents the uncertainty of life. A special day is set aside for worship to Legba.

Earth (gods) Vodun

Aagbata is the earth and thunder offspring of Mawu and Lisa. Earth is older and Sagbata is its ruler. He is associated with smallpox, which can be very severe. That ailment is a penalty for some wrongdoing.

Orishas figure into the genealogy of the people as all see themselves as descending from the divine Nana Buluku.

In **Ancient History** on November 6, 1975, we learned that literature was very important in the Middle Kingdom. Amenemhat was the first king of the 12th Dynasty. He established his capital at Thebes then moved this to Kish (south of Memphis), neutral territory.

This was a very challenging time for Amenemhat. He wrote *Instructions from Amenemhat* for his son Sesostris. In addition, he broke the power of the Nomarchs and set up a new administrative system with a Vizier and two sub-Viziers. After surveying and splitting up the nomes, the sub-Viziers administered those with governors. He sent Nomarchs as trade representatives to Crete and thus eroding their powers in the nomes. He had his son Sesostris I appointed co-regent and this was helpful for the king was later assassinated.

QUINTESSENTIAL BOOK "THE HOLY LAND"

Holy Land Photo 91. Memphis Museum. The author and photographer sits before the sign indicating the contents of this site.

From this reign comes the Story of Sinuhe. Amenemhat opened trade routes with the south and Levant. Intensive irrigation was utilized to increase crop production. He dug a canal from the Nile River and refilled the Faiyum Lake. On his monuments he claimed to be a very efficient king. This is the period of the Good Shepherd. There was great prosperity and stability, trade and a population increase. The temple lands were now taxed again. There were great achievements in the arts. Egypt experienced great influence in the entire Levant, Crete and Asia Minor.

The 12th Dynasty was a reaction to the First Intermediate Period. A new social order came into being in a consolidated central administration. The office of mayor was established as Egypt moved from a rural to urban society. Sesostris III completed the culmination of the bureaucratic structure of the state. Documents from Old Testament times are contemporary with this period. As early as the First Intermediate Period there is the concept of monotheism.

Michelliea Georges: Well done Brother. You continue to amaze me.
Regina Hendricks: Say that again! I too am amazed, my Brother.

2. Bus Ride

Michelliea Georges: George, Henrietta Potter wants to join the discussion. Though not a student, she has been aroused from the descriptions we gave her of the enormous amount of information you have shared with us.

Regina Hendricks: I must agree with my sister.
Henrietta Potter: I am honored to be a part of this. Unfortunately, I missed the early part of what you shared with these sisters. My brother, you are blessed. I think you have done a wonderful thing to complement the work of Dr. Monderson. It's a pity so few sisters were privy to this reservoir of knowledge you have shared with Michelliea and Regina.

George Washington: It is an honor for me to be able to pass on the information that I received as I sought my elevation grounded in knowledge of the ancient Africans.

On November 17, 1975, in **African Religious Thought Systems** Dr. Richards spoke of Sagbata (earth) who was associated with small pox as punishment for disobedience. This deity nourishes man by giving good harvests and punishes him when humans are not good to him. The small pox epidemic is a punishment and a general purification of the entire group is required to restore harmony with Sagbata. Sagbata is a generic term for the earth family of Vodun. Webster defines generic as pertaining to a genus, kind or class.

Sagbata equals twins Dada Zodji and Nyuoh we Ananu. His first son was Dada

QUINTESSENTIAL BOOK
"THE HOLY LAND"

Langa who was "king-person-living." Another son was Da Jokpo – king-water-watch. A third son, Da Sindji guards drinking water.

Aglosuto was a messenger of Da Sindji, carrier of diseases. Hweve was in charge of sunlight and Adowa brings famine to harborers of evildoers.

Nudjenume guards against people who conspire to do harm to others and acts in the affairs of man.

Suvinen Ga was symbolized by a vulture and brings messages from Sagbata to Mawu Lisa.

Sagbata's earth pantheon represents an expression of moral conceptions, ethics and social control.

Agbogdodji punishes by drowning.

Chanu punishes for incest.

Magba is for the ladies. He gives children to good women when needed.

Alogbwe is the youngest and many handed. He guards Sagbata's riches and guards roads. He holds a lamp and drives away darkness. He gives man knowledge of the road to travel. He gives riches where deserving. He impedes progress of evil-doers and is associated with the forest and fish.

The Thunder pantheon Xevioso included Sogbo and Agbe.
Thunder – Xevioso – punishes with an axe (Thor).

Sogbo – The children of Sogbo remain in the sky but relate to the sky.

Aden – took over Agbe's duties in the sky. He gives fine rain and makes fruit trees bear fruit. He is the guardian of the fruit tree.

Akolombe – regulates temperature of earth. He brings hail, and causes rivers to overflow.

Adjakata is the guardian of the heavens and brings strong rain and heavy showers. Then there is Gowesu, Akete, Alasa, Gbade and Abge.

Agboyu is the first child of Agbe, and watches over his parents.

Axwaga is brutal and tried to outdo his father.

FREDERICK MONDERSON

Tokpodun is female, and associated with women, religiosity and is very quiet.

Saxo inhabits the incoming waves and makes the sea rise.

Gbeyogbo is the Vodun of the receding surf and the most evil of the sea deities.

Afrekete is the youngest and very important. He is the greatest of cunning deities, most favored. He plays the role of a trickster and a great gossip.

Michael Sinclair: What of the sister who sat with us this morning?
Mrs. Alexander Pushkin: She is sick. Teddy and I visited with her earlier.

Teddy Cubia: She is going to be all right.
Dr. Alexander Pushkin: Ok.

4. Site:

ABU SIMBEL

The twin temples of Rameses II and his beautiful wife Nefertari are spectacular for being rock-hewn with colossal seated and standing statues and wonderfully decorated and colorful decorations of the king in battle, adoration and making presentations to the gods!

5. Post-Site Lecture

The 27th Dynasty was Persian with Cambyses, Darius I, Xerxes, Artaxerxes and Darius II. Cambyses tore down the temples. Darius I rebuilt some of these. Under Darius the Persians had sought to conquer the world and his army was spread too thin. Thus, Persia began to decline. Greek, Late Egyptian and Aramaic were spoken in this period.

During Darius I's reign Persians believed that Egyptian culture was good. The pursuit of philosophy during this period was considered a luxury. From their exposure to the Egyptians, the Persians adopted a new type of burial called the "Persian Pit." They also changed mummification techniques. Emphasis was on use of wet and dry natron. Perhaps mummification may go back to the beginnings of the dynasties. We know Queen Hetepheres, mother of Khufu was mummified. We don't have her mummy but the jars containing her entrails. Alexander the

QUINTESSENTIAL BOOK "THE HOLY LAND"

Great was mummified in white honey.

6. Discussion

Dr. Fred Monderson: Interestingly enough we began the last section according to my notes of Mr. Allen's lecture showing Baboons worshipping. In fact he began this last lecture with "**Baboons worshipping Sunrise at the Lake of Fire**." This was presented on Friday March 20, 1992, 6:00 P.M., in the Orientation Theater.

The rising land: Tatenen

The Step-pyramid = First rising land – Memphis

Heliopolis = Sun City, home of the true pyramids. All pyramids had a primeval origin.

The illustration is of the Primeval Mound behind with the sun's rays beyond.

The Lotus God – Nefertum – God's head appearing out of the Lotus.

Tutankhamon as the primeval hill, Nefertum.

HELIOPOLITAN

The **AENNEAD** is a group of 9. Sometimes it can be from 5 to 23 members. It is a plural of plurals. Three of three gods. We have Atum who begat Shu and Tefnut. This pair made Geb and Nut who had two sets of twins, Osiris and Isis and Seth and Nephthys. Later Horus was born.

Osiris – Principle.

The face that makes plants grow was Osiris. Primarily associated with Green = God of Vegetation.

FREDERICK MONDERSON

Black equals Black land versus Red land. This is debated and should really mean "black people." After all, when the god says "I give you the Black Land" does this mean he does not give the "Red Land" also?

Osiris is associated with the Duat or underworld. That's where the cosmic principle of life lies. Power of rebirth comes from the earth.

Osiris meant "Seat of the eye." Seth meant wildness, opposite of Osiris, desert, and disorder. However, Seth sometime does good things.

Part of Unification principle comes from the Middle Kingdom.

Isis = name not known; not a throne or seat on top of her head.

Nephthys – Lady of the House. Woman as wife. Role: companion of Isis as supporter of Osiris. They represent the male-female principle of life.

The bottom 4 of the Heliopolitan Ennead union of male and female principle.

Geb = Earth
Nut = watery one or a cosmic amniotic sack –

Atmosphere = Tefnut female counterpart of Shu. Shu empty of universal water; dry.

Atum sits at the top of the Ennead as "the Completer." To complete something not to exist.

Atum equals totality; the lord of totality; the lord to the limit.

The primeval hill is the first emanation of Atum. The totality of all existence; the source of all things.

Singularity = black hole = Atum = singularity

Amonad = a group of 1 = Atum.

Horus is the 10th god. He is not a proper member of the ennead. Horus represented the force of nature.

A natural cosmic force of kingship united with Khafre.

Horus was the sun. From the First Dynasty, there were 2 aspects of Horus.

1. He was Horus who was in his disc = Sun.

QUINTESSENTIAL BOOK "THE HOLY LAND"

2. Son of Isis, Hathor = House of Horus. The sun is the ruler of all creation. Horus is the Akhet (Horakhti) = first hour of the day before sunrise.

   Atum = Harmakhis = Sphinx

Ra, Khepri, Atum, Aten are all different gods with different centers of worship.

THE ENNEAD is:

1. Totality

2. All the things in nature

3. All things that made life possible.

Creation equals birth equals causality. There are two meanings of the Ennead (1) causality; (2) dependency.

The bottom 4 of the Osiris, Isis, Seth, and Nephthys myth are the principle of life.

Spell 176 end of the world.

Holy Land Illustration 79. Felucca in full sail on the Nile River (left); and view of the Nile at one of the Channels at the First Cataract, Upper Egypt (right).

ARE THERE ANY QUESTIONS?

Carmelitiea Shabazz: I see how at Deir el Bahari and in the Valley of the Kings they have moved vehicles back from the sites. I suppose this is to keep the fumes from these treasures. What other type of damage were the monuments subjected to?

Dr. Fred Monderson: The monuments were subject to untold damages by humans - nationals, foreigners, Christians, invaders, conquerors, Muslims, Arabs, Turks, English, French, Germans and tourists, and thieves – thieves from time immemorial, locals and foreigners. Then there were the ravages of time. More importantly, however is the water damage. Water damage with its saline content is the most destructive to the monuments. This is one reason why the temples of Nubia had to be removed because of the flooding by the dam. This involved Abu Simbel, Philae, Kalabsha, Beit Wali, and so many more.

However, the standing monuments also have had their share of salt content owing to the floods. I think it's best if I refer you to Alfred Lucas who deals with salt, sodium, chloride in "Damage Caused by Salt at Karnak" in Egypt published in *Services des Antiquities* 25, 1925.

He explained the nature and extent of damage in the temple in this statement: "The upper portions of the buildings and monuments are free from any particular surface disintegration and also from any signs of damp or of efflorescent salts. The damage is confined to two areas, namely, a) an irregular zone some distance up the walls, which marks the height to which at one time earth has been piled, and which is often well above the highest level to which any water can have risen by capillarity, and which in many cases is marked by a broad band of land; and b) a zone extending from the floor level to a height varying from about half a meter to several meters above and where there is generally a white incrustation. But both damp and incrustation, although very unsightly, are merely the outward manifestation of the presence of the powerful destructive agent salt, which is insidiously ruining the stone, beginning with a disintegration of the surface and frequently with total destruction."

Even further, Lucas (1925: 50) added: "At Karnak the conditions, although at first sight much the same as those at Luxor and Philae, are in reality very different. The water flooding Karnak, although Nile water does not come directly from the river, but is water that has irrigated and washed the land to the south and east before it reaches the temple area, and as a result it must pick up a certain amount of salt in its passage. After remaining for a short time the water subsides but as the drainage conditions are very poor, although much of the water slowly winds its way back to the river a portion remains in the subsoil and a further portion drains into the depression on the south side where it forms the sacred lake. Before the infiltration water subsides there is a certain amount of evaporation with consequent increase in salinity of what remains: in the lake too there is also evaporation of the water and concentration of the salt. This process has been going on for several thousand years with the result that salt has gradually accumulated in both the subsoil water and the lake water. In addition to this however, salt in large quantity

QUINTESSENTIAL BOOK
"THE HOLY LAND"

was undoubtedly derived from the urine of the human and animal inhabitants of the temple area during the time it was encumbered with houses and rubbish heaps and used as a dwelling place for a large colony of people. Under the imperfect conditions that exist the accumulated salt from this source would never have an opportunity to escape but remained in the temple area, and at the present time the soil, the subsoil, the subsoil water, the lake water and the foundations and lower courses of the buildings are all impregnated with salt."

Regina Singleton: What subjects were taught and how was Egyptian education structured?
Dr. Fred Monderson: Education in ancient Egypt was of three principal types, Elementary, Secondary and Professional. In addition, there was the socialization of the poor young child especially, as in so many other places in Africa that was done by the family.

Miriam Stead in *Egyptian Life* shows at birth its mother gave the child a name. After this: "the period of childhood before education, apprenticeship and work was short, but not totally non-existent. Various toys have survived, such as balls, tops, dolls and figures of animals with moving parts, not dissimilar to wooden playthings given to children today. There are also depictions of boys and girls engaged in group activities such as athletic games, mock battles with sticks, and gymnastics." In addition, the wealthy, noble and royal families practiced such sports as swimming, archery and horsemanship, sailing and hunting in the marshes, water sports.

Of the three principal types of education only the elementary was practiced in the Old Kingdom, 2680-2240 B.C. There were no public schools and education was largely in the hands of the fathers. "Boys were taught skills by their father in the hope of at least one son winning a place in the official corps of tomb-builders. Those youths who were most likely to be accepted were designated 'children of the tomb.' They were attached to one of the gangs to do odd jobs and run messages, but no doubt primarily to watch and learn until such time as a place became available for them."

By the Middle and New Kingdom, three types of schools at the elementary level had developed. The first of these were the Temple Schools, taught by the priests. The children began school about the age of five and were taught writing by copying standard texts. Much recitation was encouraged where the boys repeated poems and standard lessons. The basic primer was a book called the *Kemyt*, which meant 'completion.'

Next were the Court Schools. They were established in the court or palace to train the heirs to the throne. Also, some kingly companions were taught the duties of royalty. Likewise, there were Department Schools. They were conducted in each government department to prepare boys for official careers. This education was mainly vocational. The school day ended at noon.

In *History of Education*, S.E. Frost Jr., points out that among the subjects taught at these elementary department schools were writing, arithmetic, fairy tales, swimming, sacred songs, dancing, manners and morals.

The next level of education was taught at secondary schools. Here, teachers used copybooks to teach writing and morals. Particularly during the New Kingdom, the works studied were mainly from the Middle Kingdom. This period in Egyptian civilization marks the greatest period of literary production.

The educational principles the priest teachers taught were many. Students were taught motivation as a way to promote advancement. Next were morals. The basic qualities were bravery, good character, and social and personal responsibilities. Literature was didactic. It taught:

a. Piety towards the gods;
b. A sense of absolute submission to the supreme and overshadowing will of these Gods;
c. Abject loyalty to the king;
d. Slavish deference to the king;
e. Honor to parents.
f. Neighborliness especially towards the poor and needy; and
g. Self control.

For all Egyptians, moral actions were motivated largely by the law of reward and favor aimed at happiness in a purely worldly life.

The third type of education was of a professional nature. The temples were the schools of this higher liberal education. They taught such subjects as ancient forms of writing, geography, cosmography, astronomy, chronology, sculpture, painting, ritual dancing, and theory of music, law, medicine, morals, arithmetic, mensuration, hydrostatics, and architecture.

Education for professional careers emphasized practice rather than theory. Secrets of each profession were handed down within a family and transmitted through apprenticeship. The areas of professional training included medicine, the priesthood, the military, architecture, and the skills of the scribe.

Education continued in the practical development of the arts and crafts.

The Egyptian craftsmen attained great proficiency in –

QUINTESSENTIAL BOOK
"THE HOLY LAND"

Building: producing the pyramids, obelisks, tombs and temples.
Irrigation: growing out of the need for control of the Nile River and use of its waters.
Embalming: the preparation of the body for the judgment and existence in the afterlife.

Education was further extended and reinforced owing to the development of certain institutions and ethical concepts. Chief among these were the family, social institutions, government, and religion. The development of the sciences and higher arts evolved in vital connection with the growth of practical skills in the arts and crafts.

The development of the language arts was aided by the growth of the alphabet. It evolved from picture writing, to pictograms and phonograms. Also, the development of symbolism, drawing and writing was a subject taught. In addition, such subjects as arithmetic, geometry, astronomy, mechanics, geography and medical knowledge also grew from the practical necessity of the culture.

Egyptian education was in many ways empirical: wholly the result of experience; action preceded thought, and practice reconditioned thought. Throughout it all, the priesthood held the secrets to all learning, by their devoted reverence of the accomplishments of the Egyptian past.

The concepts of this educational experience were simply a transitional stage in the intellectual growth of man in Africa. What was accomplished in this culture was to shape education in Africa down through the ages.

Today, the same concepts encourage and motivate Africans, especially in the Diaspora, to reach back into time to learn of our cultural heritage. The creativity of the African intellectual spirit, the preservative nature of the climate, and modern scholarship has helped us salvage and teach our-selves and young the greatness of Africa's children. Africa's contribution to the world has been immense. Thus, the African whether in America or elsewhere has so much to grow with, study and teach that will help us all to overcome the many centuries of obstacles placed in our paths. And, Egypt beacons we should use her treasures to our greatest abilities to teach the young, as Egyptian education has always been a source of inspiration, knowledge and challenge to intellect.

Michelliea Georges: Did the Egyptian lose his temper often and how was swearing viewed by the society?
Dr. Fred Monderson: The ancient Egyptians frowned on any type of behavior that involved distemper. The Book of Ptah-Hotep says avoid showing bad temper and be not quarrelsome. 'If thou desirest thy conduct to be good and preserved from

FREDERICK MONDERSON

evil, keep thyself from attacks of bad temper. It is a fatal malady (which leads) to discord, and there is no longer any existence for him who entangles himself therein. For it (introduces) quarrels (between) fathers and mothers, as well as (between) brothers and sisters; it causes wife (and) husband to detest each other, it contains all kinds of wickedness, and embodies all kinds of wrongs. When a man has taken righteousness for his rule, walking in her paths and making his dwelling with her, therein is no place for bad temper.' Even further: 'It is wrong to fly into a passion with one's neighbors to the point of not knowing how to manage one's words. When there is only a little irritation, one creates an affliction for himself for the (time when he shall be) cool.' This is the same manner in which swearing was viewed. The Ka of the deceased denied that while on earth he was guilty of unnecessary swearing.

Bryce Menkheperre: Who was Thoth?
Dr. Fred Monderson: Thoth is one of the ancient gods of Egypt. He was the author of writing, logic, the inventor of music and musical instruments and a whole lot more. When his brother Set murdered Osiris, Ra sent Thoth and Anubis to aid Isis and Nephthys. He was the deity of intellectuality and maintainer of the harmony of the universe as well as the creator of the universe by means of his voice. He was the chronographer of the gods and in the Judgment he wrote down the results of the weighing of the heart.

Rev. Dr. Mc Flair: What type of relationship existed between the people and the temple?
Dr. Fred Monderson: The people held the temple in high regard, for after all, it was the residence of the god and his servants. They recognized that though they were welcome in the temple, they could enter only so far, and this was generally in the Great Court in which there was an altar for them to worship. Persons of higher stature could venture a little further, but the pharaoh and the priests of the highest order could only enter the deep inner recesses of the temple.

QUINTESSENTIAL BOOK "THE HOLY LAND"

Holy Land Photo 92. Memphis Museum. Frontal view of the alabaster Sphinx of Rameses II.

FREDERICK MONDERSON

Holy Land Illustration 80. Sepulchral stele of Akberu, a doorkeeper of a temple of Rameses II, XXth Dynasty (left); and Sepulchral stele of Un-ta-uat, a Governor of the Sudan, XXth Dynasty (right).

Robert Matthews: What have surviving texts told us about ancient Egyptian society?

Dr. Fred Monderson: The surviving texts have told us much about ancient Egyptian society. In as much as we have only a small percentage of the knowledge we should possess, we do know a great deal, much of which is based on deduction. We pretty well know of their educational system, their methods of warfare, their arts and crafts, how they built their temples and tombs. Such things as steles tell us of their titles and aspirations, while the *Books of the Dead* detail their lives on earth through the confessions they made in the Hall of Judgment of the things they held in disdain. We also know of their music, foods, sailing, working, partying and philosophic speculation.

Teddy Cubia: How did the ancient Egyptian relate to his tomb and what does this teach us?

Dr. Fred Monderson: Well, the tomb was a place where he intended to spend eternity, or where his body would repose for the duration. For the most part, he began preparing for his tomb as early as he could afford. Here he interred everything he thought he would need and be able to utilize through the use of magic. This included ushabtis for service, flowers and fruit for decoration and

QUINTESSENTIAL BOOK
"THE HOLY LAND"

delicacy. There were animals and grain for his meals and music for his entertainment. The tomb was his holy place and there was also a place in the forepart where either his family or priests would come to perform certain ceremonies in remembrance of him.

The tombs teach us he was a man of wisdom, intellect, peaceful, respectful of authority, loved and praised the gods, showed compassion and kindness to his neighbors and often tried to avoid wrongdoing. Equally too, he avoided using another person's tomb or parts thereof as building materials for his own. Many an Egyptian boasted that his tomb was hewn out of virgin soil or that his sarcophagus was specially cut from the hills so as to be pure as a place he intended to repose for eternity.

Jack Bender: How was treachery viewed or how was treason treated?
Dr. Fred Monderson: Treachery or treason against the state or the king was considered a serious offense. Killing by treachery was condemned. This was serious because it reminded of how Seth tricked and then killed Osiris. As a result, the Ka of the deceased denied committing either treason or treachery while on earth. In the *Confessions* he asserted 'I have not killed a man by treachery.'

Jessie James. What role did the 'Tree of Life' play in Egyptian mythology?
Dr. Fred Monderson: To understand the role of the 'Tree of life' is also to understand the role of the Garden in ancient Egypt, a land of little trees. The Papyrus of Ani praises the individual: "thou has made thyself a watered (irrigated) enclosure; thou hast surrounded the tilled earth before thee, with hedges; thou has planted sycamores in well arranged circles [or rows] around thy residence; thou fillest thy hands with all the flowers thine eye perceives. One is wearied (nevertheless) with all that. Happy (the one) who does not forsake it.'

FREDERICK MONDERSON

Holy Land Ceramic Art 12. Yet another colorful goose, this time he seems pecking at a budding lotus plant.

Myers (1900: 151-152) discusses the meaning of gardens to the wealthy around whose surrounding villas they adorn. "Such gardens are shown on the monuments, especially those of Tell-el-Amarna. The people, universally were fond of trees, plants and flowers, and largely used such for table decorations, the adornment of apartments, and in the form of wreaths, for the presentation to and the adornment of, guests. Everywhere on the monuments are to be found delineations of flowers and the presenting of complicated bouquets, as offerings to the deities, and the coffins of the dead are found covered with wreaths of flowers. They also made arbors of flowers, vines and plants, over the paths of their princes, and for the owners of villas to pass under, to their houses. In the old times these villas were constructed surrounded by gardens and parks, and these latter were especial subjects of pride with their owners and of devotion by the poets. There were but few wild flowers indigenous to the land, and one of the desires of the wealthy classes, was to import and cultivate many rare and exotic plants and trees for the decoration of their gardens. Among such trees and plants grown in them were the sycamore, the fig tree, acacia, mimosa, carob or locust, grape vine, palms, olive, pomegranate, *nebbek*, tamarisk, etc., some indigenous like the tamarisk, and others of these importations. The sycamore or wild fig, called to-day *Sycamorus antiquorum*, also Pharaoh's fig, will flourish even in the sand on the edge of the desert, sending its roots deep to any moisture, and although it does not grow very

QUINTESSENTIAL BOOK
"THE HOLY LAND"

high, its wide spreading branches give a dense shade which is very grateful. It occupied an important position among the Egyptian sacred trees as the Tree of life, and is frequently mentioned in the so-called Book of the Dead. In the LIX Chapter, L. 1, of this last mentioned writing, this sacred tree represents the goddess Nut, i.e., Heaven. Its wood was preferred, for making statuettes of Osiris, but whilst it is capable of being cut into large blocks and strong planks, it is so knotty and yellow, that it is not suitable for very fine work.

The Persea (*Balanites Aegyptiaca*) was also considered a sacred tree. (It was the symbol of the mysterious, "Sacred Heart.")

The lotus bud and flower, the palm, and the papyrus, were conventionalized in architecture and mural paintings. The colored columns and the capitals of the same, in the most magnificent of the ancient temples, being made in imitation of one of the other of these plants and of their buds and flowers. The indigenous flowering plants were almost confined to the lotus, papyrus, and varieties of the *colocasia, centaurea, papaver*, and desert plants.

In the gardens were ponds and tanks, filled with fish and aquatic birds, and planted with the rose-colored, white, and blue lotus, and the papyrus plant.

In the Hypostyle Hall at Karnak Temple, on the south side, both Seti I and Rameses II are depicted kneeling while Thoth and other gods write their names in the 'Tree of Life.' Thus, the "Tree of Life" is just that, it is an honor and a record of a good life and an enduring reminder of this.

Regina Hendricks: What were the Books of Hermes or Thoth?
Dr. Fred Monderson: Firstly, the Greeks Hermes, and also, Hermes Trismegistus, the Thrice Great Hermes, was called Thoth. As the inventor of writing and music and father of all wisdom, literature and knowledge, Thoth is thought to have written many books on a variety of subjects. The numbers vary according to the writers. Clemens of Alexandria says he wrote 42 books, while Iamblichus says 20,000 and Manetho said they were 36,525. Still, all this is unclear and we may be tempted to agree with the smaller number because it is more in line with the number 42, so familiar with the Nomes, Negative Confessions and the number of the steps at the entrance to Abydos Temple of Seti I.

Even further, because the Books of Thoth were held in such reverence, The *Papyrus of Ani* says Study on a subject before giving an opinion. 'If one come (to thee) in order to seek thy views (advice), let that be a reason for thee to turn to the divine books" and "One comes to seek thy views (advice), let that make thee lean upon the books." This maxim, according to Myers (1900: 119) recommends "the one from whom counsel is sought, to seek the divine books and inspire himself from them, with the experience of the past; and to fill his mind with the wisdom of the past, and with the wisdom contained in the ancient writings, before giving counsel, instead of using his own unguided thoughts." The Egyptian phrase for the old writings was 'The words of the ancients' and 'The wisdom of the ancestors.'

Mary Palmer: Perhaps you could explain the misconception about the uraeus.
Dr. Fred Monderson: The *Papyrus of Sayings* says "The transgressors rush after the uraeus; the power of the sun-god startles both lands." Confusing as this may sound, Myers (1900: 257) explained "In Egypt the uraeus asps or vipers, were considered executioners under Ra, the sun-god. They spit flames on the wicked. They annihilated their names. The symbol of sovereignty over Upper Egypt was the uraeus, and its representation was worn in time of peace on the king's crown, and in time of war on his helmet. It was thought to protect him from his enemies, and to punish them as it had done for the god Ra, of whom he was the representative."

Peter Monderson: How did the ancient Egyptians view violence and the violent?
Dr. Fred Monderson: They regarded violence and the violent as abomination of the laws of the land and the Ka of the deceased denied being violent in his earthly life. Equally too, the writings caution against using one's position to promote violence against one's fellow man.

Mrs. Mc Flair: Was there such a thing as "Holy Water" in ancient Egypt?
Dr. Fred Monderson: I am not sure but I would venture to say, water from the altar of the god that was consecrated would probably be considered holy by our standards. Then again, there was the water contained in the Sacred Lake that the priests used to purify themselves. I suppose, this could be considered holy. The Nile was also named after Osiris because it brought the land back to life.

Hattie Jones: How was Egyptian society structured? Did they have class or caste?
Dr. Fred Monderson: Egyptian society did not have a caste system that is hereditary like the Hindus of India. Theirs was a class system that encouraged initiative and intellect. An individual could rise from humble beginnings, based on industry, character, skill and intellect. Hence, the admonition, "Be a scribe! Be a scribe!"

While there were social classes of the King and nobles, there were also a middle class and a peasant class. There was also a slave class, usually people generally captured in war. The literary class was well respected and praised.

Rev. Dr. Mc Flair: How would you define the role of Christianity and Christians in ancient Egypt?
Dr. Fred Monderson: The role of Christianity in ancient Egypt is very dubious. Some believe Egyptian religion was the forerunner of Christianity. Dr. ben-Jochannan's book is entitled: *African Origins of the Major Western Religions*:

QUINTESSENTIAL BOOK
"THE HOLY LAND"

Judaism, Christianity and Islam. Nevertheless, though Christians and Christianity were welcomed in Egypt their stay in Egypt was good for Christianity but bad for Egyptian culture and history.

Christianity seems to have met with a favorable early reception in Egypt and to have taken an early hold in Egyptian thought, and many of its theological teachings were formulated from Greek ideality and Oriental mysticism in which Egyptian and Jewish ideas were blended and embedded. There was considerable overlapping. We hereafter have a *Book of the Dead* of 64 A.D., of the time of Nero, and there are Egyptian mummies in the British Museum of 400 A.D., and mummies were made in Egypt after that date.

St. Mark, according to ancient tradition, founded the Christian church in Egypt at Alexandria. Eusebius gives us the earliest record of this. It is quite clear that a regularly organized church existed there long before the close of the first century. Eusebius says that in the eighth year of Nero that is (A.D. 62) "Ammianus succeeded the apostle and evangelist, Mark, in the administration of the church at Alexandria. He was a man distinguished for his piety." There was no doubt many learned Christians in Alexandria in the first century. One Apollos, a native citizen, was a companion of St. Paul, later were Clement and his pupil Origen. The first Christians, both of that city and of Rome, were most probably Hellenist or Greek-speaking Jews, with some Greeks, and those first in Rome likely came from Alexandria, Egypt. The earliest inscriptions in the Roman catacombs are in Greek, subsequently sometimes a mixture of Greek and Latin, written in Greek letters. In any case Christians were in the first century very few, and not at first people of distinction. Hebrew inscriptions of Christian burials are not found. Such was the smallness or secrecy of the first of that sect, that neither Seneca nor Juvenal appears to have known of the Christians."

This aside, many of the Egyptian monuments were destroyed by over-zealous Christians who sought to stamp out what they thought was paganism and we see the results of their handiwork today. Still, it is agreed, the Christians did more damage to ancient Egypt than the angry and invading armies who often wrecked Egyptian cities.

Nelson Escobar: Some societies seem to recognize men sometimes need more than one woman, how was this resolved in ancient Egypt?
Dr. Fred Monderson: While everyone was encouraged to marry and remain faithful, the wealthy and the king were permitted to have concubines and a harem. However, even this pleasure had its pitfalls. Pharaohs had concubines or harems and though some concubines supplied the heir to the throne, there were times when the harem of concubines was caught in a conspiracy to kill the king so their offspring could get the throne.

FREDERICK MONDERSON

George Washington: I do a little magic myself and am really concerned about its use. how did the ancient Egyptian regard the use of magic.

Dr. Fred Monderson: The Egyptian considered magic, or *hik*, a special and useful art that gods and certain skillful men, priests especially could use for constructive purposes. Naturally the gods were the most powerful users of this art. However, it was but natural that the Egyptians should wish to employ magic for their own benefit and self-gratification, and since religion put no veto on the practice so long as it was exercised within legal bounds, it was put to a widespread use among them. When magicians made figures of wax representing men whom they desired to injure, this was of course an illegal act like any other, and the law stepped in to prevent it. One papyrus that has been preserved records the judicial proceedings taken in such a case in connection with the harem conspiracy against Rameses III of the 20th dynasty.

That is enough for today. See you folks at dinner this evening.

Michelliea Georges: I am ordering room service refreshments as we watch the sun go do. What are you having, Regina, and you, George? I will have a brandy and a local Stella beer.

Regina Hendricks: I will have a brandy also and lemon squeezes.

George Washington: You ladies can surprise me and order anything.

Ancient History - November 12, 1975.

There was a great deal of jewelry in private tombs signifying the wealth of these individuals.

The term paper topics, Due December 18, 1975, included:

(1) Religious Reforms of Ikhnaton (Akhenaten, Amenhotep IV). Use Kegan Section II, *Problems in Ancient History* Vol. I; *Cambridge Ancient History*; *Documents in Old Testament History*.

Historical Jesus. Cantor – *Problems in European History*, Vol. 1, Part IV, "The Passover Plot."

By 1750 B.C. the Ancient Near East was enjoying prosperity and this was about the time of the 13th Egyptian Dynasty. There was a tremendous increase in trade between Egypt and Byblos.

Mushily I, the Hittite King destroyed the Babylonian Kingdom, and later Kassites settled there.

(1) Indo-Europeans began their movement from the north around 2000 B.C.

QUINTESSENTIAL BOOK
"THE HOLY LAND"

(2) C. 1640 B.C. the Hyksos conquered Egypt.

At this time Indo-European influence began to spread in the Near East.
We see Hittites, Kassites, Mitanni, and Durians on the scene.

The 13th Dynasty lasted about 1785-1640 B.C. At the end of the 13th Dynasty, the Delta broke off and became autonomous forming the 14th Dynasty. This was the time of the Hyksos who conquered Egypt bringing horses and new military fortifications.

7. Free Time

Dr. Leonard James: Brother Brown, let's do a little shopping this afternoon. I noticed some hats I would like to get.
Walter Brown: Glad you mentioned that. I want to get a few cotton t-shirts for my sons and a bag for myself. My wife was out with the ladies the other night and I suppose they got everything they needed.

8. Dinner

Michelliea Georges: This afternoon was brief but the company was good.
Regina Hendricks: I say amen to that.
George Washington: Ladies, you say some of the most uplifting things. I am glad, proud and honored to be in your company and share some of this knowledge with you.

In **Ancient History** class on November 24, 1975 the instructor mentioned Hatshepsut reigned for 20 years. Thutmose III succeeded Hatshepsut and implemented a program of militarization. At that time, 20,000 men was a very large army for the ancient world. At Megiddo 330 kings waited to do battle with him. The King of Kadesh led the coalition. The King of Mitanni instigated the coalition.

FREDERICK MONDERSON

Holy Land Illustration 81. A boat for sailing into the afterlife and now reassembled and housed in the Cairo Museum of Egyptian Antiquities.

The Battle of Megiddo is mentioned in the Bible as the Battle of Armageddon. The 300 kings owed tribute to the king, not the state. Kings' sons were retained as hostages at the Egyptian court. With treaties, the losing monarch would send his daughter to marry the winning monarch. Thutmose conducted 17 campaigns in his reign. Campaigns 2, 3, and 4 were to solidify his conquered territories.

Amenhotep II succeeded Thutmose III. He was his co-regent. This king was very military minded. He was burly and very physical. During this time silver was more scarce than gold. The military and the priesthood benefited from the many tributes that were paid by the vassals of Egypt. Trade increased immensely. Egypt was the dominant power and exported all of its culture. There was a sort of *Pox Aegyptica* – or Egyptian peace. This was also a period of internationalization.

The status of women in the palace became an issue at this time. Thutmose IV married a woman from Mitanni. However, Amenhotep III married Queen Tiy, a Nubian. Still, there were major wives and minor wives and concubines.

QUINTESSENTIAL BOOK
"THE HOLY LAND"

FON COSMOLOGY

On November 20, 1975. **African Religious Thought Systems** taught, in Fon Cosmology, the calabash is a form of the universe in two halves. Water is the source of rain and it surrounds the earth. Heavenly bodies revolve around the inner surface of the calabash. Then three processes take place. First, gathering together of the earth; next, determining the position of waters; then welding all together in an ordered all whole.

DA is very important. It is a force that controls all life and motion and organizes the world for Mawu-Lisa.

Conceptions of DA

Dangbe = Serpent life or spirit of bush. Supernatural parent of founder of a particular Dahomean clan. The totem is at Wydah.

All snakes are called Da, but a deeper meaning is there. Also, Da is a special spiritual entity.

Da is a living quality that expresses in all things that are flexible, sinuous and moist. A connecting thing, rainbow or umbilical cord. This symbol of continuity or life equates the snake with tail in mouth.

Da – collective and personal fate or fortune that goes and comes mysteriously has to be watched very closely, close interaction with Da. This is very vital to the group.

9. Lounge Discussion

Michelliea Georges: I thought we should hang out in the lounge this evening and enjoy the ambience.
Regina Hendricks: A few sisters are supposed to join us. You can proceed my brother.
George Washington: Thank you ladies. It was very thoughtful of you to choose the lounge. It's good for a change. In **Ancient History** December 1, 1975

FREDERICK MONDERSON

When Amenhotep III ruled in the 18th Dynasty, Egypt was at its apogee. The capital shifted between Memphis, Thebes and Amarna. It was the height of Egyptian civilization at which time there was consolidation of the Hittites and Assyria. Amenhotep IV (Ikhnaton) succeeded his father, Amenhotep III. His mother was Queen Tiy.

During the early part of Amenhotep IV's reign, the priesthood and army had reaped the fruits of the empire's opulence. Some scholars question a co-regency between he and his father, even though co-regency was common during this dynasty.

In year 4 he changed his name to Ikhnaton (Akhnaton). Aton equals the Sun God. The High Priest of Amen-Ra was dismissed. The Temple of Amen Ra was destroyed. There was economic hardship in year 14 of Ikhnaton's reign and this was blamed on his religious revolution. The temple he built, at Karnak in year 4, to the God Aton had no roof, and so the sun could shine in.

In **African Religious Thought Systems** on November 24, 1975, we discussed:

YORUBA

Orisha or Orisa

Vodun – Supreme spirit. There are two families of spirits.

General Characteristics: They bless people with all good things. They are also vengeful if neglected by sacrifice. (Lightening, the weather)

Orishas have very specific functions. They also have taboos. They respond to specific rhythmic patterns of song and dance. So, their functions include blessings, punishing, prescribed taboos, responds to rhythms of songs and dance, they have personalities with tastes or likes and dislikes. They have favorite praise songs.

Spellings of Sango, Hango, and Chango are all correct.

      FAMILIES OF ORISA with different functions.

The House of learning offers training as part of the process of initiation.

QUINTESSENTIAL BOOK "THE HOLY LAND"

1. OLODUMARE (Olorun)

He is the creator of all Orisa. Supreme but has no shrines. He assigns destiny to individuals and gives each human characteristics.

2. ESHU – The Divine Messenger. His counterpart is Legba, Elegba, or Ananse. He is the youngest and cleverest. Delivers sacrifice to Olorun. He serves Olorun.

(Punish) – He causes trouble to people who neglect the gods. He serves to deliver blessings.

His symbol is a string of small opaque maroon or black beads. Favorite foods in offerings include palm oil, boiled corn, and beans as well as male animals and fowls. Palm wine is consumed. He represents the possibility of evil but can protect against evil and illness. He guards pathways, roads and doors.

3. IFA/ORUNMILA – God of wisdom and knowledge. Orisha of Divination (Babalawo priest) practices a system of divination.

The divining will of divination "symbolic scribe of the Orishas" teaches the Babalawo (priest) to "write" Ifa messages sent thru Orunmila. Ifa divination is the most direct contact with Olorun.

10. Hotel Room

Dr. Fred Monderson: Time to recharge all batteries.

FREDERICK MONDERSON

Holy Land Illustration 81a. Part of the offering presented at the false door in the tomb of an Old Kingdom nobleman, Nenki.

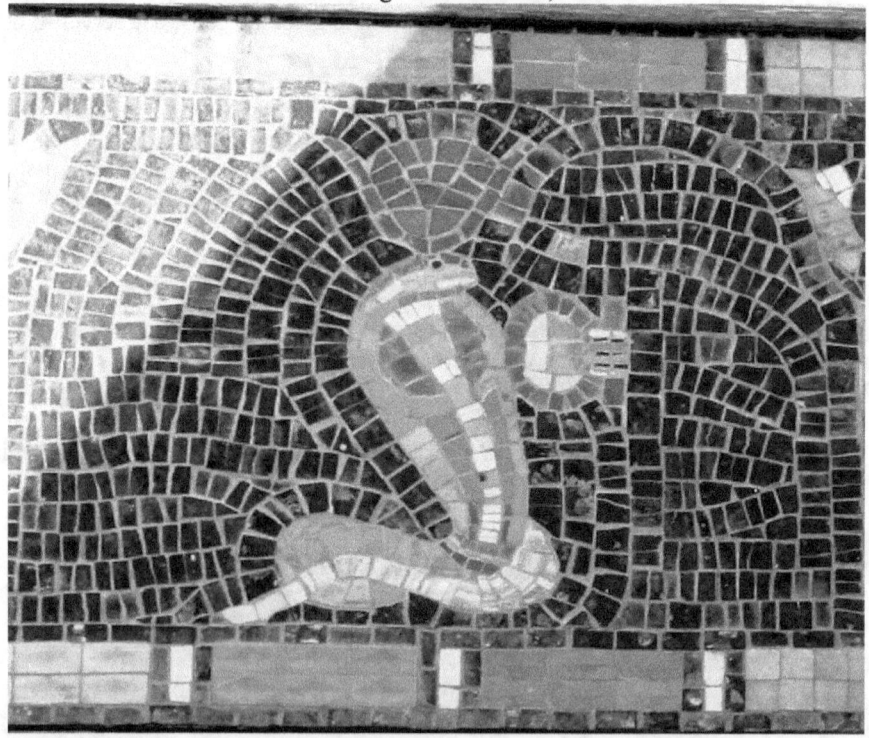

Holy Land Ceramic Art 13. The uraeus is always an interesting animal but clothed in ceramic wear, he seems more colorful than deadly.

QUINTESSENTIAL BOOK "THE HOLY LAND"

Day 9.
TEMPLE OF ISIS AND KALABSHA TEMPLE OF GOD MENDULESE

1.   Wake Up

Esperanza Rodriguez: Good Morning, Mi Amor. Your schedule for today calls for a bus and boat trip to the Temple of Isis on Agilka Island and then to the nearby Kalabsha Temple of God Mendulese. Your article is prepared for distribution.
Dr. Monderson: Thank you, my dear.

FASCINATON OF EGYPTIAN ARCHAEOLOGY
By

Frederick Monderson

Egyptian/Kemetic archaeology has proved to be one of the most fascinating subjects in the modern world. Modern archaeology has unearthed and pieced together the art and architectural history and craftsmanship, scientific accomplishments, industry and religious beliefs of early African man in Egypt. Today, what has been recovered still casts a long beam of light. This helps to illuminate and explain modern man's quest to understand and accept the promises of those long established principles, sciences and beliefs that forever has governed the world. Such is ancient African legacy to humankind. In a world of tourists, collectors, thieves, merchants of genuine and faked artifacts, attaches,' a new science struggled to establish a systematic method of retrieving and chronicling mortuary and architectural data for study of Nile Valley culture. Archaeology, principally under pioneering and widespread excavation established the principles of a new discipline on a firm footing. That age, 1870-1930, experienced an unprecedented amount of exploration, excavation, discussion, and publishing of interpretation of the evidence. However, if the great African and African-American scholars of the Twentieth Century alone, DuBois, Woodson, Huggins,

FREDERICK MONDERSON

Jackson, Rogers, G.M. James, ben-Jochannan, John H. Clarke, Van Sertima, Karenga, Carruthers, Diop, Obenga, who, after lengthy years of scholarship, research, lectures, publications, study of history and historical phenomenon, have determined that the record has been falsified, we must give this consideration! Therefore, we are forced to concede that despite the wonders of its great revelation, archaeology's practitioners may have erred in their interpretations. Hence, there is the need to identify such and educate African peoples about this fact and elicit their support in erudite efforts aimed at correcting history.

If we argue from a philosophic perspective, ancient Kemetic architecture can be perceived as living manifestations of cosmic experience. Sculpture became wood, stone and metal expressions of physical features, and official and social portraits of the society. Paintings were mainly found on walls of temples and tombs and people of ancient Kemet, today's Egyptians, generally used four colors, viz., red, blue, green and yellow. They particularly seemed to also use black. In the Cairo Museum, a display shows Amenhotep II, we know Queen Ahmes Nefertari is painted Black and Tutankhamon specifically reveals his Blackness. Elsewhere an official is shown worshipping Thutmose I who is also painted Black. Are we to believe when evidence of the Blackness of Egypt was encountered it was not tampered with, destroyed or otherwise altered? Who knows? In practically every tomb in the Valley of the Kings, broken bits of wood painted black were strewn about. Are these remnants of "Tutankhamon-like" statues? In Horemhab's (Horemheb's) tomb a defaced wooden statue painted black was found. Such, therefore, reinforces the view "Tutankhamon-like" statues were the norm!

QUINTESSENTIAL BOOK "THE HOLY LAND"

Holy Land Illustration 81a. A sacrificial altar. Notice the center depression through which the blood flowed.

Tomb depiction represented history, literature, theology, ritual and medicine. Architecture, horticulture, clothing, feasting at banquets, farming, fishing, and hunting as well as religious practices were represented as art in tombs. Literature was very extensive throughout dynastic history. The *Wise Sayings of Imhotep* was quoted for centuries. He was the Grand Vizier of King Zoser of the Third Dynasty. Imhotep built his Pharaoh Zoser's mortuary temple called the Step-Pyramid at Sakkara. The artistic and architectural conventions he introduced provided the experimental basis of the Great Pyramids at Giza that represented the great flowering of ancient Kemet's mortuary and religious praise structures, beliefs and practices, as well as forays into science, medicine, agriculture, quarrying, navigation, etc., which so characterized the Old Kingdom of dynasties 3, 4, 5, and 6.

FREDERICK MONDERSON

Holy Land Illustration 82. Sepulchral stele of the scribes Au-en-Amen and Ahauti-nefer, sculptured with scenes representing the deceased persons worshipping Osiris and Her-shefit, XXth Dynasty (left); and Sepulchral stele of Prince Auuaruath, son of Osorkon II, sculptured with a scene representing the deceased and his sister worshipping Ra-Harmachis from the XXIInd Dynasty (right).

QUINTESSENTIAL BOOK "THE HOLY LAND"

Holy Land Illustration 82a. Abydos Temple of Osiris. Seti I with empty and upraised hands in adoration of Ptah, out in the Courtyard before excavation.

Tales of Sinuhe told of an official under King Amenemhet, 2000 B.C. He fled to Palestine and longed for his native land. Finally he was welcomed home just before he died. The *Prophecies of Nefert* and the *Miracles* during the reign of Khufu are interesting pieces also. So too were *The Tale of the Two Brothers*, *The Eloquent Peasant*, and *The Shipwrecked Sailor*. These are all wonderful specimens of the literary genius of ancient African man of Egypt. The *Book of Surgery* is dated to the Old Kingdom and *Ebers* and *Edwin Smith* Papyri to the 18th Dynasty. These were copies of much older medical works and were copied by students for centuries. The *Pyramid Texts* were found in tombs of kings of the 5th and 6th Dynasties. The *Coffin Texts* are the same religious teachings and inscriptions that were written on the outside and inside of coffins that dates to the Middle and New Kingdoms. The famous *Book of the Dead* became a compilation of religious beliefs and very graphic representations of what was to be expected in the next world. These Africans were original in their intellectual adventures in sciences, arts and metaphysics. Their creative genius pioneered in establishing the parameters of today's scientific disciplines.

Kemetic/Egyptian archaeology has taught us that modern man is not unique in disturbing the resting-place of the revered ancestors. The only difference today, man's search is clouded in the dubious term science. We have learnt that most of the royal and wealthy burials were desecrated from the earliest times, especially in the twentieth through twenty-second dynasties. Celebrated investigations were conducted to focus attention on this vile practice. During the late ages of the nineteenth century, Gaston Maspero found the entire modern village Abu el Gurneh was a nest of tomb robbing despoilers. Equally, the Abu Rasul brothers knew and robbed the Deir el Bahari cache of mummy and their rich hoard.

Yet still, today, we must see Egypt/Kemet as a cultural beacon, that reinforces the genius of our African ancestral heritage.

Dr. ben-Jochannan, whom I have known since 1972, and traveled with to the "Holy Land," on several occasions, has always insisted that in the temples we should not enter the Sanctuary or "Holy of Holies." We see this being contravened by visitors and many native Egyptians, who don't fully respect the ancient culture. This is why critical scholars, our children, families and whomsoever we convert, must move tenaciously and boldly to reclaim the revered African past. We must defend it with vehemence whether in teaching or researching and writing about that glorious ancestral heritage.

Modern interest in Egypt began around 1800 when Napoleon, the French Emperor, visited Egypt with an army and a coterie of scholars who made the first systematic study of the culture of the ancient Egyptians. Their efforts produced a work entitled *Description of Egypt*. At a place called Rosetta in 1798, engineers unearthed the Rosetta Stone. This important document is a tri-lingual inscription in Hieroglyphic, Demotic and Greek. It became the key to decipherment of the ancient language allowing scholars to establish a scientific discipline called Egyptology.

The language was deciphered by Champollion in 1822 and simultaneously inaugurated antiquarian interest in Egypt. Prior to the Rosetta Stone's discovery, Count Volney had visited Egypt and in his book *Ruins of Empire* wrote, Blacks or people with "sable skin and frizzled hair," then "enslaved in the modern world, founded thousands of years ago, the principles and sciences that today govern the universe." Another distinguished French visitor, Baron Denon, was the first modern visitor to draw a picture of the Sphinx of Giza. Some claimed Napoleon's artillery shot off the Sphinx's nose for his drawing show this part of the anatomy intact.

In 1836 Sir Godfrey Higgins wrote *Anacalypsis* in two volumes. This book became a veritable reference reservoir on 'Black who's who' of the ancient world. It indicated that Osiris, Chreeshna, Jesus, Buddha, Hercules, etc., were all Black personalities. In fact, Sir Godfrey Higgins I (1836: 134-135) wrote regarding Osiris: "Mr. Maurice says, 'That Osiris, too, the black divinity of Egypt, and Chreeshna, the sable shepherd-God of Mathura, have the striking similitude of

QUINTESSENTIAL BOOK
"THE HOLY LAND"

character, intimated by Mr. Wilford, cannot be disputed, any more than that Chreeshna, from his rites continuing so universally to flourish over India, from such remote periods to the present day, was the prototype, and Osiris the mythological copy …. Again, he says, 'Now it is not a little remarkable that a dark blue tint, approaching to black, as his name signifies, was the complexion of Chreeshna, who is considered by the Hindoos not so much an avatar, as the person of great Vishnu, himself in human form. That by Osiris was meant the sun; it is now allowed by every writer who has treated on the antiquities of Egypt. Mr. Maurice, as the reader sees, states him to have been black and that the Mnevis, or sacred bull, of Heliopolis, the symbol of Osiris, was also black."

Holy Land Illustration 82b. Abydos Temple of Osiris. The king kneels (below, left, center and right) before the divinities, in Osiris' shrine and before Anubis and other gods as he presents a vase of ointment.

These pioneering works were done in the period from 1800-1875 when great scholars were engrossed in establishing the linguistic system and structures that came to characterize Egyptology.

Wilkinson's *Manners and Customs of the Ancient Egyptians*, Birch's *Records of the Past* and Bunsen' *Egypt's Place in Universal History* were all outstanding

FREDERICK MONDERSON

works. From mid-16th Century, European imperialism and colonialism emerged eventually with chattel slavery. The latter brutal system launched a physical assault against the psychic nature as well as the personality and intellectual integrity of Africa and Africans. To a great degree it was successful.

Holy Land Photo 93. Memphis Museum. Profile view of Alabaster Sphinx of Rameses II.

Samuel Cartwright, the "banana skin physician" in his classic *Slavery and Ethnology* represented a significant culture of pro-slavery advocates. He wrote in 1857, the "Nilotic monuments record Negroes were nothing but slaves in Egypt from time immemorial."

Anton's *Dictionary of Classical Antiquity* tell us 1863 the "red color is evidently intended to represent the complexion of the people, and is not put on in the want of a lighter paint or flesh color for when the limbs or bodies are represented as seen through a thin veil, the tint used resembles the complexion of Europeans."

"The Negro is a Beast" is an article Dr. Hunt wrote in 1864. This type of psychological assaults amidst physical emasculation and degradation of slavery, were typical of the backdrop of 19th Century racist scholarship regarding Africans. Imperialists excavated, controlled and molded the presentation of a distorted version of Africa and history. As late as 1897, De Rouge argued for the Asiatic origin of the Ancient Egyptians.

QUINTESSENTIAL BOOK
"THE HOLY LAND"

Holy Land Ceramic Art 14. Whether Anubis is wearing a veil or head-cloth of colored stripes is anyone's guess.

The period from 1870-1930 represented the birth and classical period of Egyptian Archaeology. European academic, governmental and private organizations sponsored archaeological expeditions to unearth early African culture. They were, at first, most interested in acquiring artifacts for private collections and museums. These academics and adventurers often swarmed all over the ancient land. Of particular interest were the numerous magazines and journals that came into being as a result and helped to record their excavations; in fact perpetuating and ossifying a false view. Nevertheless, these are treasure troves of ancient Egyptian history. Such institutions as the Smithsonian Institution, the Metropolitan Museum of Art, the Philadelphia Museum and equally its Journal, Bulletin of the Museum of Fine Arts, University of California Publications of Egyptian Archaeology and more published Journals. Academic and scholarly publications in the forefront of the newly recovered information and resultant interpretation included, *Ancient Egypt*, the *Journal of Egyptian Archaeology, Society of Biblical Archaeology Journal, Biblia, American Philological Society*, the *Journal of the Asiatic Society, Antiquity, Annals of Archaeology and Anthropology, Ancient*

FREDERICK MONDERSON

Egypt, Art and Architecture, Harvard African Studies, Modern Quarterly, Journal of Biblical Literature, Nation, Memnon, Good News, Open Court, Dublin University Magazine, The Academy, and *Annals of Medical History,* to name some sources of important documentation.

We know historical sources come in primary and secondary categories. The information was further included in *Biblical World, Journal of the Royal Anthropological Institute, Man, Biometrika, Journal of Semitic Languages* and *The American Anthropologist, American Journal of Archaeology, Isis, Journal of Near Eastern Studies,* and numerous other collections of archaeological, anthropological and scientific repositories are all extremely significant reservoirs of ancient data. They entities all published briefs, extracts and reports of archaeological finds. Africans wrote none of the reports and none had a Black editor. None of the writers or journals was systematically taken to tasks for any and all disparagement, discrepancies or distortions of the African historical past they were so significant in molding.

Holy Land Illustration 82c. Abydos Temple of Osiris. With Isis as Hathor at his rear holding the Sistrum, Seti offers a plant to Osiris grasping his emblems of power. Notice Osiris holds three scepters and flail.

QUINTESSENTIAL BOOK
"THE HOLY LAND"

Holy Land Illustration 82d. Abydos Temple of Osiris. With hand stretched forward before Anubis, Seti receives the breadth of life, or Ankh.

Several individuals excavated at the various pyramids from Giza through Meydum, Hawara and Lahun. These structures were large and inviting. They yielded interesting mathematical and technological information as well as religious and mortuary data. The pyramids of Egypt are immortal. These gigantic monoliths came to characterize a period and a culture in Egypt, Northeast Africa. The pyramids were not a new idea to Africa for several places along the Nile could be found naturally hewn stone pyramids that were shaped by wind, sand and other forces of nature. The ancient burial lands to the south of Egypt are strewn with such pyramids.

Because of the great body of knowledge unearthed in archaeological excavations of the age, a concept called the "Hamitic Hypothesis" was born. It argued, essentially "any evidence of civilization and high culture found in Africa was brought there by a people of white morphology." Since the existence of the natural pyramids, absence the remains of pyramids as burial structures of people alien to Africa, at this early age, we must conclude ancient Africans are the genuine source and inspiration of the wonderful man-made mountains we call the pyramids. The genius of their construction owes nothing, if anything to Europeans and other foreigners. In fact, they represent mountains of hope, intellect and steadfastness even resilient nature and aspirations of Africans, those at home and even in the Americas.

The idea of the pyramids grew out of the needs of the Old Kingdom to preserve the remains of a dead king who journeyed into immortality in the next world as well as establish some connection with Ra as he journeyed in the sky above. At first kings were buried in elaborate sub-structures underground that were covered with a super structure called Mastabas. The step-pyramid was a superstructure development of seven such Mastabas in decreasing size from the bottom up. The true pyramid emerged from the trial and error of the Step-Pyramid and the Bent Pyramid until the building techniques had been mastered.

In 1897, 3 theories existed as to origin of the Egyptians. 1. They came from Asia via the Suez Isthmus. 2. Another version noted they came from Asia, along the Horn of Africa and through Ethiopia, and then journeyed down the Nile. 3. That the majority of the Egyptian population, it is held, had its origin in Africa and passed into Egypt by the West and Southwest, but these were of a European origination.

That same busy year, 1897, the Frenchman Gaston Maspero, who has argued for the latter, in one of his archaeological excavations discovered a *Table of Offerings* that was a replica of these on Memphite tombs. The best examples are two Old Kingdom tombs of Ti and Pepi II. Their inscriptions listed thousands of loaves of bread, cakes, game, meat, cloths, and perfumes and so on. To be given the deceased. d A set of rites was listed on the table to be performed in five parts.

1. Two purifications, by water and incense.
2. A ceremony of Opening the Mouth with purification and a summary meal.
3. The dressing of the deceased.
4. The anointing of the deceased.
5. Two additional purifications by incense and water.

This notion of cleanliness characterized the ancient Egyptian/Kemet culture. The image of a "flea-infested Arab" scratching himself is itself alien to Africa! These excavations were made in the classical Victorian period. On one of his trips in Egypt, Dr. ben-Jochannan got a lot of mileage from a book of the time called *Dirt*. It noted an English Queen, perhaps Mary, castigation of the women of Europe. She boasted of being the cleanest woman in all of Europe because she had taken one bath that year. Thousands of years ago, the people of Kemet had constructed baths with provisions for the water to be brought and to also exit the contraption. The Temple of Rameses III at Medinet Habu had four bathrooms for the king.

QUINTESSENTIAL BOOK
"THE HOLY LAND"

Holy Land Illustration 82e. Abydos Temple of Osiris. Seti stands empty handed and wearing the lion skin before the enthroned Osiris who holds the whip and scepter, two of the symbols of his power.

Abydos and Thebes were the most extensively excavated archaeological sites in Egypt. Abydos gained fame very early in Egyptian history for a vast number of reasons. It was the cemetery of the Thinite kings of the First and Second Dynasties. In this vicinity forts were constructed. Most of their remains have disappeared. There was a great Hypostyle Hall located here as well as monuments of kings Khasekhemwy and Perabsen. There was a Stela of King Zet and a Great Stella of Ahmose. Strabo, the Greek Geographer (63 B.C. to 24 A.D.) recorded seeing a well here when he visited Abydos. In addition, there were a number of temples including that of Ahmose I, Khentiamenti, and much later Rameses II and his father Seti I. Most importantly, at Abydos the ladder to heaven was located. Petrie discovered 10-levels of temples dating back to the beginning of dynastic rule.

FREDERICK MONDERSON

Holy Land Illustration 82f. Abydos Temple of Osiris. Speaking of magic. Holding his instruments of power, Thoth administers the breadth of life to Osiris, and then one has to wonder who is the more powerful god or is it that Thoth is the faithful servant doing his bit to restore the power to his brother god, in as much as he had been his minister plenipotentiary.

Thebes was the capital of Egypt during the Middle and New Kingdoms. The twin temples of *Warit* and *Waset*, Karnak and Luxor, were located here. This city boasts the richest architectural and religious remains anywhere on earth. The site is endowed with art, architecture, religious beliefs and preparations for the otherworld. Archaeological excavations exposed records of military and other historical developments and provide geologic and botanical evidence of ancient man along the Nile River in Northeast Africa.

Generally, worship temples were located on the east bank and mortuary temples on the west bank of the Nile River. The "Colossi of Memnon" are two gigantic seated statues of Amenhotep III that stood outside a large temple that has now disappeared, from the West Bank. This was Amenhotep III's mortuary temple.
The Temple of Luxor, dedicated to Amon-Ra, was built by Amenhotep III of the

QUINTESSENTIAL BOOK
"THE HOLY LAND"

18th Dynasty and extended by Rameses II of the 19th Dynasty.

The Great Temple of Karnak was begun about 2000 B.C., in the Middle Kingdom, and successive pharaohs built here for 2000 years. The architect Senmut built Deir el-Bahari for Queen Hatshepsut who ruled as pharaoh. Both herself and later Pharaoh Amenhotep III claimed to have had divine births and these were recorded in their temples. Pharaoh Rameses II, the great statesman, and builder, military strategist, who also erected the twin temples of Abu Simbel, built the Ramesseum as his mortuary temple. These were considered the pharaoh's "Mansion of Millions of Years." Then there was Medinet Habu, a great mortuary temple, built by Rameses III, of the Twentieth Dynasty.

The Valley of the Kings became the final resting-place for the greatest pharaohs. In 1881, Maspero found 44 royal mummies in a cache at Deir el-Bahari, hidden by 22nd Dynasty priests who sought to foil the tomb-robbing agents and invading hordes of their time. Importantly, the Egyptians a subterranean passage entrance into the underworld lay at Deir El Bahari. In 1898, the Frenchman Loret found another cache of 13 mummies in the tomb of Amenhotep II. The illustrious Dr. Cheikh Anta Diop in his *Civilization or Barbarism* has pointed out that the mummies in Egypt have had their skins stripped from the flesh. The skin was the surest way to tell the race of their owners. Still, he was able to detect significant amounts of melanin in the bodies. Many of the mummies seemed like "peeled potatoes." These preserved remains were tampered with.

The Valley of the Queens, Valley of the Nobles and Valley of the Artisans are all outstanding examples of creative African genius in theology, art, mummification practice, science and other contributions to the pageantry of human and civilization drama.

This is all said to reinforce Drs. Diop, ben-Jochannan and Ivan Van Sertima's convincing arguments for the blackness of ancient Egypt/Kemet. This powerful legacy belongs to people of African descent. We must teach others especially our young, particularly during Black History Month and Women's History Month; African people have a proud and illustrious heritage. We possess a determined and resilient spirit that helps us to survive and grow. The twenty-first century must not find Africans wanting knowledge of the past. They must possess the tenacity to conduct research and engage in meaningful African historiographic reconstruction. We must set the record straight. Ancient Kemet archaeology holds the key. We must study archaeology and mold the future for our youth.

FREDERICK MONDERSON

2. Breakfast

Dr. Leonard James: The Nile River is a fascinating phenomenon of nature. From its sources in Central Africa where it's fed by several small tributaries and the White Nile and Blue Nile and Atbara River, it spans a distance of 4100 miles and empties into the Mediterranean Sea. This occurs just after the diversion of its six branches in the Delta. The Nile has been called Egypt's "Gift," "River of Life," "Osiris" because of its "resurrection" or "rebirth" culminating in the Inundation. In essence, the Nile is indispensable to Egypt. It provides Egypt's transportation highway, the waters to nurture its crops, justifies a religious belief in mirroring a calculus of life, death and rebirth. The Nile facilitated the development of boat building, and river transportation. It aided the development of mathematics in creating Nilometers to measure the volume of the river. Equally, the destructive nature of the inundation, despite its fertilizing effluence, required geometry and other measurements in the mandatory re-surveying of the land after the flood. Nile mud aided the temporary nature of domestic architecture and later encouraged quarrying of stone and building more permanent religious structures of temples, obelisk, avenues of sphinxes, sarcophagi. etc.

Holy Land Illustration 83. Third Dynasty arch (left); Diorite statue of Khafre (center); and limestone statue of Ranofer (right).

QUINTESSENTIAL BOOK
"THE HOLY LAND"

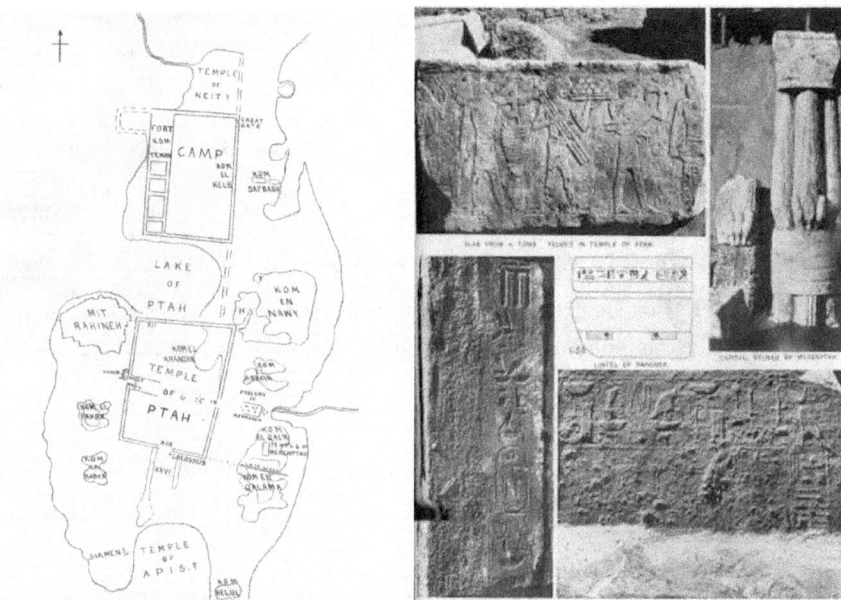

Holy Land Illustration 83a. Memphis Sketch Map showing the Temple of Ptah in the Mit Rahina area as well as the Lake of Ptah and other structures; and sculptures of the Fifth and Sixth Dynasties such as a Slab in the Temple of Ptah, Capitol reused by Merenptah, Jamb of Ranuser and Lintel of Teta.

The Nile is incomparable. It is the longest river in the world, the only major river that flows south to north and from time immemorial the inundation provided a rich, alluvial fertilizer that enabled the lucrative agriculture foundations of Egypt's cultural wealth and economic well-being. With the construction of Egypt's "old "and "new" dams, the natural fertilizing process ceased. In constructing the "damn" Dam at Aswan, Egypt created enormous hydroelectric potential for lighting, manufacturing industry to help its modern development. On the other hand, with the cessation of the Nile's natural fertilizing process, Egypt now has to manufacture fertilizer as well as contend with the perennial siltation problem that affects the ducts through which water flows in the dams.

In the earliest military engagement, Narmer mobilized his forces at Thebes, sailed northward, conquered the rival kingdom and then unified the land. From that time onward every military or major enterprise involved the Nile. Whether it was the funerary pilgrimage to Abydos, visit of the pharaoh to any temple, trade abroad and within the nomes, or imperial ventures, river traffic provided the means and this was equally for celebrating the many festivals Egyptians became famous for.

FREDERICK MONDERSON

Walter Brown: Thanks.

Michelliea Georges: Good Morning, George. How are you this wonderful day?
George Washington: Fine, my sister. Where is your roommate?
Michelliea Georges: She is ill today. I too am not feeling that great but I'm here.

George Washington: Perhaps I should not discuss today's contribution since she is not here. But then again, you can share it with her later. In **Ancient History** on December 4, 1975, we discussed how animals represent Egyptian deities. Case in point. Cattle represent Hathor; birds represent Horus; the Dog is Anubis, and the crocodile is Sobek.

Egyptian religion is principally a solar cult. So Ra, Aten and Atum are the sun, a creator force.

They have triads of human qualities, as in the case of Osiris, Isis and Horus. These are anthropomorphized gods.

Syncretism is the blending of opposite and contradictory tenets or laws. We have Amun-Re where Amun is hidden and Atum who is the totality.

Monaltry is when there is one god for you, but not denying your neighbor's god.

In year 4, Akhnaton proclaimed one god – Aton. Aton is seen as god of Egypt, Syria and Aten. Throughout in their experience, Pharaohs vied with each other to prove their loyalty to the popular god. There was a tendency of accountability on part of both man and god.

In **African Religious Thought Systems** on December 1, 1975, we continued the study of Yoruba.

Usufruct is the temporary use and enjoyment of lands and tenements belonging to another.

Special priests are trained for Ifa.

ODUDUWA (Odua) (Orisha) [Orishada Obatala] is the progenitor of all Yoruba. He is the first king of Ifa. (King) Oni of Ifa is in direct relationship with Oduduwa. Many Orisha are associated with Oduduwa. These include Obameri, Eshidale,

QUINTESSENTIAL BOOK "THE HOLY LAND"

Osanyin (Eleshije), and Oshosi (Ore).

Obameri looks out for suicide.

Osanyin is the Orisha of medicine, the owner of all herbs and patron of physicians.

Ore (Oshosi) is the Orisha of the hunt. He is concerned with atonement for incest.

Holy Land Photo 94. Memphis Museum. Bust of alabaster statue of Rameses II lying in the prone position but raised upright for this demonstration.

FREDERICK MONDERSON

ORISHADA OR OBATALA is the creator of mankind and whose symbol is a white cloth. He represents the highest moral conduct of Yoruba. He made the first man and woman and can refashion the fetus in the mother's womb. In their worship of this deity, women wear small opaque white bead necklaces also white anklets or bracelets. The symbol of his shrine is a flat piece of bone or ivory.

There are approximately 50 subordinates to Obatala. Orisha Oko is the deity of farm. Ogun is the patron of all who use iron tools. These include blacksmiths, hunters, warriors and barbers. For Ogun, whose symbol is iron, the concept of rebirth is very important. The Adinka cloth is associated with this deity.

3.   Bus Ride

George Washington: I see you made it after all.
Regina Hendricks: Yes. It was difficult. I did not come to breakfast as you probably noticed.
George Washington: Yes I did. I also gave Michelliea some work for her to share with you.
Regina Washington: You are always on point, Brother. That is what I like about you.

George Washington: Thanks. On December 12, 1975, in **Ancient History** we discussed how the Hittites were responsible for the collapse of the Egyptian empire. At this time the Egyptian population was 3 million. The Hittites occupied northern Loan, Southern Anatolia. Hurrians were very influential on the Hittite culture. The Hittites had a feudal social organization, militarism, feudalism. A council of nobles elected a king among the Hittites who led them into battle. Hittite kings were Labarna, Mattushili I in the city of Hattushash and Murshil who was murdered.

By 1525 of the Egyptian Empire, in the 18th Dynasty, Telipinn had made the kingship hereditary. Then came Tudhaliya, Shuppiluliuma and the Hittites conquered northern Levant. Then came Murshili II, Muwqatalli and Hattushili III.

The Hittite god was called by the Hurrian name Teshu. Kubaba became a major god of the Phrygians and was later renamed Kubele and later the Greek Cybele.

QUINTESSENTIAL BOOK
"THE HOLY LAND"

In Egypt, on the other hand, Thutmose III gave great tracts of land to the temples. Generals and priests held the same office. The temple of Karnak owned 40% of the land. We see the creation of a theocratic state, the total submission to the church.

Harmhab appointed Rameses (General) to succeed him. Rameses I reigned for a short time and was succeeded by his son Seti I who built the Abydos temple.

The Jewish exodus was not a single event but a set of minor exoduses, one family at a time. Kadesh was the focal point during Rameses II's reign. He built the Hypostyle Hall at Karnak and the Ramesseum, his magnificent funeral temple.

Holy Land Illustration 83b. Memphis. General collection of objects from the Temple of Merenptah (left); and Sculpture of the XIXth Dynasty (right).

4. Site:
TEMPLE OF ISIS
THE TEMPLE OF ISIS

FREDERICK MONDERSON

Holy Land Papyrus 27. Enthroned Tutankhamon, in an intimate mood, relaxes with his wife.

The Temple of Isis of Philae, "Pearl of the Nile," is an important geographical, historical and religious landmark, in the culture of ancient Kemet. Located on an island in the Nile at Aswan, it was built during the Graeco-Roman period, after 332 B.C. or *Nile Year* 3908. Along with the other temples of this period, whose structures have withstood the ravages of time as at Dendera, Esna, Edfu, Kalabsha and Kom Ombo, all are built on much older foundations. The ancient Kemetic name is "Island of the time of Ra." Old Kingdom evidence indicates these ancients believed the area around Philae and the First Cataract was the source of the Nile. This notwithstanding, West (1995: 426) explained, "Philae incorporates some work done under Nectanebo, and blocks built into its foundation name the

QUINTESSENTIAL BOOK
"THE HOLY LAND"

Nubian king, Taharka (690-664 B.C.), the earliest concrete evidence unearthed.

But it is on Philae that the last known inscription in sacred Hieroglyphs is to be found, dated 394 A.D. And the last example of Demotic graffiti, this dated 425 A.D. If knowledge of the Hieroglyphs persisted beyond this time, no record of it has been found."

On the Island of Philae a number of other temples, dedicated to various deities, were added, in the culture complex, including two Nilometers. Work on these structures lasted through the entire Ptolemaic and Roman Periods. All of these architectural masterpieces were erected as appendages to celebrating and worshiping Isis, faithful wife, mother, nurse, artificer and magician who possessed great words of enchantment. Wayne (1987: 230) states: "Isis, the sister and wife of the great Osiris was the Egyptian goddess of healing, purity and sexuality, of motherhood and women, of promise of immortality and of nature itself." Theophile Obenga (1992: 168) showing that Isis represented female equality with men, freedom of women to own land, wills and legacies, be educated, and divine femininity, mentions an extract from the Great Hymn to Isis, found on a papyrus of the Second Century B.C. which describes the lady as "Goddess of numerous games, pride of the female sex, though reigneth in the sublime and infinite, Thou wanteth women (at the age of procreation) to come and anchor with men, it is thee the mistress of the earth, Thou maketh the power of women equal to that of men."

Her home was also held in high regard, for as Ferguson, a nineteenth century writer, believed the irregularity of the Isis Temple was stupendous in its beauty. Interestingly enough, he wrote: "No Gothic architect in his wildest moments ever played so freely with his lines and dimensions, and none, it must be added, ever produced anything so beautifully picturesque as this. It contains all the play of light and shade, all the variety of Gothic art, with massiveness and grandeur of the Egyptian style; and as it is still tolerably entire, and retains much of its color, there is no building out of Thebes that gives so favorable an impression of Egyptian art as this. It is true it's far less sublime than many, but hardly one can be quoted as more beautiful."

FREDERICK MONDERSON

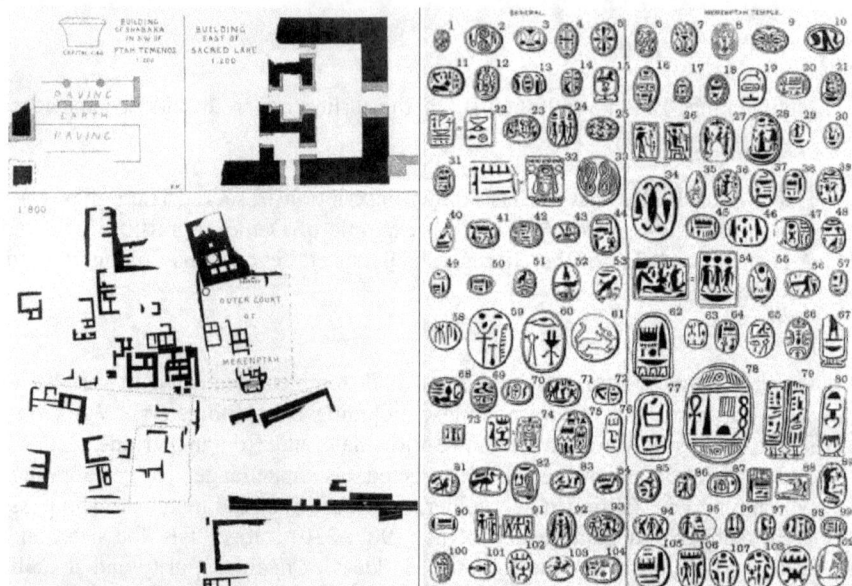

Holy Land Illustration 83c. Memphis. Plan of Town around Merenptah's Temple (left); and Scarabs, General and from Merenptah's Temple area (right).

From the earliest times, it was believed the source of the Nile was connected with the Island of Philae, making it a very special place. We may picture this from the writing of Strolocke (1965: 52) who noted: "Just before the northern tip of the island are a number of rocks with inscriptions-boundary stones marking the southernmost limits of the Pharaonic Kingdom." Of course, at different times the border extended way beyond this Aswan region. Nevertheless, this boundary mark meant the Temple of Isis was built in Nubia. However, and significantly, while the Head of Osiris was buried at Abydos, his heart was thought buried at Philae, making the Goddess's temple even more special. Morally, in the worship of Isis, such principles as Ma'at - balance, beauty, order, truth, etc., were foremost and rightfully embodied African womanhood. Here we see the essential roots of the complimentarity of the African male-female principles of cooperation, respect, love and faithfulness.

Blending the principles of nature with architecture and art, the Kemetic/Egyptian artist achieved quintessential mastery of the materials and complexity of his art form, viz., wood, stone, metal, painting, sculpture, architecture, etc. However, with Greek inventiveness came changes in size, structure, art motifs and prolific inscriptions whether in temples, or on civic projects, stelae, correspondence, etc.

QUINTESSENTIAL BOOK "THE HOLY LAND"

Underscoring this view, Smith (1981: 422) has argued: "Alexandrian artists, in general, made little more than a playful use of misunderstood Egyptian motifs, much as such Egyptian elements entered into the fashionable decorative scheme of Imperial Rome or as they were revived in Napoleonic France."

Even more so, Bratton (1987: 22) forcefully expressed: "No Sumerian, Babylonian or Persian sculpture can compare with the Egyptian in draftsmanship, mastery of form or sense of proportion. No ancient sculpture, except possibly the Greeks, has such a universal appeal. Goethe recognized the classical nature of the Egyptian sculpture in his comparison of the 'black basalt' figures with the Greek 'white marble.'"

Importantly, an obelisk found at Philae and now at Kingston Hall in Dorsetshire, England, played a significant part in the decipherment of Hieroglyphics/Medu Netcher, to which Champollion is credited with so much.

Since the Temple of Isis was close to the earliest views of the origin of the source of the Nile, King Zoser of the Third Dynasty, who built his Step-Pyramid at Sakkara, once enquired of the priests of the Temple of Isis, whether this was indeed the source of the Nile. As such, the temple must be envisioned as very early manifesting cosmic, aetiological, esthetical and ethical relevance. Therefore, clearly and significantly, evidence of African theosophy, theology, spirituality, metaphysics, linked to the Nile River in its flow from interior Africa, can be searched for and seen in this mound of genesis, where the Temple of Isis stood.

PART II

That much known, the Temple of Isis is the principal building on the island and a significant contribution of the early, but particularly Greek Period. The island measured 450 meters long and 150 meters across. During the 1960s, as the Aswan High Dam neared completion, UNESCO appealed to interested nations to help save the endangered Nubian monuments, including Philae. Agilka Island was chosen as the new home of Philae temple. Then its dimensions and contours were altered to exactly replicate Philae Island with its monuments.

FREDERICK MONDERSON

Holy Land Illustration 84. Stele recording the dedication of a building to the goddess Neith by Aahmes (Amasis) II, about B.C. 573 (left); and Stele sculptured with a scene representing Ptolemy IV, adoring Menu, or Amsu, Isis, Heru-sa-Ast, and other deities about B.C. 200 (right).

The modern boat ride to the Island of Agilka docks on the southern end of the island. Here visitors emerge with a recent Refreshment Stand to the right and the

QUINTESSENTIAL BOOK
"THE HOLY LAND"

Holy Land Ceramic Art 15. What grace and majesty is contained in this bird's expansion from wingspan to head and tailpiece.

Pavilion of Nectanebo I on the left, the first ancient building encountered. This structure has bell-shaped columns and Hathor head capitals. Leading to the Temple of Isis, it stands on the southern entrance of the Dromos or Outer Temple Court where an antique Nilometer was also located. In this majestic court, the Western Colonnade consisted of 32 composite plant-form columns with reliefs. Wayne (1987: 276) writes accordingly, the illustrations depict, "Tiberius offering gifts to the gods, the capitals of varying unfinished state plant motifs, no two alike." The East Colonnade consists of 17 columns in an unfinished manner. To the right of the court and at the southern end of the east colonnade is the Temple of Aresnufi, near midway is the Temple of Mandulis and at the northern end is the Temple of Imhotep. Deified as the Greek Aesculapius, Imhotep became the Greek/Kemetic/Egyptian God of Medicine, even though he practiced as a physician two thousand years before Hippocrates, the Western "father of medicine." To recall, he is shown at Kom Ombo on the back wall with medical instruments nearby.

Budge I (1969: 523) has written that an inscription on a door of Imhotep's Temple read: "Great one, son of Ptah, the creative god, made by Thenen, begotten by him and beloved by him, the god of divine forms in the temples, who giveth life to all men, the mighty one of wonders, the maker of time, who cometh unto him that calleth upon him wheresoever he may be, who giveth sons to the childless, the chief Kher-heb (the wisest and most learned one), the image and likeness of Thoth the wise."

At the end of the Dromos is the First Pylon of the temple with two massive towers that are 120 feet wide and 60 feet high. On the exterior face are colossal sculptures of divinities and Ptolemy Philometer swinging his battle-axe over a batch of bound prisoners. The name of Nectanebo is found left of this pylon.

A short courtyard entrances the Pylon proper to, the Temple of Isis that was commenced by Ptolemy Philadelphus and Arsinoe, and completed by succeeding monarchs; among whom are Euergetes I, Philometer, his brother Euergetes II, with two Cleopatras, and Ptolemy the elder son of Auletes, whose name is found in the area and on the pylon. Many of the sculptures of the exterior are of the later epoch of the Roman emperors, Augustus, Tiberius, Claudius, Domitian, Nerva and Trajan.

The principal entrance through the First Pylon is that of Philadelphus. The second entrance is that of Nectanebo. These portals lead into the Central Court of the Temple of Isis. To the east is the second East Colonnade with 7 columns. To the west is the Mammisi or Birth House entrance with its colonnade whose rear is seen from the river and aligned with the entrance of Nectanebo. Further east of the Mammisi is the new Nilometer leading down to the river. The average length of the cubit on the Nilometer is 1 ft. 8.9 in., being almost the same as that of the average cubit on the Nilometer of Elephantine Island.

At the northern end of the court on a different axis is the Second Pylon of the temple proper, of a much smaller size than the First Pylon. The eastern tower of the Second Pylon bears an inscription that mentions grants of land made to the temple by Ptolemy Philometer and Ptolemy Euergetes II. This Gate of Ptolemy at the Second Pylon leads to a Pronaos or Hypostyle Hall with 10 gigantic columns, all remarkable for the brilliancy of the colors still remaining on their capitals. The walls and ceiling are covered with astronomical and other subjects, and figures of divinities. In this hall, and in other parts of the temple, the presence of the cross may be taken as evidence of the existence of the church of St. Stephen, into which this temple was converted at the end of the 6th century.

QUINTESSENTIAL BOOK "THE HOLY LAND"

Holy Land Photo 95. Memphis Museum. Headless bust with mane and illustration on the back (left); and standing statue with defaced features (right).

This Hypostyle Hall entrances into three chambers in succession, of which the last is the Sanctuary, in which is a monolithic granite shrine. On the wall is a representation of Ptolemy Philadelphus, suckled by Isis. On either side of these chambers are other rooms, in the first of which on the right, will be found the latitude and longitude of the island, as taken by the scientific members of the French expedition. Near this room is the entrance to crypts and hidden passages, similar to those at Dendera. From the corresponding lateral chamber on the opposite side a staircase leads to the terrace. During the Graeco-Roman Period, the divinity's corporeal form was taken to the roof to be bathed in the rays of the Sun God Re.

On the left, at the top of the staircase, is a small room covered with interesting sculptures relating to the death and resurrection of Osiris. Flaubert's commentary, according to Wayne (1987: 278) states: "In one of the upper rooms, scenes of embalming: in the corner to the right a woman on her knees lamenting, her arms raised in despair; here the artist's observation cuts through the ritual of the conventional form." From Greek ex-votos in this chamber, we learn the interesting fact that the worship of Isis and Osiris was still carried on at Philae in

FREDERICK MONDERSON

A.D. 453, more than 70 years after the Edict of Theodosius abolishing the religion of ancient Kemet.

On the eastside of the Temple of Isis, is a small Temple of Hathor, built by Ptolemy VI Philometer and Euergetes II. Wayne's (1987: 179) description is that the: "colonnade was decorated during the reign of Augustus with amusing carvings of music and drinking - apes dancing and one playing a lute, dwarfish Bes beating a tambourine, while Augustus offers a festal crown to Isis." To the north of this are remains of what appears to have been an arched gate with steps down to the river. To the south of this is Trajan's Pavilion or Kiosk, called "Pharaoh's Bed." It is an oblong rectangular building of the late date surrounded by an inter-columnar screen with 14 columns with beautifully carved floral columns. The temple was roofed with stone slabs, supported on wooden beams, the sockets of which are still existing. Trajan is shown offering incense and wine to Isis, Osiris and Horus.

In conclusion, the Temple of Isis at Philae, called "Pearl of the Nile" by Herodotus, has also been called "vision of Paradise" as it seems to rise out of the sacred waters of the Nile. Procopius c. 540 A.D. tells, according to Keating (1975: 185), at Philae "the last stronghold of the ancient gods was reduced and their worship passed into memory. But the temples remained in romantic view for posterity to wonder at." Somewhat similar to the modern approach, Amelia Edwards wrote of the inundation at the turn of the 20th century as Keating (1975: 185) reported: "The approach by water is quite the most beautiful. Seen from the level of a small boat, the island, with its palms, its colonnades, its pylons, seem to rise out of the river like a mirage. Piled rocks frame it in on either side, and purple mountains close up the distance. As the boat glides nearer between glistening boulders, those sculptured towers rise higher and even higher against the sky. They show no sign of ruin or of age. All looks solid, stately, and perfect. One forgets for the moment that anything is changed. If a sound of antique chanting were to be borne along the quiet air - if a procession of white-robed priests aloft the veiled ark of the God, were to come sweeping round between the palms and the pylons - we should not think it strange." This observation was made following the temple's submersion as a result of the first dam at Aswan during the inundation. Even more importantly, however, Bratton (1968: 264) has quoted the words found on one of the portals of the temple.

"The Holy Mound is the sacred golden domain of Osiris and his sister Isis. It was predestined therefore from the beginning (of the world).... Let there every day be divine service by the appointed high priest; let there be a libation to Isis, Lady of Philae, when the libation of each day is poured. Let there be no beating of drums or playing of harps or flutes. No man shall ever enter here; no one, great or small, shall tread upon this spot. None here shall raise his voice during the sacred time of the days when Isis, Lady of Philae, who is enthroned, shall be here to pour the

QUINTESSENTIAL BOOK
"THE HOLY LAND"

libation each tenth day. Isis, Lady of Philae, will embark for the Sacred Mound on the holy days, in the sacred bark of which the name is ... (effaced)."

One is therefore constantly reminded of Dr. ben-Jochannan's admonition that a particular decorum must be paramount for all visitors and that African-American visitors must not enter certain parts of the temple in reverence. Still, some misguided brothers and sisters insist they enter those sacred and prohibited domains and bathe in the power of its aura. We must insist they not do so, for too often Europeans and Arabs disrespect the temple by doing just that. Nevertheless, the Temple of Isis is one of the great repositories of African spirituality, cosmic force, religiosity, artistic and architectural accomplishments as well as philosophical, epistemological and scientific knowledge that African-Americans can take great pride in. Therefore, we must teach the children to honor, worship and respect the notion of African womanhood in all its godliness and pristine beauty that the Temple of Isis came to represent for this makes us all proud and strong.

Holy Land Photo 96. Memphis Museum. A vendor's Bazaar (left); and sign indicating the Sarcophagus of Amen-Hotep Hwi of the 19th Dynasty, 1290-1224 (right).

THE BLESSING

Wilson (1901: 121) has provided the basis of the blessing in: "Of Bringing Men Back to Earth" from the *Papyrus of Ani* in the British Museum No. 10,470, sheet 18. THE CHAPTER OF CAUSING A MAN TO COME BACK TO SEE HIS HOUSE UPON EARTH [In the Saite Recension (see Lepsius, *Todtenbuch* Bl.54) the house is said to be "in the underworld."] The Osiris Ani Saith: "I am the Lion-god coming forth with extended strides. I have shot arrows and I have wounded the prey; I have shot arrows and I have wounded the prey. I am the Eye of Horus, and I pass through the Eye of Horus at this season. I have arrived at the furrows; let the Osiris Ani advance in peace." [Another papyrus adds the words: "I have advanced, and behold, I have not been found light, and the Balance is empty of my affair."]

Wilson (1901: 125) offers "FOR THE NEW MOON" which is an inspiration that comes from Lepsius' *Todtenbuch*, Bl. 55. ANOTHER CHAPTER TO BE RECITED WHEN THE MOON RENEWETH ITSELF ON THE DAY OF THE MONTH. The Osiris Auf-ankh, triumphant, saith: "Osiris unfettereth," or, as others say "openeth the storm cloud [in] the body of heaven, and is unfettered himself."

"Horus is made strong happily each day. He whose transformations are great (or many) hath offerings made unto him at the moment, and he hath made an end of the storm, which is in the face of the Osiris Auf-ankh, triumphant. Verily he cometh, and he is Ra in [his] journeying, and he is the four celestial gods in the heavens above. The Osiris Auf-ankh, triumphant, cometh forth in his day, and he embarketh among the tackle of the boat."

IF THIS CHAPTER BE KNOWN BY THE DECEASED HE SHALL BECOME A PERFECT KHU IN THE UNDERWORLD, AND HE SHALL NOT DIE THEREIN A SECOND TIME, AND HE SHALL EAT HIS FOOD SIDE BY SIDE WITH OSIRIS. IF THIS CHAPTER BE KNOWN BY HIM UPON EARTH HE SHALL BE LIKE UNTO THOTH, AND HE SHALL BE ADORED BY THE LIVING ONES; HE SHALL NOT FALL HEADLONG AT THE MOMENT OF ROYAL FLAME OF THE GODDESS BAST, AND THE MIGHTY PRINCESS SHALL MAKE HIM TO ADVANCE HAPPILY.

Wilson (1901: 125) mentions "OF TRAVELING IN THE BOAT OF RA" from the *Papyrus of Nu* in the British Museum No. 10,477, sheet 28, and is as follows: ANOTHER CHAPTER OF TRAVELING IN THE BOAT OF RA. The Osiris Nu, the overseer of the palace, the chancellor-in-chief, triumphant, saith "Behold now, O ye luminaries in Annu, ye people in Kher-aba, the god Kha (?) hath been born; his cordage hath been completed, and the instrument wherewith he maketh his way hath [he] grasped firmly. I have protected the implements of the gods, and I have delivered the boat Kha (?) for him. I have come into heaven, and I have traveled back the paths of Nut at the staircase of the god Sebek."

Wilson's (1901: 126-27) selection "OF MAKING PERFECT THE KHU" from the *Papyrus of Nu* in the British Museum No. 10,477, sheet 16 is as indicated below.

ANOTHER CHAPTER OF MAKING PERFECT THE KHU: [it shall be recited] on the festival of six. The Osiris Nu, the overseer of the palace, the chancellor-in-chief, triumphant, saith "Behold now, O ye luminaries in Annu (Heliopolis), ye

QUINTESSENTIAL BOOK "THE HOLY LAND"

people in Kher-aba, the god hath been born; his cordage (?) hath been completed, and the instrument wherewith he maketh his way he hath grasped firmly; and the Osiris Nu is strong with them to direct the implement of the gods. The Osiris Nu hath delivered the boat of the sun therewith and he cometh forth into heaven. The Osiris Nu sailed round about in heaven, he traveleth therein unto Nut, he journeyeth along with Ra, and he voyageth therein in the form of apes; [he] turneth back the water-flood which is over the Thigh of the goddess Nut at the staircase of the god Sebaku. The hearts of Seb and Nut are glad and repeat the name, which is new. Un-Neferu reneweth [his] youth, Ra is in his splendors of light, Unti hath his speech, and lo, the god of the Inundation is Prince among the gods. The taste of sweetness hath forced a way into the heart of the destitute one, and the lord of thy outcries hath been done away with, and the oars (?) of the company of the gods are in vigorous motion. Adored be thou, O divine Soul, who art endowed more than the gods of the South and North [in] their splendors! Behold, grant that the Osiris Nu may be great in heaven even as thou art great among the gods; deliver thou him from every evil and murderous thing which may be wrought upon him by the Fiend, and fortify thou his heart. Grant thou, moreover, that the Osiris Nu may be stronger than all the gods, all the Khus, and all the dead. The Osiris Nu is strong and is the lord of powers. The Osiris Nu is the lord of right and truth, which the goddess Uatchit worketh. The strength, which protects the Osiris Nu, is the strength, which protects the god Ra in heaven. O god Ra, grant thou that the Osiris Nu may travel on in thy boat in peace, and do thou prepare a road whereon [thy] boat may journey onward; for the force which protecteth thee. The Osiris Nu driveth back the Crocodile from Ra day by day. The Osiris Nu cometh even as doth Horus in the splendors (?) of the horizon of heaven, and he directeth Ra through the mansions of the sky; the gods rejoice greatly when the Osiris Nu repulseth the Crocodile. The Osiris Nu hath the amulet (?) of the god, and the cloud of Nebt shall not come nigh unto him, and the divine guardians of the mansions of the sky shall not destroy him. The Osiris Nu is a divine being whose face is hidden, and he dwelleth within the Great House [as] the chief of the Shrine of the god. The Osiris Nu carrieth the words of the gods to Ra, and he cometh and maketh his offering at the moment among those who perform the ceremonies of sacrifice."

[THIS CHAPTER] SHALL BE SAID OVER A FIGURE OF THE DECEASED WHICH SHALL BE PLACED IN [A MODEL OF] THE BOAT OF THE SUN, AND BEHOLD, [HE THAT RECITETH IT] SHALL BE WASHED, AND SHALL BE CEREMONIALLY PURE, AND HE SHALL HAVE BURNT INCENSE BEFORE RA, AND SHALL HAVE OFFERED WINE, AND CAKES, AND ROASTED FOWL FOR THE JOURNEY [OF THE DECEASED] IN THE BOAT OF RA. NOW, EVERY KHU FOR WHOM SUCH THINGS ARE DONE SHALL HAVE AN EXISTENCE AMONG THE LIVING ONES, AND HE SHALL NEVER PERISH, AND HE SHALL HAVE A BEING LIKE UNTO

FREDERICK MONDERSON

THAT OF THE HOLY GOD; NO EVIL THING WHATSOEVER SHALL ATTACK HIM. AND HE SHALL BE LIKE UNTO A HAPPY KHU IN AMENTET, AND HE SHALL NOT DIE A SECOND TIME. HE SHALL EAT AND HE SHALL DRINK IN THE PRESENCE OF OSIRIS EACH DAY; HE SHALL BE BORNE ALONG WITH THE KINGS OF THE NORTH AND OF THE SOUTH EACH AND EVERY DAY; HE SHALL QUAFF WATER AT THE FOUNTAIN-HEAD; HE SHALL COME FORTH BY DAY EVEN AS DOTH HORUS; HE SHALL LIVE AND SHALL BECOME LIKE UNTO GOD; AND HE SHALL BE HYMNED BY THE LIVING ONES, EVEN AS IS RA EACH AND EVERY DAY CONTINUALLY AND REGULARLY FOREVER.

Wilson (1901: 128-29) chooses "SAILING IN THE GREAT BOAT" from the *Papyrus of Nu* in the British Museum No. 10,477, sheet 28.

THE CHAPTER OF SAILING IN THE GREAT BOAT OF RA TO PASS OVER THE CIRCLE OF BRIGHT FLAME. The Osiris Nu, the overseer of the palace, the chancellor-in-chief, triumphant, saith "[Hail], ye bright and shining flames that keep your place behind, Ra, and which slay behind him, the boat of Ra is in fear of the whirlwind and the storm; shine ye forth, then, and make [ye yourselves] visible. I have come [daily] along with the god Sek-hra from the bight of his holy lake, and I have seen the Maat [goddesses] pass along, and the lion-gods who belong unto them. Hail, thou that dwellest in the coffer who hast multitudes of plants (?), I have seen [what is] there. We rejoice, and their princes rejoice greatly, and their lesser gods (?) are glad. I have made a way in front of the boat of Ra, I have lifted myself up into his divine Disk, I shine brightly through his splendors; he hath furnished himself with the things which are his, taking possession thereof as the lord of right and truth. And behold, O ye company of the gods, and thou ancestor of the goddess Isis, [Read "god Osiris"?] grant ye that he may bear testimony to his father, the lord of those who are therein. I have weighed the ... in him [as] chief, and I have brought to him the goddess Tefnut and he liveth. Behold, come, come and declare before him the testimony of right and truth of the lord Tem."

"I cry out at eventide and at his hour, saying, Grant ye unto me that I may come. I have brought unto him the jaws of the passages of the tomb; I have brought unto him the bones which are in Annu (Heliopolis); I have gathered together for him his manifold parts; I have driven back for him the serpent fiend Apep; I have spit upon his gashes for him; I have made my road and I have passed in among you. I am he who dwelleth among the gods, come, let [me] pass onward in the boat, the boat of the lord Sa. Behold, O Heru-ur, there is a flame, but the fire hath been extinguished. I have made [my] road; O ye divine fathers and your divine apes! I have entered upon the horizon, and I have passed on to the side of the divine princes, and I have borne testimony unto him that dwelleth in his divine boat. I

QUINTESSENTIAL BOOK
"THE HOLY LAND"

have gone forward over the circle of bright flame, which is behind the lord of the lock of hair, which moveth round about. Behold, ye who cry out over yourselves, ye worms in [your] hidden places, grant that I may pass onward, for I am the mighty one, the lord of divine strength, and I am the spiritual body (Sah) of the lord of divine right and truth made by the goddess Uatchit. His strength, which protecteth is my strength, which protecteth, which is the strength, which protecteth Ra. [Grant ye that I may be in the following of Ra], and grant that I may go round about with him in Sekhet-hetep [and in] the two lands. [I am] a great god, and [I have been] judged by the company of his gods; grant that divine, sepulchral meals may be given unto me."

Wilson (1901: 129-31) examines, "OF THE FOUR FLAMES," from the *Papyrus of Nu* in the British Museum No. 10,477, sheet 26.

THE CHAPTER OF THE FOUR BLAZING FLAMES, WHICH ARE MADE FOR THE KHU. Behold, thou shalt make foursquare troughs of clay, whereon thou shalt scatter incense, and thou shalt fill them with the milk of a white cow, and by means of these thou shalt extinguish the flame.

The Osiris Nu, the overseer of the palace, the chancellor-in-chief, triumphant, saith: "The fire cometh to the Ka, O Osiris, governor of Amentia; the fire cometh to thy Ka, O Osiris Nu, the overseer of the palace, the chancellor-in-chief, triumphant. He that ordereth the night cometh after the day. Behold, [The flame cometh to thy Ka, O Osiris, governor of those in Amentia] [Added from the Papyrus of Nebseni] and the two sisters (?) of Ra come likewise. Behold, [the flame] riseth in Abtu (Abydos) and it cometh; and I cause it to come [to] the Eye of Horus. It is set in order upon thy brow, O Osiris, governor of Amentia, [In the Papyrus of Nebseni the deceased is here addressed.] and it is fixed within thy shrine and riseth upon thy brow; it is set in order upon thy breast, O Osiris Nu, and it is fixed upon thy brow. The Eye of Horus is protecting thee, O Osiris, governor of Amentia, and it keepeth thee in safety; it casteth down headlong all thine enemies for thee and all thine enemies have fallen headlong before thee. O Osiris Nu, the Eye of Horus protecteth thee, it keepeth thee in safety, and it casteth down headlong all thine enemies. Thine enemies have fallen down headlong before thy Ka, O Osiris, governor of Amentia, the Eye of Horus protecteth thee, it keepeth thee in safety, and it hath cast down headlong all thine enemies."

"Thine enemies have fallen down headlong before thee. The Eye of Horus cometh, it is sound and well, and it sendeth forth rays like unto Ra in the horizon; it covereth over with darkness the powers of Suti, it taketh possession thereof and it bringeth its flame against him upon [its] feet (?). The Eye of Horus is sound and well, thou eatest the flesh (?) of thy body by means thereof, and thou givest praise (?) thereto."

FREDERICK MONDERSON

"The four flames enter into thy ka, O Osiris Nu, the overseer of the palace, the chancellor-in-chief, triumphant. Hail, ye children of Horus, Mesthi, Hapi, Taumautef and Webhsennuf, ye have given your protection unto your divine Father Osiris, the governor of Amentia, grant ye your protection to the Osiris Nu, triumphant. Now, therefore, inasmuch as ye have destroyed the opponent[s] of Osiris, the governor of Amentia, he liveth with the gods, and he hath smitten Suti, with his hand and arm since light dawned upon the earth, and Horus hath gotten power, and he hath avenged his divine Father Osiris himself; and inasmuch as your divine father hath been made vigorous through the union which ye have effected for him with the Ka of Osiris, the governor of Amentia - now the Eye of Horus hath avenged him, and it hath protected him, and it hath cast down headlong for him all his enemies, and all his enemies have fallen down before him - even so do ye destroy the opponent[s] of Osiris NU, the overseer of the palace, the chancellor-in-chief, triumphant. Let him live with the gods, let him smite down his enemy, let him destroy [him] when light dawneth upon the earth, let Horus gain power and avenge the Osiris Nu, let the Osiris NU have vigor through the union which ye have effected for him with his ka. O Osiris Nu, the Eye of Horus hath avenged thee, it hath cast down headlong all thine enemies for thee, and all thine enemies have fallen headlong before thee. Hail, Osiris, governor of Amentia, grant thou light and fire to the happy soul, which is in Suten-heten (Heracleopolis); and [O ye children of Horus] grant ye power unto the living soul of the Osiris Nu within his flame. Let him not be repulsed and let him not be driven back at the doors of Amentet; oh let his offerings of bread and of linen garments be brought unto him among [those of] the lords of funeral oblations, or, offer ye praises as unto a god, to the Osiris Nu, destroyer of his opponent[s] in the form of right and truth and in his attributes of a god of right and truth."

REFERENCES

Budge, E. A. Wallis. *Dwellers on the Nile*. New York: Benjamin Bloom, Inc., (1885) 1972.

_____. *The Mummy*. New York: Causeway Books, (1989) 1974.

Campbell, David. *Everyman's Guides*: *Egypt*. London: Everyman Guides, (1995) 1996.

Chalaby, Abbas. *Egypt*. Firenze, Italy: Casa Editrice Bonechi, 1989.

Clarke, Sommers and R. Engelbach. *Ancient Egyptian Construction and Architecture*. New York: Dover Publications Inc., (1930) 1990.

Diop, Cheikh Anta. *Civilization or Barbarism*: *An Authentic Anthropology*. New York: Lawrence Hill Books, 1991.

Du Bois, W.E.B. *The Suppression of the African Slave Trade to America 1638-1888*.

Eames, Andrew. *Insight Guides*: *The Nile*. Hong Kong: APA Publications, Ltd.,

QUINTESSENTIAL BOOK
"THE HOLY LAND"

1992.
Ellis, Simon P. *Graeco-Roman Egypt*. Berks: Shire Publications, 1992.
Erman, Adolf. *A Handbook of Egyptian Religion*. Trans. By A. S. Griffith. London: Archibald Constable and Co., Ltd., 1907.
Finch, Charles in Ivan Van Sertima's *Egypt: Child of Africa*. New Brunswick, New Jersey: Transaction Books, 1995.
Haag, Michael. *Guide to Egypt*. London: Michael Haag, 1987.
Habachi, Labib. *The Obelisks of Egypt: Skyscrapers of the Past*. Cairo: The American University in Cairo Press, (1984) 1987.
Hart, George. *Egyptian Myths*. London: The British Museum, 1990.
Herodotus. Trans. Aubrey de Selincourt. *The Histories*. Baltimore, MD.: Penguin Books, (1954) 1973.
Higgins, Sir Godfrey. *Anacalypsis*. 2 Vols. London: Longman, Rees, Orme, Green, and Longman, Paternoster-Row, 1836.
Hobson, Christine. *The World of the Pharaohs*. New York: Thames and Hudson, 1987.
Hoefer, Hans Johannes. *Insight Guides: Egypt*. Hong Kong: APA Publications, (H. K.) Ltd., 1991.
Kamil, Jill. *Upper Egypt: Historical Outline and Descriptive Guide to the Ancient Sites*. New York: Longman, Inc., 1983.
Langenscheidt. *Self-Guided Egypt*. New York: Langenscheidt Publishers, 1990.
Magi, Giovanni. *Aswan, Philae, Abu Simbel*. Firenze, Italy: Casa Editrice Bonechi, 1989.
_____. *Esna, Edfu, Kom Ombo*. Firenze, Italy: Casa Editrice Bonechi, 1990.
Mann, A. *Sacred Architecture*. Rockport, Massachusetts: Element, 1993.
Maspero, Gaston. *Egyptian Archaeology*. Trans Amelia B. Edwards. New York: G. Putnam's Sons, 1892.
_____. *Manual of Egyptian Archaeology*. Trans. A. B. Edwards. New York: G. Putnam's Sons, 1902.
_____. *A History of Egypt*. Vol. I and II (of XII Vol.) London: The Grollier Society, 1904.
_____. *Manual of Egyptian Archaeology*. New York: G. P. Putnam's Sons, 1926.
McGrath, Nancy. Frommer's *Dollarwise Guide To Egypt*. New York: Frommer/Pasmantier Publishers, (1980) 1982.
Murray's. *Handbook for Egypt*. London: John Murray, 1888.
Murray, Margaret. *The Splendor That Was Egypt*. New York: Philosophical Library, (1949) 1957.
Nelson, Nina. *Essential Egypt*. Boston: Little Brown, and Co., 1990.
Pemberton, Delia. *Ancient Egypt: Architectural Guides for Travelers*. San Francisco: Chronicle Books, 1992.
Petrie, W. M. Flinders. *Dendereh: 1898*. London: Egypt Exploration Fund, 1900; Kegan Paul, Trench, Trubner, and Co., 1900.

FREDERICK MONDERSON

_____. *Religious Life in Ancient Egypt*. London: Constable and Company, Ltd., (1924) 1932 (61-62).

Quirke, Stephen. *Ancient Egyptian Religion*. London: British Museum Publications, 1992.

Holy Land Papyrus 28. Isis wearing horns and disk nurses Horus in the swamps and is being tended by Amon (left) and Thoth (right) assisted by two goddesses wearing the Osiris Crown and the Double Crown. Notice only the gods not the goddesses, wear a tail behind.

Richardson, Dan and Karen O'Brien. *Egypt: The Rough Guide*. London: Rough Guides, 1991.

Sauernon, Serge in Georges Poserner's *A Dictionary of Egyptian Civilization*. London: Methuen and Co., Ltd., (1959) 1962.

Shaw, Ian and Paul Nicholson. *The Dictionary of Ancient Egypt*. London: Harry N. Abrams, Inc., Publishers, 1995.

Showker, Kay. *Fodor's 90: Egypt*. New York: Fodor's Travel Publications, Inc., 1989.

Simpkins, Splendor of Egypt. *The Temple of Dendera*. Salt Lake City, Utah: Simpkins, 1987.

Smith, Fay. *Egypt at Cost: A Traveler's Guide*. New York: Little Hill Press, 1991.

Van Sertima, Ivan. Editor. *Egypt: Child of Africa*. New Brunswick, New Jersey: Transaction Publishers, 1995.

_____. *They Came Before Columbus*. New York:

Washington, Booker T. *Up From Slavery*.

Wayne, Scott. *Egypt and the Sudan: A Travel Survival Kit*. Berkeley, Calif.: Lonely Planet Publications, 1987.

Weigall, Arthur E. P. *A Guide to the Antiquities of Upper Egypt: From Abydos to the Sudan Frontier*. New York: The Macmillan Company, 1910.

QUINTESSENTIAL BOOK "THE HOLY LAND"

White, J. E. Manchip. *Ancient Egypt: Its Culture and History*. New York: Dover Publications, Inc., (1952) 1970.
_____. *Everyday Life in Ancient Egypt*. New York: Perigree Books, (1963) 1980.
Wilkinson, Alix. *Ancient Egyptian Jewelry*. London: Methuen and Co, Inc., 1971.
Wilson, Epiphanus. *Ancient Egyptian Literature*. New York: The Colonial Press, 1901.
Woldering, Irmgard. *The Art of Egypt: In the Time of the Pharaohs*. New York: Greystone Press, (1962) 1963.

5. Post-site Lecture

From 730-663 are the years that follow Dynasty XXII. Dynasty XXVI picks up after 663 B.C. The Assyrians were at their height. Ashurbanipal appointed Necho to administer Egypt. Necho rebelled and was defeated.

Psametech 663-610 unified all Egypt to fight the Assyrians and found the XXVIth Dynasty. His daughter Nitocris was sent to Thebes to assume the title 'Divine Wife of Amon.' Married to Amon, with an earthly vow of chastity, she became almost as powerful as the Pharaoh. At this time there was a considerable influx of foreigners who settled in Egypt. Greeks in the Delta and Jews at Elephantine.

Necho II 610-595 defeated the Assyrians and fought the Babylonians Nebuchadnezzar and lost.

Psamtek II 595-589 sent trading expeditions to Phoenicia.

Apries 589-570 was asked by a Libyan king to put down a Greek revolt. He sent troops and lost to the Greeks. He was overthrown.

Amasis 570-526 usurped the throne. He rebuilt Greek temples. He wanted peace. Naucratis was the Greek trading city. He limited them to that city in an agreement forcing them to give up all other settlements. This pleased both Greeks and Egyptians who now realized the Greeks were contained at Naucratis.

Cyrus II and his son Cambyses defeated Psamtek III.

FREDERICK MONDERSON

Holy Land Photo 97. Memphis Museum. Headless seated statue as part of the gallery in this Garden Museum.

6. Discussion
Are there Any Questions?

James Morrison: I have heard of the Council. What is it and what are the rules under which it operated?

Dr. Fred Monderson: The "Great Council" consisted of thirty individuals who were wise and well respected and who advised the Pharaoh. They helped the Pharaoh govern all of Egypt. There was also a "Grand Council" of Six who were of a higher order. In sort of American parlance, these were like the House of Representatives and the Senate, except they were not elected to this position and this analogy is somewhat of a long stretch, except they were wise persons. One had to be particular careful of what is said in the Council. There was an art of speaking in the Council and an insistence that when you speak, think of what your opponent may object to before you speak. However, the Proverbs of Ptah-Hotep says: "In the Council give thy opinion to thy lord freely and without the dissimulation followed by some Councilors. Declare thy line of conduct without reticence; give thy opinion in the Council of thy Lord; whereas there are some people who turn back upon their own (words) when they speak, so as not to offend him who has put forth a statement, (and) not replying, following this reasoning: 'It is for the great to recognize error, and when he shall raise the voice so as to oppose him because of it (the error?) he will keep silent as to what I have said.'

QUINTESSENTIAL BOOK
"THE HOLY LAND"

Michael Montout: Did the ancient Egyptians have rules for conversation in different situations?
Dr. Fred Monderson: Like all forms of social interaction, Conversation demanded a certain decorum that was based on ethics and respect for the other person in whatever situation. There were rules of good manners during conversation as well as rules for conducting good conversation. Equally too, what should be discussed in a conversation was considered as well as the dangers of repeating a conversation or overhearing something and then repeating it. They frowned on idle chatter.

John Brown: How was the concept of command received and understood in ancient Egypt?
Dr. Fred Monderson: The concept of command can be viewed in a number of ways. First you had to be able to command or control yourself; you had to be careful of not over-commanding. There was a protocol when commanding men, particularly in battle. Also, in social relations, it was suggested in terms of work and so on, do more than is commanded of you.

Rev. Dr. McNair: Who makes a covenant and why?
Dr. Fred Monderson: Religion was founded on a covenant with the deity. The god asked to be propitiated and the adherents wished to win his favor in sympathy and good fortune. As long as both parties kept their part of the bargain the covenant remained viable.

In explaining this concept, Myers (1900: 117-118) wrote: "In Ancient Egypt the primitive idea seems to have been, that the divinity and the Egyptian who prayed to him, were on the same footing; the one would receive on the condition of giving, the other would give on the condition of receiving. God never came to seek the approbation of the one who prayed to him, ... We find in the Hebrew Sacred Writings, Jacob saying, "If **YHVH** Elohim will be with me and will keep me in this way that I go, and will give me bread to eat and raiment to put on and I come to my father's house in peace; then shall **YHVH** be my Elohim (i.e., God). And this stone, which I have set for a pillar, shall be the House of Elohim. And of all that Thou shalt give I will surely give the tenth unto Thee. Many others of the early sacrifices mentioned in the O.T., seem to contain the idea of a bond or covenant, entered into by the worshipper with God, through his action as the sacrificer. According to the idea in vogue in pharaonic times, the maintenance of the physical order of the universe and the preservation of society, were bound up in the performance of the religious ceremonies and worship of the deities of the land of Egypt. The imprecations of the magician of their time threatened usually, the extinguishment of the sun and the overturning of the earth, but often they only threatened the cessation of worship. The Egyptian historians always mention the greatest calamity that could happen to their country, would be the disorganization of its worship and the cessation of the proper offerings."

FREDERICK MONDERSON

George Washington: How did the Egyptians respond to change?
Dr. Fred Monderson: The ancient Egyptians frowned on change even though change is inevitable and perhaps good. They admonished persons to not change any of the precepts, but deliver the same unaltered from Father to Son. They considered teachers making change injurious to the people. Persons were cautioned to deliver any message as given and not make any changes. Of course one unchanging reality in the life of the nation was the Nile River, that though it remained constant in its annual activity, it did bring change, some bad, some good, bounty and destruction. Even in the *Negative Confessions*, the Ka of the deceased is given to say, he has not changed the waters of the Nile nor has he altered a word of any message.

Peter Monderson: Who was the Chancellor and what were his duties?
Dr. Fred Monderson: The Chancellor was generally an elderly man, who was in charge of the royal seal, and whose duties were to keep in charge the titles of the nobles, officers, etc., also the origin and names of the slaves.

Robert Matthews: Can you say the Egyptian was a benevolent man?
Dr. Fred Monderson: Yes.

Walter Brown: River life is hard, are there reports of drowning?
Dr. Fred Monderson: In the boats today, you probably noticed the youngsters swimming alongside, so they learn to swim very early and this enables their mastery of the river. I suppose people do drown, perhaps from accidents. A hippopotamus killed Narmer in the river at the start of dynastic rule.

Holy Land Illustration 84a. Luxor Temple. View of statues of the southern part of the Ramesseum Front, the Processional Colonnade and the Court of Amenhotep II further on with the Minaret of the Mosque of Abu Haggag (left); and columns of the Court of Amenhotep III with the Hypostyle Hall to its rear (right).

QUINTESSENTIAL BOOK
"THE HOLY LAND"

Dr. Leonard James: Can you elaborate on the role of balance in the lives of ancient Egyptians?
Dr. Fred Monderson: Balance in life, balance in life's highways and byways. Balance is the tool of Thoth and the baboon cynocephalus and the devourer Ammit. Remember, Thoth, weighs the heart in the balance in the Hall of Judgment before Osiris and the Maati sisters, Isis and Ma'at. In the *Negative Confessions*, the Ka of the Deceased says "I have not defrauded by means of the weights of the balance." Things must be kept in balance and harmony.

Cherise Maloney: We know the Egyptians ate bread, but what else did they eat?
Dr. Fred Monderson: Well, from time immemorial Egypt was considered a breadbasket. They ate bread and cakes, meat, fish, fruits, and vegetables. Bakeries were busy and beer was important. From the lavish breakfast and dinner spreads we have been, and I have noticed the size and variety of some of your plates, clearly any and all edibles were fair game. This then is reminiscence of some foods enjoyed by the ancient Egyptians.

Kashmoney Malone: Seems like there's a book for this and a book for that, what are some names and uses of books?
Dr. Fred Monderson: Books were important and so was literacy in ancient Egypt. The *Book of the Dead* is a compilation of some of the earliest thoughts – religious, speculative, philosophic – of the ancient Egyptians. They were enshrined in the pyramids earlier. However, we are taught Aha of the First Dynasty wrote a book on medicine. The name of the workbook comes from papyrus.

We know of the *Book of the Dead*. In fact, there were *Books of the Dead.* Then they were *Book of Funerals, Book of Knowing, Book of Opening the Mouth, Book of the Portals, Book of Respirations, Book of the Rituals, Book of the Praising of Ra* and *Book of the Sun's Journey, Book of the Duat (Underworld)*, and so on. All these books possessed some moral and ethical message designed to make a better man of the ancient Egyptian so that he could aspire to everlasting life like the gods.

Michael Sinclair: Blaspheming. Were they "communists" of their time?
Dr. Fred Monderson: No! Blaspheming was considered an offense against the gods and the Ka of the deceased, in the Hall of Judgment, denied he had done such a despicable thing.

Joshua Monderson: How much bandage was used in the wrapping of a mummy?
Dr. Fred Monderson: Lots of bandage was used in wrapping a mummy. In fact, there were several levels or layers of the white stuff, each layer covering either amulets or jewels overlaid with bitumen that helped preserve the mummy.

FREDERICK MONDERSON

Lesley Jacobs: Where did you go to school?
Dr. Fred Monderson: Interesting! I am a product of the City University of New York. An Associate in Liberal Arts from New York City Technical College, BA and MA from Hunter College in African History, BA and MPA from John Jay College of Criminal Justice, and an MA in Education Supervision and Administration from Brooklyn College. I have Doctor of the University degree from Commonwealth Open University in Spain. I did spend a year at Temple University's Afrocentric Institute under Molefi Asante and took courses on Egyptology at the New School with Bob Brier, New York University with David Moyer and even did an African Art course given by Prof Fraser of Columbia University. I spent the summers of 1976 and 1981 at Exeter College Oxford University studying British Colonial History and in the summers of 1977 and 1992 I researched Egyptian Archaeology and Architecture at Bodleian Library, Oxford University. I also researched Colonial Africa at Rhodes House Library in Oxford and the Slave Trade at the Bodleian and Public Records Office in London. I was trained by Dr. Leonard James and I have been a student of Dr. ben-Jochannan and traveled with him to Egypt many times, traveled by myself and with tours also. I studied with Dr. Donna Richards (Merimba Ani) and Prof. John Clarke at Hunter College. I have never said this before, but there was a Professor at John Jay, Bonnie Sue Morrison who taught Public Administration. I took every course she taught, about six or so. Of course, I also attended lectures at the Metropolitan Museum of Art, Fordham University and the Pennsylvania Museum as well as the Brooklyn Museum, all on Egyptian subjects. Much of this before I made my first trip to Egypt in the 1989 with "Dr. Ben" whom I have known since 1972 when Barney, a friend, first introduced me to his book *Africa: Mother of Western Civilization*. He instructed me to choose one country in Africa and specialize in that. He took me there and explained the Egyptian Collection at the Metropolitan Museum of Art. I investigated the Brooklyn Museum collection myself where I also did research at the Wilbour Library. As a student Dr. Ben took myself and others to his home in Harlem and showed us his library and told us of the importance of books and maintaining this form of knowledge. I used the New York Public Library as well as spent money on creating my own personal library on Egypt, rather than invest in clothes as many of my friends did as far back as the early 1970s. I have used Temple University's Library extensively but I have spent more time at Hunter College Library than time spent in all the other libraries combined. I go there every chance I get.

QUINTESSENTIAL BOOK "THE HOLY LAND"

Holy Land Ceramic Art 16. What more can be said of the Ankh other than it is further enraptured in love.

Of course I have written more than 1000 articles for three Black newspapers in New York City dealing principally with Egypt, Africa and a few on local politico-social events and individuals. Well, this is some of what I have done. Should I also say I have also written more than 20 books on Egyptian topics. While I have not released all of them, they are all registered with the Library of Congress. In fact at last count I had 67 Library of Congress certificates for my different works registered there. I could be more specific but that can wait.

Michelliea Georges: I see. Where does the weighing of the heart take place?
Dr. Fred Monderson: The weighing of the heart took place in the underworld, in the Hall of Judgment, also called the Hall of Double Maati, where Osiris presided with the Maati goddesses and the company of gods who sat in judgment.

Regina Hendricks: We see lots of art in tombs and temples, perhaps in the palaces, what of the homes of the common people, were they also surrounded by art?

FREDERICK MONDERSON

Dr. Fred Monderson: Inasmuch as little remains of the homes of the poorer class has survived, because they were made of perishable materials, it is reasonable to assume they were lovers of art as well and would decorate their surroundings to the extent they could afford it.

Juliet Brown: I have heard somewhere there were over 1500 obelisks erected in Egypt. Were they all quarried at Aswan?

Dr. Fred Monderson: Let me say first of all, I cannot verify this number. Perhaps this number was correct, but I doubt it. However, we must be careful of false information merchants. False by virtue of unchecked sources. The name obelisk is alien to Egypt. The Egyptians called them *Tekhen*. I can say that number is highly questionable. Not every king erected one or more. While some temples had several, it is not certain if every temple had one. There seems to have been some obelisks erected in the Old Kingdom but they were more extensively erected in the Middle and New Kingdoms. I don't recall much evidence of them in the Old Kingdom and the Graeco-Roman temples of Kom Ombo, Edfu, Dendera, Esneh, etc., do not seem to have had any. We know nearly two dozen Egyptian obelisks were removed and are scattered throughout Europe and America.

Some kings erected several. Hatshepsut erected 4 at Karnak. Thutmose I erected 4 between Pylons IV and V where one still stands; while Thutmose III erected seven there. Middle Kingdom pharaohs, perhaps Usertesen I erected two at Heliopolis and one still stands. There were two in front of Luxor Temple's "Ramessean Front" put there by Rameses II. There were two small ones in front of the Karnak temple and one still stands today.

Now, we know there were 76 kings from Narmer to Seti I. There could not have been many more kings after this. Rameses II, Merenptah and the 20th Dynasty Ramesside kings. After that I don't believe many more were built. Consider the undertaking to quarry, transport and erect these wonderful "needles" and that there were not many kings who could undertake such an expedition since the economic viability of the country was in decline. The last major New Kingdom construction was the mortuary temple of Rameses III at Medinet Habu. Therefore I ask you to do the math. I could say the Washington Monument is an obelisk. However, it is a collection of stones and steel put together whereas the Egyptian obelisk is a single piece of stone quarried, transported, decorated and erected after considerable effort. No. It is hard to imagine 1500 obelisks in Egypt!

Teddy Cubia: Can you describe the heavenly existence the ancient Egyptian aspired to?

Dr. Fred Monderson: *Encyclopedia Britannica* has pointed out: "The life of the dead man in the sky is variously envisaged in different texts; at one moment he is spoken of as accompanying the sun-god in his celestial bark, at another as a

QUINTESSENTIAL BOOK "THE HOLY LAND"

mighty king of heaven more powerful than Re himself; the crudest fancy of all pictures him as a hunter who catches the stars and gods, and cooks and eats them. According to another conception that persisted in the imagination of the Egyptians longer than any of the ideas just mentioned, the home of the dead in the heavens was a fertile region not very different from Egypt itself, intersected by canals and abounding in corn and fruit; this place was called the *Sekhet Earu* or "Field of Reeds."

Any more questions. Hearing none, I will see you at dinner.

Michelliea Georges: What do you have for us today, Brother?
Regina Hendricks: Can we take you shopping after dinner tonight? I want to pick out something special for you.
George Washington: Thanks. I would love that. I don't want to forget you two sisters. Now, on December 11, 1975, in **Ancient History** class we discussed the major reason for attacks on Akhnaton were the cessation of imperialism and the economic decline of the Egyptian empire.

Rameses II reigned for 67 years. The Battle of Kadesh is the war between Rameses II and Muwatali, the Hittite king, at the City of Kadesh. Rameses defeated Muttashili III who formed a treaty with Rameses II.

The Treaty Outlines were that there be mutual assistance if another attacked either country. They would not attack each other. Political prisoners who fled from one country to another must be extradited and returned to one's country though the prisoner must not be harmed. This clause was written in the treaty.

There is a letter from the Hittites asking the Egyptians to send grain. Period of great migration. The Sheriden people were repulsed from Egypt and they founded Sardinia.

Merneptah succeeded his father Rameses II. He repulsed the sea peoples.

Akawa = Achaeans = Greeks.

Tursha = Etruscans = Italians.

We can do the **African Thought** at dinner.
Michelliea Georges: That's fine.

FREDERICK MONDERSON

8. Dinner

Michelle George: Ok. So let's begin.
Regina Hendricks: Don't forget we're going shopping right after.

George Washington: Right. Ok. So, **African Religious Thought Systems** on December 3, 1975, we discussed:

OGUN

For Ogun iron is crucial. He is patron of all who use iron tools. The people clear a path for all Orishas with machetes.

ORANYAN (ORUNMIYAN) was the first king of Oyo. Lakange was the mother of Oranyan. He had two fathers Ogun and Oduduwa. Oranyan was a warrior and ruler of Ife after Oduduwa, the founder of Oyo.

His sacrificial animal is a ram. Wine from the raffia pine is taboo for him. His worshipers do not wear beads. His priests –Eredemi – use wooden staffs.

SANGO (SHANGO) (CHANGO) was the son of Oranyan. He was the Orisha of thunder who lives in the sky and hurls thunderstones to earth. His priests wear leather bags (laba). Houses destroyed by lightening must be ritually cleansed by one of his priests. Sese beads are taboo for him. When possessed by Shango fire must not be waved in front of those possessed.

Tastes of Shango

Bitter cola nuts, yams, bean stew, porridge are some of what he consumes. His beads are red and white and a wand is associated with his priests. They wear red clothes. Shango, son of Oranyan, succeeded his father king of Ife.

The kings are as follows:

Alafin of Oyo; Oba of Benin; Oni of Ife.

9. Lounge Discussion

Michelliea Georges: Regina will be down in a few minutes.
George Washington: Ok. Dr. James and Mr. Brown are coming with us. They will be here in a few. Let me get in some work in the meantime.

QUINTESSENTIAL BOOK
"THE HOLY LAND"

Ancient History – December 15, 1975

Rameses III of the succeeding and 20th Dynasty built his mortuary temple at Medinet Habu. This temple is a history of the king's reign and his fights against the "People of the Sea" even while there were many foreign peoples coming to Egypt. The Pelest were the Philistines. Great droves of Indo-European migrations came from the north. The Philistines were last to arrive, coming through the Levant. Repulsed, they settled northeast of Sinai.

Even though the economy declined, pharaohs continued to build great tombs. Workers on many tombs were not being paid on time for the economy was greatly shattered. There was great inflation as well.

Sheridan and Shekelesh (slaves) were incorporated in the army and when they did not get paid they raised hell.

Depiction of animals and people are a lot different since the time of Akhnaton. No daily life scenes portrayed. A decline in the economy brought about much corruption in the governmental structure in the temples and by nobles. This is the beginning of great violations of the tombs of the great pharaohs.

(*Journal of World History*) – Cerny "Wages and prices in the 20th Dynasty."

A great percentage of the army was mercenary. The eastern Sinai was lost in this dynasty. With tomb robberies gold was available in abundance and with copper being scarce, what moderns call inflation began to take its toll.

The office of Amon-Ra high priest became hereditary. A high priest is depicted on the same plane of pharaoh in the Temple of Karnak. The 20th Dynasty ends and Egypt splits into two, north and south.

Holy Land Illustration 85. Gate of Nectanebo seen from the roof of the Temple of Khonsu with sphinxes placed by Amenhotep III, leading to the temple (left); Island of Elephantine, home of the "Lords of the Southern Frontier."

The high priest was also the military chief. Egypt was thus considered a broken reed. Culturally she did not decline, but would no longer be a political power. She became secondary. In the Greco-Prussian War Egypt aided Athens.

The impact of the year 1200 – Mitanni, Hittites and the Egyptians declined. The Levant becomes a free trading area. Sea-traders, Neo-Hittites, Aramaeans, Phoenicians, Philistines, Canaanites, and Hebrews became great traders straddling the Levant. The Indo-Europeans originated in western Russia.

George Washington: Now everyone's here, let's go.

Holy Land Photo 98. Cairo Museum of Egyptian Antiquities. Isis on the side of a Sarcophagus.

QUINTESSENTIAL BOOK "THE HOLY LAND"

Day 10. HIGH DAM, UNFINISHED OBELISK, LOTUS MEMORIAL
1. Wake Up

Esperanza Rodriguez: Good Morning, Mi Amor. Your schedule for today calls for visits to the High Dam, the Unfinished Obelisk and the Lotus Memorial.

Your article on "Egypt and Africa" *Daily Challenge* June 16, 1997, is ready for distribution.
Dr. Monderson: Thank you, my dear.

EGYPT AND AFRICA
By
Fred Monderson

Today, only the most knowledgeable and culturally aware African-Americans know the accurate story about Egypt/ancient Kemet and the rest of Africa. Young people, in particularly those with parents who were civil rights activists, Black scholars, and whose teachers know the truth, have a better understanding of Egypt and Africa.

The history of Africa has been distorted to exclude the contributions of Egypt as the Voice of the Mother Continent, Africa. Academic and cultural imperialists created a mythical area called the "Middle East." They projected Egypt as being a part of that area at the expense of Africa. The fact is, from time immemorial, Egypt/Sinai has been and still is a state in Africa and the Egyptians were and still are Africans. For that matter, more than a decade ago, Egypt was the host and it's President Mubarak, Chairman of the Organization of African Unity (OAU). This clearly shows Egypt is in Africa, not the Middle East!

The great writers of antiquity including Herodotus, Strabo and Diodorus all held that the Egyptians/Kamites were Black people. This belief was accepted until interest in Egypt/Kemet was developed by c. 1800 of our era. Because Africans were enslaved and had been downtrodden in the west, at that time, pseudo-Scientists felt it necessary and natural to exclude Egypt from Africa to justify that condition as being a perpetual one. As such, Africa's true role in Egypt was omitted and the history falsified to show the superiority of Europeans and their

FREDERICK MONDERSON

culture. Why not, since White men subjugated black men in an institution of trans-Atlantic slave trade and slavery in the west. And so, successive generations accepted the false belief and systematically shaped history to justify their story.

As the Science of Egyptology developed in 19th Century Europe, aided by the disciplines of Anthropology and Archaeology, the strategy was to elevate Africa north of the Sahara and denigrate Africa south of the Sahara. This outlook was achieved by falsely analyzing and interpreting the historical record. The premise was accepted and perpetuated by innocent and ignorant scholars and writers who dared not challenge the prevailing myths about Africa, and so, timidity and ignorance reigned. Individuals who preached racism colonized the writing of history.

Holy Land Illustration 85a. Workers in the Tomb of Vizier Rekhmire.

Modern European scholars including Volney, *Ruins of Empire* (1791); Denon, *Travels in Egypt and Assyria* (1793); and Sir Godfrey Higgins, *Anacalypsis* 2 Vols. (1836) took an iconoclastic view. They shattered the myths surrounding Africa, Africans and especially Egypt/Kemet. They too, had read Herodotus, "the Father of History" and had been aware of his descriptions of Egyptians/Kamites, as having "thick lips, broad noses, wooly hair and being burnt of skin." Diodorus Siculus had said the Ethiopians claimed to have found Egypt/Kemet as a colony.

QUINTESSENTIAL BOOK
"THE HOLY LAND"

And so, a new school of thought arose.

European writers such as Volney had written, Africans now "enslaved had once founded the arts and sciences that governs the universe." Godfrey Higgins also wrote that Jesus, the Virgin Mary, and many ancient "Holy Men" and races including the Sumerians, Buddha and Hercules were also Black! Their works were only published in limited editions! Western scholarship ostracized them! Their works were excluded and publishers refused to print their research. Such iconoclastic European scholars suffered for attacking the accepted myths about Africans! Nevertheless, these iconoclasts paved the way for Africans such as Duse Mohammed, Caseley Hayford, Dantes Bellgrade and Marcus Garvey, founder of the Universal Negro Improvement Association in 1916, to take pride in the Blackness of the Egyptians/Kamites. Then in 1922, Howard Carter discovered the tomb of Tutankhamon of the XVIIIth Dynasty. To that time, his was the greatest find of any ancient cultural remains. The wealth of his tomb, found in the Valley of the Kings at Thebes, is reflected in the jewelry, furniture and ushabti figures, musical instruments and untold wealth. However, the most astonishing but overlooked discovery were two boy-like replica statues of the boy king standing guard in front of the burial chamber. The replicas were to accompany, protect and present the king in the after-life. They were painted black to physically describe how the king actually looked. Since they accompanied him into eternity he could not misrepresent how he or they looked.

This find then, aided other critical historians such as W.E.B DuBois, *The Negro* (1916), and Carter G. Woodson, the "Father of Black History," who founded the *Journal of Negro History* and wrote *The Mis-Education of the Negro*, to look more closely at Tutankhamon's roots and it helped them trace the blackness of the XVIIIth Dynasty. Then J.A. Rogers in his *Sex and Race* Vol. I and *World's Great Men of Color* Vol. I took up the mantle. They showed how great Africans had been in the past. They began to expose the distortions and to include the omissions of African history and culture systematically implanted by racist pseudo-Scientists, theologians, writers, dramatists, publicists, teachers, et al. Following these great African-American writers, the baton was passed to Dr. Clarke and Dr. ben-Jochannan, who continued the assault on the bastions of misinformation about the indigenous quality of Africa in Egypt.

Dr. John H. Clarke wrote and lectured. Dr. ben-Jochannan too, lectured and wrote *African Origins of the "Major Western Religions"* (1970); *Africa: Mother of Western Civilization* (1971); *Black Man of the Nile and his Family* (1972); and, *Cultural Genocide in the Black and African Studies Curriculum* (1972). Then Dr. Cheikh Anta Diop published his *African Origins of Civilization: Myth or Reality?* (1955, 1974); *The Cultural Unity of Black Africa* (1959, 1978); *Pre-colonial Black Africa (*1960, 1987); and *Civilization or Barbarism* (1981), now released in English translation. Dr. Ivan Van Sertima founded the *Journal of African*

FREDERICK MONDERSON

Civilizations (April 1979), with focus on Africa and that great ancient culture, Egypt. Lastly, he published *Nile Valley Civilizations* (1984), *Black Women Antiquity* (1986), *Blacks in Science* (1987), and *Great African Thinkers*: *Cheikh Anta Diop* (1986) and *Egypt Revisited* (1988). In addition, the University of Chicago scholar Dr. Bruce Williams published his findings of "Ancient Nubian Artifacts Yield Evidence of Earliest Monarchy," as reported in *The New York Times*, March 1, 1979. He showed that the symbols of power and authority which we associate with Dynastic Egypt at 3200 B.C., viz., White Crown, enthroned Pharaoh, crook and flail, incense burner, Nile Boat, palace facade, serekh, etc., were dated to at least 3400 B.C. from Qustul, Nubia. This is the land south of Egypt/Kemet. Here he struck a major blow for the anteriority of Nubia/Ethiopian cultural origins that gave further credence to Diodorus' statement that the Ethiopians founded Egypt as a colony. As Bauval and Brophy reported in Black Genesis, when the people of Nabta Playa finally migrated to the Nile they settled in the area southwards of Aswan at c. 3500 B.C.

Between these last 5 African-American writers, more than 60 books were written. They documented the greatness of Africa, Africans, and their cultural heritage. They exposed the myths, attacked the false information and introduced new approaches and methods of studying and understanding the African past. Meanwhile, they taught the African-American youth to be proud and be able to achieve for the ancestors and their posterity.

The new African scholars, mirroring the efforts of teachers like Dr. Leonard Jeffries, Dr. Leonard James, Regent Adelaide Sanford, Dr. Donald H. Smith, Merimba Ani (Donna Richards), Prof. George Simmonds, the unsung hero in our community and the 'complimentarity of the African male-female principle,' must forge ahead, research, write and teach steadfastly asserting that Egypt is African! Those who understand what is at stake must waste no time! Young and old Black-manhood is at stake! More importantly, Black cultural heritage is at stake! We must defend Egypt as African and teach the attitude of critical humanism while challenging the dehumanizing Euro-centric perspective that Africans and their descendants in Diaspora have made no significant contributions to human culture and/or civilization. We must also continue to provide for our constituency the cognitive tools of critical analysis and synthesis which will better enable them to apply their own intellect and psyche to a more systematic, rigorous and objective search for truth in all areas of study.

QUINTESSENTIAL BOOK
"THE HOLY LAND"

Holy Land Illustration 85b. Objects from Decorated Rectangular Coffin; and Objects from plain Rectangular Coffin.

The history and culture of Africans and their descendants at home and abroad, will then become a valid corrective to the omissions and distortions of that history and culture which are characteristic of Euro-centric education, which in turn wreaked such psycho/socio/cultural havoc in Western European/American societies.

2. Breakfast

Dr. Leonard James: Much as been said of the Indian Maharaja who built the Taj Mahal for the woman he loved. Yet, not much has been publicized about the African named Senmut who built a temple at Deir el Bahari, Egypt, for the woman he served and loved. Unquestionably, Hatshepsut was an assertive, intelligent, beautiful and well-loved woman who ruled as pharaoh in early 18th Dynasty of Egyptian history. In the unfolding drama of this cultural dynamic, Senmut was one of a group of significant men who served their queen and were rewarded. Senmut it is said received more than forty titles, holding some of the most significant posts in the monarchical administrative and religious domains of Egyptian culture. Nevertheless, he is remembered more for his skill as an architect in the queen's mortuary temple at Deir el-Bahari, the worship temple of Mut in Asher and the two obelisks he quarried at Aswan, transported and had erected at Karnak. However, while time has taken its toll on the temple of Mut, one of the obelisks has fallen and Deir el Bahari has remained significantly intact. This is remarkable given the fact, supporters of Hatshepsut's rival and successor, Thutmose III, attacked, defaced and destroyed much of the temple and her efforts. The temple also suffered in the Aten's attack on Amon and abandoned to become covered by the sands of time and essentially remained for modern explorers and archaeologists to discover and unearth the temple Senmut lovingly built for his queen. For decades Polish scholars have struggled to restore and preserve the Upper Terrace, the heart of the temple with its sanctuary, which suffered the most from the destroyer's wrath.

FREDERICK MONDERSON

That much said; some more on Senmut would help identify this early lover who sat behind the throne of Egypt. According to some sources, Senmut was a general in the army of Hatshepsut's father Thutmose I. When the old king neared death he chose his daughter to succeed him. It was unthinkable for a woman to be Pharaoh. Realizing the problems she would face in a male dominated society he aligned her with strong, wise and experienced males. Besides, being the tutor and guardian of Hatshepsut's daughter among his titles, Senmut boasted of being the custodian of the royal bedroom. Such close proximity of commoner to royal divinity was unthinkable, for here is the assumed lover's connection! Equally too, perhaps this is why he worked so assiduously to build religious and other structures to help justify the queen's rule. All this notwithstanding, history records Senmut as a gifted African lover who built and enshrined the fame of his queen as a testimonial of his love. All this occurred at a time when Black men loved, respected and adored their women.

Walter Brown: You're as sharp as ever, Dr. James.

Holy Land Photo 98a. Professor John Henrik Clarke sits in the chair at the 1999 ASCAC Conference at City College in New York and is surrounded by Dr. Leonard Jeffries (left) and Dr. Jacob Carruthers (right) and backed by two beautiful sisters.

Michelliea Georges: What's up, Brother Washington?
Regina Hendricks: Do you like your gift?

QUINTESSENTIAL BOOK
"THE HOLY LAND"

George Washington: It is beautiful. Such a wonderful leather sachet case. My papers will fit well in this. Now I will really remember you sisters. Regarding: **African Religious Thought Systems** on December 4, 1975, Professor Donna Richards noted: Shango is capable of great feats and mysterious acts. All Shango Orishas are special to the people of Oyo.

Orisha of River – Obo.

Obo – Orisha of the River Niger and favorite wife of Shango. She comes before him like the winds. Her taboos are rams and ewes. Fire or smoke is not to be near her shrine. Her symbol is polished stone Celts also horns of the African buffalo.

Yemoja – Sango's mother. Her symbol is river worn stones.
Fertility gives women children. Water is kept in a pot in the shrine and given to newborn children. There is an annual festival to Yemoja. In Brazil (Bahia) Yemoja worshippers wear strings of small glass beads. The Ochra leaf is taboo to this deity.

River Orishas include Erinle, Oba (wife of Shango), Yewa, Ondo, Are, and Oskun, whose worshipers wear brass bracelets that are very beautiful. They are polyandrous.

Shopona is a brother of Shango (Sakpata is the counterpart among the Fon). He is concerned with small pox. Corn cobs and wood of Ashaba tree is used to treat small pox. Death by small pox means no burial or funeral. The body is left in the forest and the clothes burnt.

When called to dedicate oneself, one goes through a process of initiation in a "house" dedicated to a particular Orisha. Initiates are subjected to a period of seclusion namely "making ocha." One goes through a symbolic "death" and reborn with a new name, speaking a new language. The initiate is now given a new birthday.

FREDERICK MONDERSON

Holy Land Illustration 86. Sepulchral Stele of Heru (left); and Sepulchral Stele of Petat-Heru of the Ptolemaic Period (right).

Initiates must learn songs and dances. There are symbolic mother and father of "houses." Initiates are taught songs and dances of their respective Orisha. The sacred compound, the shrine's most sacred area, is for secret rituals. Initiates live there. The dance area is for the public, a unified "family" of worshippers.

3. Bus Ride

Michelliea George: I have been sharing my notes with a few people who have come to our room.
Regina Hendricks: We think you won't mind one bit.
George Washington: Not at all, sisters. In fact, I am glad you are doing this. The whole idea, as Dr. Monderson said, is to learn and teach each other. That is why I am sharing with you and am pleased you are also sharing to educate us all.

In **Ancient History** December 17. 1075. The last class was Monday, December 22 and the Final, January 7, 1976, from 9-11:00. For the final we read Moscati chapters 1-7.

The Egyptians called the Phoenicians purple. They had a purple dye that was

QUINTESSENTIAL BOOK
"THE HOLY LAND"

exported. The Phoenicians were great sea traders. They brought the alphabet westward. They are associated with the Pythagorean theorem of A2 + B2 + C2. (A square + B square + C square).

There was cultural interaction after 1200 B.C. between Egypt, Mesopotamia, Greece and Rome. The Aramaeans were great inland traders. The Kingdom of Phrygia was in Anatolia. Gardium was the capital city of Phrygia. King Midas was the ruler and the cult of Cybele was practiced there. Therefore, Ancient History Phase I lasted from 3000 to 1200 B.C.

Hebrews settled around the Dead Sea.

Between 1200-1000 B.C., we see the conquest and establishment of the Kingdom of Israel. By c.1050 B.C. Saul was given religious sanctions by Samuel to form a configuration of 12 Hebrew Tribes. The Amphyctconic League was formed. David was the founder of the Kingdom of Israel. He established the 12 tribes into a state of confederation. Many trade alliances were made. One of Solomon's 700 wives was an Egyptian. Solomon died in 922 B.C. That same year Israel split into the Kingdoms of Israel and Judah.

At this time the Assyrians began their conquests. By 720 B.C., they conquered the Kingdom of Israel. In 586 the Kingdom of Judah was conquered. Assyrians (neo-Babylonians) conquered, colonized and deported Jews. By 539 the new power in the ancient world was the Persian king, Syrus.

4. Site:

HIGH DAM
UNFINISHED OBELISK

LOTUS MEMORIAL

5. Post Site Lecture

FREDERICK MONDERSON

6. Discussion

Are there any questions?

Regina Hendricks: Did the people give tithes to temples like we give to churches? Dr. Fred Monderson: Sure they did, but the state also played an initial and then ongoing part in collecting revenue for the temple. Today we call it tithes or collection. J.A. MacCulloch's "Tithes" in *Encyclopedia of Religion and Ethics* (1927, 12: 347) explained the origin and purpose of Tithes. "Tithes are connected, on the one hand, religiously, with offerings of first fruits; on the other hand, politically, with tribute and taxation. While taxation often took the form of a tenth, the amount might vary, less or more, thought the name 'tenth' (*decima*) was retained. Voluntary offerings to a deity soon became customary, and even necessary, especially where kings began to impose taxation and tribute, and where a god was now thought to be a divine monarch. To keep up his sanctuary was as much an obligation as to keep up the royal person and court .... The voluntary offerings necessarily became tribute also, as the ritual of a sanctuary became more elaborate, the sanctuary itself more splendid, and the attendant priest more numerous. Why a tithe or tenth should have been fixed on so generally is not clear, but probably it is connected with primitive views about numbers, or with methods of counting - e.g., by fingers and toes."

Holy Land Photo 99. Cairo Museum of Egyptian Antiquities. Alabaster treasure from the Tutankhamun collection.

QUINTESSENTIAL BOOK
"THE HOLY LAND"

James Madison: How did the ancient Egyptian builders pick a spot to erect a temple?

Dr. Fred Monderson: From the article "Temples" in *Encyclopedia of Religion and Ethics* (1927, 12: 237) we read: "This is obviously necessary where a sacred tree or stone stands in such a place. Sometimes sacred places are associated with the traditional appearances of spirits, gods, or ancestors, and must therefore be holy for all time. The mere fact that a religious gathering takes place in a certain spot once is enough to give it sanctity, and the gathering becomes recurrent there. Such sacred places will usually be marked by images or symbols, or by boundary-stones forming an enclosure. Single graves, often with a structure over them, and places of sculpture also become recognized places of cult .... The grove is thus a primitive holy place, which may have as an accessory a small structure for the image which later becomes a more elaborate temple. This worship in groves, which might become the seat of a temple, is also found among lower races."

Holy Land Illustration 86a. In the Tomb of Prince Amenkhepeshef, King Rameses II and Prince is received by Isis (left); and the Vizier's Audience-Chamber in the Tomb of Rekhmara (right).

Let me also give you another example of how people's perception can create the sacred. It appears that one pharaoh sent a contingent into a quarry to collect stone for a sarcophagus. As they approached, they noticed a gazelle giving birth on a stone. To them this was unusual so they chose that particular piece of stone to secure for the sarcophagus.

Peter Monderson: Did they teach music in Egypt?

FREDERICK MONDERSON

Dr. Fred Monderson: Yes they taught music in ancient Egypt. James Baikie's "Music: Egyptian" in *Encyclopedia of Religion and Ethics* (1917, 9: 33) wrote: "Strabo says 'the children of the Egyptians were taught letters, the songs appointed by law, and a certain kind of music, established by government, to the exclusion of every other; and, further, that vocal and instrumental music was usually admitted in the worship of the gods, especially at the commencement of the services, except in the temple of Osiris, where neither singers nor players on the flute or the lyre were allowed to perform. It is questionable how much of this confident assertion is the result of actual knowledge; the statement as to the limiting the kinds of music certainly does not agree with what is known from more reliable sources. Herodotus (ii, 79) speaks of his surprise at finding that the song called Maneros by the Egyptians, a dirge said to have been named after the son of the first king of Egypt, was similar to the Cyprian dirge *Lions* or *Alinios*. This, however, is practically all that can be gathered from such sources."

Juliet Brown: Ok so, how important then will you say was music in the society of ancient Egypt?

Dr. Fred Monderson: Music was very important. It was found in all walks of life. The gods loved music. James Baikie in "Music: Egyptian" *Encyclopedia of Religion and Ethics* (1917, 9: 34) explained: "Its origin was ascribed to divinity - sometimes to the goddess Isis, but more particularly to the god Thoth, or Tehuti. Among the sacred books attributed to him are two Books of the Singer. From a very early date it appears to have been the custom that a regular part of the royal establishment should consist of a band of instrumentalities and singers. Thus under the Old Empire we have mention of a certain Ra'heben, 'the Superintendent of the singing,' who was also, with a somewhat curious jumbling of duties, 'Superintendent of the singing,' and Superintendent of the royal harem. Another reference gives us the names of three 'Superintendents of the royal singing,' two of whom seem to have been singers themselves, for they observe that 'they daily rejoice the heart of the king with beautiful songs, and fulfill every wish of the king by their beautiful singing.' Some of these choirmasters appear to have been of high rank – they are called 'royal relatives' – and to have held priestly as well as musical office, being priests of the king and of his ancestors. Under the New Empire there are also references to men who were 'singers to Pharaoh' and also 'superintendent of the singing of all the gods.' This point to a regular organization of the sacred music of the whole Empire; and the probability is that there was a stereotyped form of religious music, prescribed and maintained by the priests, in which, however, part sometimes taken especially in the time of the New Empire, by lay performers – more particularly of women. Under the XVIII dynasty many women of high rank were appointed to offices connected with the worship of the temple of Amon, some of them bearing the title *Qemt en Amen*, 'singer of Amen.' Erman states that 'we scarcely meet with one lady under the New Empire, whether she were married or unmarried, the wife of ecclesiastic or layman, whether she belonged to the family of a high priest or to that of an artisan, who was not thus

QUINTESSENTIAL BOOK
"THE HOLY LAND"

connected with a temple. The chief duty of these women was to play the sistrum before the god."

Holy Land Papyrus 29. The young queen offers her husband, Tutankhamon two bouquets of lotus flowers as he stands holding his walking stick, many of which were found in his tomb.

Erik Joel: What is the tail I see hanging behind the king?

FREDERICK MONDERSON

Dr. Fred Monderson: Flinders Petrie's article on "Art: Egyptian" in *Encyclopedia of Religion and Ethics* (1909, 1: 862) explained how the 'tail I see hanging behind the king' is part of the kingly dress retinue that makes up the full power of the sovereign. "The gods are usually clad in the oldest form of close-fitting waist-cloth; it is always older forms of dress that are thought appropriate for religious or artistic purposes, and in Babylonia the oldest figures of worshippers are entirely nude. Another primitive piece of costume was the animal's tail, hung at the back from the belt. This is shown as a bushy tail, like a fox's, on the archaic hunters, carved on a slate palette. It appears on all kings from the first dynasty onward. And it gradually becomes almost universal for gods after the early ages. Here it can be seen on the figure of Horus and Thoth, in the long form, and thinner than usual. The principal religious dress was the leopard skin, as on the priest in the scene of sacrifice. It was worn before the first dynasty (Narmer), and is seen not only on scenes but also on statues in the eighteenth dynasty. It is shown on the priest when seated, or standing giving directions, or making offerings; it might be worn over a short kilt or over a long muslin dress."

Holy Land Illustration 86b. Objects from Rishi Coffins.

Leonard James: How did material availability shape building practice in Egypt?
Dr. Fred Monderson: Flinders Petrie's "Architecture: Egyptian" in *Encyclopedia of Religion and Ethics* (1909, 1: 722) supplies a description of materials used in Egyptian building practice. "The materials necessarily condition the style and decoration of all architecture. In Egypt the commonest materials used by the peasantry are maize stalks, mud, mud brick, palm sticks, and palm logs. The simplest huts are made by lashing maize stalks (stems of the *durrah*, called *bus*) together by means of palm-fiber; the flat screens thus formed are set upright at right angles, and lashed together down the corners. If the weather is cold and the wind strong, they are plastered over with mud. In this form the temporary dwellings in the field are set up for two or three months of the pasture season. Where a column is required, a bundle of maize stalks is bound together, from 4 to 10 in. in diameter, and plastered with mud, thus forming an extremely stiff and unbreakable mass. Two such columns are even used to support the shaduf, or

QUINTESSENTIAL BOOK
"THE HOLY LAND"

water-lift, which weighs two or three hundredweight, and is kept constantly in swinging motion. In ancient times the papyrus stem was also commonly used, as well as the maize stalk. Mud brick was the principal building material in Egypt in all ages; even in the rainy climates of Syria and Babylonia it was universal, and in the general drought of Egypt it is an excellent material. The mud required to be mixed with so much sand that the grains would be almost in contact, and then rain has but a slow effect upon it. Another way of making it durable was to mix it with chopped straw or even grass roots, which bind it together. The bricks down to the VIth dynasty were generally pure mud; the sandy and gravelly bricks are of later age. Another form of brick is thin and wide like a tile, and ribbed on the face, in order to build it up by adhesion of mud on the faces, in forming arches. The palm-stick is used for fences, the tops being left with side leaves to form a barrier to men and animals. The logs of the palm tree are used for roofing-beams, but never for columns."

Holy Land Ceramic Art 17. This time the Ankh is accompanied by its twin.

"The nature of these materials has led to the general features of the architecture. The constant use of a portico or verandah in front of house, temple, or tomb, result

FREDERICK MONDERSON

from the common use of bundles of maize stalk. The palm capital results from strengthening the column with a coat of the harder palm branches, whose tops were left loose around the capital. The sloping walls of the pylon result from tilting the courses of brick inward, so as to prevent them from being easily dislodged. In order to save the corners of reed huts or brickwork from being broken away, bundles of stalks were lashed on down the edge; these were the origin of torus molding marked by diagonal winding bands along the angles of the buildings. The fence, formed of palm-sticks were loose heads, lashed together near the top to a line of cross sticks, is the source of the cavetto molding with torus roll below it. The palm-log roof is copied in stone in tombs at Gizeh and Abydos. Thus the forms adopted for the stone architecture belong to the earlier materials, as in Greece."

Carmelita Shabazz: Which is the oldest temple that there are available plans for?
Dr. Fred Monderson: Clearly, "The oldest temple of which we have full plans is of Thutmose III at Medinet Habu. It is solely a processional resting-place for a sacred bark, open at both ends, with a colonnade round it for the procession to pass, and six store chambers behind. Of the same type were the subsequent temples of Amenhotep III at Elephantine, of Ramessu III at Karnak, of Alexander at Luqsor, of Philip Arrhidaeus at Karnak, and of the Ptolemaic age at Kom Ombo and Dakkeh."

Stephanie Mc Call: I noticed columns all over, what are some names of these columns?
Dr. Fred Monderson: First there were square or even oblong pillars. Those were succeeded by palm and lotus columns. Then there were "Proto-Doric" derived from the "Greek Doric." The papyrus had "closed bud" and the lotus "umbel" or open in bloom. The "capital: is the decorated apex of the column. In Thutmose III's "Akh Menu" festival temple at Karnak, having both pillars and columns, the columns are turned upside down. Finally, there's the composite column of late date in which a colonnade the capitals of the columns are all different. A good example is the Western Colonnade at Philae, the "Kiosk of Trajan" and also at Edfu, Kom Ombo and Esneh.

QUINTESSENTIAL BOOK
"THE HOLY LAND"

Holy Land Illustration 87. Coffin of Menkaure (Mycerinus) King of Egypt, builder of the Third Pyramid at Ghizeh, IVth Dynasty (left); and Gilded wooden coffin of An-Antef, King of Egypt XIth-XIVth Dynasty (right).

FREDERICK MONDERSON

Michael Montout: Who were the creator gods?
Dr. Fred Monderson: W.M. Flinders Petrie's "Cosmogony and Cosmology: Egyptian" in *Encyclopedia of Religion and Ethics* (1912, 4: 145) discusses Egyptian theology of the creator gods. Principally these were Khnum, Ptah, Osiris, Amon-Ra and Thoth. "The gods associated with creation were many. Khnum, 'the Shaper,' who shapes living things on his potter's wheel,' created all that is, he formed all that exists, he is the father of fathers, the mothers of mothers ... he fashioned men, he made the gods, he was father from the beginning ... he is the creator of the heaven, the earth, the underworld, the water, the mountains ... he formed a male and a female of all birds, fishes, wild beasts, cattle, and of all worms. He is figured always with the ram's head, to signify creative power, and was worshipped at the source of the Nile - the cataract. Ptah, 'the Great Artificer,' the Demiurge, shapes the sun and moon-eggs on his potter's wheel; he is the god of law and order who created all things by Ma'at, truth or exactness. Osiris 'formed with his hand' the earth, its water, its air, its plants, all its cattle, all its birds, all its winged fowl, all is reptiles, all its quadrupeds.' This is the development of the primitive idea of Osiris as a god of vegetation. Amon-Ra also, on the growth of his worship when Thebes was the capital, became 'the father of the gods, the fashioner of men,' and all other things. Thoth, according to Hermopolitan legend, when in the chaos of Nun, created Seb and Nut by his word; and they were parted asunder at Hermopolis. This creation by the word was the highly spiritualized idea of later times, and is seen in the *Kore' Kosmou* (500 B.C.). where Thoth-Hermes is first of the gods."

James Morrison: What is the story or Legend of Osiris?
Dr. Fred Monderson: Osiris is thought to be a deified king who was benevolent and taught the Egyptians how to be industrious. His brother Seth killed him. Gardener (1912, 5: 479) tells us: "In the doctrine of the *Psychostasia*, Osiris appeared as the perfect judge, the arbiter of human character and ruler of the virtuous dead. The origin and the early nature of Osiris are shrouded in obscurity, but at a very ancient date he became the prototype of the beneficent Pharaoh. Mythology told how Osiris had succumbed, after a long and prosperous reign, to the machinations of his wicked brother Seth, who mutilated his body and scattered his limbs. At length, Isis, the faithful wife of Osiris, succeeded in collecting his remains, and infusing new life into them by dint of her magical power; but henceforth Osiris was a shadowy being ruling among the dead, while his son Horus, having taken vengeance upon Seth, sat upon the throne of the living. It is, doubtless, owing to its human interest and pathos that the story of Osiris took so firm a hold on the imagination of the Egyptians; and, as we have seen, every Egyptian who died claimed to be another Osiris, destined at last to conquer the powers of evil, and to awake to a happier and never-ending life. Pilgrims flocked to Abydos, which had become (though not much before the Middle Kingdom) the traditional burial place of the god; and, as everyone sought to establish for himself

QUINTESSENTIAL BOOK "THE HOLY LAND"

a cenotaph in that city, it was sometimes called 'the island of the Just' (Gardiner, *Literary Texts*, Leipzig, 1911). In the temple-cults all the other gods were gradually assimilated to Osiris; and the Pharaoh, whom a fiction always represented as the chief officiant, played the part of the 'loving son' Horus (Moret). In Ptolemaic times, Osiris was blended with a newly introduced god, Serapis, and henceforth his importance waned; but at the same time the popularity of Isis increased, and it was in her shrines that the Osirian faith was kept alive throughout the length and breadth of the Roman Empire."

Joshua Monderson: How did the Egyptian regard his character or reputation?
Dr. Fred Monderson: Alan H. Gardener's "Ethics and Morality: Egyptian" in *Encyclopedia of Religion and Ethics* (1912, 5: 476) paints a picture of the Egyptian and the notion of a good reputation. He says: "In the desire for a good reputation the extreme limit of Egyptian disinterestedness is reached; it was deemed the highest possible virtue for a man to 'raise up a good name' in his city (*Shipwrecked Sailor*, 159), though, of course, the desire for approval is a self-seeking motive only a little less crass than other selfish motives. Naturally it was more profitable for a man that he should stand well with the king than that he should be respected by the people at large; the Egyptian noble, in the naiveté of his soul, esteemed himself even more for the good opinion in which Pharaoh held him than for his fair fame among his equals. Blended with protestations of his generosity, his love of justice, and so forth, we frequently find he described himself as 'beloved of his master,' or as one 'with whose excellence the lord of the two lands was content.' In such a high degree was the Pharaoh considered to be the patron and recompenser of virtue that he was known as 'the good God and the lord of Right.'"

Cherise Maloney: Were any of the gods ever sick?
Dr. Fred Monderson: Yes. Ra became sick after being bitten by the snake of Isis.

Teddy Cubia: I saw the baboon at Luxor and again at Abu Simbel, what is his role?
Dr. Fred Monderson: The baboon was a form of Thoth, the God of Wisdom. It had sharp eyes and was the first to spot the rising sun in the morning. It was also in the African Hall of Judgment where its keen eyes observed the motion of the scales and passed this on to Thoth who recorded in and relayed this information to Osiris. There is a whole story of the French cutting off the erect penis of the baboon on Rameses II's obelisk from Luxor Temple, given to the French monarch.

Esperanza Rodriguez: What did the deceased hope for or what was his view of salvation?
Dr. Fred Monderson: A warm reception and the chance to dwell as an

FREDERICK MONDERSON

imperishable star or identification with Osiris is what the deceased hoped for. Aylward M. Blackman's "Salvation: Egyptian" in *Encyclopedia of Religion and Ethics* (1921, 11: 132) informs: "Side by side with the view that their life on earth had been spent existed the idea that they could attain bliss here-after through identification with Osiris. Originally only the dead Pharaoh was identified with Osiris, who appears in the Pyramid Texts as the prototype of all dead Pharaohs, the dead Pharaoh par excellence. This identification ensued other deceased Pharaohs the same renewed and glorified existence as that of the god. As Osiris lives he also will live; as Osiris dies not, he will not die; as Osiris was not destroyed, he will not be destroyed. The gods do for the deceased Pharaoh what in the first instance they did for Osiris. Nut, the mother of Osiris, gives the dead Piopi his head, unites for him his bones, puts together his limbs for him, and places his heart in his body. Isis and Nephthys may also perform this service for him and make his eyes to shine in his head. Again, he is washed and embalmed in Anubis and revivified by Horus. As the representative or successor of Osiris, the departed is said to be a blessed one or spirit (*ikh*), and to be mighty as a god. His soul (*Bai*) is within him and his power (*sachem*) behind him. Finally, the dead Pharaoh must appear before the judicial council of the gods, by whom, like Osiris, he is pronounced 'justified,' 'righteous of voice,' thanks to the pleading of Thoth, who also made Osiris to triumph over his enemies. He can now enter upon a glorified existence – according to one conception, in heaven, or, according to another, in the west. After the VIth dynasty every dead person was identified with Osiris, and the custom then arose of appending to the deceased's name the Osirian epithet 'justified.' The tendency, therefore, was to regard the deceased as righteous or 'justified,' not on his own merits, but, owing to his identification with Osiris, his personality and acts becoming merged in those of his righteous and justified prototype."

Teddy Cubia: What were some ceremonies celebrated by the Egyptians?
Dr. Fred Monderson: Religious ceremonies celebrating the gods, funeral ceremonies, and ceremony of the opening of the mouth. There were also ceremonies marking the opening of the farming season, of civic projects and so on.

Robert Matthews: Who were the mummy gods?
Dr. Fred Monderson: There were principally three mummy gods. These are Osiris of Abydos; Ptah of Memphis; and Khonsu of Karnak, son of Amon and Mut. Khonsu was also a moon god and so too was Thoth.

QUINTESSENTIAL BOOK
"THE HOLY LAND"

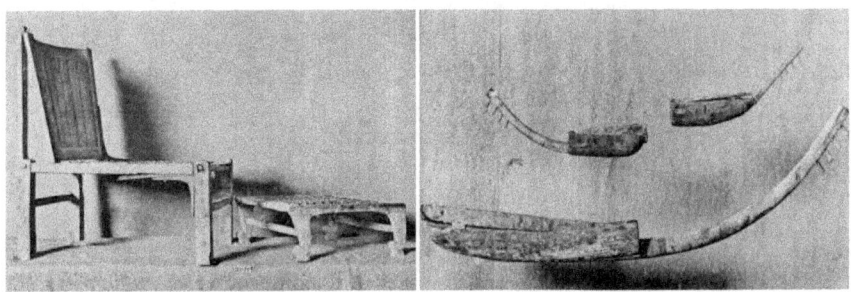

Holy Land Illustration 87b. Chair and Stool (left); and Musical Instruments (right).

Walter Brown: How did the Egyptian view criminal behavior?
Dr. Fred Monderson: F. Ll. Griffith's "Crimes and Punishment: Egyptian" in *Encyclopedia of Religion and Ethics* (1912, 4: 272) explained the attitude towards criminal behavior. "The Negative Confessions in the Book of the Dead contains a long list of moral and religious obliquities, including adultery, falsification of measure and weights, and cursing the king. More to our purpose is a list of charges brought against a shipmaster at Elephantine, preserved in a papyrus at Turin; amongst his offences are breaking into stores and stealing the grain, embezzling corn put in his charge, extorting corn from the people, burning a boat and concealing the fact, also adultery, and apparently the misuse of cattle bred by the sacred Mnevis sire. There is no record whether the charges were proved, or of the punishment. A decree of King Horemheb to repress military exactions and oppression in Egypt imposes a severe penalty on the unauthorized commandeering of boats; the offender loses his nose and ears, and is transported to the frontier city of Saru (agreeing with Diodorus' account of the city of Rhinocolura); and soldiers who stole hides were to be beaten with 100 lashes so as to open five wounds, and to restore the property to its owners. Other documents indicate Ethiopia as the place of banishment, where perhaps convicts were forced to toil in the gold mines. The condition of suspected persons after examination 'by beating on their hands and feet' must have been miserable in the extreme, but probably the law contrived to make it still worse for the convicted criminal in the end."

8. Dinner

Michelliea Georges: Regina, you get the beverages this evening.
Regina Hendricks: No doubt. Here comes the waiter. I will order for us.
George Washington: Very good, sisters. We are coming to the end of this.

In **Ancient History** for the final examination on December 22, 1975, we were given the following questions:

Discuss methods taken by Amenemhat I to establish Dynasty 12.

Discuss the Amarna Period and the reaction to it.

Discuss the development of Judaism.

Discuss the development of Christianity.

Discuss the states of the Levant after 1200 B.C. and their importance.

Give reasons for the decline of the Old Kingdom.

Give reasons for the decline of the New Empire (19th and 20th Dynasties).

Discuss Egyptian society and the role that Ma'at and kingship played in it.

Characterize the Egyptian culture and religion.

Characterize the Mesopotamian culture and religions.

What common traits were shared by the early (Primitive) Indo-Europeans? Who were they?

Mithraism has 7 stages of initiation including baptism, lustration, eating of a sacred animal. Water is substituted for wine.

Stoicism taught the brotherhood of man.

Gnosticism was a philosophy that taught that a savor would come as god incarnate in the flesh.

Judaism had Pharisees, Sadducees and Essenes.

9. Lounge Discussion

Michelliea Georges: I invited a few sisters to share in the dissemination and have a sort of party as we reminisce on the trip.

Regina Hendricks: Here come two of them now.

QUINTESSENTIAL BOOK "THE HOLY LAND"

George Washington: Ok. Let's begin.

African Religious Thought Systems on December 8, 1975.

IFA Divination

Adinkra or Dinkra is a set of symbols among the Akan people of West Africa. The symbol represents the omnipotence of Nyame.

Di means to make use of.
Nkra means to pass, to be separated, to leave one another, to say goodbye.

Adinkra cloth used at funerals is also called farewell cloths.

Esu is same as biology.

Okra means fate, destiny, predetermined.

Sun is a teachable, clever character.

I left the room and when I returned Dr. Richards was speaking of "persons able to gain access to forces that influence material being."

IFA DIVINATION

There are 16 basic figures of Ifa. These are also called chain patterns.

1. Ogbe 1111-
2. Oyeku 11-11-11-11-
3. Iwori 11-1-1-11-
4. Edu 1-11-11-1-
5. Pgbara 1-11-11-11-
6. Okanran 11-11-11-1-
7. Oransi 1-1-11-11-
8. Owonrin 11-11-1-1-
9. Ogunda 1-1-1-11-
10. Osa 11-1-1-1-
11. Irete 1-1-11-1-

FREDERICK MONDERSON

12.	Otura	1-11-1-1-
13.	Oturupon	11-11-1-11-
14.	Ika	11-1-11-11-
15.	Ose	1-11-1-11-
16.	Ofun	11-1-11-1-

Ifai = Orisha

Mathematics is considered a sacred art. (See Logical Patterns used in course 19-111.) Ifa is based on 16 basic figures or patterns and 256 derivative patterns (16 x 16) = Odu. This has very deep meaning and it is secret.

How are patterns arrived at?

There are two methods used to arrive at patterns. The manipulation of 16 palm nuts and the toss of a divining chain, chain of half-seed shells. The Babalawo is the highest order of priest. The divining tray lies in front of the Babalawo as he performs the ritual.

With palm nuts, the nuts are grasped by the right hand. He switches to the left, with one remaining in hand (magic) (manipulation, a skill).

2 nuts equal 1
1 nut equals 11. Repeat this four times and this makes one basic Ifa pattern.

16 squares equal 256 patterns.

The Chain Method (Opele)

$0 = 1$
$x = 11$
$x = 11$
$0 = 1$

PERMUTATIONS are defined in Webster's *Dictionary* as "the exchange of one thing or another; the arrangement of any determinate number of things or letters, in all possible orders, one after the other."

QUINTESSENTIAL BOOK "THE HOLY LAND"

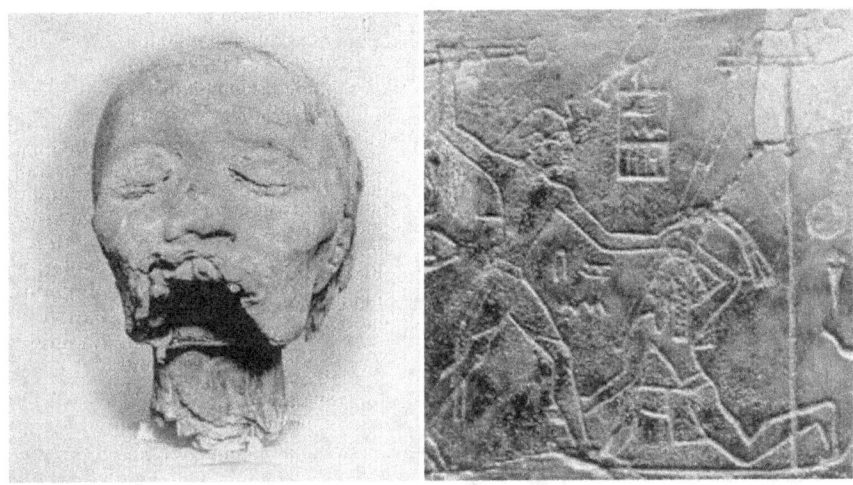

Holy Land Illustration 88. Head of King Merenre (left); and Ivory tablet of First Dynasty King Usephais, smiting an "Easterner" (right).

COMBINATIONS is also defined in Webster's *Dictionary* as "any of the different sets into which a number of individuals, numbers, patterns, may be grouped without regard to the order of arrangement to the group."

Ifa is practiced in Yoruba. It is practiced by: the Ado of Benin; the Ewe of Togo; and Fon of Dahomey.

The word Caba in Ifa is Afa in Brazil where it is also practiced. Ifa divination is also used in Madagascar. The number 16 is very important.

Readings

```
        1    11
        1    11
        11   1
        1    11
```

Left   Right
"Female"   "Male"

Eji Ogbe   (Ogbe Meji)

                Beyioku   Obatala (Orisala)

FREDERICK MONDERSON

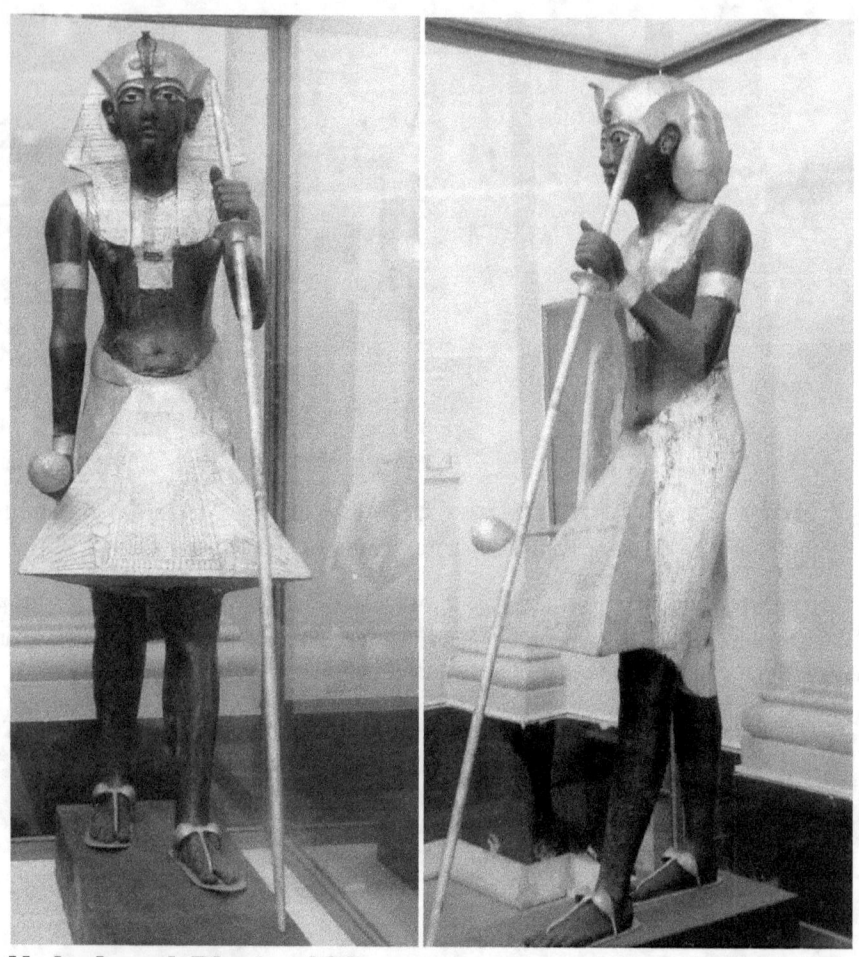

Holy Land Photo 100. Cairo Museum of Egyptian Antiquities. The two wooden lifelike statues of the boy King Tutankhamun (Tutankhamon, Tutankhamen) painted Black on display in the Cairo Museum, Hall of Tutankhamon.

Fon	Xevioso (Sango)
Ife	Orisala (For boy) (Oshun for girl)
Meko	Sango, Oya, Ogun
Verses (key)	

QUINTESSENTIAL BOOK "THE HOLY LAND"

Verses used by priests to interpret patterns and meaning can only come with profound spiritual wisdom. From this forms bodies of verbal art, myths, folktales, incantations. Praise names, songs, proverbs, psalms, and riddles. Incantations are very important. Use of special verses to call forth tranquility and keep away evil spirits as goldsmith works in Laye. Verses have an aesthetic value, which is secondary to the religious functions.

10. Hotel Room

Day 11. TOMBS OF THE NOBLES, MAUSOLEUM OF AGA KHAN, KITCHNER GARDENS, OLD CATARACT GARDENS, BOATING ON THE NILE (All Optional)

1. Wake Up

Esperanza Rodriguez: Good Morning, Mi Amor. Your schedule for today calls for visits to the *Mausoleum of Aga Khan, Kitchener Gardens* and *Boating on the Nile*. Your Article on the "Franklin Avenue Shuttle: Shuttle into the Millennium" is ready for distribution to the group.

Dr. Fred Monderson: Thank you, my dear. Oh, how beautiful you look today.

The Tombs of the Nobles is optional. This should be attempted on an off day and it is better to begin very early so as to arrive at the top before it is too late. You want to be at the top before 9:00 AM so as to avoid the tremendous heat. You should be on the way down before midday. At that time the heat is extremely dangerous. In fact, the earlier you leave and the earlier you get up there the easier it is for you. Under no circumstances do you want to be walking up there between 12:00 and 2:00 PM, for you can easily be seriously injured from sunstroke. That is why it is cautiously recommended that only the hardiest of you attempt this venture.

FREDERICK MONDERSON

FRANKLIN AVENUE SHUTTLE: SHUTTLE INTO THE MILLENNIUM
By
Frederick Monderson
in *Daily Challenge*

The Franklin Avenue Shuttle is a beauty to behold, a joy to ride, and a symbol of the revitalization possibilities of a community served by this historic rail link. However, in the dismal days when it languished on the termination altar of non-revitalization and its back-draft posed a serious economic and social blow to the Central Brooklyn communities of Bedford Stuyvesant and Crown Heights, a handful of activists and concerned community residents would not let it die. This was tantamount to the Biblical story of the individual who would not let the angel depart until he had blest him.

Some say the fight to **Save the Franklin Avenue Shuttle** struggle is traceable to the days of Fred Richman and Woodrow Lewis, State Assemblymen in the 1970s and 1980s. Indicative of one person becoming a majority, if he or she advocates their truths, a small group of activists, realizing the significance of the line to its residents, met perennially to strategize on efforts to make revitalization a reality. The Shuttle serves major Brooklyn institutions, including the Brooklyn Museum, Brooklyn Botanic Gardens, Prospect Park, Interfaith Hospital, the Center for Nursing and Rehabilitation, Prospect Heights High School and Clara Barton High School, the School for the Blind, MS 320, PS 316 and nearby religious institutions. Students and faculty from Clara Barton and Prospect Heights High Schools played a key role in urging legislators to restore funding for the shuttle. So too did students from Middle School 61 who wrote the MTA urging the reconstruction project but also requesting the adoption of an elevator at Franklin Avenue Station on Eastern Parkway to be accessible to the handicapped. The Shuttle links the A and C lines at Franklin Avenue and Fulton Street and the D and Q lines at the Prospect Park station, and offers the only transfer between the lines. The shuttle now features stations that are accessible for the disabled persons, and a free walkway between the shuttle and the 2, 3, 4, and 5 lines at the Brooklyn Botanic Garden Station.

Helmut Lesold and Lois Goring, bless their souls, led the efforts at public

QUINTESSENTIAL BOOK
"THE HOLY LAND"

hearings, Borough Consultation Meetings, Transit Advisory Meetings, petitioning of public officials, educating the community at Community Board Meetings, through and from the pulpit of religious, civic, social, educational and artistic associations. Then, Mabel Boston, Chairperson of Community Planning Board 8's Transportation Committee came aboard. She soon realized the task ahead, picked up the mantle of leadership; and baptized in the fire of activism, she led the charge. Into the citadels of Metropolitan Transit Authority and Transit Authority decision-making headed by Virgil Conway and the other big boys, the struggle was unrelenting. The banners of 'Save the Franklin Avenue Shuttle,' 'The Community Needs the Franklin Avenue Shuttle' and the *Daily Challenge* advocacy under the pen of Fred Monderson began to mobilize the community.

Former Assemblyman Joe Ferris did work on the Shuttle, Tupper Thomas has been a consistent friend of the Shuttle, so too Sophie Johnson of the Brooklyn Museum. Jennie Porter was the first chairman of Community Board 8's Transportation Committee and Ruth Goring its Community Board's Chair. Gwen Harmon of the Crown Heights Service Center, bless her soul, kept people informed. Joe Rappaport of NYPIRG's Straphangers Campaign, wrote articles, attended meetings, gave Press Conferences and distributed literature on Subway platforms. Also, the New York City Environmental Justice Alliance was a part of the struggle. Constance (Connie) Lesold, once Chair of Community Board 8's Transportation Committee, attended meetings, held press conferences and spoke out on behalf of the Franklin Avenue Shuttle and the Franklin Avenue Shuttle Garden. This perennial social activist and garden lover and her husband Helmuth have, for decades, been stalwart fixtures advocating social, psychological, transportation and environmental well being of Community Board 8 and therefore Brooklyn and New York City. Touché! Kudos! Gloria Briggs was a chief advocate for the Franklin Avenue Shuttle Garden. So, too, Bishop Owen Augustine and the Eastern Parkway Coalition. Hattie Carthan and Magnolia Tree, the Brooklyn NAACP, Sybil Holmes of HPD and 77 New York Avenue who rode the Shuttle to school as a teen, would not cooperate with MTA on the Shuttle and it's Garden. She organized friends in the struggle. Lars Larmon from Interfaith was the last of a long line of Public Relations Chiefs from 1972 to present who championed the Shuttle, and the Botanic Gardens, Prospect Park, Operation Green Thumb and the Parks Department were key institutions in the fight. When questioned on the Shuttle, Connie Lesold remarked: "People often think transportation is an issue only interesting to men but this has not been true. The Shuttle and many other transportation issues are more women's issues for they certainly get involved."

FREDERICK MONDERSON

Holy Land Illustration 88a. Karnak, Temple of Amon. The Quay, "Avenue of Sphinxes" and the Great Pylon (left); and Column of the Ethiopian King Taharka with the Second Pylon in rear in the Great Court (right).

Mary Pinkett, the social conscience of government, was at practically every meeting held. After meeting at the Lesold Residence, then Joe Richardson of the Haitian American Day Care Center's summer youths on Bedford Avenue and St. John's Place played a role and the center then became the venue. When the other elected officials were 'busy,' and some sent their representatives, Mary Pinkett was there! In the City Council, she championed the vital economic artery of her community.

Constantine (Connie) Hall, Chairman of Community Board 9's Transportation Committee was a regular fixture at those meetings that emboldened Mabel Boston in her struggles with the Citadel of MTA power. Chief Charles Joshua of the Central Brooklyn Coordinating Council was working, and the ubiquitous Ann Marie Blynn was there also. Despite his avalanche of responsibilities, Robert Matthews, in the 1990s, Chairman of Community Board 8 came out too and raised the issue from his "pulpit." Former District Manager Al Wright, and the current District Manager, Doris Alexander were in the mix.

As the Community Planning Board 8's steamroller with its allies in a number of change agencies, became mobilized and began to batter the boardroom of MTA, those 'big boys' responded by saying 'Let's study the issue.' In 1994, they sponsored a Public Hearing at Clara Barton High School in Brooklyn. Boro President Howard Golden sent his representative; Jeanette Gadsen, Deputy Boro President was there. That mountain of a community resident, Jitu Weusi was

QUINTESSENTIAL BOOK
"THE HOLY LAND"

there. Alice Wengrow and Helmuth Lesold, advocates for wheel-chair accessibility in the transit system were there. From the comfort of his vehicle, Lesold addressed the dais of MTA decision-makers. Having traveled the long road of Franklin Avenue Shuttle advocacy he beamed with a smile reminiscent of Jesse Jackson, Joseph Lowery, and et. al., present when George Wallace signed the historic bill moving Alabama forward in the Civil Rights struggle!

Holy Land Illustration 88b. Group family portrait of Official, with wife, daughter and son. Notice his right hand on her right shoulder and his daughter and son follow with theirs in the same position; and husband and wife being addressed by an individual. Notice how she embraces him with both hands and also notice the figure beside her seat.

Helmut said, "I'm happy to be here. We have come a long way. I may not live to see it, but I am confident the Franklin Avenue Shuttle will be rebuilt. I only hope they preserve the historic station house on the platform of Park Place." For his efforts on behalf of the Franklin Avenue Shuttle and the reconstruction of Eastern Parkway, some believe, Helmuth Lesold's name should be permanent, perhaps in plaque, at the Park Place stop.

Carlos Lezama of the West Indian Day Carnival Association tapped Fred Monderson of the "Save the Franklin Avenue Shuttle Coalition" to collect signatures to Save the Franklin Avenue Shuttle (and share the name Caribbean Parkway with Eastern Parkway). After 5 years of such an endeavor and more than 10,000 signatures, this issue was tabled. The 10,000 signatures are still valid, even with the Franklin Avenue Shuttle restored. This is an issue, just as vital for the economic, socio-cultural and nascent political wellbeing of the district, Brooklyn and New York.

FREDERICK MONDERSON

Nevertheless, in customary manner, the MTA promised repairs then balked. Elsewhere in other areas, particularly in the southern end of Brooklyn repairs and refurbishing of subway stations continued. The community and its activist adherents refused to accept MTA's stonewall. The activist juggernaut, experienced in the long struggle, mobilized resources and met at Restoration Center on Fulton Street in Brooklyn. The Regiment, the Brigade, Battalion, Company, Platoon and Squad of the Franklin Avenue Shuttle activism, were tried and proved on the battlefield of MTA stonewalling. Everyone was there. Community Board 3, Community Board 8's Bob Matthews, Anna Marie Blynn, Doris Alexander, Connie Lesold, Fred Monderson, and Community Board 9's Connie Hall. Joe Rappaport and several others were there for this historic gathering to force the issue to Save the Franklin Avenue Shuttle. This was like the final battle! Or, should I say the final push!

Assemblyman Al Vann stood up and drew a line in the sand. As State Assembly Chairman of Corporations in charge of their budgets he stated flatly: "No Franklin Avenue Shuttle, no Budget." Francis Byrd of Parkway Independent Democrats gave credit to "the leadership of Al Vann, Catherine Noland and Speaker Sheldon Silver for they are the reason our efforts paid off." Gene Russianoff of the NYPIRG Straphangers Campaign pointed out State Assembly Speaker Silver threatened to cut the MTA's 2000-2001 capital budget and remarked: "One lesson of the Franklin Avenue Shuttle is that the Assembly can be a powerful friend because it played a giant role in winning this battle." Mary Pinkett, the perennial social activist conscience on the City Council stood beside him. "Tell the monarch of City Hall to let our people have the Franklin Avenue Shuttle." Annette Robinson, Roger Green, Frank Boyland and Velmanette Montgomery championed the cause. Underscoring the power of the vote, Marty Markowitz admonished the group: our people must register and vote. Howard Golden's people were there, so too Jeanette Gadsen.

In jubilation the community was rejuvenated. There was a tremendous sense of inevitability this time. This was the final battle! Activists burned their boats. Victory was in sight. Faced with the potential of this experienced battering ram at its doors, Virgil and his boys acquiesced. 'We were with you all the time, they shouted.' 'Work will begin soon.' In typical corporate bureaucratic strategy, they championed the cause in their public relations spin.

Finally, after two years of restructuring, reconstruction and beautification the work was completed. However, not without community and Mary Pinkett's challenging the MTA about the closing of the Dean Street Station, and the contractor Judlau, and all concerned for jobs for local residents, and participation of local artisans in creating and designing the layout. At the Opening Ceremony and Ribbon Cutting, many who had worked hard were in attendance and Mabel Boston was very

QUINTESSENTIAL BOOK
"THE HOLY LAND"

pleased. She remarked: "This is an exhilarating day because we didn't just stop the MTA from cutting off our community; we won the complete restoration of the subway line for decades to come."

The inevitable local transportation problems had to be coped with. The TA supplied Shuttle Buses to Prospect Park. Arthur Brave, owner of the West Indian Restaurant on Franklin Avenue at Fulton Street suffered throughout the reconstruction. Still, he was optimistic and remarked: "I know there must be some inconvenience for the betterment of the community. We all stand to gain from this revitalization and beautification of the community." This notwithstanding, when the *Daily Challenge* contacted Jitu Weusi, that mountain of a man and social conscience of the Bed-Stuy community regarding his views on the newly completed multi-million dollar reconstruction, he stated clearly: "I was infuriated a week ago at Franklin Avenue, the elevator was broken and graffiti scrawled over the station. We will not let this station be treated like a ghetto station. I threatened to write the MTA" he said, "and hope the community is as displeased as I am." Further, he uttered: "I am not finished with the Franklin Avenue Shuttle."

Dr. Leonard James: Mr. Brown, how are you this morning? How are you, Mrs. Brown?
Walter Brown: I'm fine, Dr. James. How's Mrs. James this morning?
Mrs. Juliet Brown: I'm fine, Mr. and Mrs. James. Today is a wonderful day. I have learned so much on this trip. More importantly, we are so pleased to meet such a wonderful couple as the James' and you're right from Atlanta with us. You never know such wonderful people can be so nearby.
Walter Brown: Dr. James, that's Juliet letting on. But, of course, what she say is correct.
Dr. Leonard James: Marilyn and I are really flattered and besides, we are really happy to have met you. I hear you have known Dr. Monderson a long time.
Walter Brown: Yes I did and also hope we can continue this association when we return to Atlanta.
Dr. Leonard James: Let's stay in touch.

FREDERICK MONDERSON

Holy Land Papyrus 30. Tutankhamon sits in his chair while attended by his beautiful wife.

Michelliea Georges: What's happening today, Brother?

Regina Hendricks: What you are doing is so enlightening. Thanks a million.

QUINTESSENTIAL BOOK
"THE HOLY LAND"

George Washington: **African Religious Thought Systems** December 11, 1975.

Holy Land Illustration 89. Middle Kingdom coffin and mortuary furniture (above); and ducks swimming among the Lotus Flowers.

Verses constitute unwritten scriptures. They embody myths, which recount the activities of the Orishas. They help to explain the details of ritual. Babalawo is the key. He is a priest diviner and expert in Yoruba theology. He is consulted by all (even foreigners). Babalawo 'father has secrets.'

The Babalawo goes through two extended initiations and he receives two sets of 16 palm nuts. He directs sacrifices and worshipers to different families of Orishas. He liquidates evil.

FREDERICK MONDERSON

Aribu is a child, which does not want to be born.

Read *Laye* on initiation and *Mbiti* on initiation. Look for symbolism.

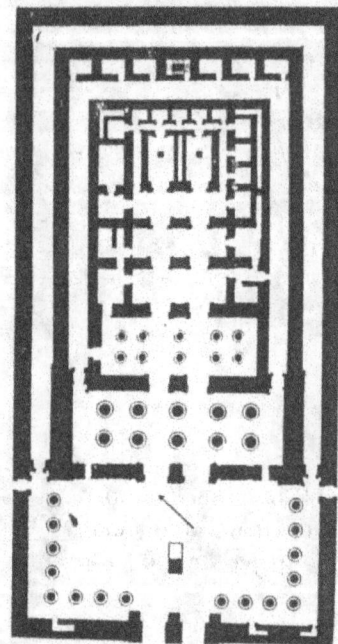

Holy Land – Plan of the Twin Temple of Kom Ombo.

Regina Singleton: How are you this morning Mr. Stewart? Are you ready for today's adventure?
Mr. John Stewart: Sure I am my dear. "It is the mind that makes the man and our vigor is in our immortal soul."
Regina Singleton: Those sayings you so vividly recounted from the Library of Congress are philosophically and intellectually penetrating, tell me how have they influenced your thinking having seen and memorized them?
Mr. John Stewart: When I first saw that wall and ceiling decoration and the writing I thought what a wonderful artistic and philosophical display of art, knowledge and intellect. Since that time either I exposed my students to the powerful message or tried to see the wisdom of those words myself. In a way, I have tried to let them influence my thinking and actions as I view the world and tried to find my place in it. Wisdom and knowledge comes from many sources and it's up to the individual

QUINTESSENTIAL BOOK
"THE HOLY LAND"

to internalize and materialize their message.

3. Bus Ride

Michelliea Georges: So what do you have for us today, Brother?
Regina Hendricks: I must continually harp, you are doing such an outstanding service to us, you add the spice to this important tour we're on.

George Washington: **African Religious Thought Systems** December 15, 1975.

Read Mbiti Chapter 12, pp. 158-164 on initiation and Laye Chapters 6, 7, 8.

Today we shall look at the significance of the blacksmith or goldsmith or metallurgy.

When working with metal one become associated with the origin of the cosmos. The aim of alchemy is freeing of the human soul and harmony of the cosmos. Through metal working individuals get close-up transcendentation of the cosmos.

Tools are hammer, bellows, anvil that are all animate and all are revered. The art of creating tools is superhuman. In the act of creation energy is released, and in the African conception, this is a mysterious occurrence.

Celt is defined in **Webster's Dictionary** as "an instrument or weapon of stone or metal, resembling a chisel or blade of an axe." Metallurgy, thunder stones, agriculture are all hooked up. Thunderstones that first came to earth were the first tools. These are signs of sacred communication between earth and heaven. The thunder symbol is very important. Ogun is the divine smith.

FECUNDITY means fertility or growth.

The smith has a spiritual sign imitating original creation or Ogun who formed the cosmos through a metallurgic process repeating original acts as done by spirits. When engaged in metallurgy, agriculture, one is engaged in a divine act. The creative process involves two things.

A ritual union or joining or marriage between realms of the cosmos.
The idea of "blood" or other sacrifices.

FREDERICK MONDERSON

Life can only come from life. The act of creating is a sacrificial process. One has to give blood, sweat and tears. Something then becomes an experience of mystical identification or sympathy with the universe. The idea of life is itself projected onto the cosmos. Earthly fertility is understood as divine workings among humans.

The Bambara are a pre-Islamic people who lived in Mali, Upper Volta and in Guinea.

DOGON of West Africa have a unique history of art and astronomy. For them, working with any natural materials, rules involve becomes a complex, philosophic system, which involves principles of power, wisdom and energy. Tools are visual metaphors. It's vitally integrated with social and religious patterns of life. They are famous for sculptural creativity. This is the domain of the blacksmith. Artistic qualifications include (1) technical expertise; (2) sensitivity to form; (3) carefully acquired religious or spiritual knowledge; (4) he receives this partly during the period of 8 years of (instruction) apprenticeship. He becomes a highly trained specialist. He also holds a key position in the society; (5) he is the head of important religious associations placed alongside of political leaders.

Religious Roles of Bambara Blacksmith:

He is the divination specialist known as Doni – Kela (Someone who knows) highly trained person. In ascertaining events involving divination he is consulted. Divination is sensitive use of spiritual forces performed by those powerful enough to control those manipulations. The individual must have power to interpret and control the energy released. Techniques involve throwing of cowrie shells (Kolon); use of small stones (Bele Jiki); and drawing lines in the sand (Cenda).

QUINTESSENTIAL BOOK
"THE HOLY LAND"

Holy Land Ceramic Art 18. Two sentinels for the Ankh?

He can make amulets or charms (Seben) which protect against harm and misfortune (Baara – Keila); person who can activate protective things and must have personal power to manipulate and use charms.

Medicine – He shares responsibility of healing people with other physicians. He is the surgeon who must have knowledge. Small pox inoculation used to contain epidemics in 1913. Knowledge of smallpox inoculation is indigenous to Africa.

POWER   WISDOM   ENERGY

4.   Site:

TOMBS OF THE NOBLES

MAUSOLEUM OF AGA KHAN

FREDERICK MONDERSON

KITCHENER GARDENS

OLD CATARACT GARDENS

BOATING ON THE NILE

5. Post-Site Lecture

Let me congratulate those of you who were able to make it to see the Tombs of the Nobles on your day off. These tombs date to the Old and Middle Kingdoms. I'm sure you saw the tomb of "Burded" of the Old Kingdom and "Sabni and Mekhu" of the Middle Kingdom. Burded received the earliest recorded letter for his expedition to inner Africa during the old Kingdom. It is inscribed at the entrance of his tomb. What a beautiful site to choose as your last resting place to look across the river and view Aswan. I am sure you found it very picturesque.

However, I would like to sketch the transition from the XIX to the XX dynasties. The 18th Dynasty came to an end after Akhenaten was deposed. Smenkare followed him on the throne and Tutankhaten followed him. When he returned to Karnak he changed his name to Tutankhamon. He was succeeded by Aye, his prime minister. Aye is pictured in Tutankhamon's tomb performing the "Opening of the Mouth Ceremony." He married the widow of Tutankhamon, Ankhesenamon, and Akhenaton's daughter. He was succeeded in turn by the general Horemheb, whose name means Horus in Festival.

Horemheb built a pylon at Karnak and hid in it many blocks associated with Akhenaten's Temple at Karnak. He felt it was too soon to discard the remnants of a god who had had a national following and so hid those remains in the pylon. Some think this was an appropriate and yet ingenious Egyptian solution to that problem. Horemheb had tombs at Memphis and in the Valley of the Kings. Rameses I was a general and Horemheb's vizier and he succeeded his king. In this he founded the XIXth Dynasty. He reigned for 2 years and was succeeded by his son, Seti I who reigned for 18 years. Rameses II succeeded his father and ruled for 67 years erecting many structures throughout the land. This was the second

QUINTESSENTIAL BOOK
"THE HOLY LAND"

longest reign in Egyptian history. The longest was that of Pepi II who reigned for 94 years to end the VIth Dynasty.

Holy Land Photo 101. Cairo Museum of Egyptian Antiquities. Tina and her Mom, two friends Kashida and I we met on the 2005 Tour (left); and a colossal head of the Goddess Hathor in the Cairo Museum Garden (right).

Rameses II built at Abu Simbel a worship temple dedicated to Ra Horakhty, Ptah, Amon and himself. Next door he built a temple to his Nubian wife, Nefertari that was dedicated to Hathor. The principal temple at Abu Simbel had 3 gods beside Rameses or 4 gods as are seated in the Sanctuary. They are 67 feet tall and are very imposing in the open court. There was an open court for the populace, an enclosed court for the nobles and the Holy of Holies. There were probably no more than two dozen priests at Abu Simbel, a structure considered a public relations propaganda feat. A text relates a solar orientation for the temple. It held that the sun would shine all the way into the Holy of Holies on Rameses II's birthday. The "Gods" in the Sanctuary were, from right to left, Rameses, Ra-Horakhty, Amon and Ptah. The sun was to shine on Rameses, Ra-Horakhty, and Amon but never touch Ptah. How remarkable! However, with all modern technology, when the temple was moved, this particular spectacular feat was never to be repeated for the alignment never duplicated.

The Ramesseum, the completion of the Hypostyle Hall at Karnak and the famous "Girdle Wall" that enclosed Thutmose III's wall, the "Ramessean Front" at Luxor, the temple of Beit Wali and at so many other places there's evidence of this king leaving his mark. He even chiseled other kings' names from their monuments to insure that his name lived forever. Many of his temples bore the illustration of the "Battle of Kadesh." There is even a papyrus that details this event.

Rameses II had more than 100 sons and 60 daughters. His 13th son, Merenptah succeeded him to the throne. He is sometimes labeled as the pharaoh of the Exodus. The city called Pi-Rameses or Pi-Tum of the Bible was built by Rameses II in the Delta as a strategic site for his efforts in Southwest Asia.

FREDERICK MONDERSON

6. Discussion
Are there any questions?

John Stewart: What are some sources for the festivals of ancient Egypt?
Dr. Fred Monderson: The Festivals of Egypt were recorded principally in temples. George Foucart's "Festivals and Feasts" in *Encyclopedia of Religion and Ethics* (1912, 5: 853) mentions two types of sources for examples of Temple Calendar. In the first type: "The specimens most worthy of mention, in order of date, are those of Karnak (XVIIIth dynasty), Medinet-Habu (XXth dynasty), Edfu (Ptolemaic), Denderah and Esneh (Roman Period). The 'Stone of Palermo' (Vth dynasty) is a good example of the second type."

"Individual mention along series of festivals (sometimes augmented by brief descriptions or explanations as to their value or aim) is made from time to time in the corpus of the Egyptian texts. As principal types we may mention: (a) historical mural inscriptions or official stelae of the temples; (b) numerous extracts of temple inscriptions of a non-historical character; (c) allusions to or enumerations of private stelae or inscriptions engraved upon private statues; so-called funerary literature adds a long list in (d) the festivals quoted in the collections known as 'Books of the Dead' (cf., e.g., chs. XVIII-XXI); (e) funerary calendars, more or less complete, written on the sides of sarcophagi (the best specimens is the coffin of Babe in the Museum of Cairo, a list of a hundred local festivals [VIIIth dynasty]); and, finally, (f) the festivals mentioned (and sometimes described) on the walls of mastaba or hypogea (cf. for the Theban series, the tombs of Einna, Monna, and Nofirhatep, all belonging to the XVIIIth dynasty)."

Jerome Smith: What are some types or classes of festivals celebrated in ancient Egypt?
Dr. Fred Monderson: The various classes of festivals celebrated for the gods at fixed times included the following: (a) anniversary of the birth of the god; (b) festivals having the character of 'seasons of the year' associated with a local god (not including the feasts of the Inundation'); (c) the legendary episodes of the life of the gods; (d) the Local Life of Divine idols; (e) a series of local festivals connected with the cycles of rejoicings proper to each region of ancient Egypt. Some of the most popular festivals during the New Kingdom are the "Opet Festival" and the "Feast of the Valley."

Shirley Palmer: How would you characterize the Egyptian family?

QUINTESSENTIAL BOOK "THE HOLY LAND"

Holy Land Illustration 90. Coffin of Ankh-f-en-Khensu, a priest of the XIXth or XXth Dynasty (left); and Inner coffin of Ankh-f-en-Khensu (right).

Dr. Fred Monderson: In his article on the "Family" H. R. Hall in *Encyclopedia of*

FREDERICK MONDERSON

Religion and Ethics, (1912, 5: 733) explained: "The Egyptian family presents many points of contrast both with the Semitic and with the Greek. Its most interesting characteristics are a distinct preservation of matriarchy, the prominent position of women, and a comparative promiscuity of sexual relations. We may, therefore, regard it as in some ways more sophisticated than the family in other countries of the ancient world. The prominent position of the women in the family led generally to a prominence of women in Egypt much greater than that allowed to them either among the Semites or in later Greece, and analogous to that apparently enjoyed in a greater degree by the women in early (Mycenaean) Greece. There also, among a people probably racially connected with the Egyptians, a matriarchal idea of the family may be assumed to have brought about a feminine prominence even more pronounced than in Egypt. It was no idea of the equal intelligence of women and men that in Egypt placed the two sexes almost on the same level, and in Minoan Crete perhaps made the women quite as important as the men. This equality arose simply from the matriarchal idea that descent is absolutely certain through the mother, but not through the father, so that the family centers in the house-mother rather than in the house-father; and woman, instead of being the man's slave, as among the Semites, is in many respects his equal or even superior. Thus, at any rate in the royal family, the Egyptians, in order to secure the succession of the mothers in the same family, often married their own sisters. In Roman times we find this practice common among ordinary people."

Even further, Hall (1912, 5: 733) continued: "The most important person in the family was, then, not the father, as among the Semites, but the mother. She was the house-ruler, the *Nebt-per*, the focus of the family. Nevertheless, she was the inferior of the man, her husband, in that she was always mentioned after him: on the tombstones she is always the wife (*hemet*) of the man, he is never the husband (*zai*) of the woman. After all, she could not become *Nebt-per* unless she was first hemet, and that, when all was said and done, depended on the pleasure of the man."

Regina Hendricks: Can you explain the ramifications of sister marriage?
Dr. Fred Monderson: Sister marriage did occur in ancient Egypt but it was generally confined to the royal families. The role of the woman naturally influenced all forms of descent and inheritance in the family. This was begun by the gods for in the initial creation, the earliest pairs were married and thus sister and brother. We must remember Isis and Osiris were married as well as Nephthys and Seth. Even earlier, the original pairs of gods, Nut and Geb and Shu and Tefnut were also married. Hall (1912, 5: 733) again explained this ancient custom as it related in: "Actual marriage with sisters was more or less confined to the royal house (with disastrous results to the Pharaohs), but the indefiniteness of the relations of the women of the family to the men is shown in the fact that the word *Senet*, 'sister' was used not only for the real sisters of a man, but also for his

QUINTESSENTIAL BOOK "THE HOLY LAND"

concubines, and even for his *hemet*, or wife. Similarly 'brother' might mean 'husband.' The woman who sits at the side of a man in some funerary sculptured group may be described as 'his sister, whom his heart loveth,' or as 'his beloved wife.' He might have many of these 'sisters' together with one wife (rarely two), or no wife at all; in that case there was no properly constituted *Nebt-per*, for this only a wife could be. If there were two wives, one was the *Nebt-per*; if two *nebut-per* are mentioned on a man's tombstone, it means either that the one succeeded the other in the dignity of housemother, or that the man had maintained two separate establishments, which had no link save the fact that the same man maintained and fathered both. This a noble might do, and besides the regular 'houses' of his 'wives' he might also possess a harim of concubines. But these had nothing to do with his family or families proper, however much he might favor his natural children. The father could, if he wished, make his son his heir, but that was somewhat opposed to usual custom, which, in accordance with the matriarchal theory, preferred that property should descend in the female line. Thus, ordinarily, it was to the eldest son of the man's eldest daughter that the goods went, and a man's maternal grandfather was considered more closely related to him than his own father. Naturally this elaboration of primitive custom was at war with all parental affection, and so the men constantly broke through it, those in high station, and, above all, the kings consistently did so. It was rarely that a dead monarch was not succeeded by his own son."

Michael Montout: How did the Egyptian atone for any transgressions he may have committed?
Dr. Fred Monderson: To atone for any transgressions he may have committed the ancient Egyptian sometimes made a "Table of Offerings" to the god. On this table, Hall (1912, 5) wrote: "The Egyptian placed fruit, cakes, and cooked meat on a mat before the painted and robed figure of his deity, and burnt incense before it, in order to feed him, please him, and ward off his wrath in case the offerer had offended him by doing something wrong. But this idea of wrongdoing was probably unknown to him originally. When he sacrificed from fear of the Divine wrath, it was because he had committed a crime 'against the king's peace' or that of the god, not because he had 'sinned' in the Bab, and Jewish sense, or seen in the less emphasized Greek sense. Wickedness for him was a sin against the society rather than against God. But the gods would punish such wickedness, and so were propitiated, if necessary, by pacifying sacrifices."

FREDERICK MONDERSON

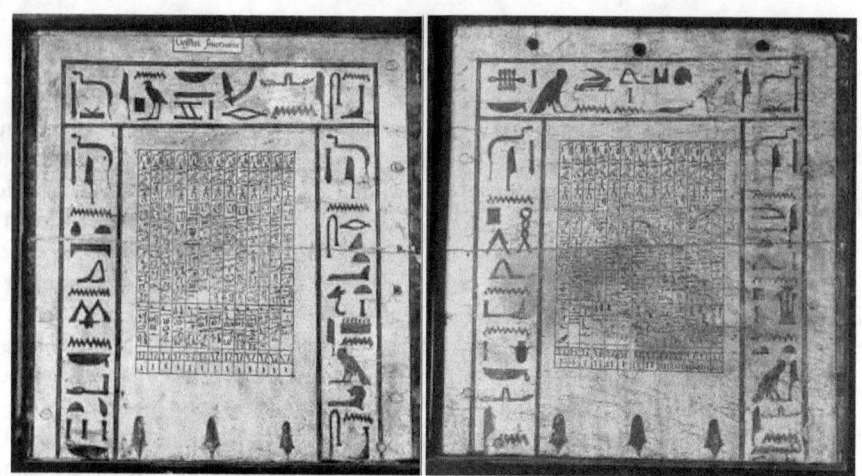

Holy Land Illustration 90a. Picture-frame representation of Egyptian Hieroglyphic writing.

Mrs. Mc Flair: How did the Egyptian view the spirit world?
Dr. Fred Monderson: The Egyptian view of the spirit world is probably like any other group, on lots of speculation though they did recognize the prevalence of good and bad spirits. H. R. Hall (1912, 5: 586) noted: "The passing allusions to a few texts seem to indicate that they were conceived under the form of 'devouring spirits' troops of monkeys, lizards, and hawks. These are, in any case, survivals of the most ancient periods. The same is true of the jackal-demons (Pyramid of Pepy II, line 849). The higher and lower 'Beings of Sit' lead us to suppose a classification of spirits into heavenly and earthly. The *rokhitu* are, according to the texts, both spirits full of wisdom and personifications of the powers opposed to (and vanquished by) Egypt or the gods of Egypt."

Glenda Stewart: Is there any way in which you can compare Osiris to Jesus?
Dr. Fred Monderson: I am certain there are many ways in which this can be done. They were both from the same region. One had been around for a great time and was widespread so knowledge of him was not wanting. In "Heroes and Hero Gods" in *Encyclopedia of Religion and Ethics* (1914, 6: 648-649) Kurt Sethe explained: "The suffering Osiris, thus conceived of as purely human, was in his origin as little a god of vegetation or of the dead as was Christ, with whom he has many points of resemblance. He, too, founded a confessional religion of a personal and ethical stamp, which forms a most decided contrast to the numerous Egyptian local cults based on fetishism, as well as to the Nature-religions indigenous to Egypt from primitive times (worship of the sun, the sky, the Nile),

QUINTESSENTIAL BOOK
"THE HOLY LAND"

and which in the course of centuries gradually extended in range, to some extent with a conscious rejection of other forms of religion (the mysteries, communal life)."

Leonard James: How old is the Osiris cult really?
Dr. Fred Monderson: Again we can look to Sethe for some clarity on this issue. In "Hero and Hero Gods" (1914, 6) he again explained: "The earliest triumphs of his cult must certainly go back to a very remote past. Even while Heliopolis was the capital of a united Egypt, and when the Heliopolitan theology instituted the 'great divine ennead of Heliopolis,' he not only found a place in that group as one of the representatives of the past-besides the great cosmic deities (sun, air, sky, earth) and the national god of the southern kingdom of Upper Egypt, which had been overthrown by the kings of Lower Egypt, and was now subject to it - but he actually became the center of the whole artificial system. He was made the son of the divine pair, Heaven and Earth. Horus again, who, as the national deity of the dominant kingdom of Lower Egypt, represented the present, and therefore remained outside the ennead, became the son of Osiris. Seth, the god of the Upper Egyptian kingdom, and now the last member of the ennead, was branded as the slayer of Osiris, and the arch-villain who had been guilty of dismembering the kingdom. These two local deities, Horus and Seth, were originally of a purely fetishistic character, and had at first no more to do with the hero Osiris than had the cosmic deities who had come to be recognized as his parents. Thus the Heliopolitan theology was even then completely under the influence of the Osirian faith."

James Morrison: What are the dynamics of Imhotep's rise to divinity status?
Dr. Fred Monderson: Well, we know he was considered a multi-genius from the time of his rise in the Third Dynasty when he built the Step Pyramid for Zoser. A millennium later with his architectural masterpiece still standing, by the time of Amenhotep III, the "magnificent" scribes when beginning their work would dip a libation honoring Imhotep, which sort of advanced him to a Demi-god status. Much later, however, he was deified. According to Sethe (1914, 6: 650) "Afterwards in the Persian period (from 525 B.C.), he became a god in the full sense, who was especially concerned with healing, and was subsequently identified by the Greeks with Asclepius as their god of medicine. His cult was attached to his tomb, which, according to Egyptian usage, was situated beside the Pyramid of his patron; and here stood the Askelpieion often referred to in Greek papyri from Sakkara."

Juliet Brown: Who is a suitable human sacrifice?
Dr. Fred Monderson: First, what is human sacrifice? Human sacrifice is "the offering up of a human individual to a divine power." It is generally understood to involve the slaughter of the victim, but that is not absolutely necessary; the "life of

FREDERICK MONDERSON

a mediaeval anchorite, walled up in a narrow cell, was sacrifice no less literally than was that of the son of Mesha." But in the Semitic world, with some exceptions and modifications, the victim was actually put to death. Still, human sacrifice is rare in ancient Egypt. Courtiers were buried alive near their king in the Archaic Period; however, by the Old Kingdom this practice had stopped completely.

Second, R.A.S. Macalister, "Human Sacrifice: Semitic" in *Encyclopedia of Religion and Ethics* (1914, 6: 864) says: "In a true human sacrifice, the victim may be (a) a young infant, the first-born of the family; (b) a criminal or prisoner of war; or (c) a person of special importance in the eyes of the person or tribe offering the sacrifice. In the first case we have, in the majority of instances, a sacrifice of primitive peoples, whereby the first fruits of the field, of domestic animals, and of the human family were sacrifices to the deity. In the second case the victim has offended against the divine majesty, either by his crimes or by fighting against the people of the divinity; the god has triumphed over his enemies, and their blood is poured out before him in celebration of the triumph. The third case is rather different: the god has to be appeased by his own people; a calamity or plague has to be averted, or some such prize or victory in battle has to be obtained; the most valuable gift that the tribe can offer has, therefore, to be presented in payment for the boon; the king's eldest son must be offered as a burnt-offering that there may be 'great wrath' against his enemies."

Holy Land Photo 102. Cairo Museum of Egyptian Antiquities. Two bronze shields depicting Tutankhamun grasping a lion by the tail (left); and as a Sphinx, attacking Nubian enemies painted Black like the previous statues of the King (right).

QUINTESSENTIAL BOOK
"THE HOLY LAND"

Rev. Dr. Mc Flair: How did the Egyptians see their God?
Dr. Fred Monderson: I suppose in the same way as everyone does, with great reverence, omniscience and benevolence. A Wiedemann in "God: Egyptian" *Encyclopedia of Religion and Ethics* (1914: 6, 275) provides this description of the subject: "From the Egyptian texts scholars have laboriously collected such passages as would imply a higher conception of deity, or such an attribute to the deity the qualities appropriate to a god regarded as One. They have also found passages which speak of a god as the creator of all life and all existing things, as one who traverses eternity, the lord of infinite time, one who cannot be grasped by the hand, whose evolutions are a miracle, the outstretch of whose being knows no limit, and who is king in Thebes, and simultaneously; prince of Heliopolis, and the great of crowns in Memphis. He cannot be seen; he listens to prayers; he turns his countenance to men according to their conduct; he is hidden, and his form is not known; he is alone, and there is none beside him. These attributes, however, were not all ascribed to the same deity, but now one now another of them was regarded as the special property of Amon, of Ra, of Ptah, or of some other member of the pantheon. Even when the texts refer to the One deity, they speak also of other independent figures. The One god is at most described, in a purely material sense, as the begetter, father, builder, conciliator, or king of the other higher powers. He is then, as such, the sovereign of the world of gods and men - one who, corresponding for the time being to the earthly Pharaoh reveals his will to his subjects by decree. In all this, however, he is never more than *primus inter pares*." That is, first among equals.

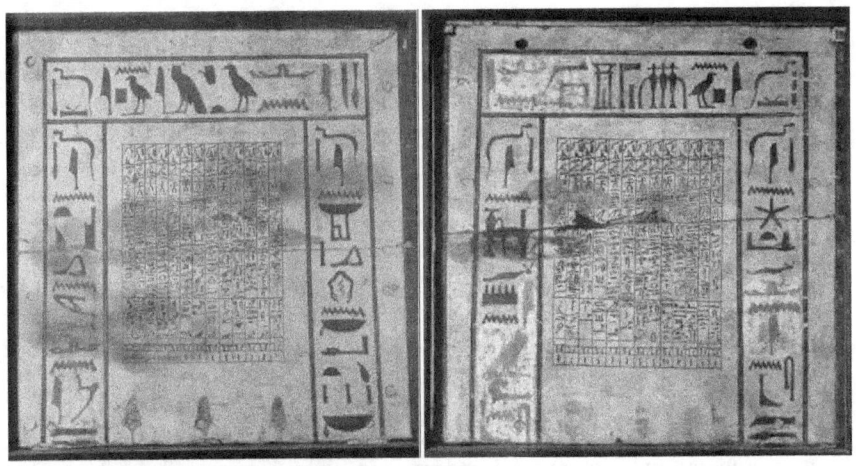

Holy Land Illustration 90b. Picture-frame representation of Egyptian Hieroglyphic writing.

FREDERICK MONDERSON

Cherise Maloney: How did the Egyptians group their gods?
Dr. Fred Monderson: Generally as a triad, father, mother and offspring, such as the Theban Triad of Amon, the father, Mut, the mother and Khonsu, the son, that is Sun, Earth and Moon. Wiedemann (1914, 6: 277) gives an answer that is more encompassing. "With a view to introducing some kind of order among the vast multitude of deities, the Egyptians attempted from a very early period to arrange them in groups. One such group after another was believed to have reigned as Pharaohs; or, again, a particular deity was regarded as the king, or as the father and lord, of others, as in the enneads of Heliopolis. In other instances we find certain smaller groups, as the Ogdoad of Hermopolis; sometimes also in the form of triads, which might appear as families (father, mother, and son, in Thebes), usually very loosely connected, or in even less coherent unions (god and two goddesses, in Elephantine) which never developed into trinities. Alongside of these we also find larger families (the Osiris cycle), and various other arrangements. But none of these systems comprised more than a relatively small number of deities, or had in general more than a local vogue. Moreover, the deities of a certain cycle in one locality might belong to an entirely different group in another. There was no single system embracing a majority of the pantheon, and, consequently, the functions of the individual deities were not everywhere defined in the same way. All the divine attributes might for the time be concentrated in a single deity, such as making war to Month, creation to Ptah, sovereignty among the gods to Ra, and procreation to the goat-deities, this arose from fortuitous and, for the most part, spasmodically operative causes, which were nowhere permanently recognized."

Joshua Monderson: In what animal forms did the ancient Egyptians represent their gods?
Dr. Fred Monderson: Thoth was an ibis and also a baboon. Horus was a falcon and Seth sometimes a pig or a hippopotamus. James Baikie, "Images and Idols: Egyptian" in *Encyclopedia of Religion and Ethics* (1915, 7: 131) mentions some of these forms of divine representations as: "In the earliest stages of Egyptian religion, the images of the gods were of the rudest and simplest description - mere fetish emblems such as pillars of stone or wood, trees, or Cairns. Thus the god of the highways, Min of Koptos, revealed himself either in a rough stake, or in a heap of stones by the wayside; the goddess Hathor dwelt in a sycamore tree; and Osiris was represented by a curious pillar apparently composed of the capitals of several pillars superimposed. An alternative method of representing divinity, which co-existed in early times with the crude fetish emblem, was that in which the god was presented in the form of an animal. Sebek, the water-god of the Fayum, manifested himself as a crocodile; Khnum, the god of the cataract district, as a he-goat; Upuat of Siut as a jackal; while Sekhmet, the goddess of Memphis, appeared as a lioness, and Hathor of Dendera as a cow. These rude early methods of representing deity maintained their influence in a modified form down to a very later period .... "

QUINTESSENTIAL BOOK
"THE HOLY LAND"

Holy Land Illustration 91. Head of King Amenemhet III, from a Sphinx found at Tanis (left); and Bust of statue of Amenemhet III (right).

"The animal form of representation was also perpetuated, in the case of many of the gods, by the curious combination of an animal's head with a human body. In the case of the Sun-god, Ra, the exploration of the Sun-temples at Abusir was made evident that, as late as the period of the Vth dynasty, this god was worshipped under the guise of his original emblem. The central object of adoration in these temples was, not an image of Ra, but a huge truncated obelisk, standing on a pedestal in the midst of an open court. The earliest divine images known to us are the three colossal figures of the god Min, found at Koptos by Flinders Petrie. These belong to the very early dynastic period, are of very rude workmanship, and, among other reliefs sculptured upon them, have representations of the fetish emblem of the god-a tall pole adorned with a garland." An interesting observation can be made here in that, these statues discovered by Petrie were all painted black but this is not mentioned here. Such is a part of the systematic omission and distortion of the historical record we need to be careful about.

Michelliea Georges: I noticed as you approached the sanctuary, the ground begins to rise. How is the "Holy of Holies" placed and protected for the ritual?
Dr. Fred Monderson: The notion of the rise of the temple represents the actual rise

of the god from the watery abyss at the beginning. The Sanctuary or Holy of Holies must sit at a high level and thus the ground rises and the ceiling declines. It is generally enclosed in surrounding buildings associated with the ritual.

Baikie (1915, 7: 132) locates the disposition of the sanctuary and how it is enclosed and protected. "The shrine of the god was in the innermost chamber of the temple, which was in total darkness save on the entry of the officiating priest bearing artificial light. It consisted generally of a single block of stone, often especially in the later periods, of enormous size, hewn into a house which surrounded with impenetrable walls the image of the god. The doorway in front was closed with bronze doors, or door of wood overlaid with bronze or gold-silver alloy; and each day, after the daily ritual had been gone through, these doors were closed, fastened with a bolt, and then tied with a cord bearing a clay seal. On either side of the sanctuary of the principal god of the temple were subsidiary sanctuaries, containing images of the other members of his triad. Thus in the temple of Amen at Thebes, Amen would occupy the central sanctuary, while his consort, Mut would be on one side, and the Moon-god Khonsu, on the other. Within the shrine the image of the god reposed in a little ark, or portable inner shrine, which could be lifted out and placed upon the barque in which the deity made his journeys abroad on stated occasions."

Kashmoney Malone: What purpose did the decoration of the tomb serve?
Dr. Fred Monderson: Magic was an integral part of the arsenal of the mortuary priests as well as the well-equipped dead man. A, Wiedemann's "Incarnation" in *Encyclopedia of Religion and Ethics* (1915, 7: 189-90) explained how this power was employed in the tomb. "By means of certain spells, a dead man, being endowed with magical powers, could, after his resurrection to life, avail himself of existing embodiments or not, having the power to assume whatever forms he liked, as that of a bird, a serpent, a crocodile, the god Ptah, etc., and was subject to no compulsion in the matter .... The dead man, moreover, had a singular power of incarnation in relation to the reliefs in his tomb. When he uttered his magic formula, the incidents portrayed in the reliefs became real. He incarnated himself in his own figure, and at the same time compelled the other persons and the animals and things depicted in the relief to become embodied in there, and to perform the actions represented. To that same mode of thought belonged the notion that a magician could by means of spells change the wax figure of a crocodile into a real crocodile."

Teddy Cubia: What materials and vessels were used in purification ceremonies?
Dr. Fred Monderson: Water was the most often used material. Natron or salts, incense for fumigation and sand regarded as purifacatory. Vessels of gold, silver and even copper vessels were used for washing the hands and for bathing and sprinkling purposes. The deity had to be bathed, its mouth purified and the feet

QUINTESSENTIAL BOOK "THE HOLY LAND"

washed, so too cleaning of the nails and shaving of the god.

Any more questions?

Well, that's all for today. See you guys for dinner.

7. Free Time:

Michelliea Georges: I am very excited today
Regina Hendricks: I will agree because of what you are doing for us, my Brother.

George Washington: **African Religious Thought Systems**. December 17, 1975.

BAMBARA

Excision is for females while circumcision is for males. In circumcision there is the removal of femaleness from man. Tremendous physical and spiritual significance is involved in this act. It is a pre-requisite to enter the society.

Jo System of religious associations that focuses on communal life. The blacksmith's surgical ability and knowledge of medicine makes him a key figure in the society. The blacksmith thus has enormous powers through his operations. There is great potentially dangerous energy released at circumcision and the blacksmith's skill is essential in this operation.

Used to direct and maintain spiritual and physical well being of the community. The system provides the hierarchy entered by each individually prescribed order that represents ever increasing levels of spiritual attainment. This is called Ntomo.

Ntomo is entered before circumcision and serves as a religious source of education. Formal education begins here. As knowledge increases the initiate enters 3 stages.

Ntomo
Komo - Nama, Kono, Ciwara
Kore

After this a person achieves full philosophical and spiritual capacity of the human intellect. Parallel for women is the Mus – Jo. Women's associations include Niagua and Kulukuyu.

The blacksmith is intermediary of disputes. He is in charge of Komo. He is also involved in social, educational and political guidance for all. The African conception of art is much deeper than Europeans.

Conception of Creative Process:

The ability to create is the process to manipulate and use spiritual energy that gives light to the universe. The ability to perform deeds is linked to an energy force (called Nyama). Nyama is the energy of action. Nyama can both protect and destroy the performer of deeds.

If the performer has sufficient Nyama then the energy released through the performance of deeds, protects him and nothing can harm him. If Nyama is not sufficient, energy released from the art will generate a disequilibrium, which he cannot control. Every individual has Nyama. Some have more than others.

Bards, griots, praise-singers and blacksmiths have a complimentary relationship that is very important. Nyama is hereditary.

Holy Land Illustration 91a. Faces in groups. No, it's not the same people.

The creator made blacksmiths as separate from other humans. They have a special social and religious role. They work with wood and iron. They forge iron or carve wood in religious symbols, signs, patterns, that are used at religious ceremonies and rituals. Only the blacksmith can control this energy. The energy released depends upon the mask created for the occasion.

When carving the Komo mask for boys, for instance, this is a very powerful mask. The energy is not merely controlled by the blacksmith; it is directed and manipulated for the benefit of the community. During circumcision Ntomo mask is used to consolidate or concentrate the energy of Ntomo boys.

QUINTESSENTIAL BOOK
"THE HOLY LAND"

8. Dinner

Michelliea Georges: Today was a wonderful day and I am feeling so different with all the knowledge I have received so far, particularly what you are giving us from your experiences.

Regina Hendricks: I agree with you. I felt so privileged and elevated from this trip. My Brother, you have played a very crucial role in the dramatic change I have experienced. I must thank you exceedingly.

George Washington: Thanks. However, I refer you back to what Dr. Monderson said when he first charged us. Learn. Grow. Exchange. Teach.

In **African Religious Thought Systems** December 18, 1975.

AFRICAN CREATION (Art)

The object of art in Africa becomes a living being and effective instrument. It has a life of its own. Uses of creation pervade African life from birth to death and are crucial parts of the life cycle. Emotions are expressed in exaggerated and ideal forms.

A combination of complex emotions expressed in African creation (art). Not meant to be representational of a man who is afraid but it represents fear itself. It becomes the emotion of love, fear, and death and expresses metaphysical reality. One's apprehension of a piece allows transcendence of the physical mask. The mask itself is a force itself.

Divine beings, human beings and animals and objects are merged in African art. A person is able to participate in a multidimensional universe. By recognizing sacred or spiritual realities allows one to have a multi-dimensional perception of the universe.

Objects eventually become animate. A mask has the ability to transform, transfigure, and transport individuals to another reality. Ritual art inspires reverence and awe. Art possesses secret power, its part of a universal force. The person who has it can invoke powers or forces, and through this man has access to the divine.

In the west there is "ritual" without meaning. In Africa there is "ritual drama" of creating and determining meaning. The mask can bring into presence ancestors and other aspects of divine being. The dominant value in Africa is the human need.

Holy Land Papyrus 31. Oh, to be entertained by musicians as beautiful as these young ladies is indeed heavenly.

"As studied from birth and initiation, the individual is immersed into a holy community, tied to a sacred rhythm of ritual, the function of which is to maintain the equilibrium of spiritual forces."

QUINTESSENTIAL BOOK "THE HOLY LAND"

Holy Land Illustration 91a. While these two torsos, the one in the Cairo Museum (left); and the one in the Ludovisi Collection in the Museum of Therese in Rome; may have been found in connection with but falsely attributed to being Hyksos, they are clearly of Twelfth Dynasty royalty.

9. Lounge Discussion

Regina Hendricks: How about a snack after this session my Brother?

George Washington: **African Religious Thought Systems** December 22, 1975.

Ok. The final was announced for January 6, 1976, Tuesday, from 9:00 to 11:00 AM

FINAL EXAMINATION REVIEW

Kondon Diara – Fear. A person has to fear danger and overcome it.
Period of seclusion – The person becomes symbolically dead and reborn as a new person. "Child"/ "Adult." The mother pretends to not know her "reborn child."
Instruction – This is an intense period of education.

FREDERICK MONDERSON

Role playing – Acting out of adult roles.
Learning the nature of communal life.

The professor wants specifics about any topic especially the blacksmith. He has mucho Nyama. Dom – Kela, Baara-Kela. He is the community surgeon who does excision and circumcision. He has a general understanding of his role in the society. He has technical skills and ability as well as religious knowledge and spiritual power. He sits alongside political leaders and heads religious associations. He is a creative artist and mask maker.

Characteristics of the Blacksmith.

The Blacksmith trade is hereditary having a divine genealogy. His wife is from a special group (potters). His is a manifestation of divine powers on earth. Involvement in agriculture, hunting and fertility makes him an intermediary between physical and spiritual worlds.

Creation involves sacrifice (part of self) with implications that are divine.

Bascom - *Yoruba of West Africa.*

FREE FOR TRAVEL TO CAIRO

CHECK IN AT ASWAN AIRPORT

Clerk will process all tickets together.

FLIGHT FROM ASWAN TO CAIRO INTERNATIONAL

Bus Ride to Hotel.

QUINTESSENTIAL BOOK "THE HOLY LAND"

Holy Land Illustration 91b. Diadem of a Twelfth Dynasty Princess, found in her tomb at Dashur.

CHECK IN AT CAIRO MENA HOUSE GARDEN HOTEL:

Bus I   —   Groups I, II and III.

Group I -   Bus Number 1.

Dr. Leonard James: Room 510
    Mrs. Marilyn James
Walter Brown: Room 512
    Mrs. Juliet Brown
Mr. Michael Palmer: Room 514
    Mrs. Mary Palmer, son Cosmos
Mr. Charles Palmer: Room 513

FREDERICK MONDERSON

Mrs. Shirley Palmer
Mr. Frank James: Room 522
   Mrs. Jessie James
Mr. John Brown: Room 526
   Mrs. Joy Brown

Group II-   Bus Number 1.

Dr. Madison: Room 616
   Mrs. Ada Madison
Mr. John Brown: Room 618
   Mrs. Joy Brown
Ms. Kashmoney Malone: Room 620
Stephaniea McCall: Room 620
Carmelitiea Shabazz: Room 622
Esperanza Rodriguez: Room 622
Peter Monderson: Room 525

Leonel Nelson Escobar: Room 625
Dr. Fred Monderson   Room 503

Group III   -   Bus Number 1.

QUINTESSENTIAL BOOK "THE HOLY LAND"

Robert Matthews: Room 626
Lesley Jacobs: Room 626
Frederick Maloney: Room 624
Henrietta Potter: Room 624
Michelliea Georges: Room 430
Regina Hendricks: Room 430
George Washington: Room 525

Group IV - Bus Number 2.

Michael Montout: Room 527
James Morrison: Room 528
Dr. McFlair: Room 610
    Mrs. McFlair
Mr. Sylvester Singleton: Room 614
    Mrs. Regina Singleton
Mr. John Stewart: Room 516
    Mrs. Glenda Stewart
Asantewaa Harris: Room 428
Hattie Jones. Room 518
Jerome Smith: Room 518

FREDERICK MONDERSON

Group V   Bus Number 2

Dr. Oswald Benjamin:	**Room 432**
Dr. John Africa:	**Room 434**
Teddy Cubia:	**Room 523**
Michael Sinclair:	**Room 523**
Dr. Alexander Pushkin:	**Room 519**
Mrs. Holly Pushkin	
Lady from California:	**Room 515**
Joshua Monderson:	**Room 624**
Cherise Maloney:	**Room 635**
Sharon Montgomery:	**Room 517**
Jack Bender:	**Room 515**

Rest of the day free

QUINTESSENTIAL BOOK
"THE HOLY LAND"

Holy Land Ceramic Art 19. Clearly the Ankh is in good company in this scene.

Day 12.   CAIRO
1.   Wake Up:

Esperanza Rodriguez: Good Morning, Mi Amor. Your schedule today calls for Sakkara and Memphis.

Your Article on "The Illustrious Queen Mother," is copied and ready for distribution.
Dr. Monderson: Thank you, my dear.

THE ILLUSTRIOUS QUEEN MOTHER
By
Frederick Monderson

With the passing of "Queen Mother Moore," African nationalism suffered a serious setback. This matriarch of African liberation left indelible impressions on the consciousness of those struggling against imperialism, colonialism, de-colonization and racism; whether through Garveyism, Nkrumahism or

FREDERICK MONDERSON

Afrocentricity as well as what is the future direction of Pan-African identification, strategy and struggle. In reflecting on a life of commitment to African liberation, this climax of her experiences is somewhat reminiscence of Marcus Garvey's classic statement: "You have caged the tiger, but the cubs are running loose out there." For certain, the Queen Mother has led an exemplary life! For sure, she has encouraged, supported, trained, and left cubs and young and old lions and lionesses, who are today committed to ideals, aspirations, and philosophic outlooks that motivate and fuel the efforts and desires of African people worldwide. As a result, she has earned her revered place in ancestral heritage and will be welcomed in the heavenly abode of the pantheon of African heroes and heroines. This state of affairs now forces us to consider the successor to the Queen Mother's august and respected place of leadership.

As an early follower of Marcus Moziah Garvey, Queen Mother Moore was influential in founding, sustaining and leading organizations such as the Universal Association of Ethiopian Women, Inc. She was the Founder of Addis Ababa, Inc; Founding Matriarch of the Ethiopian Orthodox Coptic Church; Founder and President of the African-American Cultural Foundation, Inc.; and Founder and President of the Harriet Tubman Association. She was a Life Member of Negro Women; Member of the Founding Committee 1970 Conference: Congress of African People and she was also the first woman to formally address the Organization of African Unity (OAU) in Addis Ababa, Ethiopia. Several organizations were also formed to aid her or as a result of her influence on others. She is now indeed a Great Ancestor!

Though Winnie Mandela has been crowned Queen of the Black World, candidates for the title of "Queen Mother" need to be identified, considered, chosen, and installed to provide leadership of causes affecting African people worldwide in memory of Queen Mother Moore and to keep her spirit alive and working.

To fully understand the position and significance of the title "Queen Mother," a historical reflection needs to be made of individuals who have filled this post, particularly in Nile Valley and later African culture. As such, one of the most celebrated of the "Queen Mothers" is the ancestress of the Eighteenth Dynasty, Aahmes-Nefertari, whose portrait is in the British Museum. This stately beauty, given divinity status by her people, is shown wearing a long flowing gown of red, white and blue, 1500 years Before Christ. In addition, she is bejeweled and wears the Vulture Headdress or the "Queen Mother Crown." This is a golden headdress, with uraeus, sun disk, and plumed feathers that sit atop a mortar. Another colorful portrait of a queen with the Queen Mother Crown is that of Rameses II's Nefertari of the Nineteenth Dynasty. This queen is shown in her tomb in the Valley of the Queens, where she offers two vessels in praise of the deity. However, while pictorial examples of the Queen Mother Crown may be lacking, the spirit and

QUINTESSENTIAL BOOK
"THE HOLY LAND"

personality has survived in the lives of queens who influenced their husbands, sons, grandsons, families, communities, and been forces of inspiration who in turn were praised and revered.

In the "Myth of Isis and Osiris," the king was killed by his brother Seth, while Isis his faithful wife, together with her sister Nephthys, set out to recover the body. Having found the badly dismembered body of Osiris, she was able to reconstitute the parts and through her magical divine-powers was impregnated by her dead husband. Finally she bore him a son named Horus. Horus was able to avenge his father by capturing the despicable uncle and slew him at the spot where the Temple of Edfu was built to mark the event. Some versions of the story report Horus made a claim to the gods in their great Hall of Judgment where he was defended by Thoth, the god of writing and wisdom. This intervention resulted in the great judge's ruling that Osiris was wrongfully executed and that Horus should be installed in his father's stead as King of Upper and Lower Egypt/Kemet. Through it all, Isis, granddaughter of Nut, stood by her son as she had done with her husband. Her influence, therefore, is traceable as a "Queen Mother" who gained great fame for her compassion, commitment, sincerity and faithfulness. From this mythological experience we can start with the individuals who constitute the human side of the dynastic experience.

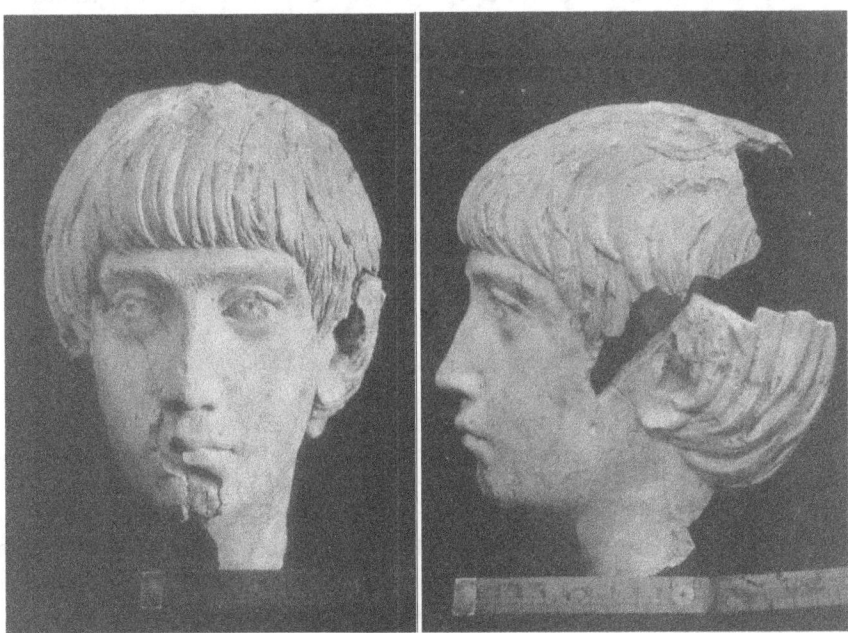

Holy Land Illustration 92. Front and side view of a head.

FREDERICK MONDERSON

If we begin with Narmer at the founding of the first dynasty, we first encounter the African queen in a majestic position of respect, certainly if not equality, within the domain of the husband and son. Narmer's wife was Queen Neithhotep, whom we encounter on the Narmer Macehead, a ceremonial weapon that has provided an enormous amount of factual information enabling scholars to arrive at some firm conclusions about this very early period. Narmer and Neithhotep's son was Hor-Aha, who followed his father as king. He built an enormous tomb for his mother, several times that of his father. We are led to believe that the influence of the Queen Mother may have begun to be exercised from this early time. In addition, because of the special role of the Queen in transmitting divine genes, she came to hold a special place in the society, as "power behind the throne" and when that august position was threatened, she exerted her influence to diminish whatever threats there may have been.

Snefru was probably the last king of the Third Dynasty and his wife was Hetep-Pheres who gave birth to a magnificent dynasty, the 4th with its illustrious kings, Khufu, Khafre, and Menkaure. These three pharaohs of the 4th Dynasty built the great pyramids on the Giza plateau.

When an expedition from the Boston Museum of Fine Arts discovered her tomb in the 1920s, they were soundly impressed with the burial remains of Queen Hetep-Pheres, mother of Khufu. Clearly the influence she enjoyed as "Queen Mother" can be deduced from her remains, including efforts at preservation of her body. This incidentally was one of the earliest examples of the process of mummification being employed. Though her mummy was never found, the viscera in canopic jars indicate the body was in fact mummified.

The First Intermediate Period followed the collapse of the Old Kingdom and power was exercised between Memphis in the North and Assuit in Middle Egypt. This period of internal disunity was comprised of the VIIth-Xth Dynasties. Theban princes who united the south before attempts were made to march northward to unify the country, began the formative era of the Middle Kingdom with consolidation of power. The German Archaeologist Von Bissing tells in the *American Journal of Archaeology* of a conflict between two of these Theban princes, Intef and Mentuhotep. Apparently, Intef had launched an attack on Mentuhotep's force and as he came out of the pass onto the Plains of Thebes, he encountered Mentuhotep with a superior force awaiting him. Intef had his mother Queen Achtothes intercede with Mentuhotep's mother Queen Aam, to bring about a cessation of hostilities to "save the day." Clearly, these "Queen Mothers" were significant political and moral influences on their respective families, for, as we know Mentuhotep was particularly successful in his efforts to unite the land. He founded the Eleventh Dynasty, defeated the northern monarchs and their allies, the Princes of Assuit, and again united the land. He consolidated his power,

QUINTESSENTIAL BOOK
"THE HOLY LAND"

reorganized the domain and expanded the cultural, economic and artistic institutions of the society and founded the Middle Kingdom. Though not much is subsequently known about his mother after this, we could well imagine the level of influence she exercised.

The next significant "Queen Mother" is considered to be Queen Tetisheri or Aahotep. At the collapse of the Middle Kingdom, the Hyksos, an Asiatic people, invaded Kemet and ruled the land from their stronghold in the Delta. The Princes of Thebes and the Upper Kingdom recognized these conquerors as their overlords and paid tribute to them. As with all such invaders, they were haughty and ruthless. After ruling as the Fifteenth and Sixteenth Dynasties, a Hyksos king sent a rather arrogant message to the Theban princes. He claimed the hippos grazing in the Nile at Thebes were making so much noise that the Hyksos rulers in the Delta, nearly 500 miles away, could not sleep at night. Therefore, "Shut up your hippopotamuses!" Such arrogance generated an intense response from the Thebans. They mobilized their forces and began a protracted war of liberation that lasted for 50 years and ended with the expulsion of the Hyksos.

Queen Tetisheri's husband was Seqenenra, who was felled in battle by an axe-wound to the head. His mummy is now in the Cairo Museum. While her husband was away fighting in the war of liberation, a palace coup broke out led by "Tety the Handsome." This gallant queen rallied the faithful and put down the rebellion. She saved the throne for her progeny. In that ongoing war of liberation, Kamose her son, expelled the Hyksos and his brother Ahmose completed the job. This latter founded the XVIIIth Dynasty and New Kingdom. Ahmose or Aahmes married his sister, Aahmes-Nefertari who became ancestress of the Eighteenth Dynasty. Clearly, for her gallantry Tetisheri was rewarded and exercised the requisite influence as "Queen Mother." We get an early glimpse of the Queen Mother or Vulture Crown being worn by her daughter Aahmes-Nefertari, whose influence was in itself far reaching. She was Black-skinned beauty who gained legendary status. Years later, when Hatshepsut was on the throne of Kemet, and faced with questions regarding her legitimacy to rule, she boasted of her heritage that was tied to this queen.

FREDERICK MONDERSON

Holy Land Photo 103. Cairo Museum of Egyptian Antiquities. Some of the numerous ushabti figures or "answerers" that followed Tutankhamun into the afterlife to continue their work of serving the King.

Hatshepsut herself was Queen or should I say "King" of Egypt/Kemet. She had a daughter named Nefru-re, whose tutor was Senmut her architect. She had another daughter named Hatshepsut and this daughter married Thutmose III. As such, Hatshepsut could be considered both Queen and Queen Mother, though her influence as the latter was very curtailed.

The next significant "Queen Mother" was Queen Tiy, wife of Amenhotep III and mother of Amenhotep IV, Ikhnaton, the revolutionary. This Queen, who looked "so Nubian," was thought to be everything but African and credited with having too much power and influence. She held a position of reverence with her husband Amenhotep III, the "Magnificent," who built Luxor Temple, the "Grand Lodge." He also built a palace called Malcata, the "place of rejoicing" for this "Queen Mother." Her influence on her son Amenhotep IV, Ikhnaton, and his religious revolution was significant, though Hayes believed reactions to the Amarna heresy absolved her of any involvement.

On a scarab she is shown wearing the vulture headdress or "Queen Mother

QUINTESSENTIAL BOOK
"THE HOLY LAND"

Crown." The queen of Tutankhamon, the next king in this dynasty, is shown wearing this crown with a menat and sistrum in a small shrine of her husband.

During the Nineteenth Dynasty, the great pharaoh, military strategist, father, husband, builder, high priest, etc., Rameses II, built the Abu Simbel temple in Nubia. Adjacent, he built another temple for his beloved Nefertari, the Nubian. Some thought he built his and her temples to solidify his relations with the people of Nubia after marrying one of their princesses.

Nevertheless, despite having several wives and untold numbers of sons, one could well imagine his favorite Nefertari as playing the role of "Queen Mother" with its attendant responsibilities and influences as their nation dominated the ancient world. Rameses II left ample evidence of their relationship.

More than two thousand years later, in the time of the empires of the Western Sudanic empires of Ghana, Mali, and Songhay, Ibn Battuta wrote of the equality, freedom and independence of the women of these societies.

Yaa Asantewaa was a respected and significant heroine in Ghanaian and West African history. In the heyday of British imperialism in Africa, she was appalled at the performance of her nation's troops against a British army who had sought to desecrate the "Golden Stool," symbol and soul of the Ghanaian people. Following their defeat in one of a series of wars, she motivated and galvanized the warriors who were ultimately victorious against the British. Here is another unique example of Black troops defeating a disciplined and more heavily armed European army. In this case, however, it was commanded by a Queen as in the case of Candace of old Ethiopia and Queen Nzinga against the Portuguese during the days of slave trade and ultimately slavery.

FREDERICK MONDERSON

Holy Land Illustration 93. Painted wooden coffin of Hu-en-Amen, an incense-bearer, about B.C. 800, XXIst or XXnd Dynasty (left); and Coffin of Katebet, a priestess of Amen-Ra at Thebes, about B.C. 800, XXIInd Dynasty (right).

In the American slave experience, the slaveholders never respected those societal

QUINTESSENTIAL BOOK
"THE HOLY LAND"

institutions as marriage and the family. Yet still, grandmothers because of their age and "uselessness" to the slave masters were the greatest assets of our people. They were the first "Queen Mothers" of our experience in the New World. My grandmother, Cherise Preville, played that crucial role of "Queen Mother" and then my mother, Mitta Monderson played a similar role in raising my offsprings. Cherise Maloney is another such "Queen Mother!" And so it had been as through the Sixteenth, Seventeenth, Eighteenth and Nineteenth Centuries. This is also the role such notables as Phyllis Wheatley, Harriet Tubman, Sojourner Truth, Mrs. Frederick Douglass, Mrs. Booker T. Washington, and Mrs. George Washington Carver played in "bringing us up" to the start of the Twentieth Century. We must not forget "Bottom Belly" and "Queen Mary" of Jamaica, who led the Maroons.

Espousing liberation, intellectual advancement, economic empowerment and cultural and historical identification, Mrs. Marcus Garvey, Mrs. W.E.B. DuBois, Mrs. Paul Robeson, Mrs. Caseley Hayford, Mrs. Nandi Azikwi, Mrs. Kwame Nkrumah, Mrs. Julius Nyerere, Mrs. Eric Williams, Mrs. Malcolm X, Betty Shabazz, and a whole host of others including Fannie Lou Hamer, Ethel Waters, Pamela Covington-Downes, Lorraine Hansberry, Ruby Dee, Jackie "Moms" Mabley, Constance Baker Motley, Ella Baker, Margaret Taylor Burroughs, Mary McLeod Bethune, Sisters Bettye Mullings, Melinda Melbourne, Rhonda Mormon, Josephine and Katie, Carmen Rudder, Sasser and Washington, and Jones, Smoke and Griffin, so too Linda Bascombe, Hyacinth Rowe and Mrs. Palmer, Rosa Parks, Mrs. Purdie, Mrs. Harper, Mrs. Woolcock, Mrs. Eileen Loncke, Listra Kangalee, Mrs. Estelle Browne, Mrs. Valma Browne, and Dorothy Dandridge, Ruth Goring, as well as Elsie Richardson and Margaret Vinson, Carol Taylor, "Sistah" Viola Plummer, Ruth Lewis, Carmen Rodriguez Alcantara, Harriet McLeod, Mavis Hill and Edith Graham, Mrs. Francis Haggler, Marilyn James, Cherise Monderson, Keisha Monderson, Kashida Maloney, Audrey Monderson, Carmen Monderson, Gracelyn Willis, Yolanda Lezama, Mable Boston, Mrs. Brown of Atlanta, Georgia; Adelaide Sandford, and Annette Robinson, Barbara Jordan, Camille Yarbrough and Gertrude ben-Jochannan. Some people would add to this Mrs. Herbert Daughtry, Mrs. Angela Jitu Weusi, Mrs. Mae Sonny Carson, and Mrs. Alton Maddox and Mrs. Cathy Jordan Sharpton, have been significant "Queen Mothers."

So as we challenge the twenty-first century, we shall go forth with a tenacious feeling of empowerment and resilience, knowing that many "Queen Mothers" have been beacons of inspiration on behalf of African people in the past and in the future. We need remember these noble women and the organizations they founded, sponsored, and supported. We must also recognize these "Queen Mothers," encourage them and support their efforts. In this way, the historic institution of "Queen Mother" will remain functional, vigilant, influential and useful in advocating economic, political, intellectual, cultural and spiritual

FREDERICK MONDERSON

liberation of our people, now and in the future.

Sakkara

Some years ago, on an educational trip to the land of ancient Kemet, now Egypt, while at Sakkara, I scaled the barriers and approached the Step Pyramid of King Zoser, built by his architect, physician and Vizier Imhotep, during the Third Dynasty. I touched this inspiring construction and said a prayer, thankful and awed to be in its reverenced and majestic presence. By the standards of eternity, this magnificent ancient African architectural structure attests to the creativity and accomplishments of the early mind of Africans. As a man-made creation, it has also defied time. Equally too, and oftentimes we are told, "time is afraid of the Pyramids," but the pyramids themselves must genuflect in the presence of their older relative, the Step-Pyramid of Sakkara, prototype of their own everlastingness. Clearly, these pathways of alpha and omega of African architecture stand as living testimony to the unconquerable force of the African mind. In their timelessness these structures beautified the majestic Nile in adoration of Africa's Gods, Kings, Women, People and Culture. Importantly, subsequent achievements of world civilization were nurtured from these creative beginnings. Therefore, this legacy is so important today it can buoy the social process and educational efforts of African people worldwide as they reflect back upon a rich cultural heritage.

In the rural and urban centers of this nation, African people need the strength and reassurance of such knowledge in their march of socialization, educational advancement, political and economic empowerment and religious, spiritual and theosophical rejuvenation. We recognize that as each generation is called upon to discover its purpose, and undergird its efforts to enhance its community, only knowledge of self, and a history of one's ancestral and cultural heritage, will enable them to read, research and conduct scientific inquiry to enlighten and educate the next link in the chain of Africa's progeny. With this knowledge base safely secured, we can then stand mightily on the threshold of the future challenges and accomplishments, knowing that effective sailing is attainable.

It's an accepted fact, in the architectural history of the world, the land and people of ancient Kemet stand supreme. Their prototypes, genesis and building practices have therefore influenced people, nations, religions, and the pageantry of history.

Architecture is considered the greatest achievement of the human mind. In its evolution from the humblest beginnings, man has sought to praise, worship and ritualize divine beings in furtherance of his cultural development. Temples as places of worship and festivities, palaces as residences and centers of joviality and administrative functions, as well as civil structures to serve the ends of humanity, and fortresses as barracks of military enterprise, and tombs as final resting places,

QUINTESSENTIAL BOOK
"THE HOLY LAND"

all are examples of experimental architecture that produced the lasting masterpieces as at Karnak, Ramesseum, Luxor, Deir El Bahari, etc., demonstrated as the crystallized building practices of African genius. In these and collateral industries, Africans excelled while the world was waking up to recognize the dawn of human consciousness and creativity. One such experiment took place at Sakkara.

The fame of Sakkara rests in its choice for tombs of everlastingness. Not simply the Step-Pyramid but massive mastabas equally tell of those significant building projects requiring even greater administrative skill to coordinate the laying out of the ground, quarrying and transportation of the massive stone, architectural genius of the constructions and the organization of the necessary manpower that expertly erected these buildings. Sakkara served as the necropolis or cemetery of Memphis during its tenure as capital. This followed Narmer's unification of the two kingdoms, and erection of the "White Wall," at c. 3200 B.C. or *Nile Year* 1040. This choice then allowed Sakkara to become a sacred resting place for pharaohs and nobles dating from the First Dynasty to the late period of Saite, Persian and Ptolemaic rule. Significantly, the ideological nucleus of this sacred cemetery was the funerary complex of King Zoser. The sprawling necropolis stretched for 8 kilometers long and one kilometer wide.

North of Zoser's structure is the North Necropolis containing the Serapeum, a number of tombs and the Pyramid of Teti, in the north-northeast. In this northern half, the massive Serapeum was the burial place of the Apis bulls, sacred to the God Ptah, deity of Memphis whose worship was inaugurated by Narmer during the First Dynasty. This structure, Strelocke (1965: 32) wrote: "consists of a series of vaults in the form of underground corridors, nearly 10 ft. wide and 18 ft. high, passing under the desert sands for 1,148 ft. Left and right in chambers dug out of the solid walls, especially in the large vault are the granite sarcophagi of the sacred Apis-bulls. The 24 monolithic sarcophagi each weigh from sixty to seventy tons. The first, 328 ft. long corridor was cut out in the time of Rameses II. Psammetichus I (26th Dynasty) extended the vaults and the Ptolemies finished the complex."

To the east of this building lay a semicircle of statues of Poets and Philosophers including Plato, Heraclitus, Protogoras, Homer and Pindarus. All were built by Ptolemy I. Further north, in a semicircle reaching towards Teti's pyramid were the Mastabas of Ptah-Hotep and Akhet-Hotep, and Ti. Next are located Baboon and Ibis galleries, and the tomb of Hesi Re whose gracefully wooden panel is now in the Cairo Museum. In addition, First Dynasty tombs of Kings Udimu, Ada, Zed, and Queen Merneith are there. Then come the Mastabas of Ankh-ma-hor, Kagemni, Mereruka and Ka-em-heset.

FREDERICK MONDERSON

Holy Land Illustration 93a. Jewelry of the Twelfth Dynasty (left); and what was considered a Sphinx of Tanis now in the Cairo Museum is actually the image of a Twelfth dynasty pharaoh (right).

To the south lies the Southern Necropolis, in front of which is the Pyramid of Unas, with its mortuary temple, monumental Gallery, causeway, sacred barks buried in large stone basins, a valley temple and its landing stage. Between the Causeway and Zoser's southern wall lie two rows of mastabas. In the first are Ha, Ishu Ef, Vizier Unefert, Unal Ankh, Princess Idut and Vizier Mehu. In the second row the tomb of Queen Khenut and Bebet are found. Further southwest lies the Funerary Complex of Sekhemket. He was successor to Zoser and also built a Step-Pyramid. His funerary complex seems as if it was finished. Within its enclosure walls are the Mastaba of Mehu-ka-irer, Mastaba of Nefer-her-ptah and tomb of Ptah-iru-ke. Its believed there were two other Step Pyramids built in addition to the great one. Watson (1987: 23-24) mentions a Step Pyramid at Zawiyet el-Aryan, between Giza and Sakkara. "A fourth step pyramid complex might be concealed within the so-called Great Enclosure at Saqqara, the rectangular outline of which has been revealed west of Sekhemkhet's complex by Arial photographs. This, however, awaits excavation."

The more significant structure, however, is the mortuary complex of Zoser containing the Great Step Pyramid, which is surrounded by an enclosure wall.

QUINTESSENTIAL BOOK "THE HOLY LAND"

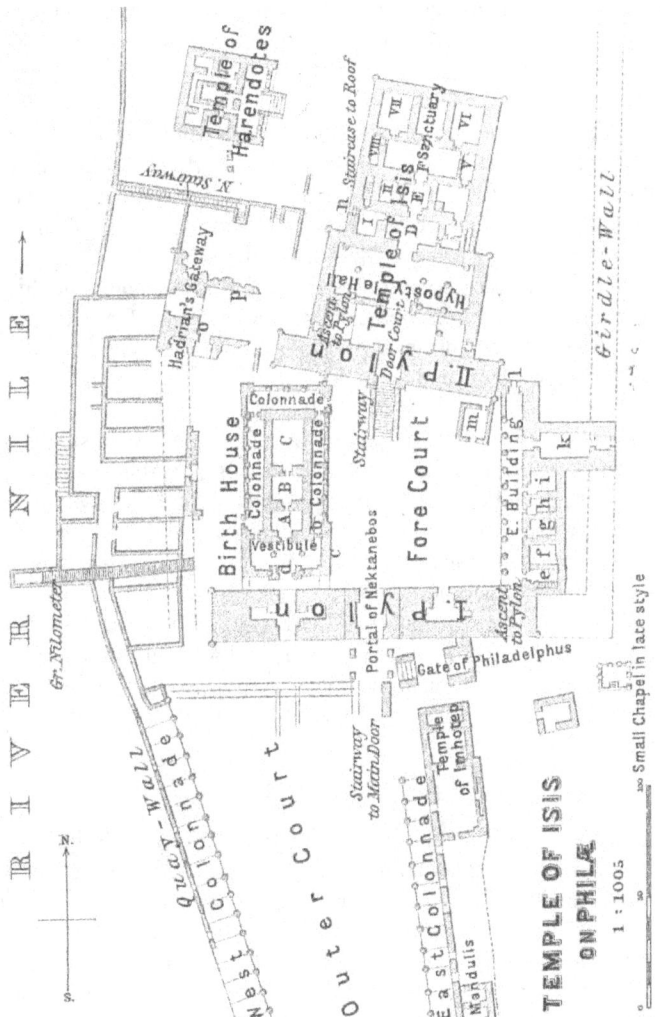

Holy Land. Temple of Isis on Philae, now Agilka Island, Aswan.

This pyramid, in six steps, is about 193 feet high. Carpiceci (1994: 74) mentions a court with altar, storehouses, and dwellings for priests; mortuary temple with the pharaoh's sirdab; "House of the North;" "House of the South;" Heb-Sed Court with buildings and altar; small temple and temple with fluted columns; entrance of the Sanctuary and entrance "colonnade;" facade of the "Cobra Palace;" storerooms and portico; and the Court in front of the Great Step-Pyramid with the three main altars. In the northeast corner of the complex, Zoser's statue was found in a walled-in stone area with two peepholes for him to look out. It is now in the Cairo Museum and a replica sits there.

While this complex boasts an architectural magnificence, its artistic beauty is itself breathtaking. The Cobra Frieze in the Great Court conveys aura. Beneath Zoser's structure are beautiful blue faience tiles and decorated panels that show the Pharaoh celebrating the Heb Sed Festival. Mereruka was a 6th Dynasty Master of Ceremonies who built a large Mastaba with some 30 rooms. He has enormous space and there are 16 rooms for his wife Sesheshet and 5 for his son Meri-tety. This Mastaba of Mereruka depicts the slaughtering of cattle and processions of offering bearers and hunting and fishing scenes showing people in boats along with birds, fishes, plants and animals.

The Mastaba of Ti was discovered by Mariette in 1865. It shows the nobleman, a royal hairdresser of the 5th Dynasty, and his family sailing through the marshes and inspecting their workers. A hippopotamus hunt is shown, with fishes in the marshes as wells as papyrus plants and birds being attacked by other animals. There are also processions of men and women bearing offerings and importantly, the first evidence of people in motion. Haag (1987: 165) mentions the dual nature of many of Ti's representations: "Literally it is a hunt in the marshes; but symbolically it is Ti against the forces of evil and chaos. The hippopotamus was particularly feared and hated in ancient Egypt, but Ti together with a helpful crocodile is killing it. Fish and birds represented chaos, but here again man and animal are subduing them."

The Mastaba of Ptah-Hotep shows this High Priest in offering scenes. There are water sports with rowers dancing in their boats. Fishes abound in the water below and individuals hold birds and animals as part of an enormous offering table before the Nobleman. The Mastaba of Kagemni has decorations showing a servant supplying seeds for birds in an aviary. Men are shown with the papyrus plant, along with birds and gazelles being led on cord as well as dancing girls. The Mastaba of Princess Idut has scenes of everyday life, administrators taking inventory, and seated scribes with their palettes and brushes making recordings. Also shown are servants butchering a bull and a water scene with men in boats holding birds, animals and fishes while crocodiles are seen in the water. However, while the art is breath-taking, the monumental architecture is timeless and awe-inspiring and set the tone for millennia to come.

Firth (1928: 463) instructs: "The perfection of the masonry makes it difficult to believe that these stone buildings are the oldest surviving in Egypt, but the imitation of brickwork and reed construction follows the law which makes every

QUINTESSENTIAL BOOK
"THE HOLY LAND"

fresh change in material imitate the forms associated with the material previously in use, a stage which precedes the generalization of the constructional properties natural to the new material. This archaic limitation was in two generations left behind by the builders of the great Pyramids of the fourth dynasty, although the Egyptians retained the end columns in imitation of the lotus and the papyrus derived from the primitive constructions of their remote ancestors."

Therefore, in looking back through time, the genius of Imhotep pioneered multi-tiered structures. These experimentations of the Third Dynasty set the stage for the True Pyramid of Giza in the Fourth Dynasty. Pyramids were built during the Fifth and Sixth Dynasties and as late as the Middle Kingdom. While these Old Kingdom structures contained both Mortuary and later Sun or Worship Temples, the transitional Middle Kingdom bequeathed to the New Kingdom a separation that encouraged Mortuary Temples erected on the west bank and Worship Temples on the east Bank of the Nile.

Though it all, African creativity proved everlasting. This magnetic attraction, whether for its art, architecture, religion or industry undergirds the drive of history. Here it needs be underscored that there is a battle for the soul of the study of Ancient Kemet/Egypt.

When asked about the significance of studies in this area, Van Sertima mentioned how he attended more than three conferences in one year underscoring the importance of this information of significance to African people. There needs to be vigorous examination of the record to make the necessary corrections as part of global African Historiographic Reconstruction. It cannot fully be underscored that the *Centenary* unearthing of a century ago of the archaeological and anthropological "ancient records" of the "Ancient Records" must become mandatory reading for our young and old, men and women, whose interests in life's pursuits are in the fields of professional enterprise that these same ancestors have provided the foundation for. The European world, by virtue of doing the research, is today more entrenched in these studies, exhibitions and writings that project a unique and powerful, yet false; nevertheless, ruling Egyptian culture with filtering of Blacks who functioned as slaves. If this is interpreted as a white society with a Black slave class, then this is distortion of the historical record! There is also much omission of this same record. What we don't know won't hurt us, it is thought! Importantly, the roots of this difficulty are traceable to the lack of knowledge at the beginnings of the nineteenth century and throughout.

Questionable European scholarship compounded and contributed to racist Global White Supremacy that dominated the world from "naked imperialism" to "enlightened imperialism." From start to the end, particularly since imperial

FREDERICK MONDERSON

Victorian England had so much influence in shaping perception and beliefs both in England and the world she vigorously pursued and controlled, scholarship may have favored White over Black people, all things being equal.

Nevertheless, despite what we know, Showker (1989: 83) informs how at the end of the Twentieth Century: "five Egyptian and eight foreign teams are excavating at Sakkara and all have made extremely valuable discoveries, including a complete burial complex from the IV and V Dynasties. In 1985 an Anglo-Dutch team rediscovered the Tomb of Maya, Minister of Finance under King Tut. It was considered a major discovery. But there is much more to be done; scholars estimate that only a third of the area has been studied."

REFERENCES

Carpiceci, Alberto Carlo. *Art and History of Egypt: 5000 Years of Civilization.* Florence, Italy: Bonechi, (1994).
"The Pyramids and Tombs." *American Journal of Archaeology,* Vol. IV, 1900, p. 480.
"The Chapel of Unas." *American Journal of Archaeology,* Vol. V, 1901, p. 332; SS *Times* July 15, 1901, Hilprecht.
"The Pyramid of Unas." *American Journal of Archaeology,* Vol. VI, 1902, p. 60. Maspero, Gaston. *C.R. Acad. Insc.* 1901, pp. 614f "A Representation of the Manufacture of Seals." *American Journal of Archaeology,* Vol. X,1906, p. 334; *Society of Biblical Archaeology,* Vol. XXVII, 1905, p.86 (pl.) P.E. Newberry.
"Sakkara." *American Journal of Archaeology,* Vol. XXXII, 1928, p. 71; *Ill. Lond. News,* November 12, 1927, p. 861, (4 figs.).
"Sakkara." *American Journal of Archaeology,* Vol. XXXII, 1928 p. 354; *Ill. Lond. News,* Jan 7, 1928, pp. 8-9 (6 figs. one in color.) Cecil M. Firth.
"Sakkara." *Ill Lond News,* Feb 27, 1937, pp. 348-49. Walter D. Emery.
"Sakkara." *American Journal of Archaeology,* Vol. XL, 1938, p. 292; *Ill. Lond. News,* June 4, 1938, pp. 1000-1001.
"Sakkara." *American Journal of Archaeology,* Vol. XL, 1938 *Ill. Lond News,* Jan 4, 1939, p. 51.
"The Season of 1938 to 1939." *American Journal of Archaeology,* Vol. VIIIL 1940, pp. 145-49, William Stevenson Smith.
"Sakkara." *American Journal of Archaeology,* Vol. IIIL, 1943 *The New Pallas,* Vol. VI, 1942, p. 26
"New Finds at Sakkarah." Jasper Y. Brinton. *Art and Archaeology,* Autumn 1949, pp. 141-144.
"The Step Pyramid at Sakkara." C. M. Firth. *Antiquity,* Vol. 2, 1928, pp. 461-463.
"Sakkara." *American Journal of Archaeology,* Vol. XL, 1936, p. 120.; *Ill. Lond.*

QUINTESSENTIAL BOOK
"THE HOLY LAND"

News, January 2, 1937, p. 3.
"Sakkara." *American Journal of Archaeology,* Vol. XL, 1936, p. 317; *Ill. Lond. News,* February 27, 1939, pp. 348-49. Walter B. Emery.
"Royal Tomb at Sakkara." *American Journal of Archaeology,* Vol. XL, 1936, p. 292; *Ill. Lond. News,* February 12, 1938, pp. 247-49. Walter B. Emery, Director of Excavations Conducted for the Egyptian Government Service of Antiquities at North Sakkara.
"Sakkara." *American Journal of Archaeology,* Vol. XLII 1938, p. 314; *Ill. Lond. News,* January 14, 1939, p. 51. Zaki Effendi Y. Saad.
"Saqqara." *American Journal of Archaeology,* Vol. XLVIII, 1944, p. 278; *Ill. Lond. News,* February 26, 1944, pp. 247-49 (9 figs.) Guy Brunton.
"Egypt." *American Journal of Archaeology,* Vol. L, 1946, p. 192.
"Egypt." *American Journal of Archaeology,* Vol. XLVII, 1951, pp. 419-24 passim.
"Egypt." *American journal of Archaeology,* Vol. LIII, 1949, pp. 40-41.
Showker, Kay. *Fodor's 90: Egypt. A Practical and Historical Guide.* New York: Fodor's Travel Publications, Inc. 1989.
Youssef, Hisham and John Rodenbeck. *Insight Guides: Egypt.* Hong Kong: APA Publications, 1991.

Holy Land Photo 104. Cairo Museum of Egyptian Antiquities. More of the numerous ushabti figures that followed Tutankhamun into the afterlife.

FREDERICK MONDERSON

Memphis

Murray's *Handbook for Egypt*, though written in 1888 still provides some useful information that helps to underscore the significance of Memphis throughout much of the three thousand years of pharaonic rule.

History of Memphis. - According to Herodotus' account of the story told him by the priests, Memphis was founded by Menes, the first recorded king of Egypt, who, by turning the Nile from its old course under the Libyan hills into a more western channel cut by him, made a large tract of dry land, on which he built the city. At the point where the river was turned off, he constructed levees to prevent its returning into its old channel and overwhelming Memphis. Of these dikes no trace remains, though Herodotus says the Persians kept them up with great care at the time of his visit: but the actual appearance of the river strongly corroborates the account. For at Kafr-el-Aiat, 14 m. above Mitrahenny, the Nile takes a considerable curve to the eastward, and would, if the previous direction of its course continued, run immediately below the Libyan mountains to Sakkarah; and the slight difference between this distance and the approximate measurement of Herodotus, who places the dykes at 100 stadia above Memphis, offers no objection. Indeed, if we calculate from the outside of the town, which the historian doubtless did, we shall find that the bend of Kafr-el-Aiat agrees exactly with his 100 stadia, or about 11-½ m. Mitrahenny being some way within the city of Memphis. It is not necessary to suppose, however, that the whole of the river was diverted from its original channel into an entirely different one. It probably divided into two arms, as is often the case in many parts of its course, which joined into one stream again some miles lower down, and Menes merely blocked up the western channel, and turned all the water into the eastern. The arm of the river was replaced by a canal, which brought water to the famous lake "on the North and West of the city" excavated by Menes; and this canal is now represented by the one, which flows through the plain between the desert and Mitrahenny, and continues on to below the pyramids of Geezeh. It is a continuation of the Bahr Yoosef, and appears here to flow through a natural depression.

Memphis is styled in Coptic *Mefi, Momf,* and *Menf,* which last are traditionally preserved by the modern Egyptians, though the only existing town whose name resembles it is Menoof, in the Delta. The Egyptians called it *Panouf, Memfi, Membe,* and *Mennefer,* "the place of the good," which Plutarch translates "the haven of good men," though it seems rather to refer to the abode of the Deity, the representative of goodness, than to the virtues of its inhabitants. In hieroglyphics it was styled 'Mennefer, the land of the pyramid,' and sometimes Ei-Ptah, 'the abode of Ptah,' as well as 'the city of the white wall.'

QUINTESSENTIAL BOOK
"THE HOLY LAND"

Holy Land Illustration 94. Three of the ten limestone statues of Amenemhet I, found in his Pyramid at Lisht.

Though the remains of Memphis lie chiefly about Mitrahenny, it is evident that the city extended considerably beyond the present mounds, which appear to have belonged to the enclosures about the temple and other sacred edifices, as well as the "palaces" that were situated, as Strabo says, on an elevated spot reaching down to the lower part of the town; and there is reason to believe that it extended from near the river at Bedreshayn to Sakkarah, which only allows a breadth East and West of 3 miles. Diodorus calculates its circuit at 150 stades, upwards of 17 English Miles, requiring a diameter of nearly 6 m; and its greatest diameter was probably North and South. But the whole of this space was not covered by houses or public buildings; much was given up to gardens, villas, and "sacred groves;" and the great Acherusian lake, "surrounded," according to Diodorus, "by meadows and canals," occupied a large portion of it. This lake was probably in the lowlands to the N.E. of Sakkarah with a canal communicating with the large reservoir constructed for the service of the temple of Ptah, in the open space to the N. of the colossus, between Mitrahenny and the long eastern mounds, in the mud of which several statues have been discovered. On the river side of these mounds is the site of what is called the Nilometer.

It may be doubted if a wall surrounded Memphis. It was not the custom of the Egyptians to include the whole of a large city within one circuit, Thebes even, with its 100 gates, had no wall; but each temple had its own circuit, generally a thick crude-brick wall, with strong gateways, sometimes within an outer one of greater extent; and the quarters of troops, or citadel, were surrounded by a massive wall of the same materials, with an inclined way to the top of the rampart. The temples of Memphis were, no doubt, encompassed in the same manner by a sacred enclosure; and the "white wall" was the fortified part of the city in which the Egyptians took refuge when defeated by the Persians. This white fortress was very ancient and from it Memphis was called the 'city of the white wall.'

Memphis had probably already suffered somewhat from the Persians when Herodotus saw it, but the account he has left of some of the principal buildings shows that it must have been the largest and most magnificent city in Egypt at the time of his visit.

Among those, which he mentions, is the Temple of Ptah or Hephaestus, said to have been founded by Menes, and enlarged and beautified by succeeding monarchs. Moeris (Amenemhat III) erected the northern vestibule; and Sesostris (Rameses II), besides the two colossal statues, one of which is still to be seen, made considerable additions with enormous blocks of stone which 'he employed his prisoners of war to drag to the temple.' Pheron (Merneptah), his son, also enriched it with suitable presents, which he sent on the recovery of his sight, as he did to all the principal temples of Egypt. The western vestibule, or propylaeum, was the work of Rhampsinitus (Rameses III), who also erected two statues, 25 cubits in height, one on the North the other on the South; to the former of which the Egyptians gave the name of summer, and to the latter winter. The eastern was the largest and most magnificent of all these propylaea, and excelled as well in the

QUINTESSENTIAL BOOK
"THE HOLY LAND"

beauty of its sculpture as in its dimensions. It was built by Asychis (Shishak). Several grand additions were afterwards made by Psammetichus, who, besides the southern vestibule, erected a large hypaethral court covered with sculpture, where Apis, was kept when exhibited in public. It was surrounded by a Peristyle of Osiride figures, 12 cubits in height, which served instead of columns; - similar no doubt to those in the Memnonium at Thebes. Many other kings adorned this magnificent temple of Ptah with sculpture and various gifts, among which may be mentioned the statues of Sethos, in commemoration of his victory over the Assyrians, holding in his hand a mouse with this inscription, 'Whoever sees me, let him be pious.' Amasis, too, dedicated a recumbent crois-sphinx, 75 ft. long in this temple, which is the more singular as there is no instance of an Egyptian statue, of early time, in that position: and the same king built a magnificent temple to the goddess Isis.

The temenos or sacred groves of Proteus were very beautiful and richly ornamented. Some Phoenicians of Tyre, settlers at Memphis, lived round it, and in consequence the whole neighborhood received the name of the Tyrian camp. Within the temenos was the temple, called 'of Venus the stranger;' whence the historian conjectured that it was of Helen, who was reported to have lived some time at the court of the Egyptian king. This is of course an idle Greek story, which, like so many others, shows how ready the Greeks were to derive everything from their own experience.

Four hundred years after Herodotus Diodorus expatiates on the size and magnificence of Memphis, which, however, had already become second in importance to Alexandria. And Strabo, a few years before the Christian era, says, 'The city is large and populous, next to Alexandria in size, and, like that, filled with foreign residents. Before it are some lakes; but the palaces, situated once in an elevated spot, and reaching down to the lower part of the city, are now ruined and deserted.' The temples, however, seem still to have been kept up in the former style of magnificence. They suffered no doubt in the reign of Theodosius from the zeal, which he displayed against idolatry and its shrines. But Memphis still continued to enjoy some consequence, even at the time of the Arab invasion; and though its ancient palace was a ruin, the governor of Egypt, John Mekaukes, still resided in the city; and it was here that he concluded a treaty with the invaders after they had succeeded in taking the strong Roman fortress at Babylon. The wealth, as well as the inhabitants of Memphis, soon passed to the new Arab city of Fustat, and the capital of Lower Egypt in a few years ceased to exist. The blocks of stone of its ruined monuments were afterwards taken to help in building the new City of Cairo; and yet notwithstanding this wholesale spoliation we find Abd el-Lateef at the end of the 12th century asserting that 'the ruins of Memphis occupy a space half a day's journey every way;' and that 'they still offer to the eyes of the spectator a collection of marvels which strike the mind with wonder, and which the most eloquent man might in vain attempt to describe.' Aboolfeda, 150 years later, speaks of the ruins as still occupying a large extent, but gradually disappearing. But from that time hardly any mention is made of them; and the waters of the inundation, long ago unrestrained by the protecting dikes, covered the plain with a gradually increasing layer of mud deposit, beneath which every trace of such ruins were left completely disappeared. It was not till the beginning of the present century that researches were made, which resulted in discovering some traces of the ancient city.

Remains of Memphis. - Some statues, a few fragments of granite and some constructions are all that can be seen of the ruins of a city, which, if there is any truth in the description given of it, 'in its glory must have exceeded any modern city, as much as the Pyramids exceed any mausoleum which has been erected since those days.' Curzon. It is possible that much may be concealed beneath the mounds, but the latest researches have been singularly un-productive. There are a few objects, chiefly statuettes of the god Ptah, at the museum at Cairo, and one interesting discovery was that of a private house.

The only object that will attract the traveler's attention is the Colossal Statue of Rameses II, which lies near the path leading from Bedreshayn to Mitrahenny. It has recently been raised out of the hollow in which it lay for many years by Major Bagnold. A wall has been built round it to protect it from injury and a small charge is made for admission. It was discovered by Signor Caviglia and Mr. Sloane, by whom it was given to the British Museum, on condition of its being taken to England; but no attempt has ever been made to do so. This is probably one of the statues mentioned by Herodotus and Diodorus as erected by, "Sesostris" in front of the Temple of Ptah. These statues were 80 cubits (45 to 51 feet) high: this one is unfortunately broken at the feet, and part of the cap is wanting; but its total height may be estimated at 48 ft. 8 in. without the pedestal. The stone is a white siliceous limestone, very hard, and capable of taking a high polish. From the neck of the king is suspended an amulet or breast-plate, like that of the Urim and Thummin of the Hebrews, in which is the royal prenomen, supported by Ptah on one side, and Pasht on the other. In the center, and at the side of his girdle, are the name and prenomen of this Rameses, and in his hand he holds a scroll, bearing at one end his name, Amen-mai-Rameses. A figure of his daughter is represented at his side. It is on a small scale, her shoulder reaching little above the level of his knee. The upper part of the statue is some-what worn away, but the under part still retains its polish. The expression of the face, which is perfectly preserved, is very beautiful: the features are sharp cut and most delicately finished.

QUINTESSENTIAL BOOK "THE HOLY LAND"

Holy Land Papyrus 32. Wearing the Queen Mother Crown of a vulture headdress surmounted by a mortar and supporting disk and feathers, Nefertari presents two jars while Tutankhamon's mask is featured at the top right and Nefertiti's bust at the bottom left.

There are some other remains of statues, and another colossus, lying not far from this one; and at the guard's house close by may be seen a few things which have been dug up at various times; among them are some statues in the sitting attitudes of the modern Egyptians, with crossed legs, or knees up to the chin. The space to the S. of the colossus is the site of the temple of Ptah, of which Mariette Pasha has discovered the foundations. In the open space to the N. are some remains only visible at low Nile. This open space, which is still a depression filled with more or less water according to the time of year, was formerly probably a reservoir in front of the temple, supplied with water by canal from the lake before mentioned situated near Sakkarah. On the borders of this pond M. Mariette discovered a small temple of Rameses II.

Holy Land Photo 105. Cairo Museum of Egyptian Antiquities. Still more of the numerous ushabti figures that followed Tutankhamun into the afterlife.

REFERENCES

Breasted, James H. *A History of Egypt*. New York: Scribner's, (1905) 1923.
Budge, E.A.W. *A History of Egypt: From the End of the Neolithic Period to the Death of Cleopatra VII. B.C.* Vol. I. *Egypt in the Neolithic and Archaic Periods*. New York: 1902.

QUINTESSENTIAL BOOK
"THE HOLY LAND"

Holy Land Ceramic Art 20. For all the Ankh has endured, a bruised companion may indeed be evidence of all the challenges posed to the sacred symbol.

Feden, Robin. *Egypt*: *Land of the Valley*. London: Michael Haag, (1977) 1986.
Campbell, David. *Egypt*. London: David Campbell Publishers, Ltd., (1994) 1996.
Wayne, Scott. *Egypt and the Sudan*. Berkeley, Calif.: Lonely Planet Publications, 1990.
Youssef, Hisham and John Rodenbeck. *Insight Guides*: *Egypt*. Hong Kong: APA Publications, 1995.

5. Post Site Lecture

The pyramid concept probably evolved from the natural pyramids we see formed by the wind against the rock and sand. The questions of origins of these structures are many but physical evidence leads to the south near Abu Simbel as the probable place. The earliest burials were sand pits. In the dry sand was natural mummification. Natural mummification may have led to the earliest belief in the afterlife. By 3100 B.C. burials were in the bedrock and adding a superstructure led

FREDERICK MONDERSON

to the mastaba concept.

Now, with a mastaba goods of the grave were added. Bedrock burials led to decay of the body. While there was natural mummification in the sand, the bedrock burials led to moisture and decay.

The nobility were buried in mastabas in the First and Second Dynasties. By the Third Dynasty, the mastaba began to be expanded upwards. Imhotep built his pharaoh Zoser's Step-Pyramid with 6 steps in decreasing size. This structure was indeed remarkable for its originality in that age.

Imhotep built the Step Pyramid at Sakkara in the IIIrd Dynasty for his Pharaoh Zoser. It had an enclosure wall with 24 doors - 1 real and 23 false. Temples were built in the enclosed Courtyard. There were representative building corresponding for the South and North. The Heb Sed Festival (Temple) Court and the Valley Temple were in this structure.

The Heb Sed Festival was a rejuvenation ceremony for the pharaoh who should die as soon as he got old or infirm. Of course, pretty soon some wise king figured out how to not be killed as he got old.

The Pharaoh was buried in the pyramid. He is shown on some illustrations in this structure, the first to have glazed tiles, doing some of the activities we associate with his Heb Sed festival. Zoser had 23 servants buried with him. This may be the only case of this practice. Most people wanted to be buried with their rulers in order to serve their king in the next life.

Zoser had 2 tombs and 2 burials. One in North Sakkara and one in South Sakkara. Most pharaohs of the Old Kingdom were buried in 2 places. One in the South and one in the North. Abydos was the burial place of kings of the First and Second Dynasties. They had cenotaphs or dummy tombs at Sakkara.

As the royal architect, Imhotep wanted to immortalize his king. He was also Zoser's Grand Vizier, the top administrative personnel in the kingdom. Imhotep was a physician, poet and astronomer. That is why they call him the world's first "multi genius." He was a maker of stone vessels. Later, Greeks deified him and associated him with their God Aesculapius mentioned in the Hippocratic Oath. Imhotep's tomb has not yet been found and many people, especially Zaki Hawass are still looking for it.

QUINTESSENTIAL BOOK
"THE HOLY LAND"

Holy Land Papyrus 33. Wearing the Blue Crown, Rameses II presents Ma'at (as his name) to enthroned Amon Ra wearing feathers.

After Zoser who ruled for 25 years, Snefru ruled for 37 years. He built the Bent Pyramid at Meydum and another Bent Pyramid at Dashur. His Red Pyramid is the closest thing to the true pyramid.

The Horus king Sekhemkhet built the "Lost Pyramid" discovered in 1955. It is the only one found intact.

The Meydum Bent Pyramid is probably the first attempt at a true pyramid. This pyramid had a mortuary temple nearby. In the XVIIIth Dynasty it was thought this was Snefru's pyramid. Snefru had two pyramids at Meydum and Dashur. The Dashur Pyramid was a second attempt at a true pyramid. The Meydum Pyramid collapsed. They changed the angel of the Dashur Pyramid. This then led to the Red Pyramid that is the first true pyramid and it is credited to Snefru.

6. Discussion

Emanuel Smith's "Egyptian Ideas of the Future Life" in *Biblical World* Vol. 19, (1902: 384-87) writes: "In regard to the realm of the dead there is a confusion of ideas and many inconsistencies, but there are three possibilities as to place: under the earth, in the sky, and on the earth: and we find inscriptional material referring to each as the abode of the dead. The rising and setting sun was a constant marvel to the Egyptians, and the phenomenon gave rise to the many solar myths. The Sun God is supposed to travel in a boat, on the celestial Nile by day, and returns through the Kingdom of darkness by night. In the Middle of the boat there is a cabin, in which the god, surrounded by his crew, keeps the heavenly court. Some myths represent him as having two boats, changing his place from one to the other at noon; others regard him as making such a change every hour. The journey ended in the west and then the boat floated back to the east. The journey of the Sun God was the symbol of man's life. The Sun God was born in the morning, grew old on his course, and died in the evening, rising on the morrow to new life again. Descriptions of the Sun-God's travels are found in the *Book of Am-Duat* and in the *Book of Gates*, in the Tombs of the kings of the Eighteenth to Twentieth Dynasties."

"Realm of the dead in the sky."

" ... the deceased person flew, there in the shape of a human-headed ba-bird. In heaven the souls partook of the joys of the gods and, strangely enough, proceeded to devour the gods, in order to acquire their excellencies."

"Before embalming the vital organs of the body, the lungs, the heart, the stomach, the intestines, and the brain, were removed. Thus, the body was fearfully mutilated."

"Threefold nature of man: The body, the Ka or the double and the ba or the soul."

Are there any questions?

Frederick Maloney: What was the purpose of magic in ancient Egypt?
Dr. Fred Monderson: Alan H. Gardiner's "Magic: Egyptian," in *Encyclopedia of*

QUINTESSENTIAL BOOK "THE HOLY LAND"

Religion and Ethics (1916, 8: 263) in explaining the purpose of magic stated: "In theory the domain of magic was as wide as men's desires themselves, magical art supplying all those things that were not procurable by simpler means. Our existing materials, which illustrate only a limited number of purposes, are probably very one-sided. The Egyptians believed, or feigned to believe, that their wizards could work all kinds of wonders; in a later tale a charm is made to bring the viceroy of Ethiopia up to Egypt, to the place where Pharaoh dwells, where he is to be beaten with five hundred blows of the sick, and returned to the land of Ethiopia again, 'all in six hours thither.' It is said to have been related at the court of Cheops how one magician fashioned a crocodile of wax that devoured an adulterer, and another parted the waters of a lake into which a jewel had accidentally fallen, and how a third cut off a goose's head and replaced it in a twinkling ...."

Holy Land Illustration 95. Bust of Khonsu, the Moon God, son of Amon-Ra and Mut of the Theban Triad (left); and Block statue of Senmut, architect of Queen Hatshepsut with his charge, the queen's daughter (right).

Hattie Jones: How many pyramids have texts and what is their purpose?
Dr. Fred Monderson: There are five pyramids with inscriptions beginning with Unas of the Vth Dynasty and the VIth Dynasty kings Teta, Pepy I, Meren-ra, and Pepy II had texts included in their tombs that modern scholars named "Pyramid Texts" because they were inscribed here.

FREDERICK MONDERSON

"The texts are, then, the oldest body of religious literature extant in the world, and a great deal of the material embodied in them carries us back to very much earlier times than their own sufficiently early date, referring to primitive customs and conditions of life which had long been extinct by the time of the Vth and VIth dynasties. The later versions show traces of editing, which has been undertaken in order to meet the new developments of religious thought arising in a period of 150 years. Broadly speaking, the object of these writings is to secure blessedness in the afterlife to the king on the walls of whose tomb they are inscribed; for there is as yet no trace of any idea that the immortality postulated of the Pharaoh may be also the property of the common people. The whole contents of the texts are directed towards the one purpose of securing entrance to the abodes of bliss for the dead king, and unification with the gods when his entrance is secured. These contents fall under the following divisions: (1) funeral ritual and ritual of mortuary offerings. (2) magical charms, (3) ancient ritual of worship, (4) ancient hymns, (5) fragments of ancient myths, (6) prayers on behalf of the king."

Stephaniea Mc Call: Why was there a conflict between Ra and Osiris worship?
Dr. Fred Monderson: Myers tells us: "The earliest form of belief represented in the text is solar; the deceased is constantly identified with Ra, and the Osiris belief I referred to in terms which show that it was held to be incompatible with, or even hostile to, the solar form. Certain prayers are designed to protect the pyramid and its temple against the intrusion of Osiris; and other passages show that 'to the devotee of the Solar faith, Osiris once represented the realm and the dominion of death, to which the follower of Ra was not delivered up.' Gradually, however, and as the texts show, even within the Pyramid Age, the Osiris faith began to assert its power and to appropriate part of the place, which the solar religion had formerly, occupied."

Michael Montout: What is the connection between the Pyramid Text and Book of the Dead?
Dr. Fred Monderson: The "Book of the Dead" is a continuation of the Old Kingdom "Pyramid Texts" with the "Coffin Texts" of the Middle Kingdom pivotal in the transition of the mortuary literature from one period to another. In fact, the proper name of these documents is "The Chapters of Pert em Hru" or "The Coming Forth by Day" (or 'Ascending by Day').

The "Pyramid Texts" are written on walls of the pyramids of the Old Kingdom; the "Coffin Texts" are written on the inside and outside of coffins in the Middle Kingdom; and the "Book of the Dead," reduced to a more portable form gained prominence in the New Kingdom. The first is continued by the second and elaborated by the third.

Peter Monderson: Was Min really created to replace the missing penis of Osiris?

QUINTESSENTIAL BOOK
"THE HOLY LAND"

Dr. Fred Monderson: Heavens no! Min was an ancient god representing fertility and had nothing to do with Osiris' phallus. Min was a fertility god who became the alter ego of Amon in the Middle and New Kingdoms. However, Min is the earliest image of a god and found in the Eastern Desert of Upper Egypt. While these were petrographs engraved on the walls of the elevated rest areas of the highlands. On the other hand, Petrie found his earliest statues at Coptos, painted black, that now reside in the Ashmolean Museum in Oxford. It's interesting that Min enjoyed prominence before Amon and thus Amon incorporated Min's attributes. The ramifications of this behavior are enormous. Imagine, that is, if we accept the "Caucasian Egypt" theory; A "White God" accepting the attributes of a "Black God" who was there before him? Then again, why would "Caucasian Egyptians" be worshipping Black Gods such as Min, Ra, Ptah, Hathor, Isis, etc.?

Marilyn James: Did brothers and sisters marry and what was the result?
Dr. Fred Monderson: Yes there was brother and sister marriage but this was not for everyone. The royal family practiced it and perhaps there were a few well off individuals who also did but for the most part the populace did not so engage. There was some justification for this practice as there was divine precedence in the marriage of Isis and Osiris and Seth and Nephthys.

F. Ll. Griffith's "Marriage: Egyptian," in *Encyclopedia of Religion and Ethics* (1916, 8: 444) reports: "The divine example of Osiris and Isis may have had special force at that period. In the First Story of Sethos Khamwese (Ptolemaic period), the ancient Pharaoh's argument about his son Nefer-keptah and his daughter Ahure seems to be that it would be impolitic, when there were only two children in the royal family, to risk the succession by marrying them together. His preference, following a family custom, would be to marry them to a son and a daughter of two of his generals in order to enlarge his family. At a banquet he questioned Ahure, and was won over by her wishes to the other plan; thereupon he commanded his chief steward to take the princess to her brother's house that same night with all necessary things; Pharaoh's whole household gave her presents, and Neferkeptah made a 'good day' and entertained them all on the marriage eve. This is the only account that we possess of an Egyptian betrothal or marriage that is not of the fairy-tale order, and it is noticeable that there is no mention in it of the writing of a contract, perhaps because this marriage was an affair within the family."

Regina Hendricks: How did the people come up with the earliest forms or symbols of power as represented by the various gods?
Dr. Fred Monderson: We must first go beyond the great magnificence we see at Luxor on both sides of the river. We must go back very early in the beginnings of the concept of the gods.

Adolf Erman (1907: 5-6) puts it best in explaining what he calls the outward form of their religion. Very early in their religious awakening and technical growth: "The people had already learnt to carve rough figures of gods either in human or animal form, and those they chose to distinguish by a variety of crowns, but as yet their imagination did not go beyond diadems formed either of handfuls of reeds, the horns of sheep or cows, or of ostrich feathers. For a scepter, their gods carried a staff such as every Bedouin cuts for himself at the present day, and their goddesses were contented with a simple reed. Their temples were mere huts with walls of plaited wickerwork, the front of the roof was adorned with projecting wooden beams. A few short posts and two high masts in front of the building were added to provide further decoration? The altar consisted of a reed mat, and for the celebration of festivals simple bowers were erected."

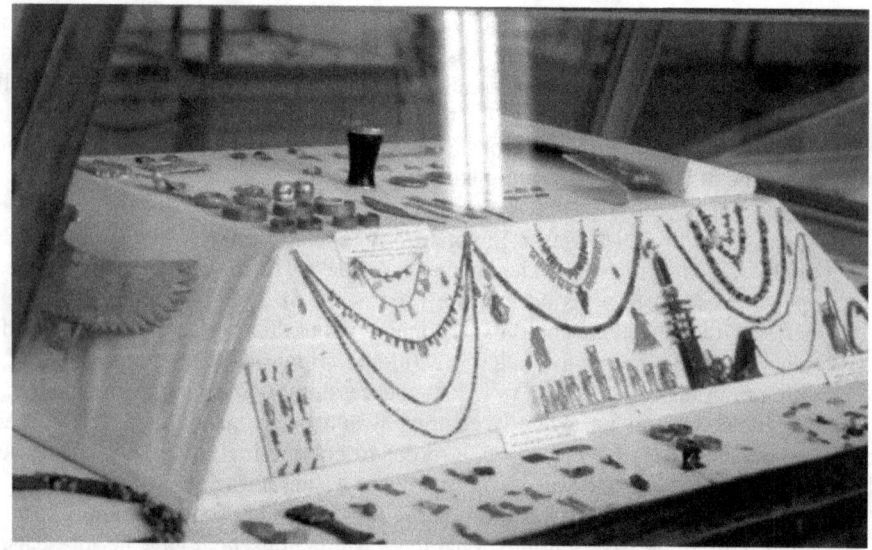

Holy Land Photo 106. Cairo Museum of Egyptian Antiquities. Gold and precious stone jewelry housed in this wonderful building.

Cherise Maloney: In their march to civilization, how did they settle on their cosmogony?
Dr. Fred Monderson: That gradual process called civilization blends different talents of its citizens and produces an ordered system that forms the great society. Erman (1907: 24) is of the view: "In its youth a nation may well be satisfied with worshipping the gods which it believes it sees on earth, and with winning their favor by means of offerings and prayers, but a mature nation becomes more intimately acquainted with the deity, and the more intimate it becomes, the more it discards the notion of his unapproachable majesty. Then it is that imagination

QUINTESSENTIAL BOOK
"THE HOLY LAND"

begins its work, and the divine is represented more and more as human deities that appear to resemble each other, or that are worshipped in the same locality, are grouped together into one family; the preferences or hatreds of gods for each other become known; the manner in which the world originated becomes clearly defined, and also the order in which the gods reigned."

Joshua Monderson: Not much has been said about the various myths of the Egyptians regarding the creation of the world and everything else? What can you tell us of religious beliefs of the early period?
Dr. Fred Monderson: There are different creation myths from different parts of the country. By the Old Kingdom attempts were made to synchronize the gods in a system but only the well-liked ones seemed to go beyond this period. We know of the principal places of worship as Heliopolis, Memphis, Abydos, and Thebes and there were other places as in Nubia.

One creation story begins in a manner as Erman (1907: 25-26) explains: "In the beginning only chaos existed, Nun, the primeval waters. Out of this in some way or other the sun god was created. He came into being *while as yet there was no heaven, when neither serpent nor reptile was formed, He came into being in the form of Khepre, and there was nothing that was with him in that place where he was ... resting in the waters of nun, and he found no place where he could stand.* Then the god bethought himself in his heart create other beings, and he begat of himself and spat it out. And what he spat out was the god Shu, and the goddess Tefnut, those two beings who according to Egyptian belief supported the heavens. Shu and Tefnut then produced Keb and Nut, the earth god and sky goddess, and Keb and Nut produced Osiris, Set, Isis, and Nephthys, *whose children are many on this earth.*

Michael Sinclair: When we saw Tutankhamon coming out of the lotus, is this an aspect of creation in process?
Dr. Fred Monderson: Yes. This may be in the water. There are a number of water versions of this myth of creation. Erman (1907: 26-27) offers that the young sun god is born out of the lotus blossom. "According to some a lotus flower sprang out of the primeval waters on which sat the young sun god as a child. In Eshmunen, however, tradition told of a mound in the waters of Desdes, and of an egg laid in a nest there, from which the sun god was hatched in the same way as the waterfowl of the Egyptian marshes. Eight primeval beings in the forms of frogs and serpents took some part in this event, and a cow (which must be connected with the celestial cow) was also present; the young god seated himself on her back, and swam across the water. Abydos boasted a birthplace of the sun, and Thebes also prided herself later on possessing the magnificent primeval mound. In Abydos the gods who issued from the mouth of Re himself were not Shu and Tefnut, but Shu and the frog goddess Hekt, *the progenitors of the gods.*

FREDERICK MONDERSON

Teddy Cubia: Why did the kings vie to build such luxury monuments to the gods of Egypt?

Dr. Fred Monderson: This is an interesting question. They were tremendously religious. The gods favored them so they built in praise of their gods. I think Erman (1907: 52) offers a good explanation as to how this worked. He says: "From the very first the rulers of Egypt considered themselves bound to present gifts to the more important temples of their dominions, and to provide for their building; this was for them a natural obligation. Furthermore it became the custom, if any temple which had been richly endowed by a king, to implore the blessing of the gods upon him before all others, while the temple inscriptions and scenes served as a perpetual reminder of him. But, strangely enough, over thousands of years the fiction arose that every temple was built exclusively by the king and was also supported by him, so that all that was contributed by the devout citizens and the revenues belonging to the temple, were entirely ignored. This continued throughout all periods, and even the Greek kings and Roman emperors were pleased to figure as the builders of all the temples that arose during their reigns."

Calif. Sister: I suppose then, I should ask that you explain what the term a "Greek or Roman temple" means?

Dr. Fred Monderson: Even though the Greeks and Romans conquered Egypt and set up their own administration, they sought to leave the religious aspects of the state in the hands of the priesthood. This nevertheless, they tried to get as much from the aura and majesty of the culture. They encouraged building in hope the gods would favor them. One slight misunderstanding here is that the priest architects still built the temples on Egyptian plans even though the foreign rulers wanted their persons to feature prominently in the inscriptions that decorated theses place. Therefore, while it may be called a "Greek" or "Roman" temple, as Kom Ombo, Edfu, Philae, Esneh, and so on, they were built by Egyptian and Nubian builders and administrators, along the plans of ancient times. However, foreign influence allowed them to be deluged with inscriptions of the ritual, which in a number of ways was a good thing. This helped to preserve some of what they did in the temples for posterity.

Marilyn James: I know you discussed the Priesthood before, but did you say the profession was hereditary?

Dr. Fred Monderson: Well, in a way, most professions were hereditary, in that the father passed it down to the son. Priestships came from many streams. The Pharaoh himself appointed whom he wanted to the priesthood. However, the "Bureaucracy" can be considered hereditary in their different orders. Erman (1907:

QUINTESSENTIAL BOOK "THE HOLY LAND"

53) in explaining some early religious customs has written: "The natural relationship imposed on the more important families by the charge of a sanctuary which had existed in their town since the memory of man, prevailed in Egypt in the earliest times, and again in the Middle Kingdom we find in the greater temples that the priesthood remained in certain families whose members generally adopted it as a secondary profession. And here we speedily arrive at another development; certain priest's orders are connected to certain professions. Thus the high judicial functionaries of the Old Kingdom are at the same time priests of the goddess of truth, the physicians are priests of Sekhmet, the great artists are priests of Ptah."

Rev. Dr. McNair: What is the function of the High Priest?
Dr. Fred Monderson: Well, the Pharaoh is the first High Priest. However, since he could not be in every temple he had to appoint a High Priest for the various gods' worship. Therefore, each temple had a high priest, and we see high priests across the nation. In the principal centers, viz., Heliopolis, Memphis, Abydos, Karnak, that sect's high priest oversaw that cult's ceremonies and rituals wherever in the country, a shrine or place of worship was set up for that divinity. Erman (1907: 53) writes: "At the head of every temple was a high-priest who acted as *overseer of all the sacred offices*, he is *initiated into divine books and divine things* and *gives directions to the priests as regulating* the festivals. He has *a loud voice when he praises the god* and *a pure hand when he brings flowers and offers water and food upon the altar*. The administration of the temple property is incumbent on him, and in war he has also to command the contingent provided by his temple."

Erman (1907: 53) explained further: "In the great sanctuaries these high priests frequently bore special antiquated titles. Thus at Heliopolis the high-priest was called "He who is great in beholding," perhaps because he could behold at pleasure the beauty of his lord, i.e., the statue of the god; while at Eshmunen he was "great of the five." At Memphis, where Ptah the god of artificers was worshipped, the title of the high-priest was the "chief of the artificers," and in the Old Kingdom he held the position of "superintendent of sculpture," and all such artistic work; it appears that originally this combination of spiritual and worldly offices was shared by two persons, but toward the end of the Old Kingdom the king transferred every divine affair, and every duty that was in charge of the two high-priests, to Teti-Sabu, because his majesty trusted him especially."

Walter Brown: How was the temple staffed?
Dr. Fred Monderson: Erman (1907: 55) tells of papyri in Berlin that shed light on the early priesthood. "In addition to eight minor officials the permanent staff of the temple consisted only of the prince and superintendent of the temple (i.e., the high-priest) and the chief Kherheb, who were thus the administrators of the temple property and the directors of the ceremonies; nine other priests took regular

turns there; a superintendent of classes, a temple scribe, an ordinary Kher heb, etc., and each time one of these classes entered on their duties, they took over the sanctuary and all its contents from the outgoing class, and relieved them of their charge."

Michelliea Georges: Who inherited property in the family?
Dr. Fred Monderson: The pre-eminence of the eldest son, which has been definitely proved for the whole of the last period of history, from Amasis onwards, is supposed, and not without reason, to have existed from the earliest times or at least from the time of the Kahun papyri. "Revillout and Maspero have shown that this peculiarity of Egyptian law persisted in modern Egypt, especially Coptic families, until the introduction of the civil law emanating from Europe. Later, in the time of Nepherites, we find that the shares to be inherited are regulated by the father, who deals exclusively with his eldest son. He, in his turn, has to settle the claims of his younger brothers and sisters. It is he that administers the hereditary domain for the common good. He is responsible for the dividing of the revenue, as his father's will has decreed, into the shares due to his brothers and sisters and the usufruct instituted for his mother's benefit, whether by will, marriage contract, or act registered during wedlock, before or after the birth of the children. The eldest, as representing his mother, brothers, and sisters, is legally bound to defend their inheritance against strangers. He acts as *nib*, or 'master.' Revillout's opinion is that he had even the right to prevent the family property from being disposed of by his father, administered the estate, pleaded in the law courts, and been generally responsible for the family estate to each of his brothers and sisters and other members of the family, including his mother, his aunts, and any children who were still minors. At his death the inheritance passed to the second oldest son, who must observe the clauses regarding usufruct for the benefit of the testator's wife, which he accepted as biding by registered act. The share to which the eldest was entitled does not seem to have been in any way larger than that given to the rest and the principle of equal shares seems to have been the rule down to the Ptolemaic period, when a law was made entitling the eldest to a larger share than his co-heirs."

Day 13. The Pyramids of Ghizeh and the Perfume Factory
1. Wake Up

Esperanza Rodriguez: Good Morning, Mi Amor. Your schedule today calls for the Pyramids of Ghizeh and the Perfume Factory.

QUINTESSENTIAL BOOK "THE HOLY LAND"

Your "Black Brooklyn" article is copied and ready for distribution to the group.
Dr. Fred Monderson: Thank you, Ms. Rodriguez. Your assistance is so invaluable.

BLACK EGYPT AND THE STRUGGLE FOR INCLUSION

By
Dr. Frederick Monderson

Recently Hollywood has again imprinted upon the minds of young people with their films on Egypt, which include *The Mummy*, *The Mummy Returns*, *The Scorpion King* as well as the Disney productions of *Prince of Egypt* and also *Tarzan*, which did not have any Africans in it. In olden times the *Ten Commandments*, *The Mummy* and several versions of *Cleopatra*, to name a few, have left indelible impressions on the mind's images regarding the people of Egypt. Equally too, *National Geographic* Magazine has done extensive writings on Egypt. More importantly, however, seeing these movies and reading *National Geographic* Magazine will not tell our people the ancient Egyptians were Black. Many of the books, particularly those written by European and European-American writers today are so sanitized they give no inclination that the Egyptians were Black people in North-East Africa along the banks of the River Nile.

For my Egyptian enlightenment I am indebted to Dr. ben-Jochannan, who in his scholarly admonition reminded me to "Get the oldest materials and work from there," when doing research. This is because of the need for a reference point in view of modern Egyptological teachings and interpretations. Importantly however, many new books are so devoid of constructive reference to the role of Black people in Egypt, there is need for vigorous re-writing, or certainly critical analysis of their content. None of these books purposely propagate the fact of Queen Aahmes-Nefertari's blackness, despite her portrait in the British Museum that depicts a "coal-black Ethiopian" wearing the fashion of the times, red, white and blue, 1500 years Before Christ and 3500 years ago. This Black queen is the ancestress of the 18th Dynasty. She was deified and worshipped with her son Amenhotep I, in their own temple at Thebes, on the West Bank as patrons of the mortuary area. His son, Thutmose I is father of Queen Hatshepsut who ruled as pharaoh. When challenged for being an "uppity woman" who ruled as pharaoh, underscored her relationship to Aahmes-Nefertari the Black Queen and Goddess.

FREDERICK MONDERSON

The modern historical record is replete with distortions and omissions. In 1903 the temple and tomb of Mentuhotep II, founder of the 11th Dynasty and the Middle Kingdom, was found at Deir el Bahari, Thebes. In it they found King Mentuhotep dressed in Heb Sed festival garment wearing the Red Crown as symbolic of King of Lower Egypt. The assumption is that there was another statue with the king wearing the White Crown as King of Upper Egypt. However, what was significant for the ethnicity of this monarch is he was painted black. This surviving statue was then moved to the Museum of Egyptian Antiquities in Cairo, where it still rests. Importantly, while this temple was described in the major archaeological and news media as being the only Middle Kingdom temple and the oldest temple at Thebes discovered, no one or anything was said about the king's color. It was 1959; 56 years later, when W. Stephenson Smith of the Boston Museum of Fine Arts in his *Art and Architecture of Ancient Egypt* did say Mentuhotep had "black flesh."

In 1922, one hundred years after the decipherment of Hieroglyphics, Howard Carter discovered the intact tomb of King Tutankhamon, the boy king. There was such a great stir about this fabulous find, because of the wonderful treasures contained in his tomb. Still, two life-like wooden statues of the king were painted "black and stood guard" over the burial chamber. These are at the entrance to the Hall of Tutankhamon in the Cairo Museum. People by-pass them unnoticeably in their hurry to view the wonderful treasures he carried to the next life. In 1978-79, the King Tut exhibition toured the United States and the symbol of that display was an alabaster bust of the boy king. Alabaster is a white marble-like material. How appropriate to show this picture or image of the young African Pharaoh. No one would suspect. All the major cultural institutions in the United States accepted the bust as symbolic of the king's representation. I don't think there was any objection, except perhaps by knowledgeable African-Americans who understood the distortion and fraud being perpetuated. However and interestingly enough, it is an Afrocentric belief it was a fraud being perpetuated against the general public who were forced to accept a distorted view.

It is my opinion and belief that the true color representation of kingly persons can only be viewed in wooden statues. These statues are the only ones painted, while others of stone or metal reflect the color of the material being used. This is significant because inasmuch as so little artifacts have survived and then the need to understand what may possibly have been destroyed for their *de-facto* link to Black ethnicity of the Egyptians, everything is suspect. In a multitude of ways, there are those who would say that we must not forget that the remains of ancient Africa are scattered throughout the capitals of Western Europe, Canada, the United States and Australia. As such then, there is so much "culture in captivity."

In his *Destruction of Black Civilization: Great Issues of a Race 4500 B.C. to 2000 A.D.*, Chancellor Williams wrote about the record being distorted to show that

QUINTESSENTIAL BOOK
"THE HOLY LAND"

despite Dynasties beginning with Black founders they end up being pictured as white. This is particularly true of the 18th Dynasty. There is a statue of Seti I in the British Museum that is made of wood. Even the untrained eye could detect this statue of the son of Rameses I, the founder of the 19th Dynasty, seemed willing to depict a Black pharaoh. There is a considered belief many such pieces are "doctored" in the "basements" of institutions willing to be in complicity with this historical distortion. Perpetuating such a fraud is to deny Rameses II, "the Great" would be Black and so too the 19th Dynasty. Which brings us to the 20th Dynasty and last but not least the 25th Dynasty.

There is talk that Egypt is building the world's largest museum to house some of its wonderful collection. Many things could be displaced, misplaced or certainly replaced. However, there is one case in the Cairo Museum, on the second floor where wooden statues are housed. Here there are small wooden statues of pharaohs painted Black alongside a particular statue of a leopard also painted black. Now, if there is no connection between these wooden pieces it is hard to fathom. However, there is a question of whether they will be placed again in such close proximity when the new museum is opened.

In the 19th century several European explorers visited and reported from all over Egypt and these appeared in some of the credible journals or newspapers of that age. An issue of the *Academy* in the 1880s mentions the discovery of a tomb of an official of King Thutmose I of the 18th Dynasty. Here the official is pictured in his tomb praying to a statue of Thutmose I, painted Black. This is lost to history and despite the numerous books being written today none contain any reference to this. Are we to believe the numbers of scholars are ignorant of this reference? How credible are they then? What has happened to it? Such statues or paintings reinforce the blackness of the 18th Dynasty. In this *The African Origin of Civilization: Myth or Reality* and *Civilization or Barbarism: An Authentic Anthropology* has shown how Egypt has been falsely represented. Underscoring the intellectual professionalism Diop brought to his studies, Cleggs' "Black Rulers of the Golden Age" in Van Sertima's *Nile Valley Civilizations* has showed us Dr. Diop relied on: "anthropology, iconography, melanin dosage tests, osteological measurements, blood groupings, the testimony of classical writers, self-descriptive Egyptian hieroglyphs, divine epithets, Biblical eyewitnesses, linguistic and various cultural data in support of his opinion regarding the ethnicity of the ancient Egyptians." In fact, Diop shows that the ancient gods and goddesses Apis, Min, Thoth, Isis, Hathor, and Horus were all Black. So too was Amon the great god of Thebes during the Middle and New Empires. Equally too, in *The African Origins*, Diop quotes Herodotus that in Egypt the "Natives are black with the heat." Even further, regarding the Greek oracle at Adelphi, Herodotus said: "By calling the dove black they [the Dodonaceans] indicated that the woman was Egyptian." Diop further said Strabo wrote "Egypt founded Ethiopia" and that Diodorus noted "Ethiopia founded Egypt." Either way we are dealing with the same people, with

FREDERICK MONDERSON

the same cultural roots.

Even further, elsewhere in his *Physiognomonica*, Aristotle, in his search for the mean wrote: "Egyptians are cowards because they are black." So too were northern Europeans who were "white." The Greeks are the mean in between. Aristotle was wrong about their courage but right about their color.

If we start with the ancient scholars, historians and priests, Herodotus, Manetho, Diodorus Siculus, Strabo, and even Aristotle and Lucan, all agree the ancient Egyptians were black. Herodotus said the "Colchians, Ethiopians and Egyptians" were essentially Negroes with "broad noses, thick lips, wooly hair and had burnt" or black skin.

Even more, when we look at the works of such brilliant scholars as Cheikh Anta Diop, the Senegalese "Pharaoh," who wrote *The African Origin of Civilization: Myth or Reality, Civilization or Barbarism: An Authentic Anthropology, The Cultural Unity of Black Africa*; Theophile Obenga's *Ancient Egypt and Black Africa* and Ivan Van Sertima's *Egypt Child of Africa, Egypt Revisited, and Nile Valley Civilizations*; then Yosef ben-Jochannan's *Black Man of the Nile and his Family, Africa: Mother of Western Civilization, African Origins of the Major Western Religions*, and *Abu Simbel to Ghizeh: A Manual and Guide Book*; and Fred Monderson's *10 Poems Praising Great Blacks for Mike Tyson and Seven Letters to Mike Tyson on Ancient Egyptian Temples, Where Are the Kamite Kings* and *Research Essays on Ancient Egypt*, the reader gets the full dimension of the issues, problems and solutions.

Therefore, the work of reclamation and rectification of Africa and African roles in ancient Egypt must continually be stressed for the young should never allow their history to be systematically and continually distorted. They must continue to assert and defend Egypt as African. Not because the valuable antiquities of this wonderful heritage are in captivity in western collections and museums, must we acquiesce in the pernicious and false position that there is no history of Africa, only a history of Europeans in Africa. Africa has a long, rich and culturally diverse and enlightening history. Mother Africa first spoke through Ethiopia, the Nile Valley and Egypt. We must continue to affirm that Egypt was Black civilization, it was peopled by Black Africans for most of its duration and trust the work of our redemptive Black scholars, researchers and historians who for many years in their careers have grappled with the questions of distortions and omissions and now have given us the tools to continue the fight for African historiographic reconstruction. Diop said the history of Africa cannot be fully told without the inclusion of Egypt. The African scholar who refuses to deal with Egypt is either a neurotic or ill-educated. We must teach and defend Egypt as African and therefore Black. Egypt was a Black civilization!

QUINTESSENTIAL BOOK
"THE HOLY LAND"

Holy Land Photo 107. Kashida Maloney of Brooklyn, New York stands beside two lifelike statues of Tutankhamun at a store near the Cairo Museum.

2.   Breakfast

Dr. Leonard James: Queen Hatshepsut ruled Egypt for two decades at a time it was unthinkable for a woman to head a major nation in the ancient world. In challenging male dominance to rule as pharaoh she had to contend with priestly and rival opposition as well as the perception that a woman's role is supportive and not leading the nation's direction. The American Egyptologist J.H. Breasted called this period, the "feud of the Thutmosids." In this, Hatshepsut found herself embroiled in a controversy involving Thutmose I, her father; Thutmose II, her husband; and Thutmose III, her nephew, some say brother, rival heir and successor.

Her father, Thutmose I was a vigorous and wise ruler with family ties to the expellers of the Hyksos and founders of the XVIIIth Dynasty of Black rulers. Up in age and realizing Thutmose II would be a weak ruler, he married him to his sister Hatshepsut, hoping they would co-rule. Then he assembled the nobles of the land, emphasizing his choice of Hatshepsut and extolling them, those who followed her rule and supported her would be favored. Those who did not would

FREDERICK MONDERSON

be held in disfavor.

In preparing her for the new role the old king had schooled his daughter in administrative practices and procedures as a co-ruler. He took her around the country for purposes of familiarity and recognition. Then he aligned her with some of his faithful followers, one of whom was Senmut and his party of loyalists. In order to justify her rule the queen undertook civil and religious architectural projects. She repaired temples destroyed or lay in disrepair during the Hyksos rule. She built herself a tomb in the Valley of the Queens and once in control of the reins of power she built another tomb in the Valley of the Kings; this was unthinkable! Her architect Senmut built her mortuary temple at Deir el Bahari, conceiving of a ceremony to internment in the tomb. He began the rebuilding of the Temple of Mut, goddess of the Theban Triad. Repairs and additions were done at Karnak Temple of Amon as well as two obelisks quarried at Aswan and erected before the Sanctuary. A pylon at Karnak, a Kiosk to the Theban Triad, Amon, Mut and Khonsu at Luxor Temple, later usurped by Thutmose III, a gate at Medinet Habu, were all part of the scheme to justify her rule.

Perhaps the earliest justification for divine intervention, the Queen denied Thutmose I was her father. She claimed in the inscriptions Amon had visited her mother in a flash of perfume and divinely conceived her. This endowed her with 12 kas or souls and the principal gods and goddesses were in attendance at her birth. Pretty soon the house of cards fell. Senmut and his people could not stop the scheming of Thutmose III who, with the complicity of Amon's priesthood deposed the queen. Little is known of her demise and end. Her works were attacked, her name erased and those who tied their fate to her were dealt with. When all is said, Hatshepsut was a daring, able and astute ruler who led an African nation at a time when such a feat was unthinkable.

Walter Brown: Well done, Dr. James.

QUINTESSENTIAL BOOK
"THE HOLY LAND"

Holy Land Papyrus 34. As Ra-Horakhty sits enthroned, Anubis adjusts the scale of judgment, Thoth records and the deceased observes his fate being determined.

3. Bus Ride

Today we will visit the Pyramids of Ghizeh and the Sphinx. These monoliths characterize the timelessness of Egyptian technology and building practice. While we are familiar with the great pyramids but there are also smaller pyramids thought to be designed for the female members of this kings who built these larger structures. There is also the Boat Museum housing a reconstituted boat of Khufu found in 1954 and reassembled. We will be able to go by bus to a site to be able have a scenic view of the pyramids. That is, we will be able to see all three of the great pyramids in a single view. There is also an opportunity to get on a camel for a photograph with the pyramid far into the background. After that we will visit one of the perfume factories where you can purchase an extract or essence of the perfume of your choice.

4. Site:

Ghizeh Pyramids – constructed during the 4th Dynasty are characteristic of the early and enduring architecture of ancient Egypt.

Khufu – built the great pyramid Herodotus says took 20 years in construction, employing 100,000 persons. Recent researches found the village of workers who built these imposing structures.

Khafre – built the second pyramid. Some scholars say the Sphinx has his features, while others think he only did repairs to it.

Menkaure – built the smallest of the three Great Pyramids. He is the third in a trio of father, son and grandson.

The Sphinx – is the enduring face of Egypt. Legend has it that Thutmose IV fell asleep in the shadows of the Sphinx and, in a dream; it told him to clear the sand encompassing it and he would be king. This he did and once king, he erected the Stele of the Sphinx recounting these events.

The Temple of the Sphinx – is an early form of religious structure used in the worship of the colossal. Its architecture is certainly timeless and represents an early form of religious architecture.

Shopping: The Khalili bazaar is a street location, several blocks long where the buses will deliver you for a three hour stroll and shopping spree. Bargain for everything so as not to pay ridiculous prices.

Perfume Factory – You can purchase some of the sweet smelling stuff or simply go along for the ride.

5. Post Site Lecture

Because of their gigantic size the Pyramids seem to epitomize Egypt, but as you have seen, the temples and tombs as well as the terrain have their place too. As noted, there were three great pyramids built by Khufu, Khafre and Menkaure. The Greeks called these rulers Cheops, Chephren and Mycerinus. I notice some effort to revert to the ancient names or to give both the Greek, and in persons, an Egyptian name. We must thank Dr. ben-Jochannan for popularizing early use of the indigenous names of Egypt in the academic community.

Earlier we spoke of art and you have a sense of the art of architecture and of decoration. The pyramids are art of gigantic proportions and exactitude. We wonder, despite what Herodotus told us, of how many men, one hundred thousand who worked on the great pyramid, how many died. We have evidence of mobile hospitals or perhaps we could use the word clinics that were set up to treat the wounded on the job. For sure, some of Imhotep's medical methodology were used

QUINTESSENTIAL BOOK
"THE HOLY LAND"

to treat those who got hurt on the job. It is not an easy thing to create something as big as the pyramids that can withstand the ravages of time. A popular refrain has been: 'Man is afraid of time but time is afraid of the pyramids.' Theophile Gautier (1811-1872) tells us: "Everything passes. Robust art alone is eternal. The bust outlasts the citadel." On the other hand, Andre Gide (1869-1951) pointed out: "Art begins with resistance - at the point where resistance is overcome. No human masterpiece has ever been created without great labor." Further, T.S. Eliot opined: "The progress of an artist is a continual self-sacrifice, a continual extinction of personality."

Now, a pyramid is a complex with other building besides the king's pyramid. As you saw today, there were smaller pyramids on that plateau. In fact, there are 82 pyramids along the banks of the Nile River.

The Great Pyramid was built by Khufu and stands at a height of 442 feet high. The base is a square and not a triangle. It has four sides and sits on 13 ½ acres. Two and a half million blocks of stone, some averaging 5 tons each, were assembled here. The blocks were put together without mortar, which is a later invention. There is no mortar between the blocks of stone. The structure is build on bedrock and not on sand. This gives a solid base. The sand does not.

Herodotus who visited Egypt around 450 B.C. gives the earliest description of the European visitors. He said it took 20 years with 100,000 men working 3 months at a time. During the Inundation period maybe 100,000 men were available since there was no work, but at other times they have been perhaps 20,000 men employed in year round work.

Limestone was quarried year round and moved to the site of construction. There are 2 theories about the construction. One is the corkscrew method of roads around the pyramid and the ramps made of mud brick. This latter seems more plausible. The Great Pyramid is not a solid structure. The Pharaoh was not buried in the pyramid.

At the base there is a well to the bedrock. The entrance was not concealed. The pyramid was robbed around 2200 B.C. The entrance was found in the 9th century of our era. There are granite plugs stored in the Grand Gallery to plug the entrance to the Burial Chamber. A pink sarcophagus was found inside. There are small chambers above the burial chamber. Khufu possibly had another burial at Abydos but this pyramid was a cenotaph. There was possibly an underground burial intended. First the Queen's Chamber and the move to the Burial Chamber.

You should know the "Battle of the Pyramids" with Napoleon did not take place at the Pyramids.

FREDERICK MONDERSON

Khafre built the second great pyramid. He like others had two temples. The first is the Mortuary Temple and the second is the Valley Temple.

In summary then, the Pyramid Complex had the following parts to it:

An Enclosure Wall.
A Valley Temple where mummification took place.
A Causeway or road that brought the body into the complex.
A Mortuary Temple where rites for the deceased were performed.
Chapels.
The Heb Sed Festival Chapel in a Heb sed Court.
Possibly a Colonnade of columns in a Hypostyle Hall.
An Obelisk.
A Sphinx.
Magazines for Storage.
Dummy Buildings representing the north and south.
Boat Pits contained boats. A 150-foot boat was buried next to the pyramid of Khufu. It was disassembled and designed to take the pharaoh into the next world. One such boat was reassembled and now is featured in the Boat Museum next to the Pyramid. There were nine boats, evidenced by nine boat pits buried near Khufu's Great Pyramid.
Subsidiary pyramids were built for queens.
The Pharaoh's Pyramid was the most imposing structure in the complex.
The God's Temple stood nearby.
There were Mastaba tombs nearby for Nobles who wanted to be buried in the shadow of the Great Pyramid.

Shepsekaf was the last king of the Fourth Dynasty. He did not build a pyramid but a mastaba tomb. His name did not contain Ra. This may signify the decline of Ra as principal god. From the valley and mortuary temple concept they moved to a mastaba and an obelisk which gave birth to the Ben Ben idea.

By the Fifth Dynasty, sun temples appear at Abu Ghorab and Unas' at Sakkara. Unas' pyramid was the first with texts of a religious nature. The step and other pyramids had no inscriptions on their walls. Unas started the tradition of the "Pyramid Texts." In most books you read about Egypt, the pyramids and hieroglyphics.

The "Pyramid Texts" are magical texts. Unas, Teti I, Teti II, Merenre, Pepi I, and Pepi II all decorated their pyramids with texts. There is no coherency to the texts. They make no connection. Each line represents a single text.

We have identified three stages in the texts. The first is protection in the tomb.

QUINTESSENTIAL BOOK "THE HOLY LAND"

The deceased has to make sure his body is intact and remain in the tomb. Second, the Journey to the Next World. In the journey to the next world Unas is guided on his "Journey to the Next World." Third, acceptance in the next world. Osiris greets Unas. Unas become one with the gods. There were some pyramid texts of the Sixth Dynasty. However, by the time of this reign, the Old Kingdom came crashing down.

There are several theories for decline of the Old Kingdom. One holds the end of pyramid building led to end of the Old Kingdom and the other says the end of the Old Kingdom led to end of pyramid building. Really, Pepi II's age led to the decline of the Old Kingdom. He reigned for 94 years and the nobles increased their power at the royal expense.

The Loeb Classical Library on Manetho mentions there were 70 kings in 70 days during the First Intermediate Period lasting from 2180 to 2134 B.C.

The Pharaohs had pyramid texts, etc., in their tombs. The nobles and commoners had scenes of daily life in their tombs. The *Pyramid Texts* of the Old Kingdom became the *Coffin Texts* of the Middle Kingdom, which became the *Book of the Dead* texts in the New Kingdom.

Holy Land Ceramic Art 21. The "Eye of Horus" has always had a message, "We're watching you!"

FREDERICK MONDERSON

6. Discussion
Are there any questions?

Cosmos Palmer: Why did they build those pyramids?
Dr. Fred Monderson: The pyramids were national monuments. In this undertaking, it is believed there were no or few slaves. Slave labor is not efficient. Essentially, the government levied people during the fallow season when the river was high. Many scholars believe the pharaohs wanted to awe their contemporaries, harness the unemployed masses of an agricultural society laid idle by the inundation to build a lasting monument. Those pharaohs were true patrons of the arts. Johann Wolfgang Von Goethe (1749-1842) ordered: "Artist create! Do not talk." This is what the pharaohs did. Even further Goethe continued: "I call architecture frozen music" and that in viewing architecture: "Three things are to be looked to in a building: that it stands on the right spot; that it be securely founded; that it be successfully executed."

James Madison: Herodotus did say Khufu was mean to his workers.
Dr. Fred Monderson: Sometimes you have to be a hard taskmaster to get something done especially something as massive as the pyramids. The proof of the pudding is in the eating. His work stands to this day. That is what is most important. His success! Leo Nikolayevich Tolstoy (1828-1910) in answering the question: "What is art?" said: "Art is human activity having for its purpose, the transmission to others of the highest and best feelings to which men have risen." Even further, Publius Virgilius Maro or Virgil 70 A.D. - 19 B.C., put it most appropriately: "Your descendants shall gather your fruits." So it is up to you to gather the fruits of knowledge and to continue to expand it. These early African artists, architects, great men, have shown the way. They have sown the seeds for us to gather the fruits. Do it!

Cherise Maloney: How does the Sun God retain his cleanliness?
Dr. Fred Monderson: Both the living and the dead undergo lustrations of purification and this seems connected to the Heliopolitan sun cult. Aylward M. Blackman presented an article in *Society of Biblical Archaeology* Vol. 40 (March 13, 1918: 57-66) entitled: "Sacramental Ideas and Usages in Ancient Egypt: I. Lustrations and the Heliopolitan Sun-God." Here it is stated:

"In the so-called Pyramid Texts, he is frequently represented as undergoing purification by washing in the Field or Pool of Earu or in the Field of Life. According to the Piankhy Stele, 1.101 F., the Sun-God was wont to wash his face in the cool pool, the stream of Nun, which seems to have been situated somewhere

QUINTESSENTIAL BOOK "THE HOLY LAND"

between Heliopolis and Kher'eha. The purification in which the text describes was apparently a daily matutional one, preceding the god's appearance above the eastern horizon. Two passages in the Pyramid Texts indicate that Horus and Thoth acted in the capacity of the Sun God's bath-attendants, rubbing his back and feet at the conclusion of his ablutions. Another passage represents the Goddess Kebhowetas emptying four pitchers of water over him. The same collection of texts informs us that after his ablutions Num, the sky-goddess, grasped the arm of the Sun-God who, with the assistance of Shu, was thus drawn up into heaven.

"The purity attributed to the Sun-God also characterizes the denizens of his celestial kingdom and the things connected with them and himself. For example: - the abodes of the Sun-God are pure, those who voyage in the boat of turn-face, the celestial ferryman, the lotus flower which the Sun-god holds to his nose, the deceased pharaoh's throne in heaven and his seat in the Sun-God's ship, neither of which he can occupy unless he is pure."

Life, good fortune, protection, stability, health, and happiness are in a special degree properties of the Sun-God. Given life like Ra is a constantly recurring pharaonic attribute, and the following phrase, or an abbreviated version thereof, occurs behind the figure of the Egyptian sovereign in almost every relief in which he appears. "All protection, life, stability, good fortune, all health, happiness, behind him like Ra every day." "Living like Ra."

According to one notion that finds constant expression in Egyptian religious texts, the Sun-God was reborn every morning. "The sun was conceived of as an infant issuing from the womb of the sky-goddess Nut, or as a calf, the offspring of the celestial cow Mehet Weret. The idea that the Sun-God bathed every morning before he appeared in the eastern sky, brought ablutions and rebirth into close connection. This connection which has been further strengthened by the attribution of life-giving quantities of water and by the belief that the Sun-God was in the first instance born out of the waters of the primeval ocean Nut."

Mehet Weret, the name of the celestial cow that gave birth to the Sun-God every morning means "great flood."

Owing to the political predominance gained by Buto over Heliopolis in the predynastic age, Horus, originally the local god of Buto came to be identified with the: "Sun-God, the local god of Heliopolis since the king was regarded as the embodiment of the Sun-God. The King would usually have been the son of the previous king and therefore the son of the embodiment of the Sun-God. In course of time the notion naturally grew up that the King was the son of the actual Sun-God, and from the reign of Isesi of the Vth Dynasty onwards it found general acceptance."

FREDERICK MONDERSON

"At death the pharaoh was said to ascend to heaven where he was assimilated to the Sun-God or identified with him or else reborn of his position of son."

"Before he could ascend to heaven the dead pharaoh, like his divine prototype had to undergo purification."

"The texts describing his lustrations emphasize the connection between him and the Sun god. They represent them as taking place in the Letopolis or Heliopolitan nome, in the water of Kher'eha, in the excellent pool ... or in the Pool of the God. The last there mentioned pools were situated in the neighborhood of Heliopolis and were closely connected with the Heliopolitan sun-cult. More often these lustrations are said to take place in mythological pools or water holes, such as the Field or Pool of Earu, and the Field of Life, which as we have seen, were used by the Sun god for the same purpose. Kebhowetas, who washed the Sun God, also washed the deceased pharaoh. Horus and Thoth, the Sun God's bath attendants are described as massaging him at the conclusion of his ablutions. Again he might be washed by Horus in the Pool of Earu along with the Sun-God himself."

"Life and good fortune."

"In the Field of Life the dead pharaoh is said to meet with Kebhowetas, who treating him like the Sun-God, empties over him the contents of her four pitchers of water and refreshes his heart therewith for life."

"The Field of Life, where Kebhowetas refreshes the heart of the deceased pharaoh for life, is called as we have already learnt, the birth place of Re."

"Ablutions of the deceased pharaoh in the sacred pools of the Letopolite and Helopolite nomes. The pool of the latter nome is possibly identical with what is called the Water of Kher'eha in the *Book of the Dead*, Chap. 169, L. 19f., and with what the Piankhi Stele, L. 102, names the Stream of Nun, and places in the neighborhood of Khereha. "Thus he has power over the body, thy foot is not held back, thou art born for Horus, thou art conceived for Seth ..."

After being washed in the Jackal Pool and the Pool of Tei, and following his ascent to heaven and reception by the gods, it is said of the deceased Nefer-Kere that the Sky-goddess '*bears thee like Orion.*'

"This passage also seems to associate the washing of the dead pharaoh with rebirth. The Waters of Life which are in the sky come. The Waters of Life, which are in the earth come. The sky burns for thee, the earth trembles for thee before

QUINTESSENTIAL BOOK
"THE HOLY LAND"

the birth of the God. Two hills are divided (the god come into being, the god takes possession of his body). The two hills are divided, this Nefer-Kere comes into being, and this Nefer-Kere takes possession of his body. Behold this Nefer-Kere – his feet are kissed by the pure waters, which are from Atum, which the phallus of Shu made, which the vulva of Tefnut brought into being. They have come; they have brought for thee the pure waters from their father. They purify thee; they cense thee, O Nefer-Kere."

"We have in the Pyramid Texts a description unhappily full of lacunae, of the fashioning of the deceased pharaoh's new body for which copper is certainly one of the materials employed."

"The Book of Breathings, after describing the washing of the deceased, by various divinities, informs us that Ptah fashions his body. In this connection it should likewise be recollected that the Sun-God, whose daily rebirth, as we have seen was associated with ablutions, was evidently thought to be reborn with a new body. One of the commonest representations in the *Book of Him Who is in the Tei* shows that god emerging reborn from the Underworld, wherein lies his discarded corpse."

Holy Land Photo 108. Cherise Maloney of Brooklyn (center and below the hat), New York, is joined by beautiful people from Detroit, Michigan, for a sit-down outside the Mausoleum of Aga Khan at Aswan, Egypt.

FREDERICK MONDERSON

Joshua Monderson: The guide is taking some of us on a trip to Alexandria tomorrow afternoon. I wonder why Alexandria is considered so important.
Dr. Fred Monderson: Its history makes it important. Alexandria was founded to commemorate Alexander the Great, though that port city had been in use from the earliest times. Its early and ancient name is *Racotis*. On the Mediterranean Sea it was an entrepot to trade in that region and with South-West Asia.

Myers (1900: vi-vii) has written: "With the passing of paganism in the Roman dominions, the early philosophy of Greece and Rome, in which religion and ethics largely emerged, tempered with the religion and religious thought of Palestine and the Orient, but above all the religious thought and ethics of Ancient Egypt, which still existed in the waning years of Greece and Rome after an origin of thousands of years in the past, met at Alexandria in Egypt, the then great center of that period of intellectual vigor in the domain of thought, and which, fostered by the Ptolemies, had been such a center for many years previous."

In Alexandria, then sprung up many new sects and religions formulated to meet the growing need in the minds of the men of that day, for something that would bring them nearer to the Supreme Deity than had been heretofore given them, through the animalism and materialism of Greek and Roman philosophy and paganism.

It has been said that the Ancient Egyptians did not have any knowledge of philosophy, if by this association the ideas set forth in Greek and Roman philosophy are to be understood we agree with it, although Greek philosophy upon which much of Latin philosophy has been based, and had an original basis in Ancient Egyptian thought, some of the greatest Greek philosophers having studied at the feet of Egyptian priests. And in the papyrus of the scribe Ani, we have perhaps the first attempt to teach philosophy in a conversational way, which was afterwards used in certain schools of Greek philosophy and by them more fully developed. We allude more especially to the method adopted by Aristotle."

Molefi Asante of Temple University has a book entitled *Ancient Egyptian Philosophers* in which he makes the connection with its early thinkers and the concept of philosophy. He argued the first philosophers were Egyptians and the Greeks and Romans inherited, developed and documented this line of reasoning.

Michael Sinclair: When I look at the green fields contrasted against the nearby desert I am amazed at how they got them that way.
Dr. Fred Monderson: Agriculture is and was the mainstay of Egypt. It was the foundation of its existence and civilization. The Nile River had been beneficial and destructive and since conquest of the waterway was the essential foundation principle of civilization, the government early developed a bureaucracy to handle this. There were government departments headed by a "Superintendent of

QUINTESSENTIAL BOOK
"THE HOLY LAND"

Agriculture," "Scribes of Agriculture" and also a "Chief of the Granaries." In the same way in a descending scale, such officers existed in the Nomes and local farms.

The *Book of Ptah-Hotep* says: "An agriculturalist should live on the produce of his own fields and not on the home of another. The powerful who seized by force the property of others, and his children, are cursed."

Teddy Cubia: I know of the popular crowns, but what are some others and where can we find them?
Dr. Fred Monderson: The Crowns were regarded as goddesses. The popular crowns are Red Crown for Lower Egypt and White Crown for Upper Egypt. The Red and White Double Crown represented a united land. The Osiris Crown, Queen Mother Crown, Amon Crown, Nemes Headdress, Blue or War Crown, are some and so much more. There is the Buttercup Crown, the Forget-Me-Not and the Lotus Crowns. Today these can be seen on either east and west outer facing at Dendera as well as on a column in the right section of the Pronaos.

Marilyn James: What is the meaning of the celestial cow?
Dr. Fred Monderson: This is associated with Nut, goddess of the sky whom you saw at Dendera, in the little cove, the chapel showing her on the ceiling. There she gives birth to the sun in the morning and swallows it up at evening time after traveling across the heavens. All this and shining her beacon on the Temple of Dendera where Hathor was worshipped.

Erman (1907: 12) explained as follows: "We meet with the goddess of the sky under various names, which prove their development from differing conceptions of her. As NUT, she retained her character as the female representative of the sky, and as the wife of the earth god KEB. The very small share is all she was accorded in the actual religion of Egypt, and in historical times she received scarcely any veneration. Under another name, however, she was extremely popular as HATHOR. Although this name, *House of Horus*, abode of the sun god, directly and unequivocally designates her as the sky, yet an almost complete change in her role occurred early. As by her position as goddess of the heavens she was the chief of the goddesses, she was also the divine representative of women, who worshipped her before all others, and thus she became the brilliant goddess of pleasure and of love. Other aspects must have grown out of her characteristic of sky goddess, but to us they remain incomprehensible. She is called the *Eye of Re*, and she appears as the goddess of the West; as such she stands on the mountain of the West and receives the setting sun and the dead. It is needless to remark that the goddess of women would necessarily have innumerable sanctuaries. One of the principal of these was Denderah in Upper Egypt, where her temple still delights us with its beauty."

FREDERICK MONDERSON

He says further, Aldred (1907: 12-13) continued: "The cow form of the goddess of heaven, to which we have already referred, appears originally to have been assigned exclusively to Hathor, but it is possible that its application to this goddess was not popular, and also that when merely the head of the cow was placed on her, it was not in agreement with her later characteristics. Therefore in very early times a remarkable head was contrived for her, human, yet at the same time animal, a broad kindly woman's face surrounded by thick plaits of hair, and retaining nothing of the cow except the ears, which preserve some trace of the animal in her aspect. Or else she was an ordinary woman's head, and a head-dress which recalls the ancient celestial cow, consisting of two horns between which appears the sun."

Frederick Maloney: Did the Egyptians really hate foreigners? Why? And how did so many foreigners make such headway in Egypt?
Dr. Fred Monderson: From the *Papyrus of Sayings*, Myers (1900: 235) quotes: "'The barbarian takes from everywhere unlawful gain: nothing remains from yesterday.' This shows great changes are happening to the old inhabitants apparently from invaders. The Ancient Egyptians called foreigners 'Barbarians.'"

Dr. Leonard James: Can you throw some light on the psychology of the Egyptians so we can seek to understand the religion of Ancient Egypt and its religious philosophy? What can we deduce from the Per-em-Hru?
Dr. Fred Monderson: We are always confronted with the question as to what happens to the person when he dies. That is, what did the Ancient Egyptians believe?

According to Myers:

I.   After death the corruptible body, as an entirety, was called the Kha or Khat. Its ideogram was a dead fish, the sign for any putrid, foul-smelling, decaying thing. This was embalmed, and then placed in the tomb. This body, in life, formed a unity of oneness. The spiritual parts which dwelt in it when it constituted the living human being, each, after death, were thought of as distinct, and although, whilst in the living man, held in combination, they only dwelt in his body. At death, on leaving it, each separated, and some left it and set out by themselves to find a way to a higher sphere; excepted, however, from this was the lower spiritual part, which held together the atoms composing the Kha or dead body.

The word Sahu was also sometimes (with a lower meaning) applied to the mummy-body in the tomb. (Comp., the *Per-em-hru*, Chap. LXXVI. L11.) The dead body itself was not thought of as either leaving the tomb or reappearing upon our earth, but its preservation intact was deemed essential. This is set forth with

QUINTESSENTIAL BOOK "THE HOLY LAND"

great positive-ness on one of the linen wrappings which surrounds the body of Thotmes III. The word Sahu was more especially applied to the spiritual body of the dead, which ascended to the Egyptian heaven, and there dwelt with the gods.

The process of embalmment required the performance of many rites and the sayings of many litanies and prayers, the extent of which depended largely on the sum given to those who knew them, and whose duty it was to do and say them. The direction for many of these has reached our day in several papyri, one of which is now termed, the *Ritual of Embalmment*. The placing of the mummy in the tomb also required rites, ceremonies and prayers, which we have in the papyrus now called, the *Book of the Funerals*, part of which has been published by Dr. Ernesto Schiaparelli.

II.   The soul was called Ba or Bai; plural, Baiu. The word really means something like sublimes or "noble," but has been usually translated by Egyptologists as "soul." This was the eternal part of the spiritual, which was thought to contain the elements necessary for the world-life of a man, such as judgment, conscience, etc.; yet it was not considered as absolutely incorporeal. It was supposed to inhabit man's heart. The idea of it seems to be similar to that termed psuke or psyche, by the Greeks. This Ba performed a pilgrimage in the Netherworld, and was judged for the conduct of the man it inhabited in this world, by Osiris and the Forty-two judges. It was usually represented as a bird, especially as a human-headed sparrow hawk. It fluttered to and fro between this world and the next, and could pass into heaven and dwell with the perfected souls therein, also, sometimes visiting and conversing with the spirit of the body or mummy, in its tomb ....

III.   The intellectual part of man's spirit was called Xu or Khu – i.e., the Luminous. It was thought to be eternal, and was considered as part of the flame detached from the upper divine fire. It was called, "Shining One," "The glorious one," the "Intelligence." Freed from mortality, it wandered through space, and had the power of keeping company with, or haunting, humanity, and even of entering into and taking possession of the body of a living man. The Egyptians spoke of being possessed with a Khu, we would say of being possessed by a spirit. We may therefore define it as "Spirit." We may assert that it was considered as an ever-living luminous spirit. It can be thought of as the Intelligence, and thus answers to the Nous of the Greeks, and the Neshamah of the Hebrew Qabbalah. In the Per-em-hru, Chap. LXXXIX, L. 3, it is mentioned in connection with the BA; in Chap. CXLIX, L, 40, with the Khaibit; and in Chap. XCII, with both.

The Khu was considered as a translucent or shining case or covering of the body, and is frequently shown in the form of a mummy. The Khus of the gods lived in heaven, and the Khu of the dead endeavored to get there as soon as the prayers, etc., said over the body of the dead and the favorable judgment at the Psychostasia enabled it. The Khus were the higher spirits, whose proper abode was heaven, and they were considered, as we have said, eternal. The idea of the Khu is very ancient; it is mentioned in the "Pyramid Texts." Thus, in the pyramid tomb of King Unas is: "Unas standeth with the Khus." And as to king Teta, the god Seb is said to give to him both his hands, and to welcome him as a brother, and to nourish him and place him among the imperishable Khus, and to Teta is said: 'He (Horus) has plucked his eye from himself; he hath given it unto thee to strengthen therewith, that thou mayest prevail with it among the Khus.' When the Baiu of the gods enter to support Unas their Khu's are with and surround him. In the description of his entrance into the Egyptian heaven, inscribed on the inner walls of the Pyramid of Pepi I (circa 3467-3447 B.C.), the Khus or ever-glorified shining ones, meet him and make obeisance to his spirit. Part of it reads: 'Hail, Osiris Pepi! Thou has come, and thou art radiant; thou rulest like the god who is seated on his throne, who is called Osiris; thy soul is with thee in thy body; thy form of strength is with thee, behind thee; thy crown is upon thy head, thy head-dress upon thy shoulders; thy face before thee and those who sing songs of adoration are upon both sides of thee; the followers in the train of a god are behind thee, and the divine forms who cause a god to come are upon each side of thee. The god cometh, this Pepe has come upon the throne of Osiris! The Shining One cometh who dwelleth in Netat, the Master who dwelleth in Tini (Thinis), and Isis speaks as to thee, Nephthys holdeth converse with thee, and the Shining Ones come up to thee, bowing down even to the ground in adoration at thy feet .... Thou does that which he doeth among the immortal Shining Ones, and thy soul sitteth upon its throne, being provided with the form, and it doeth whatever thou doest, in the presence of Him who liveth among the Living,' etc.

The Shadow or Shade was called Khaibit. The Greeks had an okia and the Romans an umbra. This Shade preserved the individuality of the deceased, and was an important part of the personality, having an independent existence. There was a valley in the Nether world in which the Shades were. The Shade was restored to the soul in the Second life. The Shades are frequently mentioned in the Per-em-hru. His shadow would early attract the attention of the primitive man. It was sometimes represented as a fan or a sunshade. The gods and spirits, it was thought, might have Shades as well as the dead, and these Shades might live independently of their owners, and this they were supposed to do, immediately upon the death of the human being to whom they had been in life attached; then the Shade went forth by itself to appear in the kingdom of the spiritual. When it visited the tomb of its former owner it spiritually partook of the funeral offerings. It was defined as early as the "Pyramid Texts."

The Egyptians divided Shadows into the Dark Shadow, or the *Khaibit,* and the Clear Shadow, such as is reflected in still water or in a mirror; the latter was considered as the *Ka* or Double. The XCIInd Chapter of the Per-em-hru reads:

QUINTESSENTIAL BOOK
"THE HOLY LAND"

"Let my heart not be shut in, let My *Khaibit* not be fettered; let the way be opened for *my Ba* and *my Khaibit;* may it see the great god." The LXXXIX Chapter says: "May I look upon my heart and my Khaibit."

The Name of the individual was called the *Ren*. Thi, was the Personality of the

Holy Land Ceramic Art 22. Egyptian artistic creative symbolism is renown, so is this eye water?

deceased, that something which continued to know itself by a designation as a distinct and separate individual through every change of the atoms and appearance of the body. In the Per-em-hru was written: "The Osiris" (then the name of the dead person was inserted). The *Repi* was restored for eternity to the soul in the second life. The Pei also retained the *Rets* in its journey through the Netherworld. It the "Pyramid Texts" we have: "This Pepi is happy with his *Ren;* this Pepi liveth with his *Ka*."

V.   The Life or Double was called the Ka, plur. *Kau*. This was the vital principle necessary to the existence of man, an animal being on this earth. It was a spiritual double, a second perfect exemplar or copy, of his flesh, blood, body, etc., but, of a matter less dense than corporeal matter, having however all its shape and features, being child, man, or woman, as the living had been. It had power to enter and leave the tomb when it pleased. Its emblem was the Kawa - something like the higher *Arephesh* of the Hebrew Qabbalah. The sacrificial food left in the tombs, and the pictures on their walls, were for the deities, who were prayed to use them for the benefit of the *Ka*, - and the smell of the burning incense was pleasant to it. The Ka corresponded somewhat to the Latin, *genius*. Its original meaning may have been image; it was like the Greek Eidolon, i.e., Ghost. The funeral ablations and prayers were made to the deities for the benefit of the *Ka*. The *Ka* was a spiritual double of the man, and had a prototype in the Upper World or real World, of the *Ka* of the man in the Lower World or World of phenomena, that of our earth.'

Peter Monderson: What is Hathor's relationship to Nubia? Or rephrasing that what is her origin?
Dr. Fred Monderson: Hathor's original home is Nubia. This has been called the Sudan. Consider that Hathor is one of the oldest gods of Egypt whose origin is Sudan as like the cow, celestial or otherwise. Consider that the origin of the Egyptians is from the area of the Sudan, then it's reasonable that they would worship a goddess of their own area. We must not forget the people of Nabta Playa early worshipped the "Cow Goddess" from the earliest times down to 3500 B.C.

Michael Montout: Has the new research refuted the descriptions of Herodotus?
Dr. Fred Monderson: No! Herodotus was essentially correct, this "father of history;" he based many of his deductions on physical observation. When he described the people it should not be compared to when he tries to explain their religion because he gets this from another source. Descriptions of the physiognomy of the people are easy to accept because he was with the people, visited, traversed their land and communicated with them, observing all the time.

Kashmoney Malone: What evidence do we have of calendars?
Dr. Fred Monderson: There is an abundance of evidence establishing the measurement of the year by the Ancient Egyptians. George Foucart's "Calendars: Egyptian," in *Encyclopedia of Religion and Ethics* (1911, 3: 92) lists the following documentary evidence about calendars in Ancient Egypt. He says: "We may note the following as real calendars in chronological order: (1) the Palermo Stone (Vth dynasty, copied partly from documents of great antiquity), (2) the Kahun Papyrus (XIIth dynasty), (3) portions of the calendar of Thothmes III at Karnak (XVIIIth dynasty), (4) portions of the same king's calendar at Elephantine, (5) calendar of Medinet Habu (XXth dynasty), (6) calendar of Sallier Papyrus (XIXth dynasty, cf. British Museum Papyrus 10,174), (7) calendar of Edfu (Ptolemaic age), (8) that of Ombos (same period), (9) that of Denderah (Roman Period), (10) that of Esneh (same period), (11) that of the Leyden Papyrus (same period)." Clearly we cannot accept any argument of the origin of Egyptian calendars with the Greeks or

QUINTESSENTIAL BOOK
"THE HOLY LAND"

Romans.

Michelliea Georges: We see the king being purified by Thoth and Horus before entering the temple. Is this the only time he is purified?
Dr. Fred Monderson: No. He is purified many times throughout his lifetime. (1) He was purified as an infant in preparation for the time he would become pharaoh. (2) He was purified before Coronation as was done with Piankhy, on his way to wash his face in the "Cool Pool." (3) He was purified at Coronation when a priest placed the diadems on his head repeating as the god would do: 'I purify thee with the water of all life and good fortune, all stability, all health and happiness." The Pharaoh, therefore, was not only purified, but endowed with the qualities which pitted him for his new position, and which he possessed, qua Pharaoh, in common with the sun god. (4) He was purified before officiating at the temple. (5) He was purified at a Sed-festival, where special attention seems to be placed on washing the Pharaoh's hands and feet.

Stephaniea Mc Call: What were the cleanliness requirements of priests?
Dr. Fred Monderson: Cleanliness or purity on the part of priests was absolutely essential. From Graeco-Roman records we learn that during this period a priest had to purify himself for several days before entering to perform his duties in the temple. Priests and priestesses had always to wash or sprinkle themselves before entering a temple or engaging in a religious ceremony; every temple seems to have possessed a tank or pool set apart for this purpose. The priest also fumigated themselves with incense before officiating at the temple ceremonies. They had to wash their hands often and the pairing of nails was absolutely necessary. They practiced depilation or shaving the body hair regularly as well as shaving the face and head. They wore cotton and leather sandals. Circumcision was also a requirement.

Carmelitiea Shabazz: How did Ra become sick and what happened?
Dr. Fred Monderson: It was a question of envy on part of Isis who wanted powers she did not have. F. Ll. Griffith's "Charms and Amulets: Egyptian" in Hastings' *Encyclopedia of Religion and Ethics* (1911, 3: 430) reports: "We hear, for instance, of the goddess Isis, who desired to be equal in power with her father Ra. The only means of having her wish fulfilled was to know the mysterious and hidden name of her father. She therefore devised a stratagem. She caused Ra to be bitten by a [scorpion or] serpent; the pain of this wound was so intolerable that the voice of the old king reached the sky and all the gods flocked around him. Ra is described as expatiating at great length upon his sufferings, which the crafty goddess does not attempt to relieve until her father consents to be searched by her, so that she may get hold of his mysterious name. Only then does she call on the venom to go out of the body of Ra. The narrative ends here; but we are told that this story is to be said to, or as the Egyptians say, over, figures of Tum, Horus, and

FREDERICK MONDERSON

Isis, which will thus be made talismans against the serpents."

Henrietta Potter: What evidence is there of circumcision?
Dr. Fred Monderson: There is lots of evidence for circumcision in Ancient Egypt. George Foucart's "Circumcision: Egyptian," in Hastings' *Encyclopedia of Religion and Ethics* (1911, 3: 670) indicated: "The documentary evidence, properly so called, is of the most varied kinds: (1) scenes representing the actual operation; (2) frescoes and bas-reliefs showing nude figures circumcised; (3) statues of the same; (4) Egyptian texts of the classical period understood to refer to circumcision, from a religious or historical point of view; (5) papyrus-texts of the Roman epoch relating to the practice of circumcision; (6) evidence of classical authors; (7) the mummies of kings, chief priests, and a great number of Egyptians of noble rank or affluent condition."

Dr. Leonard James: Following Champollion's untimely death, who filled the gap in refining the Hieroglyphic language?
Dr. Fred Monderson: A great many scholars starting with Rosellini. It has been said the early scholars began seeking Biblical justification among the Egyptian records. Nevertheless, there are many names including Lepsius, Wilkinson, Birch, Hincks, Dumichen, Ebers, Goodwin, LePage Renouf, Vassili, Zoega, Akerblad, A. Peyron, A de Rouge, Vassili, Zoega, Th. Deveria, Chabas,. Lester L'Hote, Leemans, Prisse D'Avennes, Erman, Maspero and many others.

Teddy Cubia: Can you describe two fundamental ideas that truly characterize ancient Egyptian belief systems?
Dr. Fred Monderson: The first would be that the actions of the pharaohs and all his subordinates be guided by the philosophic principle of Ma'at. The second would be the absolute necessity of building and maintaining the temple of the god and worshipping and ritualizing his essence or manifestation as part of never-ending religious practice. I suppose you could add the pursuit of science inquiry of knowledge and intellectual growth.

Well, that's all for today. See you guys at dinner. If anyone is going out shopping this evening, try to stay in groups and do be careful.

Day 14.   EGYPTIAN MUSEUM OF ANTIQUITIES
1.   Wake Up

QUINTESSENTIAL BOOK
"THE HOLY LAND"

Esperanza Rodriguez: Good Morning, Mi Amor. Your schedule for today calls for a visit to the Cairo Museum of Egyptian Antiquities. In addition, there will be a three-hour stop at the Khalili Bazaar for those interested in doing some bargaining while they shop. I have prepared today's copy of your article for the group.
Dr. Monderson: Thank you, my dear.

"Queen of Sheba in Racial Portrayal as Historical Distortion"
By
Fred Monderson

Standing in the line last month for the cashier at a local supermarket, my eye caught one of the customary tabloids with headlines that read "World's Mysteries Solved." Like any enthusiast of any such esoteric phenomenon, I purchased the paper and took it home. Such topics as a "New Discovery of Noah Ark" are recurring historical themes, and "Vatican Confirms the Existence of Angels," were some of the articles in this issue. Turning to the centerfold, my eyes caught the story, Scientists Discover the Home of the Queen of Sheba. This was a short story, juxtaposed to a large picture of the Queen of Sheba. It was a picture of a beautiful woman, white! What's wrong with this picture?

Just then a friend, Rodolfo was visiting my home. When I brought this to his attention and having some familiarity with my work, he admonished: "You should write an article on this distortion." Finally I agreed, looking at the article again it read: "British Archaeologists have discovered the home of the Queen of Sheba, located in the southern Nigerian forest region." Often times the general reading public would overlook such a report.

Many times readers have questioned the veracity of the tabloids to sensationalize their stories that in a number of instances are outright distortions of fact. Too often, Gary Byrd on WLIB, New York radio has said: "The information you don't have could kill you." Equally too, Malcolm X admonished his listeners to be skillful readers, for newspapers have a tendency to put things in a manner that denigrates Blacks, and generally distorts the truth. "They" also hide information in "their" papers placing it somewhere on page 96, where most people hardly get to.

On the eve of the 21st century and a new millennium, Blacks in America and worldwide must be concerned about the ever present problems of racism that distorts the image of Blacks whether politically, historically, culturally, psychologically or simply let's say as human beings.

The fact is, in a general sense, the information presented to Blacks and Whites, pertaining to the same issue are colored differently and there should be more concerted efforts to synchronize what both groups are being taught.

Now to present my case, I will document a few examples to show that historical truths are perennially distorted and to set the record straight, men and women of objective scholarship must constantly challenge distortions.

As a student of Professor ben-Jochannan, I have often listened to his debates and observed the ink spilled discussing a line in the Bible. Depending on the versions one consults, the question is always did the Queen of Sheba say, 'I am Black and comely.' Or, 'I am Black but comely.' In the first instance she is saying "I'm Black and beautiful" and being proud of it. In the second instance, in saying "I'm Black but beautiful," she is, if you will, denigrating her Blackness but affirming her beauty. People on a pejorative bent towards Blacks flaunt the latter affirming she was not proud of her Blackness, though they would concede she was beautiful. Did the editor of the tabloid know this or was he simply uncaring and determined to distort in the belief it would go unnoticed. Of course, if Solomon had married the Queen of Sheba and made an 'honest woman' out of her, this matter would probably have been solved. Now, in an extension of this argument, a more potent social issue is raised. Still, in the heart of Southern Nigeria, the picture presented of the Queen is that of a White woman! Some scholars have asserted that contrary to popular opinion, though Sheba was beautiful, and this is not mistaken, Solomon pursued her more because her empire was greater than his! And, if we accept the Southern Nigeria origins, then it extended clear across the Sudan to Ethiopia, with trading ventures well into Asia.

Historical distortions like forgeries are nothing new. The "Donation of Constantine" is one such example of a forgery.

People with historical consciousness know that after the decline of Egyptian/Kemetic civilization, and the rise of Greece and Rome, Jesus the Christ came, was crucified, died, was buried and rose again. In the centuries right after, early Christians were martyred through Roman rulers' fear that the promised "heavenly kingdom" was a threat to the Roman Empire. After the games and the mauling by African lions, there were martyrdoms, etc. Of course, the African had nothing to do with this. It was the Romans who took lions from Africa and had them devour Christians!

Constantine the Great became Emperor of Rome. On the eve of a major military

QUINTESSENTIAL BOOK
"THE HOLY LAND"

engagement he had a dream or vision that involved religious matters, priestly paraphernalia, the Bishop's Miter, and insignia of his vestments, etc. Succeeding in battle the next day, Constantine credited his dream with being part of his good fortune. Purportedly he declared 'We killed enough Christians,' 'Let's cage the lions,' 'Stop having Christians for lunch,' and 'End the crucifixion.' He declared Christianity would be recognized as a legitimate religion in the Roman Empire. The Church could get equal footing with the state, Christians would be respected. He called the *Council of Nicea* in 325 AD and invited all the Bishops of the Christian church to hammer out the glitches in the fundamental tenets of Christianity. Constantine was hailed as the first Christian Emperor of the Roman Empire.

A document entitled "The Donation of Constantine" later showed the Emperor had donated extensive tracts of land to the church that were tax-exempt, etc. A thousand years later, an Italian Lorenzo Valla, a linguist, while doing research made a remarkable discovery. As anyone familiar with linguistics would know language constantly changes. New words are added and old words dropped. Remember, 'where's the beef?'

Lorenzo Valla (1518) showed that the document contained words that did not come into the vernacular until centuries after Constantine; therefore, he declared the document 'Donation of Constantine' a forgery. The Bishop of Chichester and Baronius in his "Annales Ecclesiastici" (ad an. 1324) admitted that the "Donatio" was a forgery. As an example, using the same "Where's the Beef" analogy, a 1920s document purports something of significance and the above line used, when it was not yet "Born." Thus, it is considered historical fraud or misrepresentation.

The search for Prester John was one of those monumental failures that remained a perennial success. Perhaps as equally important as the riches of the east, the search for Prester John in Africa motivated Portuguese explorers for centuries. Since he was never found, it is not inconceivable that the thought of finding his kingdom is not a moot issue.

Following the decline of the Roman Empire and Rise of Islam, the Moors or Shakespeare's "Blackamoors" invaded Southern Europe. They occupied that land from 711 to 1485 A.D. providing the "Arab conduit" of ancient African intellectualism, developed in the Nile Valley. Perhaps in that age the myth of Prester John was born, yet it fueled particularly Portuguese aspirations of exploration and colonization. The notion of Prester John, a White king ruling a Black kingdom in Africa represented a phalanx of global white supremacy on that continent. Everyone came, searching, to find this individual.

As Professor Clarke liked to say "The Africans invited Europeans for lunch and we became the meal." The result was "naked imperialism" "enlightened

FREDERICK MONDERSON

imperialism" and then "intellectual imperialism." Of course, as a known fact, the missionaries were a vanguard in colonial strategy. We can thank Jomo Kenyatta for his insightful assessment of this aftermath in *Facing Mount Kenya*. "When the missionaries came" he wrote, "they gave us the Bible and taught us to close our eyes and pray. When we opened our eyes, we were holding the Bible and the Europeans the land."

As a youngster growing up in Guyana, reading was an enjoyable past time. There was not "Black History," these were not yet "born." Even though they have been manifestly evolving from time immemorial. We were taught English History 1066-1485, from the Norman Invasion to the War of the Roses and Ascension of the Tudors. We read about the Phantom in Africa. He was a masked crusader who single-handedly subdued all comers in the heart of Africa. As if that was not enough, Edgar Rice Burroughs gave us Tarzan and Hollywood had a field day in its systematic and well-choreographed denigration of the African persona. And, we all laughed heartily as one white man defeated and made fools of "tribes of Africans" portrayed and degraded as "savages." A recent article indicated there were no Africans in Walt Disney's new movie, 'Tarzan.' That's taking it to the next level!

The Western literary traditions began with Homer's *Iliad* and *Odyssey*. It is believed he visited Egypt/Kemet. The description of Thebes with its "palaces" and "hundred gates" refers to the City of Thebes in the time of Rameses III of the XXth Dynasty. However, the erudite Cheikh Anta Diop argued: "If Homer visited Egypt and this fact is attested to by Greek tradition - it was probably during the time of the XXVth Sudanese Dynasty, under Piankhi or Shabaka, around 750 B.C." Murray's handbook for Egypt (1888) informs, selections from Homer's works are engraved on walls at the 20th Dynasty Egyptian King Rameses III's mortuary temple Medinet Habu. Then again, much controversy surrounds the Greeks in Egypt. Modern scholars have accepted some of these classical writers' views on the Egyptians but they reject salient parts particularly of an ethnological nature. Herodotus visited Egypt around 450 B.C. and in his *Histories* Book II, *Euterpe* is devoted to that land. Granted he traveled the land seeking information from priests who guarded their history and culture very well. Yet he secured information from them. Nevertheless, he also observed much but he was right about their color!

In the era of the 18th century, the American, French and Haitian Revolutions, when men aspired to the nobility of freedom, of spirit and of body, Africans in American were enslaved. In that era of *les philosophes'* and free thinking, Count Volney wrote his *Ruins of Empire*, and postulated the view, 'men and women of sable skin and frizzled hair, now enslaved, founded along the banks of the Nile River, the fundamental laws of science that govern the world, while much of humanity was still in a barbaric stage.'

QUINTESSENTIAL BOOK
"THE HOLY LAND"

Holy Land Papyrus 35. The Goddess leads the Queen wearing a beautiful long flowing dress.

In 1799, Napoleon's artillery officers discovered the now famous Black basalt trilingual inscription called the Rosetta Stone. In 1822, this became the basis of Champollion's decipherment of hieroglyphics, *Medu Netcher*. In 1836, Sir Godfrey Higgins published *Anacalypsis* in 2 vols. In this masterful work he identified the ancient races and military, political, spiritual, and religious luminaries who were Black, from Osiris to Jesus. A powerful work of erudite scholarship, *Anacalypsis*, challenged all comers to contest its revelations.

In the age of political, military and economic imperialism intellectual advantage

FREDERICK MONDERSON

became an extension of that movement. Archaeological excavation in the Nile Valley got a significant boost in the years 1870-1920. Not only was that discipline placed on a systematic and scientific footing, but a number of organs of literary expression were inaugurated to chronicle the constantly unfolding spectacular discoveries. The *American Journal of Archaeology* was a prominent publication among numerous others. In the 1903-04 Archaeological Season, the "Mortuary Temple of Nebhepetra Mentuhotep II was discovered at Deir el-Bahari, Thebes. A statue of the king was found wearing his *heb sed* attire. The statue was removed and to this day resides in the Cairo Museum

A phenomenon occurred which is not dissimilar by today's standards, "All the news printed to fit." All that AJA IX (1905: 98) could say of a physio-ethnological nature was the: "thick lips with edges defaced by sharp ridges, the heavy chin and the muscles emphasized round the corners of the mouth and nose, are derived from the mannerisms of the late Sixth Dynasty." Again, remember Malcolm's admonition: "No matter what the man says, You better look into it!"

For Black readers then, in an age of slavery, civil war, and aftermath reconstruction, "Jim Crowism," "tenant farming," "separate but equal," discrimination, and racism, it was difficult for those Black readers who could not analyze AJA's description. For them it had no meaning! No major publishing vehicle in the United States carried it until W. Stephenson Smith in 1959, 56 years later, dared to say Mentuhotep II had "Black flesh.' The statue is in the same place in the museum, but for more than half century Black readers did not know the Theban Mentuhotep II of the XIth Dynasty was a Black king. That is, until Dr. ben-Jochannan began carrying Afro-Americans to Egypt. That too, is why Dr. Monderson, a student of the august elder, intends to continue the tradition of research, writing and publication and carrying our people to Egypt to expose them to the ancient African heritage and legacy. Not simply Mentuhotep's statue in the Cairo Museum but the wonderful temples of Karnak, Luxor, Deir el-Bahari, Abydos, Dendera, Edfu, Esna, Kom Ombo, Philae, and Kalabsha and Beit Wali, and Abu Simbel, invites all, with their wonderful architectural, spiritual and intellectual enlightenment.

"Tutankhamon," as Prof. Clarke liked to Say: "was a minor king who got a major funeral." In 1922, Howard Carter discovered his tomb in the Valley of the Kings. Two life-like statues of the boy king stood at the entrance to the burial chamber.

Comparative analysis is a potent tool or weapon in dismantling and destroying the myths of distortion. The French scholar Jean Yoyote in Georges Posener's *Dictionary of Egyptian Civilization* (1963: 291) speaks of Tutankhamon's treasures: "Everything was there. Nests of sarcophagi, statues of the king, golden jewelry, magical and everyday furniture, golden shrines, and alabaster and faience

QUINTESSENTIAL BOOK "THE HOLY LAND"

vases, the whole comprising an unrivalled collection of objects for the study of the arts and ritual ceremonies." Elsewhere (p. 293) he says: "The everyday requirements of a prince were buried with him, including; weapons, chariots, vessels, embroidered garments, chests and other pieces of furniture. The funerary equipment of the glorified dead was always plentiful - canopic jars, ushabtis of every material and figures of gods, to which must be added portable shrines and the *blackened wooden statues, which had been used in the funeral rite.* No scholar of merit has supplied a credible explanation of the phrase. Everything was costly and worthy of a king." Again, elsewhere (p. 75) "The red and Black Land." Red the desert, black, the valley and plain. Where the Nile "rose to flood the land and replenish it with new soil each year." Or, should I say, "red equals death and black equals Life!"

At the 1998, ASCAC Conference at City College, New York, in a taped interview, Prof. Obenga said "Kemet" or "Black Land" referred to the indigenous people and not the land. He said the word does not appear with the derivative for land and that it is for the Black people. Even further, while this may not still be, owing to the reorganization of the Museum, "Blackened wooden statues" of the Kings Amenhotep I and Amenhotep II, among others were observed by this writer. Interestingly enough, juxtaposed in the case was a Black wooden statue of a panther. The placement of the panther in the case confronts and contradicts such claims those similar statues as the two from Tutankhamon's burial chamber only had ceremonial uses.

In 1985 as the nation approached the 500th Anniversary of the celebration of Columbus' discovery of America, this in itself a distortion, Dr. Cheikh Anta Diop wrote a letter to the *Journal of African Civilization.* He discussed the finding of tobacco, a New World strain, in the Mummy of Rameses II. This mummy of the New Kingdom monarch, discovered in the late 19th Century, began to decay. It was rushed to Paris to undergo scientific surgery to arrest the decay. The Senegalese scholar Diop was qualified enough to be part of the examination team. The only Black accorded that privilege. Perhaps had he not been there, the manifestation of the discovery and the tenacity to defend its meaning and significance would probably not been made manifest. Dr. Diop was mentioned in UNESCO's final report on the 'Peopling of the Nile Valley.' They commended Cheikh Anta Diop and Theophile Obenga as being the best prepared of all the participants at the conference.

The esteemed multi-disciplinarian deduced that New World tobacco in Rameses' stomach meant he smoked the stuff or consumed some just before death. Even more important, however, it meant his emissaries visited the New World and returned! This meant Africans were in the New World nearly 3000 years before Columbus. In addition, at the 1992 Temple University Diopian Conference, papers were presented showing the Malian king Abu Bekr and a fleet of ships left

FREDERICK MONDERSON

for the New World at the start of the fourteenth century nearly 200 years before Columbus. This being so, Africans should be celebrating the 700th year of that adventure. Much of this is not known, though we celebrate 500 years of the exploration, conquest and exploitation and extermination of New World peoples and cultures. Let's not forget, records in the logs of Magellan's ships indicate as they were crossing the Atlantic, 'Africans in long canoes' were observed *returning from the New World*. Dr. Charsee Macintyre argued for the arrival of "little Africans" in the New World as early as 120,000 years ago. Prof. Betancourt questioned those dates though he did suggest "firm dates at 70,000 years" before our era in the New World.

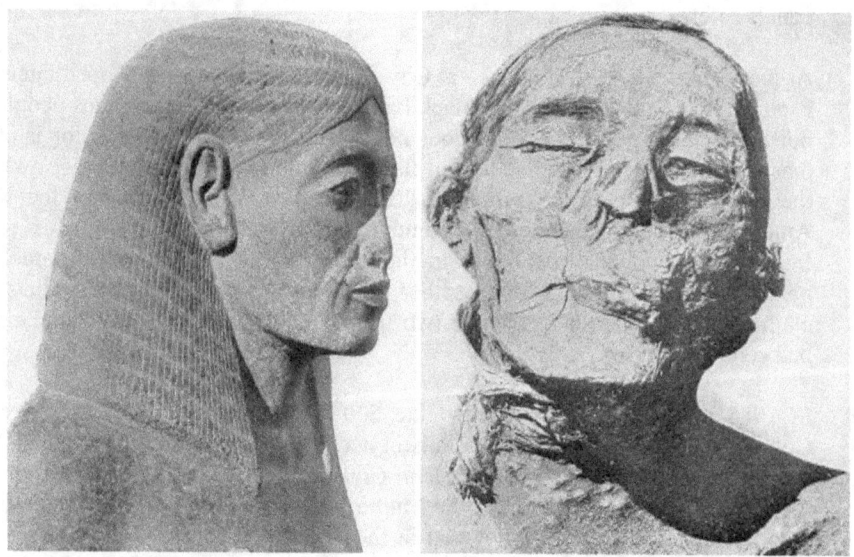

Holy Land Illustration 96. Bust of Amenhotep, Son of Hapu, 18th Dynasty (left); and mummy head of Seti I, of the 19th Dynasty (right).

Malcolm X looms so large in our history. A student at Temple University once submitted a dissertation request to show that the "Norse Epics" were those of Blacks. Also, that "Eric the Red" was not the white, full red bearded, individual so often pictured. He was like say, Malcolm as "Detroit Red." The rather articulate and well-known Professor responded, "Well, without a lot more documentation, I can't sell this to the Graduate Board." So, it got the sort of "Let's kill it in Committee" treatment!

Finally, and cut this short, Dr. Cheek Anta Diop, also with an opportunity to examine the Cairo Mummies, in his Magnum Opus, *Civilization or Barbarism: An Authentic Anthropology*, informed us the mummies had their skins peeled like

QUINTESSENTIAL BOOK "THE HOLY LAND"

potatoes to hide their blackness!

All this and so much more, distorted, omitted and hidden from Black readers.

2. Breakfast

Dr. Leonard James: Deir el Bahari is the brainchild of Hatshepsut and the architectural genius of Senmut her architect. For a decade during the late 19th century scholars and explorers speculated on the prototypical origins of this sprawling, yet magnificent architectural construction. At first, its terraced design was speculated to mirror the geographical landscape of Punt, the land to the south of Egypt. Of course, in the "hide and seek" for Egypt, Punt was rumored to be on the coast of the Red Sea and even across in Arabia. Interestingly, nevertheless, the 19th Dynasty papyrus of the nobleman Hunefer places Punt and the origins of the Egyptians in the general East Africa area in the statement: "We came from the foothills of the mountains of the moon where the God Hapi dwells." This is the plain between Mount Ruwenzori and Kilimanjaro in today's East Africa. However, with the discovery of Mentuhotep II's XIth Dynasty temple at Deir el Bahari in 1903, it was determined this was in fact the prototype of Hatshepsut's temple.

The beauty of Deir el Bahari and the genius of Senmut was the use of terraces, ramps, and colonnades, round columns, statues, square pillars and Osiride figures. Smith (1959) describes it as a blending of "open space with architectural nicety." Dedicated to Amon, it also contained shrines to Hathor (left) and Anubis (right). During the New Kingdom this site was oriented in alignment with Karnak across the river where Amon dwelt. A Valley Temple at the river's edge led up an Avenue of Sphinxes, now lost, to the temple's first Pylon where remains of two incense trees are still evident.

Beyond the first entrance pylon, the First Court entrances the Lower Colonnade of 11 columns split by the First Ramp to the Second Court. The Middle Colonnade is again split by the Second Ramp, which leads to the Upper Terrace. The Middle Colonnade contains the Punt Colonnade to the left juxtaposed against the Hathor Shrine. This colonnade depicts the Queen's inspiration and dispatch of a voyage to Punt to secure incense trees of the sacred heart used in worship of her father Amon. To the right the Birth Colonnade juxtaposes the Anubis Shrine to the right against the northern face of the cliff connecting the Northern Colonnade with these "proto-Doric" columns, so named by Champollion.

The Second Ramp esplanades the Upper Terrace with its Upper Court and magnificent hypostyle colonnade, Sanctuary and off to the right, court with open-air altar, all against the western face of the cliff of the Deir el Bahari amphitheater.

FREDERICK MONDERSON

While the Queen dedicated her mortuary temple to her father Amon, also dedicating it to the other deities, Ra-Horakhty, Hathor and Anubis, made it unique for its age. Most temples up to that time had been dedicated to one god. This does not include Karnak, were beside the Theban Triad Amon, Mut and Khonsu, each with their own temple, the National Gods were also worshipped in their own temples in the "palace" where they visited. In this temple the Aennead of 15-gods were resident. In the 19th Dynasty, Seti I worshipped seven deities at Abydos. These were from right to left Horus, Isis, Osiris, Amun, Ra Horakhty, Ptah and Seti himself. His son Rameses II built his Abu Simbel Temple and dedicated it to Ra-Horakhty, Amon, Ptah and his deified self. Not until the later Graeco-Roman period would another temple be dedicated to two gods. This is Kom Ombo dedicated to Haroeis the Elder Horus and Sobek the Crocodile god. Dendera is dedicated to Hathor but her husband Horus and son Ihy are al so resident. Naturally the gods each had their consort.

Another feature of Hatshepsut's temple is, in an age of one-story buildings, hers was three stories.

With the fall of the Queen, Thutmose III and his followers took vengeance on the temple destroying much and defacing her name and inscriptions. This nevertheless, was selective out of respect for defacing a temple dedicated to Amon. In fact Thutmose built a small temple between Hatshepsut's and the Middle Kingdom Temple of Mentuhotep II. A quick perusal of the plans of these three temples find they orient right across the river to the Karnak area.

By the end of the 19th Dynasty, Deir el Bahari had become a quarry. In the Christian era Deir el Bahari became a sanitarium with a reputation for healing and got the name "convent of the north."

Walter Brown: Getting better, Dr. James!

QUINTESSENTIAL BOOK "THE HOLY LAND"

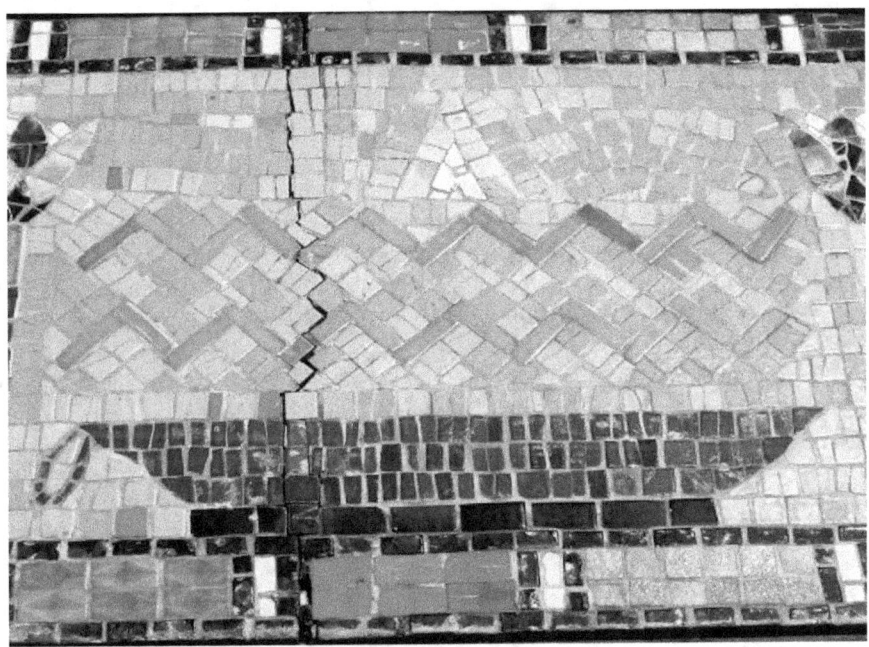

Holy Land Ceramic Art 23. Sure it could be a basket with handle but how about a bowl of soup with the vapor rising.

3. Bus Trip
4. Site

EGYPTIAN MUSEUM OF ANTIQUITIES
5. Post Site Lecture
After Site Lecturer: Dr. Oswald Benjamin

Today we visited the Egyptian Museum. I am going to give you some basic general information about trips and round about Cairo.

Color or physical appearance of the ancient Egyptians. Remember. Artifacts for the day-to-day use were not found. There is much I must say. They were of perishable materials – wooden forks, spoons, houses of mud brick, etc.

The peopling of ancient Egypt – much not shown in Museums. The nasal features, which were knocked off. Should we assume the ancient Egyptians had one nose? There were various facial expressions of the Egyptians.

The Hyksos invasion brought different peoples to Egypt and from then on it was an onslaught upon the indigenous race composition.

Herodotus – The father of historical research and analysis, anthropologically speaking.

In his Book II *Euterpe* in the *Histories*, he wrote: "The Egyptians, Colchians, Ethiopians and *Nubians*, all had thick lips, broad noses, curly hair and burnt of skin."

The Hyksos

Assyrians – Under Ashurbanipal

Cambyses

Darius II 525 B.C.

332 B.C. the Greeks overran Egypt.

The Romans and Julius Caesar

All brought no wives, but all soldiers.

Hannibal took only soldiers. We assume they had Iberian women. Or should we believe they were "doing it" with the elephants!

The same thing must be assumed for Europeans. From the time of the Hyksos Egypt became a melting pot.

The African woman bore the brunt of the burden. She had to get along. Sometimes her African man was at home but she had to get the dollar, or the coin of the day.

QUINTESSENTIAL BOOK
"THE HOLY LAND"

Holy Land Papyrus 37. Carpet Factory illustration depicting the Sky Goddess Nuit giving birth to the sun in the morning and consuming it in the afternoon, as well as a parade of gods and other wonderful colored collections.

On the Colchians: Maspero said: "The Colchians were negroid but not of negro physiognomy." That is to say the Egyptians were Negroid but not Negro. Remember, Beethoven was described by his Biographers as "Negroid" and "Negro," "swarthy," "black," and so on. See J.A. Rogers. *Sex and Race*.

6. Byzantine Period

7. Coptic

8. Christian

9. Arabs

10. Mamelukes – Turkish

11. French

12. English

There were many great, modern (20th century) largely African-American writers, who were concerned about the color problem. We have Dr. John Clarke, Dr. Yosef ben-Jochannan, Carter G. Woodson, Du Bois, Diop, Van Sertima, J. A. Rogers and some of the younger ones, Molefi Asante and Maulana Karenga, Wade

FREDERICK MONDERSON

Nobles. There are others. They wrote many things.

Chancellor Williams argued "They were mulattos!" This was because of the mule. The mule's father is the horse. The mother a donkey. Mules are hybrid. Thus this mulatto was assigned to the Egyptians.

Tutankhamon

Different peoples. The pharaoh shown with conquered people as king's foot mat.

Tut is shown black. Henna changes. Henna used on modern brides' skins. No matter what their color, they turned red after being colored with Henna.

Tut's exhibit shows people of various colors.

From the time of the Persians in 525 B.C., until 1952 when General Naguib overthrew King Farouk, for 2500 years all Egyptian rulers had at least one foreign parent.

Nasser's father was Arab and his mother Sudanese.

Sadat's father was Arab and his mother Sudanese.

Mubarak both parents Arab.

Nubians – The vast majority reflected their own self. Others reflected a mixture with Arabs and others.

The Egyptians show themselves in the resurrection as green. Are we to assume they were green? However, both blue and green are forms of Black.

We have to look at the Nile – Uganda and Nubia.

Hunefer says in his papyrus, the *Papyrus of Hunefer*, "We came from the beginning of the Nile where God Hapi dwells at the foot hills of the Mountains of the Moon." Kilimanjaro – is the mountain of the Moon. Also Rowenzori – Mountain of the moon.

This is really a mountain range. Thus they came from inner Africa. We should not argue with Europeans. The Egyptian writers told us where they came from.

Hunefer came from his Black mama's womb.

The image of Jesus that Michelangelo painted was not the real Jesus.

QUINTESSENTIAL BOOK "THE HOLY LAND"

Tut's exhibit revalidated what I learned.

Some of us are still confused about who built the pyramids.

Van Deniken said: "They came from outer space and built the pyramids from the top down." This is nonsense.

I speak Soulville English – not Shakespearean English. Jesus spoke the language of the people. The man in the street.

Tut lets us get closer to the skin, in-lays, jewelry.

Brothers and sisters, Nubians were doing the same thing, jewelry and all. It all had to do with the same thing. Rosa Parks and Sister Betty Shabazz were great Black women. The brothers must respect the Black woman.

Q. Dr. Benjamin, What do you input on Dr. Diop's melanin?

Ans. This gives us our color.

Q. Why is Seth represented as red?

Ans. The mummies were painted red because they were dead. Black is life, red is death.

Optional statements

6. Discussion

FREDERICK MONDERSON

Holy Land Illustration 97. Coffin of Bak-en-Mut, a priest of Amen-Ra at Thebes, about B.C. 700. XXI or XXIInd Dynasty (left); and Painted wooden cover from inside the inner coffin of a priest of Amen-Ra at Thebes, about B.C. 800, XXIst or XXIInd Dynasty (right).

In his second article "Sacramental Ideas and Usages in Ancient Egypt" Aylward M. Blackman in *Society of Biblical Archaeology* Vol. 409, May 1918, pp. 86-91, wrote: "Now let us consider the purifacatory ceremonies undergone by the living

QUINTESSENTIAL BOOK "THE HOLY LAND"

pharaoh. As prospective pharaoh the Sun god washed him in infancy. As actual pharaoh he was washed again during the coronation ceremony just before the diadems were placed upon his head. On both occasions, as depicted in the well-known series of reliefs at Deir el-Bahari, the water issues from the ewers which are being emptied over the pharaoh's head, as strings of Ankh symbols to god Iahes who officiates at the coronation purification [and] thus addresses the king: "I purify thee with the waters of all life and good fortune, all stability, all health and happiness."

"Piankhi, on his way from Ke-ere' ha, to Heliopolis where he was to be recognized by the Sun-god as his son and as pharaoh, stopped to 'Purify himself in the cool pool (Mer Keb hu)' and to 'wash his face in the stream of Nun in which he washes his face.' The pharaoh was also purified before he officiated in a temple, by two priests impersonating Horus and Thoth, or Horus and Seth."

"A relief at Karnak depicts Horus and Seth purifying Sethos I before officiating in the Temple of Amon." "The reigning sovereign was sprinkled by the Sun-god's bath attendants in order to confirm his identity with that divinity; for the same reason that Piankhi was thought to perform his ablutions in." "Cool Pool," was also called the "Stream of Nun," the god was doubtless supposed to be reborn through the medium of its waters.

"In the Pyramid Texts the dead pharaoh is conceived in Nun and born in Nun. "Mother of Millions and seed (or Begetter of Millions), suggests that those who washed in the pool were thought to be reborn." "The New Kingdom commentary informs us that the 'great god' to whom the pools were sacred is the Sun-god."

The living pharaoh, therefore was apparently believed to be reborn like the Sun-god, whose embodiment he was, through the medium of water being actually used for ablutions by the god himself, or being identified with the primeval ocean out of which he first came into existence." "Ceremonial ablutions would then have been looked upon as affiliative as well as regenerative; and there are indeed indications that this view of the rite actually existed."

"A pyramid text quoted [in this paper (p. 63f)] speaks of the dead pharaoh as having been purified by Atmu in the Heliopolitan name and as having come into existence and grown tall. Atum is then asked to endorse him in his embrace, for he (the pharaoh) is the son of his (Atum's) body forever. This passage suggests that the deceased king was thought to be reborn and affiliated to the Sun god by being washed in his sacred pool. Compare the already discussed washing of the infant heir-apparent by the Sun god. In Chap 17 of The *Book of the Dead*, the deceased asserts that the washing he underwent in the two pools attached to the temple of Harshef at Hieracleopolis Magna, took place on the day of his birth.'

FREDERICK MONDERSON

Again, in the "Karnak Relief" discussed above, the words "I have purified thee with life and good fortune so that thou are rejuvenated like the father Amun" point to the Pharaoh's rebirth in the capacity of the Son of the Sun-god rather than in that of the embodiment of the god.

"It should be recollected, in this connection that Piankhi, was on his way to Heliopolis, in order to be acknowledged there by Ra – as his son and as lawful Pharaoh, when we was washed in the sacred pool. Was it, therefore, through the medium of lustration such as this that the pharaoh became "Son of Ra?" If so, then the idea that the Sun god visited the queen in the guise of the reigning pharaoh and so began their heir to the throne would probably have arisen after the identification of the highly-sexual god Amon of Thebes with Re-Atum. This gross conception of the solar parentage may well have been a Theban innovation; dating from the early New Kingdom when "god's wife" appears for the first time as a title of the Egyptian queen." (91).

Holy Land Photos 109. Visitors mill around in the garden of the Cairo Museum of Egyptian Antiquities housing its wonderful collection of ancient artifacts. The entrance is the white area to the right just below the three flags flying on the roof.

Are there any questions?

Juliet Brown: How did the ancient Egyptians view infidelity or adultery on part of a woman?

Dr. Fred Monderson: They considered it a sin. The 19th Clause of the *Negative*

QUINTESSENTIAL BOOK
"THE HOLY LAND"

Confession of Chapter 125 of the *Book of the Dead* read: "I have not defiled the wife of a husband." This meant the wife of another man. But there are other instances where this issue is raised. During the reign of Rameses V, an Elephantine ship captain is accused of adultery with two women. In the Instruction of Ptah-Hotep, he tells: "If you enter a household as master, friend, or visitor, stay away from the women." There are still other instances. The *Story of Ubaner* whose wife lay with a peasant and she was burned. In the *Tale of the Two Brothers*, Bito the younger whose brother Anup's wife tried to frame him, is like Pothiphar's wife tried to frame Joseph.

Nelson Escobar: Much has been said about the Predynastic period, but can we give an estimate of how old Egyptian civilization really is?
Dr. Fred Monderson: I know we said the Sphinx may be 10,000 years old and *Science* gives a date of 14,500 before present for early agriculture along the banks

Holy Land Ceramic Art 24. "Watering" the hand that shook the world.

of the Nile. Remember, the Egyptian precession is 26,000 years. Some scholars argue to measure one means you must have two or possibly three. This presumes 26,000, 52,000 and even 78,000 years of astronomy time calculation. While the

FREDERICK MONDERSON

first precession is actual, and the other two postulated, Charles Finch III gives two actual precessions and tow postulated for a 104,000 year period. We must remember the New York Times discovery of red paint in a pot at 107,000 years. So these numbers are not that far-fetched.

The *Turin Papyrus*, which dates to the Middle Kingdom, gives 23,200 years for rule by the gods, and another 2000 years for rule by the lesser gods or "followers of Horus." Manetho does give lengthy years for rule by the gods and demi-gods before the kings took over. Manetho, whose work is credible, certainly pushes the age of Egypt back many millennia before the dynastic period began.

Walter Brown: Illustrations on temple walls and in some of the pyramids and mastaba tombs show presentations being made to the god or individual, how important would you say was the "Table of Offerings?"
Dr. Fred Monderson: Very important. What you call a "Table of Offering" is also an altar. You could not make presentation into the hands of the god so an altar was needed for the ritual offering. In the tombs, we see a raised structure with legs and flat top decorated with meat, bread, fruit, vegetables, oils, or container liquids and even flowers.

In the great court of most temples, stood an altar for services permitted for those who made it this far into the temple. Equally too, each temple's sanctuary had an altar for the ritual that also served as an eating table for the god when he had his meals. Importantly, no incense was burned on the god's altar but in an incenser on the ground nearby.

Very few altars or "Table of Offerings" were found in place or *in situ*. One made of alabaster was found at the Vth Dynasty Abusir Sun Temple of Ne-user-Re. It stood in the court before an obelisk. At Karnak, an altar stood in the Great Court and another great altar by Rameses III stood in the open Middle Kingdom Court before Thutmose III's Festival Temple, the *Akh Menu*, of the XVIIIth Dynasty. We believe Thutmose III himself dedicated a similar one. Another altar made of white limestone was found *in situ* at Deir el Bahari in the court to the right of the Upper Court. Still, another altar was found at Gebel Barkal, the Ethiopian temple, perhaps built by Taharka. The altar or "Table of Offerings" was an important vehicle upon which celebrants were able to communicate with their god.

George Washington: What is the purpose of the sacrifice and who are the people involved in making it?
Dr. Fred Monderson: The purpose of sacrifice is to secure a benefit, but the benefit may be for the donor, or the recipient, or for a third party.

R.A.S. Macalister in *Encyclopedia of Religion and Ethics* (1921, 11: 32) wrote on this subject: "The persons and materials involved, in a complete sacrificial ritual,

QUINTESSENTIAL BOOK
"THE HOLY LAND"

are four in number - either four individuals or four communities. These are (1) the person or persons offering the sacrifice; (2) the person or persons for whose benefit the sacrifice is offered; (3) the intermediary or priest, who receives the sacrifice from the person offering and disposes of it according to the rubrics governing the ritual; and (4) the person to whom the sacrifice is offered. On occasion these four may be reduced to three, (1) and (2) being identical; but as a rule the interposition of a priest between the person offering and the recipient is considered desirable, as he by his ordination and consecration is supposed to be more familiar with the unseen world, and by his special knowledge is able to avoid ritual mistakes."

Robert Matthews: Would you say the religion of Egypt was ancestor worship?
Dr. Fred Monderson: I remind you, Cheikh Anta Diop pointed out in his book, *Cultural Unity of Black Africa*, there was only one African culture but many manifestations of it. In essence, personal immortality is when living people remember the dead ancestor. Collective immortality is when no one alive remembers the individual except that he was good to the tribe or community.

Of course the good ancestor looked over and protected the village. But, while the good ancestor was friendly, the bad one or strangers were unfriendly and had to be feared. The *Golden Bough* by Frazier deals with this issue, claiming its widespread practice not only in Africa but elsewhere outside the continent.

Kurt Sethe reiterated that Manetho's prehistoric kings lived as gods and men who departed and thus can be considered ancestors who were worshipped. These individuals were not worshipped as ancestors who had passed on but as gods who ruled as kings.

The Sakkara Tablet of Tenuri or Tenroy, the *Karnak Tablet* of Thutmose III, and *Abydos Tablet* of Seti I are of ancestor kings reaching back to the earliest times. Even Osiris who was worshipped as an ancestor was really a dead king who was a god.

Mrs. McNair: How does Egyptian Baptism compare with baptism in the modern religious sense?
Dr. Fred Monderson: In the modern sense baptism is about sanctifying and welcoming one into the religious community. Baptism is generally by water, but Baptism by fire can burn. The illustrations in the temple show the pharaoh being baptized by two gods, who pour signs of ankh and uaz, life and stability, over him. This ritual purification is done before he could enter the temple and officiate at the ceremony for the god.

Michael Sinclair: What type of materials did the peasants use for building their places of dwelling?

FREDERICK MONDERSON

Dr. Fred Monderson: Petrie tells us: "In Egypt the commonest materials used by the peasantry are maize stalks, mud, mud bricks, palm sticks, and palm logs. The simplest huts are made by lashing maize stalks (stems of the durrah, called *bus*), together by means of palm-fiber. The flat screens thus formed are set upright at right angles, and lashed together down the corners. If the weather is cold and the wind strong, they are plastered over with mud. In this form the temporary dwellings in the fields are set up for two or three months of the pasture season. Where a column is required, a bundle of maize stalks is bound together from 4 to 10 inches in diameter, and plastered with mud, thus forming an extremely stiff and unbreakable mass."

Peter Monderson: What are the different types of temples built by the ancient Egyptians?

Dr. Fred Monderson: There were generally three types of temples, worship, mortuary and processional temples. The smallest is the processional with its front and back open. When the god was traveling in his barque or on the road, and had to rest, the priest would enter, deposit the ark and exit through the rear. Of course, there were chapels or kiosks to particular gods. Sometimes these were built to triads and even grottos which were small rock cut places of worship. However, all others can stand alone, the chapels and kiosks were generally attached to a larger temple. Most temples had a sanctuary deep in the recesses of the temple where darkness prevailed. However, Karnak had an open sanctuary that allowed the sun to shine through it. Perhaps I should reiterate, Dr. ben-Jochannan said we must not enter the Sanctuary.

Leonard James: Big as it was, how did the Priesthood coordinate its activities?

Dr. Fred Monderson: The Priesthood was able to coordinate its extensive activities through its organized bureaucratic structure and possessing fleets of boats that plied the river constantly establishing communication. They were very good administrators and intellectuals and teachers of intellectuals who were able to coordinate both religious and secular activities because their members were in all walks of life.

QUINTESSENTIAL BOOK
"THE HOLY LAND"

Holy Land Illustration 98. Mummy and cartonnage case of Thent-Mut-s-Kebti, a priestess of Amen-Ra at Thebes, XXIst-XXIInd Dynasty (left); and Mummy of Pa-Khat-Khart-Heru, an incense bearer of Khensu at Thebes, XXIst-XXIInd Dynasty (right).

Regina Hendricks: Why was Ra so popular with the Egyptians?

FREDERICK MONDERSON

Dr. Fred Monderson: The popularity of Ra and then Amon-Ra is based on his humaneness and his love of righteousness. He is said to create righteousness. He is said to be the Sun-god, the creator of and champion of righteousness. Baikie (1919, 10: 795) mentions "Breasted has clearly shown that 'the great god' of ... the divinity who first came to be regarded as the champion of righteousness and the judge of the dead, was not Osiris, but the Heliopolitan sun-god Re-Atum; indeed the sun-god is said to be he 'who fashioned (ms) righteousness." Accordingly we read in a Middle Kingdom Coffin Text: 'I am Re who came forth from Nun .... My detestation is wickedness, I behold it not. I am he who made righteousness.'"

James Madison: How did one triumph over death?
Dr. Fred Monderson: One triumphed over death by being a virtuous person whose life is an example for others. Blackman (1919, 10: 795) sets out a case for the development of the belief in a posthumous judgment in the following statement: "According to the earliest religious writings that we possess, the so-called Pyramid Texts, the chief qualification for admittance to the realm of the sun-god was physical purity. Magic also played a great part in furthering the welfare of the dead, the Pyramid Texts themselves being for the most part a collection of powerful spells, which enabled him for whom or by whom they were recited to enter the celestial kingdom. But even in these very ancient texts more than mere physical cleanliness or magical power is sometimes demanded; the deceased must also be righteous. Thus we find that the ceremonial washing of the dead king by the four gods who preside over the pool of Kenset, or by the Worshippers of Horus, has also an ethical significance. During or following the ablutions a spell asserting the righteousness of the deceased is recited. The ghostly ferryman who conveys the dead over to the Field of Earu is thus addressed 'O thou who ferriest over the righteous who hath no boat, ferryman of the Field of Earu, this N. is righteous before the sky, before the earth, this N. is righteous before this island of the land whiter he hath swum and whither he hath arrived.'"

"The claim of the deceased to be righteous had of course to be tested, and in the imagination of the Egyptians, with their innate love of litigation; the test naturally took the form of a legal process. There are already in the Pyramid Texts allusions to the posthumous trial; but many of the inscriptions on tomb-stones and tomb-chapel walls of officials and private persons from the VIth dynasty onwards are explicit on this subject. On the one hand, the deceased threatens with judgment at the hands of 'the great god, the lord of judgment, in the place where judgment is had, those who injure his tomb-chapel, enter it in a state of ceremonial impurity, injure its inscriptions, or violate its endowments.' On the other hand, the deceased himself claims to have been virtuous, 'because I desired that it might be well with me in the presence of the great god' or 'in order that I might offer righteousness to the great god, the lord of heaven.'"

QUINTESSENTIAL BOOK "THE HOLY LAND"

Frederick Maloney: How did the ancient Egyptian view the question of truth?
Dr. Fred Monderson: Everyone seems to know the benefit and utility of being truthful and we can pretty well believe the ancient Egyptian was also aware of this reality. A.M. Blackman's "Righteousness: Egyptian" in *Encyclopedia of Religion and Ethics* (1919, 10: 793) asserts: "Truthfulness seems to have been highly esteemed, and was particularly looked for in the great and powerful. 'Speak not falsehood, thou art great,' says the *Eloquent Peasant* to the high steward Rensi; indeed such a one must 'destroy lies and create truth [or 'right']. An Old Kingdom noble asserts that he was straightforward in the royal presence and free from falsehood. Says another: 'I spoke the truth which the god loves every day.' The sage Ptahhotep recommends one to act in accordance with right, free from falsehood. A well known XVIIIth dynasty official claims to have been free from iniquity, accurate of mind, with no lie in him. 'Speak the truth (*Ma'at*). Do right (*Ma'at*) for it is great, it is mighty, it is enduring,' - was an utterance ascribed to the sun-god Re himself. 'I have not spoken lies knowingly,' says the deceased to Osiris. 'I have not spoken lies' is one of the statements in the "assertion of Sinlessness.'"

Lesley Jacobs: How was justice administered in ancient Egypt?
Dr. Fred Monderson: Justice was the right of the people and the god, king and justices were expected to do what is right. Blackman (1919, 10: 793) says: "The viziers, Nomarchs, and high officials who governed and administered the laws were expected to exhibit a high standard of justice. We are informed that 'men expect the exercise of justice in the procedure of the vizier.' The vizier must not be wroth only with what one ought to be wroth with. He must deal with petitioners in accordance with the law and equity and help them to their rights. The petitioner must not be able to say when the verdict is pronounced: 'My right has not been given me. Again, the vizier must not be a respecter of persons or show partiality, for that is what the god abhors. He must not, however, go to the other extreme and act like the Vizier Akhthoi, who discriminated against some of his own kin in favor of strangers, in fear lest it should be wrongly said of him that he favored his kin dishonestly; 'that,' we are informed, 'is more than justice.' The ideal judge must be 'a father of the lowly (*nmh*), a husband of the widow, a brother of the forsaken, and the garment of the motherless ... one who comes forth at the voice of him who calls.' If such a one veils his face against the violent, who shall repress crime. A judge must be as unerring and impartial as the balance."

FREDERICK MONDERSON

Holy Land Photo 110. Bronze depiction of two Hathors crowning the Goddess Mut.

Walter Brown: What really are the Negative Confessions?
Dr. Fred Monderson: What has been called the 'Assertion of Sinlessness' or the *'Negative Confession'* is simply a list of things the deceased mentions he did not do while he lived on earth. "Among the sins there denied are murder, incitement to murder, robbery, theft, oppression, impiety, lying, slander, dishonesty, avarice, hasty temper, pride, loquacity, eavesdropping, impurity (adultery and masturbation), and a number of ceremonial transgressions."

Michelliea Georges: What was the Egyptian view of good qualities?
Dr. Fred Monderson: Generosity and beneficence; avoidance of slander; honesty and fair dealing, faithfulness, obedience, and deference to superiors; piety towards the dead; and sexual morality. We could add courage to this list.

Kashmoney Malone: How popular was Amon in Nubia?
Dr. Fred Monderson: Very popular! One description of him is as: "And in this

QUINTESSENTIAL BOOK
"THE HOLY LAND"

character of the all-beneficent sun god, the living lamp, which rises from out of the ocean of heaven, Amon attained real popularity. The officials prayed to him for promotion, the oppressed trust in him, for he is the vizier of the poor, who takes no bribes, and who also does not corrupt the witnesses. Any cautions person making a promise added these words: 'If Amon permits me to live.'" This popularity was carried over in Nubia where a number of temples were dedicated to the god throughout Egyptian influence and after. Erman (1907: 67) throws light on the relationship of the god to the people of Nubia. "When the Pharaohs of the Middle Kingdom conquered Nubia they left the people their god Dedwen, and associated with him the Egyptian cataract god Khnum. In the New Kingdom, when conquest extended greatly to the south and Nubia was organized as a province under the rule of a vizier, the religion of Nubia was Egyptianized. The great gods of the Empire, Amon, Ptah, and Re Harakhti, were introduced into the country with Isis and Hathor, and in addition to these the Nubians were given the Pharaohs themselves to worship as deities of the country. At Semneh the people were forced to worship Sesostris III, the first conqueror of their country, and also Thothmes III who had recently conquered them."

At Soleb, Amenophis III established himself as a god; at Abu Simbel, Rameses II was enthroned with the gods in the holy of holies in the great temple, while in like manner his wife is worshipped in the smaller temple with Hathor.

Magnificently did the government maintain the dignity of their gods before the eyes of the Nubians. In this sparsely populated, poverty-stricken country, they built temples which could bear comparison with the celebrated marvels of architecture of Egyptian towns, and when the narrow valley could not provide sufficient space, the cliffs themselves were hollowed out, and thus formed the marvelous rock temples of Abu Simbel, Gerf Hussein, or Der. Quite in the south, however, somewhere near the place where the Soudan railway leaves the desert and strikes once more into the Nile Valley, at the town of Napata in the pure mountain, a temple was founded which received the same name, throne of the two lands, which was borne by the great temple of Karnak. It was obvious that it was intended to be the southern counterpart of Karnak, the official temple of Nubia. It was a matter of course that the priesthood of this temple should receive a corresponding endowment of land and revenues; however little such a provision might be in accordance with the poverty of the country."

So therefore we can argue Amon was very popular in Nubia.

So, in summary, Brothers and Sisters, we have made a wonderful excursion into the historical and cultural origins and experience of early African man on the banks of the Nile River in Northeast Africa. For me this has always been a revitalizing and intellectual adventure as well as a reality check that bolsters my interface with the modern world. Pride in the realization that ancestral heritage is

FREDERICK MONDERSON

so profound bolsters my daily efforts as a Black man, in meeting the challenges, battles and wars I face, by the minute, daily and each and every year.

I wish every one of you will benefit each in his or her way, from what you brought in terms of preparation, what you saw and learnt and what you do with the knowledge you now have. If you read further, delve even deeper into the Egyptian adventure you can experience a profound transformation in your thinking and how you view the world.

Leaving New York, we flew into Cairo and on to Luxor. There you saw the monuments of Karnak and Luxor, the Valley of the Kings, the Mortuary temples of Deir el Bahari, Ramesseum and some of you did Medinet Habu. Then the day excursion to Abydos Temple of Seti I was the highlight of the tour, where we saw the "Immaculate Conception.". On the way back we saw Dendera, worship temple of Goddess Hathor, with the Goddess Nut (Nuit) in her chapel giving birth to the sun in the morning and swallowing it in the evening while shining her wonderful rays on the Temple of Dendera.

We then headed south by motor coach for the worship temples of Esneh, Edfu, Kom Ombo and arrived at Aswan, the city to the south of Egypt. From there we flew to Abu Simbel to experience the twin temples of Rameses II and his wife Nefertari. After that we visited Philae Temple of Isis now on Agilka Island and onto Kalabsha Temple of God Mendulese, older brother of Osiris. You saw the High Dam and Lotus Memorial, a symbol of cooperation between Egypt and the Soviet Union. The courageous ones among you challenged the arduous climb to view the Tombs of the Nobles with its magnificent view of the Aswan area. Then we crossed the river again to view the Kitchener Gardens and Mausoleum of Aga Khan. Those of you who spent the evening at the Nubian Museum must admit it's one of the best displays of its kind in the world. I also think another highlight of the trip was the visit we paid to the Nubian Village where we enjoyed their warm reception and hospitality. Again, thanks for bringing those school supplies for the children.

With this leg of the trip completed, we flew from Aswan to Cairo and checked into the Meridien Hotel. In Cairo we visited the Pyramids and Sphinx on the Ghizeh Plateau. Then we moved to the Step-Pyramid at Sakkara. On the way back, we visited the Museum at Memphis, Egypt's capital during the Old Kingdom. Finally we visited the Cairo Museum of Egyptian Antiquities, the greatest museum in the entire world. Finally, for those who could haggle, the Khalili Bazaar offered many bargains, perhaps even better than the Sook at Aswan.

Throughout the food was excellent, that in the Nubian Restaurants with its melodic entertainment was superb. I know some of you bought cartouches and other jewels, perfumes and even papyrus at the different factories. I bought and also

QUINTESSENTIAL BOOK
"THE HOLY LAND"

saw some of you buying books at the different museums. Perhaps the most exhilarating experience I enjoyed was the warm reception we received in the visit to the Nubian Village at Aswan. I'm sure you liked how they received their "Nubian American brothers and sisters." I thank you for bringing pens, pencils, notebooks and other sundry items for the children at the school. The only collection we made was for the school and I think that was a good idea. Whoever made the suggestion should be commended.

Overall, after where we have been, what we have seen, what we have learnt, what we have done, what we have experienced, I'm sure you will agree it was money well spent. I have been reading Dr. ben-Jochannan since 1972. Let me say to you what he said to me on my first trip, more than 25 years ago: "Now that you have the knowledge, what are you going to do with it?"

If you will permit me, perhaps I can make some suggestions as to what you can do with the new information. By virtue of the vast amount of knowledge contained in the monuments and sources and materials written on Egypt, interest in the subject can be a lifelong educational experience for you. You see, we want our people to be knowledgeable and reclaim Egypt in their minds, hearts, pronouncements and lectures and publications. We must claim Egypt as African and to emphatically affirm it was a Black civilization. To aid this effort we could engage in some of the following:

Holy Land Photo 111. Dr. Frederick Monderson sits beside his mentor, friend and brother, the revered Dr. Yosef ben-Jochannan, "master teacher," author, lecturer and Egyptological pioneer.

FREDERICK MONDERSON

Join and maintain consistent membership in study groups to discuss and stay abreast of unfolding research.

Do our own research and write and publish our findings. Create our own baseline essays based on our observations and deductions. Identify distortions and omissions in the African historiographic record. Correct the former and include the latter as our contribution to the general African historiographic reconstruction taking place.

Teach the young the truth about Egypt and Africa. Make them aware that Europeans did the work of recovery of Egypt. Thus, we get their spin on interpretation. Mankind traces its roots to "Black Africa" and thereafter no one knows how many cultures ended up influencing its later development.

Let us be mindful of the research, findings and pronouncements of our elders, learned scholars, who believed like Prof. John H. Clarke, the "People who preached racism colonized history." Dr. Clarke felt, their conspiracy theory, was to justify the pre-eminence of Europe at the expense of all other areas of the world.

Be mindful of Dr. ben-Jochannan's admonitions, "find the oldest materials available," become versed in it and then go from there. He felt that our aim was to justify the pre-eminence of Black Africa. However, in reality, the Europeans who developed a passion for researching ancient Egypt were enthralled with analyzing the depths of this ancient and glorious civilization. Based on deductions from literature and appearance of the people in architecture and art, plus from trade routes, they theorized as to how the Egyptians were to be. We must, therefore, be careful of more recent sanitized books on Egypt, regardless of whether written by Black or White scholars and writers. This is because modern scholarship, particularly American, White or Black, has become very sloppy and poorly researched.

Challenge modern interpretations of Egyptian history by examining the contents of their references and referents.

Cheikh Anta Diop's works are absolutely essential as part of the overall equation in assessing Egypt, its creators and their creations.

Become more versed on where the materials are housed in museums world-wide to be able to sew together the disparate threads of truth scattered in this African cultural diffusion, being mindful that our descendants will continue the effort centuries from now. As we stand on the shoulders of Delaney, Perry, Garvey, DuBois, Woodson, Huggins, Jackson, Williams, ben-Jochannan, Clarke, and even Van Sertima, Karenga, Asante, Nobles, Carruthers, Akbar, Leonard James, Browder and so many others, then our progeny will benefit from our courageous

QUINTESSENTIAL BOOK
"THE HOLY LAND"

efforts and insights. That being so, may the great African divinities smile and be pleased with our work, even if it just begins with this one visit to the Holy Land, Alkebu-Lan, Mother Africa, in Northeast Africa.

Forward Ever. Backward Never.
Peace.
Dr. Fred Monderson.
Brooklyn, New York
April 5, 2014

Ok. That's it for today. I wish to thank you for your patience, understanding, insightful questions and comments and for your overall support. Again, Thank You!

Holy Land Illustration 99. The "true" Northern Colonnade at Hatshepsut's Temple at Deir el Bahari.

Mr. John Stewart: While I agree with much of what has been seen and said, I must

FREDERICK MONDERSON

also agree with the Library of Congress' wise saying that "There is but one temple in the Universe and that is the body of man."

9. Lounge Discussion

GOOD-BYE CELEBRATION

My friends, it was a privilege to take you through this experience in adventure of an intellectual and spiritual nature. I'm pretty well assured you got more than you bargained for, in many respects.

When we landed; instead of stopping in Cairo we flew on to Luxor, the southern city. This was the capital of Egypt during the Middle and New Kingdoms. While the pyramids are stupendous, I thought the archaeology, art and architecture of Luxor would have a more immediate and lasting impression. As you experienced the check in process and became familiar with the routine, many of you just fell in step. That was good. The first temple we visited was Karnak, the magnificent "palace" of Luxor where the gods visited.

Holy Land Illustration 99a. Tomb of Horemhab. With Ra-Horakhty at his back, Horemhab meets Hathor who grasps his hand (left); and he offers two jars to Anquetor Hathor and stands before Osiris (right).

QUINTESSENTIAL BOOK
"THE HOLY LAND"

Holy Land Ceramic Art 25. May there be many such jars full of success in this important venture.

This temple took nearly two thousand years to build and equally too suffered at the hands of the invader. The twin temple of Luxor has been a repository of great esoteric and artistic knowledge and is principally the work of two great Pharaohs. The Valley of the Kings and Queens, and Abydos and Dendera, then the Ramesseum and Medinet Habu, represent the greatest ages of ancient Kemet, today's Egypt. Esneh, Edfu and Kom Ombo, then Temple of Isis, Kalabsha, Unfinished Obelisk and Mausoleum of Aga Khan and for those of you who visited the Tombs of the Nobles, these were eye opening and challenging experiences. The return to Cairo with its stupendous pyramids, sphinx, local repertoire and even the Khalili shopping were adventures in themselves added to the Step Pyramid of Sakkara and the Memphis Museum, and many of you were surprised and enlightened beyond your wildest imagination. I'm sure you often wondered how a single institution could house some 120,000 pieces of ancient treasure and 1

FREDERICK MONDERSON

replica, the Rosetta Stone, and how this image will affect your thinking for some time to come. Nevertheless, the experiences you take back to America should be shared with others, and let this begin an even greater search for more knowledge and truth and let it reflect the new you. Always remember what Dr. Ben-Jochannan asked of his students, "Now you have the knowledge, what are you going to do with it?" It was a pleasure to be with you on this trip. God bless and take care.

Day 15. CAIRO AIRPORT FLIGHT TO NEW YORK

1. Wake Up

Esperanza Rodriguez: Good Morning, Mi Amor. Your schedule for today calls for a bus ride to the Cairo Airport and flight back to New York. The review of your books under "Education and Books" in the *Daily Challenge* newspaper is reproduced and ready to be handed out to the group.

Dr. Fred Monderson: Thank you so much for everything, my dear.

Holy Land Photo 112. Wonderful ceiling raised relief painted depiction of the protective Vulture Goddess wearing the Osiris White Crown with feathers and the Red Crown.

QUINTESSENTIAL BOOK "THE HOLY LAND"

Holy Land Illustration 99b. Tomb of Horemhab. King offers two jars to Osiris; he greets Hathor in horns and disk; offers two jars to Ra-Horakhty in Double Crown (left); and, again the two jars to Ra-Horakhty, greets Isis and offers two jars (right).

"SPREADING THE KNOWLEDGE - EDUCATION AND BOOKS" REVIEW

Daily Challenge Tuesday, October 10, 2000. New York City's only Black daily.

In "Ten Poems Praising Great Blacks for Mike Tyson" and "Seven Letters to Mike Tyson on Egyptian Temples," Dr. Fred Monderson has accomplished a difficult task.

Written between March 10, 1999 and May 22, 1999, the two works were completed during the former heavyweight champion's imprisonment, and were sent to him in the Montgomery County Detention Center in Maryland.

A New York City public school teacher, former college instructor and researcher on ancient Egypt, the author has served as a tour guide to Egypt under the renowned Dr. Yosef ben-Jochannan. He has also written several other title including "Glory of the Ancestors," "Essays on Ancient Kemet," "The Colonnade," "Architectural Fragments: From Here and There," "Reflections of Ancient Kemet and Other Essays," "Where are the Kamite Kings," "Karnak Temple: The Majestic Architecture of ancient Kemet," and "An Ancient Egyptian Architectural Kaleidoscope."

FREDERICK MONDERSON

In addition, Monderson has penned nearly 1000 articles in the *Daily Challenge*, *Afro Times* and *New American* newspapers.

In "Ten Poems," Monderson reaches out to Tyson during the period of his most serious challenge assuring the fighter that he could be "as tall as Queen Hatshepsut's standing obelisk at Karnak temple." The poems use references to Egyptian gods and personalities, viz., Amon, Osiris, Imhotep, Thoth, Isis, Hathor, Senmut's Praise of Queen Hatshepsut, Nephthys, Ode to Queen Tiy and Cleopatra- with compelling effect.

The author's "opening the firmaments" and "unlocking of the pillars of wisdom of the ancients," is worthy of recognition. A slim book of 15 pages, "Ten Poems" is nevertheless a significant work that should be read.

In the much larger "Seven Letters" (576 PPG) the author captures the essentials and fundamentals of the architectural history of ancient Nile Valley Africans who gave so much to the beginnings of civilization, government, art, craft, religion, administration, mathematics, science, medicine, etc. There are now 237 photographs in this book.

The author informs Tyson of the wonderful history of the ancient Africans along the Nile River; this work serves not simply as an informative history but also a guidebook for travelers to Egypt, the land of ancient Kemet.
[ISBN 1-58721-002-9].

DR. FRED MONDERSON EGYPTIAN TOURS – CONTACT

Orleane Williams-Brooks CTC of Travel Nostrand Travel Bureau, Inc., 730 Nostrand Avenue, Brooklyn, NY, 11216, handles Dr. Fred Monderson's tours to Egypt (718) 756-5300, 01, 02. Toll-free: 1-800-344-7220 Fax (718) 773-4906. The next scheduled tour to Egypt/ancient Kemet is July 10-July 24, 2014 for 15 days. The easiest way to access information on Dr. Monderson's books is to visit Amazon.com book section. Type Monderson for Author. In addition, the website FredsEgypt.com, net, org; blackfolksbooks.com and blackegypt.com are his personal websites. SuMon Publishers, PO Box 160586 Brooklyn, New York 11216

LOVE
DR. FRED MONDERSON

QUINTESSENTIAL BOOK
"THE HOLY LAND"

PEACE

Holy Land Papyrus 37. As he wears the lion skin and side locks and backed by his Queen holding a sistrum, the young King presents a plant to Osiris.

2. Breakfast

Dr. Leonard James: The pyramids are synonymous with ancient and modern Egypt. Famous for their monumental organizational and administrative cohesiveness and mystical wonderment, they defy the lapse of time. But what do these monuments truly represent? Some say tombs of the pharaohs. Others that

FREDERICK MONDERSON

these were national monuments with astronomical and religious implications. Still others say they were designed to awe the pharaoh's contemporaries and to harness the unemployed labor force lying idle by the inundation of the Nile. All this notwithstanding, the pyramids represent early African man's conscious application of the principles of science, labor, geometry, religion, bureaucratic organizational form and a labor force willing to construct a national project in praise of their monarch and deity.

Nonetheless, careful perusal of the landscape expresses the phenomenon of natural pyramids. In a desert environment, wind and sand against the natural highlands create erosion that forms a natural pyramid. Perhaps, this may be the origin of these houses of eternity. Nevertheless, it is difficult to argue against nature's influence on the man-made creations. Whatever, man's attempt to create the pyramids is a process began in the Third Dynasty with Imhotep's step-Pyramid at Sakkara for Pharaoh Zoser. In the first two dynasties, the kings were buried at Abydos, the nation's earliest religious capital, with cenotaph or dummy tombs at Sakkara.

In his bold experiment, Imhotep innovated a multi-storied building, using engaged and free standing columns and the false door façade. Whether end of the third or beginning of the Fourth Dynasty, Snefru gets credit for the bent and then the true pyramid. The art advanced rapidly and within a generation Khufu, Khafre and Menkaure built the great pyramids Ghizeh group. By the Fifth Dynasty, Unas had the Pyramid Texts inscribed in his structure. By the end of the Old Kingdom nearly 80 pyramids had been built in Egypt. A few were built in the Middle Kingdom but by this period, the age of pyramids had passed. The Ethiopians of the Twenty-fifth Dynasty built numerous pyramids at this later date. They were, however, on a less grandiose scale.

Walter Brown: Well done. Brief, accurate and insightful, Dr. James.

Mr. John Stewart: The last thing I may say to my brethren is as I saw on the walls of the Library of Congress: "There is one only good namely knowledge and one evil namely ignorance" and "Wisdom is the principal thing. Therefore get wisdom and with all thy getting get understanding."

Asantewaa Harris: I seem to remember Alfred Lloyd Tennyson (1809-1892) said that same thing in *Locksley Hall*, Line 127. He also said: "Self-reverence, Self-knowledge, Self-control, these three alone lead life's sovereign power," in *The Two Voices*, line 142 and "My strength is as the strength of ten because my heart is pure," in *Sir Galahad*, Stanza 1 (1842).

QUINTESSENTIAL BOOK "THE HOLY LAND"

CAIRO AIRPORT: Check in

CAIRO AIRPORT RETURN TO NEW YORK FLIGHT

Customs: Security requires that everyone and everything be checked. It's a little slow but we are very good at this.

Immigration: Please have your passport handy and evidence that you had checked your video camera when you arrived.

Holy Land Illustration 99c. Tomb of Horemhab. The King holds hand with Anubis; offers two jars to Hathor; meets Ra-Horakhty in Double Crown (left); offers two jars to Amentit or Hathor; stands before Osiris and finally stands before Ptah (right).

The Bus Ride home:

Dr. Fred Monderson: Brothers and sisters. By the grace of God we are returning home after a wonderful and tremendously enlightening experience. Dr. ben-Jochannan always said now you have the knowledge 'What are you going to do with it?' As we cross the Atlantic Ocean heading for our shores let us take a few minutes within our own consciousness and reflect where we have come from, where we are and where we are going. I wish each of you would think of some important saying whether you read it somewhere or heard it said, whether it was

FREDERICK MONDERSON

grandmother, mother or the neighbor who said it. Let it reflect your consciousness. In fact, just so it's remembered, write it down. Then begin anew the new you. Read even more to expand what you have learned. Buy books, certainly buy Dr. ben-Jochannan's books and Dr. John Henrik Clarke's books and speeches and teach the young, old and anyone who will listen. Boast of and share your photographs. It was a pleasure for me to be with you. I am pretty sure you would want to return. God Bless you. Remember, Mrs. Coretta Scott King in 1983 said: "When aroused the American conscience is a powerful force for reform."

Boarding the plane and being seated.

ON BOARD AIR EGYPT

The Captain: Ladies and Gentlemen, this is Captain Mohammed Farouk. We will be flying at a speed of 556 miles an hour at an altitude of 35,500 feet. The duration of our flight is 10 hours, 52 minutes. We should arrive in New York at 2: 57 PM. The weather in New York is beautiful, 84 degrees, sunny and clear. We will serve hot breakfast and lunch, and a cold serving before landing. Movies are scheduled and they will be between flashes of our progress across the Atlantic, for those people tracking our flight on the TV monitor. I will remove the seatbelt sign but if it comes on again, please return to your seat. No smoking on this flight. The flight assistants will be glad to help you in any way. Thanks for flying Egypt Air. I will come back on before we land in New York. Enjoy your flight.

REFLECTIONS OF *Characters* on *Board*:

Dr. Leonard James: Paul Robeson, in *Paul Robeson Speaks about Art and the Negro*, the *Mill gate*, December 1930 offered: "Having been given I must give. Man shall not live by bread alone. And what the farmer does I must do. I must feed the people with my song."

Walter Brown: I am so amazed by what I saw I must bring my sons on one of these trips so they would see and grow from it.

Mr. Peter Palmer: Mahabharata c. 5 B.C. extolled: "Be master of yourself, if you

QUINTESSENTIAL BOOK
"THE HOLY LAND"

will be the servant of duty."

Mr. John Brown: Education is the answer for any people if they want to be meaningful, much less contributors for their families and the society.

Dr. Madison: We must fight against injustice and falsity.

Ms. Malone: I now see the possibilities and will endeavor to explore them.

Holy Land Ceramic Art 26. All glory and praises be to the almighty!

Stephaniea McCall: Education is clearly the only choice for me and for my family. Hopefully I will be able to raise my children and tell them of all the

FREDERICK MONDERSON

wonderful things I experienced on this trip.

Carmelitiea Shabazz: This has been such a wonderful experience that I will always remember and recommend to all my friends and family. I saw so much yet still there is so much more to see.

Esperanza Rodriguez: I was so privileged to be Dr. Monderson's assistant for I experienced things beyond the ordinary imagination. I have come to realize, as Carlyle said there are two ways to obtain knowledge: "Properly, there is no other knowledge but that which is got by working; the rest is yet all a hypothesis of knowledge; a thing to be argued of in schools; a thing floating in the clouds, in endless logic-vortices, till we try and fit it." What I have learned on this trip is as Cowper believed: "Knowledge and wisdom, far from being one, Have oft-times no connection. Knowledge dwells, In heads replete with thoughts of other men;

Holy Land Illustration 100. Tomb of Horemhab. The king stands before Ra-Horakhty in Double Crown (left); and offers two jars of ointment to Anubis (right).

QUINTESSENTIAL BOOK
"THE HOLY LAND"

Wisdom in minds attentive to their own."

Peter Monderson: I have heard about Egypt for years and my parents insisted that I come and experience it for myself. I am so thankful for my parents' insistence. Now I must use the knowledge I gained on this educational trip.

Robert Matthews: For the many years I was a community servant and never dreamed my eyes would be opened so much as they have on this short excursion. Only heaven know why I did not get here before. The pyramids, temples, tombs, the people, the Nile River, obelisks, columns, if my mind was not grounded it would have been blown away with what I experienced from the sights as well as what I learned from my colleagues.

Lesley Jacobs: I am thoroughly convinced that the layout of many of the temples resemble that of some of the most advanced technological machines. One has to wonder, how did they know this so many thousand years ago. Early and ancient African man was indeed a genius.

Frederick Maloney: As a physician it was indeed a wise choice to come here and see where medicine first got its start. I am even more emboldened to know that at the head of medical history stands an African, Imhotep also called Aesculapius. In fact, on the entrance to the hospital where I work, Kings County, the name Aesculapius is engraved and I never realized that this was an African. Now I am so much more enlightened.

Henrietta Potter: When I walk the wards there will be a new sense of who I am, knowing my ancestors pioneered the discipline I practice every day.

Michelliea Georges: I now see what Harriet Tubman meant when she said freedom is worth fighting for. I am now free from the prejudices of ignorance and evil sayings against my people.

Teddy Cubia: I have always said one two ears will outlast a thousand lips, but now I realize the eye is the most important organ for it feeds the brain. I will never ever be able to forget what I saw on this trip for while I believed; now I know ancient Africans were great and industrious people who have left us a wonderful legacy. I am reminded of what Dr. Middleton said regarding his search for knowledge: "I persuade myself that the life and faculties of man, at the best but short and limited, cannot be employed more rationally than in the search for knowledge, and especially of that sort which relates to our duty, and conduces to our happiness. In these inquiries therefore, whenever I perceive any glimmering of truth before me, I readily pursue and endeavor to trace it to its source, without any reserve or caution of pushing the discovery too far, or opening too great a glare of it to the public. I

FREDERICK MONDERSON

look upon the discovery of anything which is true as a valuable acquisition to society; which cannot possibly hurt or obstruct the good effect of any other truth whatsoever; for they all partake of one common essence, and necessarily coincide with one another, and like the drops of rain which fall separately into the river, mix themselves at once with the stream, and strengthens the general current."

Dr. Alexander Pushkin: James Weldon Johnson stated in his speech at the NAACP Annual Conference in 1991, "All things in the universe move in cycles; so who knows but that in the whirl of God's great wheel the torch may again flame in the upper valley of the Nile."

Mrs. Alexander Pushkin: Jean Toomer in Kerman and Eldridge *The Lives of Jean Toomer* (1987) explained: "One must rise above the earth to become universal" and as Dr. Johnson believed: "All knowledge is of itself of some value. There is nothing so minute, or inconsiderable, that I would not rather know it than not."

Michael Sinclair: How valid is a perspectivist vision based on historical experiences and social conditions of a people? The answer is that: The perspectivist view limits the scope of its adherents. You can have a worldview based on historical experience. No perspective is ever static. They are always dynamic. There are five points I wish to make in closing this argument, or should I say discussion. Dr. Asante taught us always ask 5 questions.

1. "How valid is a perspectivist vision based on historical experiences and social conditions of a people?"

2. Ask yourself - "What orientations to data are necessary in order to sustain a legitimate inquiry into knowledge?" You must merge the notion of thought to social action.

Holy Land Illustration 101. "Avenue of Sphinxes" at Karnak Temple, looking towards the west, away from the entrance.

3. Quickly determine which modalities of location can be used to interpret, and in

QUINTESSENTIAL BOOK
"THE HOLY LAND"

recognition, location, orientation to data of historical significance. However, you must have concepts of analysis.

4. Explain how the time/space domain shattered by the quantum theory of evidence of particle wave behave that may give us a mere flexible frame of reference for human understanding.

5. Whites – (1) Are whites able to teach African-American history in this age of multiculturalism?

(2) Should whites teach African-American history? Yes.

(3) Is this politically correct? Well, who knows, maybe?

Always remember what Karenga said: "We need motif, history, mission, and ethos." Consciousness precedes unity. Self-consciousness and awareness are important. Only self-conscious awareness gives a sense of agency.

ABOARD AIR EGYPT

The Captain: Landing in New York: Ladies and Gentlemen, this is the Captain. We are now making the turn for our final approach and we will be landing in New York in 15 minutes. The weather is fine, 83 degrees and clear.

Pursuer. Ladies and Gentlemen, we are on the ground, please remain seated until the Captain removes the seatbelt signs. Thank you for flying with Egypt Air. When flying again please consider Egypt Air. For those passengers who are traveling on to our West coast destination, we will be on the ground for 45 minutes. Those passengers making other connections, after your baggage check, immigration and customs, please confirm your flights as soon as possible. Thank you for flying Egypt Air.

Immigration: Stamp of Passports upon entering the country.

Customs: Declaration of items brought into the country.

Esperanza Rodriguez: Well Mi Amor, with God's Grace we have made it back home. It was indeed a wonderful experience and I was proud to be your assistant.

FREDERICK MONDERSON

If you need my services again, please do not hesitate to call on me.

Dr. Fred Monderson: Thank you very much for the wonderful assistance you rendered, my dear. Thank you sincerely. Mi Amor. Gracious!

THE DISPERSAL
Taxi!

Holy Land Illustration 101a. Tomb of Horemhab. The King meets Isis (left); and presents two jars of ointment to Amentet as Hathor (right).

QUINTESSENTIAL BOOK "THE HOLY LAND"

RECOMMENDED READING FOR FURTHER ENRICHMENT

Asante, Molefi Kete. *The Afrocentric Idea*
_____. *Kemet, Afrocentricity and Knowledge*. Trenton, New Jersey: Africa World Press, Inc., (1990) 1992.
_____.
Bartlett, John. *Bartlett's Familiar Quotations*. Fourteenth Edition, Revised and Enlarged. Emily Morison Beck Editor. Boston: Little, Brown and Company (1882) 1968.
Ben-Jochannan, Yosef A. A. *Black Man of the Nile and his Family*. New York: Alkebu-Lan Publishers, 1972.
_____. *Africa: Mother of Western Civilization*. New York: Alkebu-Lan Publishers, 1970
_____. *African Origins of the Major Western Religions*. New York: Alkebu-Lan Publishers, 1971.
_____. *Abu Simbel to Ghizeh*. Baltimore, M.D.: Black Classics Press, 1989.
Breasted, James H. *The Conquest of Civilization*. New York: Harper and Brothers Publishers, 1926.
Carruthers, Jacob H. *Essays in Ancient Egyptian Studies*. Los Angeles, Calif.: University of Sankore Press, (1984) 1992.
_____. *Mdw Ntr: Divine Speech*. Lawrenceville, New Jersey: Red Sea Press, 1995.
Diop, Cheikh Anta. *The African Origin of Civilization: Myth or Reality*. Edited and Translated by Mercer Cook. Brooklyn, New York: Lawrence Hill Books 1974.
_____. *The Cultural Unity of Black Africa*. Chicago, Illinois. Third World Press (1959) 1978.
_____. *Pre-Colonial Black Africa*. Translated by Harold Salemson. Westport, Connecticut. Lawrence Hill and Co., 1987.
_____. *Civilization or Barbarism*. Translated from the French by Yaa-Lengi Meema Ngemi. Edited by Harold J. Salemson and Marjolijn de Jager. Brooklyn, New York: Lawrence Hill Books, (1981) 1991.
Finch, Charles S. III. M.D. *Echoes of the Old Darkland*. Decatur, Georgia. Khenti, Inc., (1991) 1996.
James, George G.M. *Stolen Legacy*. New York: Philosophical Library, 1954.
Karenga, Maulana and Jacob Carruthers. *Kemet and the African Worldview*. Los Angeles: University of Sankore Press, 1986.
King, Richard. M.D. *African Origin of Biological Psychiatry*. Hampton, Virginia. U.B. and U.S. Communications Systems, September 7, 1994.
Massey, Gerald. *Book of the Beginning*. 2 Vols.
_____. *Natural Genesis*. 2 Vols. Baltimore, M.D.: Black Classics Press,

FREDERICK MONDERSON

(1883) 1989.
_____. *Ancient Egypt: Light of the World.* 2 Vols. New York: Samuel Weiser, Inc., (1907) 1974.
Monderson, Frederick. *Glory of the Ancestors* (17 Vols.)
_____. *Seven Letters to Mike Tyson on Egyptian Temples.*
_____. *Ten Poems Praising Great Blacks for Mike Tyson*
_____. *Karnak: The Majestic Architecture of Ancient Egypt.*
_____. *The Colonnade: Then and Now* (5 Vols.).
_____. *Images of Ancient Egypt.*
_____. *The Majesty of Egyptian Gods and Temples.*
_____. *Egypt Essays on Ancient Kemet.*
_____. *Research Essays on Ancient Egypt.*
_____. *Where are the Kamite Kings?*
_____. *Medinet Habu: Mortuary Temple of Rameses III.*
_____. *The Ramesseum.*
_____. *Intrigue Through Time.*
_____. *Hatshepsut's Temple at Deir el Bahari.*
_____ *Grassroots View of Ancient Egypt*
_____. *Barack Obama: Ready, Fit to Lead.*
_____. *Barack Obama: Master of Washington, DC*
_____. *Obama: Master and Commander*
_____. *Celebrating Dr. Ben-Jochannan*
_____. *Who Were The Ancient Egyptians*
_____. *The Awesome Egyptian Temple*
Myers, Isaac. *Oldest Books in the World: An Account of the Religion, Wisdom, Philosophy, Psychology, Manners, Proverbs, Sayings, Refinement, etc., of the Ancient Egyptians.* New York: Edwin W. Dayton, 1900.
Obenga, Theophile. *Ancient Egypt and Black Africa.* Chicago: Karnak House, 1992.
Riley, Dorothy Winbush. Editor. *My Soul Looks Back, 'Less I Forget: A Collection of Quotations by People of Color.* New York: Harper Perennial (1991) 1995.
Van Sertima, Ivan. *Journal of African Civilizations.* New Brunswick, New Jersey: Transaction Publisher,
_____. *Egypt Revisited.* New Brunswick, New Jersey: Transaction Publisher,
_____. *Egypt: Child of Africa.* New Brunswick, New Jersey: Transaction Publisher, (1994) 1995.
_____. *Black Women in Antiquity.* New Brunswick, New Jersey: Transaction Publisher, (1984) 1996.
_____. *Great African Thinkers: Cheikh Anta Diop.* New Brunswick, New Jersey: Transaction Publisher, (1986) 1987.
_____. *Great Black Leaders: Ancient and Modern.* New Brunswick, New Jersey: Transaction Publisher, 1988.

QUINTESSENTIAL BOOK "THE HOLY LAND"

Woodson, Carter G. *Mis-education of the Negro*. Washington, D.C.: Associated Publishers, (1933) 1969.

INDEX

Aahmose (Ahmose, Ahmosis, Amosis) 106-107
Abarry, Abu at Temple University 394-397
Abydos 69, 421-422
    Home of Osiris 405
    Royal Tombs at, 69
Abydos and Sakkara tombs 229
Adams, Barbara 66
    (1988) *Predynastic Egypt* 66
Adultery 428-430, 766-767
Aeschylus (525-456 B.C.) 55
African Art 365-393
African American intellectual nationalists 52
African Religions 209-210, 259-260, 334-334, 361-362, 443-448, 452-456, 488, 494-496, 532-534, 551-552, 554-556, 575-576, 595-596, 624, 633-634, 661-662, 663-665, 679-680
African scholars, great 210
Afrocentric Course of Study 281
Afrocentric scholarship 207-208
Afrocentricity 61, 77, 78
    Components of 353-359
    Challenge to 491-493
Age of Predynastic Period 767-768
Agricultural beginnings along the Nile 24
Akh Menu 133-134
Akhnaton with ear-holes 91
Akhnaton and knowledge 92
Aldred, Cyril 51, 85, 95, 105, 107
    (1965) Egypt to the End of the Old Kingdom
    (1987) *The Egyptians*
Alexandria 507-514
Alexandria, name of 740
Amenhotep (107)
Amon and Amon-Ra 272-273
Amon's Ennead 103
Amon in Nubia 774-775
Amon's Second Home 145
Amarna Revolution 524-526

Ancestor Worship 769
Ancient History 234-235, 266-267, 268-269, 315-316, 331-332, 362,
 397-398, 451-452, 534-536, 552-554, 556 571-572, 572-575, 594, 596,
 615, 623, 624-626, 633-634, 666-667,
Annals of Thutmose III 134
"Architecture: Egyptian" in *Encyclopedia of Religion and Ethics* 642-844
Aristotle 40, 483
    *Metaphysics*40
    Physiognomonica 50
Armour, Robert A 124
    (1989) *Gods and Myths of Ancient Egypt*
Art 460
"Art: Egyptian" 642
Art in people's homes 622
Articles by Dr. Fred Monderson
    "Dr. Yosef A.A. Ben-Jochannan" 6-13
    "The Nile Valley" 23-39
    "Egypt, Kush, Ethiopia 49-53
    "Flow of the Nile" 62-63
    "Temple of Karnak: Majestic Architecture of
    Ancient Kemet" 79-145
    "Temple of Luxor" 145-164
    "The Ramesseum" 236-255
    "Technology in a Global Community" 309-313
    "Medinet Habu: Mortuary Temple of Rameses III" 335-337
    "The Dance, Music and Musical Instruments" 457-473
    "The Priesthood" 474-487
    "Abydos: Home of Osiris" 405
    "Temple of Dendera" 406-408
    "The Nile Valley in Antiquity History" 539-551
    "Fascination of Egyptian Archaeology" 578-591
    "Egypt and Africa" 627-631
    "Franklin Avenue Shuttle: Shuttle into the Millennium" 654-659
    "The Illustrious Queen Mother" 689-698
    "Black Egypt and the Struggle for Inclusion" 725-728
    "Queen of Sheba in Racial Portrait as Historical Distortion" 749-757
    "Spreading the Knowledge" 783-784
Asante, Molefi 74, 256-257, 261-262 301-305, 399, 740
    (1999) *Ancient Egyptian Philosophers* 740
    (1991) "Afrocentricity and the Human Future" 317-326, 399-403
Asante's name 261
ASCAC 53, 88
Atone for transgressions 671
Authority 226-227

QUINTESSENTIAL BOOK "THE HOLY LAND"

Avenue of Sphinxes 113, 152
Ba 227, 433
Bacon, Sir Francis (1561-1626) 40
    The Advancement of Learning 57
Badawy 81
    (1990) *A History of Egyptian Architecture*
Baikie, James 466-467
    (1917) "Egyptian Music"
Baines, J and J. Malek 65, 85, 86, 87123
    (1980) *Atlas of Ancient Egypt* 65
Balance 619
Baldwin, James 264
    (1963) *Nobody Knows My Name*
Barnett, Mary 93
    (1996) *Egypt: Gods and Myths of Ancient Egypt*
Battle of Kadesh 154
Bekenkhonsu 135
    Boast 151
Behaviors Egyptians frown upon 426
Belzoni 85
Ben-Jochannan, Dr. Yosef A.A. 6-13, 41. 120, 151, 463, 425
    (1970) *African Origins of the Major Western Religions* 59
    (1971) *Africa: Mother of Western Civilization* 59
    (1972) *Black man of the Nile and his Family* 59
    (1989) *Abu Simbel to Ghizeh* 59
Benjamin's, Dr. Lecture on Cairo Museum Visit 759-763
Bierbrier, Morris 92
    (1989) *The Tomb Builders of the Pharaohs*
Bishop Thomas Brigham 71
Black Egyptians 219-220
Blacks removed from Egypt 201
Black History 393-394
    Importance of 203
Blacksmith, characteristics of 684
Blasphemy 619
Blessing, the 607-612
Bonechi 237
    (1994) *Art and History of Egypt*
Book of the Dead editions 223-225
Book of Thoth 277
Bovill, E.W. 391-392
    (1970) *Golden Trade of the Moors*
Bratton, Fred Gladstone 103, 119, 149, 238
    (1968) *A History of Egyptian Archaeology*

Breasted, James Henry 246-247, 248-249, 460
    (1923) *A History of Egypt*
Budge, E.A. Wallis 70, 114, 116, 125-127, 134, 249, 460-462
    (1904) *The Gods of the Egyptians*
    (1911) *Osiris and the Egyptian Resurrection*
    (1972) *Dwellers on the Nile*
Builders of Luxor Temple 147
Breasted, J.H. 135
    (1923) *A History of Egypt*
Brightness of Aton, the Great 92
Broderick, Matthew
    (1902) *Dictionary of Egyptian Archaeology* 32
Brown, John 55
Brugsch, H.
    (1902) (1996) *Egypt Under the Pharaohs*
Building materials 769-770
"Cachette Court" 102, 103
Cairo Museum 218
Calendars 32, 112, 528-530, 746-747
"Calendars, Egyptian" 748-749
Campbell, David 238
    (1996) *Egypt: Everyman's Guide*
Canon of proportion 382-383
Carpiceci, Alberto Carlo 70
    (1994) *Art and History of Egypt*
Carruthers, Dr. Jacob on Hegel 214-215
Celestial cow 741
Centers of Civilization 24
Centers of Religious Worship 34, 111
Ceremonies 646
Champollion 85, 234
Chancellor 618
Change 618
Chappell 465
    (1874) *The History of Music*
Character, Egyptian 645
"Charms: Egyptian" 749-750
Chevier, H. 101
Childe, V. Gordon 24
    (1938) *New Light on the Most Ancient East* 24
Christianity and Christians in Egypt 569-570
Circumcision 748
"Circumcision: Egyptian" 750
Clarke, John H. Prof/Dr. 25, 51, 68, 202

QUINTESSENTIAL BOOK
"THE HOLY LAND"

Clarke and Engelbach 134
    (1930) (1990) *Ancient Egyptian Construction and Architecture*
Class in Egypt 569
Cleanliness of priests 747
Clemens of Alexandria (2nd Century A.D.) 86
Color of Egyptians 216
Columns, names or types of 642
"Coca Cola temple" 68
Command 617
Compte, Auguste (1798-1857) 41
    System of Positive Philosophy 41
Confucius (541-479) 57, 75
Conversation 617
Contributions of Africa 317
"Cosmogony and Cosmology: Egyptian" 644-647
Council, the 617
Court of the Bubastites 115
Cottrell 136, 139
    (1965) *Egypt*
Covenant 617
Creator Gods 644
Creation myths 721
"Crimes and Punishment: Egyptian" 649
Criminal behavior 647
Criteria for Critical Reading 203
Critical African historians 52
Crowns of Egypt 741
Cubia, Teddy 78
    "Black is Light" 78
    "The Game" 61-62
    "Battle Cry" 232
    "Black Love" 283-284
    "Red, Black and Green" 360
    "Now's the Time to Kill the Swine" 497-498
    "What is a Brother" 537
Culture 330
Culture of ancient Egyptians 351-352
Damage to monuments 559-561
Danquah, J.B. 264
    (1924) *Africa at the Bar of Nations*
    (1928) *Akan Law and Customs*
David 150, 154, 157-158
    (1993)

FREDERICK MONDERSON

Death, view of 427
Deir el Bahari 279-272, 631-632, 757-758
      Temples at 419-420
Dendera 69
Description of Egypt 100
Deity, supreme 523-524
Diodorus Siculus 50, 466
Diop, Cheikh Anta 42, 51, 59, 217, 265, 398
      (1974) *The African Origin of Civilization:*
           Myth or Reality 42
      (1991) *Civilization or Barbarism*
Divine lineage of kings 344
Dr. Monderson's schooling *620-621*
DuBois, W.E.B. 52, 115, 262,
      (1903) *The Souls of Black Folks*
      (1915) *The Negro* 52
      (1946) *The World and Africa* 52
Eames 82, 242
      (1990) (1992) *Insight Guides*: *The Nile*
Eastern Desert 25
Egyptian agriculture
Egyptian baptism 769
Egyptian books 619
Egyptian capitals 72
Egyptian chronology 347
Egyptian collections, most significant 530
Egyptian columns 73
Egyptian education
Egyptian family 668-670
Egyptian ideas of the future life 716
Egyptian magic 716-717
Egyptian marriage 719
Egyptian origin of Greek-Doric Column 74
Egyptian philosophy 490-491, 493
Egyptian myths 84
Egyptian sayings 514-516
Egyptian society 565
Egyptian symbolism 42, 84, 86
Egyptian Universe 435-441, 526-528, 556-559
Eliot, Charles William (1834-1926) 41
Eliot, Thomas Stearns (1888-1969) 75
Ellis, Havelock (1859-1939) 74
      Dance of Life
Engel 470

QUINTESSENTIAL BOOK "THE HOLY LAND"

(1864) *History of Music*
Erman, Adolf 93, 118, 238
    (1907) *A Handbook of Egyptian Religion*
    (1995) *Ancient Egyptian Poetry and Prose*
Esneh, Edfu, Kom Ombo temples 499-507
"Ethics and Morality: Egyptian" 647
Ethiopians, history 415-418
Ezekiel 40
Fagan, Brian 150
    (1975) *The Rape of the Nile*
Fage, Bernard 388-389
    (1976) *History of West Africa*
Fairservis, Jr., Walter A. 39?
    (1962) *The Ancient Kingdoms of the Nile* 24
"Family: Egyptian" 671-672
Fedden 122, 146
    (1986) *Egypt: Land of the Valley*
Festivals in Ancient Egypt 668
"Festivals and Feasts" 700
"Fighting Province" 90
First Intermediate Period 488
First Three Nomes 65
Foodstuff 34, 619
Fragner, Benjamin 83
    (1994) *The Illustrated History of Architecture*
Frankfort 58
    Before Philosophy 58
Friendly, Alfred 370
Garvey's classic statement 690
Geography of the Gods 212
Geographical lists 128
Gladstone Atwell Middle School No. 61 298
"God: Egyptian" 677
Gods, animal forms 676-677
Gods, group of 676
Gods, sick 645
Gods, view of 675
Golden Section (phi) 84
Good-bye celebration 780-782
Good qualities 774
Goodwin 96
    (1876) *Records of the Past*
Great Hymn to Aton 92
Greek and Roman temples 722

"Grand Lodge" 147
Gregorian, Dr. Vartan 198
Grimal, Nicholas 135
    (1992) *A History of Ancient Egypt*
Gympel 83
    (1996) *The Story of Architecture*
Haag 151, 152, 242
    (1987) *Guide to Egypt*
    Josephine's brazen request of Napoleon 151
Habachi 86, 125, 127, 152
    (1987)
Hall of Ancestors 133
Hart, George 104, 113, 150
    (1990) *Egyptian Myths*
    (1996) *Ancient Egypt*
Hatshepsut 109, 123-129, 153, 694, 729-730
    Temple building foundation 153
    Punt 420
Heavenly existence 622-623
Heb Sed Festival 714
Helmholtz (1821) 1894) 76
    Academic Discourse 76
"Hero and Hero Gods" 675
Herodotus 59, 465
    Histories
        Euterpe 50
Hieroglyphics 273
High Priest, function of 723
History, earliest fixed 348-349
Hobson 150
    (1987) *The World of the Pharaohs*
Youssef, Hisham and John Rodenbeck 406
    (1991) *Egypt: Insight Guides*
Horemhab (Horemheb) 136
Human sacrifice 673-674
"Human Sacrifice" 676
Huxley, Thomas Henry (1825-1895) 70
Hyksos 105-106
Hymn to Amon 96-98
Hypostyle Hall 119-121
Ifa Divination 649-653
"Images and Idols" 678
Imhotep 714
Imhotep's rise to divinity status 673

QUINTESSENTIAL BOOK
"THE HOLY LAND"

Imperial pharaohs 111
"Incarnation" 680
Inherited property 724
Inundation 431-432
James, T.G.H. 109
    (1984) (1985) *Pharaoh's People*
James, Leonard 203
Jewelry and tools 66
Job 71
Jordan, Paul 138
    (1976) *Egypt: The Black Land*
Joubert, Joseph (1754-1824) 41
Judges in the Hall 518
Justice administered 773
Ka 227, 433
Kamil 66, 115, 148, 149, 243, 406, 478, 481
    (1980) *Luxor: A Guide to Ancient Thebes*
    (1996 *Upper Egypt and Nubia*
Karnak temple 68-69
    Builders at 81
    "Most select of places" 68-69, 87
    Temples at 85
Kemetic pantheon 104
King list 349
King, names of 346-347
Kings, oldest name of 345
King and the Gods, relationship 347
Kiosk of Senwosret I (1970-1936) 65
King Lists 100
    Abydos 100
    Karnak 100
    Sakkara 100
    Second Abydos 100
King's Titles (Names) 65
    Horus 65
    Suten Bat 65
    Golden Horus 65
    Two ladies 65
    Son of Ra 65
Knopf, Alfred A. 87
    (1995) *Egypt*
Knowledge, possession 228
Kush, Indus Kamit 49
    (1983) *What They Never Taught You in History Class* 49

Langenscheidt 82, 239
    (1990) (1993) *Egypt: Self Guided*
Leakey, Mary and Louis 368-369
Legend of Osiris 644
Le Grain's work at Karnak 103
Lepsius 72-74
L'Hote, Henry 366-368
    (1938) "Tassili Frescoes"
Library of Congress 75, 263
Libraries in ancient Egypt 273-274
Locke, John (1632-1704) 75
    Second Treatise on Civil Government 75
Lord Burleigh (1592) 40
Love 275
Lumumba, Patrice 265
    Congo: My Country
Lurker, Manfred 84, 131, 151
    (1991) *The Gods and Symbols of Ancient Egypt*
Luxor Temple 433-434
    Pylon 154
    Visitors to 150-151
Ma'at, Goddess 227
Magic 33, 571
"Magic: Egyptian" 718-719
Manetho 276
Mann, A.T. 83, 84
    (1993) *Sacred Architecture*
Manners 276
Marriage 277
"Marriage: Egyptian" 721
Maspero, Gaston 91, 92, 95, 121-122, 149, 150-151, 153, 236, 245-246, 249-250, 400 407-408
    (1904) *History of Egypt, Assyria, Chaldea*
    (1926) *A Manual of Egyptian Archaeology*
Mastabas 277, 280
Materials for building 640-642
Maulana Karenga 260-261
Maxims 277
McGrath 103, 240
    (1982) *Frommer's Dollarwise Guide to Egypt*
Medinet Habu: Mortuary Temple of Rameses III 335-337
Memphis 706-713
Milky Way 349-350
Merenptah (1221-1214 B.C.) 103

QUINTESSENTIAL BOOK
"THE HOLY LAND"

Messenger, the 278-279
Michalowski 124, 384-387
    (No Date)
Medinet Habu 96
Mentuhotep's temple at Deir el Bahari 279
Min 719
Mineral Resources 37
Mortuary temples of pharaohs 67
Mortuary temple, essential components 433-434
Moscati 58
    Faces of the Ancient Orient 58
Moses - Who was he? 350-351
Mother and child 431
Muller, Wolfgang 123, 129, 132
    (1963) "Egyptian Art" in *Encyclopedia of Art*
Mummy bandage 619
Mummies, color of 763
Mummy gods 646
Murder 430-431
Murnane, William C. 118, 128, 132
    (1983) *The Penguin Guide to Ancient Egypt*
Murray, Margaret 108, 109, 125, 138
    (1957) *The Splendor that was Egypt*
Murray, John 132
    (1888) *Handbook for Egypt* 132
Music 637-639
"Music: Egyptian" 640-641
Myers 221, 423-425
    (1900) *Oldest Books in the World*
Myth of Isis and Osiris 691
Narmer 64
    Palette 64
    Macehead 64
Naumann, Emil 464, 468-469
    (1882) *The History of Music*
Nefertiti 343
Nefertiti and Nefertaris 343-344
Negative Confessions 774
New Kingdom 337-342
Newberry 93
    "An Egyptian Gardener: The Tomb of Nakht"
Nile River 592-593
Nkrumah, Kwame 207
Nomes 63

Nomarch responsibility 65
Nubian temples 441
Obenga, Theophile 92
	(1992) *Ancient Egypt and Black Africa*
Obelisk 622
Offerings 432
Open Middle Kingdom Court 129
Opet Festival 136, 157, 158
	Purpose of Luxor Temple 150
Osiris to Jesus, comparison 672-673
Osiris cult 673
Osiris myth 523
Owens, Major 202
Palermo Stone 348-349
Panel Discussion 408-413
Parks, Gordon 42
	(1990) *Voices in the Mirror* 42
Payne, Elizabeth 92, 113
	(1964) *The Pharaohs of Ancient Egypt*
Pemberton, 238
	(1992) *Ancient Egypt: Architectural Guide for Travelers* 203
Period of Egyptian history
Petrie, W.M. F. 468, 478
	(1923) *Egyptian Religion*
	(1940) *Wisdom of the Egyptians*
	(1909) "Egyptian Art" 372-375
Pier, Garrett Chatfield 112, 129
	(1916) "The Great Temple of Amon-Ra at Karnak" in *Art and Architecture*
Plants 36
Plato (427-347) 55
	Republic 55
	Philosophers as Kings 55
Poem of Pentaurt 95
Polygamy 570
Polyglot 81, 462
	(1965) *Egypt Travel Guides*
Portman, Ian 103, 119, 123, 153
	(1989) *Luxor: A Guide to the Temples and Tombs of Ancient Egypt*
Precession, 26,000 years 25
	The Conquest of Peru 74
Priesthood 722-723
	Priesthood activities 770
Prisse D'Avennes 133

QUINTESSENTIAL BOOK "THE HOLY LAND"

Proscription of Amon 92-93
Psalms 41
Psychology of the Egyptian 742
Purification of the king 747
Pylon, First 114
    Second 119
    Third 123
    Fourth 123-124
    Fifth 127
Pyramids of Gizeh 731-735
Pyramids with inscriptions (Pyramid Texts) 717-718
Queen 104
    Aahmes-Nefertari 106-107, 108, 694
    Aam (Mentuhotep's Mother) 693
        Achtothes (Intef's Mother) 693
    Hatshepsut
    Mother Moore 690
        Influences 690
    Nefertari 107
    Nzinga 695
    Neithhotep 693
    Teti-Sheri 104, 107
    Tiy 695
    Queen Mother 697
Queen Mother Crown 694
Question of truth 773
Quirke, Stephen 113, 125
    (1992) *Ancient Egyptian Religion*
Ra and Osiris conflict 778
Ra's popularity 771-772
Racist pseudo-scientific writers 202
Rameses II (1279-1213 B.C.) 83
    Temple of, 118
    Regiments 95
Rawlinson 213
    (1896) *The Story of Egypt*
"Records of the ancient records" 103
Religion of Egypt, message of 60
Religious (Books) inscriptions 718
Religious ritual in *Book of the Dead* 522-523
Resurrection 432-433
Richards, Donna (Merimba Ani) 57
Richardson, Dan and Karen O'Brien 238, 241
    (1991) *Egypt*: *The Rough Guide*

"Righteousness: Egyptian" 775
Riley, Dorothy Winbush 42
    (1995) *My Soul Looks Back* 42
Robbins, Gay 107
    (1993) *Women in Ancient Egypt*
Rogers, J.A. 464
    (1944) *Sex and Race*
Rohl, David 117
    (1995) *Pharaohs and Kings: A Biblical Quest*
Ruffle 121, 243
    (1977) *The Egyptians*
Sacrifice 514
Sacrifice, purpose of 768-769, 770-771
Sacramental ideas and usages 764-766
Sacred Lake 134
Sakkara 257-259, 698-705
Salvation 646-646
"Salvation: Egyptian" 648
Samkange, Stanlake 106
    (1971) *African Saga: A Brief Introduction to African History*
Sanctuary 129
    Approach to 677-678
Sauernon 85, 114
    (1962) *A Dictionary of Egyptian Civilization*
Scarab at the Sacred Lake 516-517
Scheel, Bernard 381
    (1989) *Egyptian Metalworking and Tools*
Scholz, Piotr 89
    (1997) *Ancient Egypt: An Illustrated Historical Overview*
Schwaller de Lubicz 149
Science 225-226
Scientific American Supplement 137
    (1899, Feb 25) 137
    (1899, Dec 30) 137
Second birth 517
Selden, John (1584-1654) 75
Senmut 109, 271-272
Serpent, role of 519-520
Shaw, Ian and Paul Nicholson 79, 82
    (1995) *The Dictionary of Ancient Egypt*
Shishak 115
Showker 102
    (1989)
Silence, notion of 520

QUINTESSENTIAL BOOK "THE HOLY LAND"

Simpkins 114, 134
    (1982) *The Temple of Karnak*
Sister marriage 670-671
Sites for temple erection 637
Slander, laws against 521
Smith, Fay 82, 238
    (1991) *Egypt at Cost*
Sneferu 715-716
Soul, construction of the 520-521
Soul, parts of the 742-746
South African Iron Ore industry 25
Speech, pros and cons 521
Sphinx 732
Spirit world 672
Steindorff and Seele 89
    (1971) *When Egypt Ruled the East*
Strabo 466
Stratham 72
Summary of trip 775-779
Sun God cleanliness 736-739
Swearing 563-564
Syncretism 89
"Table of Offerings" 673, 768
Taharka 115-117
    Column 116
Tarik es-Sudan 390
Tarik al-Fattah 390
Temple building foundation 153
Temple of Isis 597-607
Temple of Mut in Asher 147
Temple plans 642
"Temples" 639
"Tety the Handsome" 104
Theban Triad 79, 85
Thoth 564, 568-569
Thutmose I 123, 127
    Thutmose I and Valley of the Kings 280
Thutmose III 123, 127, 132-133
Time-Life Books 134
    (1997) *What Life Was Like on the Banks of the Nile*
Tithes 636
"Tithes" 638
Tomb, the 565-566
    Purpose of 228-229

FREDERICK MONDERSON

Tomb decoration 678
Tomb painting 432
Traunecker, Claude and Jean Claude Golvin 99
    (1992) *History and Archaeology*
Treachery 566
"Tree of Life" 566-568
Trees 37
Trigger, Et. Al. 136, 138
Triumph over death 772
Types of temples 770
Unas' Pyramid 279
Uniters of Egypt 69
Unity of the Deity
Uraeus 569
Vercoutter, Jean 99-100, 101
    (1992) *The Search for Ancient Egypt*
Violence 569
Washington, D.C. Cultural Institutions 60
Watterson, Barbara 100
    (1997) *The Egyptians*
Wayne, Scott 238
    (1990) *Egypt and the Sudan*
Weigall, A.E.P. B. 80, 86, 145, 147, 151
    (1910) (1996) *A Guide to the Antiquities of Upper Egypt*
Weighing of the heart 621
Weights and measures 278
West, J.A. 148-149, 154
    (1987) *Serpent in the Sky*
Western Desert – Nabta Playa 25
Western Necropolis 68
White, J.E Manchip 244
    (1970) *Ancient Egypt: Its Culture and History*
    (1980) *Everyday Life in Ancient Egypt*
Wilkinson, J. Gardner 55, 89
    (1850) (1996) *The Architecture of Egypt*
Wilkinson, Alix 91, 107
    (1971) *Ancient Egyptian Jewelry*
Williams, Bruce 51, 375-376
    (March 1, 1979) "World's Earliest Monarchy" 51
Williams, Chancellor 86, 244
    (1996) *The Destruction of Black Civilization*
Wilson, J.A. 58, 475, 476, 477l 484
    (1959?) *The Culture of Ancient Egypt* 58
Winnie Mandela 690

QUINTESSENTIAL BOOK "THE HOLY LAND"

Holy Land Photo 112a. Temple of Karnak. The "White Chapel" of Senusert I, 12th Dynasty, reconstructed and now in the "Open Air Museum."

Wisdom of Ancient Egypt 487-488
Woldering 101, 243, 462
    (1963) *The Art of Egypt: Time of the Pharaohs*
World's first university 221-222
Worship of Amon-Ra 114
Worship temples, essential components 434
Wright, Richard 264
    (1941) *12 Million Black Voices*
Yaa Asantewaa 695
Yoyote 241, 242
    (1962) *A Dictionary of Egyptian Civilization*
Zoological Gardens 133
Zoser 714

www.ingramcontent.com/pod-product-compliance
Lightning Source LLC
Chambersburg PA
CBHW071229300426
44116CB00008B/963